Code-IT Primary Programming

Crumble Creations

Affordable STEM Computing Projects for the Primary Classroom

A complete scheme of work for primary classrooms using the cheap Crumble Microcontroller.

Phil Bagge

First published in Great Britain in 2018 by

The University of Buckingham Press

Yeomanry House

Hunter Street

Buckingham MK18 1EG

CIP catalogue record for this book is available at the British Library.

ISBN 978-1-912500-01-7

Acknowledgements

Thank you:

Thanks to my wife Rachael, who has put up with our house being crammed with Crumble & DT kit for the last two years and who has also read every chapter and made endless grammar recommendations any final mistakes are all mine.

Thanks to my children, Antonio and Marissa, for often been the first ones to test new Crumble ideas and give me their honest feedback.

Thanks to the staff and children at Ringwood Junior School and Otterbourne Primary School, who have tried lots of new projects in many forms and have inspired me with their inquisitive questions and great problem solving attitudes.

Thanks to Professor Les Carr from the University of Southampton for all his friendship and encouragement over many years. I wouldn't be doing any of this without you.

Thanks to the CAS South East regional centre for all their support.

Thanks to Sue Savory for all her support over many years.

Thanks to Simon Walters @cymplecy for all his great programming resources and for correcting some of my misconceptions about electronics.

Thanks also to Jane Waite and Chip Chippindall, excellent primary computing science educators, who both wrote a foreword for this book.

Thanks to CAS, a fantastic grassroots organisation, for opening my eyes to the possibilities that computing science holds.

Thanks to all the subscribers of my code-it website who offered to read and comment on this book and to Karen Laggan, Darren Bungay, Phil Coulson & Stewart Dunn for providing useful feedback on specific chapters.

Final thanks go to Truffles, my daughter's hamster who lives in my office. Without his late night wheel spinning keeping me awake, it would have taken me even longer to finish this book!

Phil Bagge

12th February 2018

Forewords

From autonomous cars and delivery drones, to checkout-less supermarkets and self-landing rockets, some of the most exciting developments in the world of technology today are the engineering challenges of physical computing.

In this book, Phil helps bring that awe and wonder of 'making stuff that does stuff' into your classroom. Presenting a vast array of creative cross-curricular projects, from 'Animating animals' to 'Robot drag races', Phil provides detailed guidance so 'people with no experience of electronics or programming' can get started in this exciting area of the curriculum.

As a fellow CAS Master Teacher, I've had the pleasure of knowing and speaking alongside Phil for several years now. A Computing Inspector for Hampshire's Inspection and Advisory Service and someone who has been sharing resources with school for over 10 years, Phil is undoubtedly one of the foremost experts in the world on computing in primary schools. One or his (many) great strengths is translating potentially tricky concepts and ideas into understandable, engaging and doable lessons - and that is exactly what this book is bursting with!

The early sections present a wealth of information to support the reader in undertaking these projects, including an overview of the kit used, namely the Crumble, Crumble Playground and their various inputs and outputs. Also included are informative discussions on teaching methods, computational thinking and progression in programming - all hugely valuable for teachers, enthusiastic parents and computing volunteers alike.

The project chapters which follow strike an ideal balance of step-by-step instruction whilst still leaving room for pupils' own ideas, approaches and creativity. This is a tricky balance to achieve, which has been managed through the provision of extension ideas to challenge, and 'Maker Cards' to support.

Seeing Phil share a variety of exciting snippets of Crumble based projects across Twitter this last year or so, I was hoping a book was on its way and it's a privilege to have be asked to write this foreword, but I do question why you might be stopping to read it... there are such great ideas in the pages to come just go ahead and get stuck in!

Dr Jon (Chip) Chippindall @drchips_ Barefoot Computing Science Resource Creator

This is a long awaited, and much needed book. It will help primary teachers deliver computing lessons using the crumble microcontroller. Phil has been sharing his computing experience and expertise with the teaching community for well over ten years. When he mentioned the crumble I had to get one and try it out. I was instantly hooked.

I used the crumble with my big box of electricity resources. The crocodile clips, leds, motors and buzzers, that we used year in and year out, were all I needed to add to the crumble and power pack to start combining science, design and technology and computing. The joy that children got from making a simple light come on amazed me and by adding a whirring motor resulted in endless creative opportunities.

There are significant opportunities for collaborative work and once you and your pupils get a handle of the basics you'll be doing cross-curricular history, art, geography, maths topics, you won't be able to stop.

But HOW should we teach physical computing? We need to be brave, teach slowly and carefully, build progression and help learners become independent and creative developers.

Whether you are using the Crumble or other microcontrollers, this book is invaluable for lesson ideas and instructional techniques. Phil provides practical guidance and a scheme of work! Everything you need, all tied together and tried and tested in school, by Phil with his pupils.

Great job and thank you Phil!

Jane Waite CAS London Regional Manager Barefoot Computing Science Resource Creator

Table of Contents

Chapter 1 Introduction

A. How to use this book

This book is written for primary teachers who want to introduce an element of physical computing into their curriculum, home schooling parents of primary age children, parents who want to make things with their children and people who run coding and making clubs.

It is written for people with no experience of electronics or programming.

It seeks to guide schools into how they can resource, integrate and use the very affordable Crumble control board to provide elements of computing science through programming and design and technology whilst enriching other curriculum areas.

The scheme is designed for pupils between the ages of 5 and 11; it may also be useful for older pupils with special educational needs.

Encouraging children to think beyond the project is always to be promoted. How could they adapt the idea to make something else? What do they want to make? Most children need to make something first before they can adapt it to do something else later. Computer scientists call this generalisation and there is an explanation of the thinking skills you will be promoting later on in this chapter.

Many of the projects use 4x4x4 inch cardboard boxes as a stable platform to mount the technology on. Larger or slightly smaller boxes would work just as well and a thrifty school or parent can often find suitable boxes already at home. 4x4x4 boxes can be purchased in bulk very cheaply.

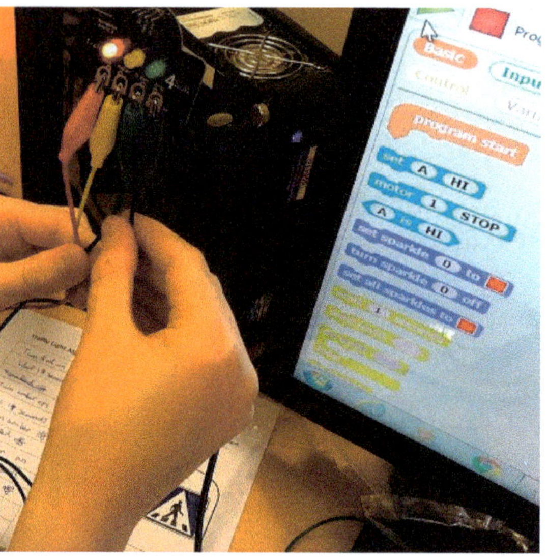

Classic Crumble programming traffic lights

New to Programming

I suggest you read the first chapter and then buy a single kit from one of the two suppliers mentioned, so that you can make some of the projects described. Then choose a simple project to make with your children and purchase enough equipment for them to make something in pairs. Remember to read pages 13-15 to help you decide what level of support to provide your pupils. Start simple but increase complexity and challenge as you and your pupils grow in confidence and competence.

Experienced Block Based Programmer

There are real differences in programming with physical equipment. The sections on how the Crumble works on page 3 & 4, issues around electronic assembly on page 16 and the discussion of the differences between Scratch and Crumble on page 22 will all be useful starting points. You can always increase the programming complexity by reducing the scaffolding as outlined on pages 14 & 15.

Experienced Design & Technology Educator

You can increase the design and technology elements by allowing children a much wider choice of materials and construction methods. Additionally, most of the early chapters have next step design sheets for pupils to plan their own projects based on a small range of equipment. Chapter 13 has some additional design sheets to encourage the children to think about aesthetics and construction issues.

Share with the Author

There is a copy of the maker cards available online. Email or tweet me with a picture of yourself holding the book and I will send you the web address and the password. Additional Crumble Creations related resources and corrections can be found at **http://code-it.co.uk/crumblecreations/**

I love seeing what children have created and adapted so please share your creations with me.

I am **@baggiepr** on Twitter or you can get in touch via email on my code-it.co.uk website at **http://code-it.co.uk/contact/**

Have fun designing, creating, building, wiring, programming and testing.

Phil Bagge

B, Crumble Programming in a Nutshell

Decide what you want to make.

Attach the accessories to the Crumble board.

Connect the Crumble board into a Windows, Mac or Linux computer using a USB wire.

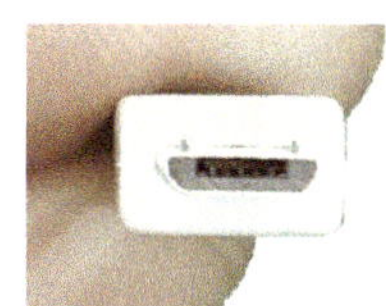

Program your devices on Crumble software using the free block based programming language.

Press the green arrow to send the program from the computer to the Crumble board.

Turn the batteries on and see if your programming works.

You can run the program while it is attached to the computer or away from the computer.

Redfern Electronics have a great programming overview document at https://goo.gl/j7bCkF

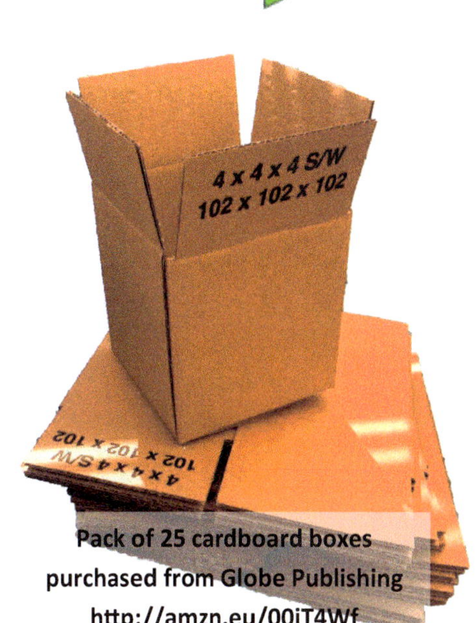

Pack of 25 cardboard boxes purchased from Globe Publishing http://amzn.eu/00jT4Wf

C, Crumble & Crumble Playground

The **Crumble** is a very cheap control board designed to enable young children to design, make and program digital creations.

Up to two motors can be programmed and attached to it, along with other **outputs** such as LED lights, buzzers and servo motors (0-90 degree turns).

The Crumble can also accept a variety of **inputs** such as buttons, sliders, dials, distance sensors, PIR sensors and touch sensors.

The Crumble is limited to four inputs or outputs excluding the two motors which use their own dedicated output connections.

Output –Something that comes out of a digital device

Crumble Classic connected to a battery pack and Sparkle programmable light

Input –Something that goes into a digital device

The USB cable, plugs into the Crumble here. When it is connected to a PC, Mac or Linux computer, programs can be sent to the control chip via this connection.

Referred to in this book as the Crumble Classic to distinguish it from the Crumble Playground.

Power is provided to the crumble board through these connections. Both Redfern Electronics and 4tronix provide a 3xAA battery holder with an on/off switch. A standard 3xAA battery pack can be used although the on/off switch is very useful.

Four inputs or outputs can be connected to A, B, C or D

These connections control **Motor 1**. The DC motor wires can be swapped to reverse the motor or reversed using the Crumble Software. It accepts 3-6v DC motors.

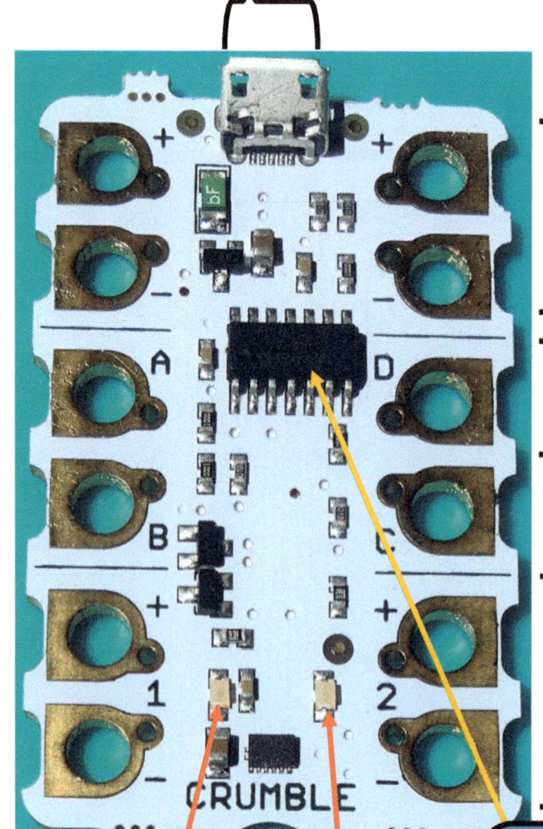

Some inputs and outputs need their own power source. They get this through these connections or directly from the battery pack.

D can be used as a standard input or output connector or to connect up to 32 programmable lights in a daisy chain.

These connections control **Motor 2**, the DC motor wires can be swapped to reverse the motor or reversed using the Crumble Software. It accepts 3-6v DC motors.

Red lights show when motors 1 or 2 are activated

The black chip stores the program once it has been sent to the Crumble from the Crumble software (Green arrow).

The **Crumble Playground** provides an easier method to connect inputs and outputs to the Crumble and comes with a built in battery pack on the underside. Users can still use crocodile clip attachments allowing them to move on from easier headphone cables when they are ready. The cable simplification allows children in Upper KS1 (6-7 years old) and Lower KS2 (7-9 years old) to program their own creations and provides a method of scaffolding older pupils who struggle with a tangle of crocodile clips. The extra power out connections at the top of the playground are a real advantage for projects that use multiple inputs and outputs.

They are also a big hit with less confident teachers as there are fewer issues that arise from connections touching each other due to crocodile clip covers slipping off.

Downsides are that the headphone cables mask the scientific principles of circuits and the black jack plug sockets can be knocked off by less than careful pupils although they are easily soldered back on by a parent volunteer.

Unlike the Crumble Classic, the playground has a light to show the user when input or output A, B, C or D are being used (D & C are activated in the picture).

Some **crocodile clip** inputs and outputs need their own power. They get this through these connections (the extra one is really useful).

Crumble Playground users must buy a crumble to screw onto the top as shown in the picture.

Four inputs or outputs can be connected to A, B, C or D. These can be either connected via the headphone cables or via the crocodile clip holes.

D can be used as a standard input or output connector or to connect up to 32 programmable lights in a daisy chain

These connections control **Motor 1**, the DC crocodile clip motor wires can be swapped to reverse the motor or reversed using the Crumble Software. It accepts 3-6v DC motors.

These connections control **Motor 2**. The DC crocodile clip motor wires can be swapped to reverse the motor or reversed using the Crumble Software. It accepts 3-6v DC motors.

The on/off switch turns the battery pack on the underside on and off. A blue light shows when it is switched on.

Input or Output connections as well as motor connections can only accept one item. You can't plug in a buzzer via headphone socket A and an LED via crocodile clip A. In some cases you could use the same type of item into both sockets but the power would be halved.

Battery pack on the reverse side of the Crumble Playground

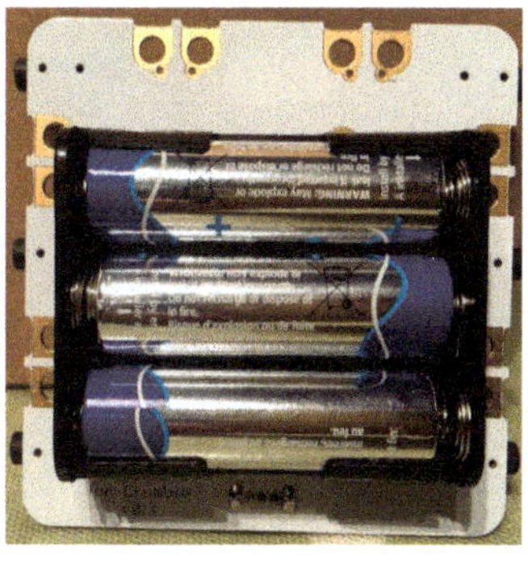

D. Crumble Inputs & Outputs

Name	Crocodile Clip (Crumble Classic)	Headphone (Playground)	Notes
Programmable Light Sparkle Flame			These can be easily programmed to display a full range of colours.
LED Light	 		These are very cheap but you do need the right voltages.
Motor			Motors between 3-6 volts will work with the Crumble (You probably have a lot in a science or DT cupboard).
Stepper (Servo) Motor			Program movement between –90-0-90 degrees. 180 degree arc
Dial & Slider	 	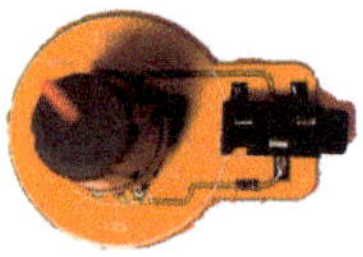	These need a variable to work well so are mainly used with older pupils.
Traffic Lights		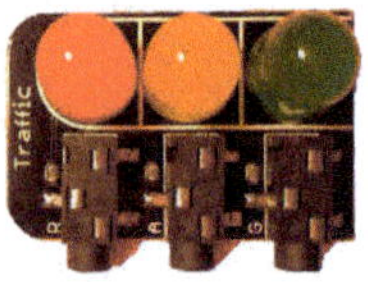	Traffic lights are great for lots of starter projects.
Buzzer	  		Beware! A classroom full of buzzers will drive you slightly crazy.
Distance Sensor	 		Detects between 2cm and 400cm. It won't always detect cloth objects.
PIR Sensor			Often used as motion detectors in house security systems. These can be a bit temperamental.
Push Button	 	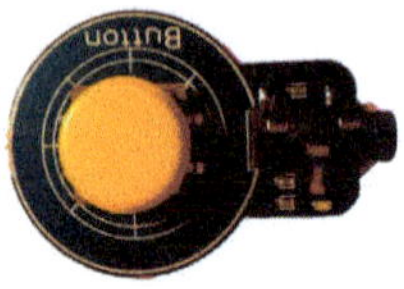	One of the most used inputs.

Name	Crocodile Clip (Crumble Classic)	Headphone (Playground)	Notes
Battery Pack		Battery Pack is built in on the reverse side	Buy ones with an on/off switch
Geared Motors			Metal geared motors are more expensive but are more hard wearing as the gears last longer.
Light Dependent Resistor (Measure amount of light)			Hold them up to light source for a higher number input.
0-99 Number Counter			Used for outputting sensor information from distance, motion, LDR, slider or dials
Tilt Sensor X, Y, or Z			Tilt the device on X, Y or Z and it inputs a number that can be used in many ways.
Close Proximity Sensor			Detect an object between 3-4cm away.

E. Crumble Equipment and Software Stockists UK

Name	Notes	Contact Details
Redfern Electronics	Redfern Electronics created the Crumble and the Crumble software and sells Crumble Accessories	**Web** https://redfernelectronics.co.uk/ **Software Download** (Free) https://redfernelectronics.co.uk/crumble-software/ **Twitter** @RedfernElec
4Tronix	Makes the Crumble Playground and an extensive range of Crumble accessories	**Web** https://4tronix.co.uk/store/ **Twitter** @4tronix_uk

Both Redfern Electronics and 4tronix have been helpful over many years when addressing the authors questions and misconceptions and they are both examples of great British enterprises that seek to make a difference in education.

Please note that the author hasn't listed every available Crumble accessory as the list is continuously growing.

F, Buying Guide to Crumble & Accessories

Disclaimer

The author has never been paid by the manufacturers of the Crumble and Crumble Playground or by any of their associates.

Crumble V Crumble Playground

Crumble-Crumble Playground Combination

If you are going to use the Crumble with 5-9 year olds in a classroom situation then the Crumble attached to the Crumble Playground combination is an absolute must. The easy headphone connections and the built in battery pack make simple projects achievable. They are also really useful for less confident teachers of older pupils.

If you are only going to use the Crumble with older 9-11 year old pupils, then you could keep your costs down and go for the Classic Crumble.

Buttons, Motors & Lights

As to which accessories to buy, it is worth choosing your projects and starting from there. Those projects that are for 5-9 year olds will benefit from the easier headphone connections of the Crumble Playground. Projects that are for older pupils will benefit from the electrical circuit knowledge which crocodile clip accessories illuminate on the Classic Crumble.

4Tronix buzzer with power in and power pass through

Many of the Crumble Classic Crocodile Clip Accessories made by 4tronix have an extra power pass through which enables them to pass power on to other inputs and outputs. These can be very useful for more complicated projects. However, simple accessories such as this push button switch supplied by Redfern Electronics are much better for electrical understanding. The basic servo/stepper motor supplied by Redfern is also easier to use in DT projects as it can be easily mounted through cardboard.

Redfern Electronic simple push button switch

Spares

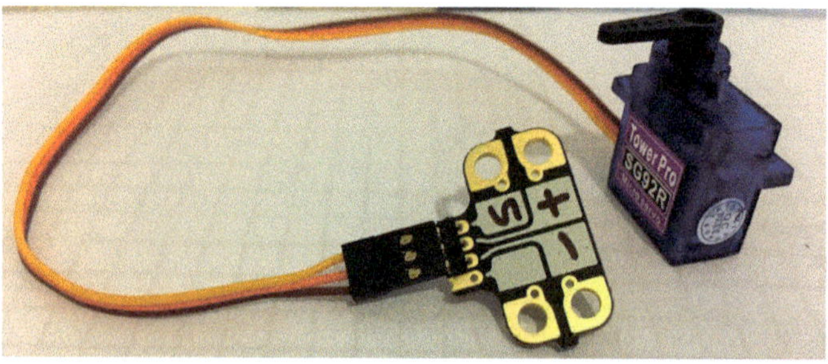

Servo motor supplied by Redfern Electronics

Spares are also essential. Despite good rugged design electronic components will fail, bulbs will blow and cables will lose their connections. Treating these as long lasting consumables will also help school managers to appreciate that some equipment will need to be replaced every year. On average my schools replace one full Crumble/Crumble Playground set every year which is good going.

Servo motor mounted through cardboard

G, Crumble and the English Computing and Design and Technology National Curriculums

Computing National Curriculum Key stage 1

Pupils should be taught to:

- **NCC1A** understand what algorithms are; how they are implemented as programs on digital devices; and that programs execute by following precise and unambiguous instructions
- **NCC1B** create and debug simple programs
- **NCC1C** use logical reasoning to predict the behaviour of simple programs

Computing National Curriculum Key Stage 2

Pupils should be taught to:

- **NCC2A** design, write and debug programs that accomplish specific goals, **including controlling** or simulating **physical systems**; solve problems by decomposing them into smaller parts
- **NCC2B** use sequence, selection, and repetition in programs; work with variables and various forms of input and output
- **NCC2C** use logical reasoning to explain how some simple algorithms work and to detect and correct errors in algorithms and programs

Design and Technology National Curriculum KS1

When designing and making, pupils should be taught to:

Design

- **NCD1A** design purposeful, functional, appealing products for themselves and other users based on design criteria
- **NCD1B** generate, develop, model and communicate their ideas through talking, drawing, templates, mock-ups and, where appropriate, information and communication technology

Make

- **NCD1C** select from and use a range of tools and equipment to perform practical tasks [for example, cutting, shaping, joining and finishing]
- **NCD1D** select from and use a wide range of materials and components, including construction materials, textiles and ingredients, according to their characteristics

There is nothing in the Computing National Curriculum that can't be covered through the Crumble controller.

However, it is important that pupils experience a variety of different programming genres and a balanced curriculum might also include opportunities to program games, music and maths projects with onscreen outputs.

Controlling physical systems is where the Crumble is superior to any other form of programming in the primary classroom.

The sense of achievement and excitement in designing, wiring and programming their creations and observing their output in lights, buzzers and motors can be very tangible in the classroom.

Evaluate

- **NCD1E** explore and evaluate a range of existing products
- **NCD1F** evaluate their ideas and products against design criteria

Technical knowledge

- **NCD1G** build structures, exploring how they can be made stronger, stiffer and more stable
- **NCD1H** explore and use mechanisms [for example, levers, sliders, wheels and axles], in their products.

Design and Technology National Curriculum KS2

When designing and making, pupils should be taught to:

In the rest of this document National Curriculum coverage will be referred to using the codes at the start of each statement

Design

- **NCD2A** use research and develop design criteria to inform the design of innovative, functional, appealing products that are fit for purpose, aimed at particular individuals or groups
- **NCD2B** generate, develop, model and communicate their ideas through discussion, annotated sketches, cross -sectional and exploded diagrams, prototypes, pattern pieces and computer-aided design

Make

- **NCD2C** select from and use a wider range of tools and equipment to perform practical tasks [for example, cutting, shaping, joining and finishing], accurately
- **NCD2D** select from and use a wider range of materials and components, including construction materials, textiles and ingredients, according to their functional properties and aesthetic qualities

Evaluate

- **NCD2E** evaluate their ideas and products against their own design criteria and consider the views of others to improve their work

Technical knowledge

- **NCD2F** understand and use mechanical systems in their products [for example, gears, pulleys, cams, levers and linkages]
- **NCD2G** understand and use electrical systems in their products [for example, series circuits incorporating switches, bulbs, buzzers and motors]
- **NCD2H** apply their understanding of computing to program, monitor and control their products.

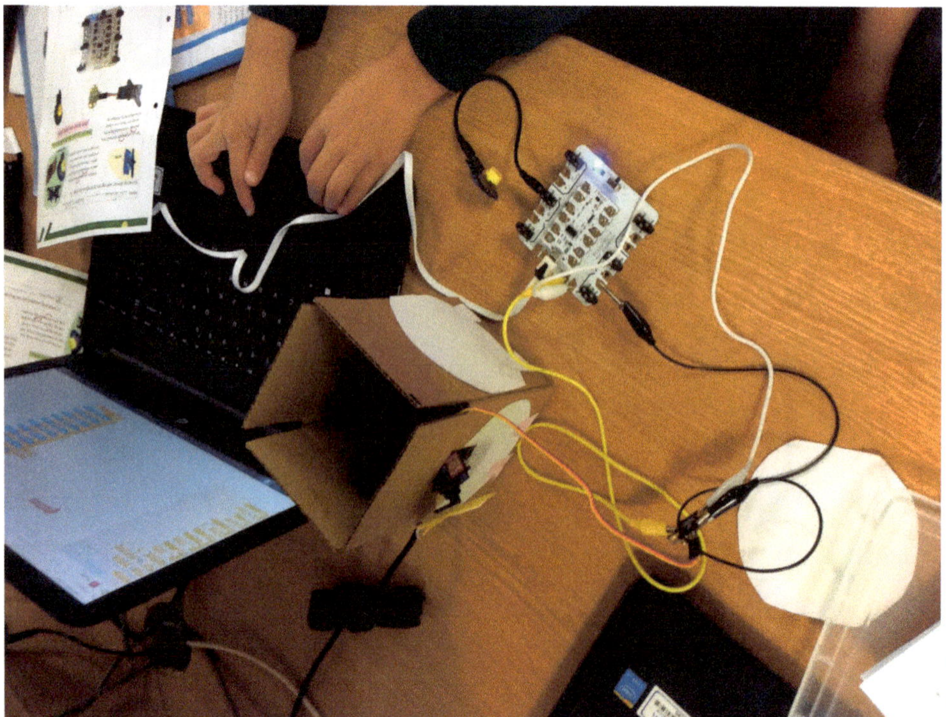

Whilst this book is aimed at the primary sector the later chapters could very easily be adapted and used with older pupils.

8-9 year old pupils programming an animated animal head using the Crumble Playground

H₁ Interaction between Computing & Design & Technology

The more complex and open ended the computing aspects, the more it is worth considering reducing the complexity or open ended nature of the DT and vice versa, **especially if time is constrained.**

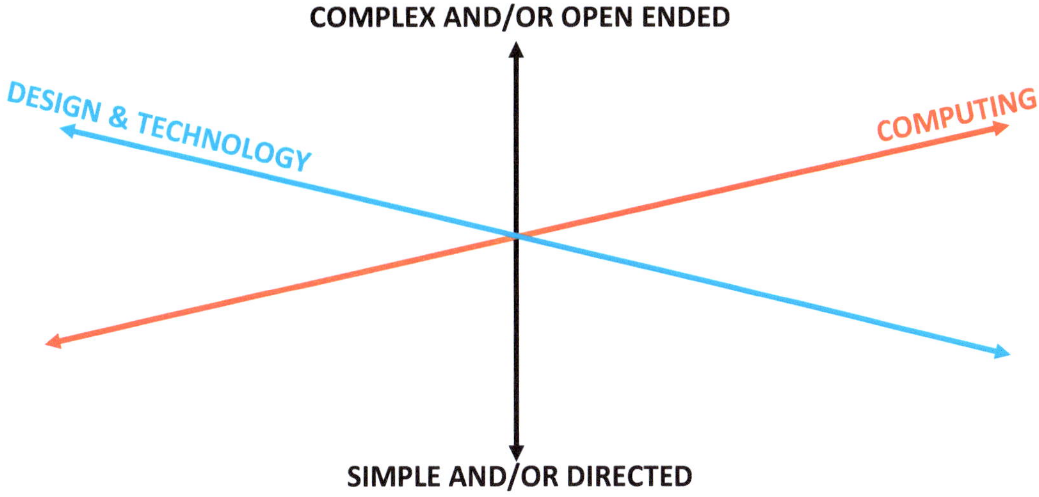

Linking to the National Curriculum

In every project the computing and possible DT national curriculum targets will be referenced using the codes written on the previous two pages.

Minimal Design & Technology

It is possible for every project apart from the robot challenges to be completed without any DT elements, although these would be the poorer for the absence of any DT element. It is also possible to provide a much greater focus for design and technology which may include much more complex mounts and housings for the electronics beyond the simple box ones suggested in this book. **Chapter 13** has a few extra planning templates to help teachers increase the design and technology element of any chapter if they so wish.

Chapter 11, the robot challenges, cannot be completed without a significant design and technology element. In this chapter the design and technology challenges and solutions are discussed in detail.

Year 6 pupils designing an automatic hypnotiser

1. Progression of Programming Skills

Programming Progression

Simple programs mainly sequence NCC1B NCC2A NCC2B

- Create a **nightlight** which is programmed to turn off after a set period of time
- Create a **flashing Christmas or Diwali** light that changes colour
- **Illuminate correct answers** in green and incorrect answers in red on a museum interactive display
- Light up different parts of a map or picture to go with an ordered description

```
program start
set sparkle 0 to [green]
wait 120 seconds
turn sparkle 0 off
```

Nightlight

```
program start
set sparkle 0 to [orange]
wait 1 seconds
set sparkle 0 to [green]
wait 1 seconds
set sparkle 0 to [yellow]
wait 1 seconds
set sparkle 0 to [light blue]
wait 1 seconds
set sparkle 0 to [purple]
wait 1 seconds
set sparkle 0 to [orange]
```

Flashing Christmas or Diwali light

```
program start
set sparkle 0 to [orange]
set sparkle 1 to [orange]
set sparkle 2 to [green]
wait 3 seconds
turn sparkle 0 off
turn sparkle 1 off
turn sparkle 2 off
```

Correct question

Programs that include simple sequence and repetition NCC2A NCC2B NCC2C

- Animate a part of a favourite **book character** to move (nodding head, wagging tail, waving arm, kicking leg)
- **Animate a part of a diorama** (moving flames on picture depicting the Great Fire of London)
- **Send an SOS from the Titanic** using a buzzer

```
program start
do forever
  servo A 0 degrees
  wait 1 seconds
  servo A 40 degrees
  wait 1 seconds
loop
```

Animate a book character

```
program start
do forever
  do 3 times
    set A HI
    wait 1 seconds
    set A LO
    wait 1 seconds
  loop
  do 3 times
    set A HI
    wait 2 seconds
    set A LO
    wait 2 seconds
  loop
  do 3 times
    set A HI
    wait 1 seconds
    set A LO
    wait 1 seconds
  loop
  wait 5 seconds
loop
```

Titanic SOS using a buzzer

Programs that include conditional selection NCC2A NCC2B NCC2C

- Any of the previous projects triggered by a button
- Crumble buggy/robot with push button steering
- Doorbell triggered by a button
- Human proximity detector triggered by a close proximity sensor

```
program start
do forever
  if C is HI then
    servo A 0 degrees
    wait 1 seconds
    servo A 40 degrees
    wait 1 seconds
  end if
loop
```

Animation triggered by a button

```
program start
do forever
  if A is HI then
    motor 1 FORWARD at 60 %
  else
    motor 1 REVERSE at 60 %
  end if
  if B is HI then
    motor 2 FORWARD at 60 %
  else
    motor 2 REVERSE at 60 %
  end if
loop
```

Crumble buggy steering

Programs that include variables

NCC2A NCC2B NCC2C

- Adjust the animation movement angle using a dial or slider
- Adjust the motor power on the buggy using a slider or dial
- Translucency meter

```
program start
do forever
  servo A 0 degrees
  wait 1 seconds
  let angle = analogue B
  servo A angle degrees
  wait 1 seconds
loop
```

Animation angle using a dial

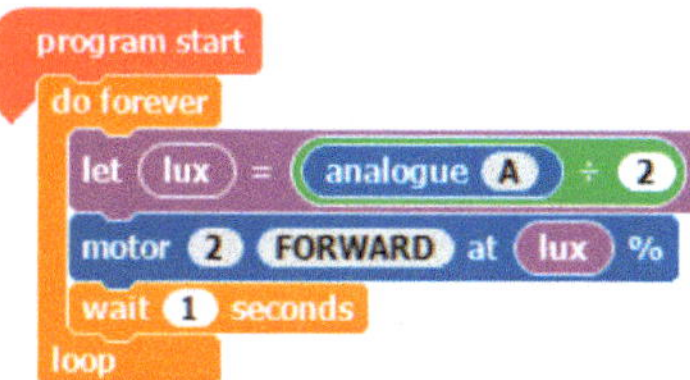

Light sensor which outputs to a number counter

J. Progression of Complexity and Independence

Many of the projects in this guide can be adjusted for complexity and independence. Complexity meaning the amount of inputs and outputs being used in the project, the difficulty of the programming and the amount of Design and Technology needed. Independence indicates the amount of choice pupils have in either adapting or choosing the project and/or choice over materials and design.

COMPLEX

Create an illuminated Christmas tree that is started by proximity to a PIR sensor or distance away from a distance sensor. Teacher chose the project ideas. Pupils choose the trigger device and materials to make the tree.

Triggering an output with a button. Pupils choose the overall theme of the project, the outputs which will be triggered and the DT framework the electronics will interact with.

Create three Christmas tree lights that flash in a child directed sequence. Teacher directs how to make the tree but children decide how to decorate it.

SIMPLE

Create a single flashing Christmas tree light using sequence only following teacher instruction.

GUIDED INDEPENDENT

In designing a curriculum we should seek to move pupils from simple to complex and from guided to independent. Teachers should note that the greater the independence, the longer the project will take.

K₁ An Examination of Teaching Methods Using the Crumble Block Based Programming Language

Programming Process

- What does the program need to do? **(Task)**
- What will the user see or do? **(User)**
- What inputs and outputs does it need to use? **(Inputs and outputs)**
- In what order does it need to do these things? **(Algorithm)**
- What part of the algorithm converts into which code? **(Algorithm to Code)**

Creating a good task, thinking about what the user will see and do as well as what each input or output will do, is all part of **decomposing** the program into parts and creating an **algorithm**.

Task

In the early chapters, the initial **task** is given by the teacher. However, there are extension opportunities in every chapter for pupils to adapt the project in order to make what they want based on what they have already made. These simple sentence scaffolds help those who struggle to create their own project idea.

- What will the program do? **My program will** ________________**by** ______________

My program will make the stars on my picture twinkle **by** replacing them with lights (Lights, Lights, Light).

My program will make the dog look alive **by** making its tail wag and making its eyes blink (Animated Animal).

My program will check if someone is in the corridor **by** detecting movement using a PIR sensor and turning a light red when it does (Maker Lab One).

User

Thinking about what the end user will see or do helps pupils to identify what they need to design, make and program. These are good questions to ask pupils and useful prompts as pupils' projects become more independent. If pupils are not sure, of their thinking then a sentence scaffold can help.

Asking the questions

- What will the user do? **The user will** __________________
- What will the user see? **The user will see the (object)** _______________ **(action)** _________

The user will turn the program on. **The user will see** the lights flashing on the picture. (Lights, Lights, Lights)

The user will see the dog wagging its tail and the light in its eye blinking (animated animal)

The user will start the program by turning on the battery pack.

Inputs & Outputs

Simple outputs are the most basic physical programming device. An output is something that is **put-out** from a digital device such as the Crumble. In most block based programming languages the main output is the screen. In Crumble programming, lights, buzzers and motors are the most basic outputs.

Inputs are things that **put-in** information into the digital device. In programming, if we asked the user to type into the program that would be a keyboard input. If we asked the user to tilt the tablet to control something, that would be a gyroscopic input. Buttons are our most used input device on the Crumble.

We can help pupils to understand inputs and outputs by encouraging them to list the inputs and outputs they are using in a table. As projects become more complex and independent, it becomes more important to design and document where everything goes and what it does. Every project asks pupils to think about what goes where.

Letter	Name of the device	Input or Output
A	Button	Input
C	Buzzer	Output

Example Input & Output Table

Algorithm Order

In many cases, thinking about the task provides enough information to program it. However, some projects need more thought around precise order. Planning a traffic light sequence is a good example of this as the precise order is very important for road safety.

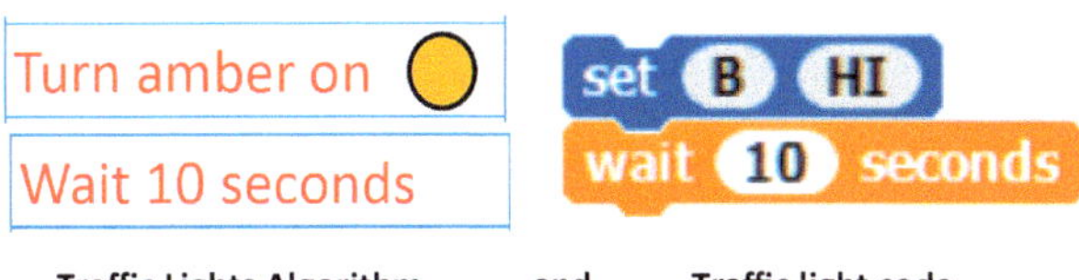

Traffic Lights Algorithm and **Traffic light code**

Scaffolding Methods for Algorithm to Code

Ultimately we are aiming for pupils to have programming agency; To be able to independently convert their ideas into code that works on the Crumble microcontroller. The Maker Lab chapters expect pupils to complete the whole process with much less support. The earlier chapters use a variety of scaffolding methods to help pupils who are new to programming and to support less confident teachers. Here are some of the scaffolding methods used, roughly graduated from more support to less.

Examples

The simplest way to support pupils is to show them what to do in order to give them a starting point that they can adapt and work with. Sometimes this can be a few blocks of simple code such as that used in Lights, Lights, Lights.

```
program start
set all sparkles to [red]
wait 1 seconds
set all sparkles to [green]
wait 1 seconds
set all sparkles to [orange]
wait 1 seconds
turn all sparkles off
```

Answering Questions About the Code Before Using or Adapting it

This is an adaptation of the examples method. Pupils are given the code and asked logical questions about it to enable a deeper connection between what processes it entails and what those processes do. Pupils may be allowed to experiment with the code whilst answering the questions or they can just work from the sheet. This may only be the first step before they need to adapt the code to meet further challenges more independently.

Starting with Similar Code that needs to be Adapted

In this method, the pupil is provided with similar code to that which they will ultimately need. They are then asked to adapt the code to make it do something similar. In this buggy steering example, pupils are given physical movement code before being asked to program a motor to go forward when a button is

```
program start
do forever
  if arm touched then
    turn right slowly
  else
    turn left slowly
  end if
loop
```

pressed and back when it is depressed. We can see that the code they will need shown on the right is very similar in both shape and logical construction.

```
program start
do forever
  if A is HI then
    motor 1 FORWARD at 75 %
  else
    motor 1 REVERSE at 75 %
  end if
loop
```

Motor 1 controlled by a button plugged into A

Recognising the same Process used in Another Block Based Programming Language

Pupils might also be asked to remember where similar code has been used in other block based programming languages such as Scratch. This is not a method included in this book as it depends on the varying programming experiences of pupils but a good teacher will help pupils to make these links.

Useful Blocks Scaffold

Providing pupils with a limited set of blocks can be a useful scaffolding method. The drawback to this method is that it tends to promote only one solution where there may be many that pupils might discover given time.

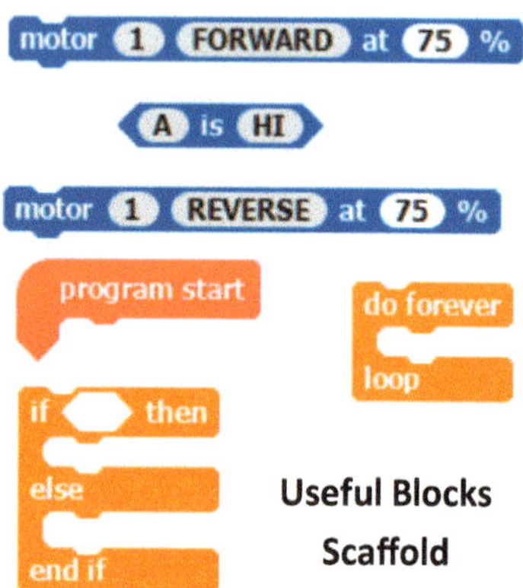

Useful Blocks Scaffold

Programming Role Play

Another method used in this book is to roleplay more complex programming examples. You can find examples of this method in the maker lab projects. The processes that pupils role play are rarely exactly the same as those they will need for their own project but they are a useful starting point.

Linking Algorithm to Code

Another method is to ask pupils to link code blocks to a well designed algorithm. This helps them to identify the connection between these two things and a possible order for the code. It is also a subtle way of reinforcing the importance of a well thought out algorithm.

Support Cards Method

All the support cards have examples of programming blocks that are useful to use with specific outputs or input devices. Puzzling out how to use these can be initially frustrating but ultimately very rewarding.

B is HI B is LO

HI means the button is pressed LO means de-pressed

wait until B is HI

Wait until the button attached to B is pressed down

```
if B is HI then
  ←
end if
```

If the button attached to B is pressed down (HI) then do something

Support Card Example

The Choice is Yours

If you and your pupils are very new to programming, some of the earlier scaffolding techniques outlined above will be exactly what you both need. However, do stretch your pupils by increasing the challenge as they become more competent. Remember you can always start with less scaffolding, keeping an easier scaffold in reserve for whoever needs it.

L₁ Electronic Assembly

All projects require some form of electronic assembly. These might be as simple as one wire going to a programmable light from a Crumble Playground and one wire going to the computer from the Playground to send the programs to the board. At the other end of the complexity scale pupils may have both motors wired and all four input/output connections used in the maker lab projects.

To PC
USB

Batteries must be switched on

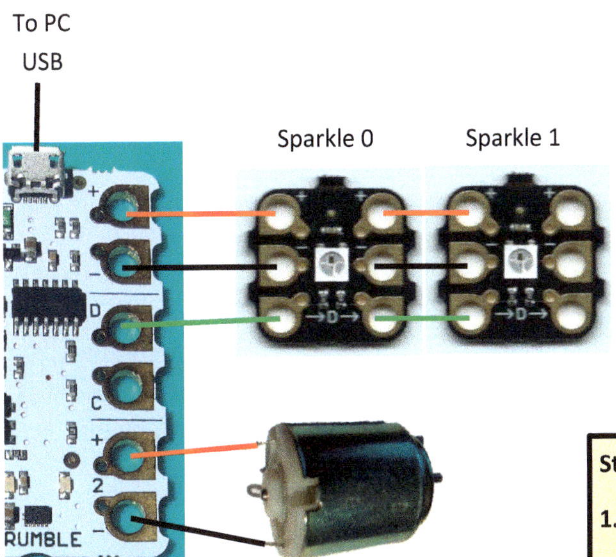

Half of the Classic Crumble wired up for a more complex project

Must be connected to D

Simple wiring Project

Steps to Wiring Independence	
1.	**Teacher wires device**
2.	**Teacher part wires and pupils add an output after being shown how**
3.	**Teacher models wiring then pupils copy**
4.	**Pupils use maker cards and teacher checks wiring before allowing programming**
5.	**Pupils use maker cards no teacher checks**

Steps 1-3 are more appropriate for younger pupils. Pupils from 7-11 should be working using steps 3-5.

Maker cards are a great way of encouraging independence. Pupils use these to work out the wiring order and blocks that are useful for programming their inputs or outputs. It helps to remind pupils to orient their Classic Crumble or Crumble Playground as shown in the card. If pupils have not covered enough science, they can believe that the colour of the lead is important rather than just a form of insulation. The colour of the leads make no difference but using a wide variety of different coloured wires aids pupils and teachers in spotting errors.

As a teacher, you will have an example wiring pattern for each project in this scheme that you can use to spot errors. When pupils have wired the Crumble incorrectly don't tell them exactly what they have done wrong, give them a hint and challenge them to find it themselves. Finding and fixing errors themselves is an important skill.

Wiring Sheets

It can really help pupils to puzzle out the wiring away from the computer. They can then take the completed sheet and use it as a guide. Most of the projects have wiring sheets to help pupils complete this vital stage correctly.

M, Computational Thinking & Doing

What is Computational Thinking Like?

Computational thinking is the ability to think about solving problems with a computer. This is like scientific thinking (how to use experimental methods) or mathematical thinking (using equations, logic, algebra and trigonometry) or historical thinking (using documentary evidence and cross-checking written sources). Although programming (or coding) is often talked about, it is the wider ability to use a variety of programming, analysis and modelling techniques that is important.

What Thinking Skills are Included?

A CAS working group included algorithmic thinking, evaluation, decomposition, abstraction and generalisation in their framework document[1]. These are specific thinking skills that have particular meanings for primary pupils and teachers. (Note that they are important for other areas of the curriculum too!)

Algorithmic Thinking

Algorithmic thinking is the ability to define a precise set of instructions or rules to achieve an outcome or solve a problem. A recipe can be an algorithm; musical notation can be an algorithm; instructional writing can be an algorithm. All working computer programs started life as human ideas that were expressed as algorithms in thoughts, words, symbols or flow charts. Programming is the challenge of turning precise ideas (algorithms) into code that can be read by a machine. When we define a precise set of instructions we save time as this algorithm can be reused to solve a problem over and over again and adapted (generalised) to solve similar problems.

Algorithmic Evaluation

Evaluation is how we look at algorithms and determine how useful they are, how adaptable, how efficient, how correct. There may be many algorithmic solutions to a problem; evaluation asks which one was best and why. Evaluation is also concerned with the people who use an algorithm. Did it solve their problem? Was it better on paper than in practice? Evaluation is also a very useful skill to extend into programming as well. Getting pupils to think about an end user in the design (algorithm) stage can help focus ideas.

Decomposition

Decomposition is the skill of breaking a complex problem up into smaller manageable chunks and solving these chunks separately. When controlling specific physical outputs such as buzzers, motors and lights and using physical inputs such as buttons and distance sensors, decomposition can often be separated into what each specific output does or what effect each specific input triggers. Pupils can also decompose a project by testing individual part of it work first before combining them at a later stage.

Abstraction

Abstraction is the skill of reducing complexity by hiding irrelevant detail and focussing on the most important element. This is a really useful computational skill as once the irrelevant detail has been stripped away computer scientists can focus on what really needs doing. Simple physical input and output projects such as those in this book don't lend themselves to complex abstraction. However, we can still start the process by asking pupils to prioritise parts of their projects.

1 Professor Paul Curzon, Mark Dorling, Thomas Ng, Dr Cynthia Selby & Dr John Woollard (2014) Developing computational thinking in the classroom: a framework http://community.computingatschool.org.uk/resources/2324 (second document link on right)

Generalisation

Generalisation is adapting a solution that solved one problem to solve another. Many of our early Crumble programming projects involve an input that constantly checks to see if it is activated (HI) or deactivated (LO). Pupils might encounter this idea and then adapt it to do many things.

A five second red light

```
program start
do forever
    if A is HI then
        set all sparkles to [red]
        wait 5.0 seconds
        turn all sparkles off
    end if
loop
```

A flashing light for 4 seconds

```
program start
do forever
    if A is HI then
        do 10 times
            set all sparkles to [red]
            wait 0.2 seconds
            set all sparkles to [yellow]
            wait 0.2 seconds
        loop
    end if
loop
```

A door bell

```
program start
do forever
    if A is HI then
        set B HI
    else
        set B LO
    end if
loop
```

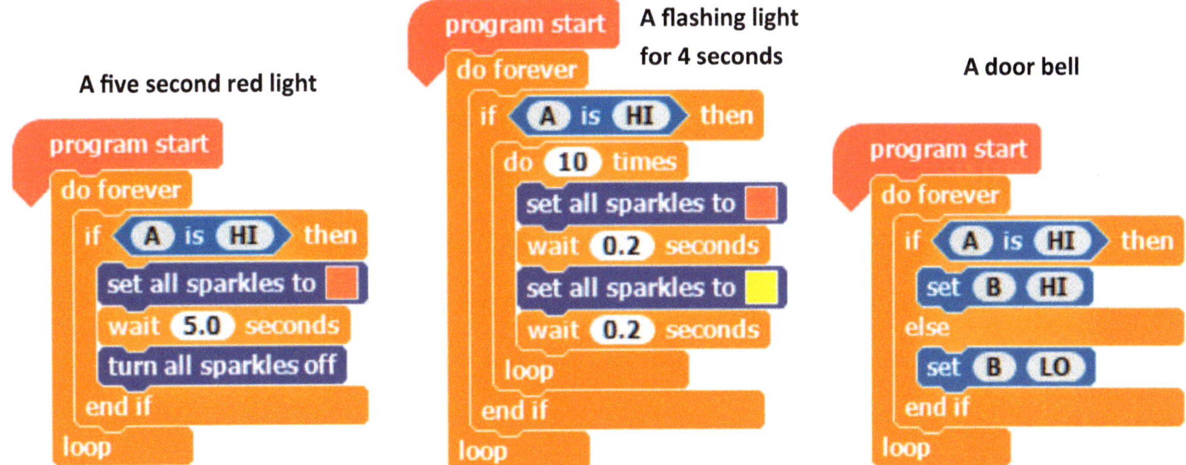

Computational Doing - Debugging and Resilience

Computing isn't just about thinking, it's also about doing. Learning to program means learning how to think about a problem, design an algorithm and then translate that algorithm into a form that the computer will understand. Like any creative process, it has lots of steps and many potential mis-steps. One of THE MOST IMPORTANT skills in programming is to be able to spot your errors, the wrong block, your logical errors and your wrong assumptions and to correct them. Debugging (so-called because of the story that errors in 1940s computer programs were caused by bugs and moths flying into the computers and short-circuiting the valves) is a learned skill of logical thinking and deduction. EB White (the author of Charlotte's Web) said that "writing is rewriting" – it's just as true that "programming is debugging".

Debugging in the English National Curriculum

Finding and fixing errors in algorithm and code is a key part of the computing curriculum. Pupils are exhorted to 'create and debug simple programs' in KS1 and 'detect and correct errors in algorithms and programs' in KS2. This emphasis on the importance of a process is in stark contrast to many pupils' experiences in ICT where the finished product was often seen as paramount. Debugging is an excellent way to promote independence, resilience and move pupils away from learnt helplessness.

Don't debug for pupils

Everywhere I teach I have seen teachers jump in and debug things for pupils. I think this often comes from the fear that something really has gone wrong, combined with too heavy a focus on the finished product over the process. If you do this you are denying your pupils essential problem solving experiences and the opportunity to develop resilience. When I first started teaching computing science, I had to train myself out of doing this. We need to facilitate pupils' debugging themselves by suggesting strategies and giving them time to find errors themselves. Make it clear that you or their peers debugging their code, fixing their algorithms or fixing their circuits is not an option. The sense of achievement when they find errors is tangible. On a technical note, we only debug code but I use the term when pupils are struggling with a wiring problem as well.

It is Normal to Make Mistakes in Programming

When I first started teaching programming a Y6 pupil in one of my classes burst into tears. When I enquired as to what was wrong, she informed me that she had never made a mistake in ICT before. Apart from the obvious horror at discovering a pupil who had gone through the whole of primary education without ever having been stretched enough in ICT to make a mistake, there is the need to reassure pupils that it is ok to make mistakes. I often find this can take quite a few weeks before pupils really believe me. As always they are judging to see if my words match up to my actions in the classroom. Once they realise that it is acceptable to make mistakes they take more risks and become better problem solvers.

Praise Debugging and Problem Solving

I save my highest praise for pupils who debug and problem solve. I reward their resilience and problem solving with perseverance stickers. On occasion, I have had younger pupils deliberately make and fix bugs just to get stickers but as long as the habit of debugging combined with the idea of personal responsibility to fix things themselves is ingrained I am happy.

Combatting Learnt Helplessness

In my experience learnt helplessness is particularly prevalent in Computing/ICT. Learnt helplessness is a strategy for getting other people to solve problems for you. In the classroom, for pupils, these others may be the teacher, LSA, teaching assistant or other pupils.

In computing/ICT learnt helplessness can be seen in various ways. Sweet helplessness often manifests to the teacher as a pupil putting on a sweet helpless voice and declaring they are stuck. Aggressive helplessness manifests with a cross tone and the implication that they think the work is 'stupid' or they don't get it. Being stuck is never a problem but if you ask what they are stuck on and the pupil cannot tell you or describe the problem or they give vague indications that they are stuck on everything then there is a good chance they are using learnt helplessness to get you to solve their problem. Similar strategies will often be used with their peers, tailored to make the problem solver feel valued, superior or pressured into helping.

The problem is that many teachers and pupils will respond to this strategy in Computing by solving the problem for the pupil. Often excellent teachers, who wouldn't dream of doing work for pupils in other areas of the curriculum, will jump in and solve the problem for the pupil. The fact that so many pupils use learnt helplessness suggests that it has been a successful strategy for many.

Getting someone else to do your work for you would be an issue in any subject, but it is the antithesis of computing science with its emphasis on problem solving and debugging. In fact, to solve a problem for a child is to deny them the opportunity to debug code or fix an algorithm and as such is debilitating.

How has it become so prevalent in computing/ICT? I suspect that it has grown out of teacher fear or unfamiliarity with the subject material, coupled with a belief that pupils know more about technology than adults, combined with an emphasis on the finished product rather than the process. All of these factors lead teachers to fix things for pupils rather than steer them to find solutions for themselves.

Steps to Counter Learned Helplessness

1, Establish a positive class attitude towards problem solving. Computing science is very useful in that it calls errors bugs and finding errors debugging. Although all bugs are caused by humans, the language is much more impersonal than mistakes which imply blame or fault. Using bug and debugging language is helpful. It is also important to let pupils know that mistakes/bugs are a normal part of computing, that they are to be expected, that professional programmers write code that have bugs all the time and that you will not be cross or upset if their work has bugs/ mistakes. This for me is a mantra for new classes for the first few weeks and once they know I mean it there is collective sigh of relief!

2, Promote the idea that it is not your job to fix their algorithms or debug their code. It is your job to promote useful strategies that they can use to fix things themselves and we will come onto those very soon. So when they come to you they know they are looking for strategies to find and fix things themselves.

3, Challenge pupils helplessness and expose it for what it is. I have asked pupils, 'are you trying to get me to fix your code?' 'Are you trying to get me to solve the problem for you?' In the same way that we couldn't move on until we recognised the issue, some pupils won't either. Of course good teachers do this tactfully and with regards to pupils known concerns but an element of challenge is inevitable to identify and tackle the problem.

4, Recruit your pupils to combat helplessness. Encourage the class to join you in this by putting a ban on doing things for other people. They can describe what to do but are not allowed to do it for them or give them a full solution to programming solutions. As you model this, they will reflect this attitude to their peers. Having a ban on touching anyone else's mouse, keyboard or touchscreen is a good start. I often compare this to writing in someone else's maths or literacy exercise book.

5, Move pupils away from language that personifies digital machines. "My computer hates me," is typical. Computers are deterministic which means that if all the inputs are the same you will always get the same output. Personification encourages pupils to think that an answer might not be available due to the capriciousness of the machine, an attitude that is anti-problem solving and frankly incorrect.

6, Don't neglect the other adults in the class, all your good work could be being undone by your LSA or teaching assistant. Train them to help using good strategies and hints rather than solutions. If you are providing training on the curriculum don't neglect your teaching assistants, they are important.

Finally, you may notice learnt helplessness in teachers and learning support assistants. Is it worth the hassle to challenge this? As a parent I know that my children don't do what I say but what I do. I lead mostly by example or lack of it as my wife will testify! This is just as true in the classroom or computer suite. Of course we need to be tactful and recognise the good practice of teachers and the excellent problem solving strategies in other curriculum areas, but if we don't identify the problem, nothing will change. I have found that talking about my own struggle to change has enabled others to do likewise.

N. Computational Attitudes

Whilst all computational thinking skills are concerned with problem solving, there exists a wider series of dispositions and attitudes that we want to inculcate in our students. Mark Dorling & Thomas Stephens have a very useful behaviour rubric that you can find at https://goo.gl/EbRdD9 the author has shortened this into the following primary attitudes and behaviours for younger pupils.

I recognise there is more than one way to solve/describe a problem

I don't just accept the first solution

I look for a range of solutions to the same problem

I look for how a project can be extended

Handles Ambiguity

Open Ended Problem Solver

I can evaluate my solutions against a set criteria

I can design criteria to evaluate my creations

I can break complex problems into parts

I can discover / concentrate on the most important part of a problem

Evaluates

I can contribute useful ideas to a partner or group

Copes with Complexity

I can identify patterns in problems and solutions

Computing Problem Solver

I can encourage others to share their ideas

I can adapt existing ideas to solve new problems

Adapts

Communicates

I can develop, test and debug until a product is refined

I lead using all the people talent in my group

Investigates

I learn from setbacks and don't let them put me off

I make predictions about what will happen

Perseveres

I can persevere even if the solution is not obvious

I repeatedly experiment through predicting, making, testing & debugging

This book will seek to reference these problem solving skills both in the planning and in the assessment process.

There are also problem solving stickers that can be printed out onto A4 sheets of stickers sheets and given to pupils as they demonstrate these behaviours.

Complexity	I can break complex problems into parts **(De)**	I can discover / concentrate on the most important part of a problem **(Ab)**	I can explain how I used decomposition & abstraction **(De Ab)**
Ambiguity	I recognise there is more than one way to solve a problem **(AE A)**	I recognise there is more than one way to describe a problem **(AE A)**	I can explain how I managed ambiguity **(AE A)**
Open Ended	I look for a range of solution to the same problem **(AE A)**	I don't just accept the first solution **(AE A)**	I can describe how a**(AE A)** project can be extended
Adapt	I can adapt existing ideas to solve new problems **(Ge)**	I can identify patterns in problems & solutions **(Ge)**	I can explain how I adapted a solution to solve a new problem **(Ge)**
Evaluate	I can evaluate my solutions against a set criteria **(AE)**	I can design criteria to evaluate my creations **(AE)**	I can explain how evaluation helped me improve a project **(AE)**
Experiment & Debug	I can develop, test and debug until a product is refined	I repeatedly experiment through making, testing & debugging	I can explain how using the iterative cycle improves my work
Persistence	I can persevere even if the solution is not obvious	I learn from setbacks and don't let them put me off	I can describe how I overcame problems
Communicate	I can contribute useful ideas to a partner or group	I can encourage others to share their ideas	I can lead using all the people talent in my group
(De)composition (Ab)straction (Ge)neralisation Algorithmic Evaluation(AE) (A)lgorithm			

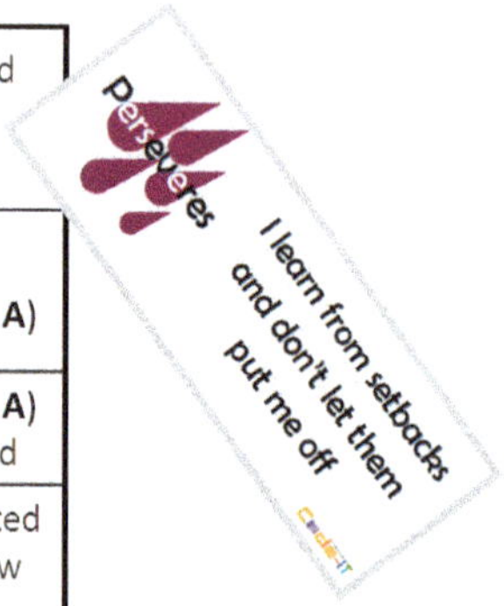

Perseveres

I learn from setbacks and don't let them put me off

In this diagram we can see the relationship between computational thinking and these problem solving skills.

O. Assessment

Quality formative assessment is one of the principle pillars on which great teaching and learning rests. It is important to identify points of development within the lesson for children and identify who is on task but not finished yet, who is genuinely stuck (not being helpless) and needs a corrective activity to clarify or re-focus and who needs an enrichment activity to stretch their thinking within the bounds of the subject under study.

As each project has a massive possible age range, depending on the technology chosen, it is not possible to provide every detailed formative assessment identifier and corresponding corrective and enhancing activity but each project will provide some examples to help teachers grow in this vital area.

Self Assessment and Summative Assessment

Each project has pupil self assessment forms to complete at the end of the project and places to stick in problem solving stickers gained throughout the project and to record how these were gained. These self assessment criteria will reflect specific attainment tasks as well as problem solving skills.

P. Scratch and Crumble Compared

The Crumble programming language was heavily influenced by Scratch. It uses the same drag and snap together block design and loops expand to fit more or less code. This makes it very easy to believe that pupils will quickly be writing programs of the same complexity on the Crumble as they do using Scratch. Whilst pupils with prior programming experience using block based languages are at a significant advantage there are significant differences which need to be understood.

Firstly, many Scratch blocks need less interpretation than Crumble code. Read this Scratch code to move a sprite forward or backwards depending on if it is touching the colour red.

Forever if touching colour red move 1 step else move -1 step.

A basic reader can make sense of the code up until the word Else and many will be able to puzzle out the second part of the programming by testing it on the screen.,

Compare this to simple code that switches a buzzer on or off using a button on the Crumble.

Do Forever if A is HI set B HI Else set B LO.

The Crumble user needs more than literacy decoding as soon as they encounter A. What is A? They need to know what is plugged into A and what is plugged into B. They also need to know that HI means pressed down for a push button and LO means de-pressed. For a buzzer HI means creating a sound and LO means quiet.

Scratch programming allows pupils to naturally decompose their program using multiple starting blocks, they can spread code out having a section for moving and another for steering, in for example a simple game. This might not lead to the most efficient code but it does allow for ideas to be broken up and for code sections to be tested separately. Crumble coding only allows one starting block, code has to be more efficient and it has to make all elements work together.

Crumble projects require pupils to cope with multiple disciplines and make these work together. Project design, electronic wiring, programming and on occasions engineering and art are some of the most common. By contrast screen only Scratch projects often need project design and programming skills.

Conversely Scratch projects have a much wider range of programming blocks whilst the Crumble is limited to four standard input/outputs A-D and two motor connections. Ultimately screen based Scratch will stretch pupils programming understanding much more than the Crumble but the multi disciplinary Crumble projects develops a better multi disciplinary 'engineering' approach.

If we take programming complexity to progress from sequence, repetition, selection through into variables, it is often worth removing one layer of complexity than pupils have achieved in screen based programming to allow for the complexity of including more disciplines. So a pupil in Year Five who might be proficient is sequence, loops and simple selection and variables, would benefit from projects that didn't include variable use.

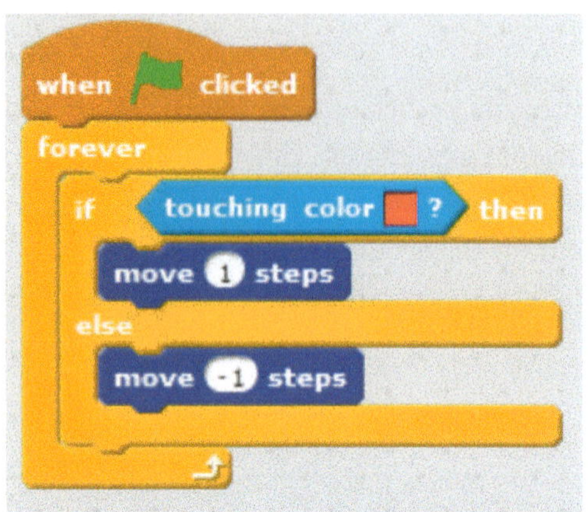

Scratch code to make a sprite move forward or backwards depending on if it is touching the colour red

Compare these two code examples

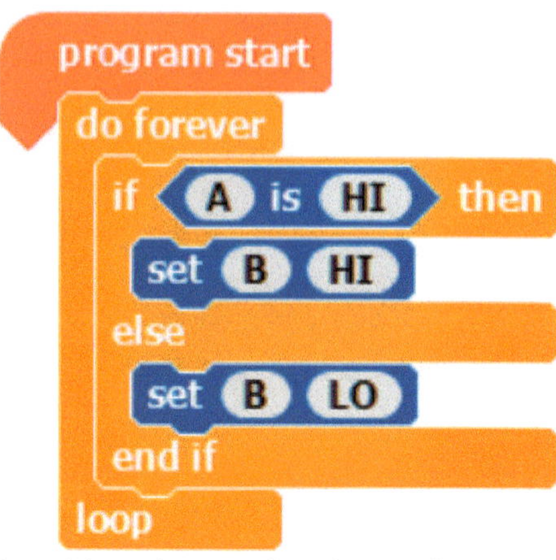

Crumble code to make a buzzer (attached to B) buzz if the button (attached to A) is pressed down (HI)

Q. Programming Project Overview at a Glance

	Sequence	Repetition	Selection	Variables
Lights Younger	Green			
Lights Older	Green	Green		
Night Light Younger	Green			
Night Light Older	Green	Green	Green	
Door Bell	Green	Green	Green	
Animated Animal Younger	Green	Green		
Animated Animal Older	Green	Green	Green	
Traffic Lights without Extension activities	Green			
Traffic Lights with Extension activities	Green	Green	Orange	
Easy Buggy	Green	Green		
Easy Buggy with Steering	Green	Green	Green	
Quiz Buzzer	Green	Green	Green	
Translucency Meter	Green	Green	Green	Green
Maker Lab One	Green	Green	Green	
Robot Challenges	Green	Green	Green	Orange
Maker Lab Two	Green	Green	Green	Green

Green = Used Orange = Could be used but not essential

2. Lights, Lights, Lights

Module Aim

Add lights to a pupil created picture.

Curriculum Links

Literacy & Art Think of a light or lights in a story. Pupils draw the picture which includes the light. Then a real light is projected through the page and programmed to flash, change colour or go on and off. A picture of the worst witches cat could have its eyes light up. A dark night scene where the moon or stars shines could twinkle with real lights. Any picture with a car could have the headlights illuminate and the indicators flash orange. Pictures with fireworks can program the lights to briefly illuminate before changing colours. Better programming experiences come from the possibility of different colours or flashing lights.

Construction

Pupils of ages 5-7 cope well with the Crumble Playground and Flame lights as shown on the right.

Small holes the size of the bulb can be poked through the picture to allow the light through. Although many pictures look really good with the lights shining through the page. This gives a more diffused light such as in fog or mist. It also reduces the complexity of the project which can be useful for younger pupils.

The lights can be taped onto the back of the paper with masking tape which makes them easy to remove and re-use.

Stars twinkling in the night sky, Crumble Playground and Flame lights

If the school has purchased the short headphone type cables, then care needs to be taken that the distance between lights is not too wide for the cable length. 15cm-20cm is a good maximum length for the short headphone cables.

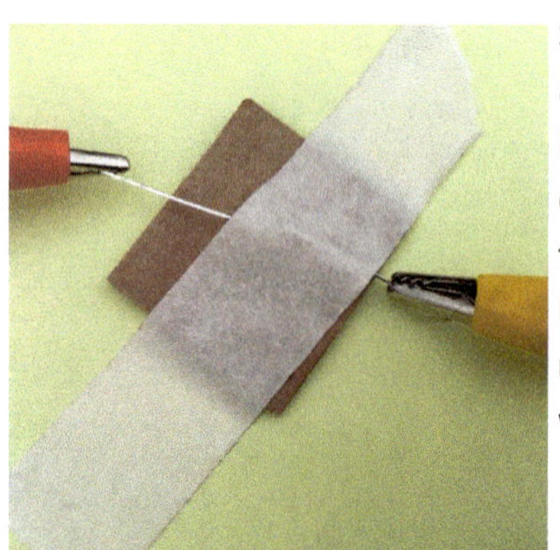

LED lights on back of picture

Smaller holes can be punched where they are needed on the picture. If using LED lights, It is worth cutting out small squares of cardboard and boring holes in these so that the LED bulb can be fitted securely. Doing this helps the bulbs sit well and reduces the chance of damage to the LEDs when pupils are wiring them.

LED set in a cardboard mount

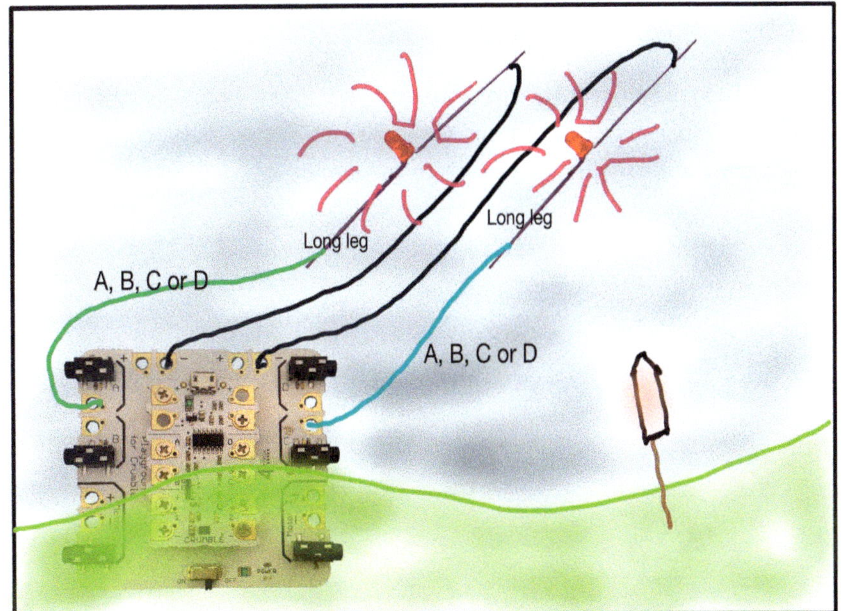

Fireworks picture using LED lights and Crumble Playground

If using crocodile clips, pupils often pull the crocodile sheath away from the metal so they can get a better grip on the clip. Unfortunately this can leads to wires touching and shorting. A pencil can be a great way of getting the plastic sheath back on.

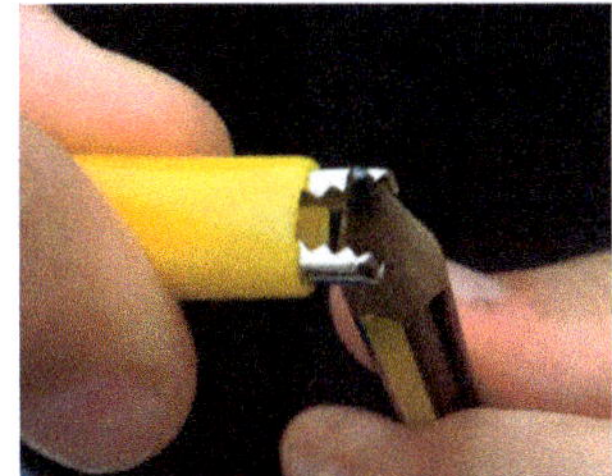

Putting the plastic sheath back on

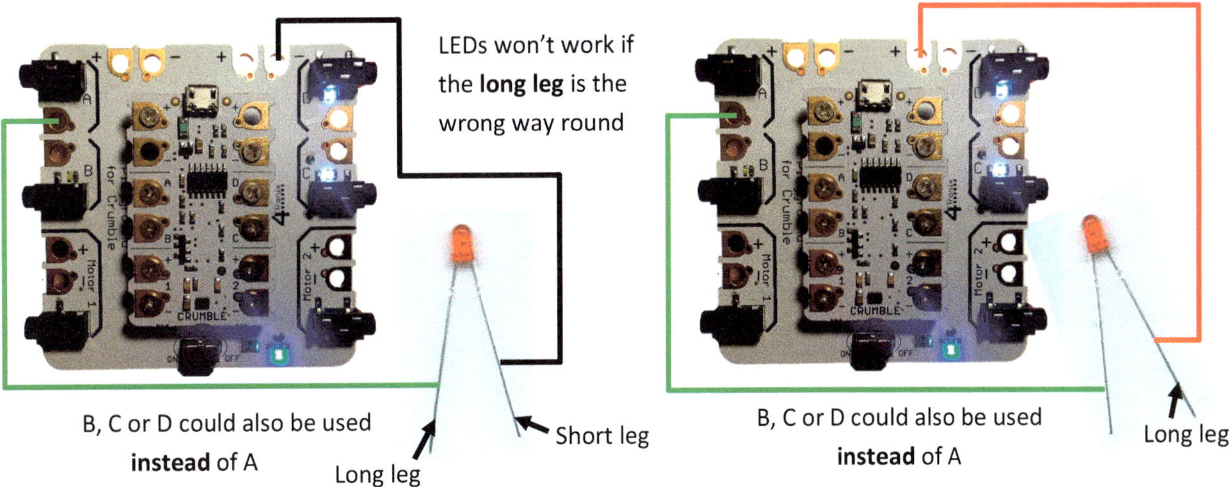

LEDs can be wired to negative or positive power out but the long LED leg must be swapped over. It doesn't harm the LED if it is wired the wrong way round, it just won't light up.

Users could also wire one leg of the Classic Crumble through the extra power outputs found on the Redfern Electronic or 4tronix power pack as shown in the diagram opposite.

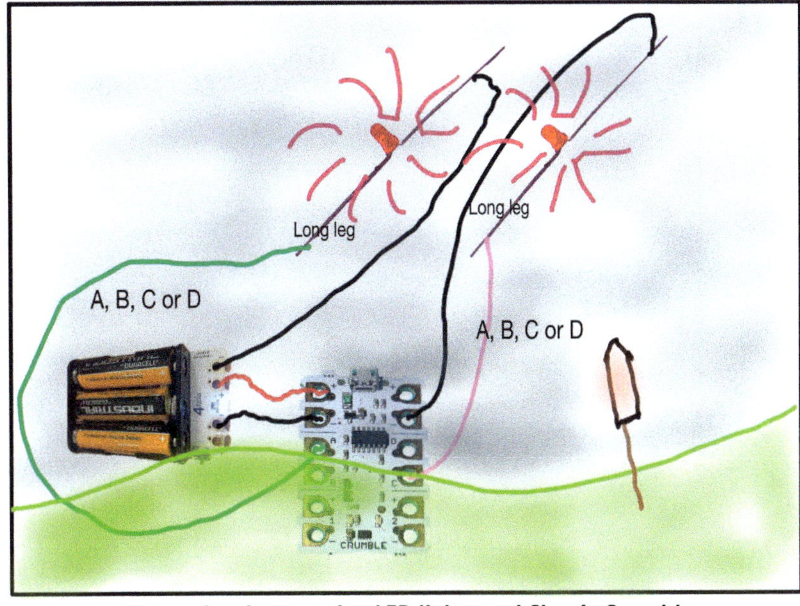

Fireworks picture using LED lights and Classic Crumble

Programmable Light Complexity

For a slightly harder challenge you might choose to use the crumble control board and original sparkles wired with crocodile clips. This is easily the cheapest option which might allow pupils to use more than two lights, leading to larger more exciting projects such as a Christmas tree picture or light up letter.

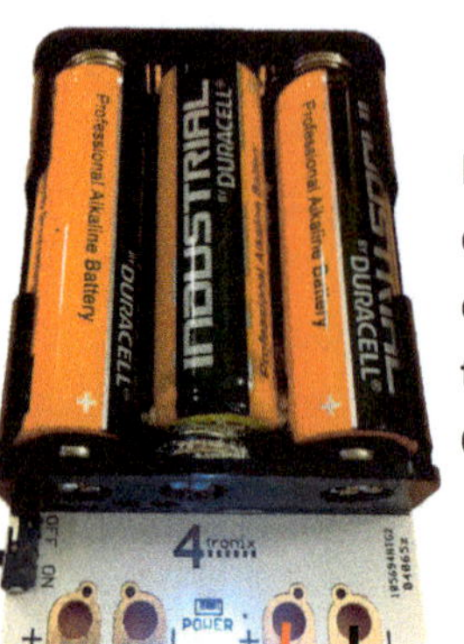

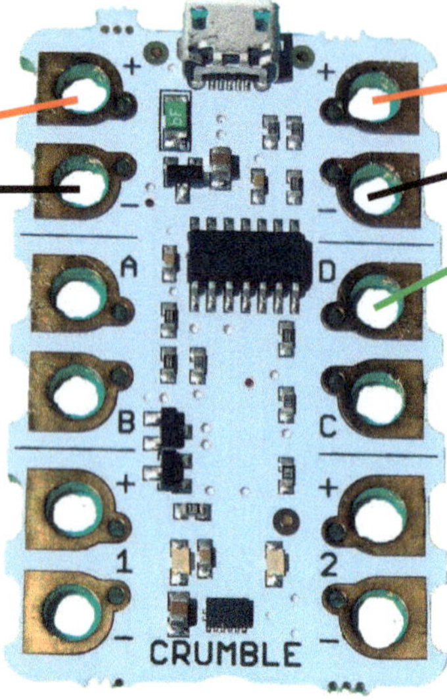

Complexity

Complex

Simple

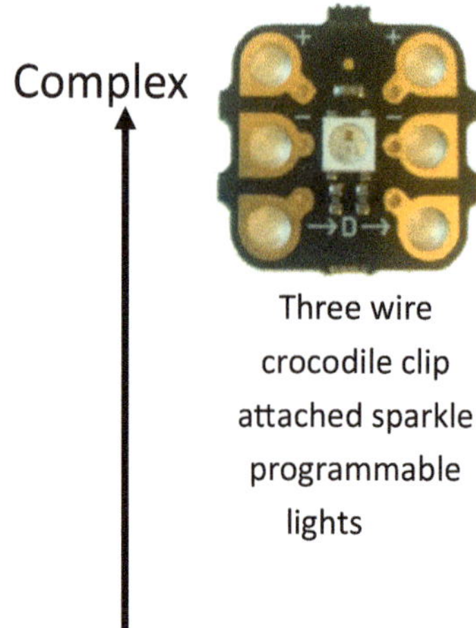

Three wire crocodile clip attached sparkle programmable lights

One wire attached flame programmable lights

Wiring

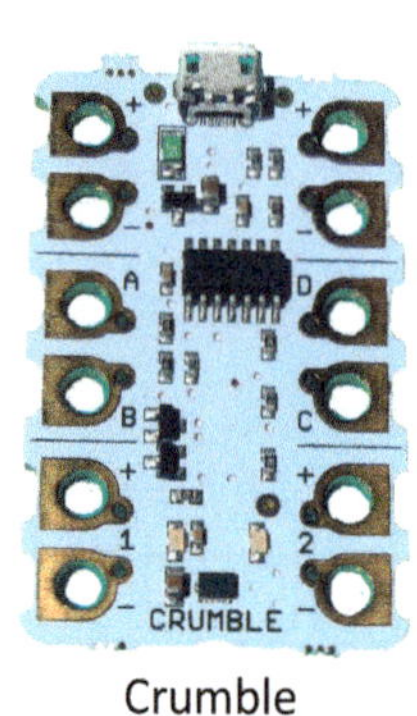

Crumble

Crumble playground

Device

Many lights

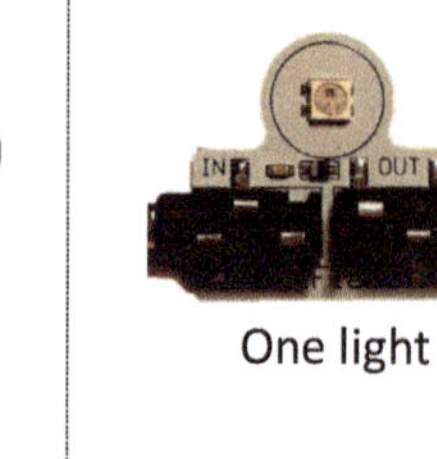

One light

One or Many

Programmable with any colour

One colour

Colour Range

Design

Younger pupils could tell their teacher what picture they would draw and what the light or lights would be and where they would be on their picture. Older pupils could sketch an outline of their picture, showing where the components would be and which connections they would use on the Crumble. Teachers might also choose to forego formal design as this is a very simple idea.

Picture Design

Teachers might choose artistic materials and techniques that fit in with the Art National Curriculum to make the most of the artistic benefits of the project.

Candle created by a 6-7 year old pupil

Useful Maker Card

MC01	**MC09**	**MC10**	**MC11**
MC43	**MC44**	**MC49**	

National Curriculum Coverage

NNC1A	**NCC1B**	**NCC1C**	**NCC2A**	**NCC2B**
NCC2C	**NCD1A**	**NCD2H**		

Suggested Module Outline for Younger Pupils

1, Introduce the idea

Introduce the idea of making a light to shine through a picture. Demonstrate how this might look with a picture you have created.

Necklace created by Year 2 pupil

2, Create a picture

Pupils create a picture and teachers ask them to point out where their light will go.

3, Plan the wiring

Show pupils how to wire up their Crumble Playground and Flame as shown in earlier pages. You may want to do this step by step together or you may want them to use the maker card and get pupils to fill in sheet LL1 first. The second method will aid future independence.

4, Pupil Wire up the Crumble

If pupils have used sheet LL1 they can put their equipment on the sheet when wiring it.

5, Check the wiring

Check pupils wiring and give hints if it is incorrect. Common errors are the flame wired into **out** instead of **in,** plugged into A, B or C instead of D & plugs not pushed all the way in and the battery not switched on.

6, Programming

Demonstrate how to attach the Crumble to a computer via a USB port. Drag out the program start block. Explain that these are like the Scratch starting blocks but that in a Crumble program we can only use one of them for the whole program. Then drag out the *'set all sparkles to red'* block and snap it to the program start. Point out the little arrow that appears when blocks are about to be connected. Explain that as you press the green triangle the program goes to the Crumble board and now sits inside the black chip waiting for the battery to be switched on to trigger the instructions.

Start the program by switching on the battery and switch it off by switching off the battery.

Demonstrate dragging out another colour block and changing the colour by left clicking inside the colour box, select a new colour and click on ok. Make sure you include a wait command and mime waiting. Now give them time to experiment with their light before creating their picture program.

7, Positioning lights behind the picture

Pupils use masking tape to place their lights onto the back of their pictures to test them. If younger pupils are only using one light then just positioning the picture is often enough.

Picture created by a year 4 pupil

8, Summative assessment

Give pupils time to complete the summative assessment sheet LL7 found at the end of the chapter.

Adaptations for Extending Lights, Lights, Lights With Older Pupils

- Pupils can cut out a **Christmas Tree** shape from rigid card, punch holes where the lights will go and tape the lights to the back. Pupils can experiment with trying to program different light patterns such as all flashing or the lights following each other. This works best with the programmable lights.
- **Diwali Light Pattern**. Pupils look up Diwali lights on Google Images and look for the type of patterns that people make. They then design their own and cut out the holes to show where the lights will go. They either use black card to represent the night or paint the backdrop black. The lights could be combined with Rangoli sand decorations. This works best with the programmable lights.

Picture created by a year 4 pupil

- **Name or initial in lights**. Pupils investigate the least number of lights needed to create their name or initials. They draw this out on card before punching holes for the lights. This works best with the programmable lights.
- **Pupils own ideas** around a teacher inspired theme such as lights in the night or around a book recently read such as the *The Firework Maker's Daughter*.
- **Wearable tech**, Pupils might even want to sew lights onto material using conductive thread. This works better with the original sparkles and crumble as pupils can loop their thread through the crocodile clip holes.

Suggested Module Outline For Older Pupils Using More Than One light

1, Introduce the Idea

Introduce the idea of making lights shine through a picture. Demonstrate how this might look with a picture you have created.

2, Draw a picture which includes lights

Pupils create a picture teachers ask them to point out where their lights will go.

3, Pupils plan the wiring

There are different plans to choose from to help pupils plan their wiring, depending on which equipment you have chosen.

LL2 Crumble playground with two flame lights

LL3 Crumble playground with two original sparkle lights

LL4 Crumble playground with two LED lights

LL5 Classic Crumble with two LED lights

LL6 Classic Crumble with two original sparkle lights

There are answer sheets to go with each version.

Sparkle showing the correct direction from the board

Give pupils the maker cards and equipment and let them follow the instructions to wire it up. Give hints rather than direct reasons why things don't work. Point to parts of the card or get them to check in and out etc. Common errors are the flame wired into **out** instead of **in** or the sparkles not following the arrows in on the light**,** plugged into A, B or C instead of D, headphone plugs not pushed all the way in and more than one program start block.

4, Programming

Demonstrate how to attach the Crumble to a computer via the USB wire and drag out the code on the right. Send it to the Crumble using the green triangle. Explain that the program is now inside the black chip on the Crumble. We can start the program by switching on the battery and switch it off by switching off the battery.

If using Sparkles /Flames

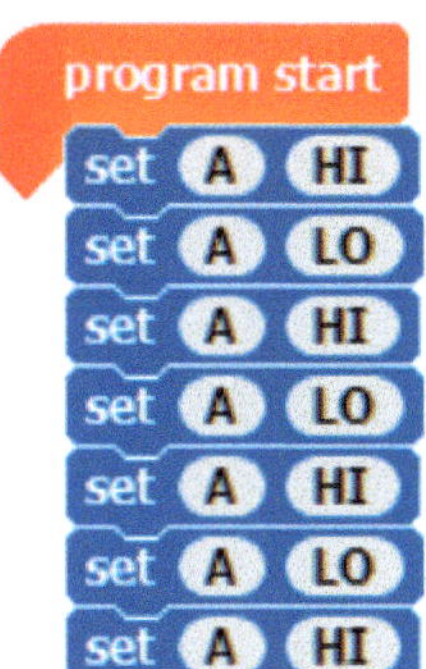

If using LED attached to output A

wait 1 second

Ask pupils what they think the code will do? Run the code. Pupils will observe that only the last colour lights up or with the LED the light goes straight on and stops. This happens because there is no instruction to wait between lights. Ask them why they think this happens. Let them investigate why and drag out a wait 1 second as a hint if no one gets it.

5, Programming the lights in the picture

Now give them time to experiment with the lights before creating their picture program.

wait 100 milliseconds

Depending on pupil ability and the nature of the project, you may want to drag out the wait 100 milliseconds block and explain how instead of using decimal fractions of a second (latest version of Crumble software now allows decimal fractions of a second) they could use milliseconds.

6, Adding lights to their picture

Pupils use masking tape to attach their lights onto the back of their pictures to test and display them.

7, Repeating light sequences

Introduce pupils to the concept of repeat loops. A simple physical activity that pupils have to repeat because they are inside a do forever loop works well such as standing and sitting. Demonstrate this simply using the Crumble software before allowing them time to investigate how they can use this in their work. The most common error when using repeat loops is that the wait so many seconds blocks is missing from the last wait block, as shown on the bottom right picture which would only show red.

```
program start
do forever
    set all sparkles to [orange]
    wait 1.0 seconds
    set all sparkles to [red]
    wait 1.0 seconds
loop
```

```
program start
do forever
    set all sparkles to [orange]
    wait 1.0 seconds
    set all sparkles to [red]
loop
```

8, Assessment

This will depend on the age of the child and the complexity of the projects (number of lights, what the lights did etc) The teacher and pupil would be looking for a number of problem solving skills as well as computing, DT and Art outcomes. These are listed in the project assessment sheet LL7. Teachers would then use this knowledge coupled with their knowledge of the child to determine if they are operating above, within or below age expectations.

9, Design your own lights program

Sheets LL8 & LL9 are available to help pupils think through and design their own lights programming project. Sentence scaffolds mentioned in the introduction on page 13 can be useful if pupils are struggling to think this through independently.

Problem Solving Skills Used in This Project

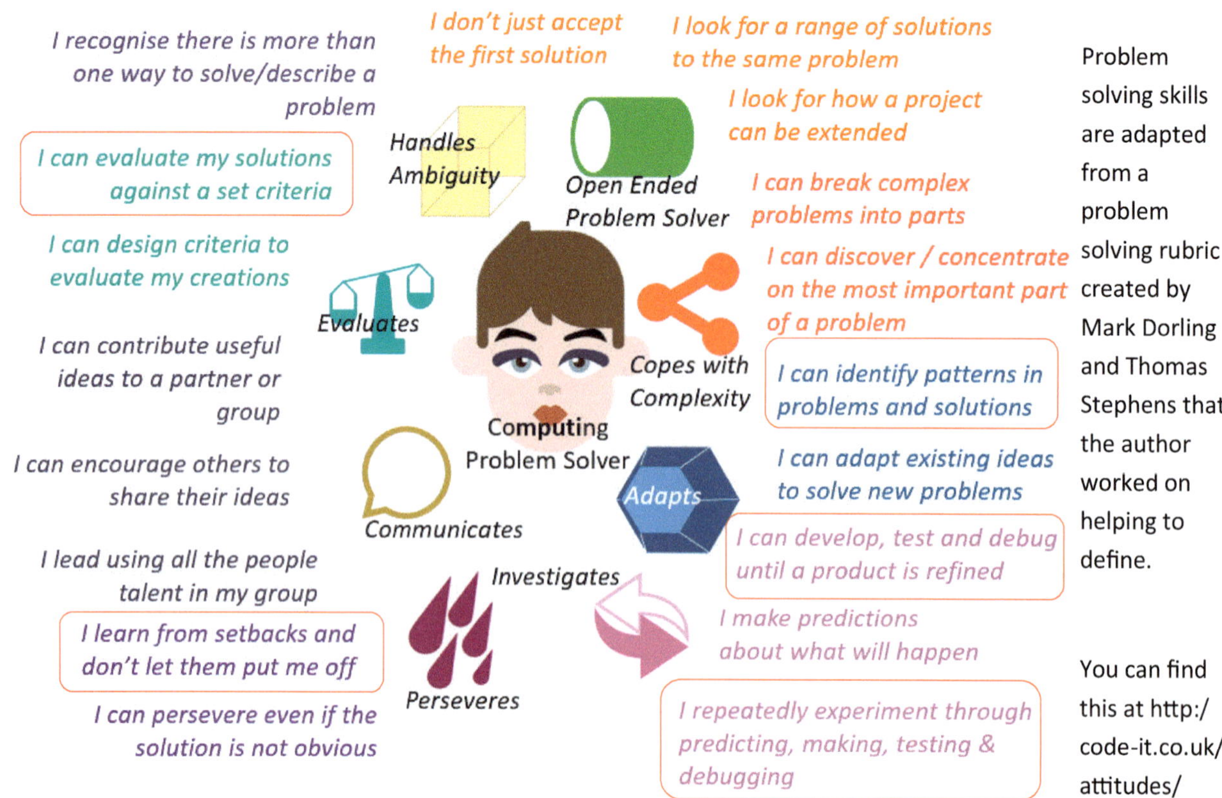
I recognise there is more than one way to solve/describe a problem
I don't just accept the first solution
I look for a range of solutions to the same problem
I look for how a project can be extended
Handles Ambiguity
Open Ended Problem Solver
I can evaluate my solutions against a set criteria
I can break complex problems into parts
I can design criteria to evaluate my creations
I can discover / concentrate on the most important part of a problem
Evaluates
I can contribute useful ideas to a partner or group
Copes with Complexity
I can identify patterns in problems and solutions
Computing Problem Solver
I can encourage others to share their ideas
I can adapt existing ideas to solve new problems
Adapts
Communicates
I can develop, test and debug until a product is refined
I lead using all the people talent in my group
Investigates
I learn from setbacks and don't let them put me off
I make predictions about what will happen
Perseveres
I can persevere even if the solution is not obvious
I repeatedly experiment through predicting, making, testing & debugging

Problem solving skills are adapted from a problem solving rubric created by Mark Dorling and Thomas Stephens that the author worked on helping to define.

You can find this at http:/ code-it.co.uk/ attitudes/

Lights, Lights, Lights Assessment Sheet LL7 Name Class

☺ I did this well

😐 I did this ok or I did this a little

☹ I tried this but it didn't work or I didn't do this at all

I created a picture that has lights in it.	
I drew a picture to show how my wiring connects together.	
I wired up my lights correctly.	
I replaced my picture lights with real lights.	
I programmed my lights.	
I listened to my partner's ideas.	
I contributed a good idea to my partner or group.	
I persevered when the wiring or programming didn't work.	

Sticker	I got this sticker for
Sticker	I got this sticker for
Sticker	I got this sticker for

Name ____________________________ Class ____________

Thinking about wiring my crumble LL1

Draw lines to join the computer, crumble and light
Use the maker card to help you

Computer

Light

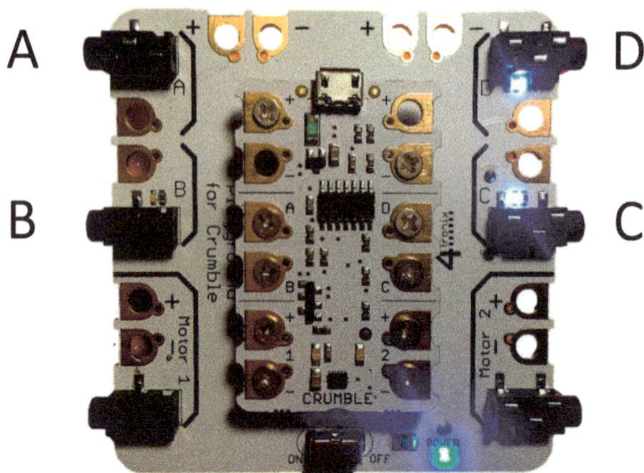

Power Switch

Crumble

Name ______________________________ Class _____________

Thinking about wiring my crumble LL1A

Draw lines to join the computer, crumble and light

Use the maker card to help you

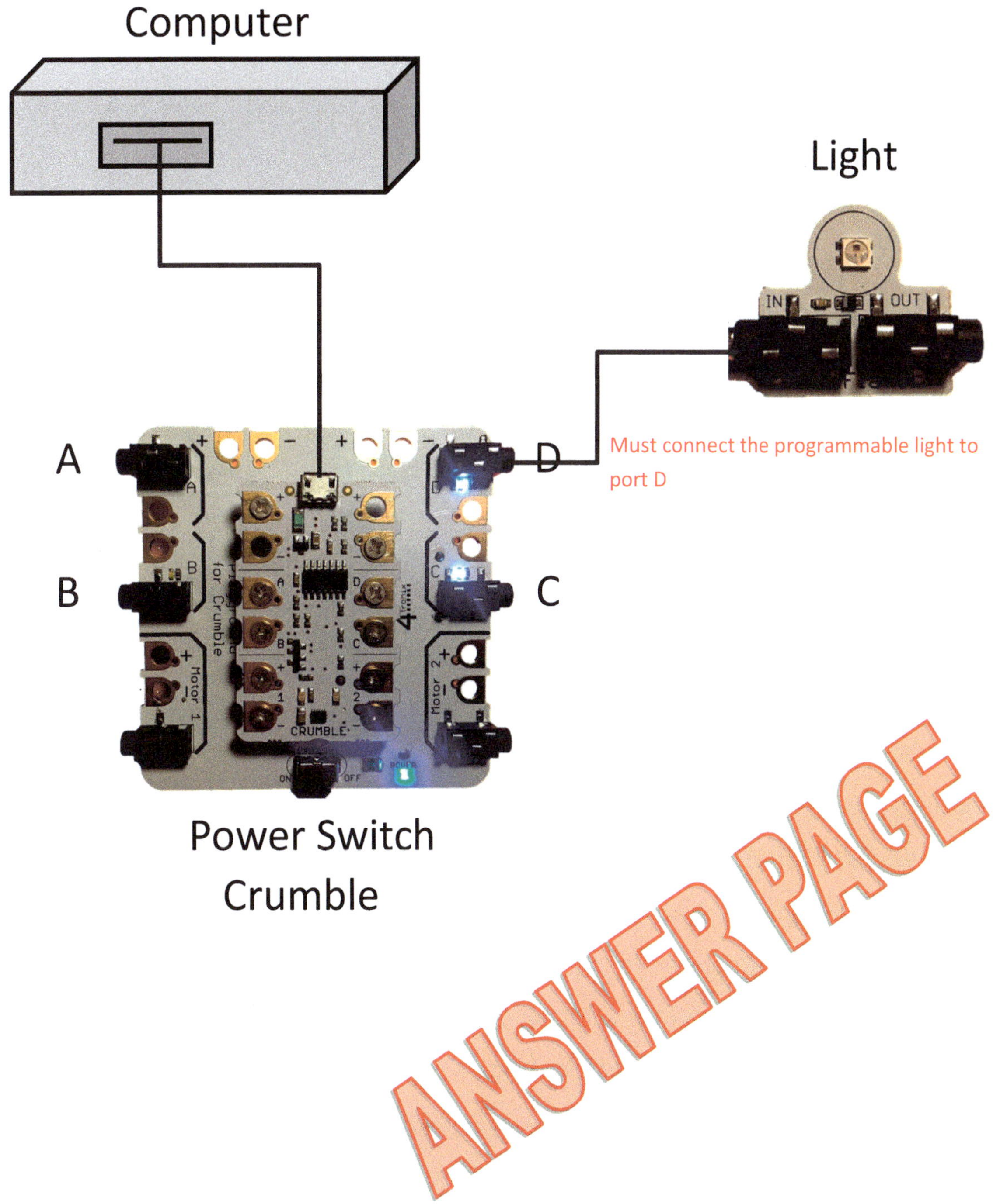

Name ______________________ Class __________

Thinking about wiring my crumble LL2

Draw lines to join the computer, crumble and lights
Use the maker card to help you

Computer

Second Light

Called Sparkle 1

First Light

Called Sparkle 0

Power Switch

Crumble

Can the programmable lights be plugged into port A, B or C? Yes or No [ ]

Name ______________________ Class __________

Thinking about wiring my crumble LL2

Draw lines to join the computer, crumble and lights
Use the maker card to help you

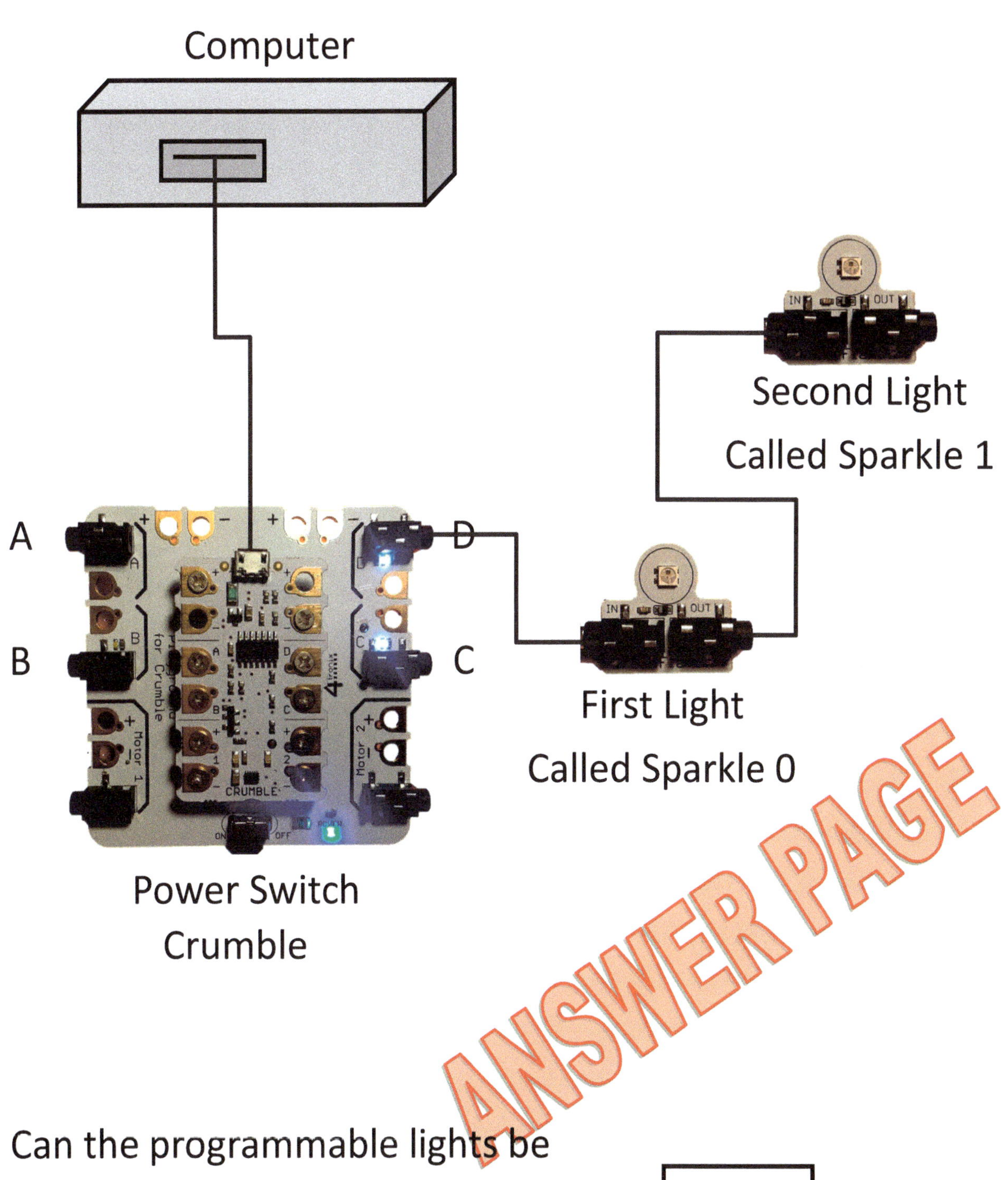

Can the programmable lights be plugged into port A, B or C? Yes or No NO

Name ______________________ Class __________

Thinking about wiring my crumble LL3

Draw lines to join the computer, crumble and lights
Use the maker card to help you

Computer

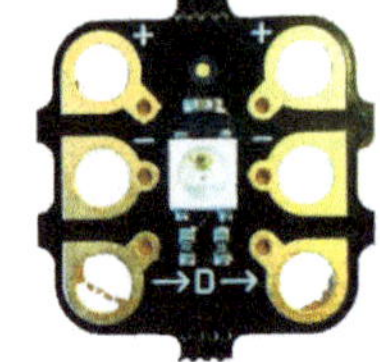

Second Light
Called Sparkle 1

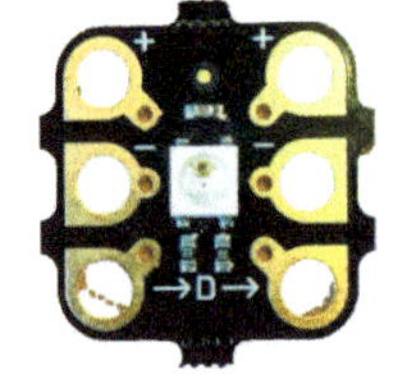

First Light
Called Sparkle 0

A D

B C

Power Switch
Crumble

Can the programmable lights be plugged into port A, B or C? Yes or No

Name ______________________________ Class ____________

Thinking about wiring my crumble LL3A

Draw lines to join the computer, crumble and lights
Use the maker cards to help you

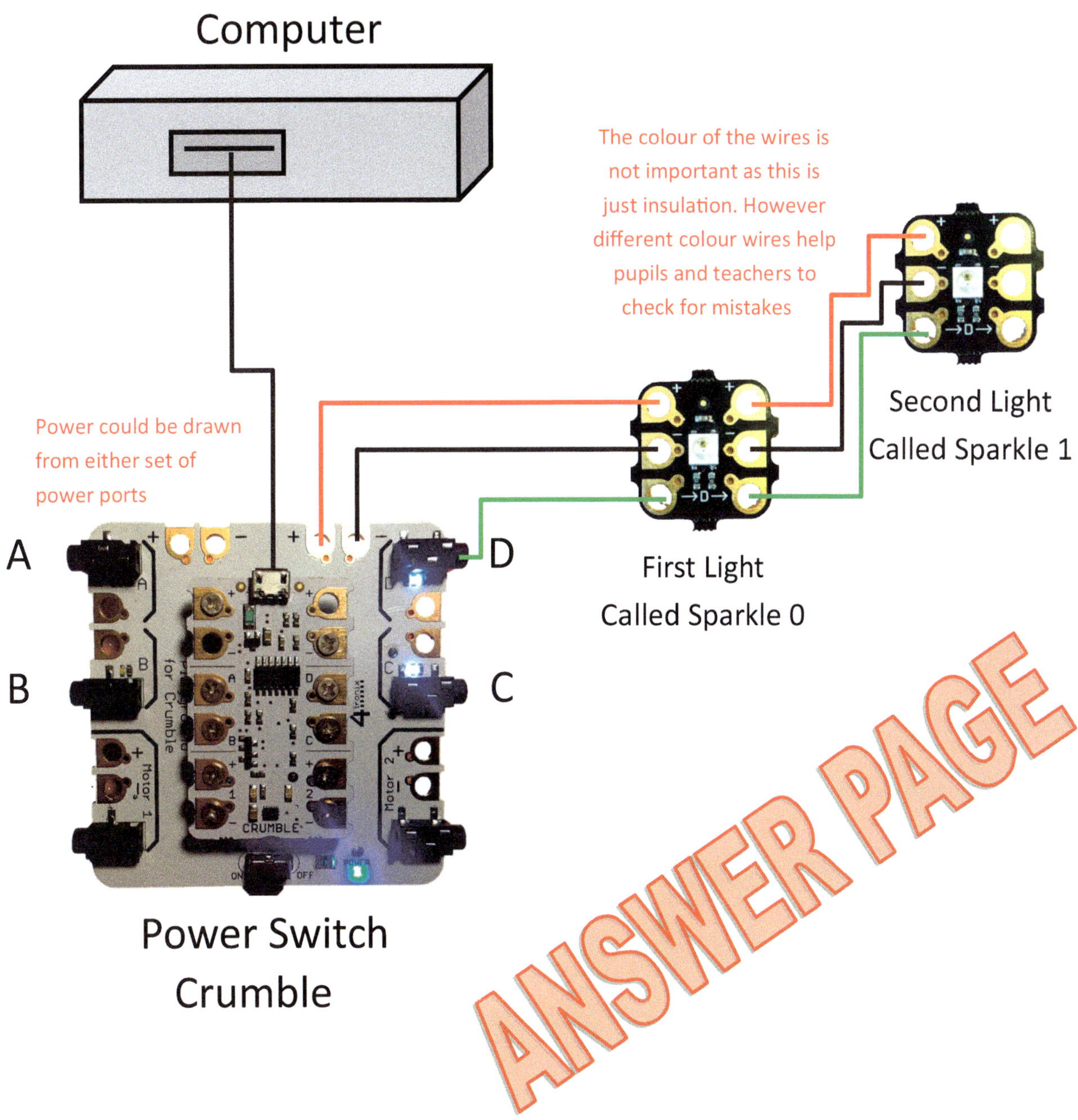

Computer
The colour of the wires is not important as this is just insulation. However different colour wires help pupils and teachers to check for mistakes
Power could be drawn from either set of power ports
A
B
D
C
Second Light
Called Sparkle 1
First Light
Called Sparkle 0
Power Switch
Crumble
ANSWER PAGE

Can the programmable lights be plugged into port A, B or C? Yes or No

NO

Name ______________________ Class __________

Thinking about wiring my crumble LL4

Draw lines to join the computer, crumble and lights
Use the maker card to help you

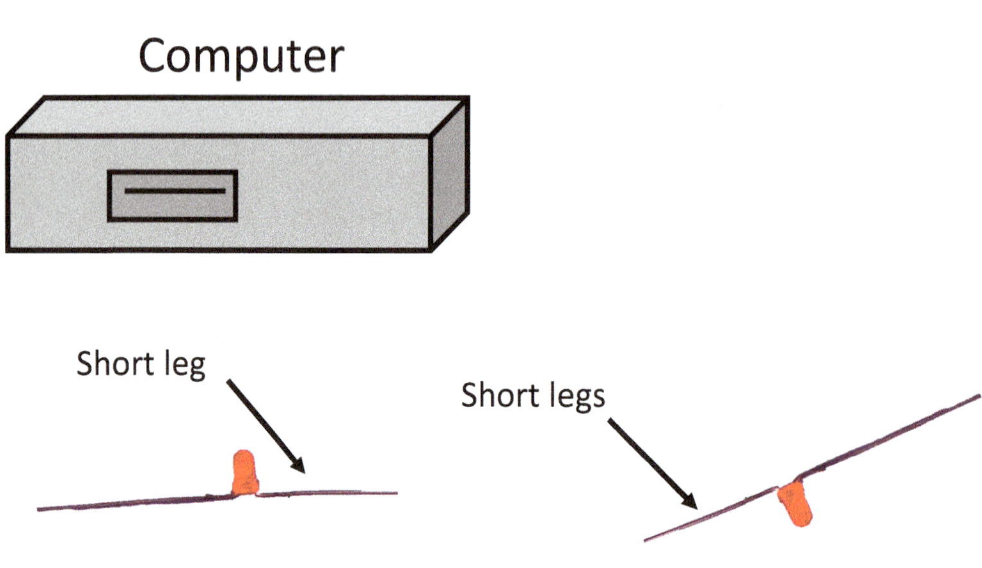

Power Switch
Crumble

Can the LED lights be plugged into ports A, B, C or D? Yes or No

Name ______________________ Class __________

Thinking about wiring my crumble LL4A

Draw lines to join the computer, crumble and lights
Use the maker card to help you

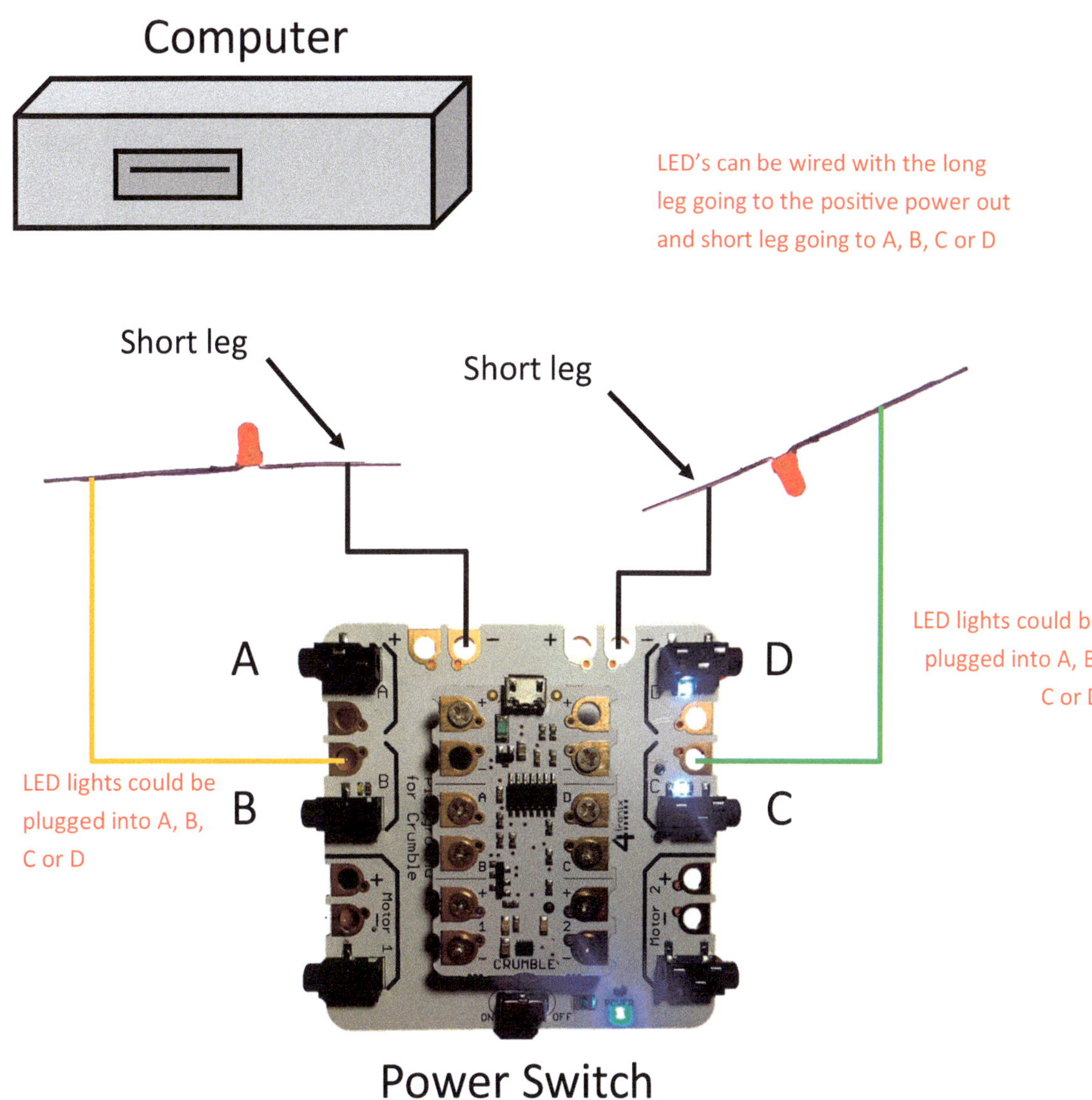
Computer
LED's can be wired with the long leg going to the positive power out and short leg going to A, B, C or D
Short leg
Short leg
A
D
B
C
LED lights could be plugged into A, B, C or D
LED lights could be plugged into A, B, C or D
Power Switch
Crumble

Can the LED lights be plugged into ports A, B, C or D? Yes or No

Yes

Name ______________________ Class __________

Thinking about wiring my crumble LL5

Draw lines to join the computer, crumble and lights

Use the maker card to help you

Computer

Short leg

Short leg

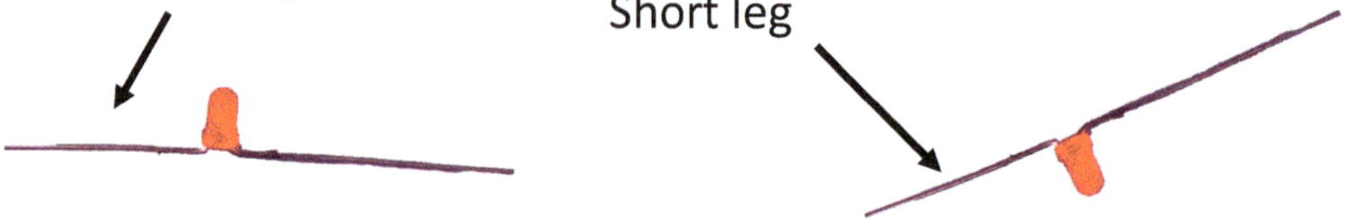

Crumble

Battery Pack

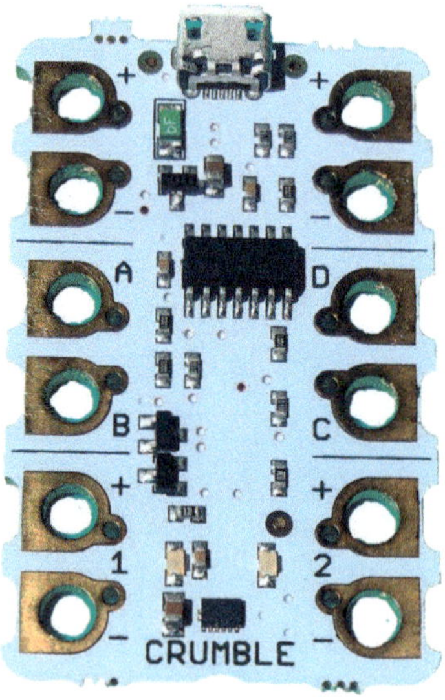

Can the LED lights be plugged into ports A, B, C or D? Yes or No

Name ______________________ Class ___________

Thinking about wiring my crumble LL5A

Draw lines to join the computer, crumble and lights
Use the maker card to help you

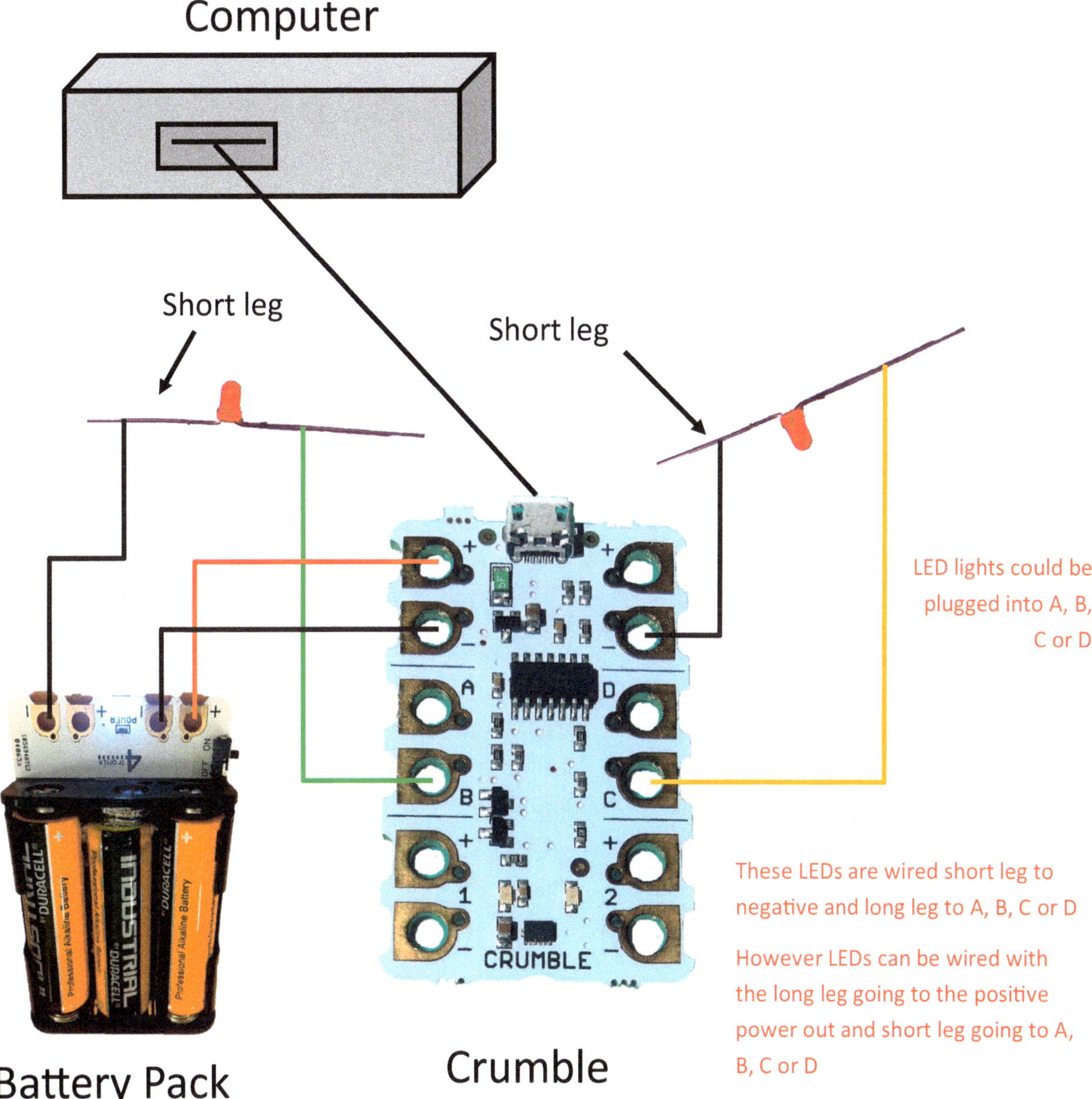

LED lights could be plugged into A, B, C or D

These LEDs are wired short leg to negative and long leg to A, B, C or D

However LEDs can be wired with the long leg going to the positive power out and short leg going to A, B, C or D

Can the LED lights be plugged into ports A, B, C or D? Yes or No

YES

Name ______________________ Class __________

Thinking about wiring my crumble LL6

Draw lines to join the computer, crumble and lights
Use the maker cards to help you

Computer

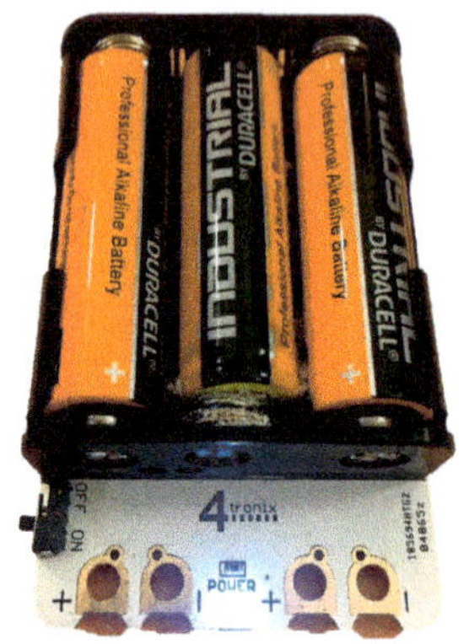

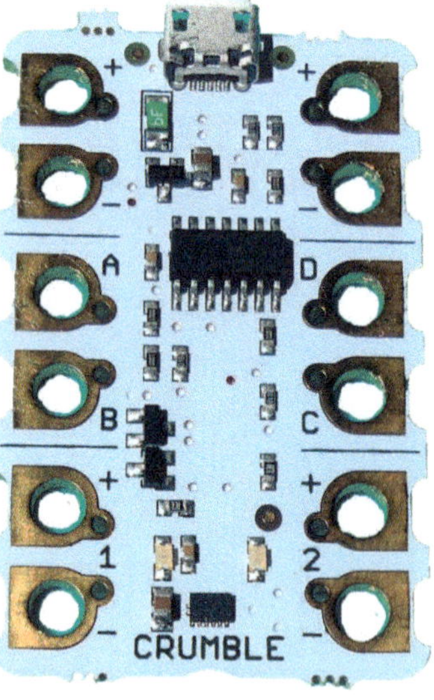

Crumble

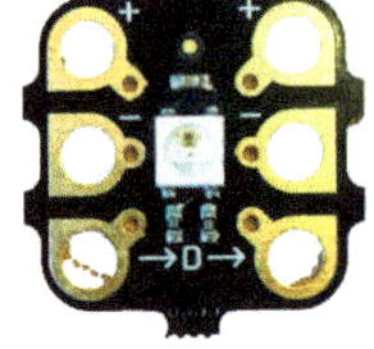

First Light
Called Sparkle 0

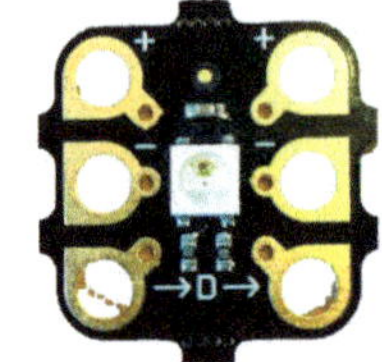

Second Light
Called Sparkle 1

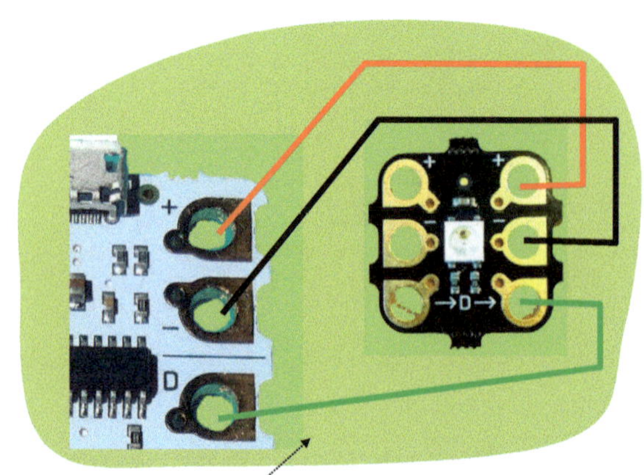

Could the wires be attached from the right hand side of the sparkle into the crumble as shown on the right?

Name ______________________ Class __________

Thinking about wiring my crumble LL6A

Draw lines to join the computer, crumble and lights
Use the maker cards to help you

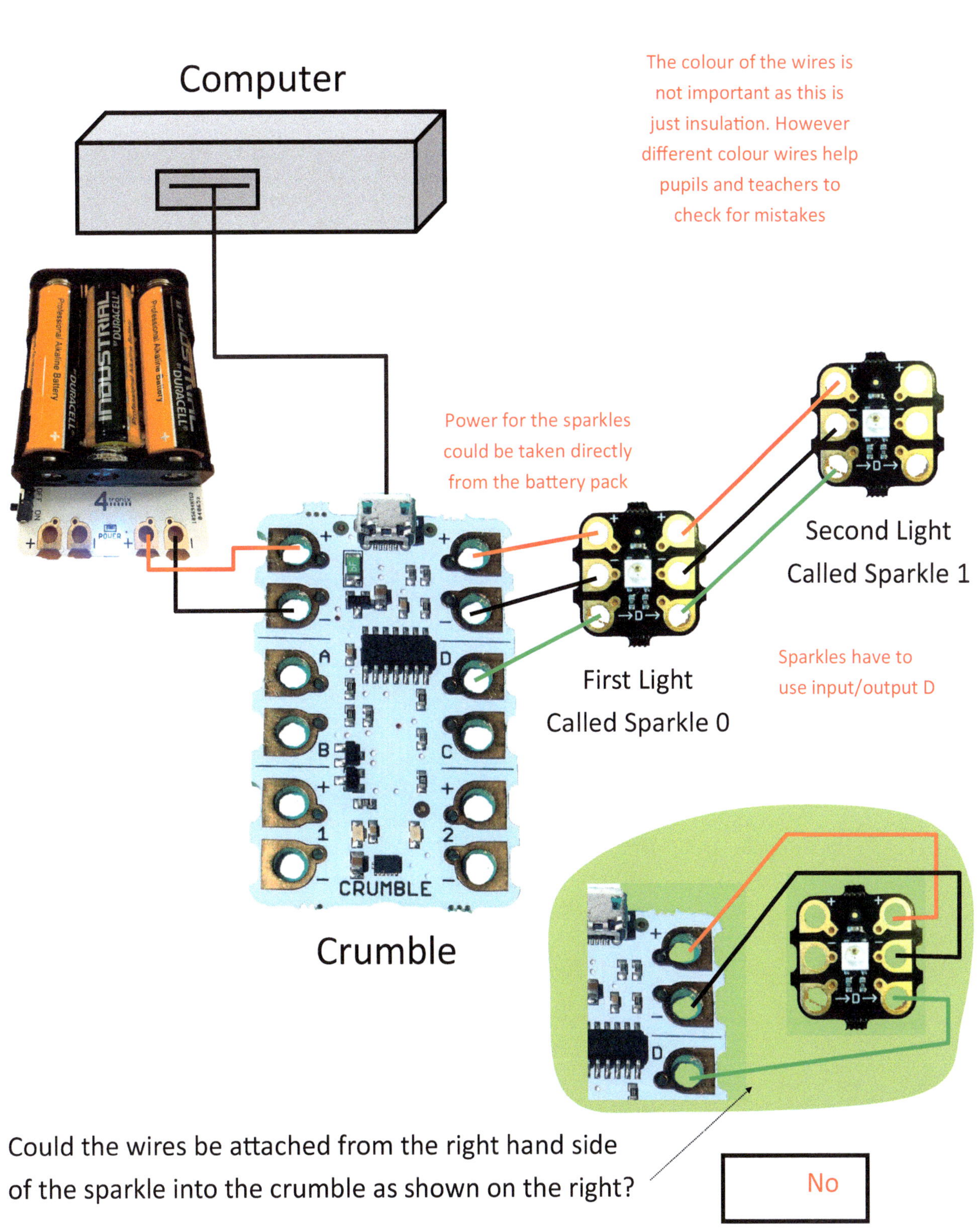

Computer
The colour of the wires is not important as this is just insulation. However different colour wires help pupils and teachers to check for mistakes
Power for the sparkles could be taken directly from the battery pack
Second Light
Called Sparkle 1
First Light
Called Sparkle 0
Sparkles have to use input/output D
Crumble
CRUMBLE

Could the wires be attached from the right hand side of the sparkle into the crumble as shown on the right?

No

Name ______________________________ Class _____________ LL8

Thinking about designing my own project that uses lights

Fill in your idea and add your inputs and outputs to the chart.

My program will

by

What will the user see and do?

Input/ Output	Name of device attached	What the device does (include as much detail as possible)
D output	Seven Programmable Lights	Flash in an arrow pattern to point to an important notice.
A		
B		
C		
D		
Motor 1		
Motor 2		

Draw your devices and the wires that connect them.

Name ______________________________ Class ____________ LL9

Thinking about designing my own project that uses lights

Fill in your idea and add your inputs and outputs to the chart.

My program will

by

What will the user see and do?

Input/ Output	Name of device attached	What the device does (include as much detail as possible)
D output	Seven Programmable Lights	Flash in an arrow pattern to point to an important notice.
A		
B		
C		
D		
Motor 1		
Motor 2		

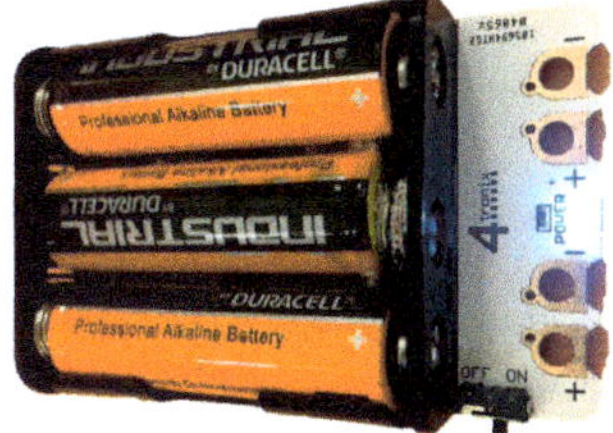

Draw your devices and the wires that connect them.

3. Night Light

Project Overview

Create a gentle night light that will stay on whilst a child goes to sleep for a set period of time before going out automatically to conserve battery power.

Trigger the night light through a button input. If you want to keep this project simpler and more accessible to younger pupils, dispense with the button. The night light is started by the battery switch and would only need simple sequence programming.

Cross Curricular Links

Science -Pupils can use their night lights to test materials to see if they are opaque, transparent or translucent. They can investigate whether the colour of the light makes any difference to the translucency of the material.

Design and Technology –Design a housing for the light that maximises the light amplification.

Art –Exterior box design

Materials Crumble Playground, programmable light, button crumb **OR**
Crumble, battery box, sparkle, button

Construction

For the quickest build, the programmable light can be mounted on or inside a pre-made cardboard box. 4 inch ones are a perfect size and can be purchased very cheaply. Holes can be pre-punched through the card-board for younger pupils. A blunt pencil is perfectly adequate for doing this. Double sided sticky tape or standard tape folded over can be used to temporarily affix the light and button to the inside or outside as needed.

The brown rectangle shown in the picture is there to allow different materials to be tested easily without touching the bulb for the science challenge. It could be made out of thick cardboard or if you had the time, sawn wood spar. It is not essential for the basic Night Light.

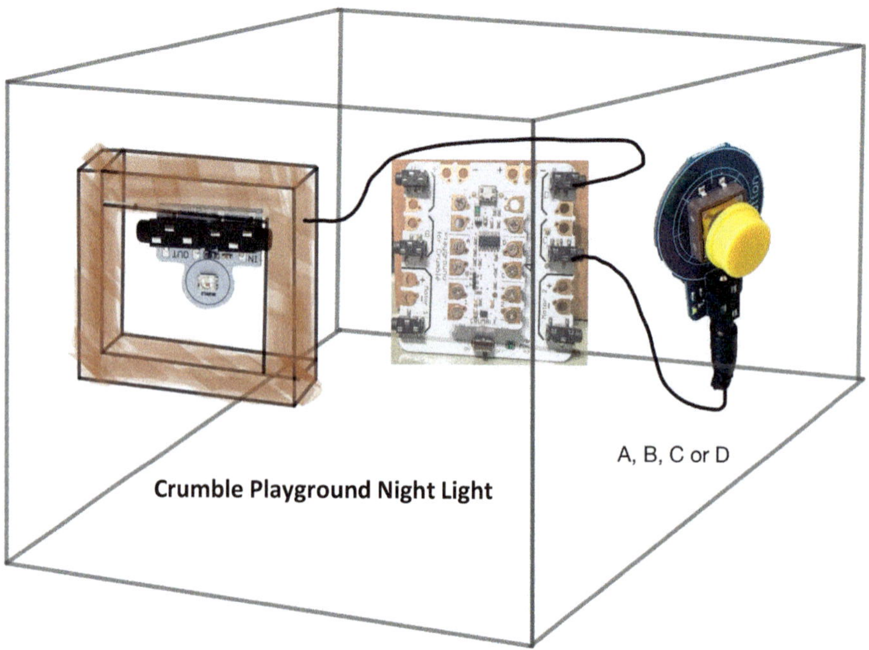

Crumble Playground Night Light

The same project can be created using the classic Crumble, battery box, button and sparkle light as shown in the diagram on the right of this page.

Classic Crumble Night Light

Art

Decoration suitable for a child's night light could be added to the box if you choose to consider art design principles around the objects purpose. This would probably lead to sleep and night themes such as clouds, stars, moon etc.

Night Light Pattern

Alternatively the light can be mounted inside the box on one of the box walls and pupils can experiment with different hole sizes and spacings as shown here. In a very dark room these will make patterns on the wall or ceiling.

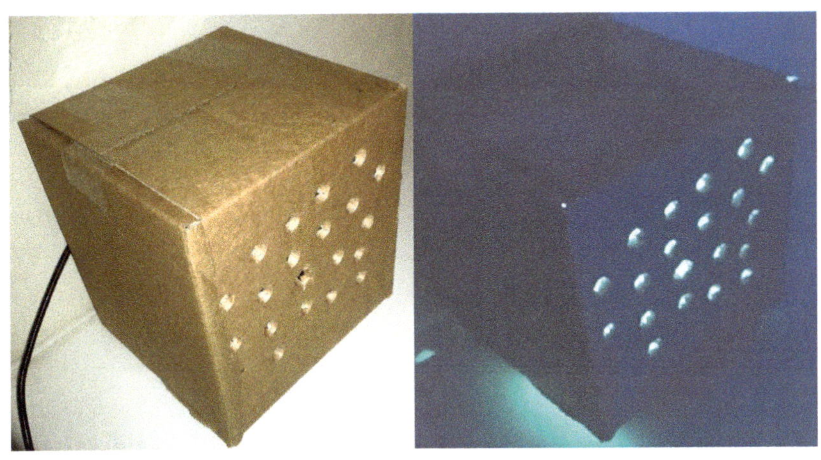

Alternatively you may wish to build a night light that uses a translucent bottle to spread the light.

The Redfern Electronic blog has a great description of this at https://goo.gl/Q39Cdk by Helen Roberts

Curricular Coverage

Design & Technology NC

No Button

Design NCD1A, NCD1B, NCD2G, NCD2H

With Button

NCD2A, NCD2B, NCD2G, NCD2H

Computing NC

No Button

NCC1A, NCC1B, NCC1C

With Button

NCC2A, NCC2B, NCC2C

Useful Maker Cards

Programmable Lights

MC01 MC09 MC49

Button

MC06 MC18 MC19

MC50 MC51

Suggested Module Outline for Younger Pupils (without the button)

1, Make a Teacher Example

Make a simple night light yourself before the introductory lesson and mount it in a cardboard box. This will help you discover all those little things such as where to poke the wire though the box and the best way to stick the light to the box.

2, Prepare pupil boxes

If your pupils are very young, you may want to prepare some boxes before the session by sealing the bottoms.

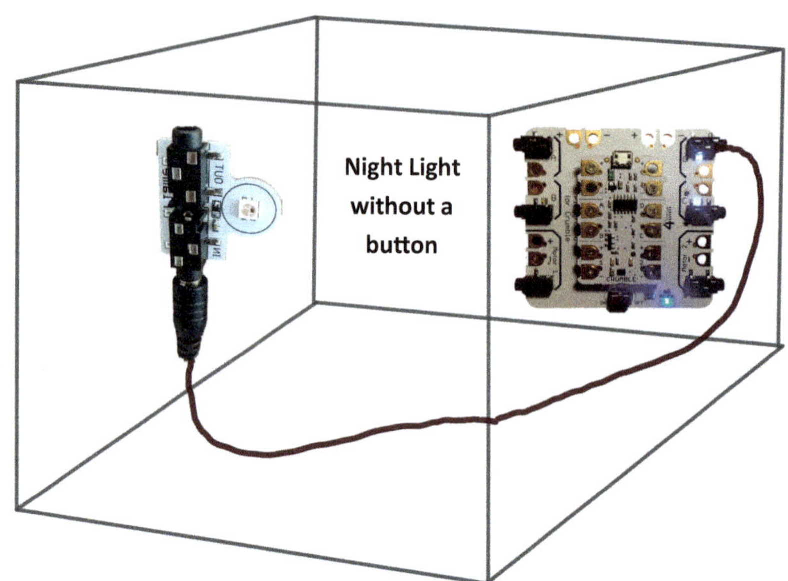

3, Introduce the project

Introduce the project by starting a discussion about sleeping with no light or some light. What are their preferences? Does anyone have a specific light that they like to keep on? Is it a special light designed to stay on all night? What does it look like? Where is it? What colour is it?

4, Pupils decorate the box

Give pupils time to decorate the box using whatever art techniques you are seeking to develop in your art curriculum. If they are making a light pattern they could poke the holes using a blunt pencil.

5, Connecting the night light

Show pupils your night light and explain/show how it is connected. Allow them time to connect their night lights. Pupils could also look at the programmable light maker card. If using the maker cards, it helps to get pupils to put the Crumble Playground on the other side of the card orientated the same way as in the card.

6, Connecting the USB

Show pupils how to connect their crumble playground to the USB on a computer and open the Crumble software.

Formative assessment	Corrective	Enrichment
Is the wire correctly connected into output D and into the in end of the programmable light? Is the USB plugged into the correct place on the computer?	Ask them which letter the output was meant to connect to? Ask if they have their **in** and **out** sides the right way round?	Ask them where they might add another flame light if their night light was going to have two lights (Answer into **out** of the first flame light) Give them the maker card to help them answer the question.

7, Starting the program

Drag out a program start block. Explain that the program can only have one of these. Encourage them to do likewise.

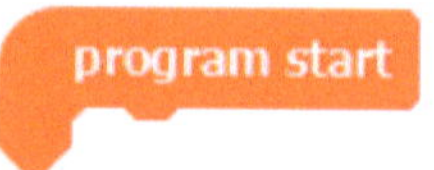

8, Changing sparkle colour

Explain that their light is a programmable one and you are going to show them how to get it to shine with a colour. Demonstrate how to change the colour by clicking on the coloured block and selecting another colour (as shown in the diagram on the right). Explain that they can send their program to the crumble by pressing the green arrow button. Can they get it to change colours?

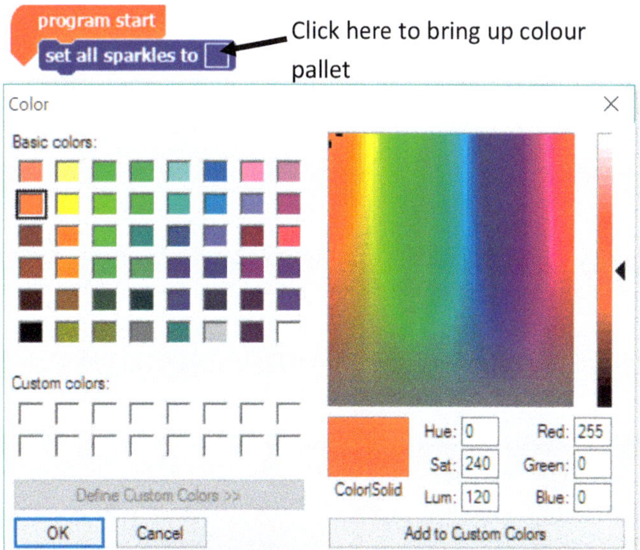

Changing the colour on the sparkle / flame

9, Light off after a period of time

Can they program it to turn on a colour before waiting 3 seconds and then turn the light off? If they are struggling with this after a while drag out these blocks unconnected at first as a hint to help them. You are looking for a program similar to this one.

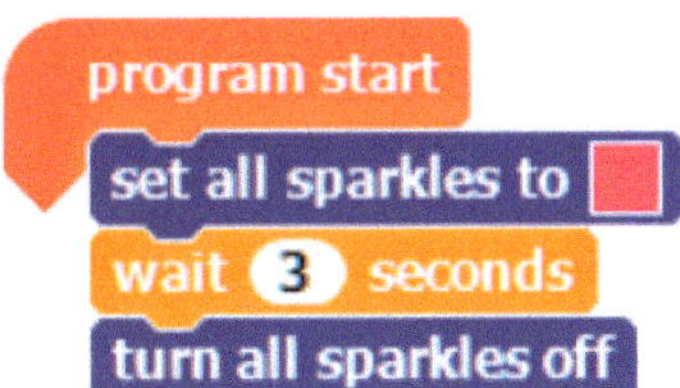

Light off after a period of time

10, Lights that change colour

Lots of children like lights that can change colour. Can they program a night light that changes colours after a period of time and still goes off after a set period of time? There is a simple example on the right.

Lights that change colour

11, Assessment

Complete the reflection and assessment sheet NL5

Suggested Module Outline
Older Pupils (with the button)

1, Make a teacher example

Make a night light yourself before the introductory lesson and mount it on a card board box. This will help you discover all those little things such as where to poke the wires though the box and the best way to stick the light to the box. There are two wiring examples at the start of the chapter. Try out all three programs on sheet NL1 or NL2.

2, Introduce the project

Introduce the project by starting a discussion about sleeping with no light or some light. What are their preferences? Does anyone have a specific light that they like to keep on at night? It can help to normalise this for older children by talking about your own children or children you know or what light they had when they were little. Is it a special light designed to stay on all night? What does it look like? Where is it? What colour does it shine? Explain that they are going to make a working night light and program it to turn on when the button is pressed and turn off again after a period of time. If you are going to use the light for a science experiment you might mention this as well.

3, **Thinking about wiring & programming**

Either use thinking sheet, NL1 for Crumble Playground or NL2 for the Classic Crumble, before checking their answers using either NL1A or NL2A, or If pupils have already programmed using conditional selection you may wish to use NL7 which gives all the code blocks with explanations of what they do but leaves pupils to puzzle out a useful order.

Formative assessment	Corrective	Enrichment
Are the lines joined to the right or wrong idea, algorithm and program? (NL1 & NL2)	Encourage them to follow key words such as **on/off**, **period of time** or **colour**. Give them time to puzzle this through.	Which algorithm and program would they adapt if they wanted to make the button switch between two patterns of lights? (A, top one)
Can they verbally tell you what an input or output is ?	Get pupils to read the information about inputs and outputs at the top of the page	Can pupils name any other things that could be outputs? (A, Buzzer, Motor, servo motor)

4, **Wiring**

Pupils wire up the night light using the maker cards provided before having their work checked by their teacher.

5, **Programming**

Pupils test their programs they reasoned about on their sheet. They could also try the following extensions.

- Program the button to turn the light off instead of on
- Create a pattern of lights that are switched on by the button and last for three minutes
- Create two patterns of lights that last for a minute toggled by the button

Common Bugs and Errors

- The battery is not turned on
- The USB is not plugged into the same computer
- Bare metal on the crocodile leads are touching creating a short circuit
- The button is plugged into a different letter on the Crumble than the one chosen in the programming
- The do forever loop is missing
- The do forever loop has been placed inside the conditional selection block not outside
- There are no wait time blocks between colours

6, **Assessment**

Pupils fill in their assessment sheet NL6

Independent Extension

The planning includes two sheets to encourage pupils to come up with their own ideas which use lights and buttons NL3 and NL4, these could be used as homework or as the next class project. Adapting an idea and using it for a different purpose significantly increases the transference of knowledge and skills from one domain to others. A Research summary is available at https://goo.gl/y65uhC . You can use the sentence scaffolds outlined on page 13 to help pupils think through the task and what the user will see and do.

Useful Problem Solving Skills to Assess

I recognise there is more than one way to solve/describe a problem
I don't just accept the first solution
I look for a range of solutions to the same problem
I look for how a project can be extended
I can evaluate my solutions against a set criteria
Handles Ambiguity
Open Ended Problem Solver
I can break complex problems into parts
I can design criteria to evaluate my creations
I can discover / concentrate on the most important part of a problem
Evaluates
I can contribute useful ideas to a partner or group
Copes with Complexity
I can identify patterns in problems and solutions
Computing Problem Solver
I can encourage others to share their ideas
I can adapt existing ideas to solve new problems
Adapts
Communicates
I can develop, test and debug until a product is refined
I lead using all the people talent in my group
Investigates
I make predictions about what will happen
I learn from setbacks and don't let them put me off
I can persevere even if the solution is not obvious
Perseveres
I repeatedly experiment through predicting, making, testing & debugging

Problem solving skills are adapted from a problem solving rubric created by Mark Dorling and Thomas Stephens that the author worked on helping to define. You can find this at http://code-it.co.uk/attitudes/

Name ___________________________ Class/Form ____________ NL1

Thinking about wiring and programming a night light

Buttons are **inputs** because they **put in** information into the program. They can do two things one when they are pressed and one when they are not pressed

Push Buttons

Programmable Lights Programmable lights are **outputs** because they **put out** information from the program. These can output lots of different colours depending on the programming.

1, Connect the program idea to the correct algorithm and the correct programming block using lines

program idea	algorithm	programming block
Switching the light on or off with a button	When the button is pressed down the light goes on. When the button is de-pressed the light goes off.	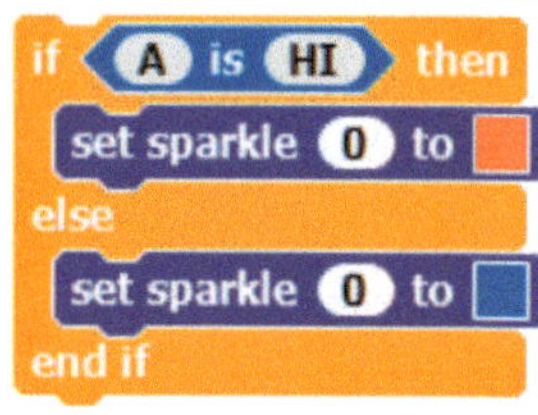 (A is input the button is plugged into)
Switching the light from one colour to another colour using the button	When the button is pressed down the light goes on for 2 minutes before going out.	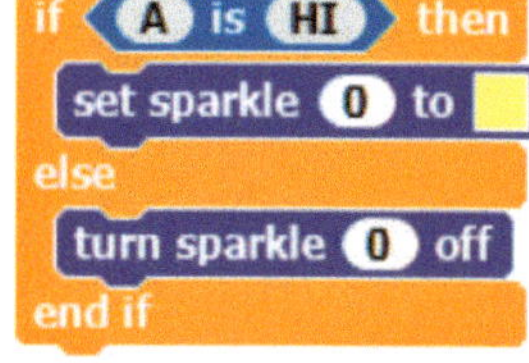 (HI is pressed down LO is de-pressed)

Switching the light on for a period of time with a button before it goes off automatically	When the button is pressed down the light goes red. When the button is de-pressed the light goes blue.	if A is HI then
		set sparkle 0 to
		wait 120 seconds
		turn sparkle 0 off
		end if

All three programs need to be wrapped inside a forever loop so the program checks if the button is pressed continually

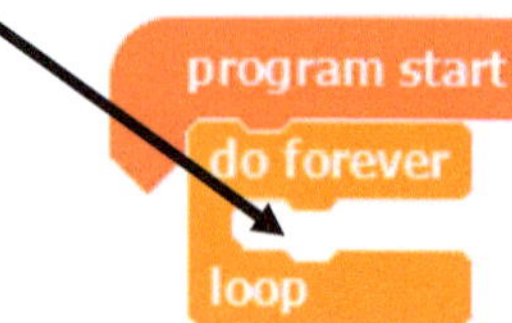

Draw your light, button & wires

Name ______________________________ Class/Form ______________NL1A

Thinking about wiring and programming a night light

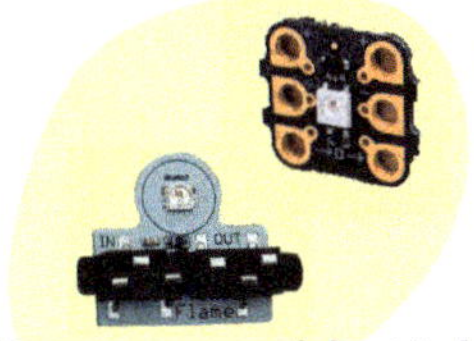

Buttons are **inputs** because they **put in** information into the program. They can do two things one when they are pressed and one when they are not pressed

Push Buttons

Programmable Lights

Programmable lights are **outputs** because they **put out** information from the program. These can output lots of different colours depending on the programming.

1, Connect the program idea to the correct algorithm and the correct programming block using lines

program idea	algorithm	programming block
Switching the light on or off with a button	When the button is pressed down the light goes on. When the button is de-pressed the light goes off	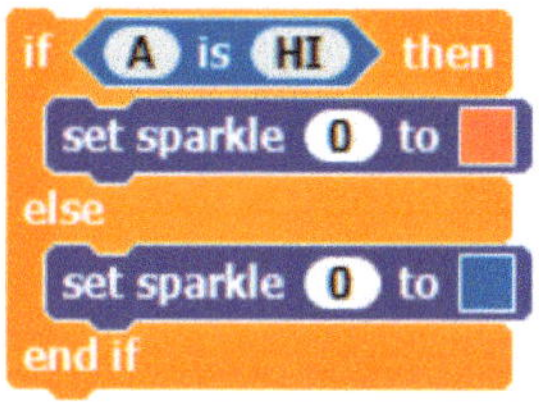 if A is HI then / set sparkle 0 to [orange] / else / set sparkle 0 to [blue] / end if (A is input the button is plugged into)
Switching the light from one colour to another colour using the button	When the button is pressed down the light goes on for 2 minutes before going out.	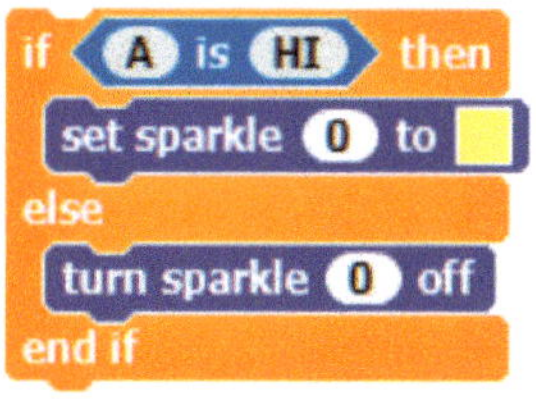 if A is HI then / set sparkle 0 to [yellow] / else / turn sparkle 0 off / end if (HI is pressed down LO is de-pressed)
Switching the light on for a period of time with a button before it goes off automatically	When the button is pressed down the light goes red. When the button is de-pressed the light goes blue	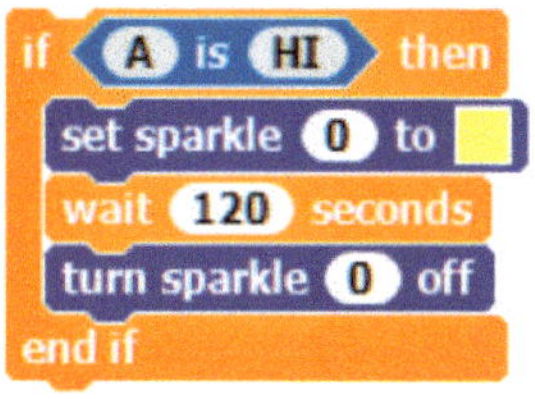 if A is HI then / set sparkle 0 to [yellow] / wait 120 seconds / turn sparkle 0 off / end if

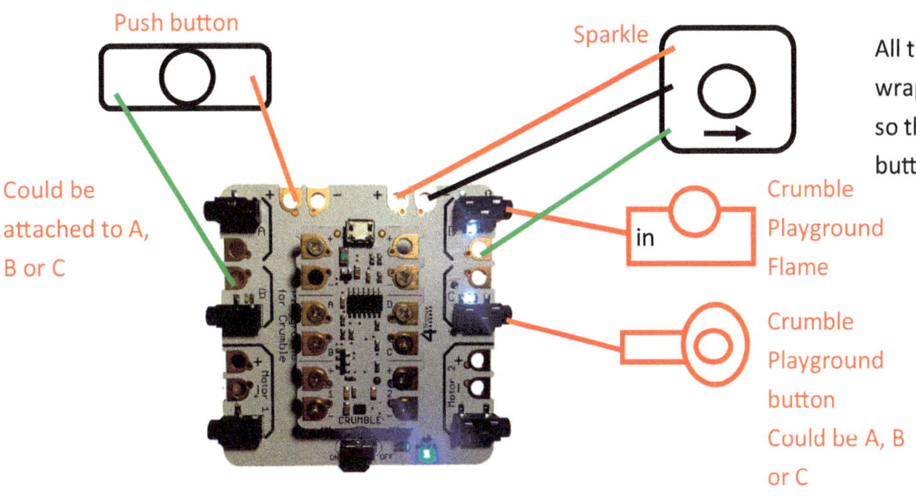

Push button

Sparkle

Could be attached to A, B or C

Crumble Playground Flame

in

Crumble Playground button Could be A, B or C

All three programs need to be wrapped inside a forever loop so the program checks if the button is pressed continually

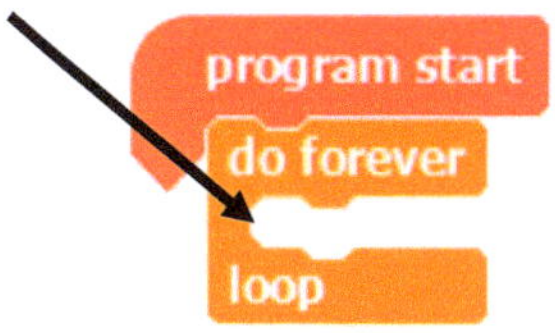

program start
do forever
loop

Draw your light, button & wires

Name ___________________________ Class/Form ____________ NL2

Thinking about wiring and programming a night light

Buttons are **inputs** because they **put in** information into the program. They can do two things one when they are pressed and one when they are not pressed

Push Buttons

Programmable Lights

Programmable lights are **outputs** because they **put out** information from the program. These can output lots of different colours depending on the programming.

1, Connect the program idea to the correct algorithm and the correct programming block using lines

program idea	algorithm	programming block
Switching the light on or off with a button	When the button is pressed down the light goes on. When the button is de-pressed the light goes off	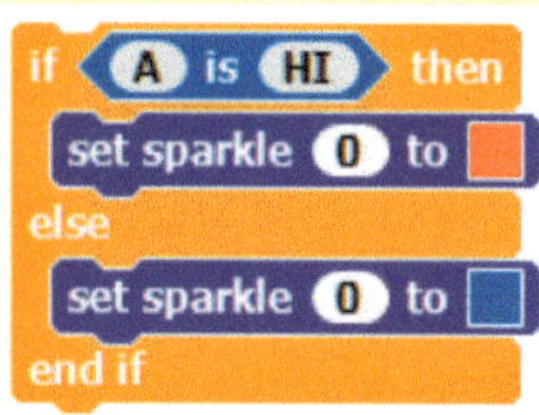 (A is input the button is plugged into)

Switching the light from one colour to another colour using the button	When the button is pressed down the light goes on for 2 minutes before going out.	if A is HI then
		set sparkle 0 to
		else
		turn sparkle 0 off
		end if
		(HI is pressed down LO is de-pressed)

Switching the light on for a period of time with a button before it goes off automatically	When the button is pressed down the light goes red. When the button is de-pressed the light goes blue	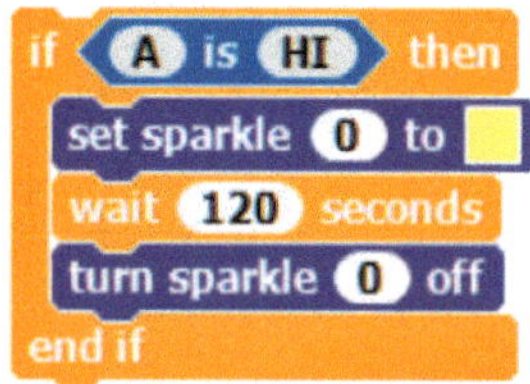

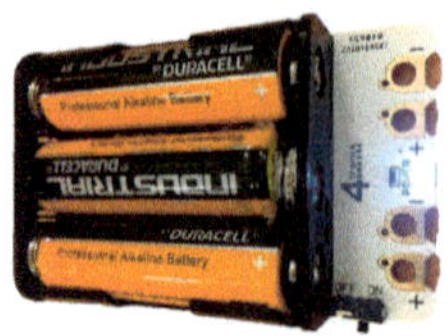

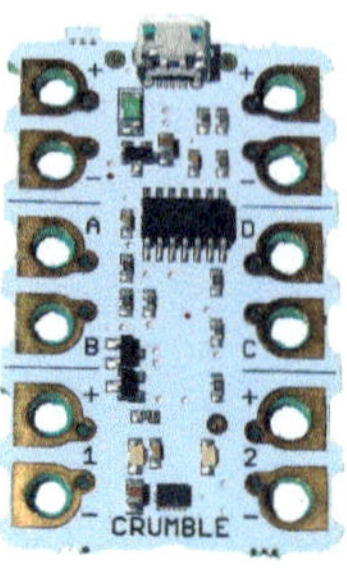

All three programs need to be wrapped inside a forever loop so the program checks if the button is pressed continually

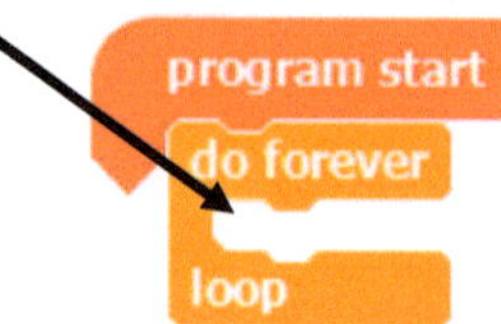

Draw your light, button & wires

Name ____________________________ Class/Form ____________ NL2A

Thinking about wiring and programming a night light

Programmable Lights

Push Buttons

Buttons are **inputs** because they **put in** information into the program. They can do two things one when they are pressed and one when they are not pressed

Programmable lights are **outputs** because they **put out** information from the program. These can output lots of different colours depending on the programming.

1, Connect the program idea to the correct algorithm and the correct programming block using lines

program idea	algorithm	programming block
Switching the light on or off with a button	When the button is pressed down the light goes on. When the button is de-pressed the light goes off	if A is HI then / set sparkle 0 to [orange] / else / set sparkle 0 to [blue] / end if (A is input the button is plugged into)
Switching the light from one colour to another colour using the button	When the button is pressed down the light goes on for 2 minutes before going out.	if A is HI then / set sparkle 0 to [yellow] / else / turn sparkle 0 off / end if (HI is pressed down LO is de-pressed)
Switching the light on for a period of time with a button before it goes off automatically	When the button is pressed down the light goes red. When the button is de-pressed the light goes blue	if A is HI then / set sparkle 0 to [yellow] / wait 120 seconds / turn sparkle 0 off / end if

All three programs need to be wrapped inside a forever loop so the program checks if the button is pressed continually

Diagrams could be different to this one depending on the button types used.

Draw your light, button & wires

Name ______________________ Class/Form __________ NL7

Thinking about programming a night light

Buttons are **inputs** because they **put in** information into the program. They can do two things one when they are pressed and one when they are not pressed

Programmable lights are **outputs** because they **put out** information from the Crumble. These can output lots of different colours depending on the programming.

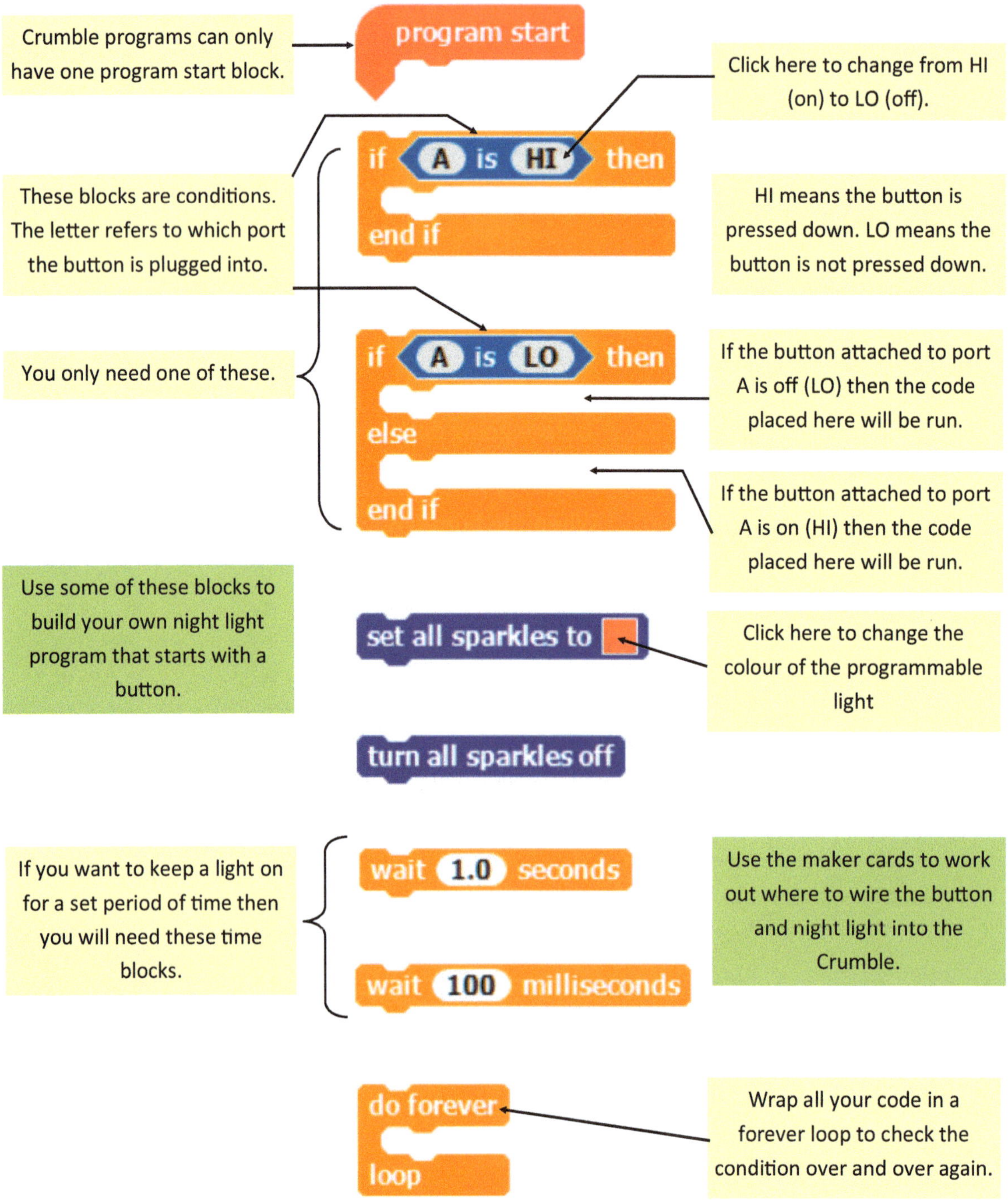

Crumble programs can only have one program start block. → **program start**

Click here to change from HI (on) to LO (off).

These blocks are conditions. The letter refers to which port the button is plugged into.

if A is HI then / **end if**

HI means the button is pressed down. LO means the button is not pressed down.

You only need one of these.

if A is LO then / **else** / **end if**

If the button attached to port A is off (LO) then the code placed here will be run.

If the button attached to port A is on (HI) then the code placed here will be run.

Use some of these blocks to build your own night light program that starts with a button.

set all sparkles to ■

Click here to change the colour of the programmable light

turn all sparkles off

If you want to keep a light on for a set period of time then you will need these time blocks.

wait 1.0 seconds

wait 100 milliseconds

Use the maker cards to work out where to wire the button and night light into the Crumble.

do forever / **loop**

Wrap all your code in a forever loop to check the condition over and over again.

Name ____________________________ Class ____________ NL3

Thinking about designing my own project that uses lights and buttons

These are programmable lights

Fill in your idea and add your inputs and outputs to the chart

My program will

by

What will the user see and do?

Input/ Output	Name of device attached	What the device does (include as much detail as possible)
A output	LED red light	The red LED lights up when the button is not being pushed (LO).
A		
B		
C		
D		
Motor 1		
Motor 2		

Draw your devices and the wires that connect them

Name ______________________________ Class _____________ NL4

Thinking about designing my own project that uses lights and buttons

These are programmable lights

Fill in your idea and add your inputs and outputs to the chart

My program will

by

What will the user see and do?

Input/ Output	Name of device attached	What the device does (include as much detail as possible)
A output	LED red light	The red LED lights up when the button is not being pushed (LO).
A		
B		
C		
D		
Motor 1		
Motor 2		

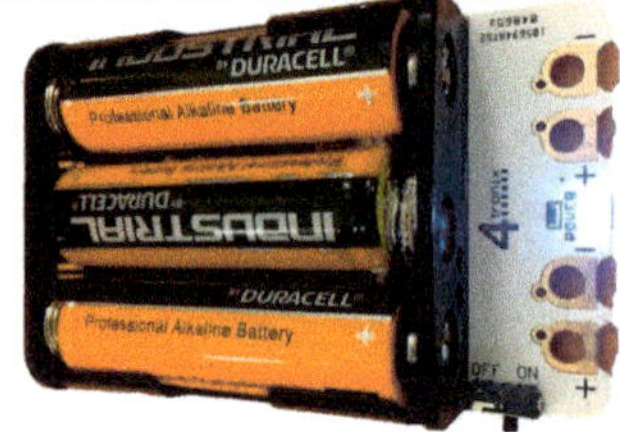

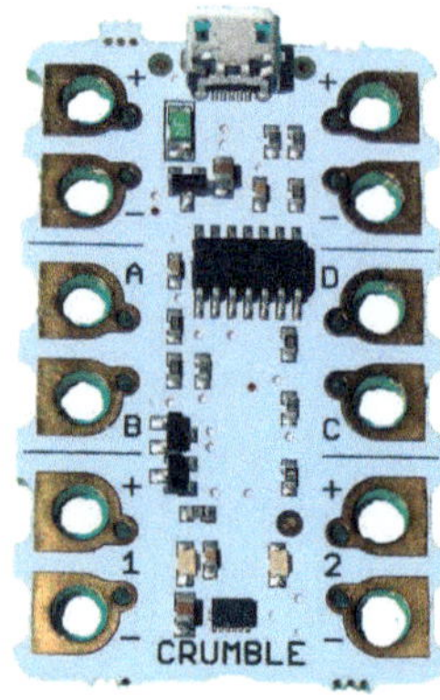

Draw your devices and the wires that connect them

Night Light Assessment Sheet

Project without Button NL5

Name ______________ Class ______

☺ I did this well

😐 I did this ok or I did this a little

☹ I tried this but it didn't work or I didn't do this at all

I wired up my night light.	
I programmed my light to turn on.	
I programmed my light to turn off after a period of time.	
I programmed my light to change colours.	
I listened to my partners ideas.	
I contributed good idea to my partner.	
I persevered when the wiring or programming didn't work.	
I thought of my own project that uses a light and shared it with my partner & teacher.	
I created my own project on my own or with my partner.	

Sticker	I got this sticker for
Sticker	I got this sticker for
Sticker	I got this sticker for

Night Light Assessment Sheet Name ____________ Class ______

Project with Button NL6

I did this well

I did this ok or I did this a little

I tried this but it didn't work or I didn't do this at all

I wired up my night light.	
I programmed my light to turn on using a button.	
I programmed my light to turn off after a period of time.	
I programmed my light to change colours.	
I listened to my partners ideas.	
I contributed good idea to my partner.	
I persevered when the wiring or programming didn't work.	
I adapted the program on the sheet to make a new program.	
I broke the problem up into inputs and outputs.	

Sticker	I got this sticker for
Sticker	I got this sticker for
Sticker	I got this sticker for

4. Door Bell

Create a door bell for your house or bedroom.

Trigger the bell through a button input.

Crocodile Clips
Buzzer attached

Cross Curricular Links

Science -Pupils could use their door bells to investigate sound proofing materials. Install the buzzer within the box, leave one end open and cover it with the material to test. Use a decibel meter held at the same distance away from the material to determine volume.

Materials

Crumble Playground, buzzer ,button **OR**
Crumble, battery box, buzzer, button

Construction

This project is easily mounted on a pre-made cardboard box. 4 inch ones are a perfect size and can be purchased very cheaply. Holes can be pre-punched through the cardboard for younger pupils. A blunt pencil is perfectly adequate for doing this. Double sided sticky tape or standard tape folded over can be used to temporarily affix the buzzer and button to the outside.

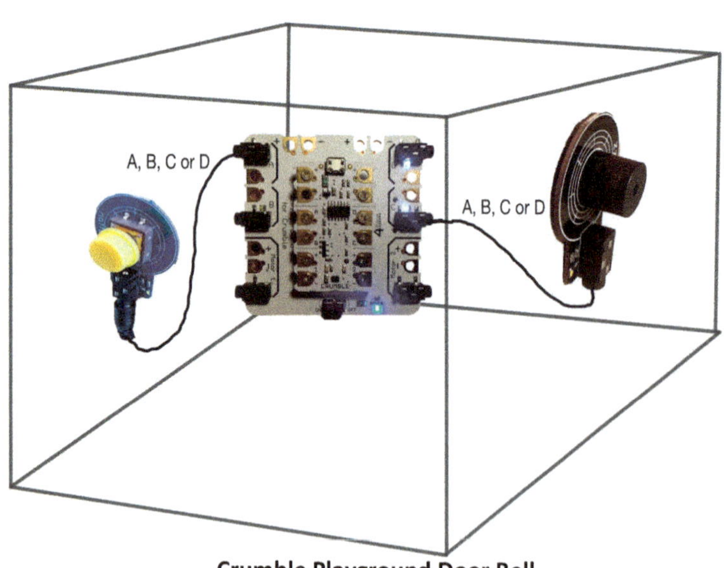

Crumble Playground Door Bell

If using crocodile clip accessories, line up the holes in the box and make them bigger than the ends of the clips, nearly all the wire can be hidden and no tape is necessary as shown in the pictures above and below.

Recycle

If you don't leave time to add decoration to the box it could be re-used in later projects.

Extending Construction

Pupils could also investigate which materials would amplify of reduce the volume of sound and use these in their construction.

Caution

Buzzer projects are noisy and can be especially distracting and in some instances disruptive for some pupils, especially ones sensitive to noise such as autistic children or those prone to migraines.

Fortunately, buzzer vibrations can be picked up by touch allowing some pupils to take part with ear defenders.

If you are making the sound insulation tester, it is a good idea to pre-test the best distance away from the buzzer to measure sound readings from. Doing this outside in the playground can improve teacher and class wellbeing.

One alternative method is to put the buzzers inside the box, which significantly reduces the amount of sound generated,

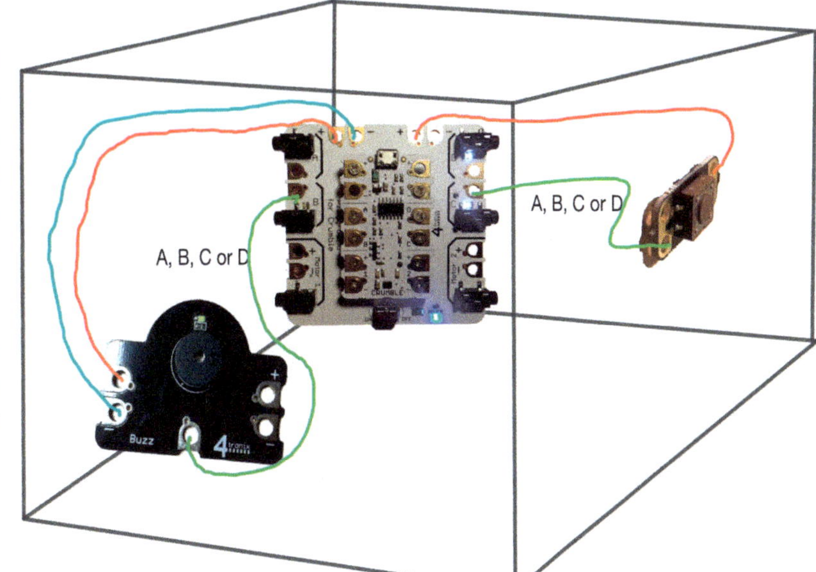

Crumble Playground Door Bell Crocodile Clip Crumbs

Maker Cards

MC05	**MC06**
MC23	**MC24**
MC18	**MC19**
MC33	**MC34**
MC50	**MC51**

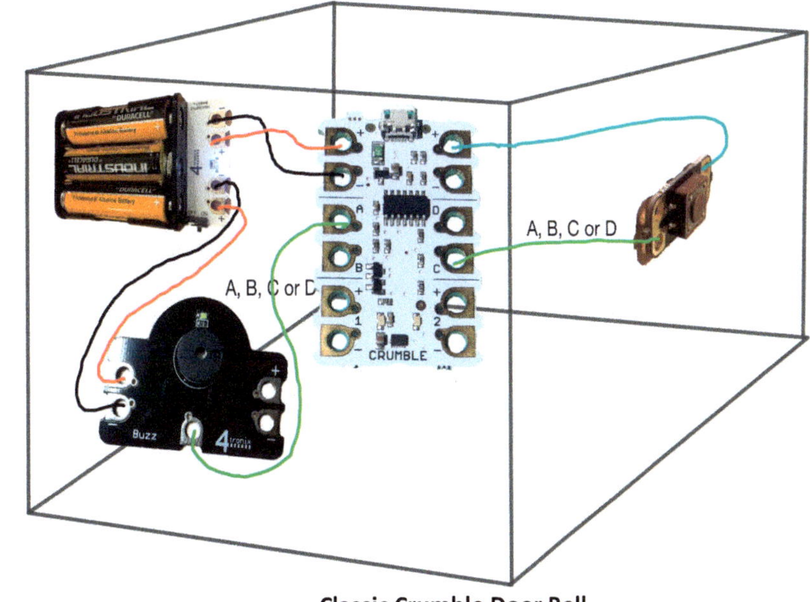

Classic Crumble Door Bell

Curricular Coverage

Design & Technology NC
NCD2A, NCD2B, NCD2G, NCD2H

Computing NC
NCC2A, NCC2B, NCC2C

Target Pupils

In this module there will only be one module outline. Doorbells can't be created without some sort of switch or button input which makes the project less useful for very young pupils.

Suggested Module Outline

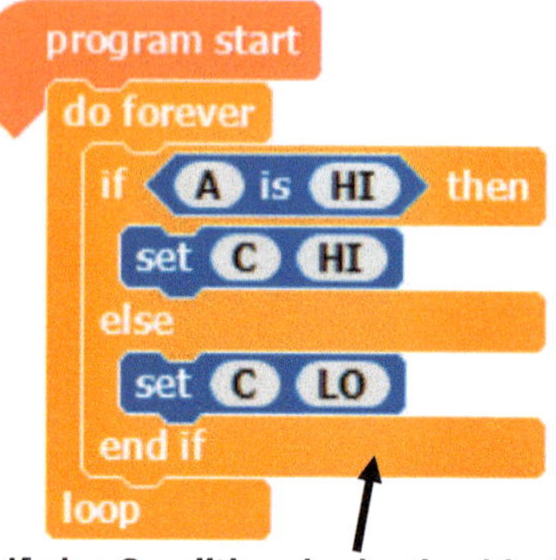

If else Conditional selection block

1, Create a teacher example

Make a door bell yourself before the introductory lesson and mount it on a cardboard box. This will help you discover all those little things such as where to poke the wires though the box and the best way to stick the buzzer to the box. There are three wiring examples at the start of the chapter.

2, Create the programming yourself

Try out the programming using this basic program on the right.
In this example the button is attached to input A and the buzzer to output C. However both could use A, B, C or D as you prefer, left click on the letters to change them. The **do forever loop** continually loops through the conditional selection **if else** block inside. The **if else** block is like a switch. If input A is pressed down it will register as HI and the code after **then** and before **else** will run. In this case it will set the buzzer output attached to output C to HI which is on. If button attached to input A registers as LO/de-pressed then the code after **else** will be run. In this case the buzzer at output C will be switched to LO/off.

2, Introduce the project

Introduce the project by starting a brief discussion about doorbells. Explain that they are going to design, make and program their own doorbell although due to lack of space these will be attached to a small box instead of a door.

3, Introduce the wiring thinking sheet

This book has the following wiring thinking sheets available. Choose the one that fits your resources or alternatively just use the maker cards. Emphasise one letter one device only before they start.

- DB1 & DB1A Crumble Playground and Crumble Playground accessories (easiest wiring)
- DB2 & DB2A Crumble Playground and 4tronix crocodile clip accessories
- DB3 & DB3A Crumble Playground and Redfern Electronic crocodile clip accessories
- DB4 & DB4A Classic Crumble and 4tronic crocodile clip accessories
- DB5 & DB5A Classic Crumble and Redfern Electronic crocodile clip accessories
- DB6 Classic Crumble with space to draw own accessories
- DB7 Crumble Playground with space to draw own accessories

5, Introduce the Programming thinking sheet DB8 & DB8A or DB12

DB8 is designed to help pupils understand the thinking behind creating a program to control a door bell. The logic question at the end can only be completed if pupils understood how the programming works. Alternatively pupils could try and puzzle the programming out for themselves first using DB12 and the maker cards to help them and DB8 could be used to help those who need more support.

It really helps if pupils wiring and programming sheets have been checked before the lesson is allowed to proceed as most errors come from incomplete wiring.

6, Time to wire and program the door bell

Armed with their wiring diagrams and example programs, pupils need to be given time to connect, program and test their programs. This is a good opportunity for some formative assessment as outlined in the following chart.

Formative assessment	Corrective	Enrichment
Is the buzzer and button correctly wired? If using a Classic Crumble is the battery pack wired correctly?	Highlight which area on the support card or device they need to check/ change. Don't just give them the answer	Ask them where they might add another buzzer if they could find one with a different tone (Answer A, B, C or D).
Are pupils communicating and persevering?	Challenge them using the problem solving and the reward of earning a sticker	Give out stickers where pupils are modelling these behaviours and get them to write them on their assessment sheets

7, What does a good one look like?

Once pupils are some way through the project, gather them together and group source a set of criteria for what a good doorbell looks, sounds and works like (WAGOLL what a good one looks like). Agree the criteria together and add these into the self assessment sheet DB9 . Pupils can then use these to assess their projects. You might want to show pupils the problem solving skills on the chart below and ask which ones pupils need to use.

8, Summative assessment

Finally allow pupils time to fill in their self assessment sheet DB9

9, Creating their own buzzer project

The last sheets DB10 & DB11 are designed to help pupils think through their own buzzer creations. You might also allow them to use other outputs they have used in previous projects such as programmable lights or LEDs. You can use the sentence scaffolds outlined on page 13 to help pupils think through the task and what the user will see and do.

Useful Problem Solving Skills to Assess

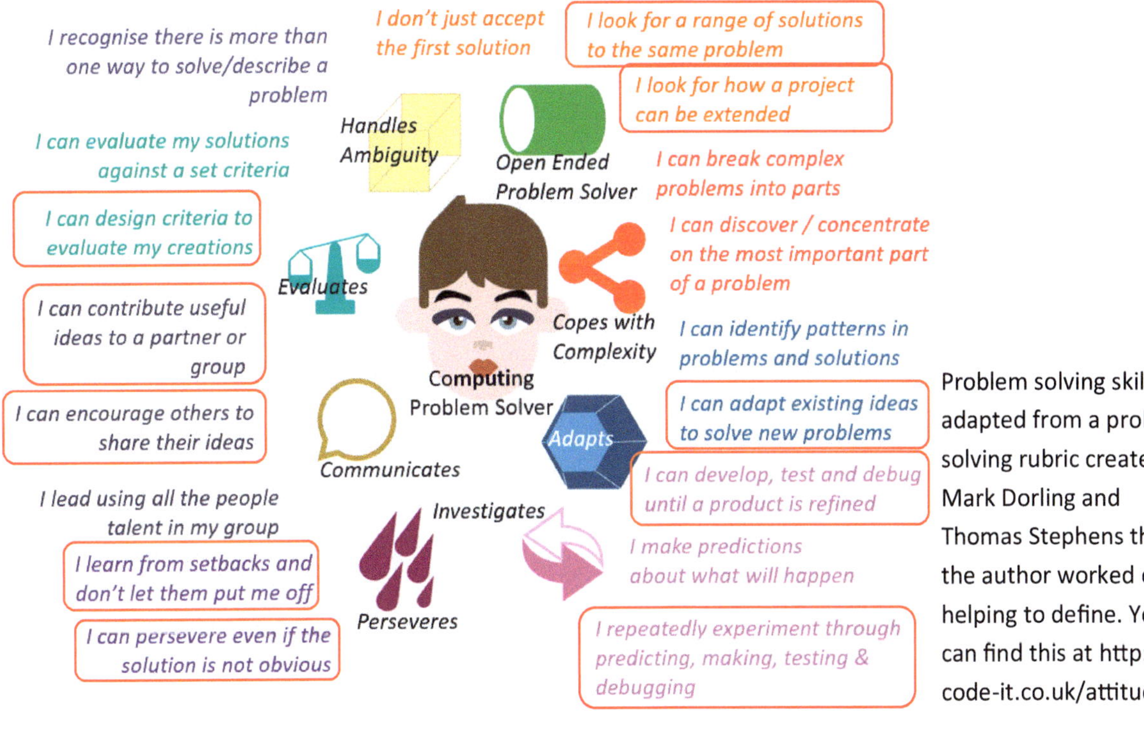

I recognise there is more than one way to solve/describe a problem
I don't just accept the first solution
I look for a range of solutions to the same problem
I look for how a project can be extended
Handles Ambiguity
Open Ended Problem Solver
I can evaluate my solutions against a set criteria
I can break complex problems into parts
I can design criteria to evaluate my creations
I can discover / concentrate on the most important part of a problem
Evaluates
I can contribute useful ideas to a partner or group
Copes with Complexity
I can identify patterns in problems and solutions
Computing Problem Solver
I can encourage others to share their ideas
I can adapt existing ideas to solve new problems
Adapts
Communicates
I can develop, test and debug until a product is refined
I lead using all the people talent in my group
Investigates
I make predictions about what will happen
I learn from setbacks and don't let them put me off
I can persevere even if the solution is not obvious
Perseveres
I repeatedly experiment through predicting, making, testing & debugging

Problem solving skills are adapted from a problem solving rubric created by Mark Dorling and Thomas Stephens that the author worked on helping to define. You can find this at http://code-it.co.uk/attitudes/

Name ______________________ Class __________

Thinking about wiring a door bell DB1

Buzzers

Buttons are **inputs** because they **put in** information into the program. They can do two things; one when they are pressed and one when they are not pressed.

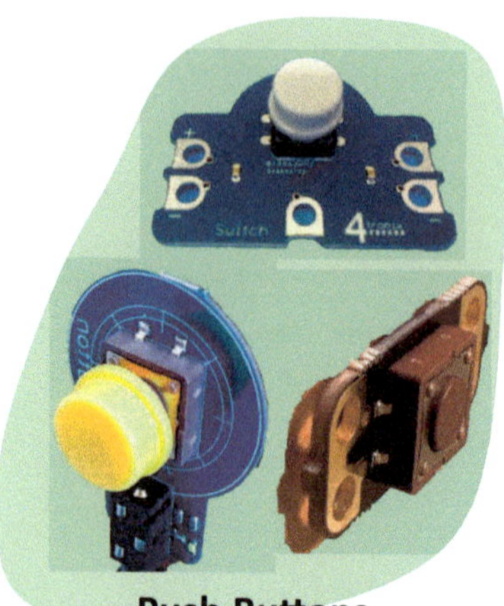

Push Buttons

Buzzers are **outputs** because they **put out** information from the program. These can output a single sound tone.

The electrician's job is to wire these up so they can work properly. The programmer's job is to make the button turn the buzzer on or off.

Draw the wires to show what connections you will use

One letter one device only!

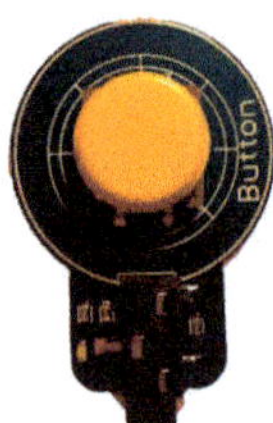

Fill in the chart to show your wires

Letter	Name of the device	Input or Output

Name ______________________________ Class ___________

Thinking about wiring a door bell DB1A

Buzzers

Buttons are **inputs** because they **put in** information into the program. They can do two things; one when they are pressed and one when they are not pressed.

Push Buttons

Buzzers are **outputs** because they **put out** information from the program. These can output a single sound tone.

The electrician's job is to wire these up so they can work properly. The programmer's job is to make the button turn the buzzer on or off.

Draw the wires to show what connections you will use

One letter one device only!

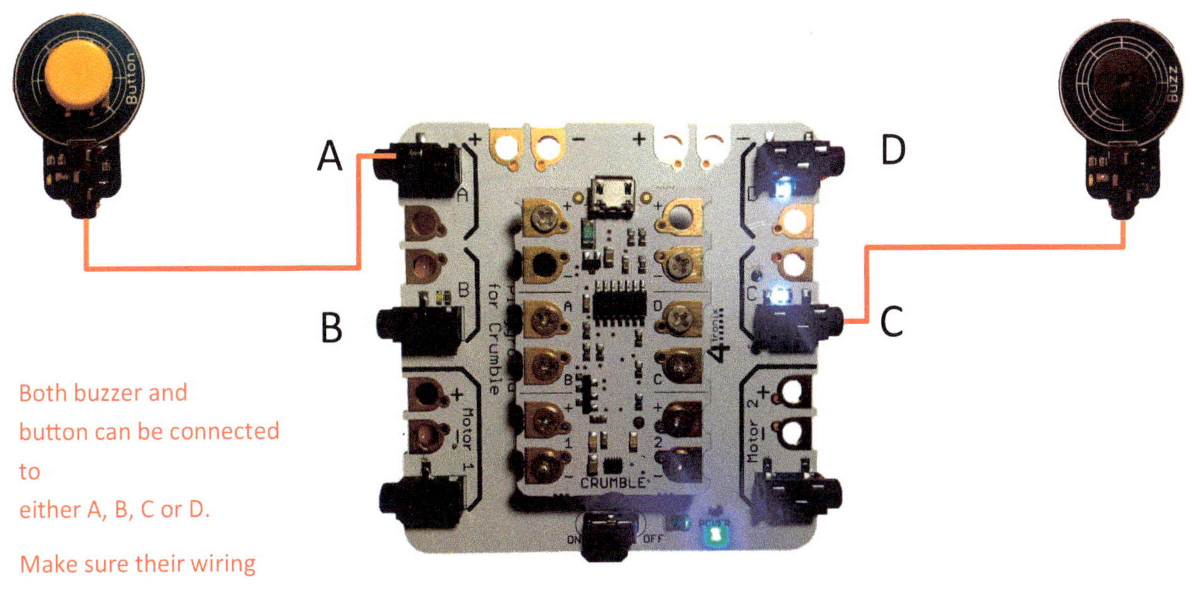

Both buzzer and button can be connected to either A, B, C or D.

Make sure their wiring matches their chart

Fill in the chart to show your wires

Letter	Name of the device	Input or Output
A	Button	Input
C	Buzzer	Output

Name ______________________________ Class _____________

Thinking about wiring a door bell DB2

Buzzers

Buzzers are **outputs** because they **put out** information from the program. These can output a single sound tone.

Buttons are **inputs** because they **put in** information into the program. They can do two things; one when they are pressed and one when they are not pressed

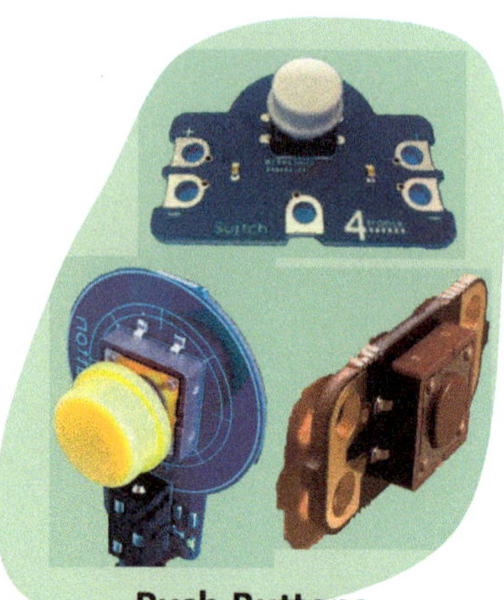

Push Buttons

The electrician's job is to wire these up so they can work properly. The programmer's job is to make the button turn the buzzer on or off.

Draw the wires to show what connections you will use

One letter one device only!

Fill in the chart to show your wires

Letter	Name of the device	Input or Output

Name ______________________________ Class ____________

Thinking about wiring a door bell DB2A

Buzzers

Buzzers are **outputs** because they **put out** information from the program. These can output a single sound tone.

Buttons are **inputs** because they **put in** information into the program. They can do two things; one when they are pressed and one when they are not pressed.

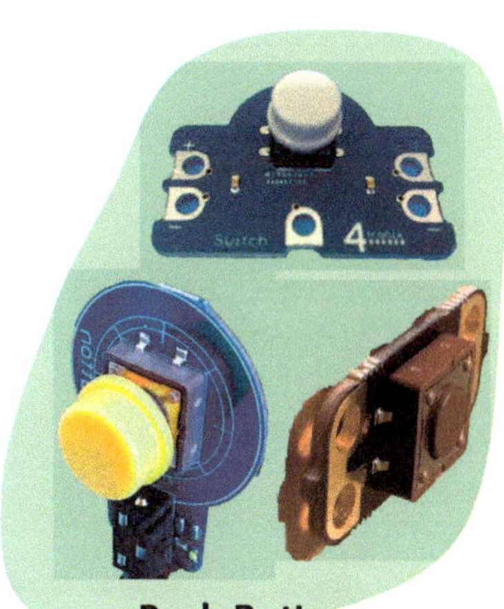

Push Buttons

The electrician's job is to wire these up so they can work properly. The programmer's job is to make the button turn the buzzer on or off.

Draw the wires to show what connections you will use

One letter one device only!

Both buzzer and button can be connected to either A, B, C or D.

Make sure their wiring matches their chart

Fill in the chart to show your wires

Letter	Name of the device	Input or Output
A	Button	Input
C	Buzzer	Output

Name ____________________________ Class ____________

Thinking about wiring a door bell DB3

Buzzers

Buttons are **inputs** because they **put in** information into the program. They can do two things; one when they are pressed and one when they are not pressed.

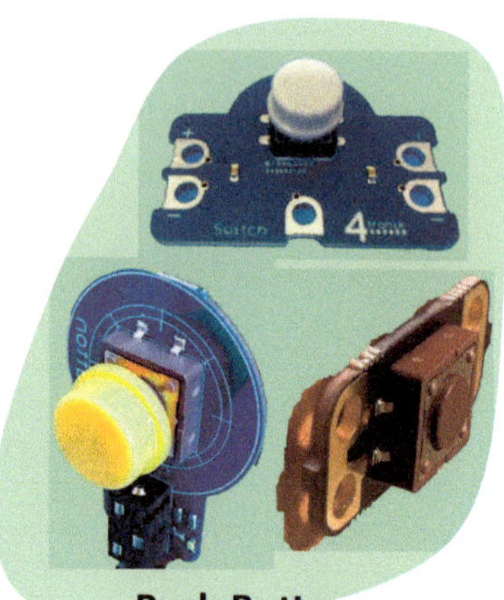

Push Buttons

Buzzers are **outputs** because they **put out** information from the program. These can output a single sound tone.

The electrician's job is to wire these up so they can work properly. The programmer's job is to make the button turn the buzzer on or off.

Draw the wires to show what connections you will use

One letter one device only!

A

D

B

C

Fill in the chart to show your wires

Letter	Name of the device	Input or Output

Name ______________________________ Class ____________

Thinking about wiring a door bell DB3A

Buzzers

Buttons are **inputs** because they **put in** information into the program. They can do two things; one when they are pressed and one when they are not pressed.

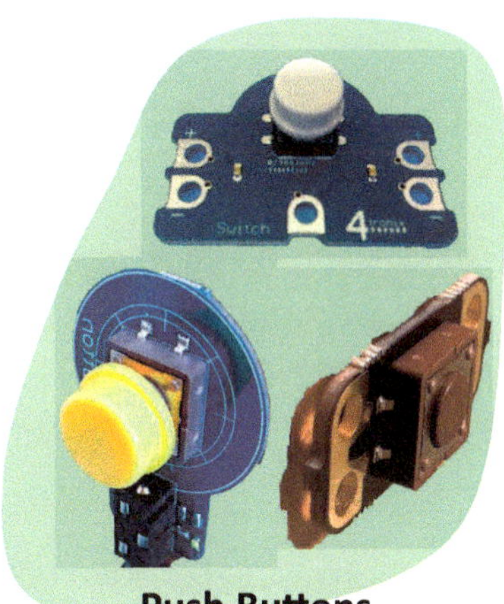

Push Buttons

Buzzers are **outputs** because they **put out** information from the program. These can output a single sound tone.

The electrician's job is to wire these up so they can work properly. The programmer's job is to make the button turn the buzzer on or off.

Draw the wires to show what connections you will use

One letter one device only!

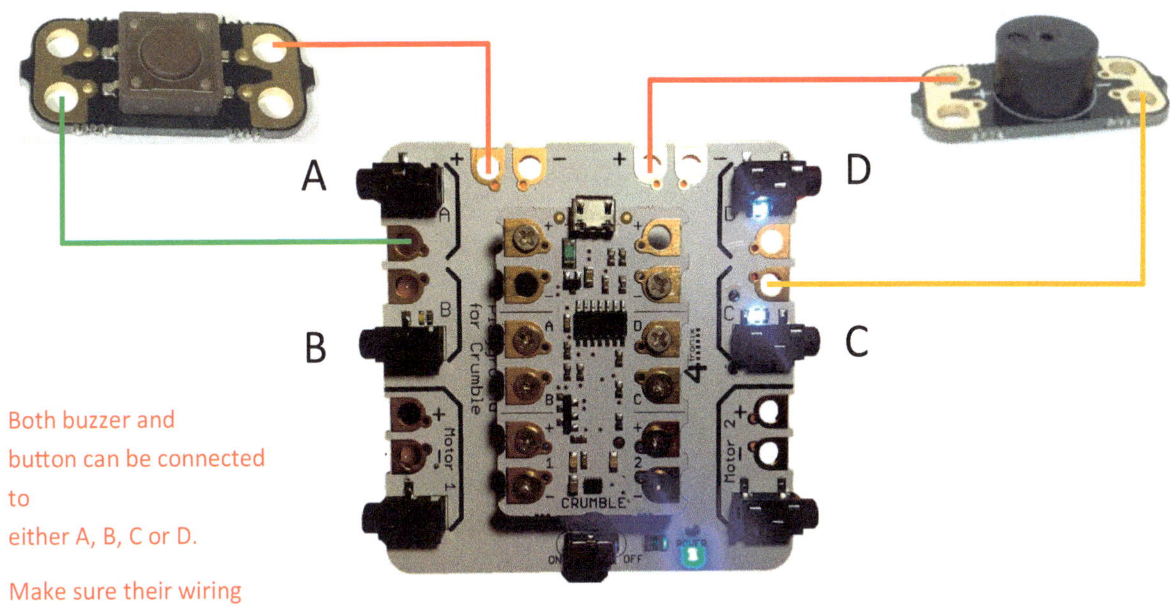

Both buzzer and button can be connected to either A, B, C or D.

Make sure their wiring matches their chart

Fill in the chart to show your wires

Letter	Name of the device	Input or Output
A	Button	Input
C	Buzzer	Output

Name ______________________ Class __________

Thinking about wiring a door bell DB4

Buzzers

Buttons are **inputs** because they **put in** information into the program. They can do two things; one when they are pressed and one when they are not pressed.

Push Buttons

Buzzers are **outputs** because they **put out** information from the program. These can output a single sound tone.

The electrician's job is to wire these up so they can work properly. The programmer's job is to make the button turn the buzzer on or off.

Draw the wires to show what connections you will use

One letter one device only!

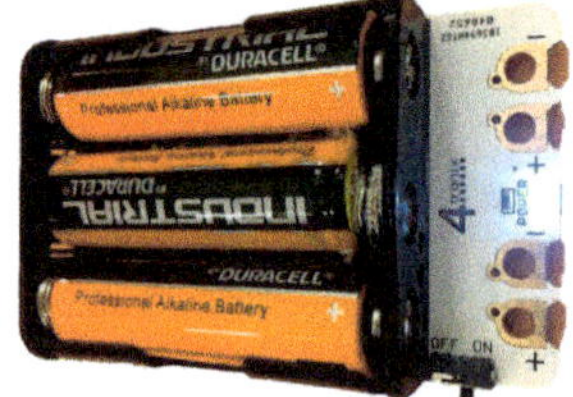

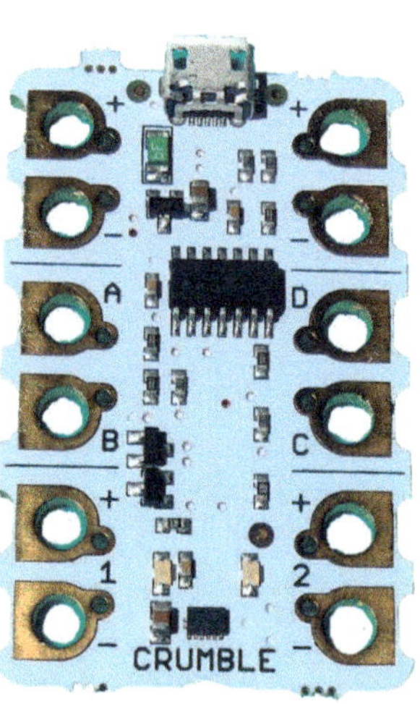

Fill in the chart to show your wires

Letter	Name of the device	Input or Output

Name ____________________________ Class ___________

Thinking about wiring a door bell DB4A

Buzzers

Buttons are **inputs** because they **put in** information into the program. They can do two things; one when they are pressed and one when they are not pressed.

Push Buttons

Buzzers are **outputs** because they **put out** information from the program. These can output a single sound tone.

The electrician's job is to wire these up so they can work properly. The programmer's job is to make the button turn the buzzer on or off.

Draw the wires to show what connections you will use

One letter one device only!

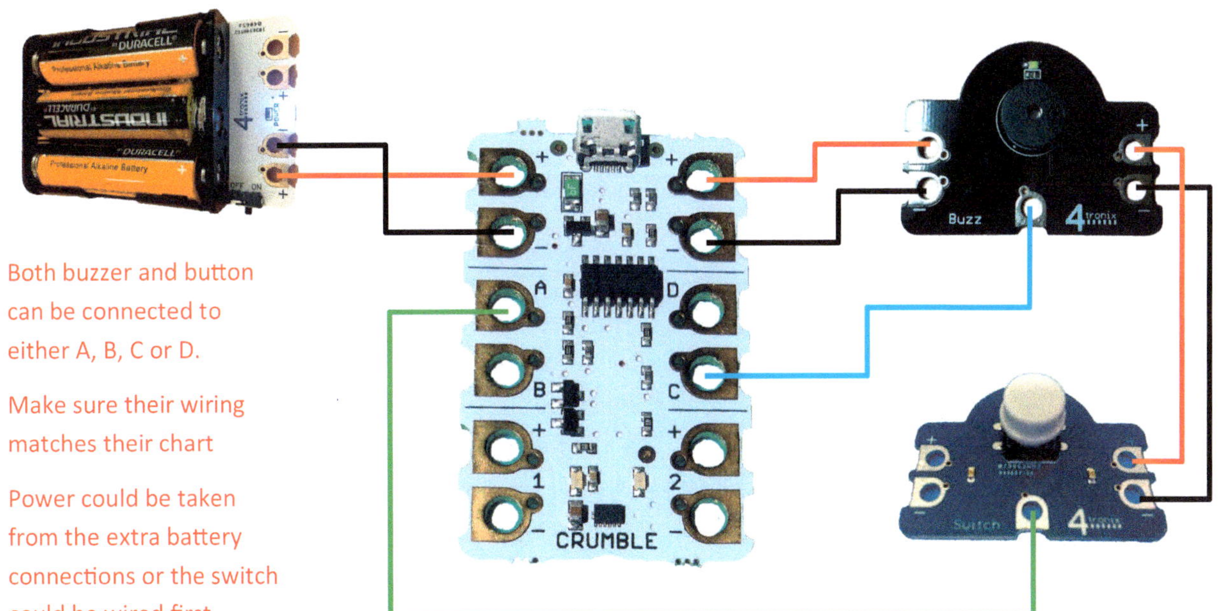

Both buzzer and button can be connected to either A, B, C or D.

Make sure their wiring matches their chart

Power could be taken from the extra battery connections or the switch could be wired first.

Fill in the chart to show your wires

Letter	Name of the device	Input or Output
A	Button	Input
C	Buzzer	Output

Name ________________________ Class __________

Thinking about wiring a door bell DB5

Buzzers

Buttons are **inputs** because they **put in** information into the program. They can do two things; one when they are pressed and one when they are not pressed.

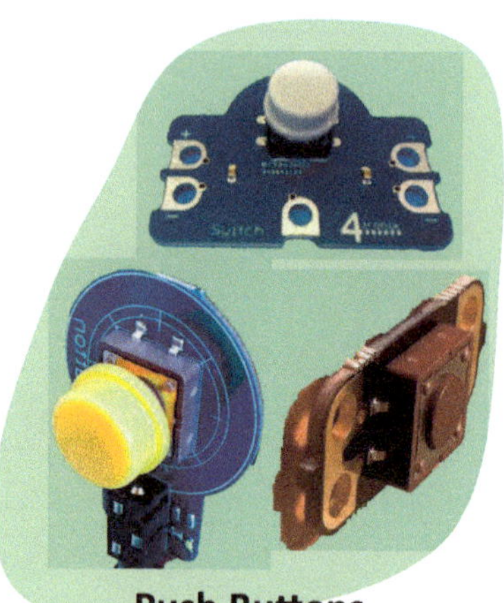

Push Buttons

Buzzers are **outputs** because they **put out** information from the program. These can output a single sound tone.

The electrician's job is to wire these up so they can work properly. The programmer's job is to make the button turn the buzzer on or off.

Draw the wires to show what connections you will use

One letter one device only!

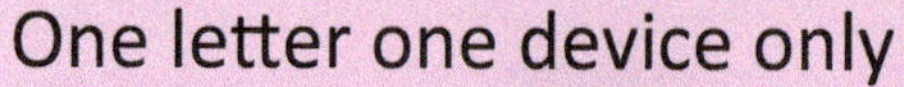

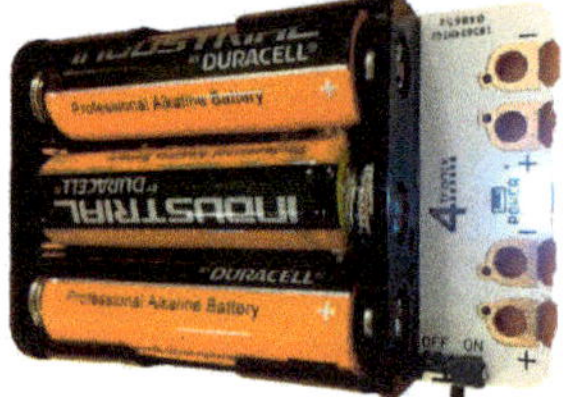

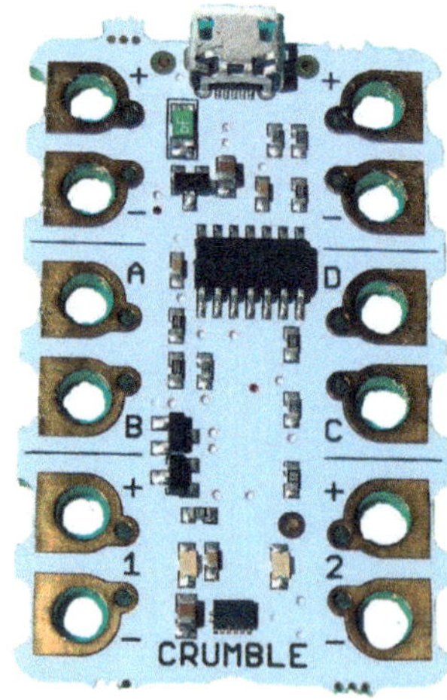

Fill in the chart to show your wires

Letter	Name of the device	Input or Output

Name ______________________________ Class ____________

Thinking about wiring a door bell DB5A

Buzzers

Buttons are **inputs** because they **put in** information into the program. They can do two things one when they are pressed and one when they are not pressed

Push Buttons

Buzzers are **outputs** because they **put out** information from the program. These can output a single sound tone.

The electricians job is to wire these up so they can work properly. The programmers job is to make the button turn the buzzer on or off

Draw the wires to show what connections you will use

One letter one device only!

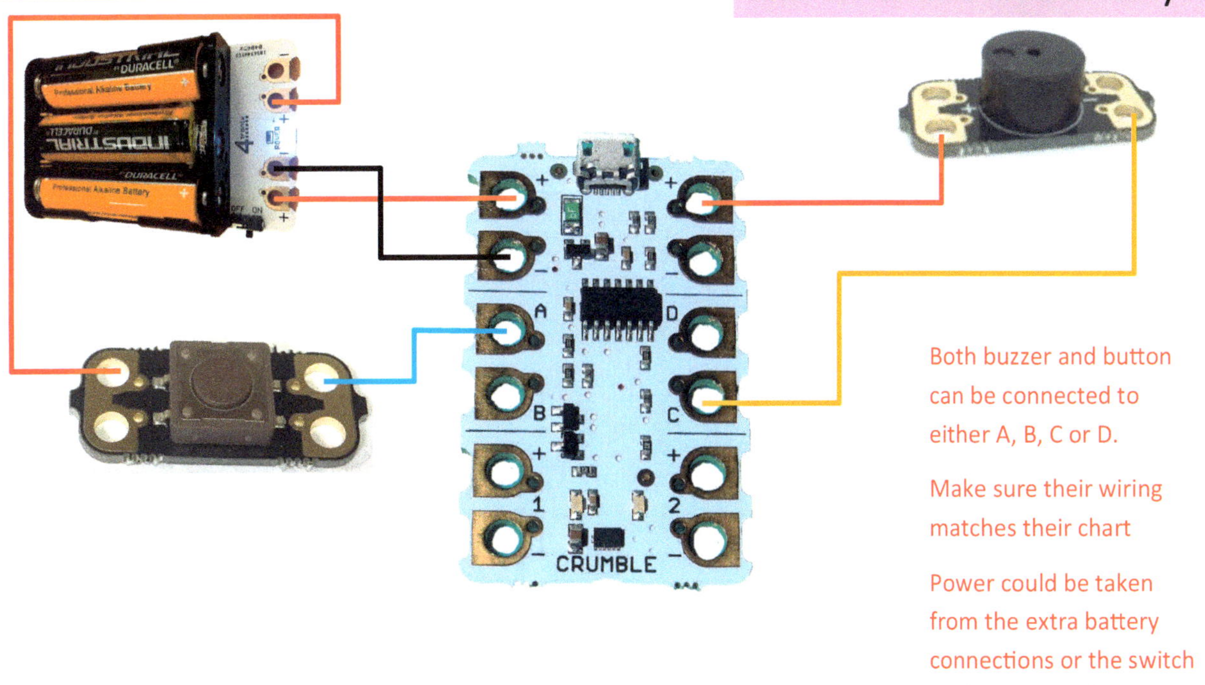

Both buzzer and button can be connected to either A, B, C or D.

Make sure their wiring matches their chart

Power could be taken from the extra battery connections or the switch could be wired first.

Fill in the chart to show your wires

Letter	Name of the device	Input or Output
A	Button	Input
C	Buzzer	Output

Name ______________________________ Class ____________

Thinking about wiring a door bell DB6

Buzzers

Buttons are **inputs** because they **put in** information into the program. They can do two things; one when they are pressed and one when they are not pressed.

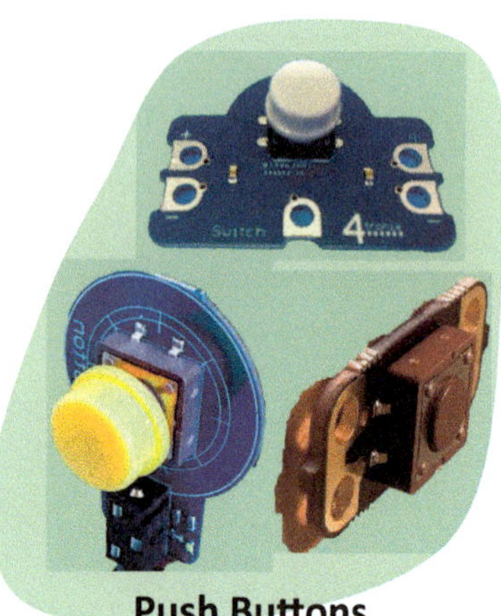
Push Buttons

Buzzers are **outputs** because they **put out** information from the program. These can output a single sound tone.

The electrician's job is to wire these up so they can work properly. The programmer's job is to make the button turn the buzzer on or off.

Draw the wires to show what connections you will use

One letter one device only!

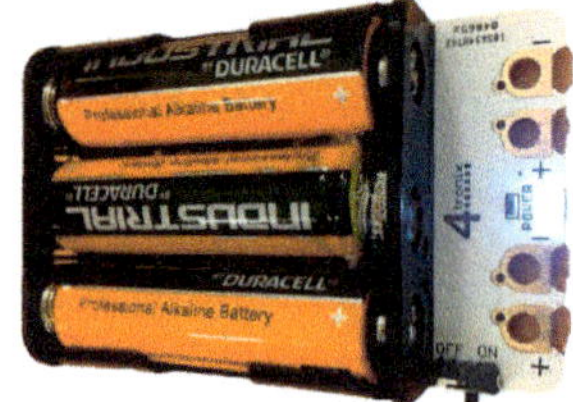

Fill in the chart to show your wires

Letter	Name of the device	Input or Output

Name ______________________ Class __________

Thinking about wiring a door bell DB7

Buzzers

Buzzers are **outputs** because they **put out** information from the program. These can output a single sound tone.

Buttons are **inputs** because they **put in** information into the program. They can do two things; one when they are pressed and one when they are not pressed.

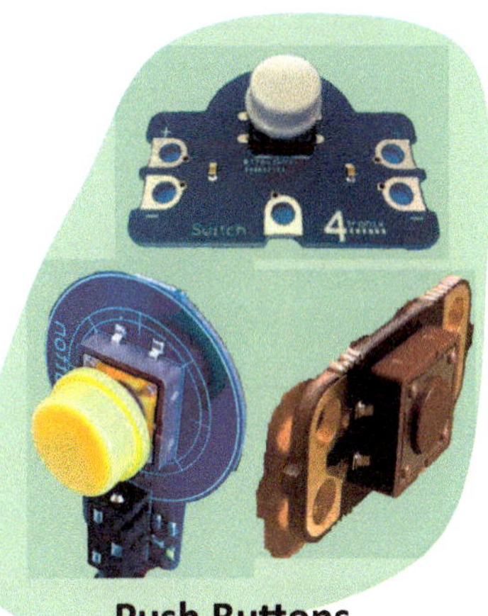
Push Buttons

The electrician's job is to wire these up so they can work properly. The programmer's job is to make the button turn the buzzer on or off.

Draw the wires to show what connections you will use

One letter one device only!

Fill in the chart to show your wires

Letter	Name of the device	Input or Output

Name ____________________________ Class ____________ DB8

Thinking about programming a door bell

Buzzers

The electrician's job is to wire these up so they can work properly. The programmer's job is to make the button turn the buzzer on or off.

Push Buttons

Antonio came up with an idea for his program first.

Program Idea
Switching the buzzer on or off with a button

He then thought about it in more detail and came up with an algorithm.

Algorithm
When the button is pressed down the buzzer will sound, when the button is de-pressed the buzzer will be silent.

Because there was a choice in his program he used a conditional selection block.

```
program start
  if <button is pressed> then
    Turn buzzer on
  else
    Turn buzzer off
  end if
```

Conditional selection block

It would only run the choice once, straight after the program was started. He then added a forever loop to check if the button is pressed over and over again.

```
program start
  do forever
    if <button is pressed down> then
      Turn buzzer on
    else
      Turn buzzer off
    end if
  loop
```

Forever loop

Turn buzzer on | set C HI
Button is pressed | A is HI
Button is de-pressed | A is LO
Turn buzzer off | set C LO

The Crumble need to know where things are plugged in (A, B, C or D) and if they are on (HI) or off (LO).

Can you decide where the programming blocks will go in these two doorbell programs? Draw arrows to show.

Make the button, attached to input A, turn on the buzzer attached to output C when pressed (HI) and off (LO) when depressed.

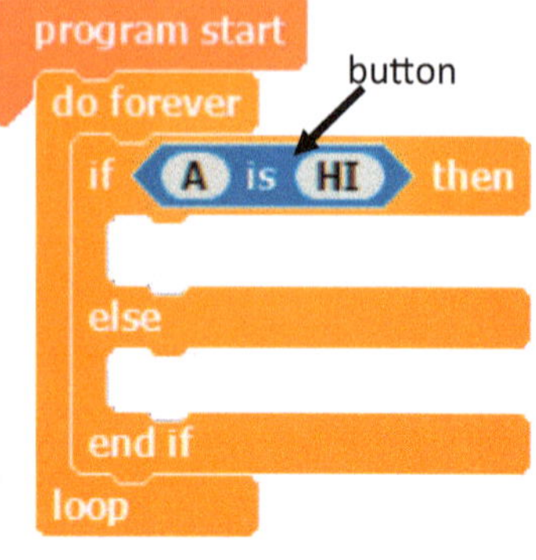

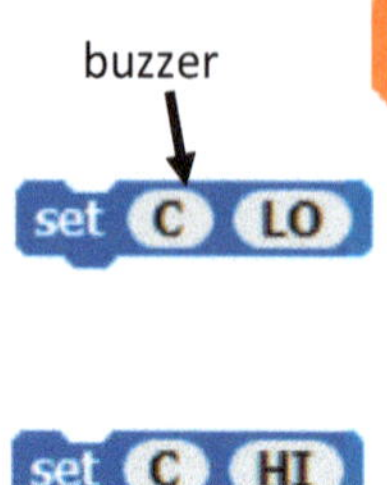

Make the button, attached to input A turn off the buzzer attached to output C when pressed (HI) and on (LO) when depressed.

```
program start
  do forever
    if <A is HI> then

    else

    end if
  loop
```

set C LO

set C HI

Tick the best program for a house bell.

Name ______________________ Class __________ DB8A

Thinking about programming a door bell

Buzzers

The electrician's job is to wire these up so they can work properly. The programmer's job is to make the button turn the buzzer on or off.

Push Buttons

Antonio came up with an idea for his program first.

Program Idea

Switching the buzzer on or off with a button

He then thought about it in more detail and came up with an algorithm.

Algorithm

When the button is pressed down the buzzer will sound, when the button is de-pressed the buzzer will be silent.

Because there was a choice in his program he used a conditional selection block.

```
program start
if <button is pressed> then
  Turn buzzer on
else
  Turn buzzer off
end if
```

Conditional selection block

It would only run the choice once, straight after the program was started. He then added a forever loop to check if the button is pressed over and over again.

```
program start
do forever
  if <button is pressed down> then
    Turn buzzer on
  else
    Turn buzzer off
  end if
loop
```

Forever loop

Turn buzzer on | Button is pressed | Button is de-pressed | Turn buzzer off

set C HI | A is HI | A is LO | set C LO

The Crumble need to know where things are plugged in (A, B, C or D) and if they are on (HI) or off (LO).

Can you decide where the programming blocks will go in these two doorbell programs? Draw arrows to show.

Make the button, attached to input A, turn on the buzzer attached to output C when pressed (HI) and off (LO) when depressed.

Make the button, attached to input A turn off the buzzer attached to output C when pressed (HI) and on (LO) when depressed.

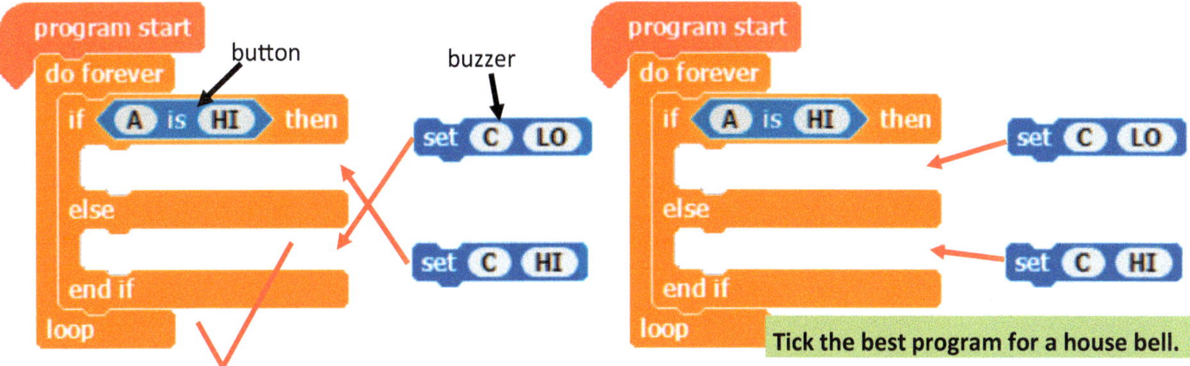

Tick the best program for a house bell.

Name ______________________ Class __________ DB12

Thinking about programming a door bell

The electrician's job is to wire these up so they can work properly. The programmer's job is to make the button turn the buzzer on or off.

Crumble programs can only have one program start block. → **program start**

Click here to change from HI (on) to LO (off).

set C HI

If you plugged your buzzer into C then you won't need to change the letter

HI means the buzzer is on. LO means the buzzer is off

set C LO

Use some of these blocks to build your own night light program that starts with a button.

if ⬡ then / else / end if

If the button attached to port A is on (HI) then the code placed here will be run.

If the button attached to port A is off (LO) then the code placed here will be run.

This block is a condition. The letter refers to which port the button is plugged into. → **A is HI**

Use the maker cards to work out where to wire the button and night light into the Crumble.

do forever / loop

Wrap all your code in a forever loop to check the condition over and over again.

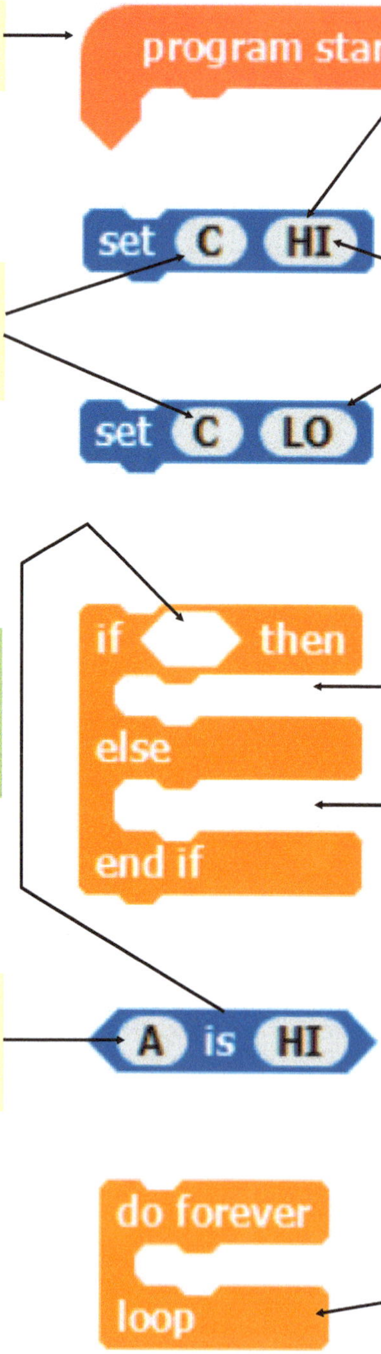

Doorbell Assessment Sheet DB9 Name ________ Class ____

☺ I did this well

😐 I did this ok or I did this a little

☹ I tried this but it didn't work or I didn't do this at all

I wired up my doorbell.	
I programmed my doorbell to turn on or off using the button.	
I listened to my partners ideas.	
I contributed good idea to my partner.	
I persevered when the wiring or programming didn't work.	
I came up with criteria to decide what a good doorbell looks, works and sounds like.	

Sticker	I got this sticker for
Sticker	I got this sticker for
Sticker	I got this sticker for

Name ____________________________ Class ____________ DB10

Thinking about designing my own project that uses a buzzer

These are buzzers

Fill in your idea and add your inputs and outputs to the chart

My program will

by

What will the user see and do?

Input/ Output	Name of device attached	What the device does (include as much detail as possible)
A output	A buzzer	Buzz in a pattern when the button is pressed.
A		
B		
C		
D		
Motor 1		
Motor 2		

Draw your devices and the wires that connect them

Name ______________________ Class __________ DB11

Thinking about designing my own project that uses a buzzer

These are buzzers

Fill in your idea and add your inputs and outputs to the chart

My program will

by

What will the user see and do?

Input/ Output	Name of device attached	What the device does (include as much detail as possible)
A output	A buzzer	Buzz in a pattern when the button is pressed
A		
B		
C		
D		
Motor 1		
Motor 2		

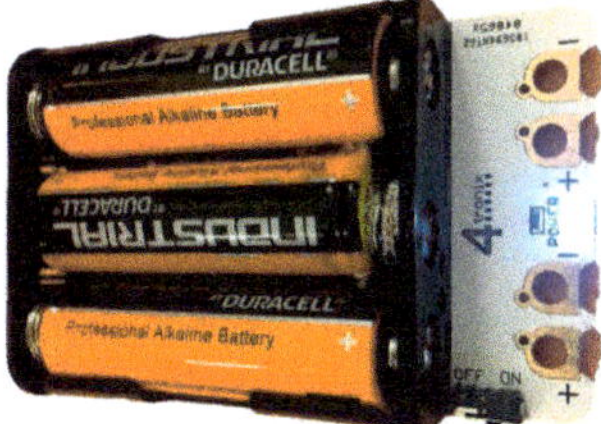

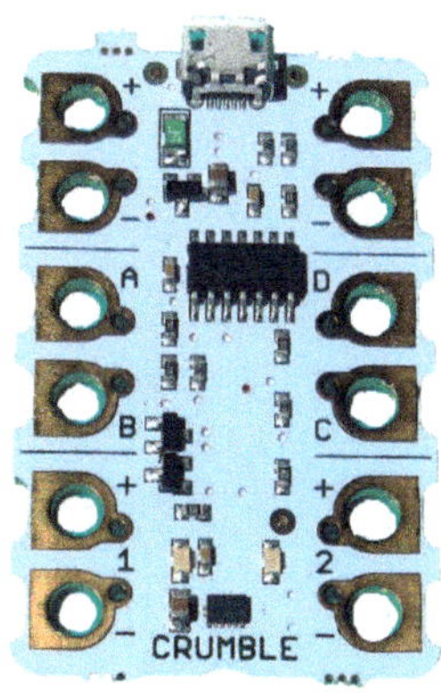

Draw your devices and the wires that connect them

5. Animated Character

Module Aim

Create a character, animating one or more limbs to move using a servo motor.

Servo driving two arms using linkages

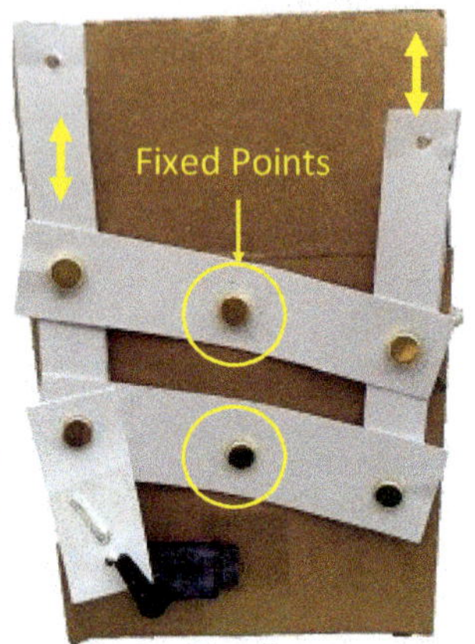

Cross Curricular Links

Literacy –Animate a story animal from your favourite book such as Tabby the cat from The Worst Witch or Peter Rabbit from Beatrix Potter, Babe from The Sheep Pig or Iorek Byrnison the polar bear from Philip Pullman's Dark Materials books. Make the tail wag, front paw wave, back paw thump or eye wink using lights.

History –Chop off the head of one of Henry VIII's wives, perpetuate George Washington's cherry tree myth or wave a banner proclaiming female emancipation.

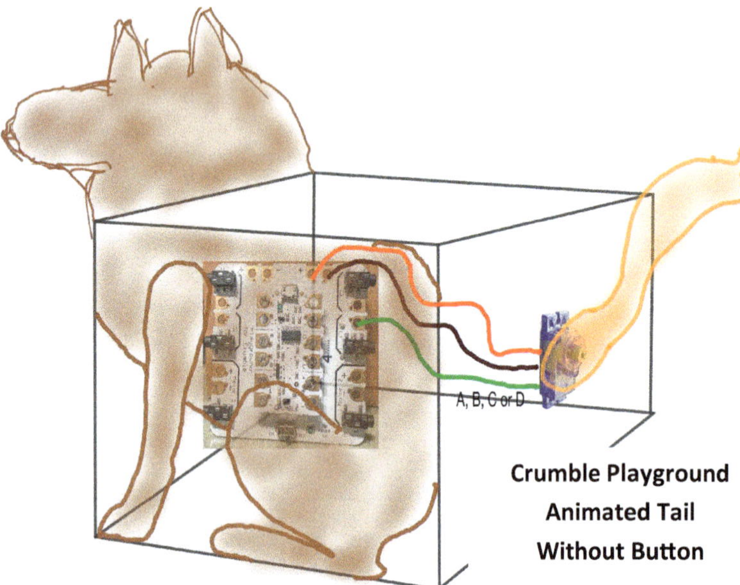

Crumble Playground Animated Tail Without Button

Design & Technology - Combine with simple levers to make multiple characters move or create a diorama.

Materials

Crumble playground, button, servo motor or Crumble, battery box, Button, servo motor

Construction

This animated character project is best mounted on a pre-made cardboard box. 4 inch ones are a perfect size and can be purchased very cheaply.

Simple templates for the cat, cow and pig, found in the book, can be decorated before being stuck on or pupils can draw their own animal on the box.

Teachers could get pupils to draw their own animal from the side view, mount it on card and stick it to one side of the box only.

Teachers could allow pupils to experiment with different types of material coverings to simulate animal fur.

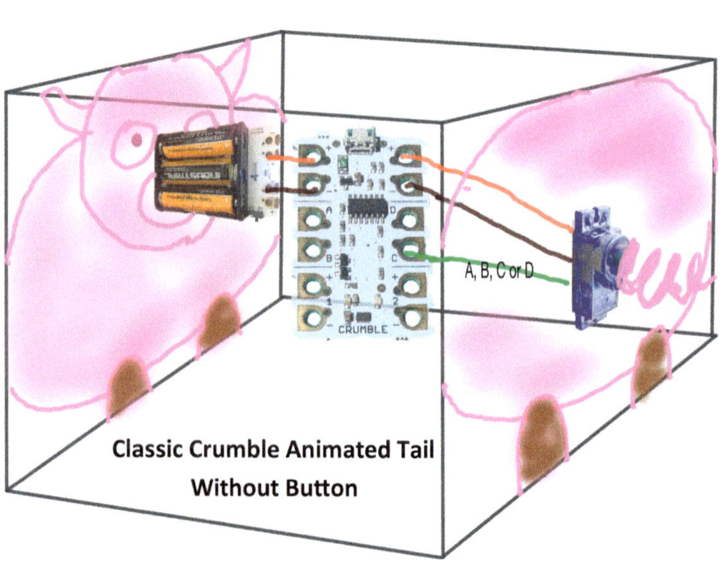

Classic Crumble Animated Tail Without Button

A rectangle can be pre-cut through the side of the cardboard box to mount the servo motor.

Observers will notice that we haven't included a playground headphone connection servo . This is due to the mounting plate making it more difficult to mount the servo through the wall of a cardboard box.

Historical simulations often work best on flat card, mounted on one side of the box only.

In this mock up you can see the servo motor controlling the protesters banner

Front and back view of servo mounted on box side

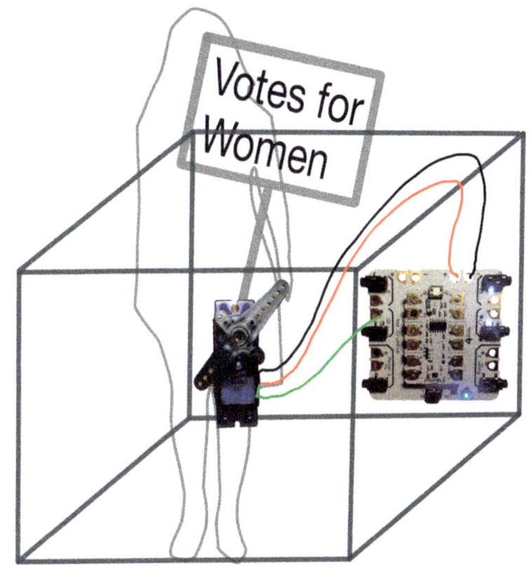

Crumble Playground Animated Banner Without Button

Versions

The most basic version of this model would only have one servo. The next version up would have the servo triggered by a button whilst at the most advanced level the model might include multiple moving limbs as well as programmable lights for eyes triggered by a distance or PIR sensor.

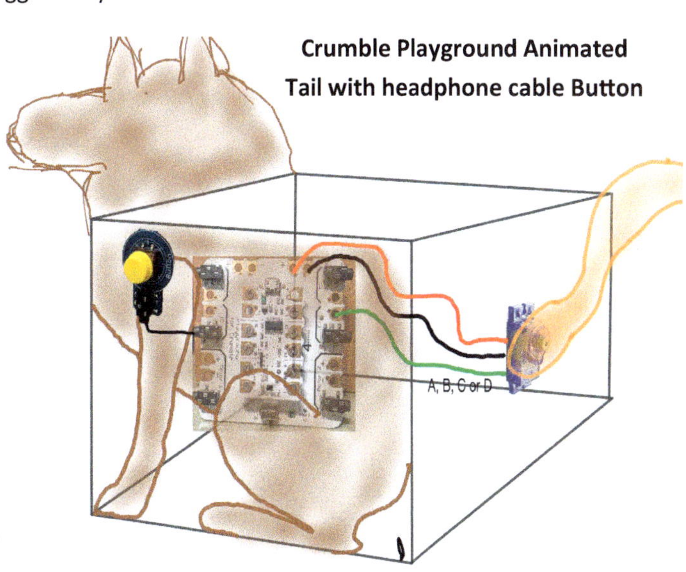

Crumble Playground Animated Tail with headphone cable Button

Programming planning includes a basic single servo version for younger children as well as a button controlled version. There is code for a distance sensor controlled version if teachers wish to leave one displayed somewhere prominent.

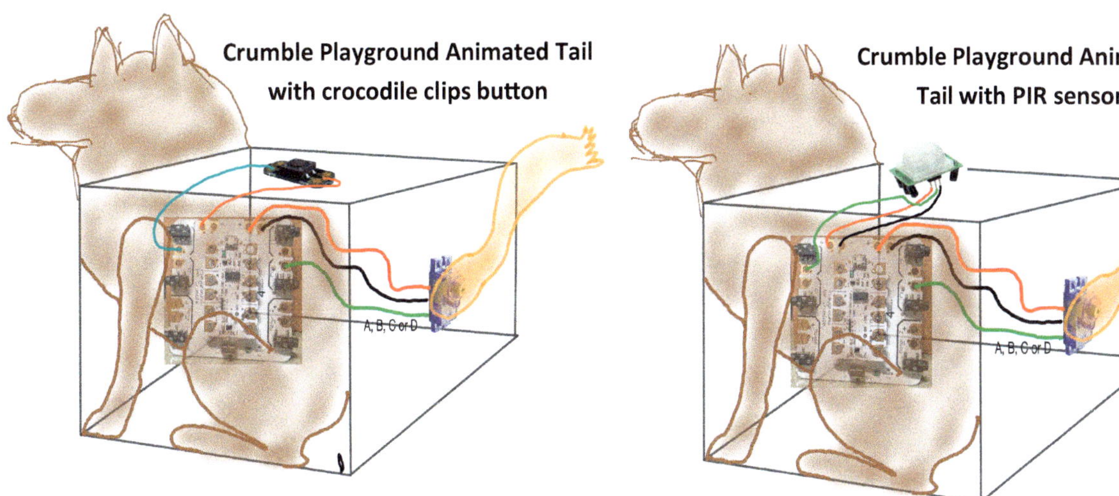

Crumble Playground Animated Tail with crocodile clips button

Crumble Playground Animated Tail with PIR sensor

Suggested Module Outline for Younger Pupils

(without the button)

1, Create an example

Make a simple animated character mounted on a card board box yourself before the introductory lesson. This will help you discover all those little things such as where to poke the wires though the box and the best way to fix the servo motor through the box side.

2, Pre-cut holes

If your pupils are very young, you may want to prepare some boxes before the session by sealing the bottoms and cutting servo size holes through the side. Make sure that the cut is only around three sides so that the cardboard can be bent back into the box and used to help fix the servo firmly. The pig and cat heads are higher so the servo hole should be cut about 10mm from the top; the cow head is more central so the servo hole should be cut more centrally.

3, Introduce the topic

Introduce the topic linked to whatever theme you have chosen. Give pupils the prepared boxes. If you are using the simple templates, pupils can colour these in or select appropriate material to cover them. Don't allow anyone to stick their template sheets onto the box until they have shown you on which side of the box they will attach it to. Make sure they fold the lid and don't stick any part of the template to the lid yet.

4, Create Templates

Glue the templates onto the box sides. If you are making the head move as shown in the photos below make sure you glue the head onto card before cutting it out.

Formative assessment	Corrective	Enrichment
Are the servo wires correctly attached?	Highlight which area on the support card or Crumble Playground that they need to check/change. Don't just give them the answer	Ask them where they might add another servo if their animated character was going to have two moving limbs. (A, B, C or D plus power positive and negative)

Animated character using the Pig Template

5, Wiring & Mounting

Show pupils how to attach and wire the servo as per one of the examples shown earlier in this chapter or use the wiring sheet AC3 and servo maker card.

Then add the head onto the server arm using a piece of double sided sticky tape or rolled up tape.

Animated character using the Cow Template

6, Thinking programming

There are two animated character thinking sheets for pupils to fill in while their glue dries. On the sheet they are introduced to the servo motor and some of the basic code to make it run. The first AC1 & AC1A is simpler and more suitable for younger pupils. The second, AC2 & AC2A has more reading and comprehension and is suitable for older children or better readers.

You might also choose to demonstrate the software or work through the thinking sheets as a class or a mixture of both of these methods.

7, Programming

If this is your pupils first Crumble project then show them how to attach the crumble to the USB lead and where to plug it into their computers. Give them plenty of time to experiment with their servo motor programs. After a while you may wish to encourage them to include a wait block before the rest of their program starts to give them time to close the box after the program has started.

8, Assessment

Fill in the assessment sheet AC12.

Suggested Module Outline for Older Pupils
(with the button)

1, Teacher Example

Make a simple animated character mounted on a card board box triggered by a single button yourself before the introductory lesson. This will help you discover all those little things such as where to poke the wires though the box and the best way to fix the servo motor and button through the box side.

2, Preparation

If time is lacking, you may want to prepare some boxes before the session by sealing the bottoms.

3, Introduce the topic

Introduce the topic linked to whatever theme you have chosen. Give pupils the boxes. If you are using the simple templates, pupils can colour these in or select appropriate material to cover them. Speak to your school art manager to see if there are any art objectives that can be covered through this part of the project.

4, Planning the wiring

Although pupils could just be given the maker cards and equipment, a much larger proportion of pupils will achieve wiring success independently if they have planned where the wiring will go before hand.

Pupils can fill in wiring thinking sheets to help them identify which input and output connections they are using and where each connection will go.

AC4 & AC4A Crumble Playground, 4tronix button and Redfern Electronic Servo
AC5 & AC5A Crumble Playground, Redfern Electronic Servo & Button

Formative assessment	Corrective	Enrichment
Is the wiring correctly attached?	Highlight which area on the support card or Crumble Playground that they need to check/change. Don't just give them the answer	Ask them where they might add another servo if their animated character was going to have two moving limbs. (A, B, C or D plus power positive and negative)

AC6 & AC6A Crumble Playground & 4tronix Playground button
AC7 & AC7A Classic Crumble, Redfern Electronic button & servo
AC8 & AC8A Classic Crumble, Redfern Electronic servo & 4tronix button

5, Thinking about the programming

Before pupils move on to coding, you may wish to use the thinking sheets to help pupils think through what they want the program to do (algorithm) and how this might be achieved (coding).

AC9, AC9Q & AC9A show how another child programmed her device. Children are asked questions based on her code example. These are a good place to start if you and your pupils are new to physical programming.

AC10, AC10Q & AC10A are another alternative with more complex questions. These may be useful for stretching your more able pupils as there are more questions that need pupils to logically reason.

AC11 could also be used instead of the previous two examples This provides two forms of algorithm and the necessary blocks to convert these into Crumble code. This sheet is suitable for more experienced programmers who just need a hint to get started.

Experienced primary programmers could also use the maker cards to help them work out a solution.

Formative assessment	Corrective	Enrichment
Are pupils communicating and persevering?	Challenge them using the problem solving attitudes and the carrot of earning a sticker.	Give out stickers where pupils are modelling these behaviours and get them to stick them on their assessment sheets describing why they got them.

6, Assessment

Allow time for pupils to complete the assessment sheet AC13

7, Own project

Giving pupils time to plan their own adapted project which uses servo motors is an important part of the process towards pupil agency. Sheets AC14 and AC15 can be used as a framework alongside questions outlined on page 13 in the introduction.

Suggested Module Adaptations for Older Pupils

The following adaptations will increase the time needed for the projects and the complexity of the coding and in some cases the cost.

```
program start
do forever
  if distance (cm) T: D E: C < 30 then
    servo A 0 degrees
    wait 300 milliseconds
    servo A 30 degrees
    wait 300 milliseconds
  end if
loop
```

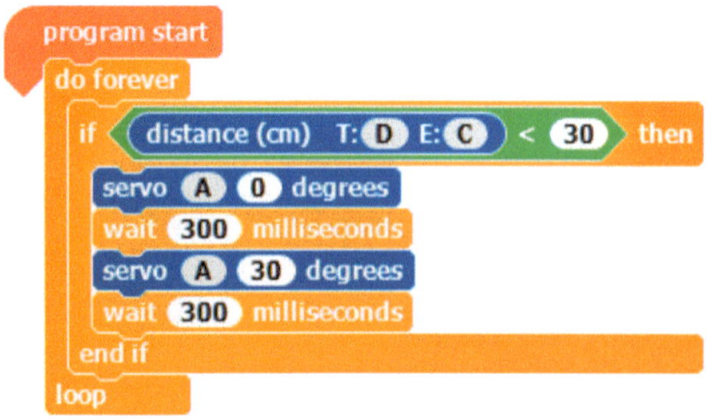

Code example if a distance sensor is plugged into D & C and a servo is plugged into A

- More than one moving limb. Pupils choose which limbs to animate and might have a paw, head and tail.
- Triggering the module using a distance sensor. Instead of using a button pupils trigger the device from a distance.

Movement is triggered when an object is detected at less than 30cm

Useful Problem Solving Skills to Assess

I recognise there is more than one way to solve/describe a problem
I don't just accept the first solution
I look for a range of solutions to the same problem
I look for how a project can be extended
Handles Ambiguity
Open Ended Problem Solver
I can evaluate my solutions against a set criteria
I can break complex problems into parts
I can design criteria to evaluate my creations
I can discover / concentrate on the most important part of a problem
Evaluates
I can contribute useful ideas to a partner or group
Copes with Complexity
I can identify patterns in problems and solutions
Computing Problem Solver
I can encourage others to share their ideas
I can adapt existing ideas to solve new problems
Adapts
Communicates
I can develop, test and debug until a product is refined
I lead using all the people talent in my group
Investigates
I learn from setbacks and don't let them put me off
I make predictions about what will happen
I can persevere even if the solution is not obvious
Perseveres
I repeatedly experiment through predicting, making, testing & debugging

Maker Cards

MC02	**MC06**
MC14	**MC13**
MC18	**MC19**
MC26	**MC27**
MC28	**MC29**
MC32	**MC35**
MC37	**MC38**
MC39	**MC48**
MC50	**MC51**
MC52	**MC53**

Curricular Coverage

Design & Technology NC

NCD2A, NCD2E, NCD2G, NCD2H

Computing NC

NCC1B, NCC2A, NCC2B, NCC2C,

I like it because I think it makes my brain churn, like a work out! *Soraiya 10*

I loved doing the animal project because it gave us a chance to work independently with our own design. I would be happy to do it again *Maddie 10*

There were a few bugs but we managed to do it in record time. Really fun would recommend. *Eve 10*

1, Servo motors can move 180 degrees from –90 to 0 to 90 degrees. I have chosen to exclude –90 from the scaffolded examples although it is included on the maker cards

Name ______________________________ Class ____________

Thinking about programming an animated character AC1 (no input)

Servo Motors

This servo motors has been programmed to turn no more than a quarter turn.

Can you turn a quarter turn?

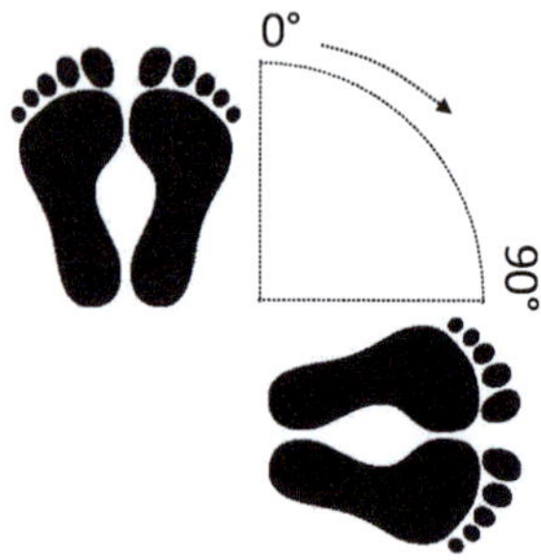

Look at the programs and answer the questions

Tick the program that turns the most.

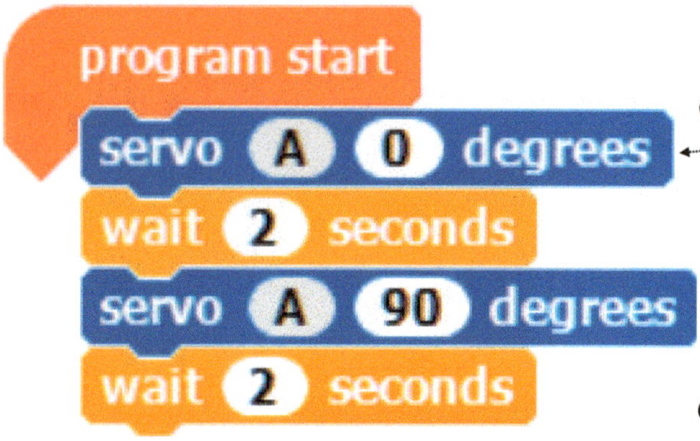

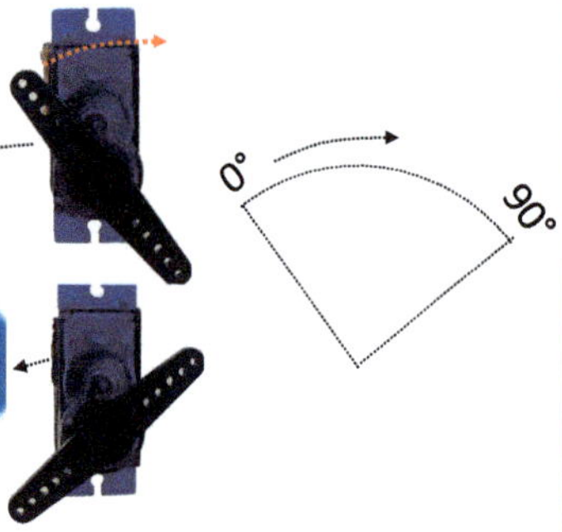

program start
servo A 0 degrees
wait 2 seconds
servo A 90 degrees
wait 2 seconds

0°
90°

How many seconds are there between moving from 0 to 45 degrees?

A, 1 second

B, 2 seconds

C, 3 seconds

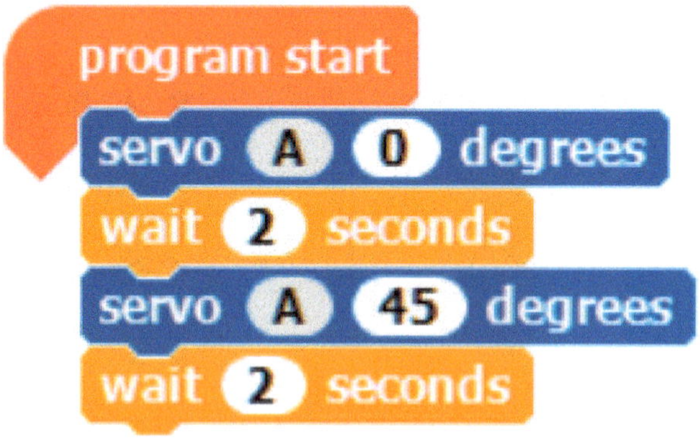

program start
servo A 0 degrees
wait 2 seconds
servo A 45 degrees
wait 2 seconds

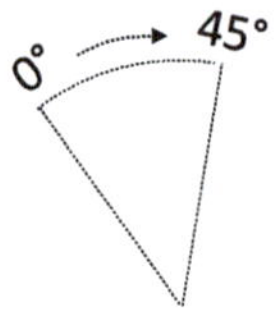

0°
45°

You can make it turn any number between 0 and 90 degrees.

What number will you try first?

Write it on the program

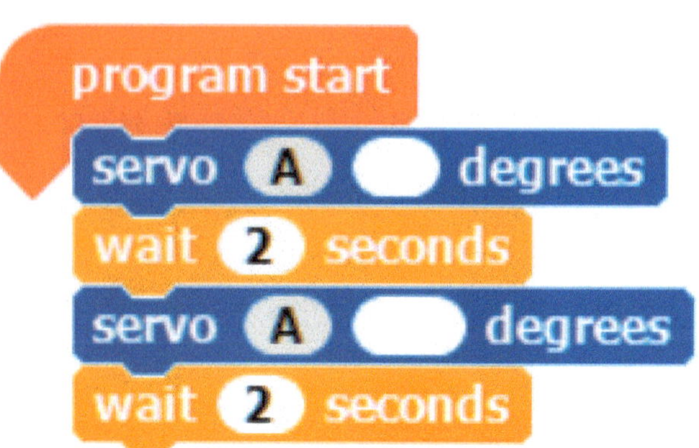

Name ______________________________ Class _____________

Thinking about programming an animated character AC1A (no input)

Servo Motors

This servo motors has been programmed to turn no more than a quarter turn.

Can you turn a quarter turn?

ANSWERS

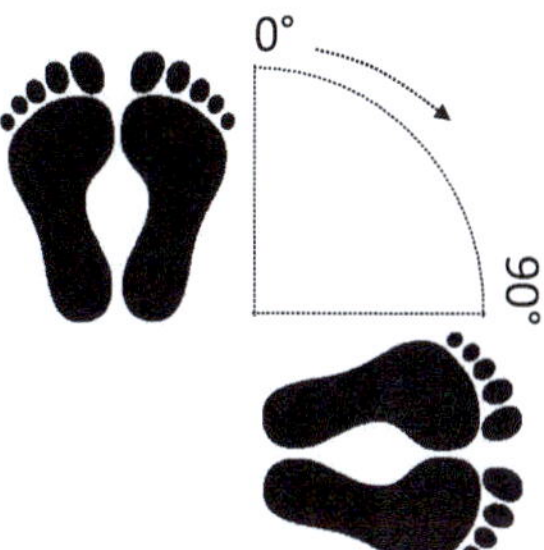

Look at the programs and answer the questions

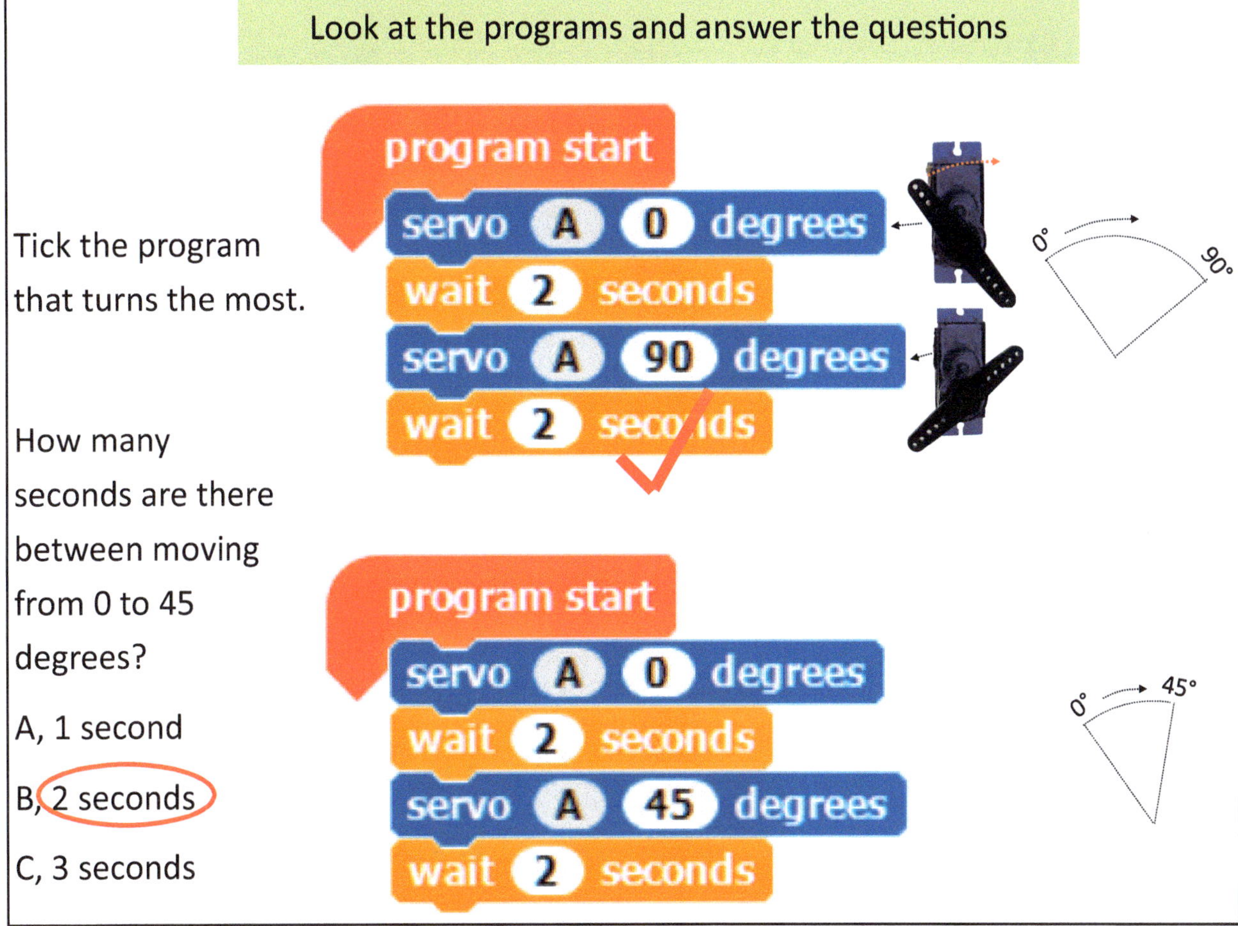

Tick the program that turns the most. ✓

How many seconds are there between moving from 0 to 45 degrees?

A, 1 second

B, 2 seconds (circled)

C, 3 seconds

You can make it turn any number between 0 and 90 degrees.

What number will you try first?

Write it on the program

Any number between 1 and 90

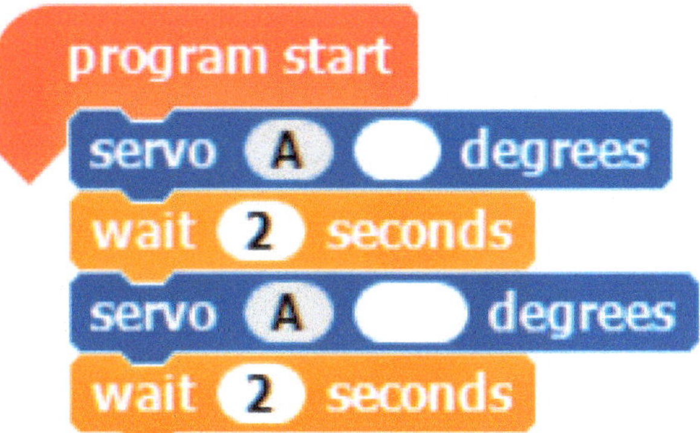

Name ______________________________ Class ____________

Thinking about programming an animated character AC2 (no input)

Motors

servo

Motors are **outputs** because they **put out** information from the Crumble. The basic motor outputs spinning motion. The servo motor only turns part way through a circle. Both motors can run forward or backwards. Our animated character uses a servo motor.

Look at the program and answer the questions

program start
servo A 0 degrees
wait 2 seconds
servo A 90 degrees
wait 2 seconds

1, Which output is the servo plugged into (A, B, C or D)? [ ]

2, Fill in the next four blocks to continue the waving motion

3, What would you change to make a smaller wave? [ ]

4, Is the servo motor an input or output? [ ]

5, Can you think of anything else you could use a servo motor for?

do forever / loop

if then / end if

do 6 times / loop

if then / else / end if

6, Tick the block that you would use to repeat the wave six times

7, Put a cross in the block you would use to repeat the wave forever

Name ______________________________ Class __________

Thinking about programming an animated character AC2A (no input)

Motors are **outputs** because they **put out** information from the Crumble. The basic motor outputs spinning motion. The servo motor only turns part way through a circle.

Both motors can run forward or backwards. Our animated character uses a servo motor.

Look at the program and answer the questions

```
program start
servo A 0 degrees
wait 2 seconds
servo A 90 degrees
wait 2 seconds
```

1, Which output is the servo plugged into (A, B, C or D)? A

2, Fill in the next four blocks to continue the waving motion

Servo A 0 degrees
Wait 2 second
Servo A 90 degrees
Wait 2 seconds

3, What would you change to make a smaller wave? Degrees

4, Is the servo motor an input or output? output

5, Can you think of anything else you could use a servo motor for?

Please accept any reasonable idea that involves a servo that moves back and forward

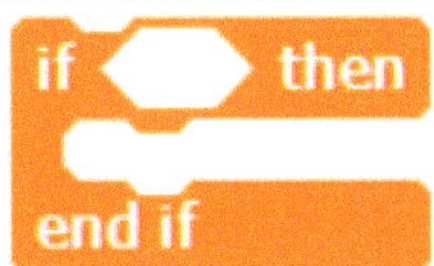

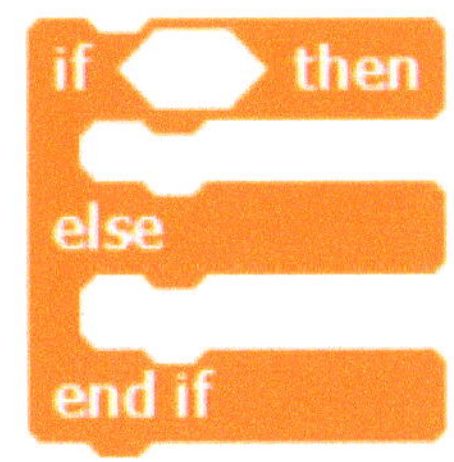

6, Tick the block that you would use to repeat the wave six times

7, Put a cross in the block you would use to repeat the wave forever

Name ______________________ Class/Form __________

Thinking about wiring an animated character AC3

Draw in the wires. Use the maker card to help you.

Fill in the chart to show your wires.

Letter	Name of the device

Name ______________________________ Class _____________

Thinking about wiring an animated character AC3A

Draw in the wires. Use the maker card to help you.

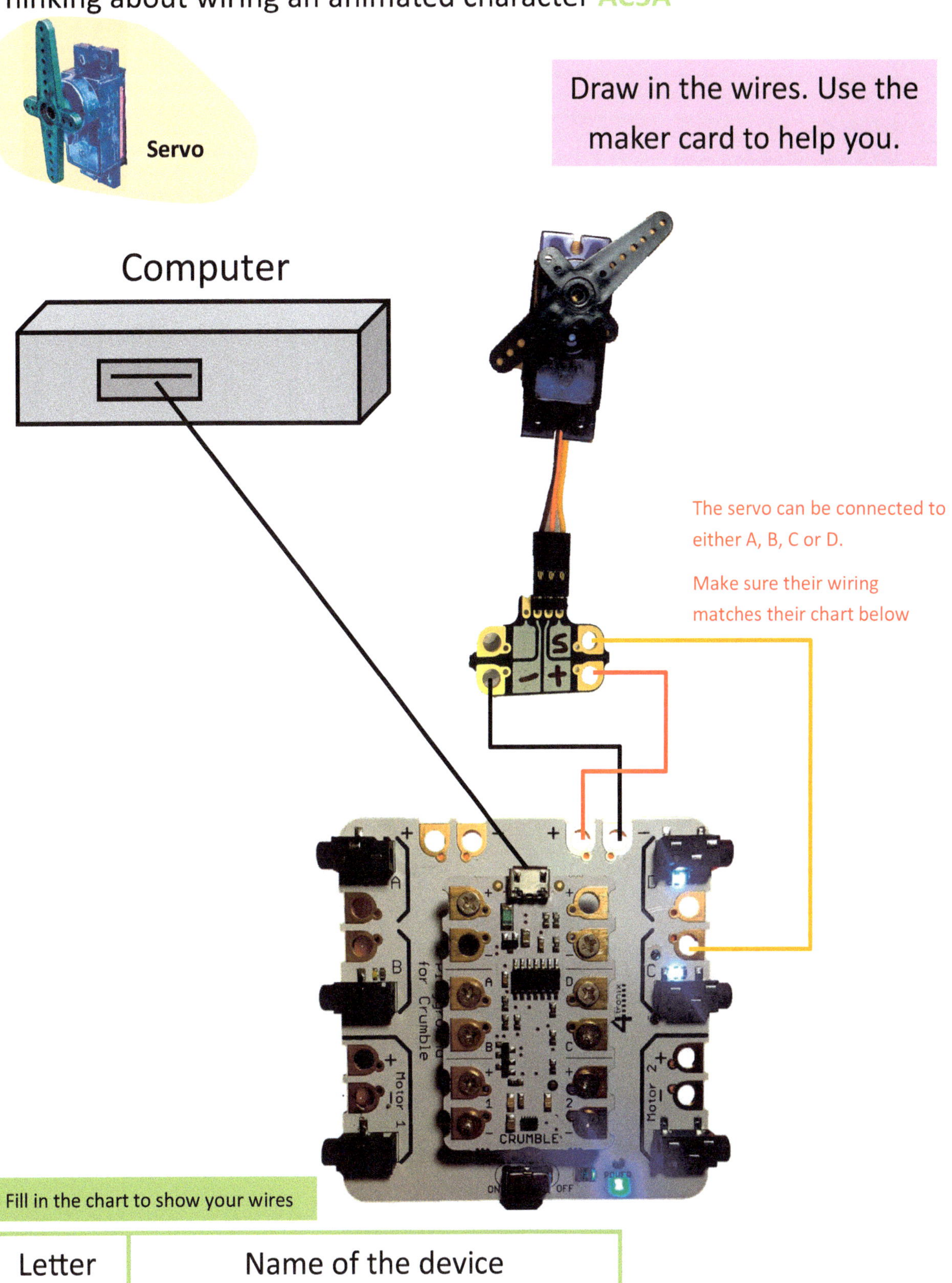

Fill in the chart to show your wires

Letter	Name of the device
C	Servo

Name ______________________________ Class _____________

Thinking about wiring an animated character AC4

Servo

Buttons are **inputs** because they **put in** information into the Crumble. They can do two things; one when they are pressed and one when they are not pressed.

Push Buttons

Servos are **outputs** because they **put out** information from the Crumble. These can output movement up to 90 degrees.

Draw the wires to show what connections you will use.

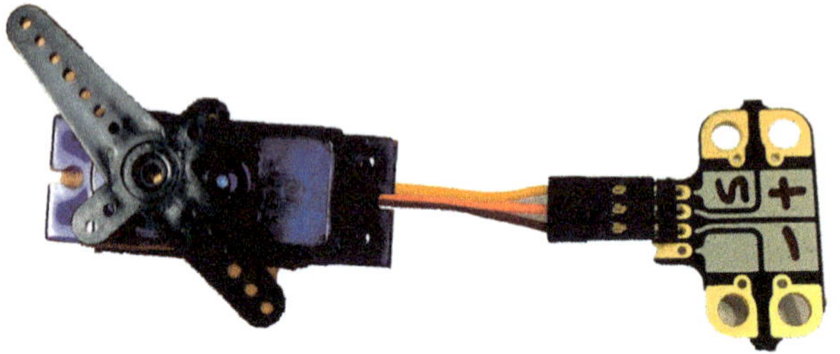

Fill in the chart to show your wires

Letter	Name of the device	Input or Output

Name ______________________ Class/Form __________

Thinking about wiring an animated character AC4A

Servo

Buttons are **inputs** because they **put in** information into the program. They can do two things; one when they are pressed and one when they are not pressed.

Push Buttons

Servos are **outputs** because they **put out** information from the Crumble. These can output movement up to 90 degrees.

Draw the wires to show what connections you will use

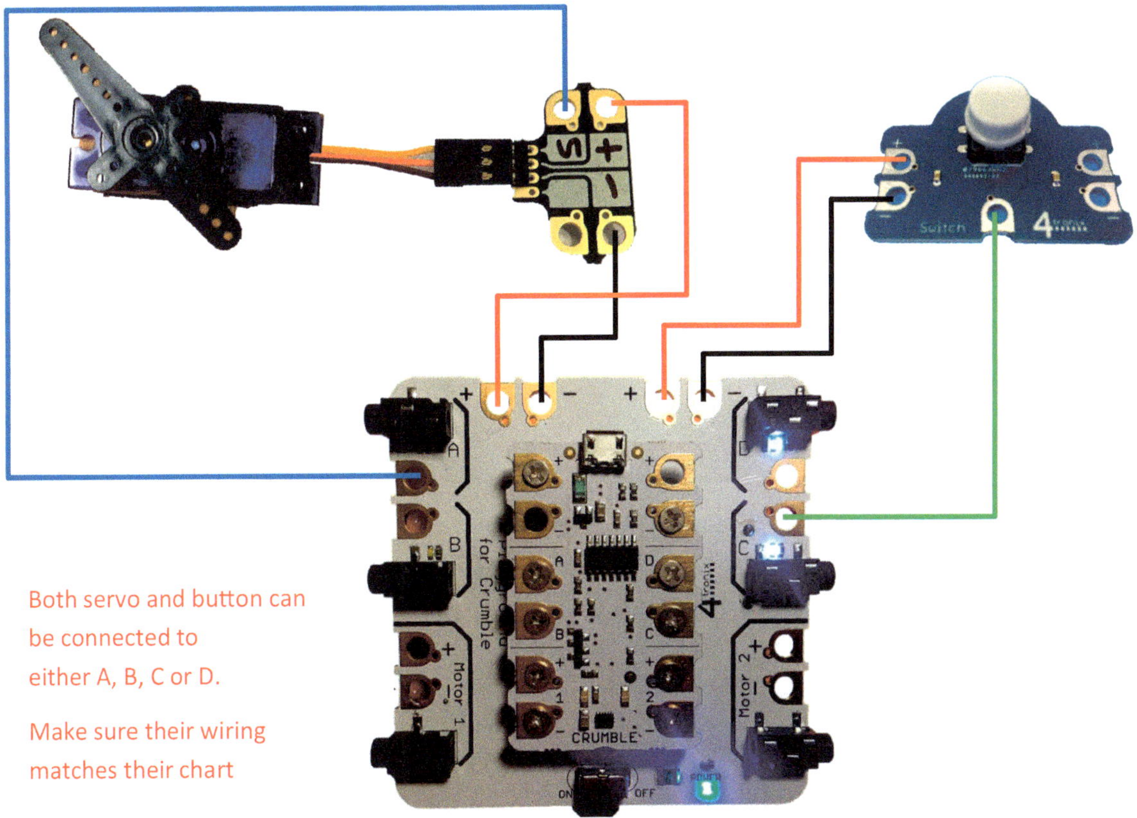
Both servo and button can be connected to either A, B, C or D.
Make sure their wiring matches their chart
CRUMBLE

Fill in the chart to show your wires

Letter	Name of the device	Input or Output
A	Servo	Output
C	Button	Input

Name ______________________________ Class ____________

Thinking about wiring an animated character AC5

Buttons are **inputs** because they **put in** information into the program. They can do two things; one when they are pressed and one when they are not pressed.

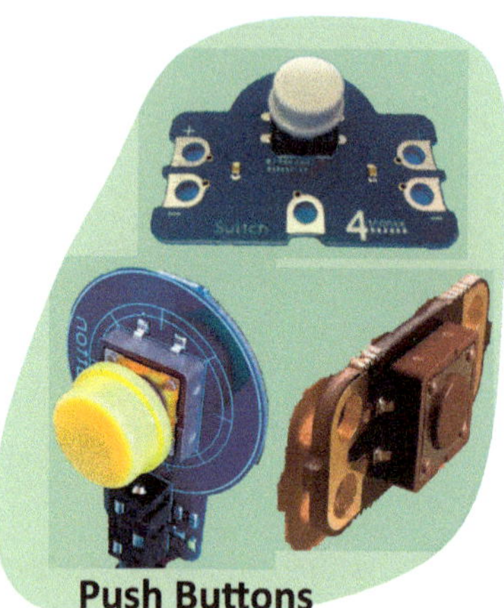

Servos are **outputs** because they **put out** information from the Crumble. These can output movement up to 90 degrees.

Draw the wires to show what connections you will use.

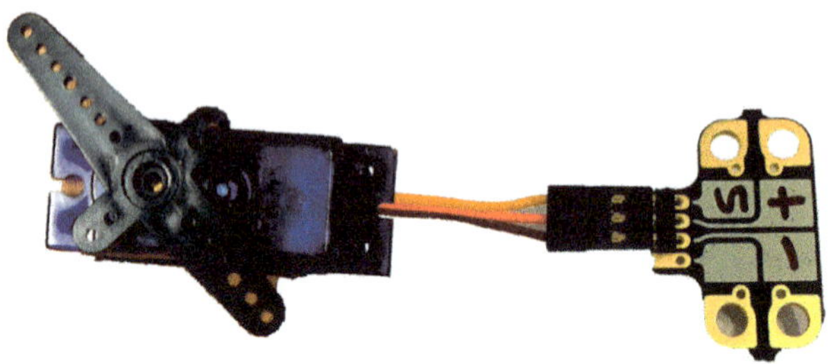

Fill in the chart to show your wires.

Letter	Name of the device	Input or Output

Name ____________________________ Class ____________

Thinking about wiring an animated character AC5A

Buttons are **inputs** because they **put in** information into the Crumble. They can do two things; one when they are pressed and one when they are not pressed.

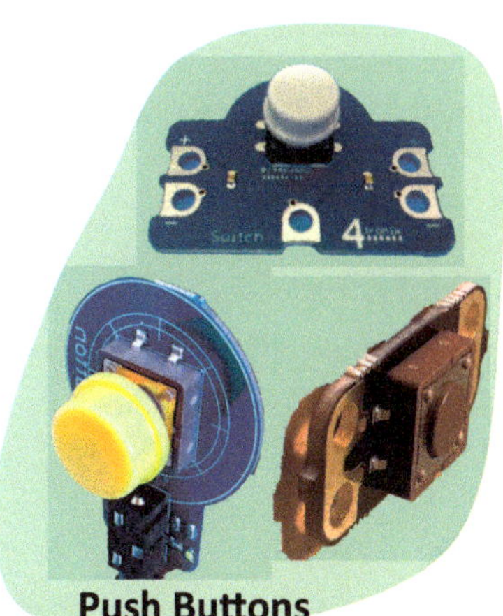

Servos are **outputs** because they **put out** information from the Crumble. These can output movement up to 90 degrees.

Draw the wires to show what connections you will use.

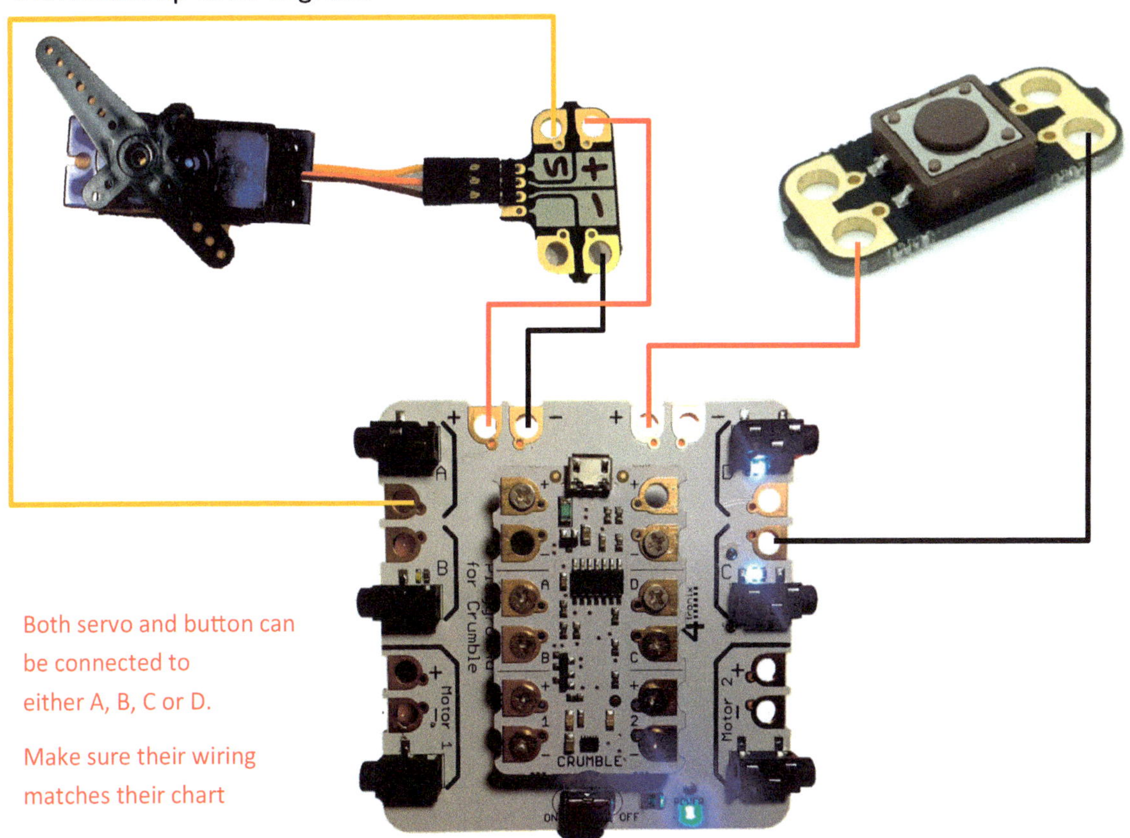

Both servo and button can be connected to either A, B, C or D.

Make sure their wiring matches their chart

Fill in the chart to show your wires.

Letter	Name of the device	Input or Output
A	Servo	Output
C	Button	Input

Name ______________________________ Class _____________

Thinking about wiring an animated character AC6

Buttons are **inputs** because they **put in** information into the Crumble. They can do two things; one when they are pressed and one when they are not pressed.

Push Buttons

Servos are **outputs** because they **put out** information from the Crumble. These can output movement up to 90 degrees.

Draw the wires to show what connections you will use.

Fill in the chart to show your wires.

Letter	Name of the device	Input or Output

Name ______________________________ Class ____________

Thinking about wiring an animated character AC6A

Servo

Buttons are **inputs** because they **put in** information into the Crumble. They can do two things; one when they are pressed and one when they are not pressed.

Push Buttons

Servos are **outputs** because they **put out** information from the Crumble. These can output movement up to 90 degrees.

Draw the wires to show what connections you will use.

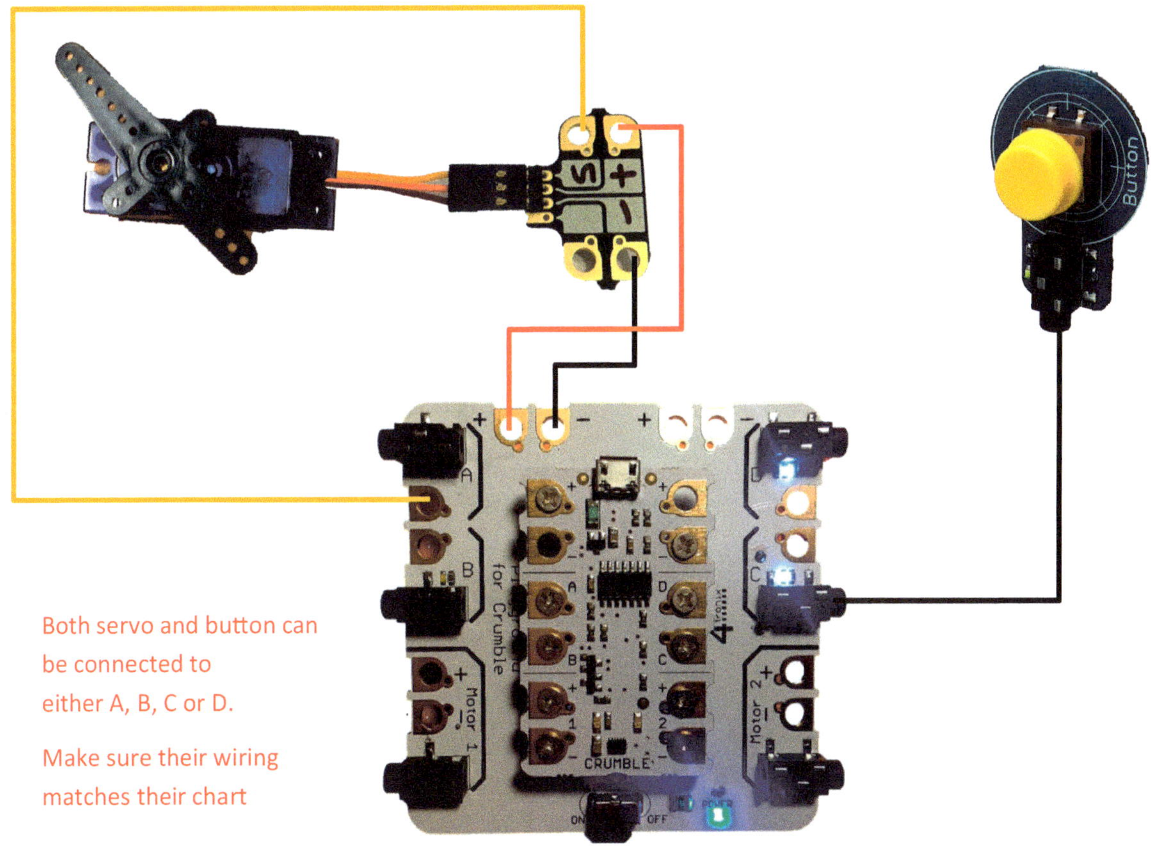
Both servo and button can be connected to either A, B, C or D.
Make sure their wiring matches their chart
Button
CRUMBLE
Motor 1
Motor 2
ON
OFF

Fill in the chart to show your wires.

Letter	Name of the device	Input or Output
A	Servo	Output
C	Button	Input

Name ______________________________ Class _____________

Thinking about wiring an animated character AC7

Buttons are **inputs** because they **put in** information into the Crumble. They can do two things; one when they are pressed and one when they are not pressed.

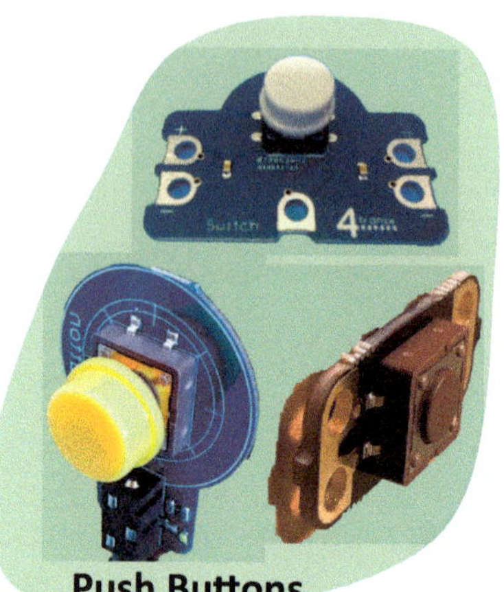

Push Buttons

Servos are **outputs** because they **put out** information from the Crumble. These can output movement up to 90 degrees.

Draw the wires to show what connections you will use.

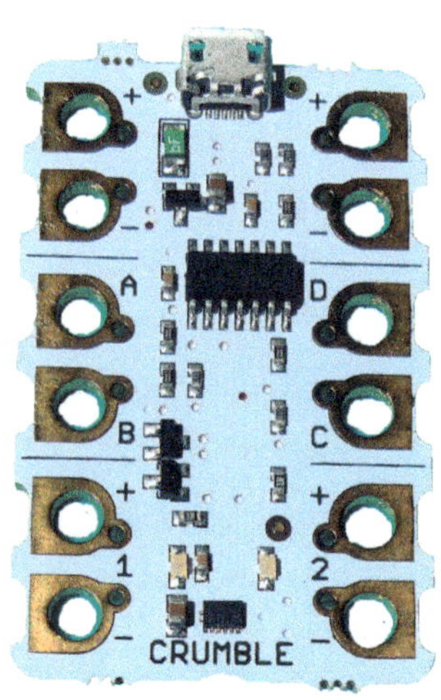

Fill in the chart to show your wires.

Letter	Name of the device	Input or Output

Name ____________________________ Class/Form ____________

Thinking about wiring an animated character AC7A

Servos are **outputs** because they **put out** information from the Crumble. These can output movement up to 90 degrees.

Buttons are **inputs** because they **put in** information into the Crumble. They can do two things; one when they are pressed and one when they are not pressed.

Push Buttons

Draw the wires to show what connections you will use.

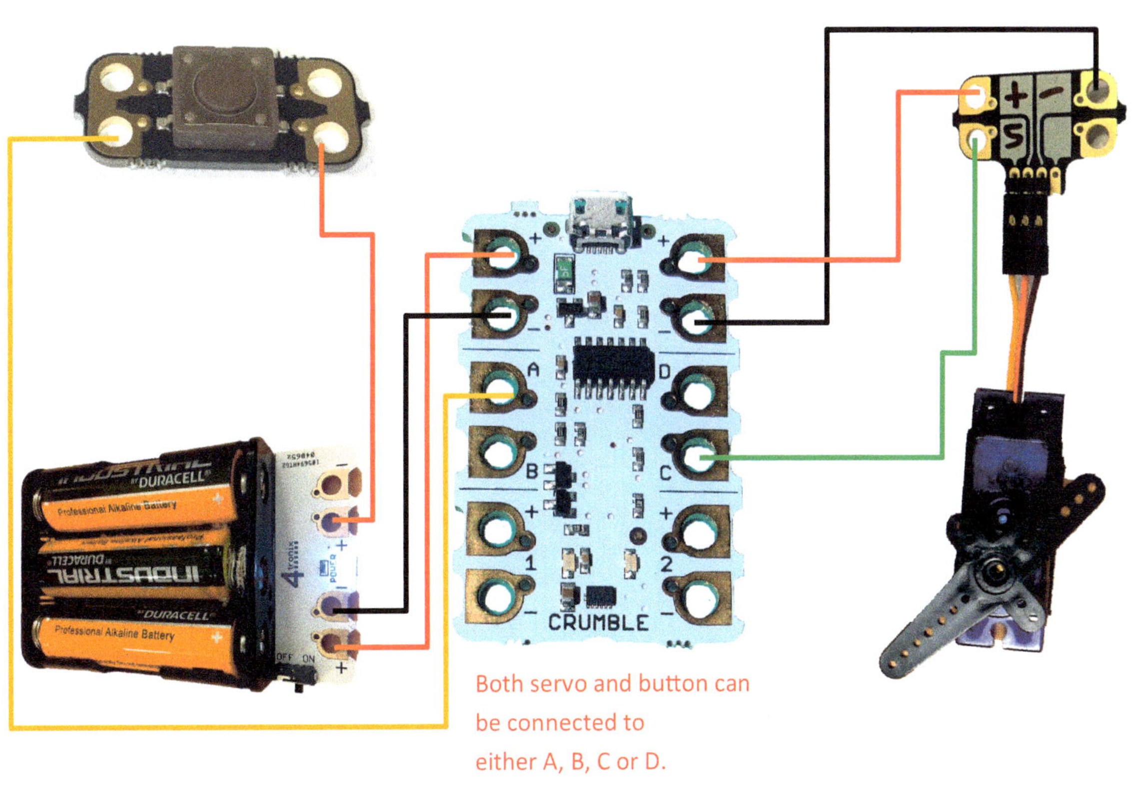

Both servo and button can be connected to either A, B, C or D.

Make sure their wiring matches their chart

Fill in the chart to show your wires.

Letter	Name of the device	Input or Output
A	Button	Input
C	Servo	Output

Name ______________________________ Class _____________

Thinking about wiring an animated character AC8

Servo

Buttons are **inputs** because they **put in** information into the Crumble. They can do two things; one when they are pressed and one when they are not pressed.

Push Buttons

Servos are **outputs** because they **put out** information from the Crumble. These can output movement up to 90 degrees.

Draw the wires to show what connections you will use.

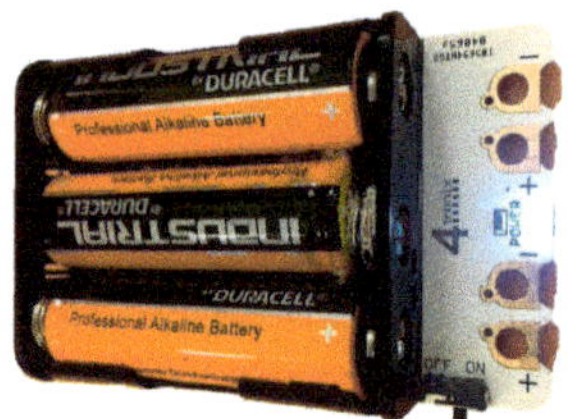

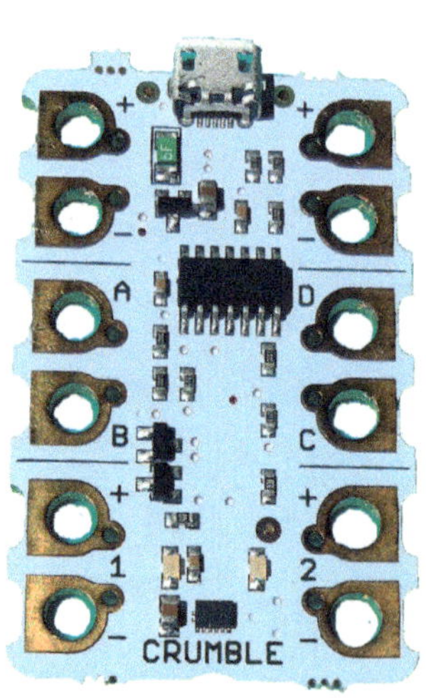

Fill in the chart to show your wires.

Letter	Name of the device	Input or Output

Name ______________________ Class __________

Thinking about wiring an animated character AC8A

Buttons are **inputs** because they **put in** information into the Crumble. They can do two things; one when they are pressed and one when they are not pressed.

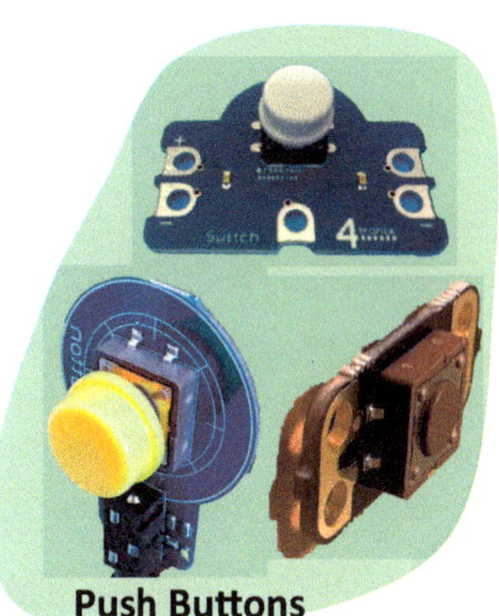

Servos are **outputs** because they **put out** information from the Crumble. These can output movement up to 90 degrees.

Draw the wires to show what connections you will use.

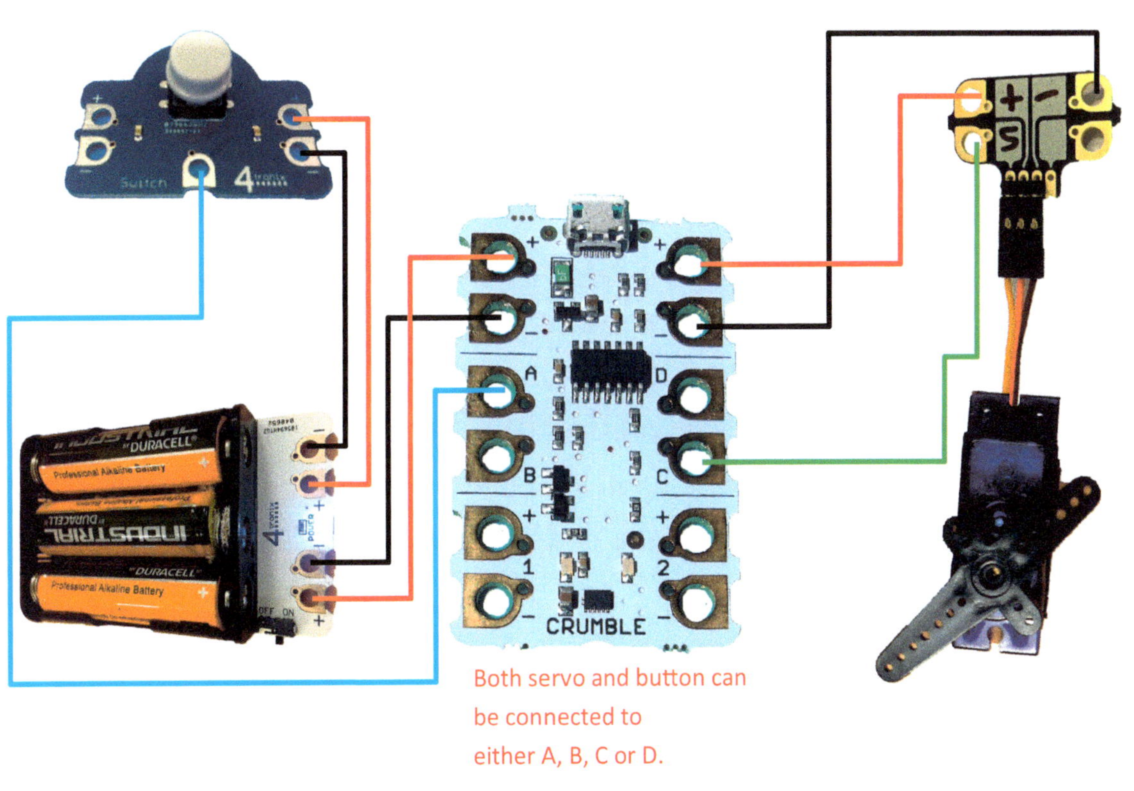

Both servo and button can be connected to either A, B, C or D.

Make sure their wiring matches their chart

Fill in the chart to show your wires.

Letter	Name of the device	Input or Output
A	Button	Input
C	Servo	Output

Name ______________________ Class __________ AC9

Thinking about programming an animated character started by a button

Marissa's Programming Example

Marissa created her program like this

I want my servo motor to move back and forwards first. I plugged the servo into output A but the maker card said it could go into A, B, C or D. I tried it without the waits first but there was not enough time for the motor to turn so it didn't work well.

```
program start
servo A 0 degrees
wait 1 seconds
servo A 40 degrees
wait 1 seconds
servo A 0 degrees
wait 1 seconds
servo A 40 degrees
wait 1 seconds
```

Servo Motor

Push Buttons

I want my servo motor to work if you press a button. I wired up my button and attached it to input C. I set the condition to start when the button is pressed (HI). The button only works once if you are pressing it down when the battery pack is turned on.

```
program start
if C is HI then
  servo A 0 degrees
  wait 1 seconds
  servo A 40 degrees
  wait 1 seconds
  servo A 0 degrees
  wait 1 seconds
  servo A 40 degrees
  wait 1 seconds
end if
```

I want the button to work all of the time so I put the conditional selection if then block inside a forever loop. It checks over and over again to see if the button is pressed or not.

```
program start
do forever
  if C is HI then
    servo A 0 degrees
    wait 1 seconds
    servo A 40 degrees
    wait 1 seconds
    servo A 0 degrees
    wait 1 seconds
    servo A 40 degrees
    wait 1 seconds
  end if
loop
```

Use this sheet to answer the questions

Name ______________________________ Class _____________ AC9Q

Thinking about programming an animated character started by a button

Read **Marissa's Programming Example** then answer these questions

1, What did Marissa want to make work first? [ ]

2, Which outputs **could** Marissa plug the servo into? [ ]

3, How many degrees has Marissa programmed her servo to turn? [ ]

4, Draw lines to match the code description to the correct block.
The first one has been done for you.

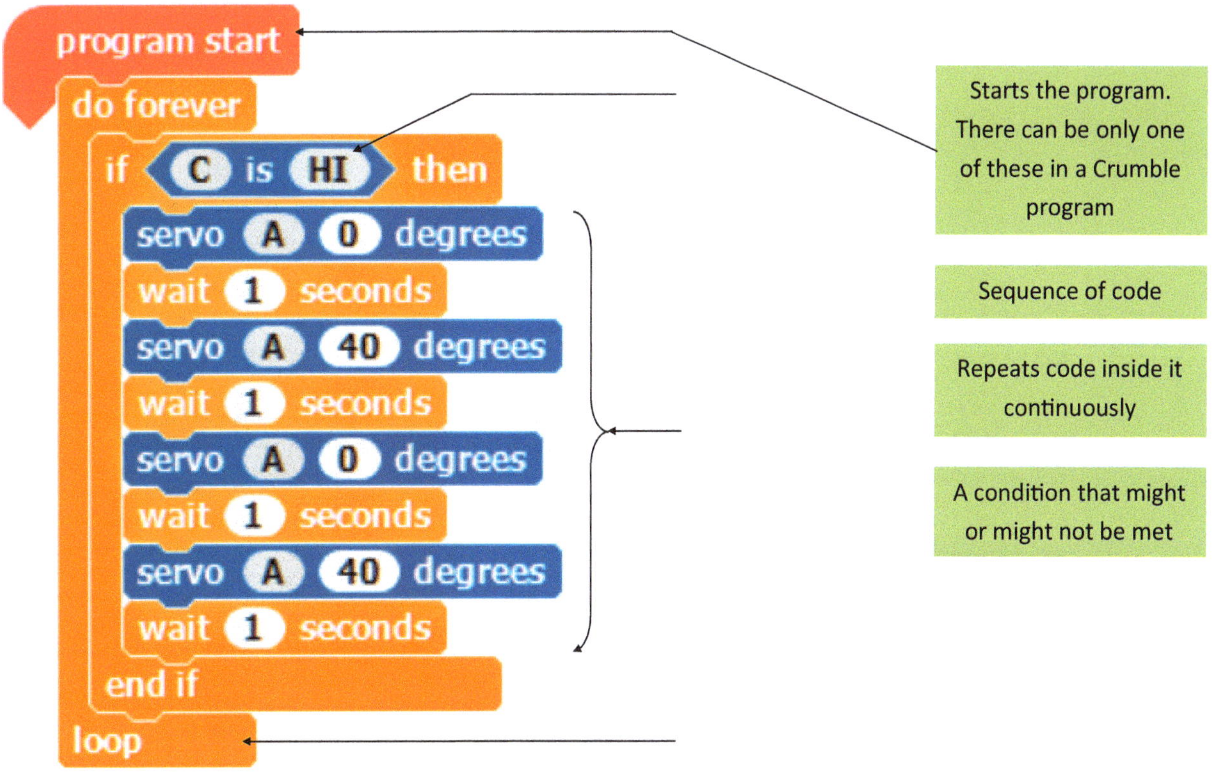

```
program start
do forever
  if C is HI then
    servo A 0 degrees
    wait 1 seconds
    servo A 40 degrees
    wait 1 seconds
    servo A 0 degrees
    wait 1 seconds
    servo A 40 degrees
    wait 1 seconds
  end if
loop
```

Starts the program. There can be only one of these in a Crumble program

Sequence of code

Repeats code inside it continuously

A condition that might or might not be met

5, Marissa used eight blocks of code to make her servo motor move four times. Her teacher challenged her to make it move forty times in five blocks.

Write or draw how you think she did it.

Name ______________________________ Class ____________ AC9A

Thinking about programming an animated character started by a button

Read **Marissa's Programming Example** then answer these questions

1, What did Marissa want to make work first? Servo motor

2, Which outputs **could** Marissa plug the servo into? A, B, C or D

3, How many degrees has Marissa programmed her servo to turn? 40 Degrees

4, Draw lines to match the code description to the correct block.
The first one has been done for you.

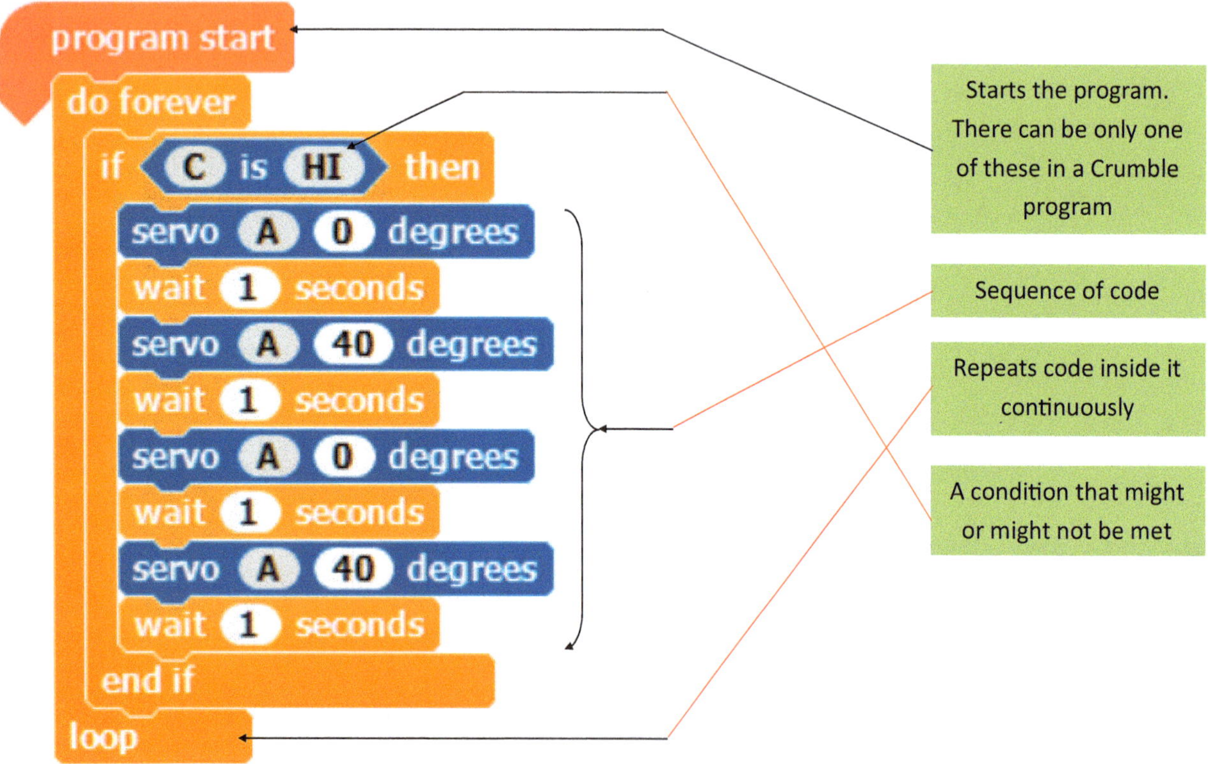
program start
do forever
if C is HI then
servo A 0 degrees
wait 1 seconds
servo A 40 degrees
wait 1 seconds
servo A 0 degrees
wait 1 seconds
servo A 40 degrees
wait 1 seconds
end if
loop
Starts the program. There can be only one of these in a Crumble program
Sequence of code
Repeats code inside it continuously
A condition that might or might not be met

5, Marissa used eight blocks of code to make her servo motor move four times. Her teacher challenged her to make it move forty times in five blocks.

Write or draw how you think she did it.

Any answer that indicates that a repeat loop would be used 20 or 40 times with four code blocks (2 servo and two waits).

20 or 40 is acceptable as some pupils will include there and back as one move and others as two moves.

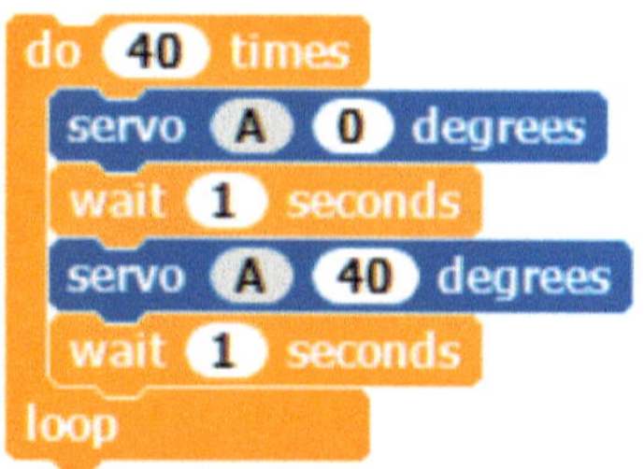
do 40 times
servo A 0 degrees
wait 1 seconds
servo A 40 degrees
wait 1 seconds
loop

Name ______________________________ Class _____________ AC10

Thinking about programming an animated character started by a button

Programming Example in Detail

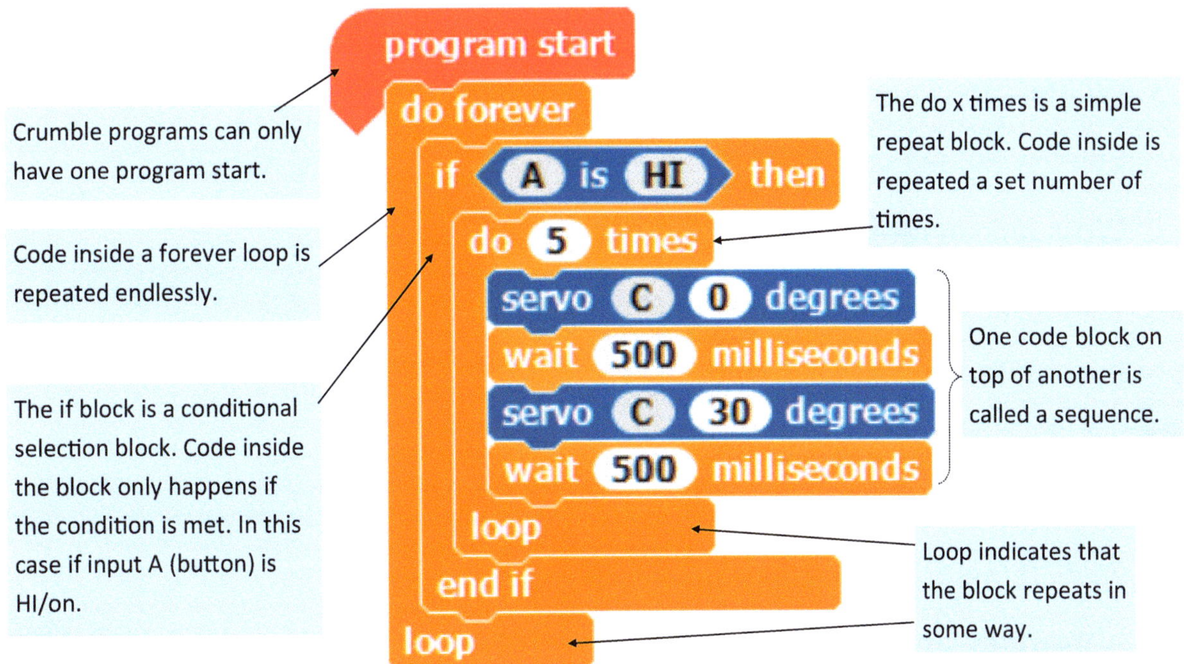

program start
do forever
if A is HI then
do 5 times
servo C 0 degrees
wait 500 milliseconds
servo C 30 degrees
wait 500 milliseconds
loop
end if
loop
Crumble programs can only have one program start.
Code inside a forever loop is repeated endlessly.
The if block is a conditional selection block. Code inside the block only happens if the condition is met. In this case if input A (button) is HI/on.
The do x times is a simple repeat block. Code inside is repeated a set number of times.
One code block on top of another is called a sequence.
Loop indicates that the block repeats in some way.

Flowchart Algorithm

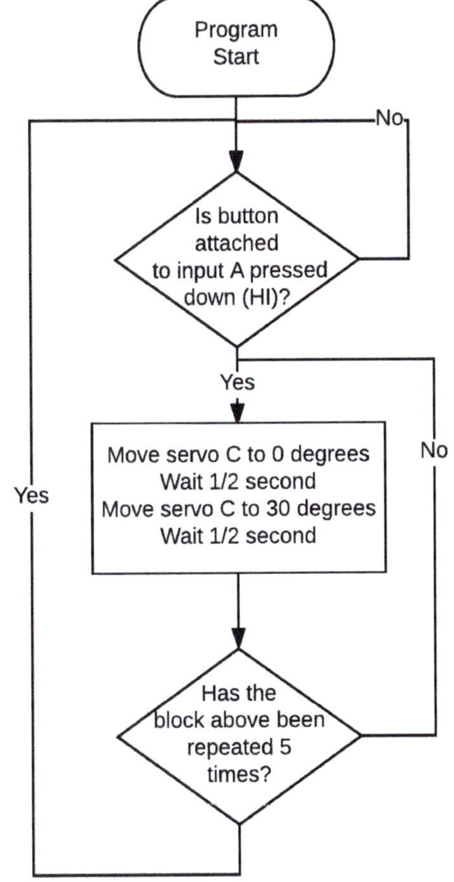

Written Algorithm

When the program starts, check forever that the button attached to input A is HI/Pressed down. If it is pressed down, repeat the code sequence in the middle five times. If it is LO/de-pressed, check again.

Read this sheet carefully.

If possible discuss it with a partner.

Then answer the questions on the sheet.

Name ______________________________ Class _____________ AC10Q

Thinking about programming an animated character started by a button

Read **Programming Example in Detail** then answer these questions

1, What is one code block on top of another called? [ ]

2, Conditional selection blocks often start with a short word. What is it? [ ]

3, What type of loop repeats endlessly? [ ]

4, What input/output is the servo connected to? [ ]

5, If a button is LO does it mean it is pressed or de-pressed? [ ]

6, What is 500 milliseconds in seconds? [ ]

7, In the flowchart algorithm which shape indicates a question? (oval, rectangle, diamond) [ ]

8, How would the program change if the forever loop was removed?

[ ]

9, If the ⟨A is HI⟩ block was changed to ⟨A is LO⟩ 1, What would the servo do when the program is started and the button in not pressed? 2, What would happen when the button is pressed?

[ ]

10, What do you think might happen if the wait 500 millisecond blocks are removed?

[ ]

11, Which type of device (blocks, flowchart algorithm or written algorithm) did you find most useful? Explain your answer.

[ ]

Name ______________________ Class __________ AC10A

ANSWERS

Thinking about programming an animated character started by a button

Read **Programming Example in Detail** then answer these questions

1, What is one code block on top of another called? sequence

2, Conditional selection blocks often start with a short word. What is it? if

3, What type of loop repeats endlessly? forever

4, What input/output is the servo connected to? C

5, If a button is LO, does it mean it is pressed or de-pressed? De-pressed

6, What is 500 milliseconds in seconds? 1/2 second

7, In the flowchart algorithm which shape indicates a question? (oval, rectangle, diamond) diamond

8, How would the program change if the forever loop was removed?

It would only check if the button was pressed once when the program was started. Accept any answer that indicated that the program would only run once.

9, If the ⟨A is HI⟩ block was changed to ⟨A is LO⟩ 1, What would the servo do when the program is started and the button de-pressed? 2, What would happen when the button is held down?

1, Accept any answer that indicates that the servo motor would run backwards and forwards.
2, Accept any answer that indicates that the servo would stop when the button is pressed.

10, What do you think might happen if the wait 500 millisecond blocks are removed?

Accept either that there wouldn't be enough time to run the servo or that the servo would move very fast. The first is what happens, the second is a logical deduction.

11, Which type of device (blocks, flowchart algorithm or written algorithm) did you find most useful? Explain your answer

Pupils need to make a choice or say all of them and justify their answer with a reason.

Name ______________________ Class/Form ___________ AC11

Thinking about programming an animated character started by a button

Programming Example in Detail

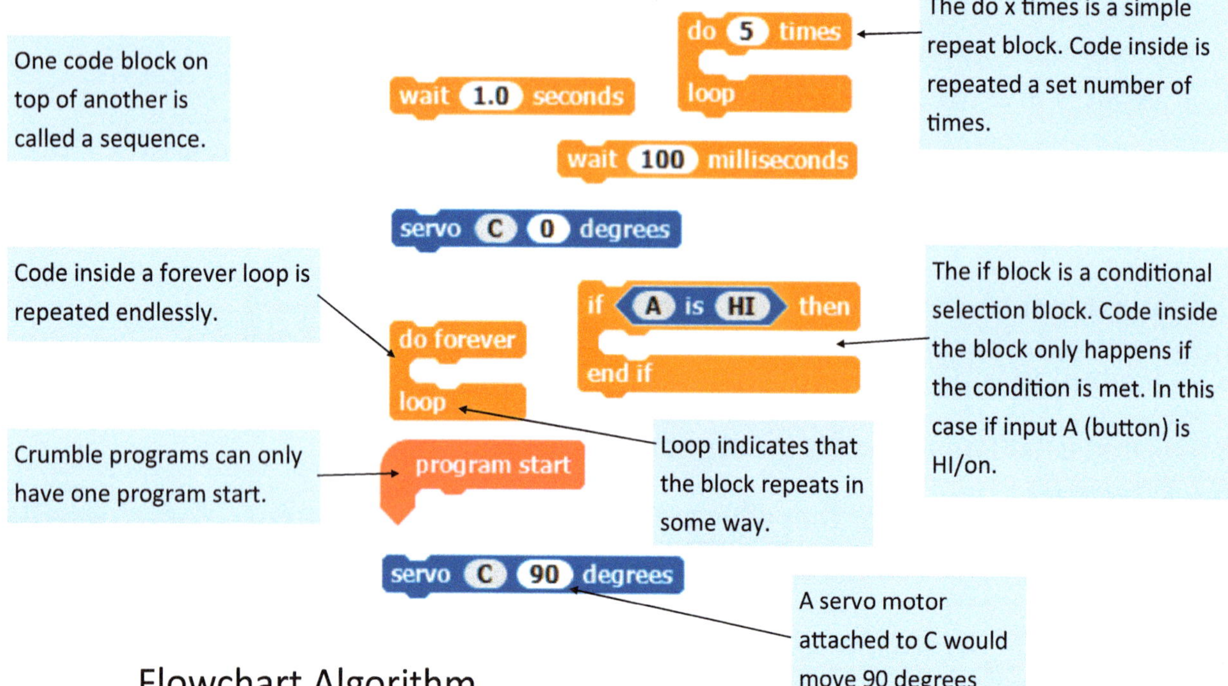

One code block on top of another is called a sequence.
wait 1.0 seconds
do 5 times
loop
The do x times is a simple repeat block. Code inside is repeated a set number of times.
wait 100 milliseconds
servo C 0 degrees
Code inside a forever loop is repeated endlessly.
do forever
loop
if A is HI then
end if
The if block is a conditional selection block. Code inside the block only happens if the condition is met. In this case if input A (button) is HI/on.
Crumble programs can only have one program start.
program start
Loop indicates that the block repeats in some way.
servo C 90 degrees
A servo motor attached to C would move 90 degrees

Flowchart Algorithm

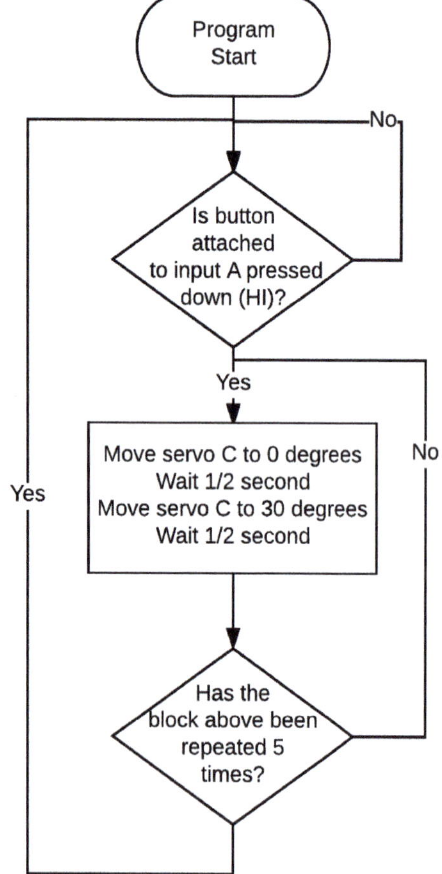

Written Algorithm

When the program starts, check forever that the button attached to input A is HI/Pressed down. If it is pressed down, repeat the code sequence in the middle five times. If it is LO/de-pressed, check again.

Read the flowchart and written algorithm

Can you convert these into working Crumble code using the blocks above?

You may need more than one of each block

Pig Template

Head

Bottom

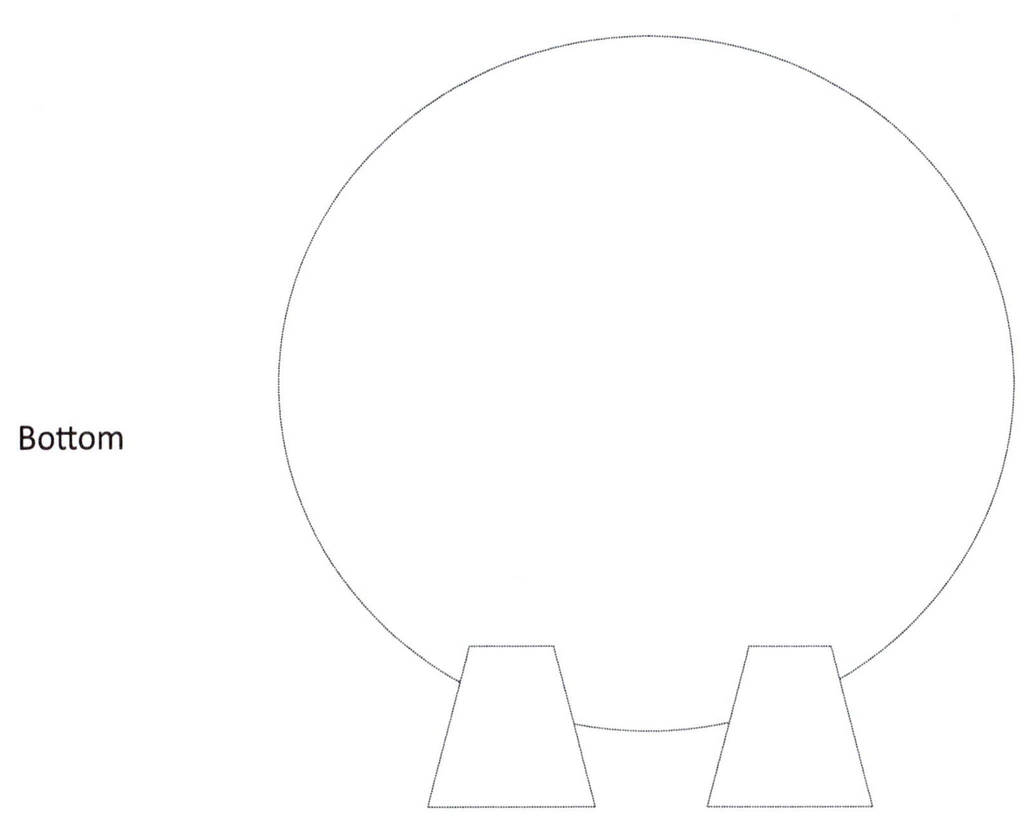

Pig Template

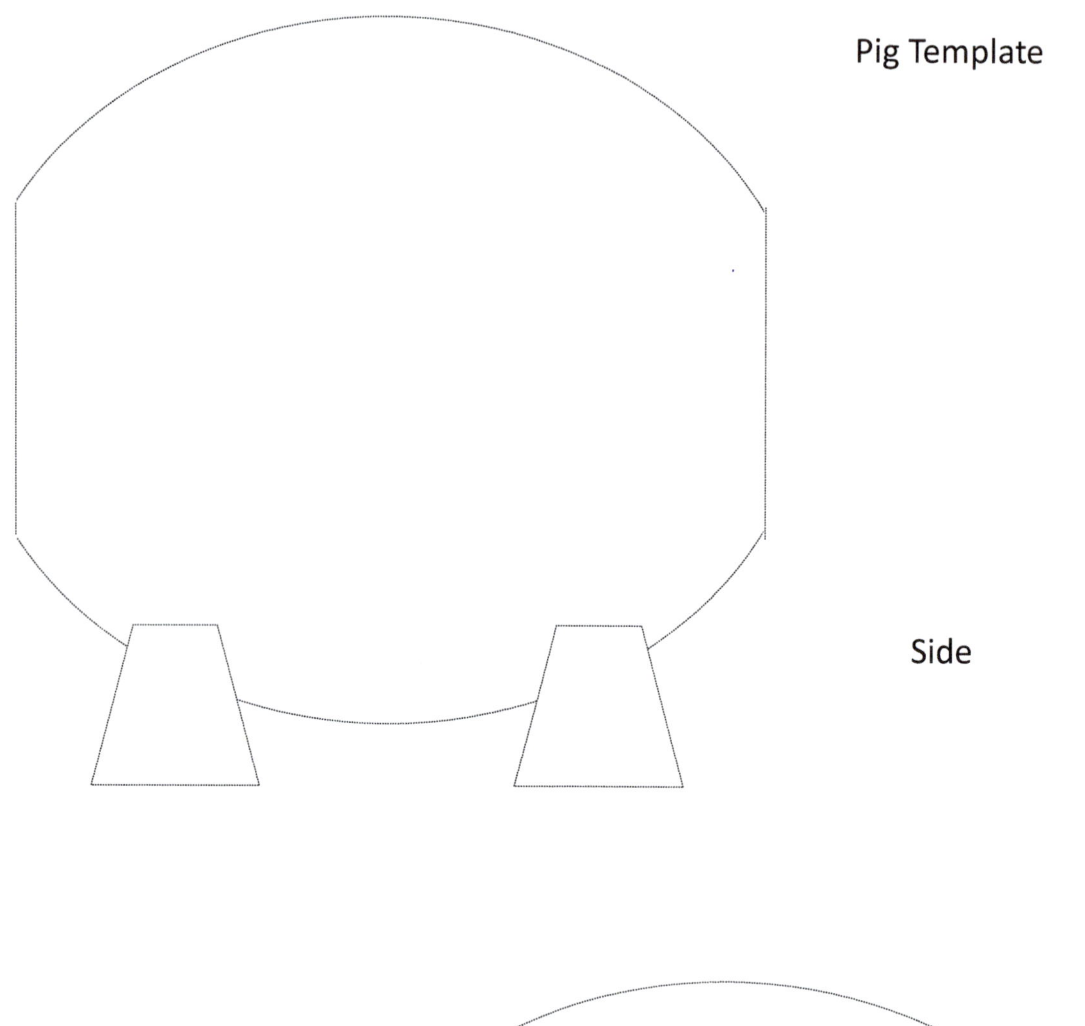

Side

Side

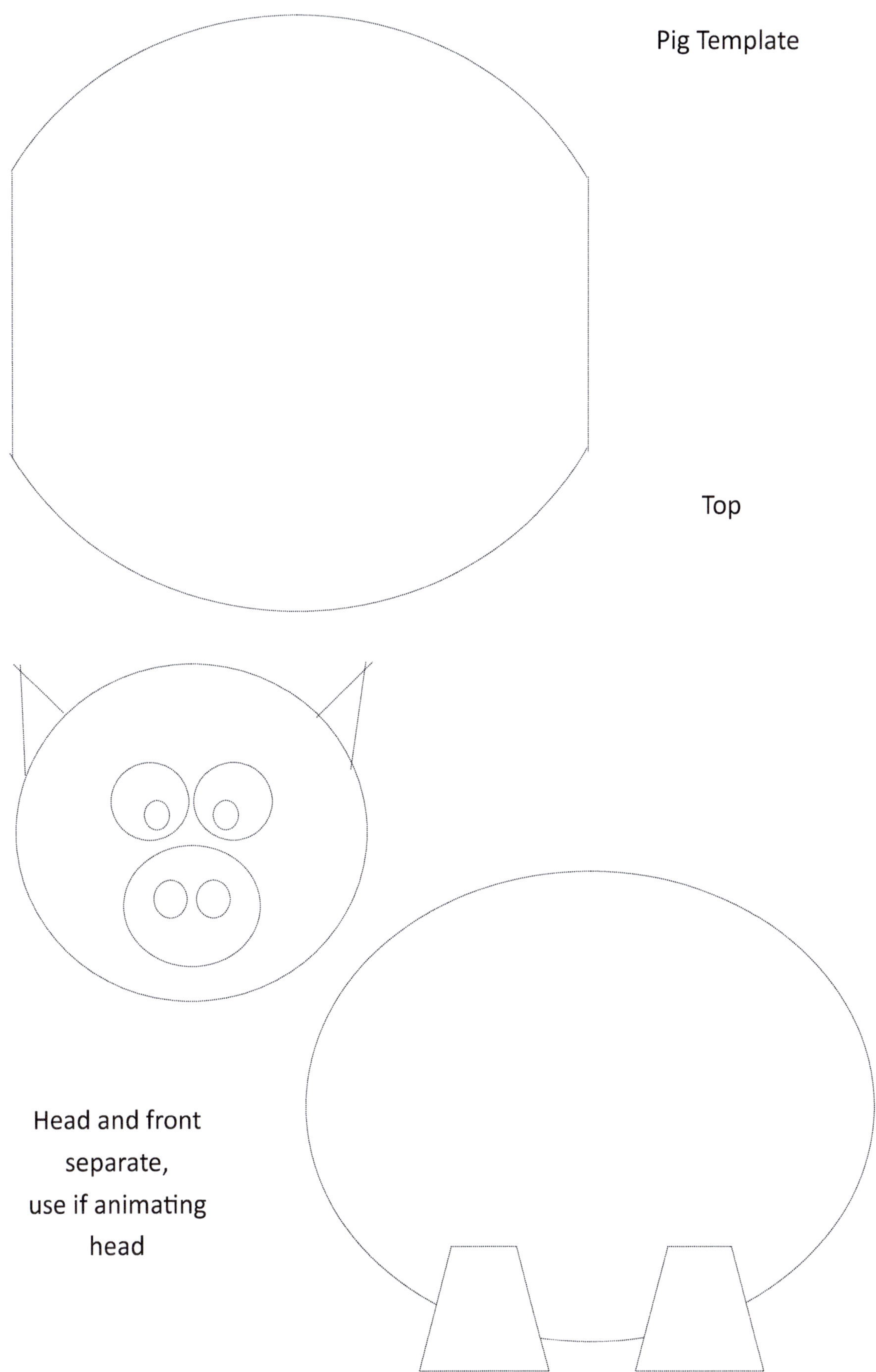
Pig Template
Top
Head and front
separate,
use if animating
head

Cow Template

Head with face use if animating tail or legs

Bottom

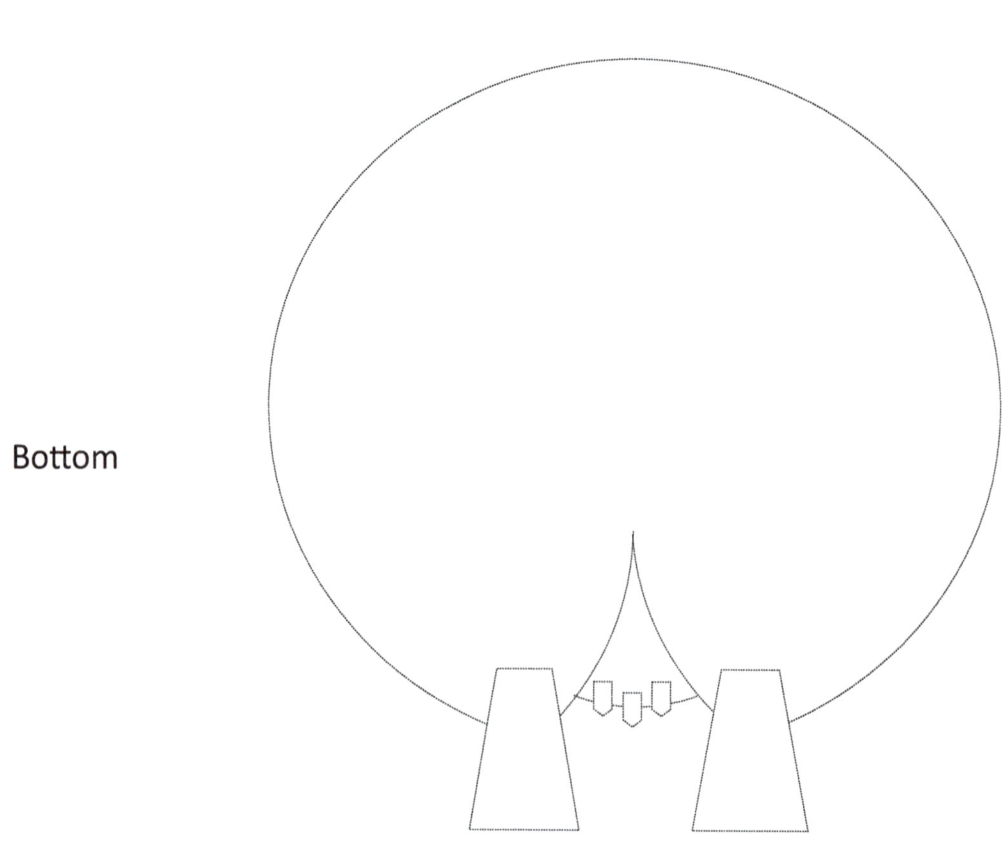

Cow Template

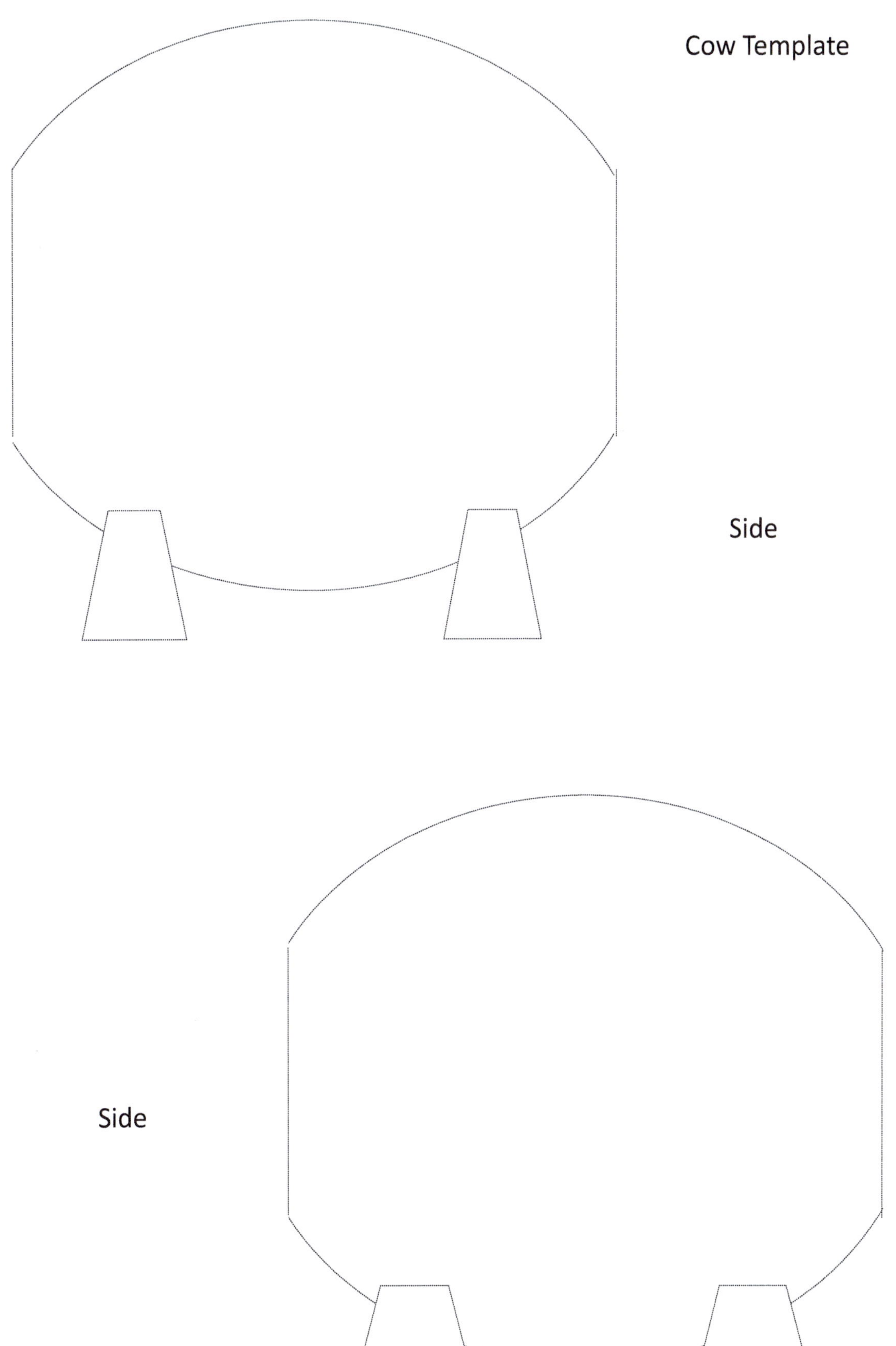

Cow Template

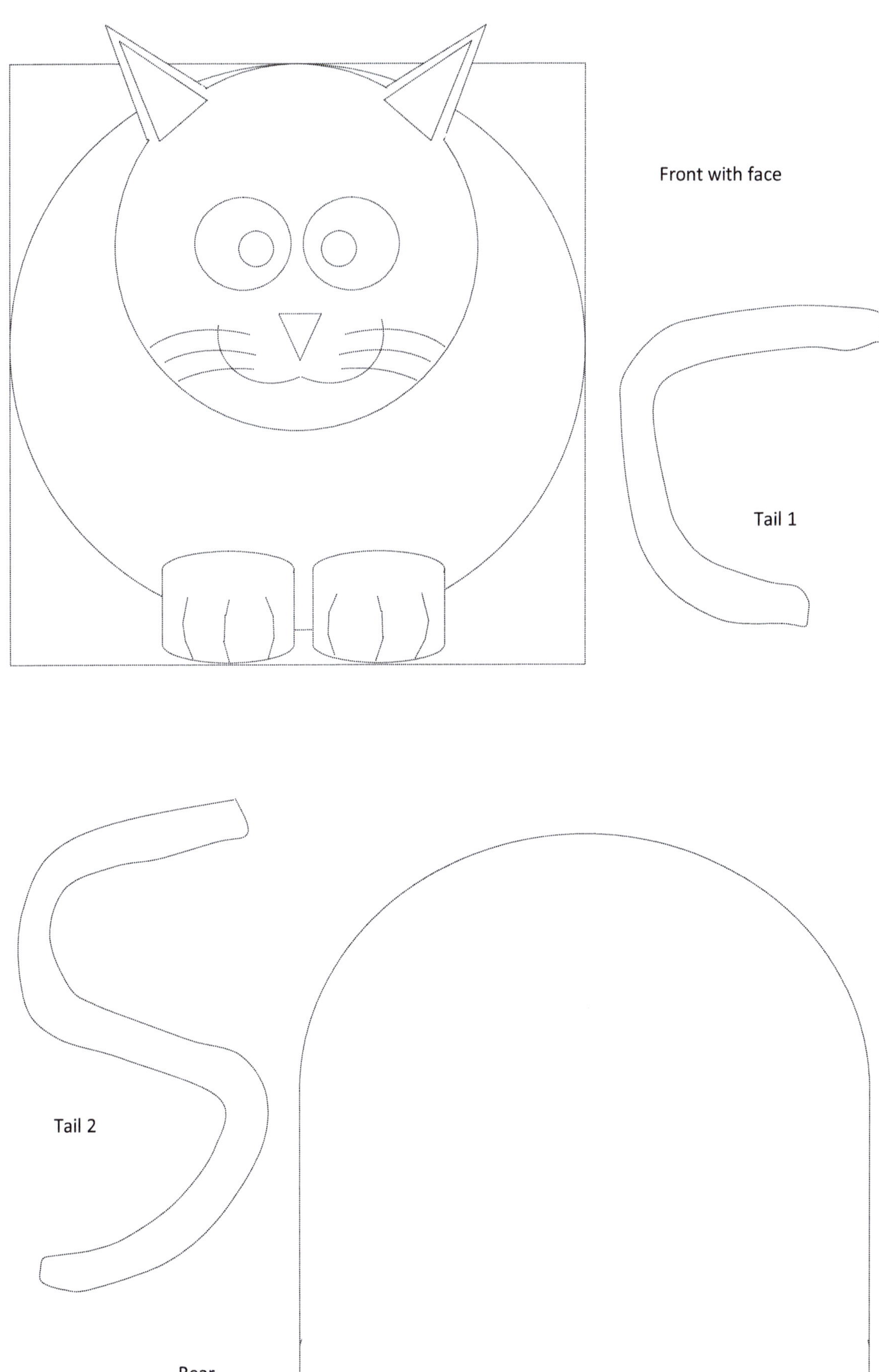
Front with face
Tail 1
Tail 2
Rear

Side

Side

Head and front separate.
Use if animating head.

Top

Animated Animal Assessment Sheet AC12 Name __________ Class ____

(no button)

☺ I did this well.

😐 I did this ok or I did this a little.

☹ I tried this but it didn't work or I didn't do this at all.

I wired my servo to the Crumble.	
I programmed my animal (head/tail/paw/hoof) to move backwards and forward.	
I listened to my partners ideas.	
I contributed good idea to my partner.	
I persevered when the wiring or programming didn't work.	

Draw what you would like to make next using a servo

Servo

Sticker	I got this sticker for
Sticker	I got this sticker for
Sticker	I got this sticker for

Animated Animal Assessment Sheet AC13 Name ________ Class ____

With a button

☺	I did this well.
😐	I did this ok or I did this a little.
☹	I tried this but it didn't work or I didn't do this at all.

I created an accurate wiring diagram using the maker cards.	
I followed my wiring diagram to connect my button and servo to the Crumble.	
I programmed my animal (head/tail/paw/hoof) to move backwards and forward.	
I programmed my animal to respond to a button input.	
I adapted my programming by.... (Say what you did).	
I listened to my partner's ideas.	
I contributed a good idea to my partner.	
I persevered when the wiring or programming didn't work.	

Sticker	I got this sticker for
Sticker	I got this sticker for
Sticker	I got this sticker for

Name ______________________ Class __________ AC14

Thinking about designing my own project that uses servo motors

My program will

by

What will your user see and do?

Input/ Output	Name of device attached	What the device does (include as much detail as possible)
A output	A Servo Motor	Is attached to an axe to chop off Anne Boleyn's head.
A		
B		
C		
D		
Motor 1		
Motor 2		

Fill in your idea and add your inputs and outputs to the chart.

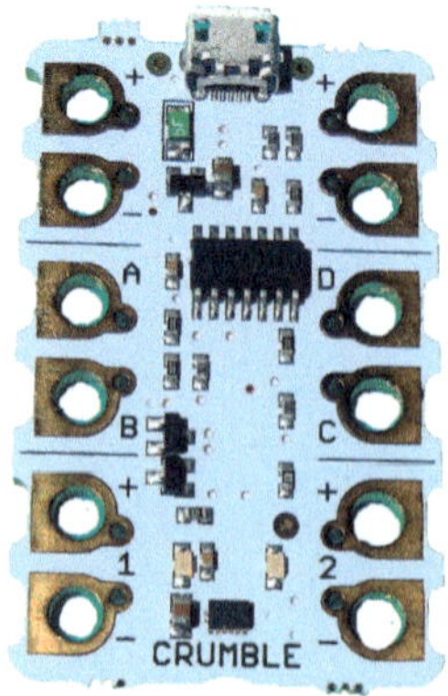

Draw your devices and the wires that connect them.

Name ______________________________ Class ____________ AC15

Thinking about designing my own project that uses servo motors

My program will

by

What will your user see and do?

Input/ Output	Name of device attached	What the device does (include as much detail as possible)
A output	A Servo Motor	Is attached to an axe to chop off Anne Boleyn's head.
A		
B		
C		
D		
Motor 1		
Motor 2		

Fill in your idea and add your inputs and outputs to the chart.

Draw your devices and the wires that connect them.

6. Traffic Lights

Module Aim

Create a working set of traffic lights

Different Methods

This module could be constructed in many ways. In the diagrams on this page you see the pre-prepared traffic light modules by 4tronix. These modules are the easiest way to wire traffic lights. Pupils could also use three LED lights mounted simply on a card as shown in the lights, lights, lights chapter. They could also use three programmable lights.

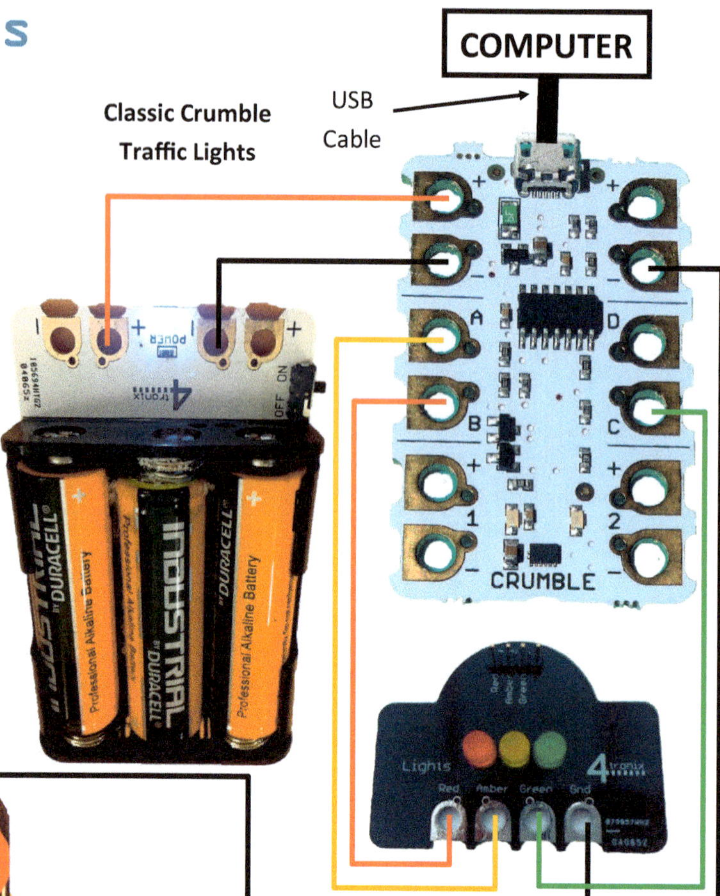

Crumble Playground
Traffic Lights

COMPUTER

Cross Curricular Links

Design and Technology –Challenge pupils to create a large traffic light that could be used by pupils out in the playground. The programmable lights, that are very bright, are far better for this Design & Technology and Computing project.

You could give the children a head start by looking at how a torch is constructed and drawing out how most lights use a cone of reflective material to increase the bulb output.

After the planning that uses the traffic lights modules there is a breakdown of how you might build the larger traffic lights project.

Materials

Crumble playground, playground traffic lights module, Crumble, Battery box, Traffic lights crumb or three programmable lights

Suggested Module Outline

1, Build a teacher example

Construct the traffic light circuit yourself before the session and test the programming needed.

2, Introduction

Recap that an algorithm can be a step by step sequence of instructions to achieve something. Explain that they are going to work out the precise algorithm for a sequence of traffic lights and once they have completed it they can turn their algorithm into code that works on a set of real lights. Hold up the traffic light module by 4tronix, don't connect it as puzzling that out later is part of the challenge.

Hand out an algorithm sheet TL3 (older pupils writing) or TL2 & TL3 (younger pupils cut out and order) and go through the Belisha Beacon example on TL3. Emphasise how the algorithm needs a wait so there is enough time to see the light and enough time for it to remain off.

Go through the algorithm commands they can use on the top right of the sheet TL3 or on the cut out sheet TL2.

Scratch Traffic Light online https://goo.gl/8fwXu1

Load the Scratch traffic light, making sure it is in full screen mode, so the code cannot be seen. Explain how the traffic light changes down then up. Draw out that up is different from down. Can they spot why? Answer Red and Amber are on together when changing down.

3, Creating an Algorithm

Give pupils plenty of time to work on the algorithm. If you are doing this with younger pupils, allowing them to work in pairs helps. When pupils think they are finished, check their algorithm with the answers sheet TL3A.

Scribing for particularly slow writers is perfectly acceptable as the thinking is more important than being able to write it or you may want to consider giving them cut out sheet TL2.

Formative assessment	Corrective	Enrichment
Is the algorithm correct? Check it with the answers sheet TL3A.	If a part of the algorithm is incorrect highlight this with pupils so they know which parts to work on. Go over a small part of the traffic light sequence using the constantly repeating Scratch file.	Once they have created an accurate algorithm give them the maker cards and appropriate wiring plan to create the circuit diagram. (TL4, TL5, TL6, TL7, TL8 or TL9)

4, Planning the wiring

Older pupils or those more used to using the Crumbles could proceed directly to wiring the Traffic lights using the maker cards only. However most pupils will benefit from planning the wiring circuit before they try to connect it.

5, Wiring the device

Formative assessment	Corrective	Enrichment
Is the Crumble wired correctly? Is the USB plugged into the correct computer? Are they wiring the Crumble upside down with black chip on the bottom? This only happens with the Classic Crumble.	Point them to the wiring diagrams on the maker cards. Trace the lead and show them where it goes so they can change it. Point out the error and turn the Crumble Classic over.	Ask pupils what other inputs and outputs might be deployed with a traffic light. Answers: Buzzer output to alert hard of hearing when it is safe to cross. Button input to check if road is safe to cross. Red and green light outputs to show pedestrian when it is safe to cross.

6, Algorithm to Code

The programming content is mainly sequencing with a forever loop once they have the sequence in the correct order.

If they have used Scratch they may think that they can create parallel blocks of code that run at the same time. Crumble only works with one script. Inform pupils that they can only use one program start block.

Successful code built using the Scratch Traffic light algorithm and the LED lights could look this

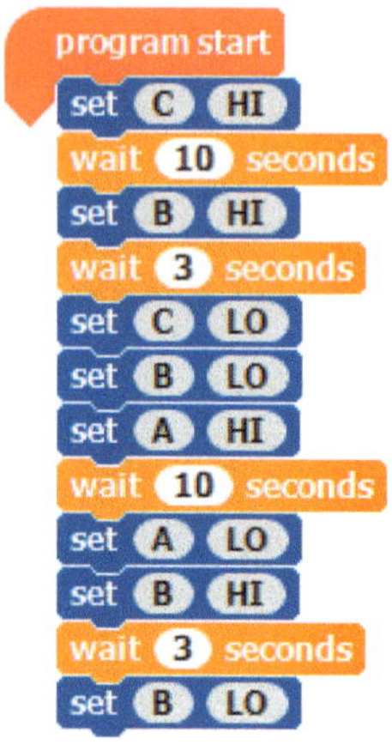

```
program start
set C HI
wait 10 seconds
set B HI
wait 3 seconds
set C LO
set B LO
set A HI
wait 10 seconds
set A LO
set B HI
wait 3 seconds
set B LO
```

Traffic Light Algorithm

Turn red on Turn walk buzzer on
Wait 10 seconds
Turn amber on Turn walk buzzer off
Wait 3 seconds
Turn red off
Turn amber off (Order not important)
Turn green on
Wait 10 seconds
Turn amber on
Turn green off
Wait 3 seconds
Turn amber off
(Repeat all forever)

7, Programming extension activities

Partially Sighted Crossing

Ask pupils, who have created a successful traffic light program how a partially sighted person, who can't see the lights would know when to cross the road.

Once they have figured out that they can use a noise of some sort show them the buzzer crumb. Challenge them to mark on their algorithm when the buzzer would go on and off.

Check that this is similar to the example shown on the left.

Then challenge them to use the buzzer crumb maker card to turn this algorithm into code.

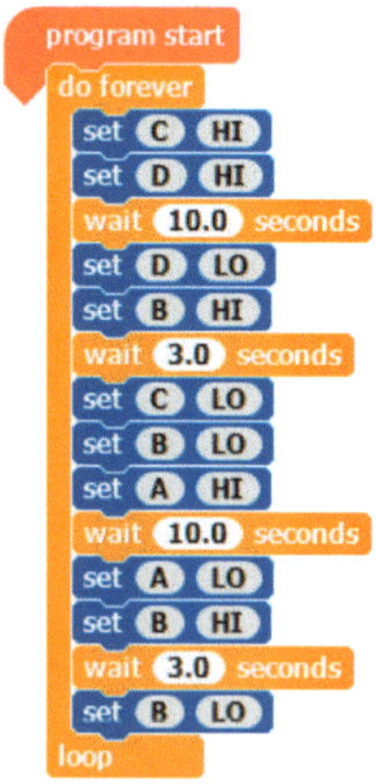

```
program start
do forever
  set C HI
  wait 10.0 seconds
  set B HI
  wait 3.0 seconds
  set C LO
  set B LO
  set A HI
  set sparkle 0 to [red]
  wait 10.0 seconds
  set A LO
  set B HI
  wait 3.0 seconds
  set sparkle 0 to [green]
  set B LO
loop
```

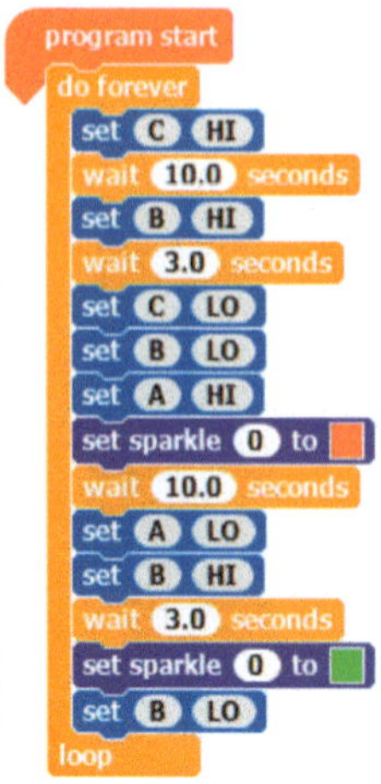

You could also have a pedestrian light that shows red when people can cross and green when it safe to do so.

```
program start
do forever
  set C HI
  set D HI
  wait 10.0 seconds
  set D LO
  set B HI
  wait 3.0 seconds
  set C LO
  set B LO
  set A HI
  wait 10.0 seconds
  set A LO
  set B HI
  wait 3.0 seconds
  set B LO
loop
```

D marks where a buzzer could be turned on (HI) and off (LO) to signal to people that it is safe to cross

C is red, B is amber and A is green
D is a buzzer

Level Crossing Extension

Add a level crossing or car park barrier using a simple servo motor to raise and lower the barrier.

As the Crumble is limited to only four input/outputs, you will need to disconnect the buzzer or programmable lights from earlier extensions to complete this activity.

Like many other projects in this book, you can mount it easily on a small cardboard box.

Simple Servo Barrier mounted on the edge of a cardboard box

Traffic Light Level Crossing Algorithm

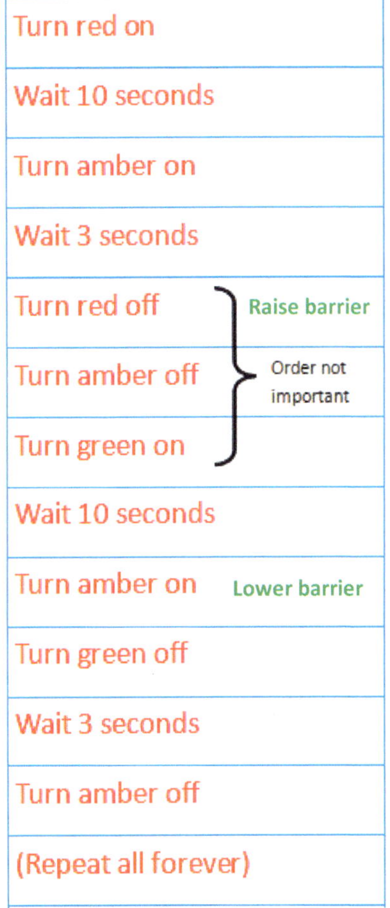

Turn red on	
Wait 10 seconds	
Turn amber on	
Wait 3 seconds	
Turn red off	Raise barrier
Turn amber off	Order not important (Turn red off, Turn amber off, Turn green on)
Turn green on	
Wait 10 seconds	
Turn amber on	Lower barrier
Turn green off	
Wait 3 seconds	
Turn amber off	
(Repeat all forever)	

Adding the level crossing raise and lower the barrier commands into the traffic light algorithm

Before pupils start to code, ask them to tell you where on their algorithm the barrier would go up and where would it go down?

There is some flexibility as to the precise place where the barrier goes up and down but while the traffic is being stopped and the train is passing the barrier must be down. When the train has passed, the traffic light is green to allow the cars to pass over the railway and the barrier needs to be up to let them pass.

Please note that 0 degrees is just where the barrier starts from; it is not a specific direction.

```
program start
do forever
  set C HI
  wait 10.0 seconds
  set B HI
  servo D 45 degrees
  wait 3.0 seconds
  set C LO
  set B LO
  set A HI
  wait 10.0 seconds
  servo D 90 degrees
  set A LO
  set B HI
  wait 3.0 seconds
  set B LO
loop
```

Level crossing program

Button Triggered Crossing

Design a pedestrian crossing where the traffic lights are always green until a pedestrian pushes a button to trigger the red light and an opportunity for them to cross the road.

One way to solve this program is to use the wait until code block to hold the program on a green light until a button is pressed. An example of the code necessary to achieve this is shown on the right.

```
program start
do forever
  set C HI
  wait 10.0 seconds
  set B HI
  wait 3.0 seconds
  set C LO
  set B LO
  set A HI
  wait until D is HI
  wait 10.0 seconds
  set A LO
  set B HI
  wait 3.0 seconds
  set B LO
loop
```

In this code a button is attached to D whilst C is red, B is amber and A is green.

8, Assessment

Use Sheet TL10 for pupils to evaluate their work at the end of every session and stick in their computational aptitudes stickers.

Large Traffic Light

This module variation can be very open ended where you provide a few resources, point pupils in the direction of some research and allow them to come up with their own traffic light designs.

I would recommend providing three boxes, three programmable lights (sparkles or Flames) and encourage the children to research what is inside a torch and/or traffic lights ignoring the battery aspect as the Crumble will provide this.

At the other end of the scale you could work pupils through each aspect, deciding on the construction methods as well as the materials.

If time is limited, I recommend a balance of both. Talk the children through how to create a reflective cone and why that might be important. They can use the cone template on TL1 which you can photocopy onto card. Stick tin foil onto one side before making it into a cone. I also recommend stressing that the programmable light will need to be in the middle and that they may need to insulate the wires from the tin foil using sticky tape. Leave them to puzzle out how to fix this inside the boxes and how to create a translucent cover.

If you are focusing on the programming and want a step by step build then here are the basic steps.

1. Make up three boxes and tape one end shut.
2. Staple all three boxes together in a row or stick them together.
3. Punch some holes through the rear of the boxes using a blunt pencil. If you are using the headphone cables then the holes will need to be quite far apart. If you are using crocodile clips they could be nearer.
4. Roll up some sticky tape and use it to fix the lights centrally inside the boxes.
5. Cut out three cone templates printed onto card and stick tin foil, shiny side up, onto the card as shown.
6. Cut the slit on the cone as shown on the template.
7. Position the cones inside the boxes so that the light shines through the hole in the bottom. Use sticky tape to position it firmly
8. Add a transparent material such as acetate over the cone and inside the box.

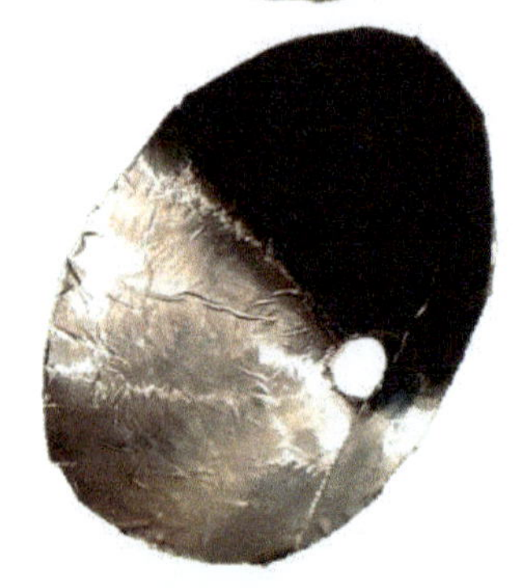

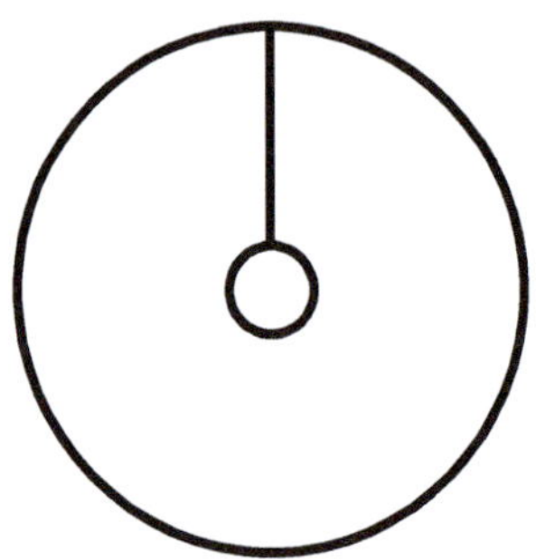

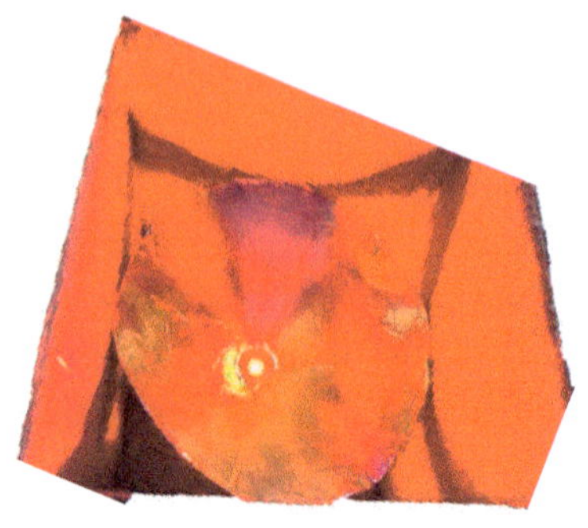

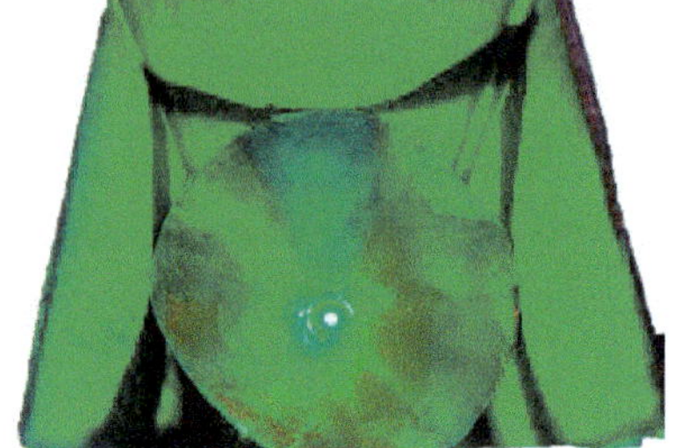

Useful Problem Solving Skills to Assess

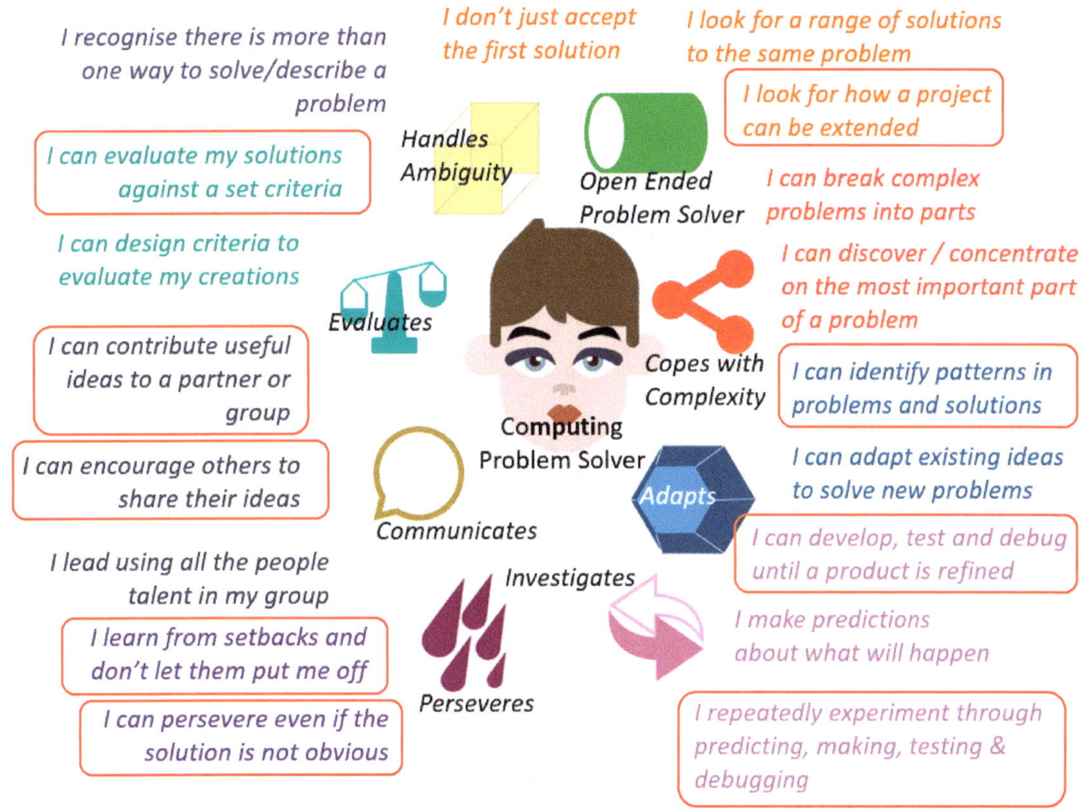
I recognise there is more than one way to solve/describe a problem
I don't just accept the first solution
I look for a range of solutions to the same problem
I look for how a project can be extended
I can evaluate my solutions against a set criteria
Handles Ambiguity
Open Ended Problem Solver
I can break complex problems into parts
I can design criteria to evaluate my creations
I can discover / concentrate on the most important part of a problem
Evaluates
I can contribute useful ideas to a partner or group
Copes with Complexity
I can identify patterns in problems and solutions
Computing Problem Solver
I can encourage others to share their ideas
I can adapt existing ideas to solve new problems
Adapts
Communicates
I can develop, test and debug until a product is refined
I lead using all the people talent in my group
Investigates
I learn from setbacks and don't let them put me off
I make predictions about what will happen
I can persevere even if the solution is not obvious
Perseveres
I repeatedly experiment through predicting, making, testing & debugging

Maker Cards

MC01	**MC23**
MC02	**MC24**
MC04	**MC33**
MC05	**MC34**
MC28	**MC49**
MC06	**MC50**
MC09	**MC38**
MC17	**MC51**
MC18	**MC52**
MC19	**MC53**
MC56	

Curricular Coverage

Design & Technology NC

NCD2A, NCD2E, NCD2G, NCD2H

Computing NC

NCC2A, NCC2B, NCC2C,

TL1

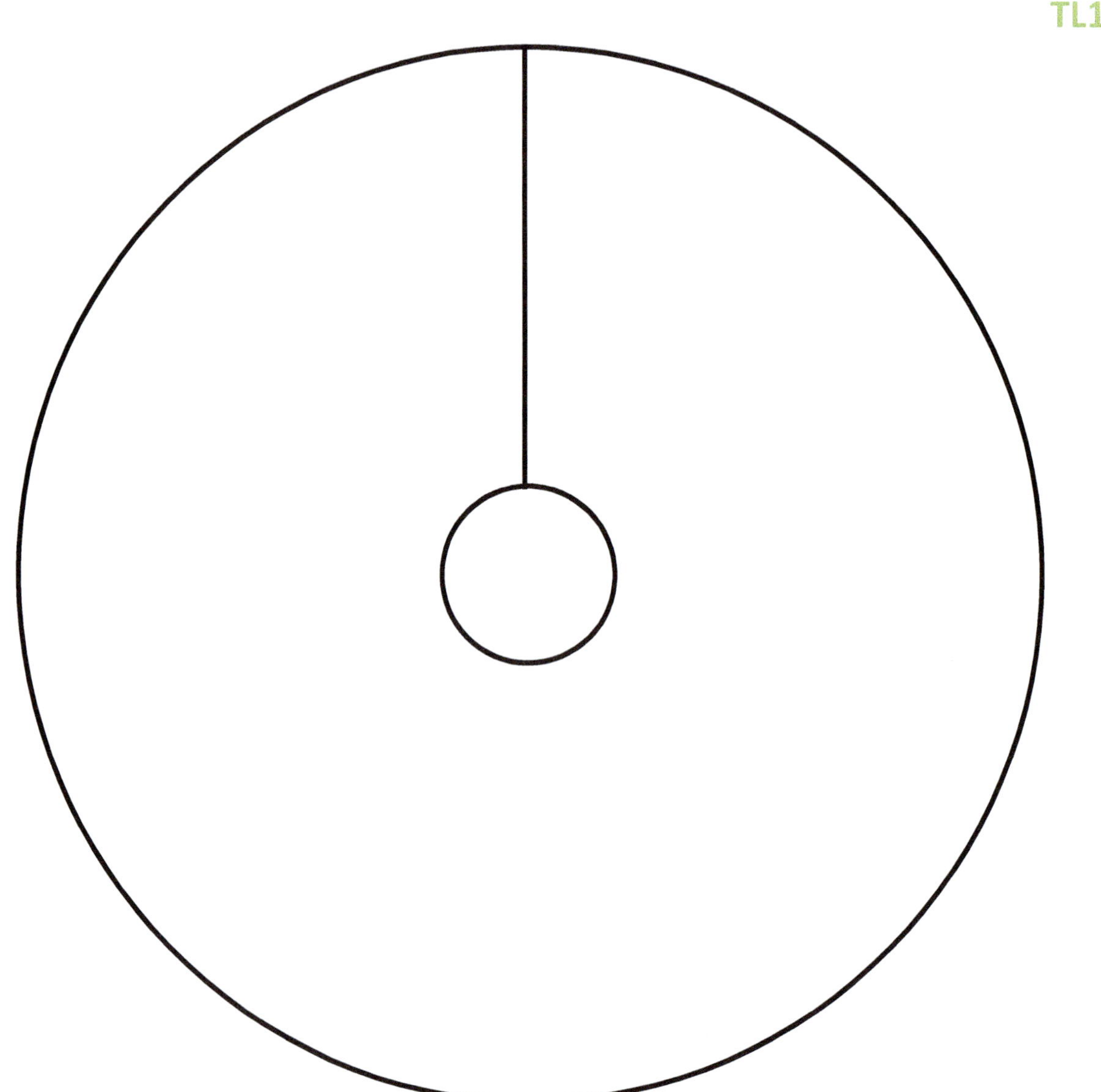

Large Traffic Light Reflection Cone

(designed to fit in a 4 inch x 4 inch box)

Traffic Light Algorithm

TL2

Wait 10 seconds
Turn red on
Turn amber on
Turn red off
Turn amber on
Turn green off
Turn green on
Turn amber off
(Repeat all forever)
Wait 3 seconds
Wait 10 seconds
Turn amber off
Wait 3 seconds

Creating an algorithm

- Cut out the algorithm instructions on the left
- Watch the traffic lights
- Order the instructions into the right order.
- Check the order with your teacher.
- Stick them onto sheet TL3.

Traffic Light Algorithm

Traffic lights algorithm example commands to use TL3

Turn red on
Turn red off
Turn amber on
Turn amber off
Wait 15 seconds

Turn Green on
Turn Green off
Wait 2 seconds

Name__________

Class__________

Turn amber on
Wait 1 second
Turn amber off
Wait 1 second
Turn amber on
Wait 1 second
Turn amber off
(The first four commands could be repeated)

Have a look at this Belisha Beacon light algorithm

TL3A

Traffic Light Algorithm
Answer Sheet

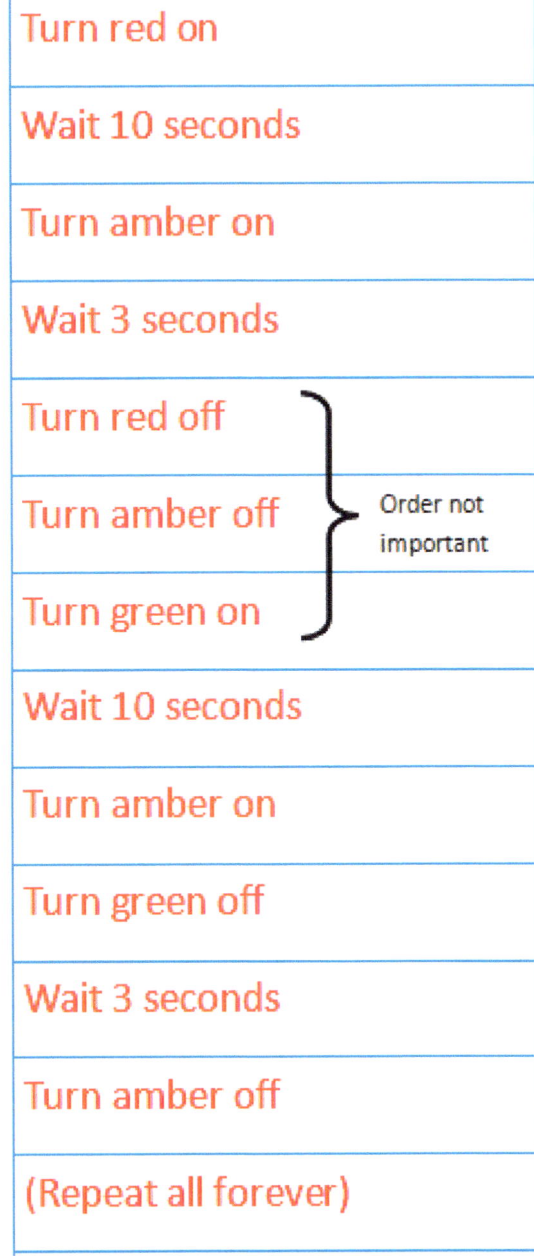

Turn red on	
Wait 10 seconds	
Turn amber on	
Wait 3 seconds	
Turn red off	Order not important
Turn amber off	Order not important
Turn green on	Order not important
Wait 10 seconds	
Turn amber on	
Turn green off	
Wait 3 seconds	
Turn amber off	
(Repeat all forever)	

The order assumes pupils have started from the red light rather than the other way round. It is worth reinforcing this before the activity.

Name ______________________________ Class _____________

Thinking about wiring a Traffic Light TL4

Traffic lights are **outputs** because they **put out** information from the program. These can output three colours.

Draw the wires to show what connections you will use

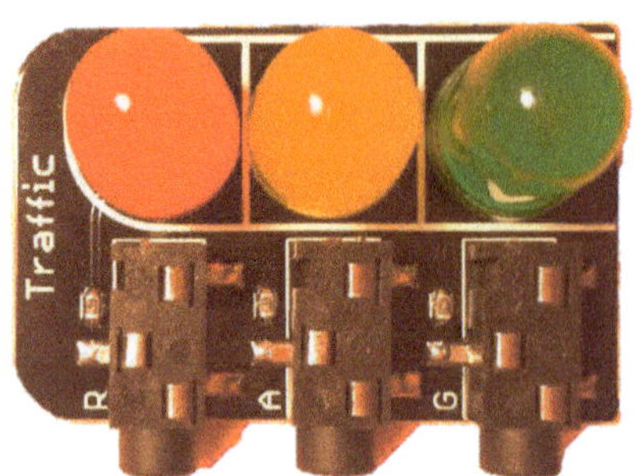

Fill in the chart to show which letters your lights are plugged into

Letter	Colour of the light	Input or Output

Name ______________________________ Class ____________

Thinking about wiring a Traffic Light TL4A

Traffic lights are **outputs** because they **put out** information from the program. These can output three colours.

Draw the wires to show what connections you will use

LED lights can be joined to A, B, C or D

Fill in the chart to show which letters your lights are plugged into

Letter	Colour of the light	Input or Output
A	Amber	Output
B	Red	Output
D	Green	Output

Name ______________________________ Class _____________

Thinking about wiring a Traffic Light TL5

Traffic lights are **outputs** because they **put out** information from the program. These can output three colours.

Draw the wires to show what connections you will use

Fill in the chart to show which letters your lights are plugged into

Letter	Colour of the light	Input or Output

Name ____________________________ Class ____________

Thinking about wiring a Traffic Light TL5A

Traffic lights are **outputs** because they **put out** information from the program. These can output three colours.

Draw the wires to show what connections you will use

LED lights can be joined to A, B, C or D

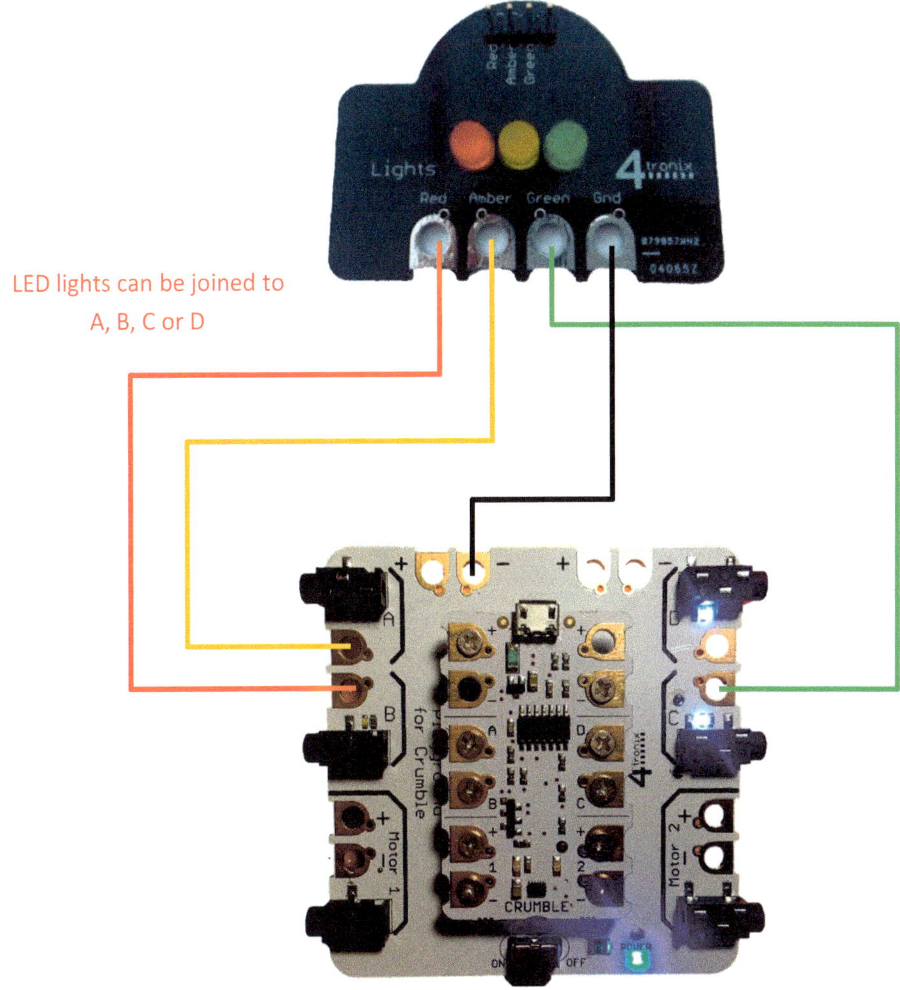

Fill in the chart to show which letters your lights are plugged into

Letter	Colour of the light	Input or Output
A	Amber	Output
B	Red	Output
C	Green	Output

Name ______________________________ Class ____________

Thinking about wiring a Traffic Light TL6

Traffic lights are **outputs** because they **put out** information from the program. These can output three colours.

Draw the wires to show what connections you will use

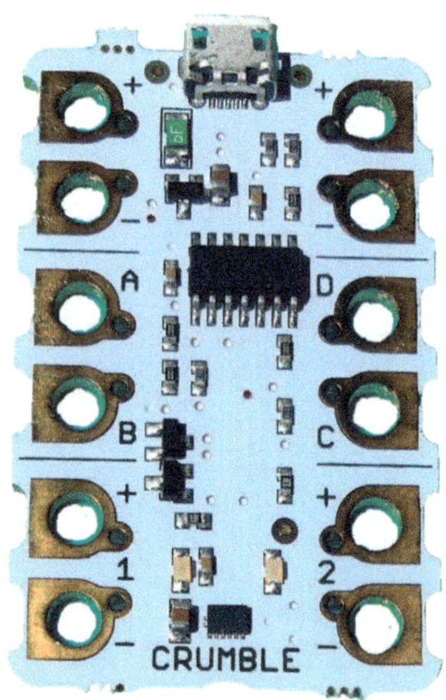

Fill in the chart to show which letters your lights are plugged into

Letter	Colour of the light	Input or Output

Name ______________________________ Class ____________

Thinking about wiring a Traffic Light TL6A

Traffic Light

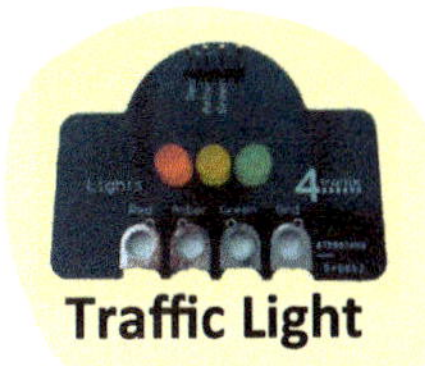

Traffic lights are **outputs** because they **put out** information from the program. These can output three colours.

Draw the wires to show what connections you will use

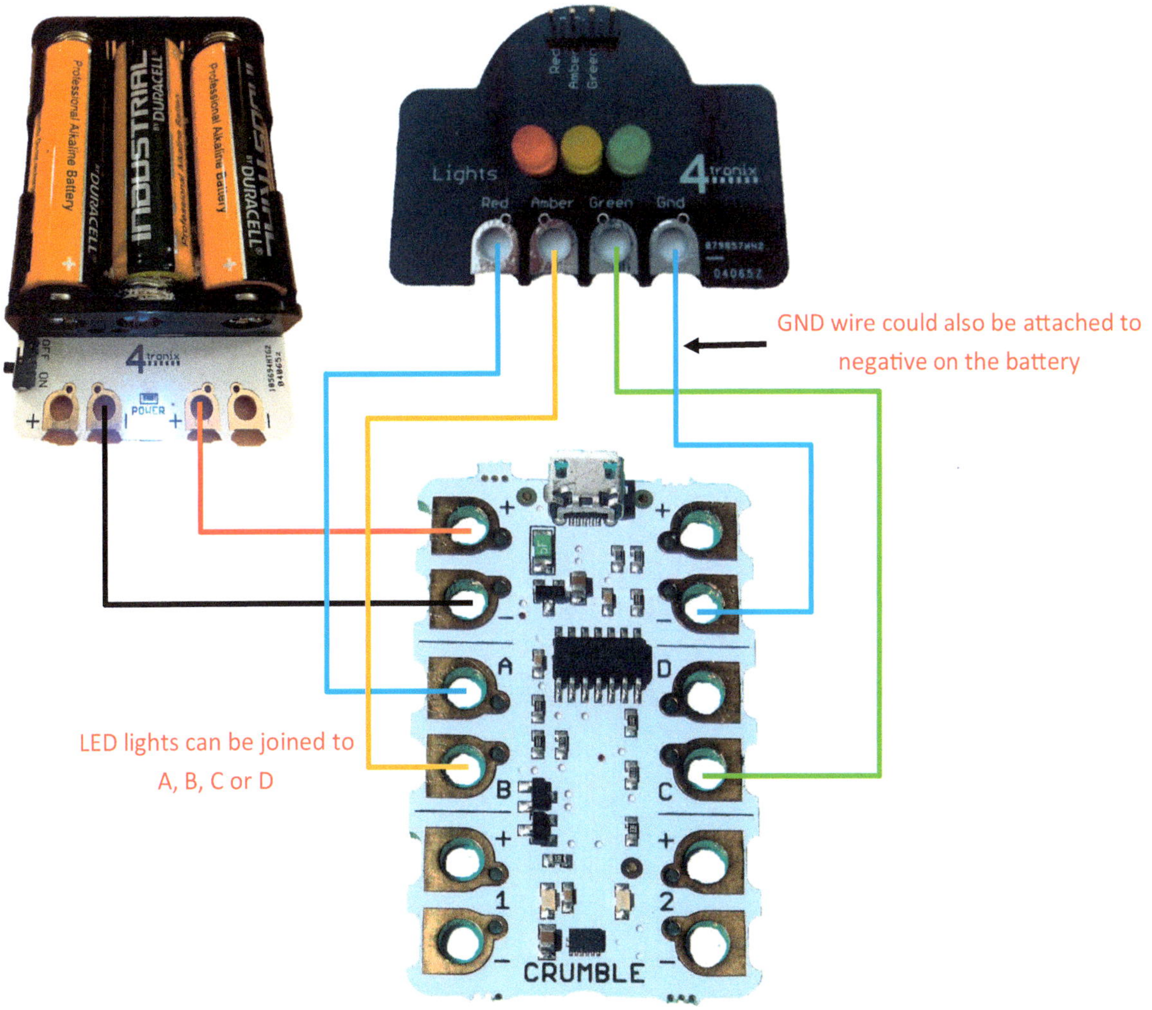

Lights
Red
Amber
Green
Gnd
GND wire could also be attached to negative on the battery
LED lights can be joined to A, B, C or D
POWER
A
B
C
D
1
2
CRUMBLE

Fill in the chart to show which letters your lights are plugged into

Letter	Colour of the light	Input or Output
A	Red	Output
B	Amber	Output
C	Green	Output

Name ______________________ Class __________

Thinking about wiring a Traffic Light TL7

Sparkle lights are **outputs** because they **put out** information from the program. These can output many colours.

Draw the wires to show what connections you will use

Don't forget to name each sparkle 0, 1 & 2

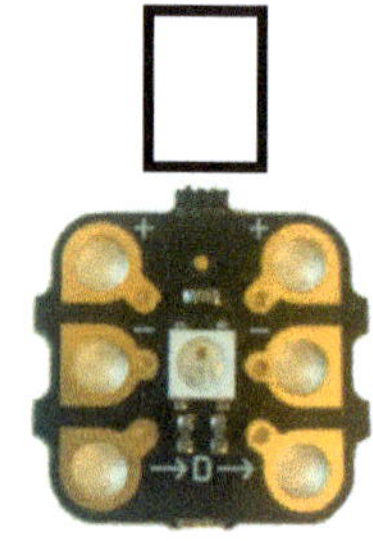

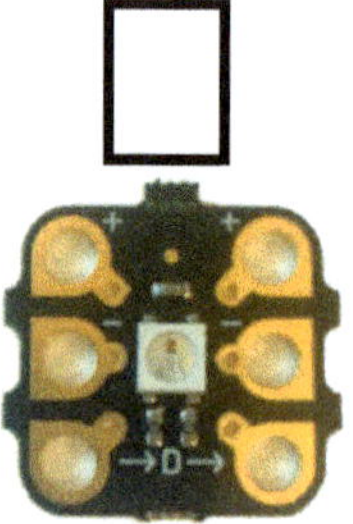

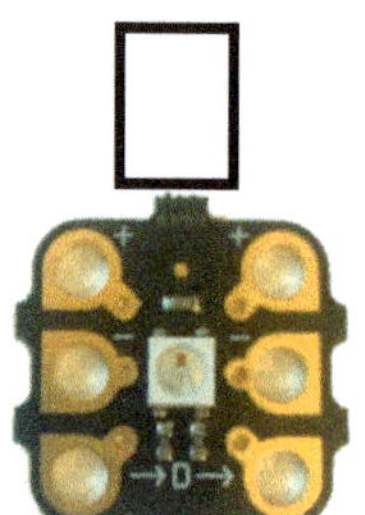

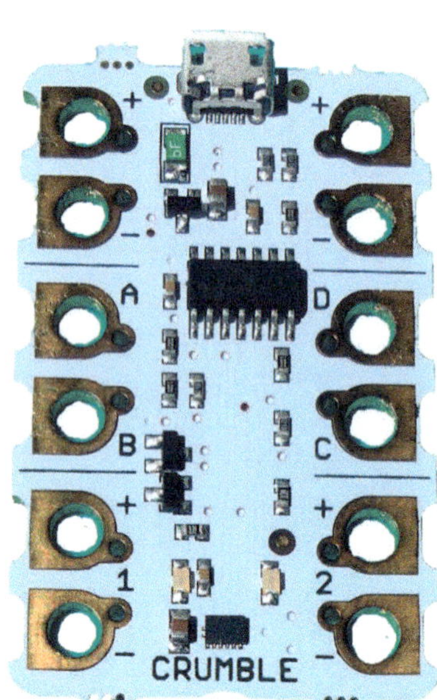

Fill in the chart to show which letters your sparkles are plugged into

Letter	Type of device	Input or Output

Name ______________________________ Class/Form _____________

Thinking about wiring a Traffic Light TL7A

Sparkle lights are **outputs** because they **put out** information from the program. These can output many colours.

Draw the wires to show what connections you will use

Don't forget to name each sparkle 0, 1 & 2

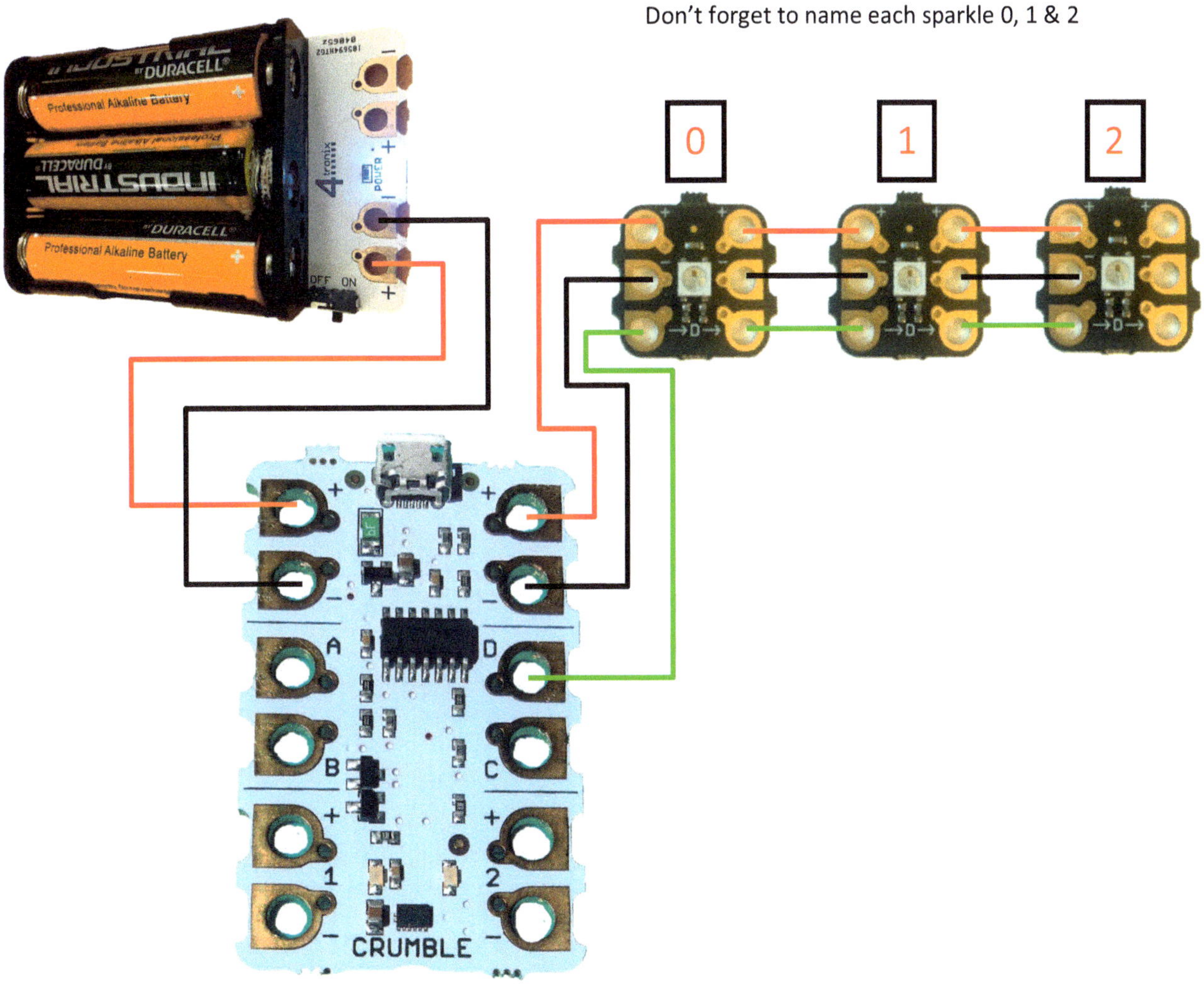

0 1 2

Fill in the chart to show which letters your sparkles are plugged into

Letter	Type of device	Input or Output
D	Sparkles 0, 1 and 2	Output

Name ______________________ Class __________

Thinking about wiring a Traffic Light TL8

Sparkle lights are **outputs** because they **put out** information from the program. These can output many colours.

Draw the wires to show what connections you will use

Don't forget to name each sparkle 0, 1 & 2

Fill in the chart to show which letters your sparkles are plugged into

Letter	Type of device	Input or Output

Name ______________________________ Class _____________

Thinking about wiring a Traffic Light TL8A

Sparkle lights are **outputs** because they **put out** information from the program. These can output many colours.

Draw the wires to show what connections you will use

Don't forget to name each sparkle 0, 1 & 2

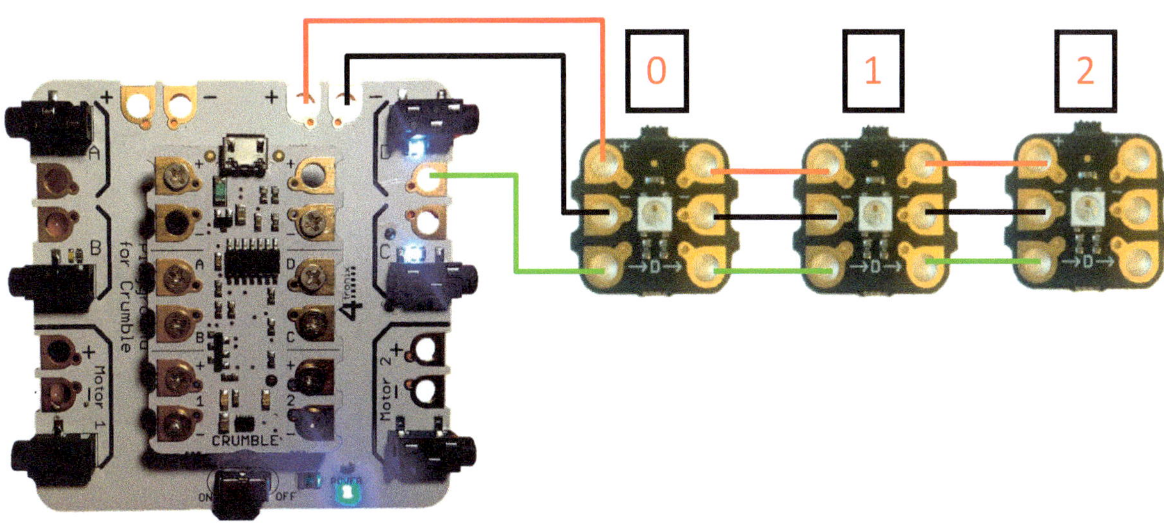

Fill in the chart to show which letters your sparkles are plugged into

Letter	Type of device	Input or Output
D	Sparkles 0, 1 and 2	Outputs

Name ____________________________ Class ____________

Thinking about wiring a Traffic Light TL9

Flame lights are **outputs** because they **put out** information from the program. These can output many colours.

Draw the wires to show what connections you will use

Don't forget to name each sparkle 0, 1 & 2

Fill in the chart to show which letters your flames are plugged into

Letter	Type of device	Input or Output

Name ______________________________ Class ____________

Thinking about wiring a Traffic Light TL9A

Flame lights are **outputs** because they **put out** information from the program. These can output many colours.

Draw the wires to show what connections you will use

Don't forget to name each sparkle 0, 1 & 2

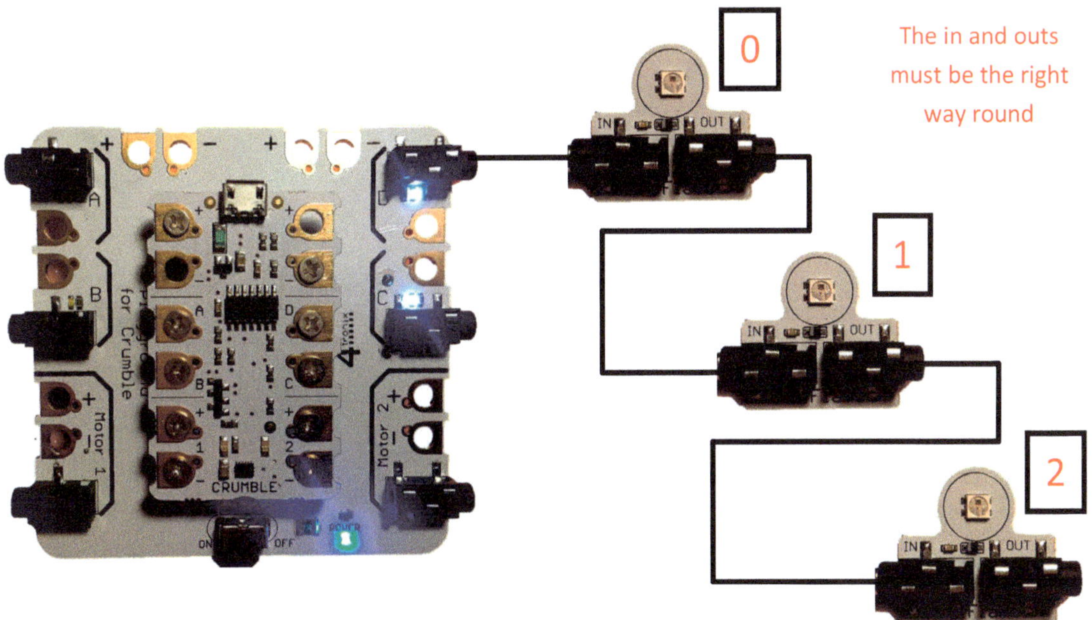
0
1
2
The in and outs must be the right way round

Fill in the chart to show which letters your flames are plugged into

Letter	Type of device	Input or Output
D	Sparkles 0, 1 and 2	Outputs

Traffic Lights Assessment Sheet TL10 Name __________ Class ___

☺ I did this well

😐 I did this ok or I did this a little

☹ I tried this but it didn't work or I didn't do this at all

I created a traffic lights algorithm.	
I persevered when my traffic lights algorithm was incorrectly ordered.	
I used the maker cards to draw a neat wiring diagram.	
I used the maker cards and my wiring diagram to wire up my traffic lights.	
I persevered when my wiring didn't work.	
I create a working traffic lights program.	
I adapted my program so it repeated endlessly.	
I debugged my code to make it mirror my traffic lights algorithm.	
I added a ...	

Sticker	I got this sticker for
Sticker	I got this sticker for
Sticker	I got this sticker for

7. Easy Buggy

Module Aim

Program a vehicle to overcome a progressively harder series of driving / programming challenges.

Cross Curricular Links

Design and Technology This is a great project to do before creating your own open ended Robot Challenges design build and program module (Chapter 11)

Materials

Crumble Playground, two geared motors and wheels, takeaway carton, plastic motor mounts, two buttons Crumble, battery box, two geared motors and wheels, takeaway carton, plastic motor mounts, two buttons

Construction

The building method shown in the pictures shows the Crumble Playground but this project works just as well with the classic Crumble. It is recommended that the teacher pre-builds the vehicle bases and attaches the motors before pupils use them to program with. The motors are awkward to slot into the engine mounts and children often break the wires trying to attach them.

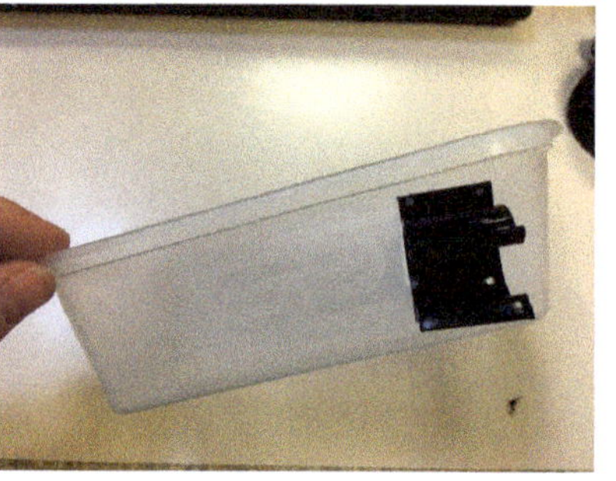

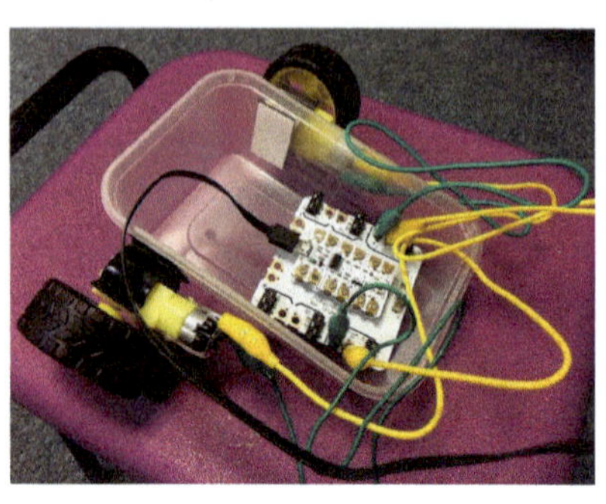

If you decide to use other geared motor types then you will need to build a different chassis. It is perfectly achievable but might cost a little more money than the method shown.

Computing

All the challenges marked up on the floor with masking tape need sequence and repetition programming knowledge to solve them. If you choose to add the steering element (section 7) then pupils will use conditional selection as well.

Useful Maker Cards

MC06	**MC07**	**MC18**
MC19	**MC26**	**MC27**
MC28	**MC37**	**MC38**
MC39	**MC50**	**MC51**

Curricular Coverage

Design & Technology

NCD2H (If they later went on the build their own programable vehicle)

Computing

NCC2A **NCC2C**

Suggested Module Outline

1, Preparation before the lesson

Prepare the buggies before the lesson as shown in the construction section on the previous page. Attach the motors but don't wire them to the Crumble or Crumble playground. Mark out the following challenges on the floor.

- Two parallel lines between 70cm and 100cm apart. This is the there and back challenge. Buggies must cross both lines twice. (Draw two per class per class if 1 buggy between 2 pupils)
- A square roughly 70cm length. Buggies must go round the square. (Draw x2 per class)
- A series of ever smaller squares within each other with the largest being about a 100cm in length. About 200cm away set a starting line. This is the parking challenge. Who can park in the centre square? Pupils are allowed three attempts. They are not allowed to touch the buggy once it has started moving. (x1 per class)

- You can also add an obstacle course if you intend to add button steering later in the lesson.

Print and cut up EB2 if you are going to add button steering later in the project.

Print EB4 if you are going to add the automated vehicle challenge extension.

2, Introduce the challenges

Explain that pupils are going to work in pairs to program their buggy to meet the challenges. Explain that the first challenge is to make their buggy go in a straight line. Then go through the other challenges which they can do in any order.

3, Algorithm Stage

Explain that pupils will need to give instructions to both wheels. Wheels can go forward or backwards for lengths of time. It is a little like steering a manual wheel chair. If you have a pupil in a wheel chair in your class, they can describe how it works. Have they noticed how the wheel chair athletes steer in basketball? Mime moving one wheel forward and the other back. You could also stop one wheel and only move the other. Now give pupils ten minutes to walk over the challenges and plan what sequence of instructions they are going to give. They can record their algorithm instructions on whiteboards. Write up simple shorthand notation such as right motor forward = RMF, wait 10 seconds = W10, left motor backwards = LMB etc.

Formative assessment	Corrective	Enrichment
Have pupils included waits in their algorithms?	Explain that if they don't have any waits the code will execute in less than a second and then run the next command.	Explain that pupils could use tenths of a seconds or milliseconds to use less than one second when waiting.

4, Introduce and wire the buggies

Show pupils a buggy and explain why it might not go in a straight line because the wheels are only held on by pressure in the clips and pupils could put the Crumble equipment in different parts of the buggy which will change where the weight is. Get them to work out the wiring using the relevant maker cards.

5, Introduce the programming

```
program start
wait 3.0 seconds
motor 1 FORWARD at 50 %
motor 2 FORWARD at 50 %
wait 3.0 seconds
motor 1 STOP
wait 1.0 seconds
motor 2 STOP
```

Start by explaining that they will program the buggies using the Crumble software. When they want to try their program they plug the buggy into the computer and build a program using only one program start and send it to the buggy by pressing the green arrow. Their buggy battery pack must be off or the buggy will drive off the table and crash on the floor when the instructions are sent to the Crumble. They must start the program with a wait 3 seconds which allows them time to get their hands away from the buggy before it moves. To test their program they detach the USB cable from the Crumble, place the buggy on the floor and turn on the battery pack. After three seconds the program will start. You may want to demonstrate this simple program. Ask them to predict what the buggy will do. They can write it on the other side of their whiteboard and hold it up. The buggy will go in a straight line before turning in one direction. Explain also that if their buggy turns on the spot when both motors are programmed to go forward, that they can just swap the positive for the negative wire on one motor. All pupils must start with only 50% power. This is because some motors trip a temporary fuse if too much power is used.

If no motor moves at all, check the following:

- Is the battery pack turned on? *Turn it on*
- Are the metal parts of the crocodile clips touching each other (short circuit)? *Stop them touching*
- Do the batteries have enough power? *Change them for new ones.*
- Is there only one program start in the programming? *Remove extra ones so there is only one program start.*
- Does the programming have waits? *Without waits the program would start and stop so quickly that no motor movement would be noticed. Add waits.*

```
program start
wait 3.0 seconds
motor 1 FORWARD at 50 %
motor 2 FORWARD at 50 %
motor 1 STOP
motor 2 STOP
```

This program would start and stop so quickly that no motor movement would be noticed.

- If you move the wheel gently, is it loose? This is a sign that the gears have stripped. *Replace the motor for another one, the cheaper plastic motors will do this but it is rare on the more expensive metal ones.*
- Occasionally a wire is faulty but you won't see anything wrong. If it is the USB wire then the program won't work at all and you will get the error message *ERROR: Crumble not found!*. If one motor works but the other doesn't, change one motor wire at a time until you find the faulty wire.
- Is the Crumble plugged into the computer they are programming. *This happens more often than you would think but it does give you a quiet chuckle. Plug the USB into the computer on which they are writing their programming.*

6, Track progress

After pupil have been on task for a reasonable period of time, point out the whole class progress tracker sheet EB1 and get each group to record their progress as they go. You can then use this to help you with summative assessment.

7, Optional Button Steering

When pupils finish the last challenge, give them the extra challenge of programming one (motor) wheel so that it goes forward when a button is not pressed and back when it is pressed down. If pupils struggle with this, you can print out and ask them to try the physical programming challenges on sheet EB2. This gives them the necessary programming but in another form.

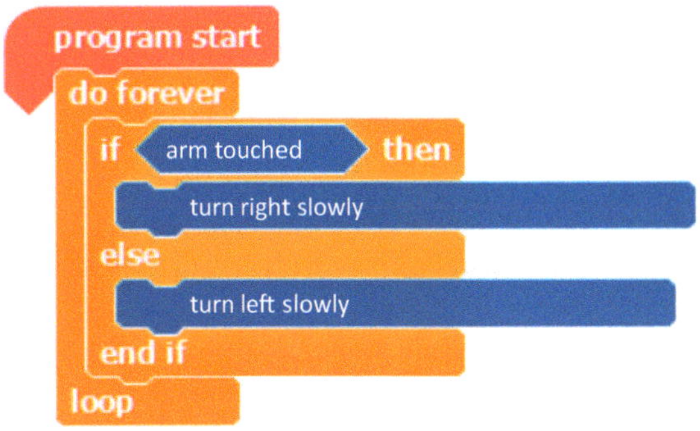

```
program start
do forever
  if arm touched then
    turn right slowly
  else
    turn left slowly
  end if
loop
```

Physical challenge hint example EB2

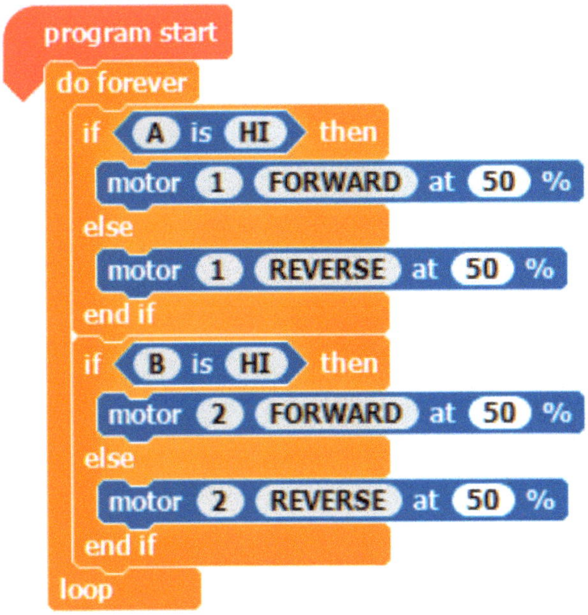

```
program start
do forever
  if A is HI then
    motor 1 FORWARD at 50 %
  else
    motor 1 REVERSE at 50 %
  end if
  if B is HI then
    motor 2 FORWARD at 50 %
  else
    motor 2 REVERSE at 50 %
  end if
loop
```

Two motor example if the buttons are plugged into A and B

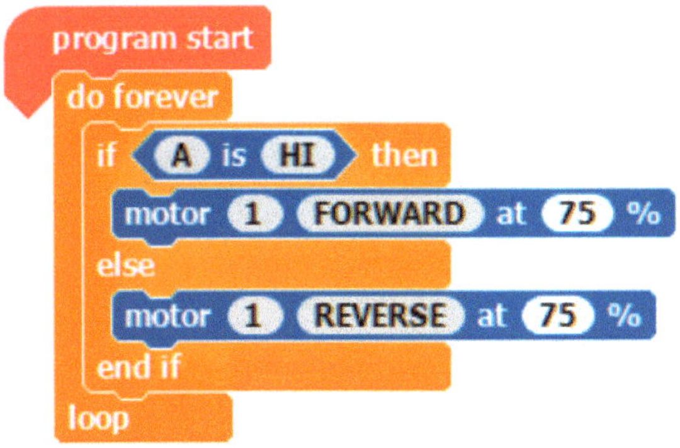

```
program start
do forever
  if A is HI then
    motor 1 FORWARD at 75 %
  else
    motor 1 REVERSE at 75 %
  end if
loop
```

One motor example if the button is plugged into A

Can they then adjust the programming to make the other wheel do the same thing using another button?

These examples are not the only way to program this and some pupils may make versions that include AND OR & NOT but this is the simplest way.

Sometimes pupils struggle to convert one motor to two and there is a physical hint example that you can print from Maker Lab One to help them.

7, Further challenges

There are lots of extra challenges that pupils can develop from the easy buggy module. They could make an automated vacuum cleaner using a distance sensor or a buggy that turns right or left when it detects motion. There

```
program start
do forever
    motor 1 FORWARD at 50 %
    motor 2 FORWARD at 50 %
    wait 3.0 seconds
    motor 1 STOP
    motor 2 STOP
    wait 100 milliseconds
    let (distance) = distance (cm) T:D E:A
    if (distance) < 10 then
        motor 1 REVERSE at 50 %
        motor 2 REVERSE at 50 %
        wait 1.0 seconds
        motor 1 STOP
        motor 2 STOP
        wait 100 milliseconds
        motor 1 FORWARD at 50 %
        wait 3.0 seconds
        motor 1 STOP
    end if
loop
```

is a code scaffold for the automated buggy EB4 and an example of programming that works on the left. These type of projects are also covered in the Maker Lab Two chapter.

8, Assessment

If pupils are working in pairs then the whole class tracking sheet EB1 is available for them to feedback on their general progress in solving the challenges. There is also a one page question sheet EB3 & EB3A to help determine their understanding after the practical programming is finished. If pupils have not attempted the button steering then you can instruct them that the fourth question is optional. If you are using stickers, then pupils can stick them on the back of the sheet.

9, Creating pupils own project

EB5 & EB6 are useful scaffolds to help pupils think through and design their own projects. The sentence scaffolds outlined on page 13 can be useful to help pupils think through the task and what the user sees and does.

Useful Problem Solving Skills to Assess

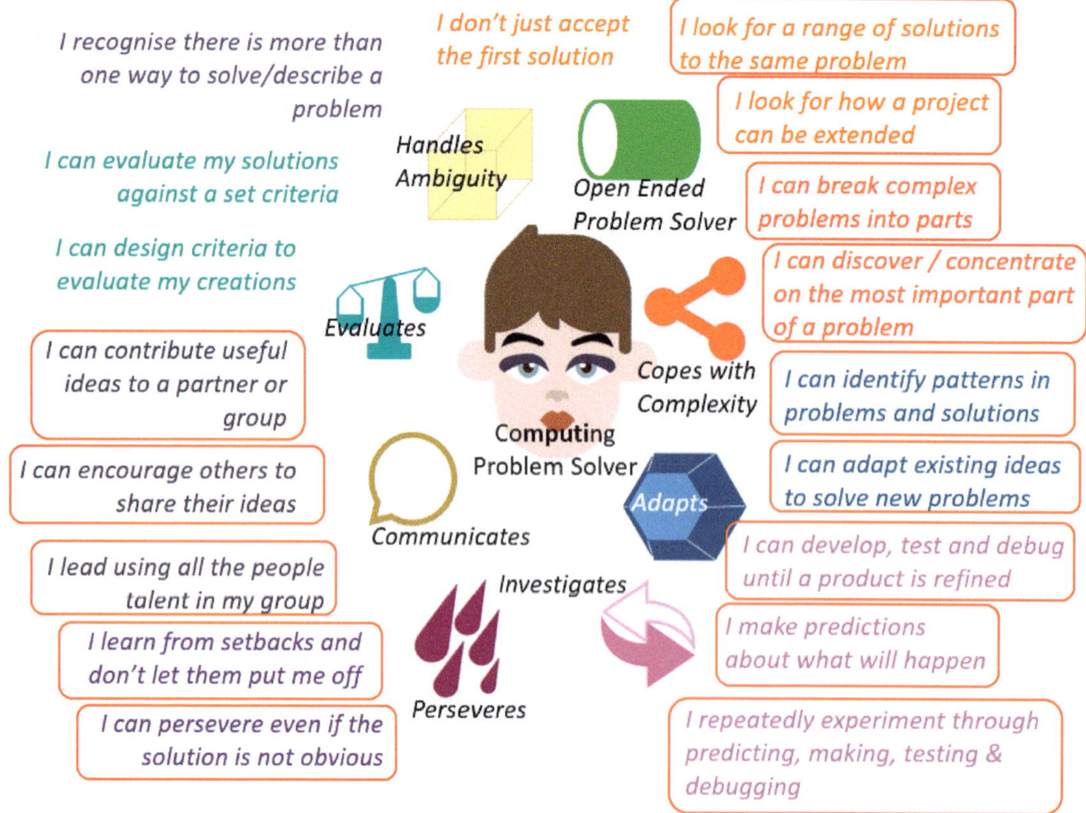

I recognise there is more than one way to solve/describe a problem
I don't just accept the first solution
I look for a range of solutions to the same problem
I look for how a project can be extended
Handles Ambiguity
Open Ended Problem Solver
I can evaluate my solutions against a set criteria
I can break complex problems into parts
I can design criteria to evaluate my creations
Evaluates
I can discover / concentrate on the most important part of a problem
I can contribute useful ideas to a partner or group
Copes with Complexity
I can identify patterns in problems and solutions
Computing Problem Solver
I can encourage others to share their ideas
I can adapt existing ideas to solve new problems
Adapts
Communicates
I can develop, test and debug until a product is refined
I lead using all the people talent in my group
Investigates
I learn from setbacks and don't let them put me off
I make predictions about what will happen
I can persevere even if the solution is not obvious
Perseveres
I repeatedly experiment through predicting, making, testing & debugging

Problem solving skills are adapted from a problem solving rubric created by Mark Dorling and Thomas Stephens that the author worked on helping to define. You can find this at http://code-it.co.uk/attitudes/

Class Progress Tracker

☺ Completed easily
😐 Completed with a struggle
☹ Still trying to work it out

EB1

Names	Motors Work	Straight Line	Cross line & Return	Square	Parking Score	Steering

```
program start
  do forever
    if head touched then
      walk forwards slowly
    else
      walk backwards slowly
    end if
  loop
```

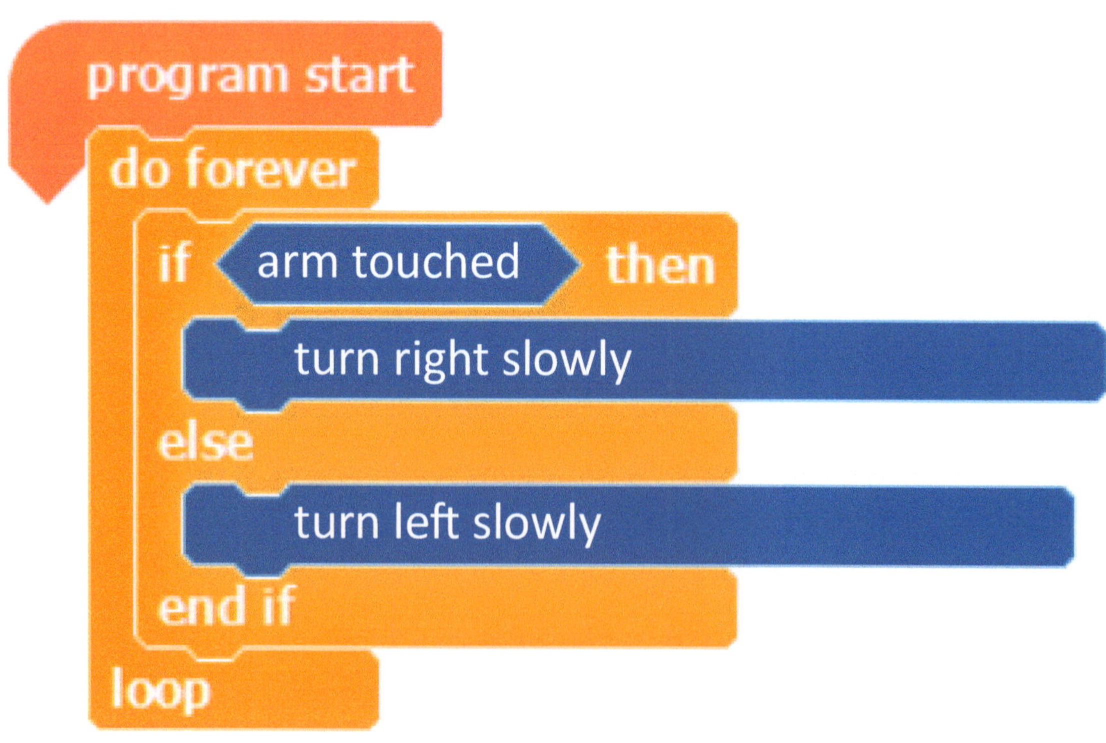

Easy Buggy Assessment   Name____________ Group_____   EB3

Can you spot and describe the bugs in these Easy Buggy Programs?

```
program start
  wait 3.0 seconds
  motor 1 FORWARD at 50 %
  motor 2 FORWARD at 50 %
  motor 1 STOP
  motor 2 STOP
```

```
program start
  wait 3.0 seconds
  motor 1 FORWARD at 50 %
  motor 2 FORWARD at 50 %
  wait 2.4 seconds
  motor 1 STOP
  motor 2 STOP
  wait 1.0 seconds
  motor 1 FORWARD at 50 %
  motor 2 REVERSE at 50 %
  wait 0.4 seconds
  motor 1 STOP
```

What shape might this draw? What clues are there?

```
program start
  wait 3.0 seconds
  do 3 times
    motor 1 FORWARD at 50 %
    motor 2 FORWARD at 50 %
    wait 3.0 seconds
    motor 1 STOP
    motor 2 STOP
    wait 0.2 seconds
    motor 1 FORWARD at 50 %
    wait 0.4 seconds
    motor 1 STOP
    wait 0.2 seconds
  loop
```

```
program start
  if A is HI then
    motor 1 FORWARD at 50 %
  else
    motor 1 REVERSE at 50 %
  end if
  if B is HI then
    motor 2 FORWARD at 50 %
  else
    motor 2 REVERSE at 50 %
  end if
```

You may choose to leave question four if you didn't use button steering.

Easy Buggy Assessment Name____________ Group_____ EB3A

Can you spot and describe the bugs in these Easy Buggy Programs?

```
program start
  wait 3.0 seconds
  motor 1 FORWARD at 50 %
  motor 2 FORWARD at 50 %
  motor 1 STOP
  motor 2 STOP
```

There is no wait between the motor starting and stopping so nothing will move.

```
program start
  wait 3.0 seconds
  motor 1 FORWARD at 50 %
  motor 2 FORWARD at 50 %
  wait 2.4 seconds
  motor 1 STOP
  motor 2 STOP
  wait 1.0 seconds
  motor 1 FORWARD at 50 %
  motor 2 REVERSE at 50 %
  wait 0.4 seconds
  motor 1 STOP
```

The final motor stop for motor 2 is missing which means this will stay on until the batteries run out or the Crumble is switched off.

```
program start
  wait 3.0 seconds
  do 3 times
    motor 1 FORWARD at 50 %
    motor 2 FORWARD at 50 %
    wait 3.0 seconds
    motor 1 STOP
    motor 2 STOP
    wait 0.2 seconds
    motor 1 FORWARD at 50 %
    wait 0.4 seconds
    motor 1 STOP
    wait 0.2 seconds
  loop
```

What shape might this draw? What clues are there?

Triangle

Clues

The program is repeated three times.

There is a straight route and a turn.

```
program start
  if A is HI then
    motor 1 FORWARD at 50 %
  else
    motor 1 REVERSE at 50 %
  end if
  if B is HI then
    motor 2 FORWARD at 50 %
  else
    motor 2 REVERSE at 50 %
  end if
```

The forever loop is missing so the conditions will be checked once only and the buggy will be stuck in reverse.

You may choose to leave question four if you didn't use button steering.

Automated Vehicle Code Scaffold

EB4

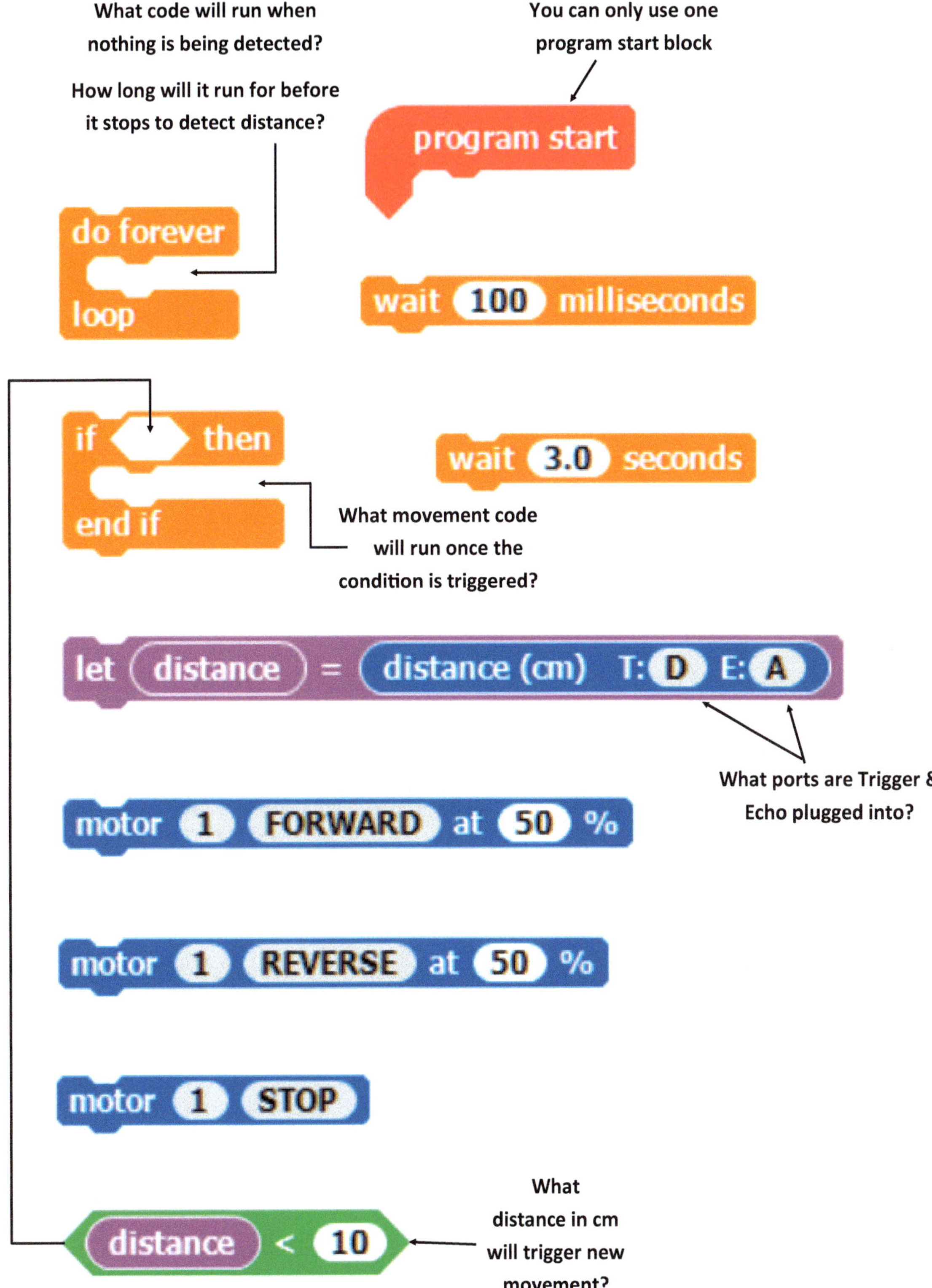

What code will run when nothing is being detected?
How long will it run for before it stops to detect distance?
You can only use one program start block
program start
do forever
loop
wait 100 milliseconds
if then
end if
wait 3.0 seconds
What movement code will run once the condition is triggered?
let distance = distance (cm) T: D E: A
What ports are Trigger & Echo plugged into?
motor 1 FORWARD at 50 %
motor 1 REVERSE at 50 %
motor 1 STOP
distance < 10
What distance in cm will trigger new movement?

Name ______________________________ Class ____________ EB5

Thinking about designing my own project that uses motors

My program will

by

What will your user see and do?

Input/ Output	Name of device attached	What the device does (include as much detail as possible)
Motor 1 Output	Motor	A fan blade which spins to move air through it
A		
B		
C		
D		
Motor 1		
Motor 2		

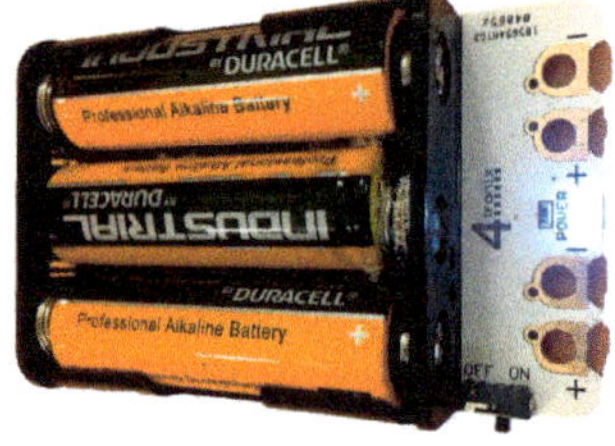

Fill in your idea and add your inputs and outputs to the chart.

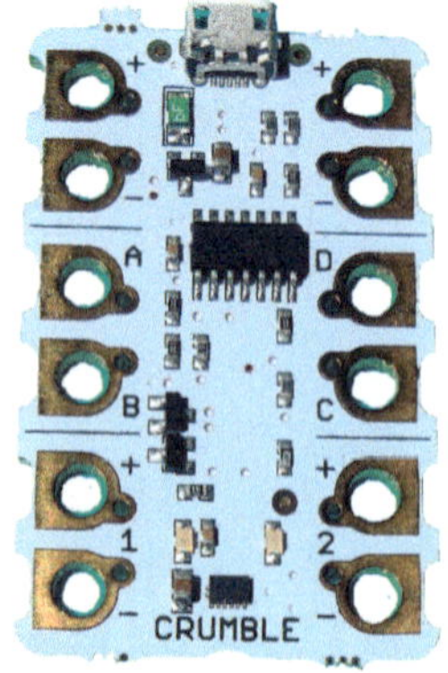

Draw your devices and the wires that connect them.

Name ______________________________ Class ____________ EB6

Thinking about designing my own project that uses motors

My program will

by

What will your user see and do?

Input/ Output	Name of device attached	What the device does (include as much detail as possible)
Motor 1 Output	Motor	A fan blade which spins to move air through it
A		
B		
C		
D		
Motor 1		
Motor 2		

Fill in your idea and add your inputs and outputs to the chart.

Draw your devices and the wires that connect them.

Chapter 8, Quiz Buzzer

Module Aim

Design a quiz buzzer to see who wants to answer a quiz question first. Each buzzer will have to have a unique signature sound. You can do this through adjusting the amount of electricity that goes through a piezo buzzer attached to motor 1 or 2. This is also a useful element that pupils can use independently in other projects.

Cross Curricular Links

Any Subject –You could link this to a quiz in any subject.

Materials

Crumble Playground, piezo buzzer, button **OR** Crumble, battery box, piezo buzzer and button

Construction

This project is most easily mounted on a pre-made cardboard box. 4 inch ones are a perfect size and can be purchased very cheaply. Pupils can punch holes very easily through the sides using a blunt pencil. Double sided sticky tape or standard tape folded over can be used to temporarily affix the piezo buzzer and button to the outside. Turn the box on its side with the opening facing the player, the buzzer facing the audience and the button on what is now the top.

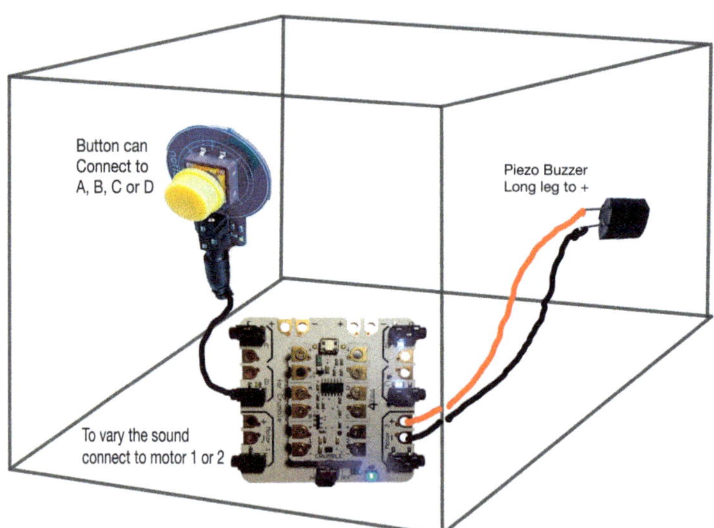

Crumble Playground Quiz Buzzer using Piezo

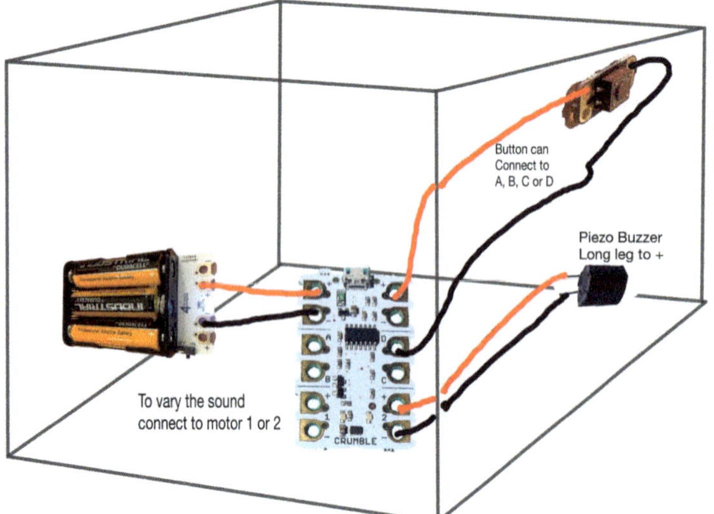

Classic Crumble Quiz Buzzer using Piezo

Punch two small holes in the box for the piezo legs to pass through. If you get these the right size the piezo can be held outside the box whilst the crocodile clips are inside the box.

The box can also be used to reduce the sound volume of the piezo during testing.

Maker Cards

MC06	MC18	MC19
MC25	MC47	MC50
MC51		

Curriculum Coverage

Computing National Curriculum

NC22A **NCC2B** **NCC2C**

Design & Technology National Curriculum

NCD2G **NCD2H**

NCD1A (If using section 9)

Suggested Module Outline

1, Preparation before the first lesson

Decide on an approach to thinking through how the button part of the programming works. QB1 & QB2 have a written algorithm and all the code blocks that pupils will need to create the code. QB3 & QB4 are similar but they ask pupils to draw lines between the code blocks and the algorithm before coding, forcing them to examine the connection between the algorithm and the code. If pupils have extensive programming knowledge you may wish to just use the maker cards. Print the sheet out that matches your Crumble type, pupils experience and preferred methodology.

2, Introducing the challenge

Introduce the idea of a quiz buzzer that will identify who has pressed the button through the unique sound it makes. Explain that if they use a standard buzzer it only produces one standard sound but if they attach a piezo element to the motor connection, they can vary how much electricity passes through the piezo and this will change the tone of the sound.

3, Making a prediction

Give out your pre-chosen sheet and read through the top half with your pupils. Explain that they will need to make a prediction by circling any of the words in capitals. Instruct them to only read the top half of the sheet.

4, Wiring the Crumble

Using the maker cards and the information on the sheet can they wire the Crumble and replicate the program on the top part of the sheet? They will need a starting block. Was their original prediction correct?

5, Signature sound

Instruct them to create a signature sound using only sequence and repeat x type loops. They might want to use decimal fractions of a second or the milliseconds block to determine how long their sounds lasts for before it fades.

Formative assessment	Corrective	Enrichment
As pupils create sounds, look for examples that duplicate the same code repetitively without using a repeat x times loop.	Challenge these pupils to keep the same sound whilst using the least blocks.	If you have enough piezo buzzers you might challenge pupils to include another one wired into the other motor.

6, Adding a button

Hand out buttons and the maker cards to go with their type of button. Instruct pupils to wire their button into input A. Direct pupils back to the sheet and ask them to read the bottom half of the sheet carefully. If pupils are using QB3 or QB4 they will need to draw lines from the code blocks to the algorithm. Using this information ask the children to create code where the signature sound is triggered by the button?

7, **More than one method**

Challenge pupils to find more than one method to make the button turn on the piezo buzzer sequence. You may wish to point out other blocks that they might use. Make sure they only keep one program start block per screen.

8, **Checking the code solutions**

One of the advantages of simple physical programming using a device like the Crumble is that it has less permutations than a more general programming language like Scratch. This makes it easier to identify possible correct solutions and likely bugs.

```
program start
do forever
  if A is HI then
    motor 2 FORWARD at 20 %
    wait 1.0 seconds
    motor 2 FORWARD at 35 %
    wait 1.0 seconds
    motor 2 FORWARD at 80 %
    wait 1.0 seconds
    motor 2 STOP
  end if
loop
```

Simplest correct solution and the one the sheets QB1-4 identify

```
program start
do forever
  if A is HI then
    motor 2 FORWARD at 20 %
    wait 0.1 seconds
    motor 2 FORWARD at 35 %
    wait 0.1 seconds
    motor 2 FORWARD at 80 %
    wait 0.1 seconds
  else
    motor 2 STOP
  end if
loop
```

```
program start
do forever
  if A is LO then
    motor 2 STOP
  else
    motor 2 FORWARD at 20 %
    wait 1.0 seconds
    motor 2 FORWARD at 35 %
    wait 1.0 seconds
    motor 2 FORWARD at 80 %
    wait 1.0 seconds
    motor 2 STOP
  end if
loop
```

Two alternate correct solutions using the if else conditional selection block

```
program start
do forever
  do until A is LO
    motor 2 FORWARD at 20 %
    wait 0.1 seconds
    motor 2 FORWARD at 35 %
    wait 0.1 seconds
    motor 2 FORWARD at 80 %
    wait 0.1 seconds
    motor 2 STOP
  loop
loop
```

An alternate correct solution using the do until block

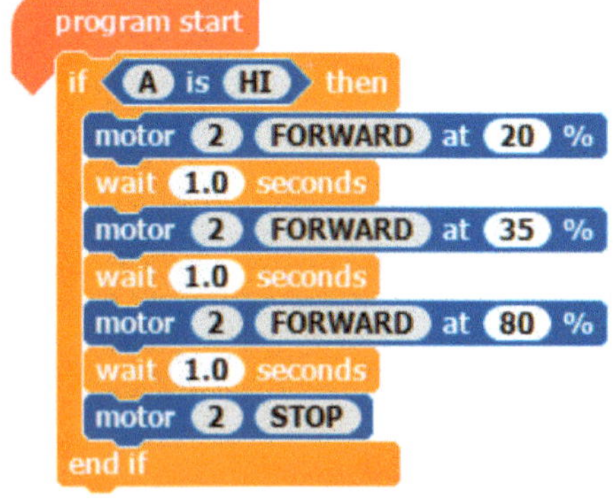

Very common bug where the forever loop has been left out. Ask pupils, "How many times will your condition be checked?"

```
program start
do forever
  if A is HI then
    do forever
      motor 2 FORWARD at 20 %
      wait 1.0 seconds
      motor 2 FORWARD at 35 %
      wait 1.0 seconds
      motor 2 FORWARD at 80 %
      wait 1.0 seconds
      motor 2 STOP
    loop
  end if
loop
```

Remember in the pupils code the sequence of motor power commands will look very different as they strive for individuality.

Common bug where another forever loop has been introduced in place of a do x times loop. This results in endless buzzing.

9, Mounting on the box

You may decide to complete this project without the box as a mount. However, it can help pupils to think about the aesthetics of their creation when they are encouraged to mount it on a structure. You may also like to encourage pupils to have a freer choice over other mounting materials if they are available.

Practical design considerations

- How easy will it be for the user to hit the button, which is the prime purpose of the quiz buzzer?
- How easy will it be for the user to switch the batteries on and off? Will they have to open the box and rummage around inside every time to find the battery switch?
- Is the piezo in a position to make the loudest sound?
- How durable is the mounting, considering that it will be used in a tense situation?

10, User Testing

Group three or four buzzers groups together and get them to answer some quiz questions to trial the buzzers in action. Could one person film the operation? How well did the buzzers work? Is any one sound more distinctive and easily recognised than any other sound? Could pupils adapt their project in light of their peers' evaluations?

11, Adapting the Project

QB5 & QB6 can be used to encourage pupils to adapt the quiz buzzer project to make their own device. Pupils come up with their own idea and work out which ports they attach accessories before building it. It is designed as a simple adaptation of the main project. If pupils want to make much more complex projects, then Maker lab one and two are better.

12, Assessment

Sheet QB7 can be used by pupils to assess their own understanding and used by teachers, alongside the finished project. to determine attainment.

Purchasing Piezo Buzzers

A pack of 30 12mm diameter DC 5V buzzers can be purchased from Amazon directly.

http://amzn.eu/dVVEIDQ

Useful Problem Solving Skills to Assess

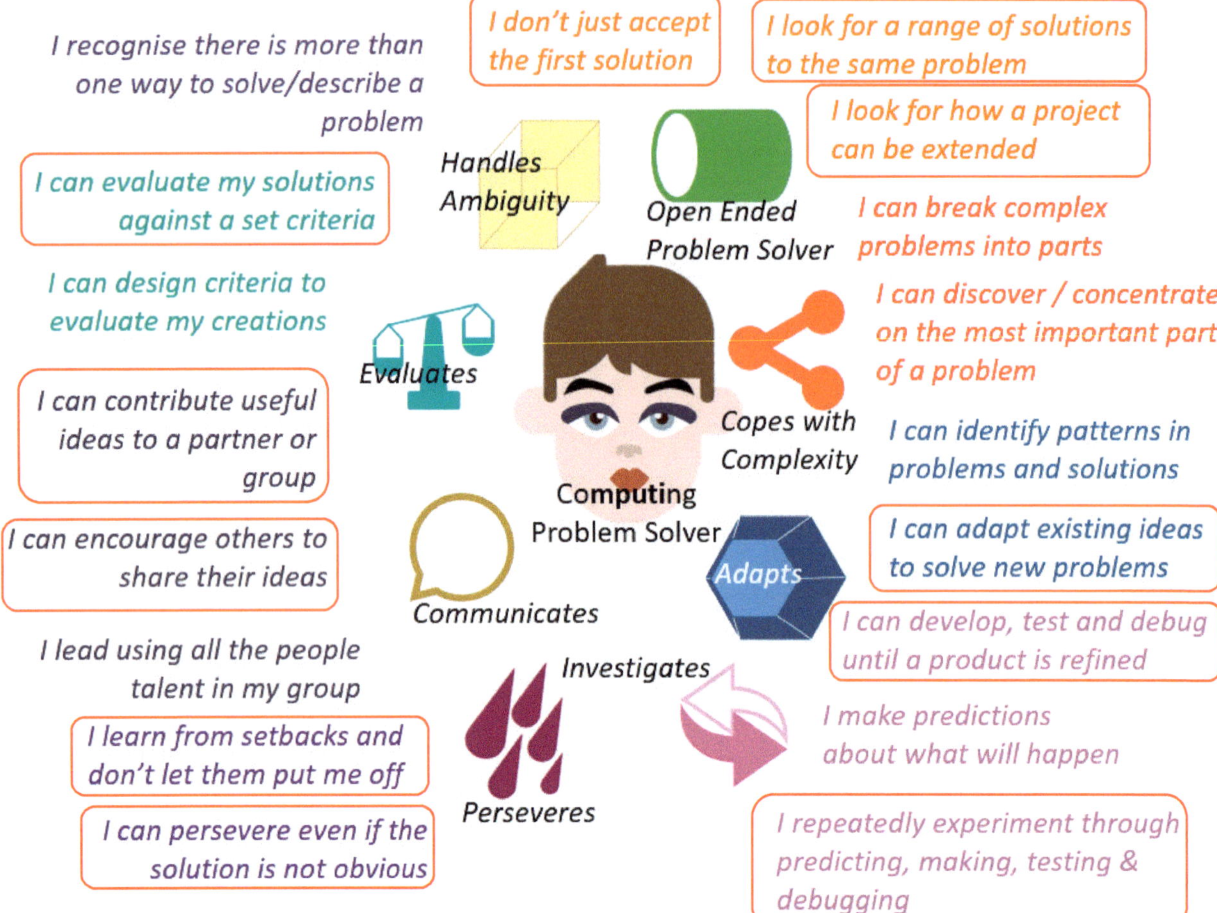

I recognise there is more than one way to solve/describe a problem
I don't just accept the first solution
I look for a range of solutions to the same problem
I look for how a project can be extended
Handles Ambiguity
Open Ended Problem Solver
I can evaluate my solutions against a set criteria
I can break complex problems into parts
I can design criteria to evaluate my creations
I can discover / concentrate on the most important part of a problem
Evaluates
I can contribute useful ideas to a partner or group
Copes with Complexity
I can identify patterns in problems and solutions
Computing Problem Solver
I can encourage others to share their ideas
I can adapt existing ideas to solve new problems
Adapts
Communicates
I can develop, test and debug until a product is refined
I lead using all the people talent in my group
Investigates
I learn from setbacks and don't let them put me off
I make predictions about what will happen
Perseveres
I can persevere even if the solution is not obvious
I repeatedly experiment through predicting, making, testing & debugging

Problem solving skills are adapted from a problem solving rubric created by Mark Dorling and Thomas Stephens that the author worked on helping to define. You can find this at http://code-it.co.uk/attitudes/

Name ____________________________ Class ____________ QB1

Thinking about programming a quiz buzzer (Classic Crumble)

This is a piezo buzzer. We pass electricity through it to make a sound.

```
motor 2 FORWARD at 20 %
wait 1 seconds
motor 2 FORWARD at 35 %
wait 1 seconds
motor 2 FORWARD at 80 %
wait 1 seconds
motor 2 STOP
```

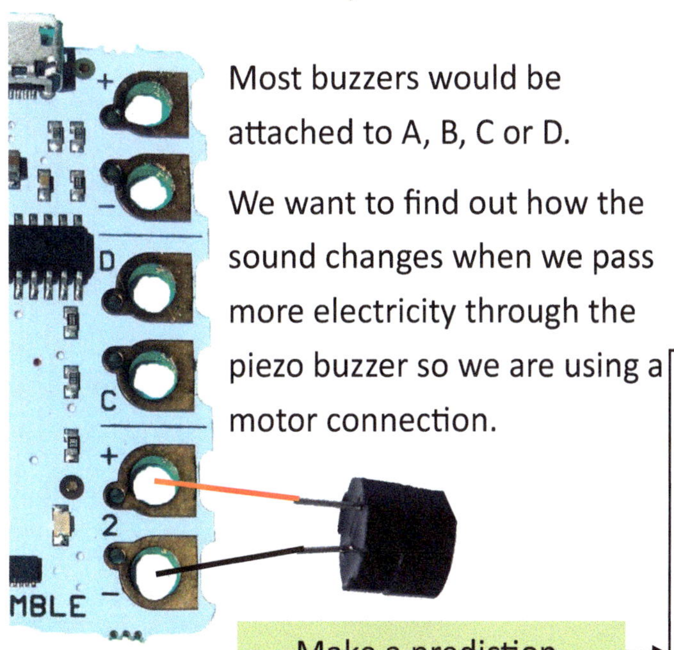

Most buzzers would be attached to A, B, C or D.

We want to find out how the sound changes when we pass more electricity through the piezo buzzer so we are using a motor connection.

Make a prediction. →

Circle the change that you predict will happen as the program above increases the power through the piezo from 20% to 35% and then to 80%. QUIETER, LOUDER, HIGHER PITCH, LOWER PITCH

Attach your piezo buzzer to motor 2. Make sure the longer leg is attached to the +. Attach your button to input A.

Algorithm

When the program starts, check forever to see if the button attached to A is pressed down.

If button A is pressed down, make the piezo buzz at 20% power for a second before increasing to 35% and 80% for one second each before stopping.

```
program start
motor 2 STOP
if ⬡ then
end if
do forever
loop
motor 2 FORWARD at 20 %
motor 2 FORWARD at 35 %
wait 1.0 seconds
motor 2 FORWARD at 80 %
wait 1.0 seconds
A is HI
wait 1.0 seconds
```

Use the algorithm, the code blocks and maker cards to help you build the quiz buzzer program. Can you design your own unique sound?

Name ______________________________ Class ____________ QB2

Thinking about programming a quiz buzzer (Crumble Playground)

This is a piezo buzzer. We pass electricity through it to make a sound.

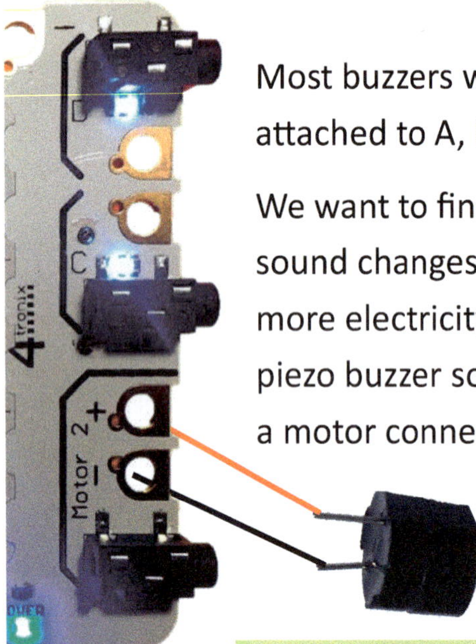

Most buzzers would be attached to A, B, C or D.

We want to find out how the sound changes when we pass more electricity through the piezo buzzer so we are using a motor connection.

```
motor 2 FORWARD at 20 %
wait 1 seconds
motor 2 FORWARD at 35 %
wait 1 seconds
motor 2 FORWARD at 80 %
wait 1 seconds
motor 2 STOP
```

Make a prediction. →

Circle the change that you predict will happen as the program above increases the power through the piezo from 20% to 35% and then to 80%. QUIETER, LOUDER, HIGHER PITCH, LOWER PITCH

Attach your piezo buzzer to motor 2. Make sure the longer leg is attached to the +. Attach your button to input A.

Algorithm

When the program starts, check forever to see if the button attached to A is pressed down.

If button A is pressed down, make the piezo buzz at 20% power for a second before increasing to 35% and 80% for one second each before stopping.

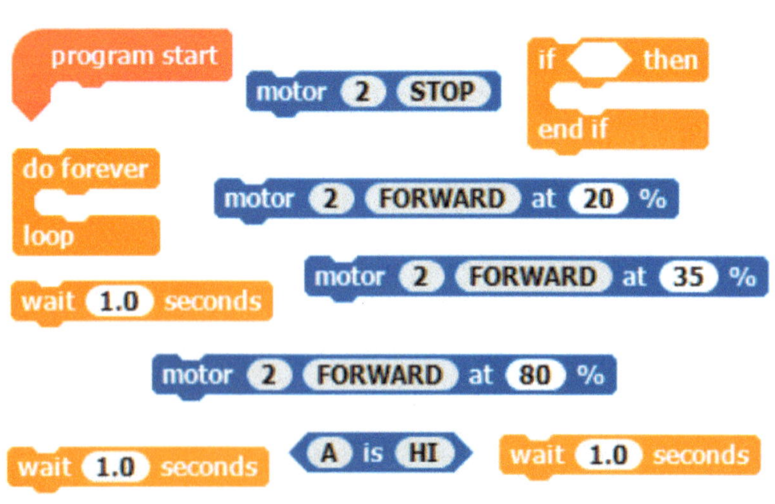

Use the algorithm, the code blocks and maker cards to help you build the quiz buzzer program. Can you design your own unique sound?

Name ______________________________ Class ____________ QB3

Thinking about programming a quiz buzzer (Classic Crumble)

This is a piezo buzzer. We pass electricity through it to make sounds.

Most buzzers would be attached to A, B, C or D

We want to find out how the sound changes when we pass more electricity through the piezo buzzer so we are using a motor connection.

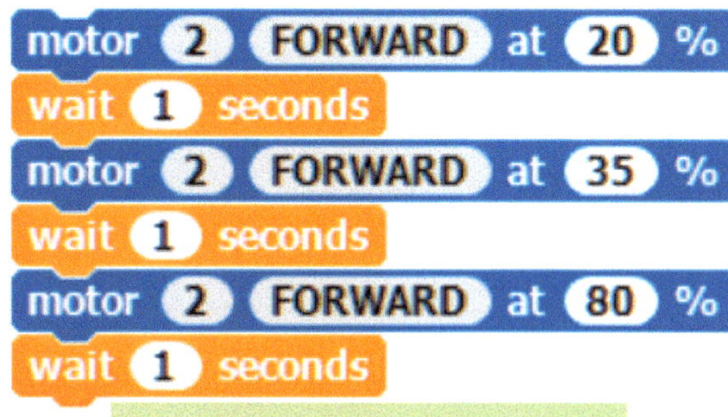

Make a prediction

Circle the change that you predict will happen as the program above increases the power through the piezo from 20% to 35% and then to 80%. QUIETER, LOUDER, HIGHER PITCH, LOWER PITCH

Attach your piezo buzzer to motor 2. Make sure the longer leg is attached to the +. Attach your button to input A.

Algorithm

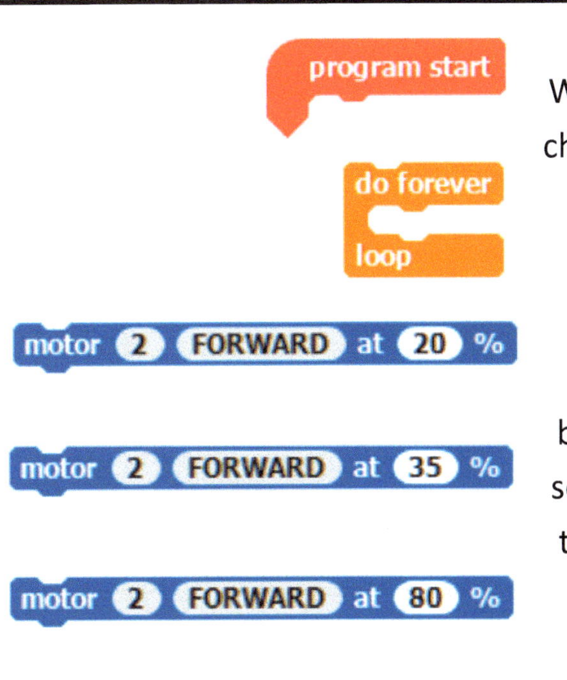

When the program starts check forever to see if the button attached to A is pressed down.

If button A is pressed down, make the piezo buzz at 20% power for a second before increasing to 35% and 80% for one second each before stopping.

motor 2 STOP

wait 1.0 seconds

wait 1.0 seconds

wait 1.0 seconds

Draw lines to match the algorithm to the code blocks. Build the program on the Crumble. Can you adapt the program to build your own unique sound?

Name ______________________________ Class_____________ QB4

Thinking about programming a quiz buzzer (Crumble Playground)

This is a piezo buzzer. We pass electricity through it to make sounds.

Most buzzers would be attached to A, B, C or D

We want to find out how the sound changes when we pass more electricity through the piezo buzzer so we are using a motor connection.

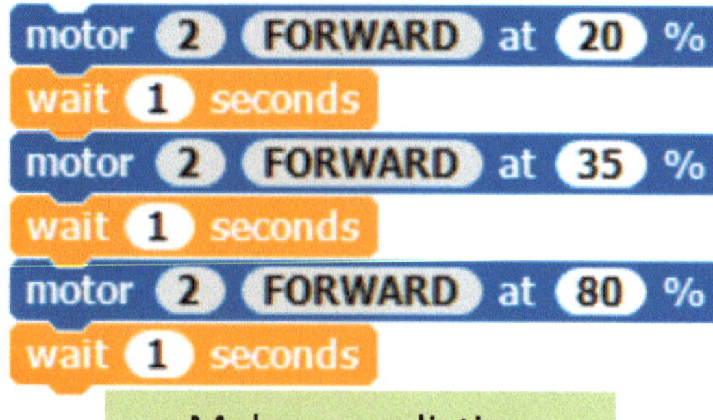

Make a prediction

Circle the change that you predict will happen as the program above increases the power through the piezo from 20% to 35% and then to 80%. QUIETER, LOUDER, HIGHER PITCH, LOWER PITCH

Attach your piezo buzzer to motor 2. Make sure the longer leg is attached to the +. Attach your button to input A.

Algorithm

program start

do forever
loop

motor 2 FORWARD at 20 %

motor 2 FORWARD at 35 %

motor 2 FORWARD at 80 %

When the program starts check forever to see if the button attached to A is pressed down.

If button A is pressed down, make the piezo buzz at 20% power for a second before increasing to 35% and 80% for one second each before stopping.

if then
end if

A is HI

motor 2 STOP

wait 1.0 seconds

wait 1.0 seconds

wait 1.0 seconds

Draw lines to match the algorithm to the code blocks. Build the program on the Crumble. Can you adapt the program to build your own unique sound?

QB3A & QB4A Lower Half Answer Sheet

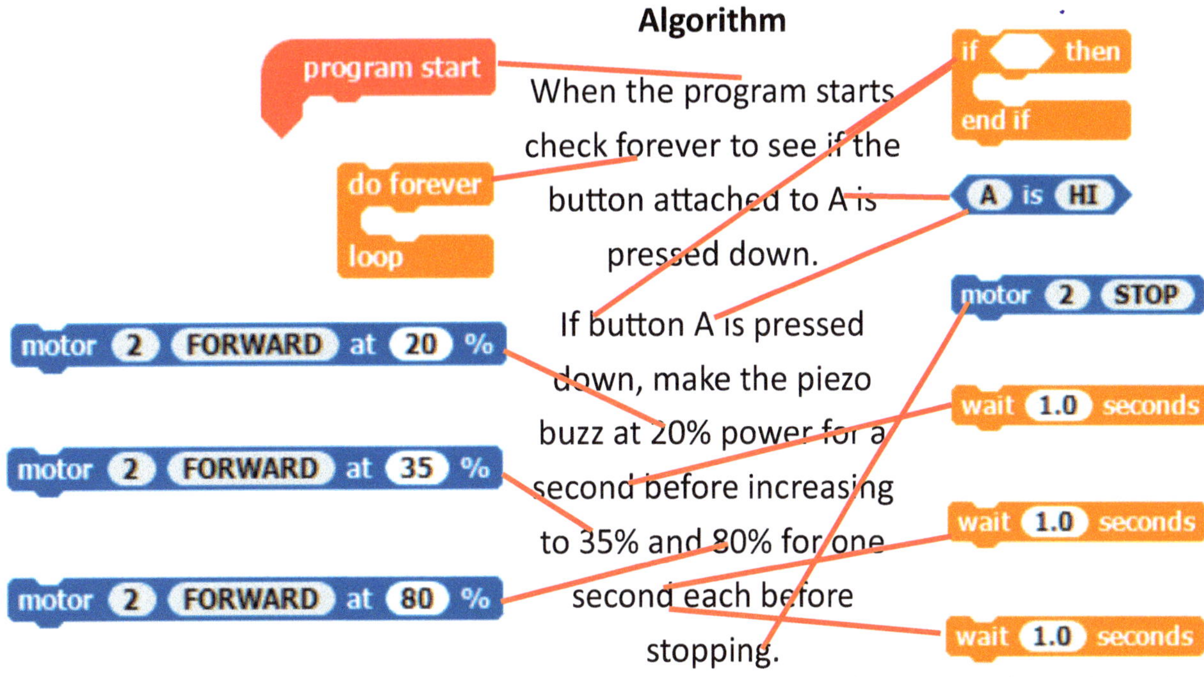
Algorithm
program start
When the program starts check forever to see if the button attached to A is pressed down.
If button A is pressed down, make the piezo buzz at 20% power for a second before increasing to 35% and 80% for one second each before stopping.
do forever
loop
if then
end if
A is HI
motor 2 STOP
motor 2 FORWARD at 20 %
motor 2 FORWARD at 35 %
motor 2 FORWARD at 80 %
wait 1.0 seconds
wait 1.0 seconds
wait 1.0 seconds

Draw lines to match the algorithm to the code blocks. Build the program on the Crumble. Can you adapt the program to build your own unique sound?

Name ____________________________ Class ____________ **QB5**

Thinking about designing my own sound project using a piezo buzzer.

This is a piezo buzzer. We pass electricity through it to make a sound.

Fill in your idea and add your inputs and outputs to the chart.

My program will

by

What will the user see and do?

Input/ Output	Name of device attached	What the device does (include as much detail as possible)
A INPUT	Push button	When the button is pushed, it stops the buzzer attached to Motor 2.
A		
B		
C		
D		
Motor 1		
Motor 2		

Draw your devices and the wires that connect them.

Name ______________________ Class ___________ QB6

Thinking about designing my own sound project using a piezo buzzer.

This is a piezo buzzer. We pass electricity through it to make a sound.

Fill in your idea and add your inputs and outputs to the chart.

My program will

by

What will the user see and do?

Input/ Output	Name of device attached	What the device does (include as much detail as possible)
A INPUT	Push button	When the button is pushed, it stops the buzzer attached to Motor 2.
A		
B		
C		
D		
Motor 1		
Motor 2		

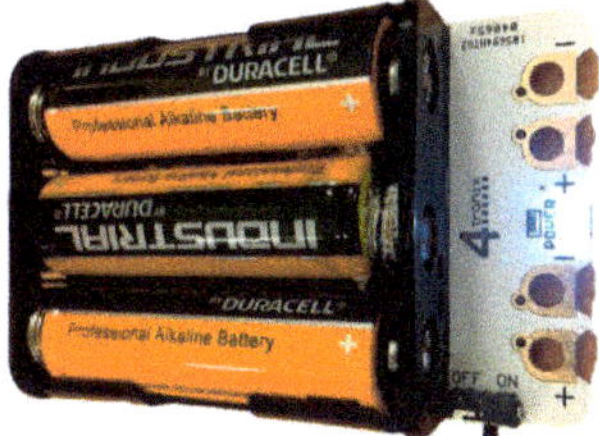

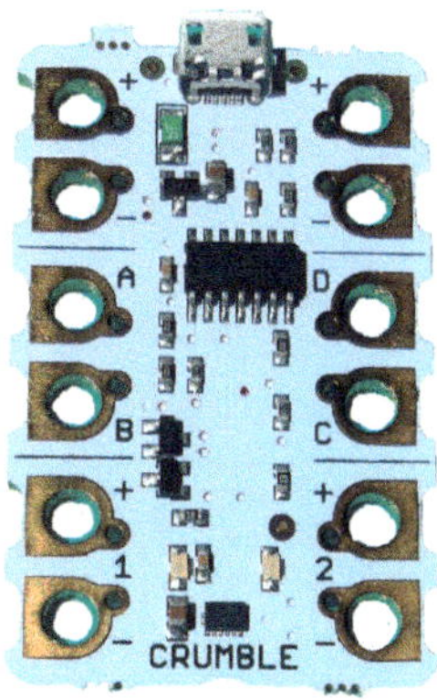

Draw your devices and the wires that connect them.

Quiz Buzzer Assessment Sheet QB7 Name ________ Class ____

☺ I did this well

😐 I did this ok or I did this a little

☹ I tried this but it didn't work or I didn't do this at all

I predicted what would happen to the buzzer sound when electricity is increased.	
I created my own unique signature sound.	
I used a repeat x times loop to repeat my signature sound.	
I turned the algorithm on my sheet into working code.	
I look for a range of solutions to the same problem.	
I debugged code that didn't work.	
I tested my code regularly to see if the changes I made worked.	
I looked at how I could extend my project.	
I extended my project by....	

Sticker	I got this sticker for
Sticker	I got this sticker for
Sticker	I got this sticker for

9. Translucency Meter

Module Aim

Create a device that will measure the amount of light detected and output the amount of light as a number on a number display.

Cross Curricular Links

This project links best to Science. Pupils can create the meter and then use it to measure the translucency of different materials. It could also be adapted to measure how dirty water is by placing the water inside a transparent vessel and placing the light dependent resister pointing through the transparent vessel[1].

Computing

Pupils will need to be able to use sequence, repetition, conditional selection and variables to program their projects.

Materials

If there isn't time to allow pupils to build a case for their electronics, then the four inch box shown in the picture works really well.

Construction

The pictures on this page and the next show the bare LDR but you could easily use the Redfern Electronic LDR or either 4tronix LDRs.

At time of publishing only 4tronix produce a number counter.

Mounting a bare LDR on the bottom of a four inch box through a sheet of cardboard. LDR crumbs from Redfern Electronics or 4tronix are even easier to mount

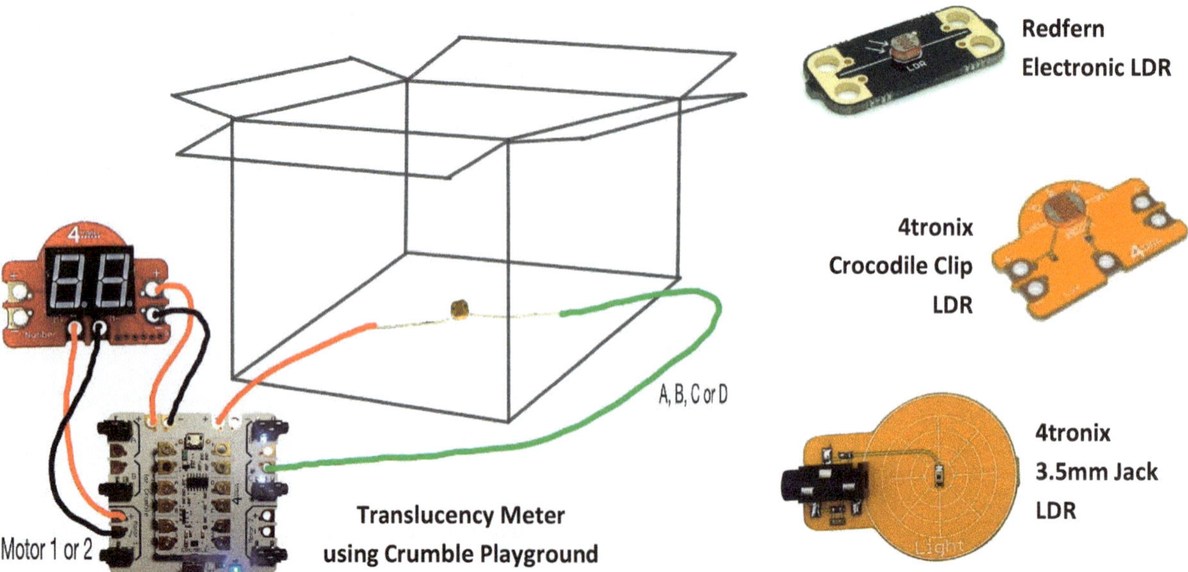

Suggested Module Outline

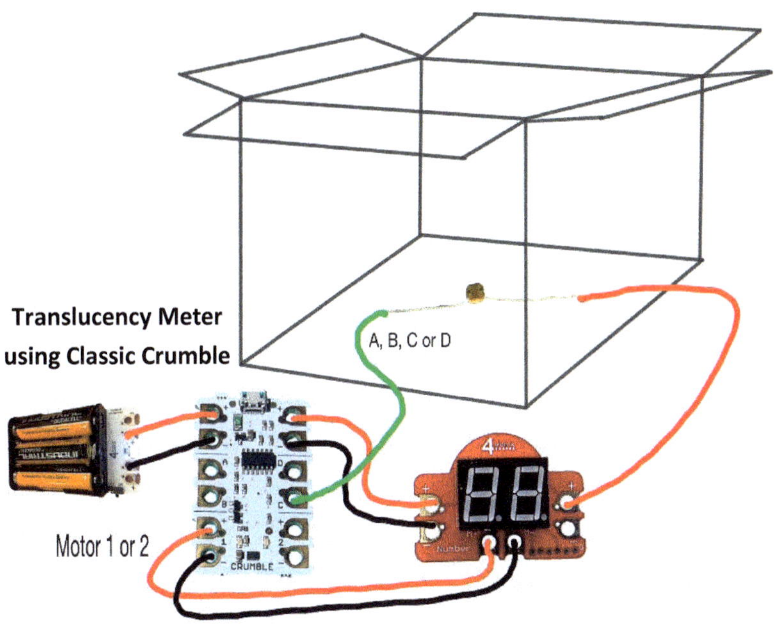

1, Preparation before the module

Build the project yourself and decide on the approach you are going to take outlined in section 3 and print the relevant support sheets.

2, Introduce the project

Explain that in this project pupils are going to create a meter that will measure the amount of light that passes through objects and provide a reading. Once this has been created pupils can use it to test translucency themselves or ask younger pupils to use their creations.

Outline how this works by sensing the amount of light through a light dependent resistor. This is passed into the Crumble as a numerical value between 0 and 255. 0 being no light and 255 being very bright light. The Crumble then takes this information and through the power of their programming, outputs it as a number between 0 and 99 on the number counter.

3, Three possible approaches to thinking the project through

A. Use TM1 or TM2. These sheets are the easiest to use as they provide a working copy of the programming needed. Pupils read about how someone else created the project before answering questions. There are answer sheets to go with both sheets TM1A and TM2A.

B. Use TM3 or TM4 to go from algorithm to code. Pupils are given a detailed algorithm and the code blocks that they would need for one solution. They are asked to build the code by following the algorithm.

C. TM5 gives the big idea and asks pupils to convert this into a written or flowchart algorithm. TM5A gives a marked example although it is important to note that there are other possible solutions. This is the hardest option.

4, Wiring Diagram

Use either sheets TM6 or TM7 to enable pupils to plan their wiring. Although lots of the thinking sheet starters have examples of the wiring, they are unlikely to be exactly the same light dependent resistors.

5, Programming

If pupils are struggling with the programming, there are two support sheets available which show which blocks could be used. TM8 is the simpler version as some of the code is already pre built. TM9 is harder as there are no pre built blocks.

6, Check their plans

Before pupils go on and connect their devices and start turning their idea into programming, it can be a really good idea to mark their thinking starters and wiring diagrams.

7, Wiring and programming

Pupils are now ready to wire and program. They will be able to do this independently using the maker cards and the thinking sheets from part 3 of the module.

Common debugging hints

- Are you sure your input/output letters on your programming match where you have wired them?
- Have you checked to see if your wiring diagram matches your wiring? All pupils say they have but have they checked it wire by wire?
- Are all your 3.5mm jack connections firmly pushed in?
- Have you checked to see if the metal on the crocodile clips are touching the metal on other crocodile clips? (short circuit)
- Is your battery pack switched on?
- Did you line up and turn the Crumble in the same manner as the maker card?
- Do your batteries need replacing?
- Are your batteries in the right way round?
- Did you send the program to the Crumble by clicking on the green arrow?
- Did you plug the Crumble into the computer using the USB cable?
- Did the program say it was running successfully?
- Did you use more than one starting block?

8, Assessment

The assessment sheet TM10 has a place for pupils to record their progress and space to record problem solving stickers if they are awarded.

Useful Maker Cards

MC08	**MC20**	**MC21**
MC22	**MC30**	**MC40**
MC41	**MC42**	**MC46**

Curricular Coverage

Design & Technology NC
NCD2G **NCD2H**

Computing NC
NCC2A **NCC2B** **NCC2C**

Useful Problem Solving Skills to Assess

I recognise there is more than one way to solve/describe a problem

I don't just accept the first solution

I look for a range of solutions to the same problem

I look for how a project can be extended

Handles Ambiguity

Open Ended Problem Solver

I can evaluate my solutions against a set criteria

I can break complex problems into parts

I can design criteria to evaluate my creations

I can discover / concentrate on the most important part of a problem

Evaluates

I can contribute useful ideas to a partner or group

Copes with Complexity

I can identify patterns in problems and solutions

Computing Problem Solver

I can encourage others to share their ideas

I can adapt existing ideas to solve new problems

Adapts

Communicates

I can develop, test and debug until a product is refined

I lead using all the people talent in my group

Investigates

I make predictions about what will happen

I learn from setbacks and don't let them put me off

I can persevere even if the solution is not obvious

Perseveres

I repeatedly experiment through predicting, making, testing & debugging

Problem solving skills are adapted from a problem solving rubric created by Mark Dorling and Thomas Stephens that the author worked on helping to define. You can find this at http://code-it.co.uk/attitudes/

[1,] Measuring dirty water was an idea by Pete Gaynord one of our featured Crumble Educators in Chapter 14

Thinking about the Translucency Meter Name________ Class ___ TM1

Program Decomposed

Martha connected her Crumble playground, number counter and light dependent resistor together as shown in the diagram on the right.

She tested the number crumb separately using a motor block. When she put 60% in the motor block, it read 60 on the number crumb.

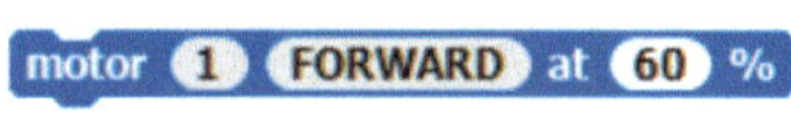

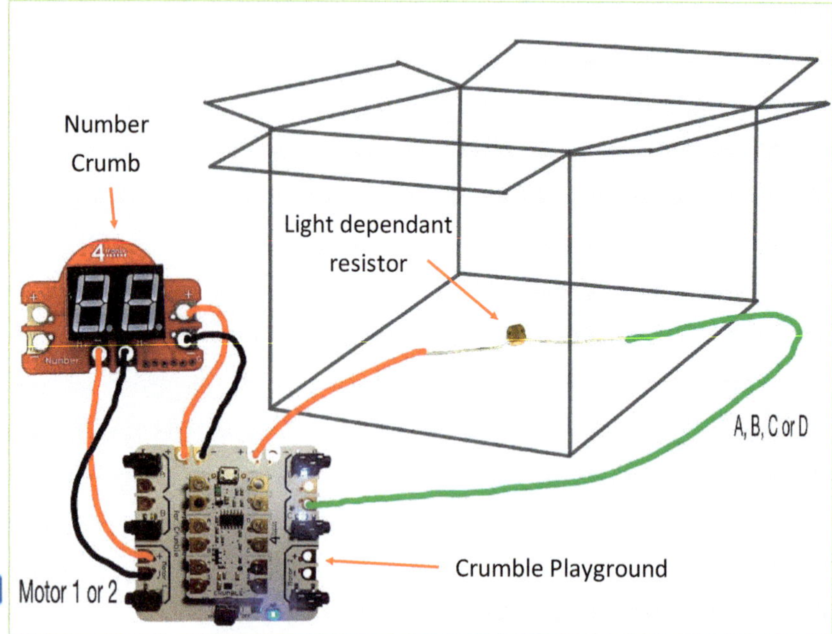


```
program start
  do forever
    let light = analogue C ÷ 3
    motor 1 FORWARD at light %
    wait 3.0 seconds
  loop
```

0-255 input from light dependent resistor

A number from 0 to 85 will now be in the light variable

Then she wrote this program. She knew that the light dependant resistor would input between 0 and 255 so she divided it by 3. This means there will only be between 0 and 85 in the light variable, which is a low enough number for the number crumb to display.

Read the information above and study the programming. You can discuss the top part with a partner. When directed answer the questions below.

1, Which block inputs the light dependent resistor sensor information? ________________

2, Which block outputs the sensor reading to the number crumb? ________________

3, Why is some information divided by 3? ________________________________

4, If the program was changed to read ***motor 2 forward at light %*** would it still work? Give a reason for your answer. ________________________________

5, If the number crumb read between 0 and 999, what would Martha change in her program?

____

6, Why do you think Martha has added a 3 second wait after the number crumb output?

____

Thinking about the Translucency Meter Name________ Class __ TM1A

Program Decomposed

Martha connected her Crumble playground, number counter and light dependent resistor together as shown in the diagram on the right.

She tested the number crumb separately using a motor block. When she put 60% in the motor block, it read 60 on the number crumb.

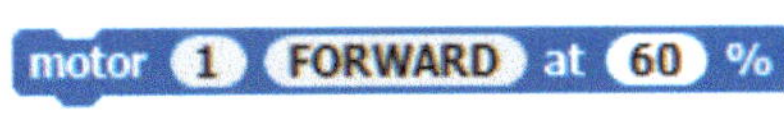

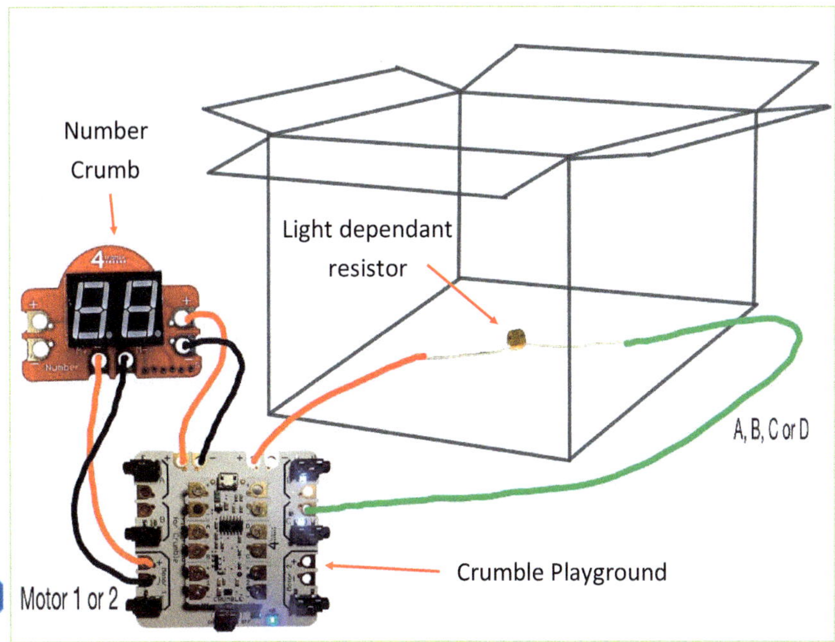


```
program start
  do forever
    let light = analogue C ÷ 3
    motor 1 FORWARD at light %
    wait 3.0 seconds
  loop
```

0-255 input from light dependant resistor

A number from 0 to 85 will now be in the light variable

Then she wrote this program. She knew that the light dependent resistor would input between 0 and 255 so she divided it by 3. This means there will only be between 0 and 85 in the light variable, which is a low enough number for the number crumb to display.

Read the information above and study the programming. You can discuss the top part with a partner. When directed answer the questions below.

1, Which block inputs the light dependent resistor sensor information? Analogue

2, Which block outputs the sensor reading to the number crumb? Motor 1 forward at light %

3, Why is some information divided by 3? Any answer that indicates that the input number may be too high for the number crumb to display all the time.

4, If the program was changed to read ***motor 2 forward at light %*** would it still work? Give a reason for your answer. Any answer that indicates that it would only work if the wires were switched round and plugged into motor 2 or that it won't work because it is not wired into motor 2.

5, If the number crumb read between 0 and 999 what would Martha change in her program?

Any answer that indicates that she would want to change the divide by 3 either to remove it or multiply it.

6, Why do you think Martha has added a 3 second wait after the number crumb output?

Any answer that indicates that she has given herself time to read the output on the number crumb.

Thinking about the Translucency Meter Name________ Class ___ TM2

Program Decomposed

Martha connected her Crumble playground, number counter and light dependent resistor together as shown in the diagram on the right.

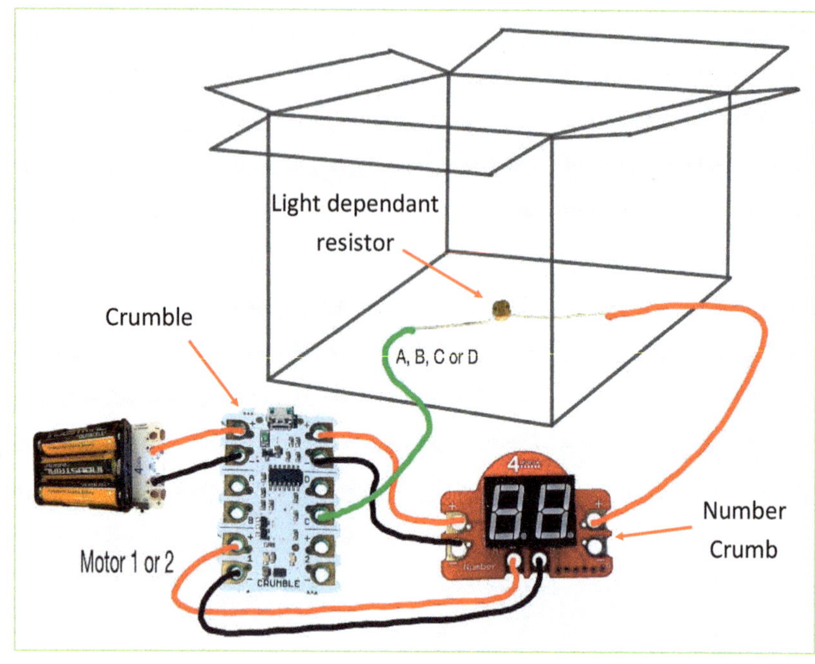

She tested the number crumb separately using a motor block. When she put 60% in the motor block, it read 60 on the number crumb.

```
program start
  do forever
    let light = analogue C ÷ 3
    motor 1 FORWARD at light %
    wait 3.0 seconds
  loop
```

0-255 input from light dependant resistor

A number from 0 to 85 will now be in the light variable

Then she wrote this program. She knew that the light dependant resistor would input between 0 and 255 so she divided it by 3. This means there will only be between 0 and 85 in the light variable, which is a low enough number for the number crumb to display.

Read the information above and study the programming. You can discuss the top part with a partner. When directed answer the questions below.

1, Which block inputs the light dependent resistor sensor information? ____________________

2, Which block outputs the sensor reading to the number crumb? ____________________

3, Why is some information divided by 3? ____________________

4, If the program was changed to read ***motor 2 forward at light %,*** would it still work? Give a reason for your answer. ____________________

5, If the number crumb read between 0 and 999, what would Martha change in her program?

____

6, Why do you think Martha has added a 3 second wait after the number crumb output?

____

Thinking about the Translucency Meter Name_______ Class ___ TM2A

Program Decomposed

Martha connected her Crumble playground, number counter and light dependant resistor together as shown in the diagram on the right.

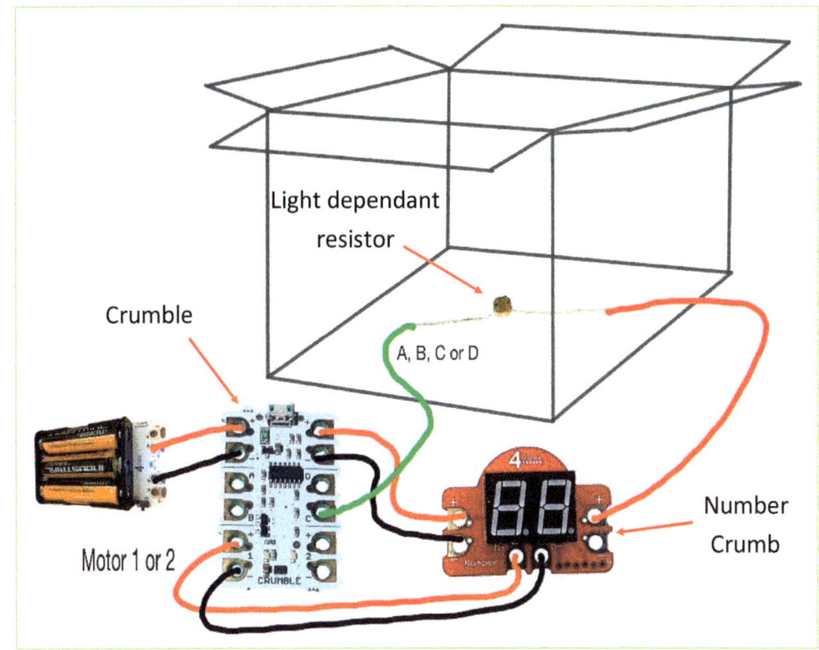
Light dependant resistor
Crumble
A, B, C or D
Motor 1 or 2
Number Crumb

She tested the number crumb separately using a motor block. When she put 60% in the motor block, it read 60 on the number crumb.

motor 1 FORWARD at 60 %

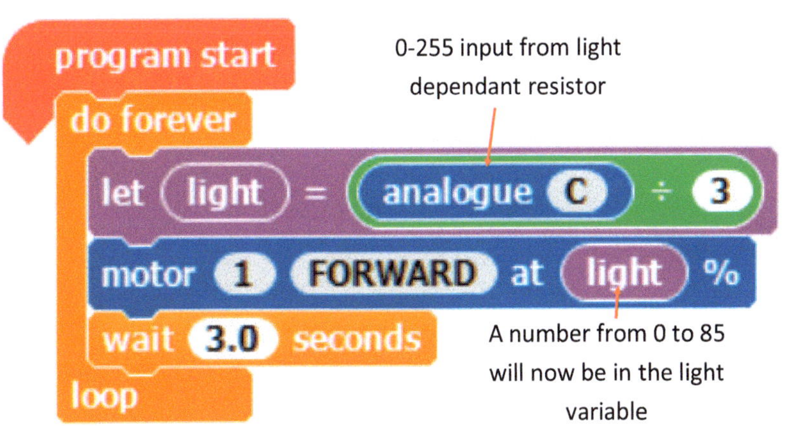
program start
do forever
let light = analogue C ÷ 3
motor 1 FORWARD at light %
wait 3.0 seconds
loop
0-255 input from light dependant resistor
A number from 0 to 85 will now be in the light variable

Then she wrote this program. She knew that the light dependent resistor would input between 0 and 255 so she divided it by 3. This means there will only be between 0 and 85 in the light variable which is a low enough number for the number crumb to display.

Read the information above and study the programming. You can discuss the top part with a partner. When directed answer the questions below.

1, Which block inputs the light dependent resistor sensor information? Analogue

2, Which block outputs the sensor reading to the number crumb? Motor 1 forward at light %

3, Why is some information divided by 3? Any answer that indicates that the input number may be too high for the number crumb to display all the time.

4, If the program was changed to read ***motor 2 forward at light %,*** would it still work? Give a reason for your answer. Any answer that indicates that it would only work if the wires were switched round and plugged into motor 2 or that it won't work because it is not wired into motor 2.

5, If the number crumb read between 0 and 999 what would Martha change in her program?

Any answer that indicates that she would want to change the divide by 3 either to remove it or multiply it.

6, Why do you think Martha has added a 3 second wait after the number crumb output?

Any answer that indicates that she has given herself time to read the output on the number crumb.

Thinking about the Translucency Meter Name_______ Class ___ TM3

From Algorithm to Code

Martha connected her Crumble playground, number counter and light dependant resistor together as shown in the diagram below.

She tested the number crumb separately using a motor block. When she put 60% in the motor block, it read 60 on the number crumb.

motor 1 FORWARD at 60 %

Her Algorithm was

1. Take a reading from the light dependant meter (0-255).
2. Divide it by three and put it in a variable called light.
3. Output the result using the variable called light to the number crumb (0-99).
4. Wait three seconds so a human can read the result.
5. Repeat steps 1 to 4 continuously.

These are the code blocks she used

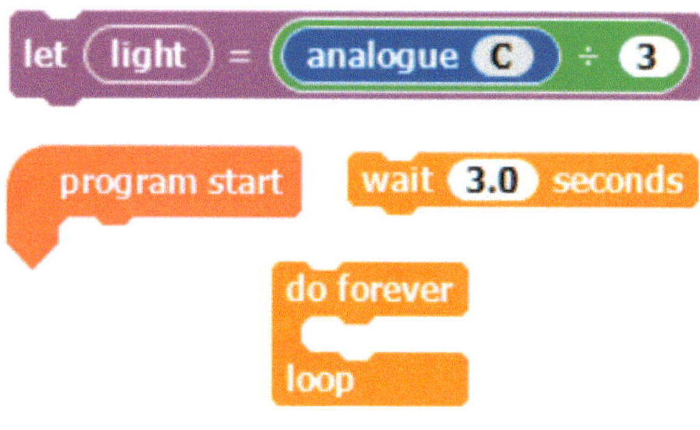

motor 1 FORWARD at light %

Analogue is the code block that brings information from 0 to 255 from the light dependent resistor sensor into the Crumble. 0 would mean no light and 255 would mean maximum brightness.

The number crumb uses the motor blocks to output a number between 0 and 99.

Instructions

Test your number crumb as Martha did.

Can you convert her algorithm into code?

Which blocks go with which steps?

Draw arrows from the code blocks to the algorithm to help you match them

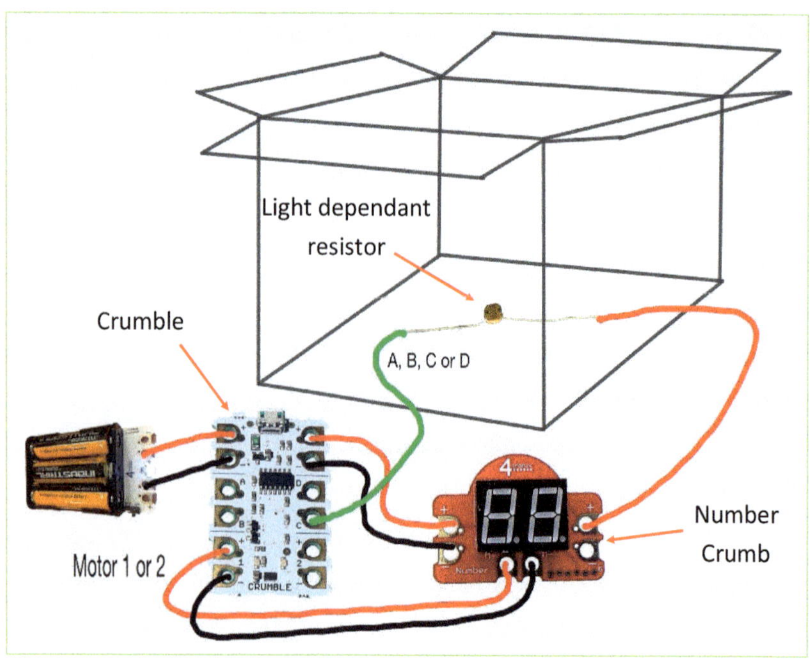

Thinking about the Translucency Meter Name_______ Class ___ TM4

From Algorithm to Code

Martha connected her Crumble playground, number counter and light dependant resistor together as shown in the diagram below.

She tested the number crumb separately using a motor block. When she put 60% in the motor block, it read 60 on the number crumb. motor 1 FORWARD at 60 %

Her Algorithm was

1. Take a reading from the light dependant meter (0-255).
2. Divide it by three and put it in a variable called light.
3. Output the result using the variable called light to the number crumb (0-99).
4. Wait three seconds so a human can read the result.
5. Repeat steps 1 to 4 continuously.

These are the code blocks she used

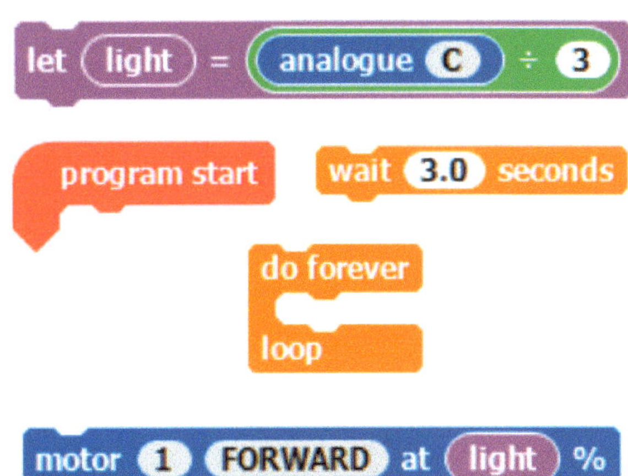

let light = analogue C ÷ 3
program start
wait 3.0 seconds
do forever
loop
motor 1 FORWARD at light %

Analogue is the code block that brings information from 0 to 255 from the light dependent resistor sensor into the Crumble. 0 would mean no light and 255 would mean maximum brightness.

The number crumb uses the motor blocks to output a number between 0 and 99.

Instructions

Test your number crumb as Martha did.

Can you convert her algorithm into code?

Which blocks go with which steps?

Draw arrows from the code blocks to the algorithm to help you match them

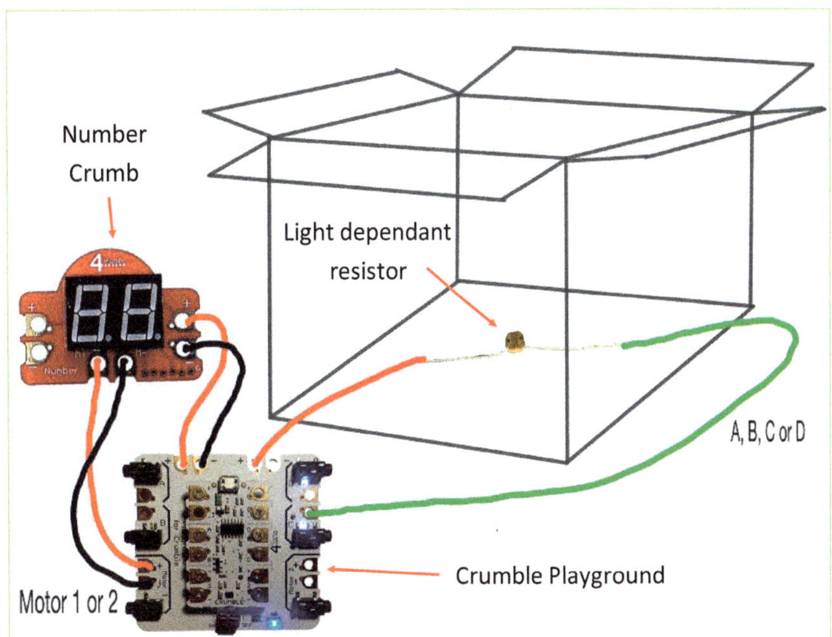

Number Crumb
Light dependant resistor
A, B, C or D
Crumble Playground
Motor 1 or 2

Thinking about the Translucency Meter Name_______ Class ___ TM5

Writing an Algorithm

Big idea

Martha came up with the following big idea

"I want to detect how bright the light is so I can use it to test how much light passes through materials. It would be great if I could get it to output as a number on the number counter."

Her research

The light dependant resistor takes a reading between 0 and 255. 0 is no light, 255 is very bright. It inputs information into the Crumble using an analogue block.

The number crumb outputs between 0 and 99. It uses the motor programming blocks.

Programmers use a variable to pass information from one part of the program to another. I will call my variable light or brightness.

Write or draw an algorithm

Write or draw Martha's big idea as a written algorithm or as a flow chart.

Thinking about the Translucency Meter Name________ Class ___ TM5A

Writing an Algorithm

Big idea

Martha came up with the following big idea.

"I want to detect how bright the light is so I can use it to test how much light passes through materials. It would be great if I could get it to output as a number on the number counter."

Her research

The light dependant resistor takes a reading between 0 and 255. 0 is no light, 255 is very bright. It inputs information into the Crumble using an analogue block.

The number crumb outputs between 0 and 99. It uses the motor programming blocks.

Programmers use a variable to pass information from one part of the program to another. I will call my variable light or brightness.

Write or draw an algorithm

Write or draw Martha's big idea as a written algorithm or as a flow chart.

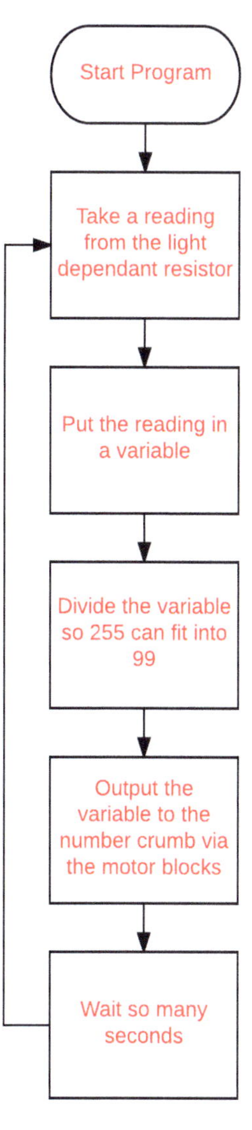

Start Program
Take a reading from the light dependant resistor
Put the reading in a variable
Divide the variable so 255 can fit into 99
Output the variable to the number crumb via the motor blocks
Wait so many seconds

A possible written algorithm

1. Take a reading from the light dependant meter (0-255).
2. Put it is a variable called light.
3. Divide it by three (or some of other number that converts 255 to 99).
4. Output the result using the variable called light to the number crumb (0-99).
5. Wait three seconds so a human can read the result.
6. Repeat steps 1 to 4 continuously.

(Step 5 is optional)

A possible flow chart

Note pupils may combine some blocks or split other commands or write them in a very different way.

Is the order correct?

Can they convert it into code?

Can someone else follow it?

(The wait step is optional)

Name ______________________________ Class _____________

TM6

Translucency Meter

Draw your devices and the wires that connect them.

Name ___________________________ Class/Form ___________ TM7

Translucency Meter

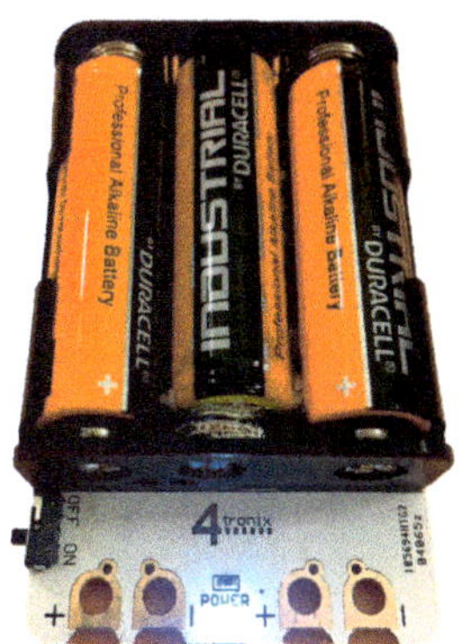

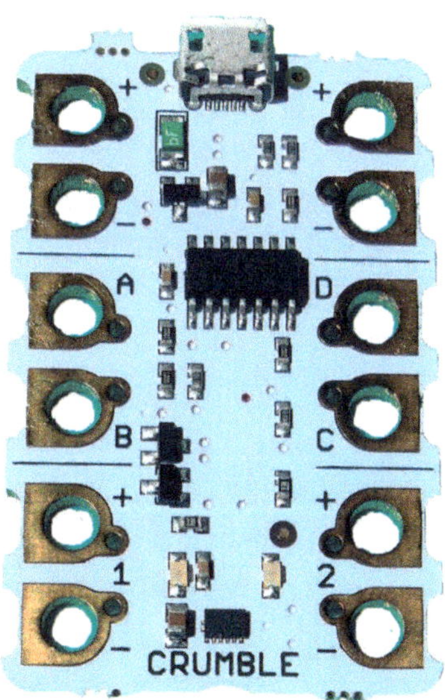

Draw your devices and the wires that connect them.

TM8

What have you called your variable?

What port have you plugged the light dependant resistor into?

let (light) = (analogue (C) ÷ (3))

program start

wait (3.0) seconds

do forever

loop

What motor have you plugged the number crumb into?

motor (1) (FORWARD) at (light) %

TM9

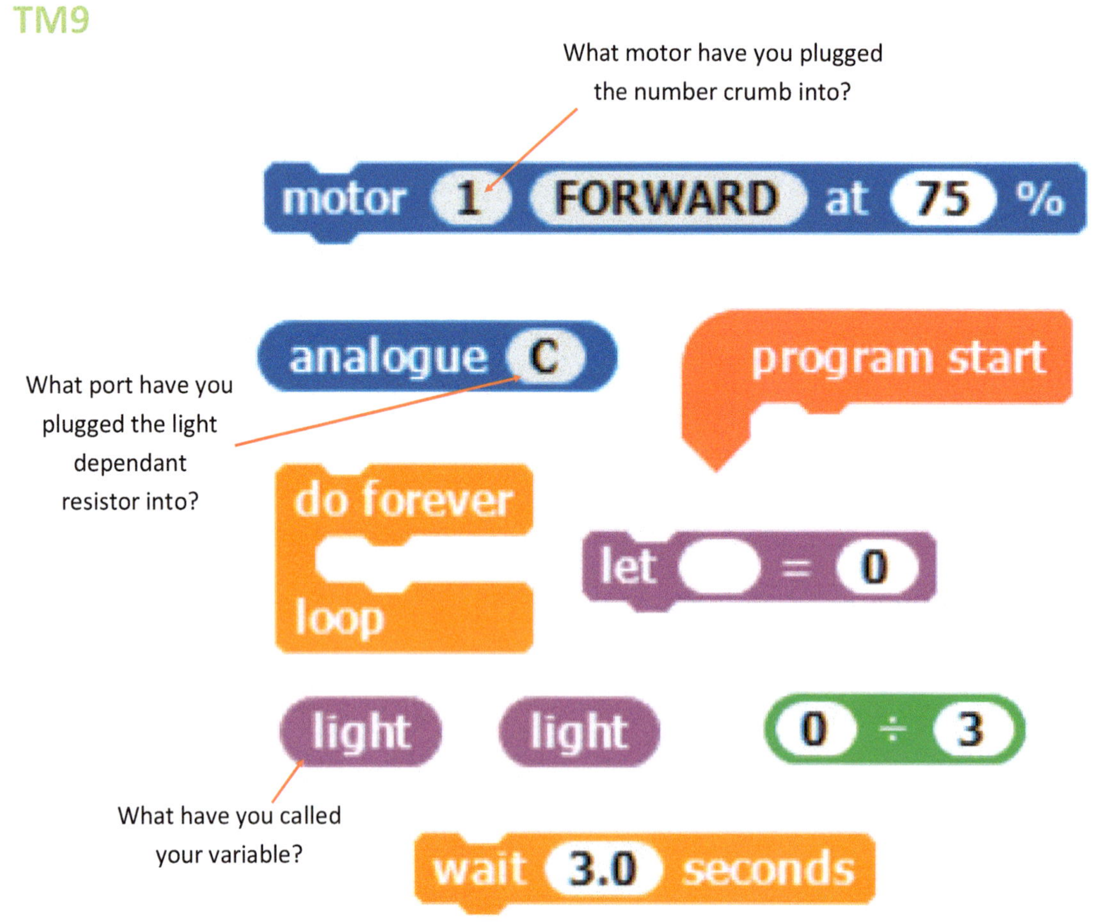

Translucency Meter Assessment Sheet Name____________Class_____

TM10

I did this well

I did this ok or I did this a little

I tried this but it didn't work or I didn't do this at all

I thought through how the programming could work.	
I drew an accurate wiring diagram.	
I wired up my Crumble, number crumb and light dependant resistor.	
I fixed any part of the wiring that wasn't working.	
I created a working program.	
I tested my programming to see if it worked.	
I fixed a programming bug.	
I looked for good computational attitudes in my peers.	
I persevered when aspects needed fixing or debugging.	

Sticker	I got this sticker for
Sticker	I got this sticker for
Sticker	I got this sticker for

10. Maker Labs One

Module Aim

Design an electronic device that involves multiple outputs changed by simple inputs. Pupils think of a range of big ideas that involve output devices, such as motors, buzzers and lights controlled by a simple input that inputs either on or off such as a button or close proximity sensor[1]. After choosing their best idea, they decompose it into its parts and create a circuit diagram before building, programming and testing it.

```
program start
  do forever
    if A is HI then
      set sparkle 0 to
      wait 5.0 seconds
      set sparkle 0 to
      wait 5.0 seconds
      set sparkle 0 to
      wait 5.0 seconds
    end if
  loop
```

The big idea here was a button to show your teacher that you needed help without putting your hand up and to inform the teacher how long you had been waiting. Input A was connected to a button.

Cross Curricular Links

Teachers could ask pupils to link their ideas to a school topic or a real life situation, such as designing a device to solve a problem in a shop or supermarket, or they could allow pupils free choice of project theme within the confines of the Crumble medium.

Computing

Pupils will need to be able to use sequence, repetition and conditional selection to program their projects. There is a very useful roleplay starter to help those pupils who are not yet fully independent when using conditional selection.

Construction

This project will benefit from Design & Technology elements such as design research, design planning and a wider choice of available materials to chose from. If there isn't time to allow pupils to plan, design and scratch build a case for their electronics, then the use of a four, five or six inch cardboard box allows pupils to think about what parts are internal or external, where to position them and how the user will interact with the device.

Very few schools will have all the equipment found in the Maker Lab One table. Teachers will need to go through the sheet and cross out equipment that is not owned by the school before giving pupils a copy of the sheet.

Useful Maker Cards

MC01	**MC02**	**MC04**	**MC05**	**MC51**
MC06	**MC07**	**MC09**	**MC10**	**MC52**
MC11	**MC12**	**MC13**	**MC14**	**MC53**
MC17	**MC18**	**MC19**	**MC23**	**MC56**
MC24	**MC25**	**MC32**	**MC33**	
MC34	**MC35**	**MC43**	**MC44**	
MC45	**MC47**	**MC49**	**MC50**	

Curricular Coverage

Design & Technology NC

NCD2G **NCD2H**

Computing NC

NCC2A **NCC2B** **NCC2C**

To the casual observer this project seems very open ended but in reality the number of possible projects are limited by the equipment and the use of a simple on or off input.

Suggested Module Outline

1, Preparation before the module

Have a good look at the MLO1 sheet. Photocopy one, preferably in colour, and cross out any equipment that you don't have in school. If there are any other outputs that you have which are not on the sheet, write them on the top of the sheet. If you have a very limited amount of equipment, you might want to put a x1 or x2 next to some equipment to show that pupils should only include one or two of these in their project. Photocopy this adapted sheet, one per group or pair of pupils. Two pupils per project is deal.

Do the same for the MLO2 sheet. If you are going to allow pupils to cut these out and stick them on their circuit diagrams (MLO4 or MLO5 sheets), photocopy one per pupil. If pupils are going to use these to help them draw the inputs and outputs themselves, then one sheet per group is plenty.

You will also need to photocopy MLO3 and either MLO4 or MLO5 for each pupil. Whilst pupils may only be able to build one project between each group or pair due to the amount of equipment available, I recommend that they all plan one project each, before choosing the best one or a composite of the best ones to make.

Print out the conditional selection role play cards ML6–13 so that there are enough sheets for one sheet between each pair. Two sets works for classes which have 32 pupils or under.

2, Role play conditional selection

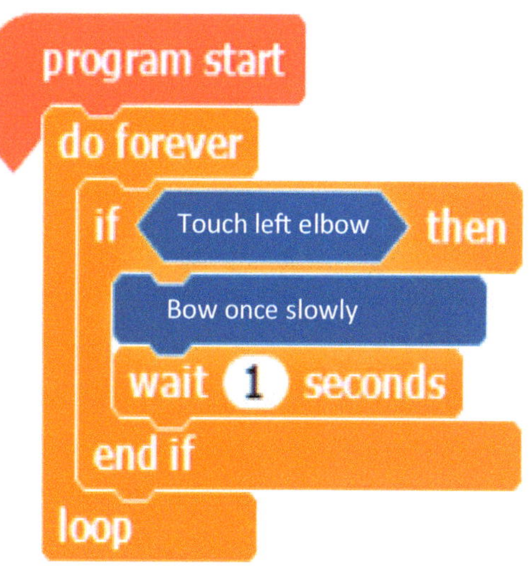
program start
do forever
if
Touch left elbow
then
Bow once slowly
wait
1
seconds
end if
loop

Explain that in this project they are going to be using lots of conditional selection programming where there are outputs that respond to triggers such as buttons. Show them the example on the right (ML06). Get a pupil to be the program and another to be the input trigger. The condition trigger touches the other pupil's left elbow to start them bowing. As soon as the trigger stops touching the left elbow, the bowing stops. Ask them what would happen without the forever loop? Make sure they realise that the condition would only be checked once without the loop. It is helpful to demonstrate an example with **AND** and one with **OR**. Explain that **AND** means both conditions have to be fulfilled for the code to work and **OR** means either condition can be met to start the code. Direct pupils to work in pairs and encourage them to swap roles so they both get an opportunity to read and be the code and trigger the conditions.

Formative assessment	Corrective	Enrichment
Pupils using parallel if sheets (MLO7) are not running all the conditions at the same time.	Point out that these are cycling quickly through all the loops so all conditions triggered will happen.	Ask if anything will happen if none of the conditions are triggered? Answer: Nothing as there are no ELSE sections.
Pupils using IF ELSE blocks don't do anything when condition are not met.	Point out that the ELSE part happens when conditions are not met.	Ask what blocks they would use if they didn't want anything to happen when the conditions were not met? Answer: The IF THEN block.

Move the class round eight times so that everyone gets to work with each example condition. Get some of the groups to demonstrate their code cards before moving on.

3, Introduce the project

Explain that pupils can design their own Crumble projects that use buttons or a close proximity sensor and a full range of outputs. If you intend to program a buggy later, exclude geared motor and wheels from their options. You may wish to go through some of the equipment if it has been a while since pupils last used it.

4, Generating big ideas (Top section MLO3)

Give out MLO1 & MLO3 and get pupils to start thinking of big ideas. It helps if they are allowed to discuss ideas with a partner or small group. Encourage pupils to fill in the big ideas top section of MLO3.

5, Breaking the project up (decomposition) (Middle section MLO3)

The section underneath the big idea is for pupils to take one idea and break it down further by asking questions such as

- What outputs will be changed, started or stopped by which input?
- In what order will things happen in?
- How long will each part of the program last?
- Will anything happen when the input is not triggered?

TOP TIP

Test every output works before attempting to wire/program the full project.

Some pupils will have written a really precise big idea and this section is less useful for them but many will have been quite vague when explaining their big idea. This section encourages them to break their idea into parts and think about how each part works.

6, Breaking the project up by hardware (Bottom section MLO3) and creating a wiring diagram

Pupils will need the relevant maker cards to help them decide which ports to use and how they need to connect their wires.

Part of the design phase for their project is to make sure that they can plug in all the inputs and outputs that they need into the one Crumble board. Completing the bottom section of MLO3 allows them to check if they have enough ports. Occasionally, pupils who are using the Crumble playground, forget that there is only one A, B, C & D port and they try and plug in something to crocodile clip A and something else into the 3.5mm jack plug for A. A quick reminder that only one device can be plugged into any one port can be helpful before they fill in this section.

They also need to use MLO4 or MLO5 to create a wiring diagram. You can either encourage pupils to draw the equipment or get them to cut out the devices they need from MLO2. Lines need to be drawn with a ruler and a pencil. It can be tempting to encourage the use of colouring pencils but due to the possibility of mistakes I would recommend plain pencils.

Producing detailed wiring diagrams allows them to check if their project is achievable with the hardware they have available and many faults can be avoided or fixed.

7, Check their plans

Before pupils go on and connect their devices and start turning their idea into programming it can be a really good idea to mark their work, paying real attention to their original idea and the answers they gave to the middle section (section 5 above). Have they linked a specific input (button or close proximity sensor) to specific outputs? Remember one button can trigger multiple outputs. Do they have an idea of the order for their programme? If they wired using a playground accessory, did they use a playground socket? If they wired using the classic Crumble, did they use the crocodile clip connections?

8, Wiring

Pupils are now ready to wire and program. They will be able to do this independently using the maker cards and their wiring diagram they created in step 6.

9, Programming

Every project will be different but it can help pupils to look at the conditional selection roleplay sheets (MLO6-13) that are similar to the idea that they want to achieve. I have also put some examples below including common misconceptions.

Common debugging hints

- Are you sure your input/output letters on your programming match those on the Crumble?
- Have you checked to see if your wiring diagram matches your actual wiring?
- Are all your wires firmly pushed in (for 3.5mm jack leads on playground)?
- Have you checked to see if the metal on the crocodile clips is touching the metal on another crocodile clip (short circuit)?
- Is your battery pack switched on?
- Did you line up and turn the Crumble in the same manner as the maker card?
- Do your batteries need replacing?
- Are your batteries the right way round?
- Did you send the program to the Crumble by clicking on the green arrow?
- Did you plug the Crumble into the computer using the USB cable?
- Did the program say it was running successfully?

```
program start
  do forever
    if A is HI then
      set B HI
    else
      set B LO
    end if
  loop
```

Simple button attached to A turning a buzzer attached to B on (HI) and off (LO).

Many programs will look like this or are similar.

```
program start
  do forever
    if A is HI then
      do forever
        set sparkle 0 to [pink]
        wait 1.0 seconds
        set sparkle 0 to [orange]
        wait 1.0 seconds
      loop
    else
      turn sparkle 0 off
    end if
  loop
```

This is a very common bug. The programmer wants the sparkle to run lots of times but instead of using a repeat so many times loop they have used a forever loop. When button A is pressed, the forever loop is started. However, there is no way of exiting the forever loop so the program will continue the sparkle loop until the battery is turned off.

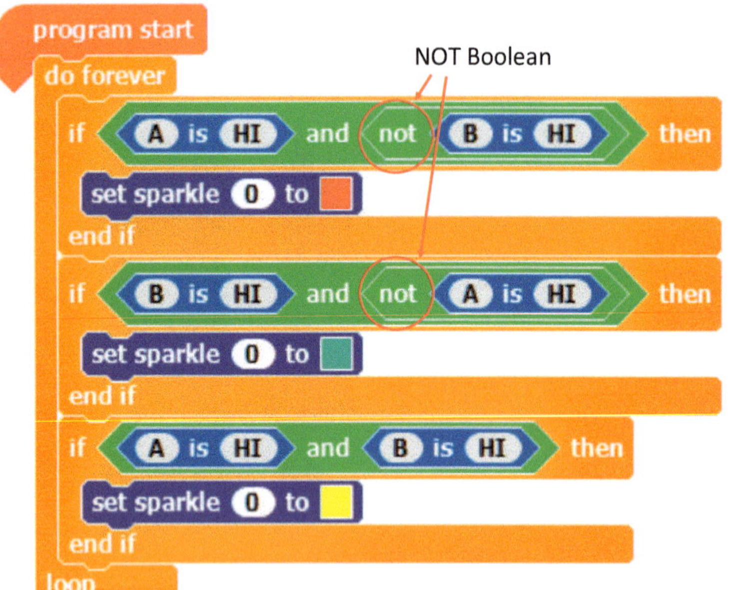

program start
do forever
NOT Boolean
if A is HI and not B is HI then
set sparkle 0 to
end if
if B is HI and not A is HI then
set sparkle 0 to
end if
if A is HI and B is HI then
set sparkle 0 to
end if
loop

10, Multiple input extension

If pupils are easily achieving success with this project challenge them to add more inputs. This will increase the complexity.

This more complex example uses two buttons to create three different colours.

A simpler version can look like it is working with just A is HI on the top if block and B is HI on the middle if block but when both are pressed it tries to do all three colours at the same time.

Using the **NOT** blocks excludes the program from running the top and middle block when both buttons are pressed.

Some upper KS2 pupils are capable of using these Boolean operations successfully, especially if they have had lots of practical experience programming.

A further challenge to this might be to see how many more colours might be triggered using just two buttons. Might the if else block be useful somewhere?

11, Assessment

There are two assessment sheet options for you. The first MLO14 follows the standard formula of many other modules of having a response form so that pupils can assess their own learning using faces and stick on any problem solving attitude stickers that they gain.

The second sheet MLO15 assesses all their problem solving skills mentioned below. Pupils assess where they are before and after the project. They can stick stickers on the bottom and back of the sheet.

Useful Problem Solving Skills to Assess

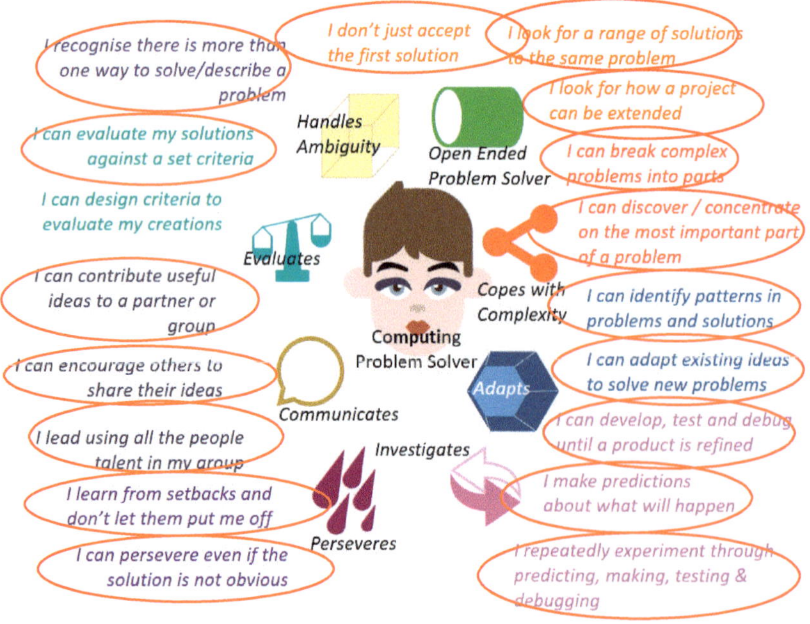

I recognise there is more than one way to solve/describe a problem
I don't just accept the first solution
I look for a range of solutions to the same problem
I look for how a project can be extended
Handles Ambiguity
Open Ended Problem Solver
I can evaluate my solutions against a set criteria
I can break complex problems into parts
I can design criteria to evaluate my creations
I can discover / concentrate on the most important part of a problem
Evaluates
I can contribute useful ideas to a partner or group
Copes with Complexity
I can identify patterns in problems and solutions
Computing Problem Solver
I can encourage others to share their ideas
I can adapt existing ideas to solve new problems
Adapts
Communicates
I can develop, test and debug until a product is refined
I lead using all the people talent in my group
Investigates
I learn from setbacks and don't let them put me off
I make predictions about what will happen
Perseveres
I can persevere even if the solution is not obvious
I repeatedly experiment through predicting, making, testing & debugging

Problem solving skills are adapted from a problem solving rubric created by Mark Dorling and Thomas Stephens, that the author worked on helping to define. You can find this at http://code-it.co.uk/attitudes/

[1], *The PIR sensor also meets that criteria but I have excluded it as it can be temperamental.*

Maker Lab One

Equipment you can use MLO1

Output Name	Crumble Classic (Crocodile Clip)	Playground (Headphone)	Connections	Notes
Programmable Light			OUTPUT D	OUTPUTS COLOURS CAN CONNECT 32 LIGHTS TO ONE OUTPUT (D)
LED Light	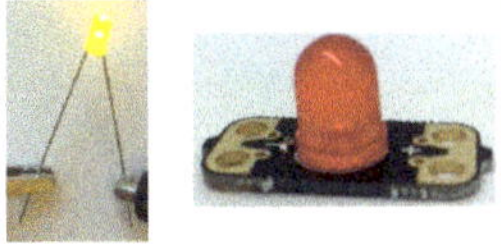		OUTPUT A, B, C or D	OUTPUTS A COLOURED LIGHT ON HI OFF LO
Motor			MOTOR 1 OR 2	OUTPUTS FORWARD OR REVERSE POWER 0-100%
Servo Motor			MOTOR 1 OR 2	OUTPUTS MOVEMENT BACK AND FORWARDS 0-90 DEGREES
Geared Motors			MOTOR 1 OR 2	OUTPUTS FORWARD OR REVERSE SPIN POWER 0-100%
Traffic Lights		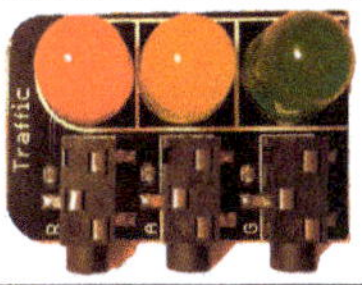	OUTPUT A, B, C or D	OUTPUTS RED GREEN AMBER ON HI OFF LO
Buzzer	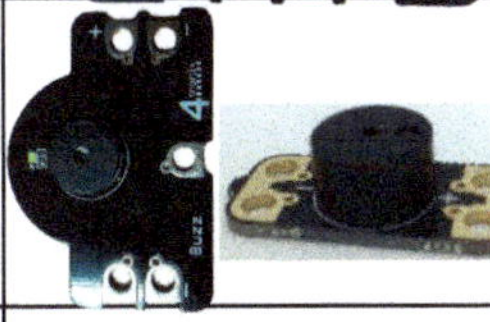	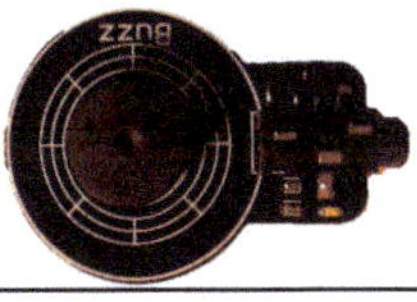	OUTPUT A, B, C or D	OUTPUTS ONE TONE SOUND ON HI OFF LO
Piezo Buzzer			MOTOR 1 OR 2	OUTPUTS DIFFERENT TONE WHEN POWER 0-100% PASSED THROUGH
Input Name	**Classic Crumble**	**Playground**	**Connections**	**Notes**
Push Button Switch		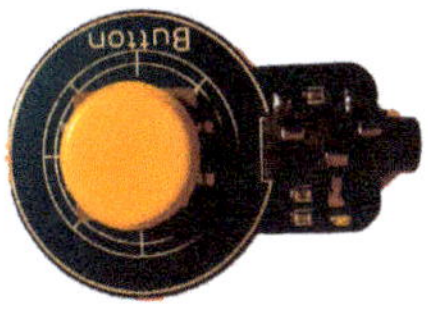	INPUT A, B, C or D	CAN BE USED TO START, STOP OR CHANGE OUTPUTS LISTED ABOVE
Close Proximity Sensor			INPUT A, B, C or D	CAN BE USED TO START, STOP OR CHANGE OUTPUTS LISTED ABOVE

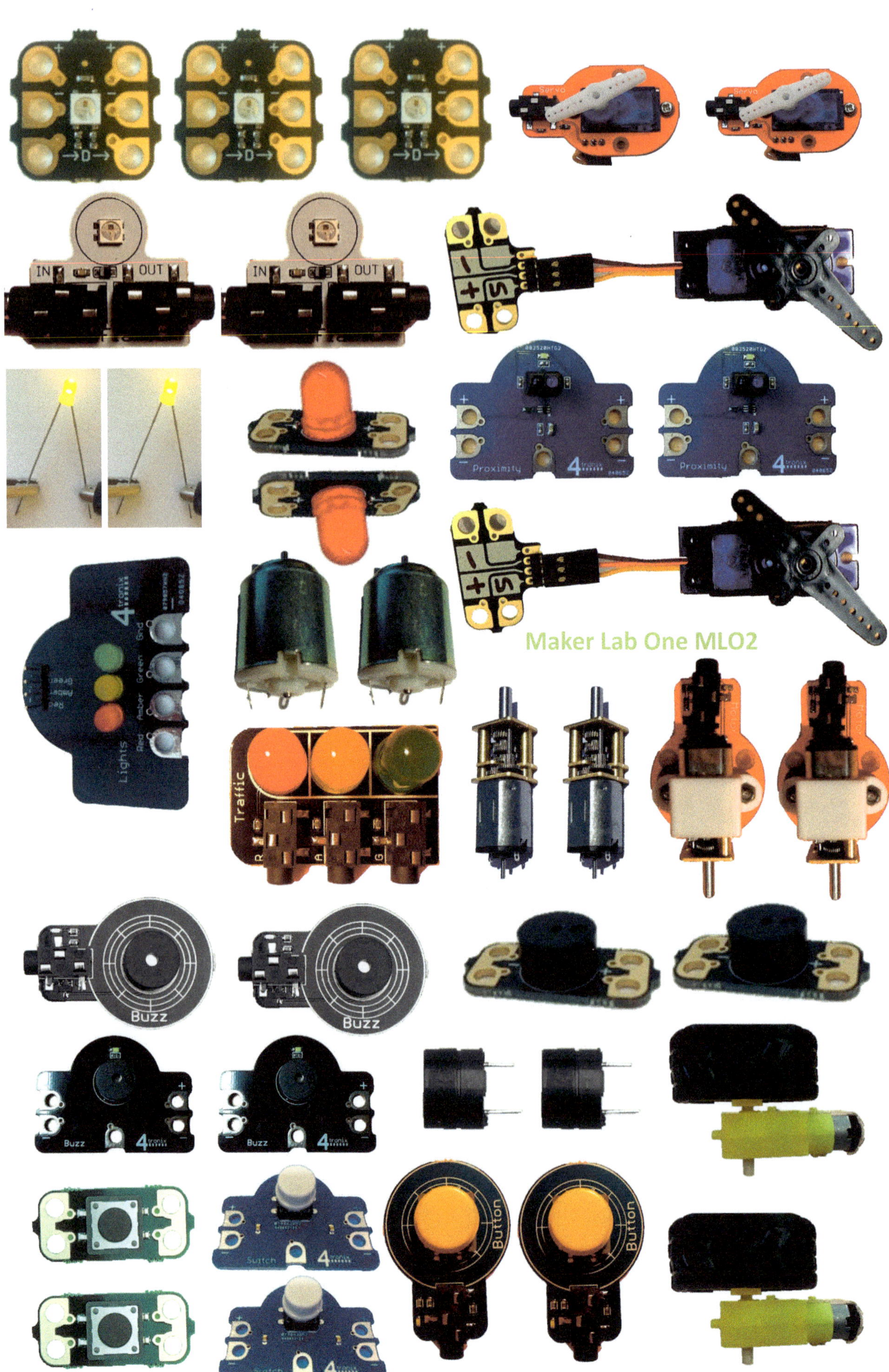
Servo
IN
OUT
Proximity
Maker Lab One MLO2
Lights
Red
Amber
Green
Gnd
Traffic
Buzz
Switch
Button

Name ____________________________ Class ___________ Maker Lab 1 MLO3

Planning my maker lab one project

Big idea 1	Big idea 2
What outputs will be changed, started or stopped by which inputs (button/close proximity sensor)?	How long will each part of your program last?
In what order will things happen? 1 2 3 4 5	Will anything happen when the input is not triggered?

PORTS	DEVICE	INPUT OR OUTPUT
A		
B		
C		
D		
MOTOR 1		
MOTOR 2		

Name ______________________________ Class _____________

MLO4

Maker Lab One Wiring Diagram

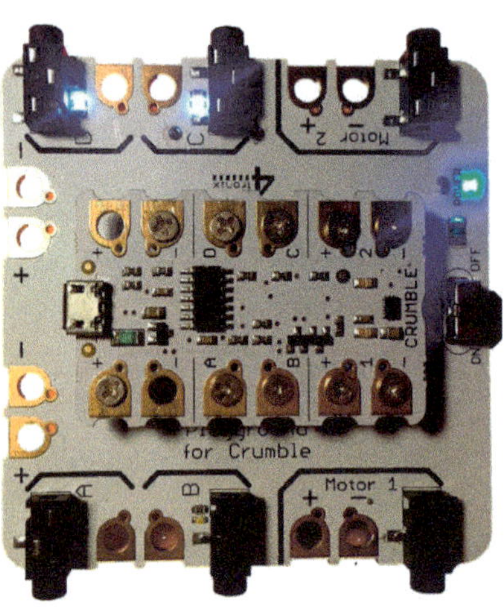

Draw your devices and the wires that connect them.

Name ______________________ Class __________ MLO5

Maker Lab One Wiring Diagram

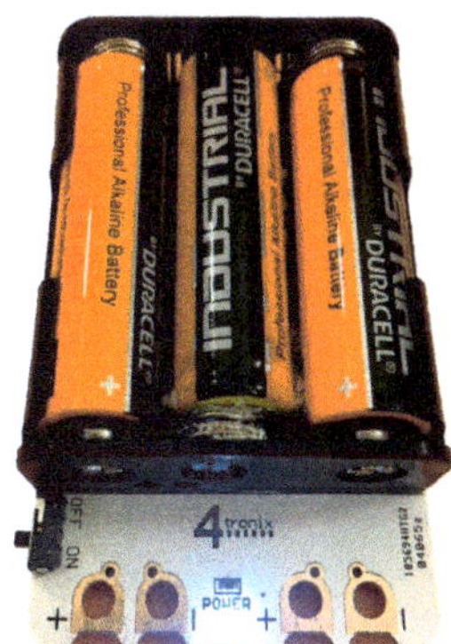

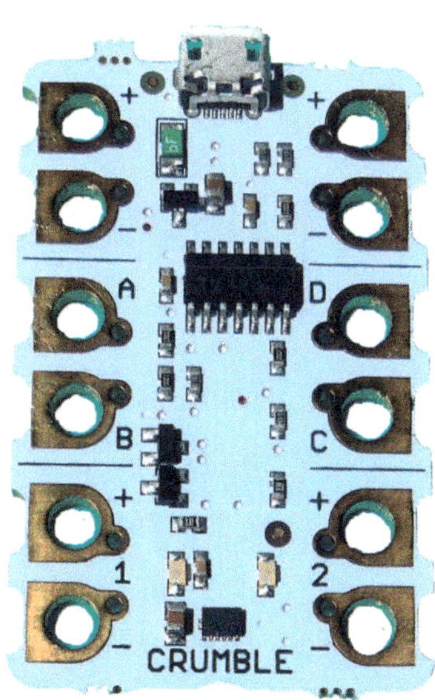

Draw your devices and the wires that connect them.

Work in pairs

One person is the **Program** and does what the code instructs.

One person is the **User** who triggers the condition through their actions.

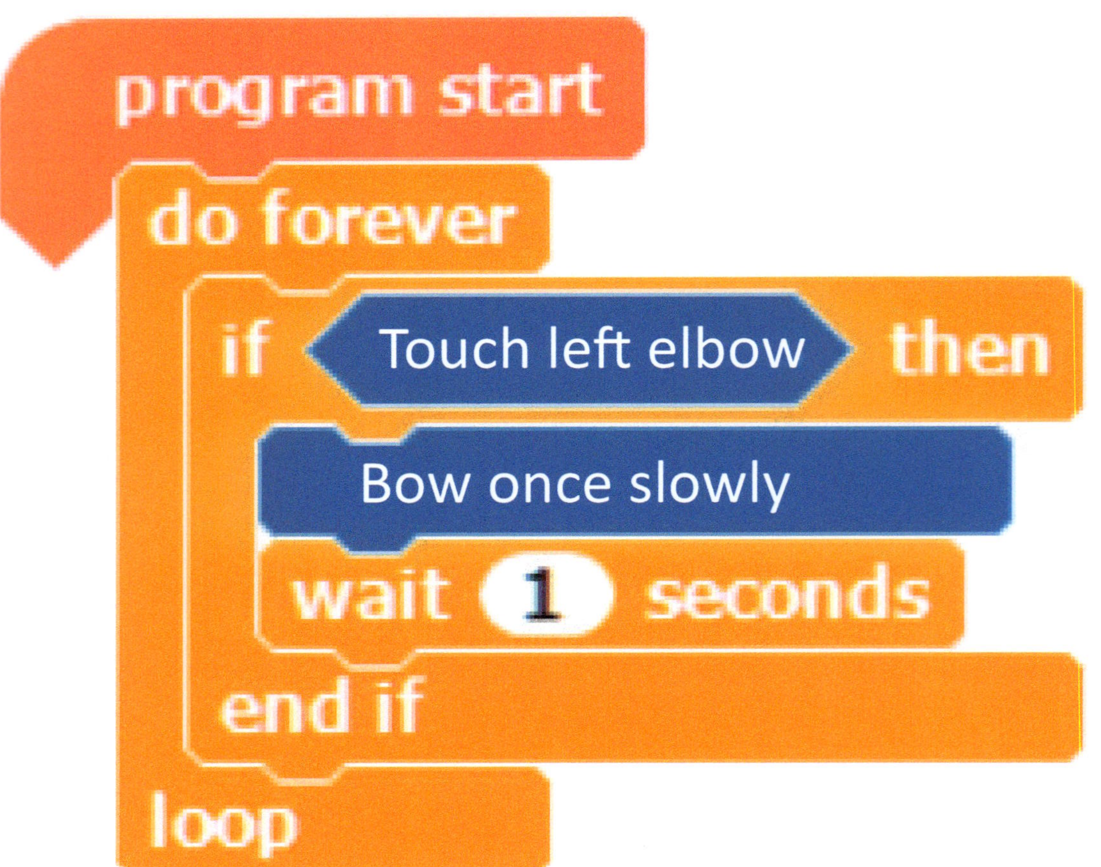
program start
do forever
if
Touch left elbow
then
Bow once slowly
wait 1 seconds
end if
loop

Don’t forget to swap roles.

Work in pairs

One person is the **Program** and does what is in the code below.

One person is the **User** who triggers the conditions.

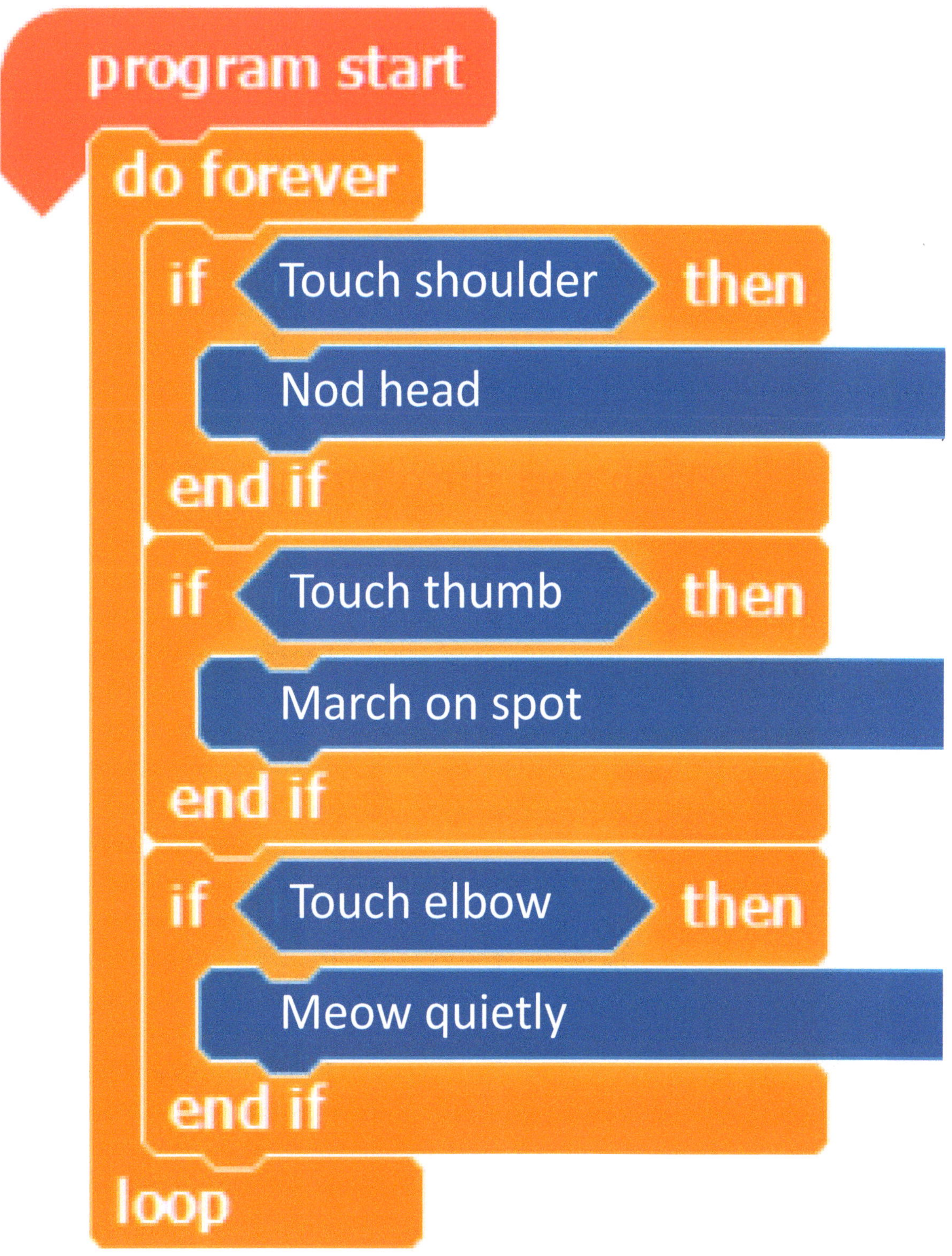
program start
do forever
if
Touch shoulder
then
Nod head
end if
if
Touch thumb
then
March on spot
end if
if
Touch elbow
then
Meow quietly
end if
loop

MLO7

Don't forget to swap roles.

Work in pairs

One person is the **Program** and does what is in the code below.

One person is the **User** who triggers the conditions.

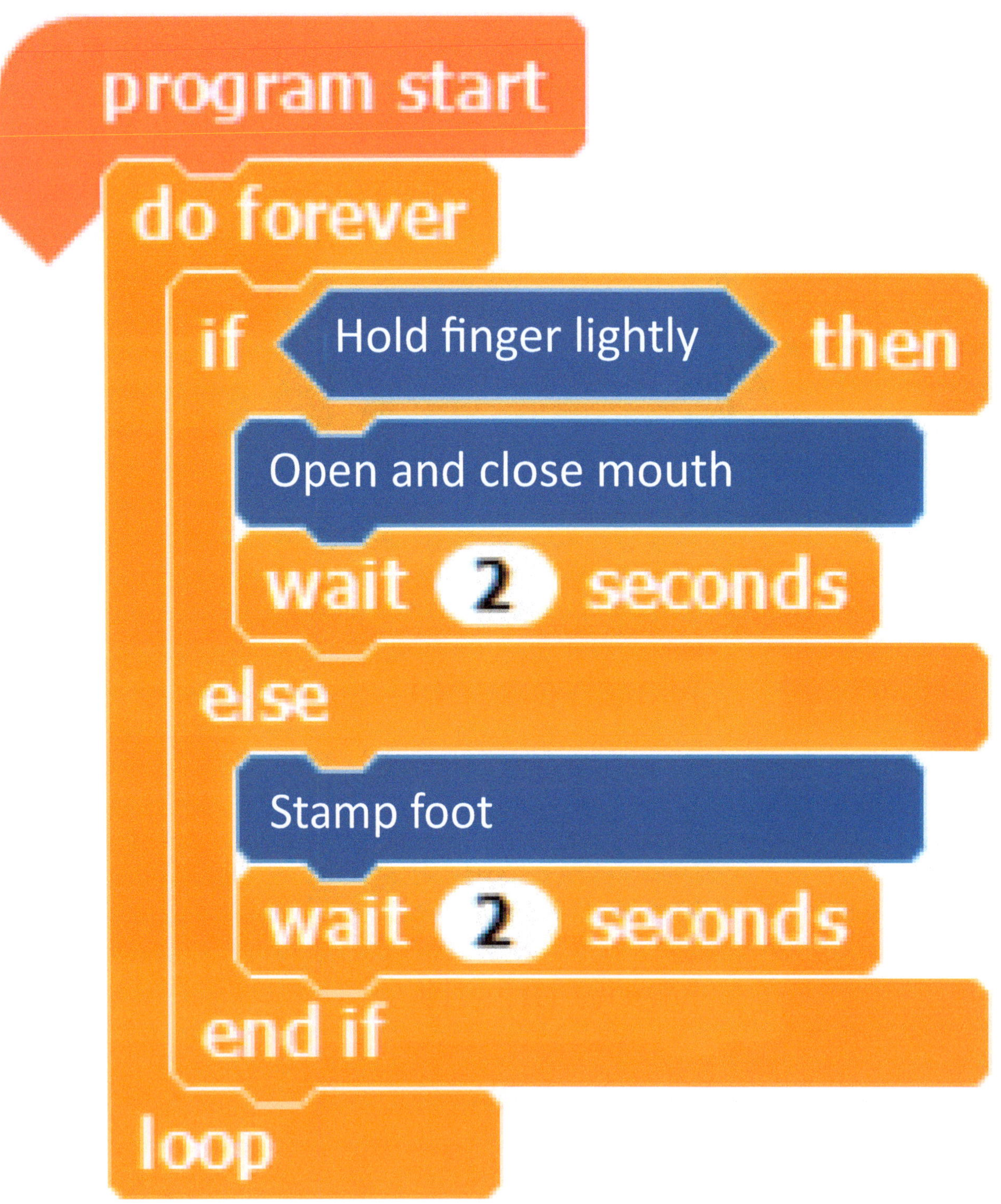
program start
do forever
if
Hold finger lightly
then
Open and close mouth
wait
2
seconds
else
Stamp foot
wait
2
seconds
end if
loop

MLO8

Don’t forget to swap roles.

Work in pairs

One person is the **Program** and does what is in the code below.

One person is the **User** who triggers the conditions.

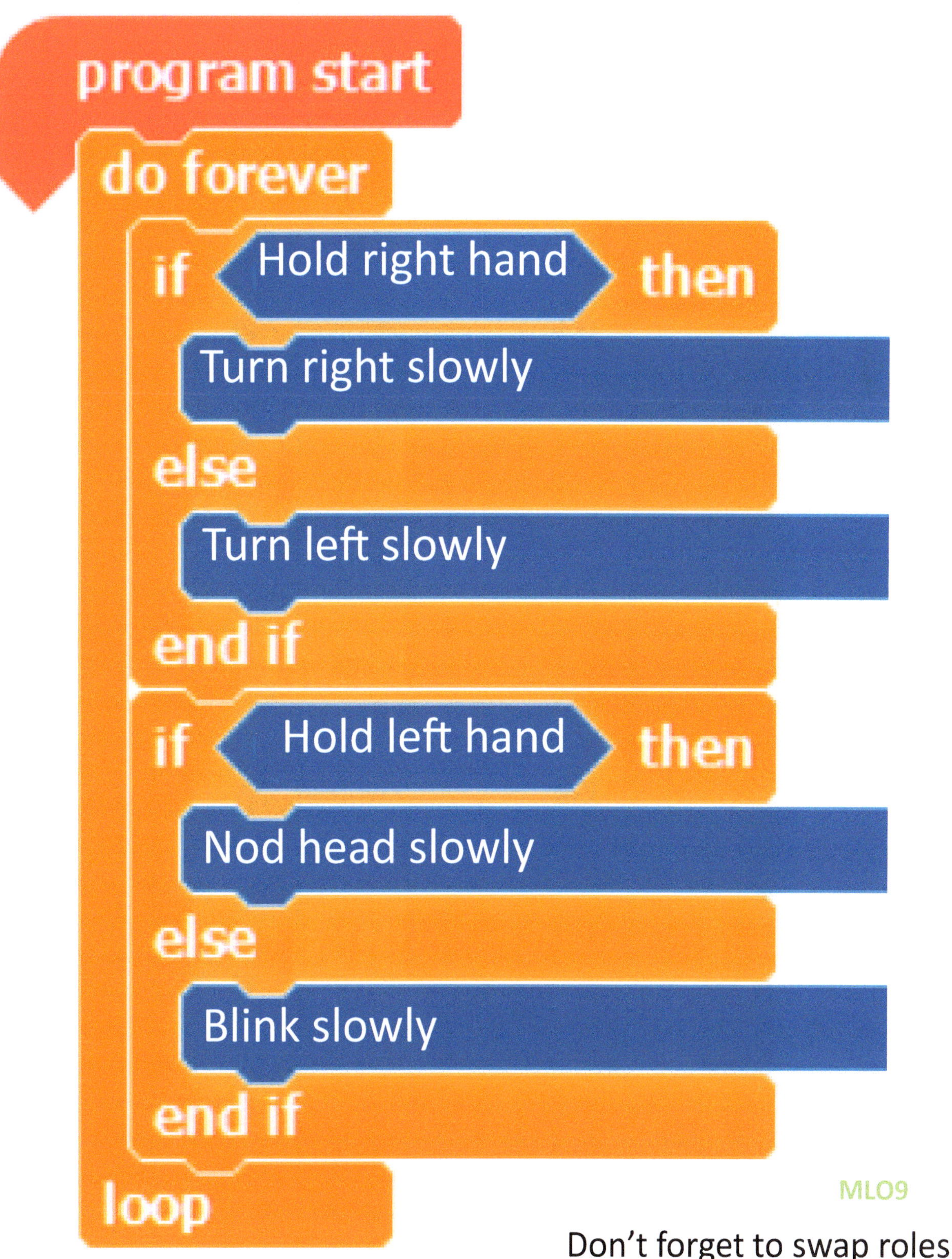
program start
do forever
if
Hold right hand
then
Turn right slowly
else
Turn left slowly
end if
if
Hold left hand
then
Nod head slowly
else
Blink slowly
end if
loop

MLO9

Don't forget to swap roles.

Work in pairs

One person is the **Program** and does what is in the code below (they hold this sheet).

One person is the **User** who triggers the conditions.

AND Means that both conditions have to be met for the code to start.

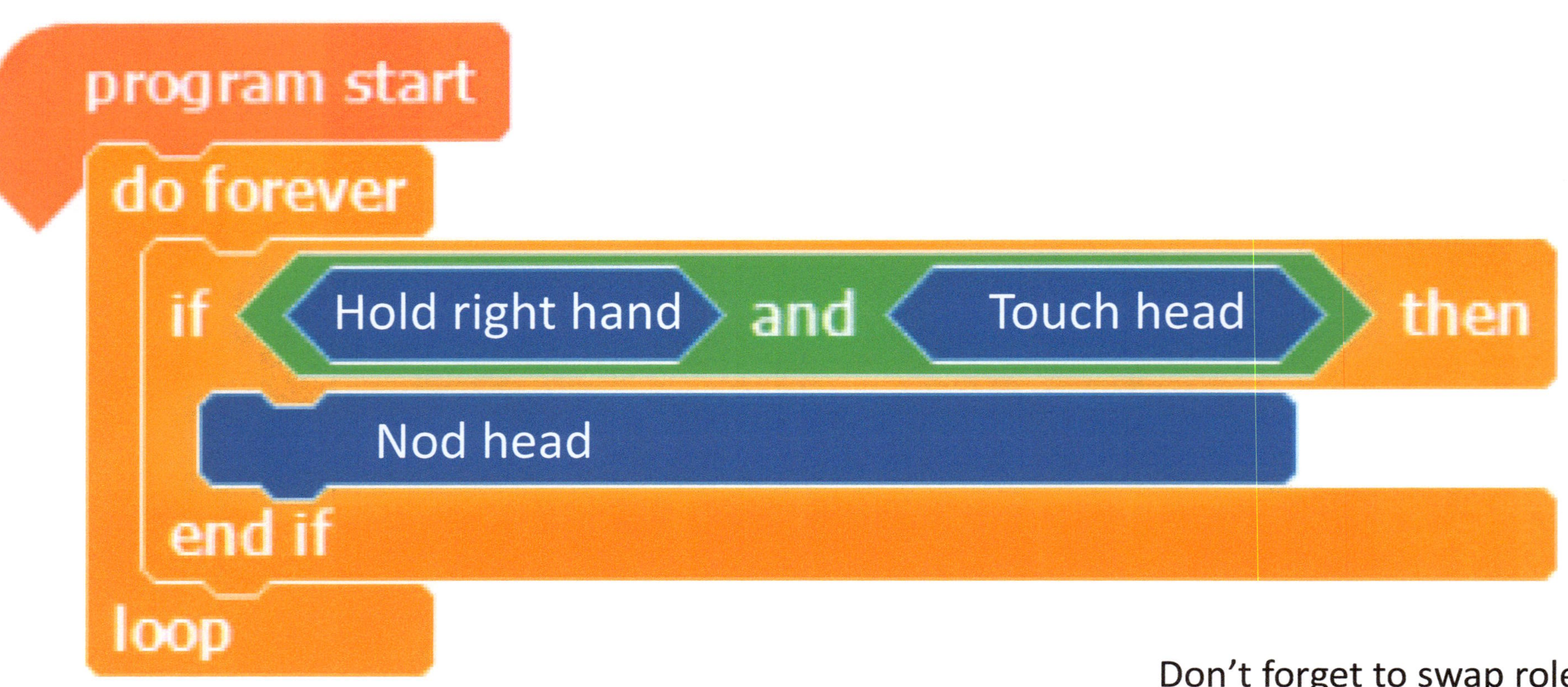
program start
do forever
if
Hold right hand
and
Touch head
then
Nod head
end if
loop

Don't forget to swap roles.

Work in pairs

One person is the **Program** and does what is in the code below (holds code).

One person is the **User** who triggers the conditions.

program start
do forever
if
Hold thumb
and
Touch elbow
then
Wave right hand
else
Wave left hand
end if
loop

Don’t forget to swap roles.

Work in pairs

One person is the **Program** and does what is in the code below (holds code).

One person is the **User** who triggers the conditions.

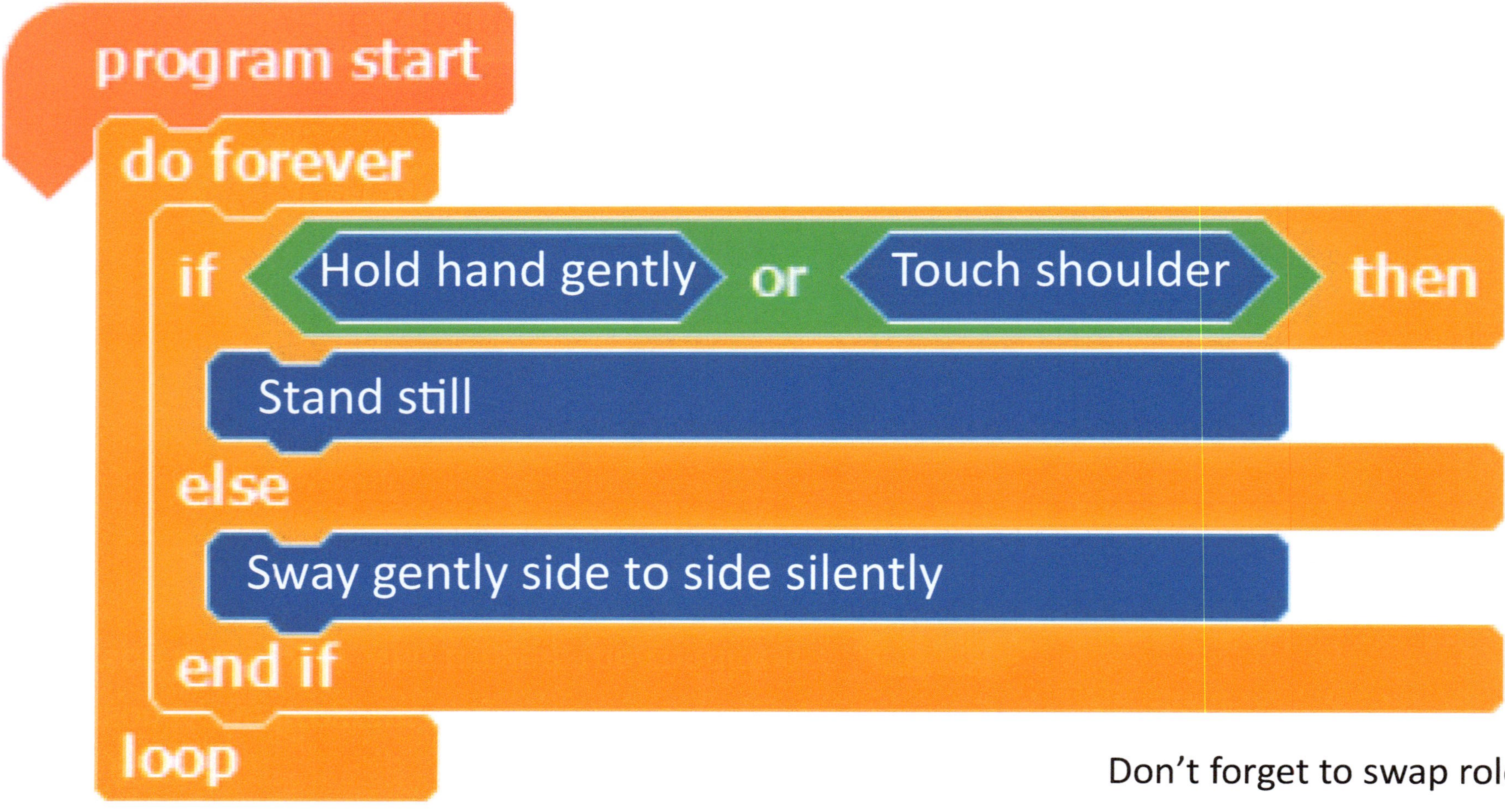
program start
do forever
if
Hold hand gently
or
Touch shoulder
then
Stand still
else
Sway gently side to side silently
end if
loop

Don't forget to swap roles.

Work in pairs

One person is the **Program** and does what is in the code below (holds code).

One person is the **User** who triggers the conditions.

```
program start
do forever
  if Touch back and Touch shoulder then
    Nod head
  end if
loop
```

Don’t forget to swap roles.

Maker Lab One Assessment Sheet Name ____________ Class ______

MLO14

I did this well ☺

I did this ok or I did this a little 😐

I tried this but it didn't work or I didn't do this at all ☹

I thought of some big ideas.	
I added more detail to one of my ideas.	
I drew an accurate wiring diagram.	
I wired up my Crumble and accessories.	
I fixed any part of the wiring that wasn't working.	
I programmed my idea independently.	
I tested my idea to see if it worked.	
I added something new after I got my initial idea working.	
I debugged a part of my program.	

Sticker	I got this sticker for
Sticker	I got this sticker for
Sticker	I got this sticker for

Maker Lab One Assessment Sheet

Name ______________ Class ______

MLO15 B = Where you are **before** the project A = Where you are **after** the project		I don't understand what it is yet	I know what it is but don't do it yet	I do it a little	I do it a lot	I do it a lot and can explain how
1	I can evaluate my solutions against set criteria.					
2	I can design criteria to evaluate my creations.					
3	I can contribute useful ideas to a partner or group.					
4	I can encourage others to share their ideas.					
5	I lead using all the people talent in my group.					
6	I learn from setbacks and don't let them put me off.					
7	I can persevere even if the solution is not obvious.					
8	I look for a range of solutions to the same problem.					
9	I look for how a project can be extended.					
10	I can break complex problems into parts.					
11	I can concentrate on the most important part of a problem.					
12	I can identify patterns in problems & solutions.					
13	I can adapt existing ideas to solve new problems.					
14	I make predictions about what will happen.					
15	I experiment through predicting, making, testing & debugging.					
16	I can develop, test and debug until a product is refined.					

11. Robot Challenges

Module Aim

Pupils design, build and program a steerable robot which is able to overcome a series of challenges.

Possible Challenges

- This project started life as **Robot Wars**. I have renamed it as not every teacher wishes to encourage battling robots. Attacking another robot and scoring points for damage, aggression or just hitting another robot is one possible challenge. In truth, the low voltage batteries limit the amount of damage. If you decide to make this one of your challenges, leave the challenge until last in case robots are damaged.
- **Fastest robot from A to B**. A timed event easy to adjust to the space you have available.
- **Obstacle Course**. Robots have to negotiate a twisting course. You can include ramps if you tape them to the floor and agree the incline. Pupils will need one ramp to test their creation on. If obstacles are physical ones, then the width of the narrowest part of the course must also be agreed.
- **Drag the most weight**. A ready supply of weights can be found in most Maths departments. You will need to specify how the weights will attach to the robots. A tray with a hook on the end might be one solution.
- **Races**. An oval shaped track where robots compete against each other to compete x number of laps first. Set up wide lanes and insist that robots keep inside their lane. Make sure you measure the length of each lane to keep them the same.

A simple obstacle course made using photocopier boxes and PE cones

- **Drag Race**. Fastest robots from A to B competing against other robots at the same time.
- **Best Looking Robot**. Add an aesthetic element to encourage great design.
- **Most innovative design**. Encourage young designers to push the boundaries by adding this challenge. You will need to agree what innovative means and how you or they will judge it.

It really helps to make the project pupil centred by giving them a say in the choice or design of the challenges. The best looking robot and the drag race were suggested by my pupils.

Cross Curricular links

Design and Technology

It would be fair to say that this is actually a design and technology project with an essential programming element. Every Key Stage 2 Design & Technology national curriculum program of study can be covered in part at some level through this project.

Art

If you opt for a best looking robot as one of your challenges, then you can easily develop the art aspect of the project. Velcro fastenings combined with detachable card panels allow pupils to concentrate on the art work separately before displaying it on their robot. You might decide on a specific art theme or give pupils choice.

Pupils to Model Ratio

I recommend that pupils research and come up with ideas and proto-type plans individually before working in groups on detailed planning, task lists, construction and programming. Groups could be as many as four pupils to each robot.

Materials

This is an ideal project to provide pupils with a wide choice of materials and encourage them to make choices based on the type of challenges they wish to do well in.

http://amzn.eu/0ReBL91
These 30mm diameter swivel castor wheels work well with the larger geared motors

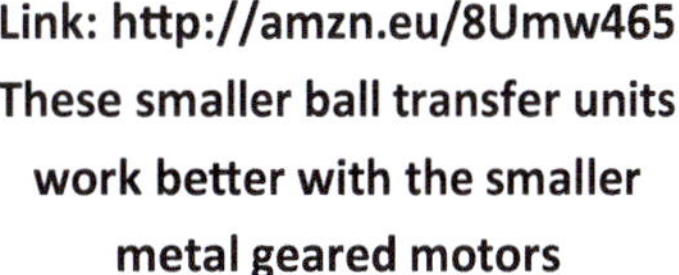

Link: http://amzn.eu/8Umw465
These smaller ball transfer units work better with the smaller metal geared motors

The following would be my minimum list per model:

- Classic Crumble, battery pack and wires or Crumble Playground.
- Two buttons and 1 metre long wires.
- Two geared motors and attached wheels.
- Plenty of 7mm or 10mm width wooden spar.
- A3 white card.
- One or two small castor wheels or ball transfer units. These are crucial as the project steers by increasing or decreasing power to the left or right motor. Ball castor units work best on flat non carpeted surfaces.

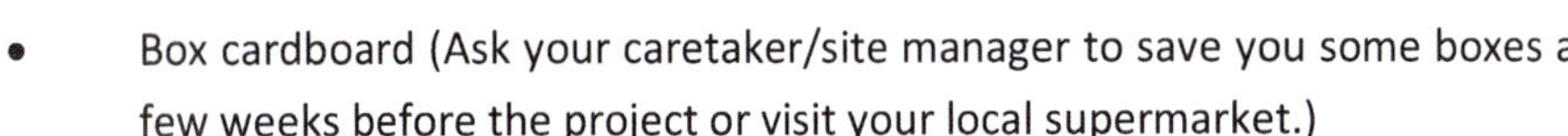

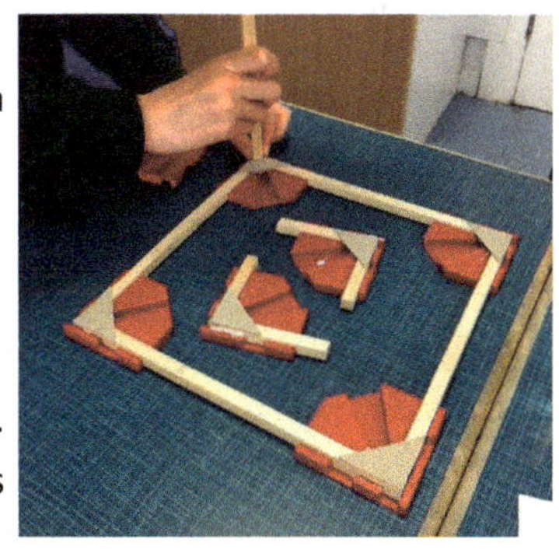

- Box cardboard (Ask your caretaker/site manager to save you some boxes a few weeks before the project or visit your local supermarket.)
- Cardboard corner triangles and cardboard axle supports.
- Wooden dowel 4mm or 5mm.
- Wooden or plastic wheels where their centre holes match the dowel size. (Although these are not necessary for the project, it is good to give pupils choice.)

Optional Materials if adding Robot wars weapons:

- Servo motor and wires.
- Ordinary 4.5v motor.
- Extra buttons and wires.
- More spa and dowel.
- Distance Sensor and wires.
- Tilt sensor and wires.

(only include the items in red if pupils have completed a maker lab two project first)

Construction Tools

- Hand saw
- Hand drill with various size drill bits
- Cutting block
- Metal ruler
- Glue gun and glue
- Scissors
- Gluing frames as shown above

- You may want to consider having an extra battery pack to power the extra motor without programming.
- You could also provide an extra Crumble or Crumble Playground to power and program weapons separately although this is not necessary for the project to work.
- It is useful to provide other craft materials such as lolly sticks and elastic bands as well as a range of small screws if you have them to provide more design choices.

NCD2D Select from and use a wider range of materials and components, including construction materials, textiles and ingredients, according to their functional properties and aesthetic qualities.

Construction

Construction choices are very much down to the pupil but as the materials provided restrict the type of construction to wooden frames with card panel sides most pupils will choose this classic construction type.

Time Needed

The planning and detailed preparation for this project takes about four hours which could be split over many weeks. The build programming and testing takes about two days. The competition takes between 1 and 3 hours depending on how you manage it.

Suggested Module Outline

1, Preparation before the module

Preparation is crucial for a project of this size. Order all the materials well in advance. It can really help pupils to see and handle the materials and electronics during the design phase so get it all in before you start. If you are going to share the competition with parents, then negotiate a date well in advance.

2, Introduce the project

Explain that pupils will design, build and program their own steerable buggy before taking part in a number of challenges (see the Challenges section above). You may wish to download and adapt the introduction slides which are located at http://code-it.co.uk/crumblebook. You might wish to impose a few key challenges and get the class to vote on additional ones. There is a video of some part finished buggies here:
https://www.youtube.com/watch?v=1Qz_BBUPIz0
These are great for helping pupils to see what others have done and to see possible construction methods.

3, Generating big ideas

Give out sheet RC1 and instruct pupils that they have 40 minutes to come up with some rough robot sketches. After 10 minutes encourage pupils to start a new idea. Stress the idea that these are only rough sketches. Can they design each robot sketch to beat one challenge?

NCD2A Use research and develop design criteria to inform the design of innovative, functional, appealing products that are fit for purpose, aimed at particular individuals or groups.

4, Choosing teams and negotiating a final design

Either choose teams yourself or let pupils choose teams themselves. Explain that in each phase there will be a different team captain. Design Captain, Build Captain, Programming Captain & Competition Captain. Captain's jobs are not to boss others about but to make sure the following things happen:

- Encourage everyone in the group to share their ideas.
- Use everyone's talent in the group.
- Be the casting vote if any decision is tied and the group can't agree the way to proceed.

Once captains are chosen, pupils need to examine the sketch ideas to come up with a rough idea of what they would like to include in their final design. They should circle parts of the sketches they are going to include in the detailed design. They also need to agree the following. The length, width, height, position of the wheels, shape of the robot and roughly what materials it will be made out of. The Design Captain will designate one team member to sketch these basic ideas onto RC2 with help from the rest of the team (10 minutes only) once the team have agreed the basics.

NCD2E Evaluate their ideas and products against their own design criteria and consider the views of others to improve their work.

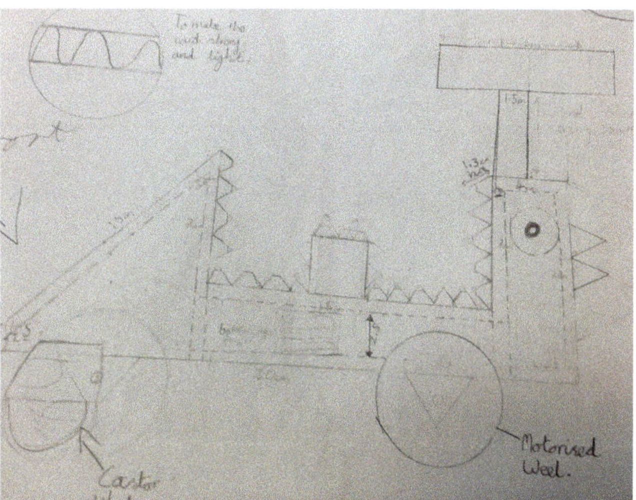

A detailed side view drawn in 1:1 scale on A3 paper

It can really help if the teacher has decided some maximum sizes before the project. I recommend using the length and width of an A3 piece of paper as the maximum size.

5, Detailed plans

Give out a piece of A3 plain paper to every pupil. Before anyone can build anything the team needs to create a detailed plan view from the top, side, front and back. Team members can split these views between them and draw them separately. Drawings need to be on a 1:1 ratio. There is an example on the Robot Challenges PowerPoint.

Encourage pupils to mark lengths on using arrows, show things that are underneath using a dotted line and write on extra information in pencil.

Pupils will need to work on parts of the plan individually but also talk to their teams if they spot issues that will affect the whole project.

NCD2B Generate, develop, model and communicate their ideas through discussion, annotated sketches, cross-sectional and exploded diagrams, prototypes, pattern pieces and computer-aided design.

6, Examine the detailed plans

Pupils are going to spend a considerable amount of time creating these robots. A small amount of teacher time examining every design for obvious issues and communicating these back to pupils will aid their build process. You may wish to do this with the schools Design and Technology lead teacher.

7, Optional task list (Construction Captain Leads)

The group has 30-60 minutes to produce a detailed list of all the jobs that will need doing and who is going to do them. This could be done on a computer. This can really help pupils to make the most of precious build time. It helps if the teams splits the list into parts and each team member or pair works on a separate part. Assigning people to tasks helps once the build has started.

<u>Base</u>

- Saw the spar to:
  - 4x 30cm
  - 4x 15cm
- Sand paper the ends of the spar
- Stick the spar pieces together to create a rectangle
- Stick the triangles to the corners of the spar
- Surround the spar with cardboard

8, Construction

Pupils need to know that it is normal to adjust their design in light of issues that arise from the construction process, as long as a majority of the group agree, with the construction captain having casting vote if there is a tied vote.

If you can encourage **parent helpers** to come in over the build time this can significantly smooth the process. Specific jobs or processes that helpers can supervise works best. Don't forget, as the teacher, to go over the processes in which you want pupils to be supported, including how much help should or should not be provided.

Good **resource and tool layouts** help the process. Do pupils know where equipment is and what they should do when they have finished with the tools or left over resources?

If one group of pupils finish the construction aspects of the build and want to start programming how can the computers be used without risking damage by tools or glue?

A large part of the teachers job is asking probing questions about pupils builds which enable them to improve their construction

These are just a few possible questions

- Where the Crumble Playground/Crumble Classic be positioned in the robot?
- How will you stop the Crumble Playground/Crumble Classic moving around inside your robot?
- How will your geared motors be attached to the frame?
- How will you tidy up your wires?
- Is that structure strong enough?

NCD2C Select from and use a wider range of tools and equipment to perform practical tasks [for example, cutting, shaping, joining and finishing], accurately.

NCD2D Select from and use a wider range of materials and components, including construction materials, textiles and ingredients, according to their functional properties and aesthetic qualities .

9, Programming

If pupils have completed the optional steering module from the Easy Buggy chapter they shouldn't need anything more than a quick reminder.

If pupils are new to steering, give them the challenge of programming one (motor) wheel so that it goes forward when a button is not pressed and back when the button is pressed. If pupils struggle with this, you can print out and ask them to try the physical programming challenge RC3 . This gives them the necessary programming but in another form. Once they have one motor working, ask them to adapt the program so that the other motor does the same using a new button. It is important to note that the method shown on the next page is not the only way of programming the steering using two buttons.

```
program start
do forever
  if arm touched then
    turn right slowly
  else
    turn left slowly
  end if
loop
```

Physical challenge hint example EB2

Students need to start with their power at 50%. They can adapt it to use higher percentages but they should be aware that some Crumble Boards will stop working for a short period of time when changing higher voltage motor from 100% forward to 100% backwards.

```
program start
do forever
  if A is HI then
    motor 1 FORWARD at 50 %
  else
    motor 1 REVERSE at 50 %
  end if
  if B is HI then
    motor 2 FORWARD at 50 %
  else
    motor 2 REVERSE at 50 %
  end if
loop
```

The simplest steering program

Useful Maker Cards

MC02	**MC06**	**MC07**	**MC12**	**MC13**
MC14	**MC18**	**MC19**	**MC26**	**MC27**
MC28	**MC31**	**MC37**	**MC38**	**MC39**
MC45	**MC50**	**MC51**	**MC52**	**MC53**
MC55				

NCD2F understand and use mechanical systems in their products

NCD2G understand and use electrical systems in their products [for example, series circuits incorporating switches, bulbs, buzzers and motors]

NCD2H apply their understanding of computing to program, monitor and control their products.

10, Optional Robot Wars Weapons

If you choose to allow weapons then introduce firm rules. Pupils can only use materials that the school has provided and are not allowed to bring in additional items. Weapons tend to fall into categories: Simple servo driven weapons, motor driven weapons and unpowered attachments such as spikes on the vehicles. For safety reasons, all poking or slashing weapons have to be blunt. Steer pupils away from lifting or flipping weapons as these often need CO^2 gas to function and are outside of the build capabilities of most primary classes. An easy but mainly harmless weapon is the direct driven servo axe. You can see a basic video of one at https://youtu.be/EGlYb7sdlnI A more effective but very difficult build is the crank https://youtu.be/oHzg7y3bjVg Of the three groups who tried to build one in my class none managed a working one in the time. More successful but less destructive is the spinner. Even a simple 4.5 volt motor with a piece of wood attached can become a fearsome looking spinner. As few of these will be geared, the destructive power is very limited. Roboteers should wear goggles to protect their eyes and the audience should be further away from the arena. A camera feeding the fight through a data projector onto a large screen is a great safe way for everyone to watch the action.

Common debugging hints

- Are you sure your input/output letters on your programming match where you have wired them on the Crumble?
- Have you checked to see if your wiring matches that on the card?
- Are all your wires firmly pushed in (for 3.5mm jack leads on playground).
- Have you checked to see if the metal on the crocodile clips are touching the metal on other crocodile clips (short circuit)?
- Is your battery pack switched on?
- Did you line up and turn the Crumble in the same manner as the maker card?
- Do your batteries need replacing?
- Are your batteries in the right way round?
- Did you send the program to the Crumble by clicking on the green arrow?
- Did you plug the Crumble into the computer using the USB cable?
- Did the program say it was running successfully?
- Did you use more than one starting block?

A simple spinning bar powered by a 4.5volt motor and a 4.5 volt battery pack with no programming.

NCD2E Evaluate their ideas and products against their own design criteria and consider the views of others to improve their work.

11, Assessment

There are two assessment sheet options for you. The first RC4 follows the standard formula of many other modules of having a response form so that pupils can assess their own learning using faces and stick on any problem solving attitude stickers that they gain.

The second sheet RC5 assesses all their problem solving skills mentioned later. Pupils assess where they are before and after the project. They could stick stickers on the bottom and back of the sheet.

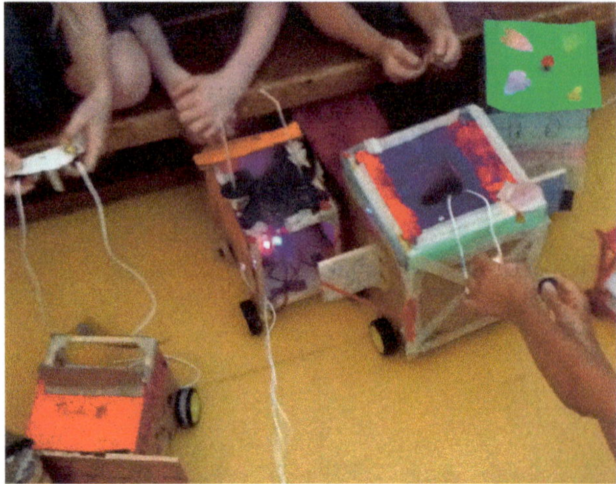

Mass robot rumble

Two spinning bars powered by a 4.5 volt motor programmed to start and stop using a button.

Useful Problem Solving Skills to Assess

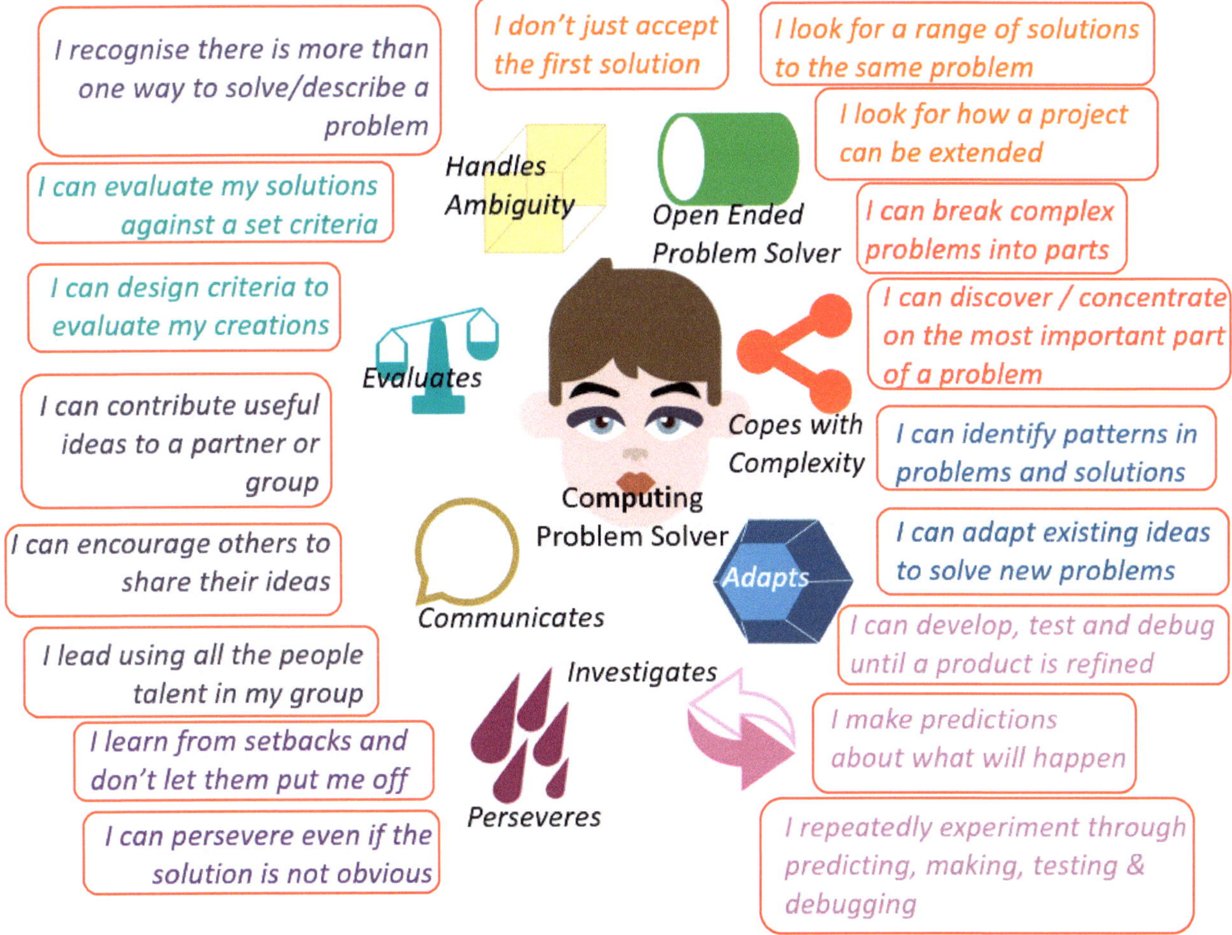

I recognise there is more than one way to solve/describe a problem
I don't just accept the first solution
I look for a range of solutions to the same problem
I look for how a project can be extended
I can evaluate my solutions against a set criteria
Handles Ambiguity
Open Ended Problem Solver
I can break complex problems into parts
I can design criteria to evaluate my creations
I can discover / concentrate on the most important part of a problem
Evaluates
I can contribute useful ideas to a partner or group
Copes with Complexity
I can identify patterns in problems and solutions
Computing Problem Solver
I can encourage others to share their ideas
I can adapt existing ideas to solve new problems
Adapts
Communicates
I can develop, test and debug until a product is refined
I lead using all the people talent in my group
Investigates
I make predictions about what will happen
I learn from setbacks and don't let them put me off
I can persevere even if the solution is not obvious
Perseveres
I repeatedly experiment through predicting, making, testing & debugging

Problem solving skills are adapted from a problem solving rubric created by Mark Dorling and Thomas Stephens that the author helped to define. You can find this at http://code-it.co.uk/attitudes/

Curricular Coverage

Design & Technology NC

NCD2A **NCD2B** **NCD2C**

NCD2D **NCD2E** **NCD2F**

NCD2G **NCD2H**

Computing NC

NCC2A **NCC2B** **NCC2C**

Name ____________________

Class ______________

Robot Challenge Sketches

You will have:
wooden spar,
thick and thin cardboard,
two geared motors,
buttons,
crumble to control them,
castor wheel,
wooden wheels,
axles

Only spend 10 minutes on each sketch.

Aim to beat one challenge in every sketch.

Go onto the back if you want to create a fifth or sixth sketch.

RC1

Names

Class/Form

Robot

Challenge

Group Choice

Design Considerations

Shape

Length

Width

Height

Wheel Type

Wheel Position

RC2

```
program start
  do forever
    if <back touched> then
      walk forwards slowly
    else
      walk backwards slowly
    end if
  loop
```

```
program start
  do forever
    if <arm touched> then
      turn right slowly
    else
      turn left slowly
    end if
  loop
```

Robot Challenges Assessment Sheet Name____________ Class ______

RC4

I did this well ☺

I did this ok or I did this a little 😐

I tried this but it didn't work or I didn't do this at all ☹

I worked with my team to evaluate ideas and choose the best features to make.	
I drew a detailed robot design.	
I worked with my team to construct our robot.	
I listened to other members of my team, taking their ideas seriously.	
I lead my team as ____________ captain, helping everyone to play a part.	
I tested and debugged our robot and programming.	
We took part in the competition and learnt (fill in what you learnt).	
I debugged a part of my program or fixed a part or our construction.	

Sticker	I got this sticker for
Sticker	I got this sticker for
Sticker	I got this sticker for

Robot Challenges Assessment Sheet

Name __________ Class ____

RC5 B = Where you are **before** the project A = Where you are **after** the project		I don't understand what it is yet.	I know what it is but don't do it yet.	I do it a little.	I do it a lot.	I do it a lot and can explain how.
1	I can evaluate my solutions against set criteria.					
2	I can design criteria to evaluate my creations.					
3	I can contribute useful ideas to a partner or group.					
4	I can encourage others to share their ideas.					
5	I lead using all the people talent in my group.					
6	I learn from setbacks and don't let them put me off.					
7	I can persevere even if the solution is not obvious.					
8	I look for a range of solutions to the same problem.					
9	I look for how a project can be extended.					
10	I can break complex problems into parts.					
11	I can concentrate on the most important part of a problem.					
12	I can identify patterns in problems & solutions.					
13	I can adapt existing ideas to solve new problems.					
14	I make predictions about what will happen.					
15	I experiment through predicting, making, testing & debugging.					
16	I can develop, test and debug until a product is refined.					

12. Maker Labs Two

Module Aim

Pupils think of some big ideas that involve a range of output devices such as motors, buzzers and lights controlled by a range of input devices such as buttons, distance sensors, PIR sensors, light dependant resistors and tilt sensors. After choosing the best idea they decompose it into its parts and create a circuit diagram before building, programming and testing it.

Cross Curricular Links

This project tends to work best if pupils start from an understanding of what the inputs can do and develop ideas that link to specific inputs affecting specific outputs.

Computing

Pupils will need to be able to use sequence, repetition, conditional selection and variables to program their projects. There is a useful roleplay starter to help those pupils who are not fully independent when using variables.

Materials

If there isn't time to allow pupils to scratch build a case for their electronics then the use of the four inch box as a case allows pupils to think about what parts are internal and what needs to be external.

Very few schools will have all the equipment found in the Maker Lab Two table. Teachers will need to go through the input and output sheets and cross out equipment that is not owned by the school before giving pupils a copy.

Construction

This project is very open ended but the limited number of ports (6 in total) and the limited number of input and output devices reduces the number of possible combinations considerably.

```
program start
do forever
    let (distance) = (distance (cm) T:(A) E:(B)) ÷ (3)
    motor (1) (FORWARD) at (distance) %
loop
```

The big idea here is a proximity sensor that changes the beep tone as it gets nearer to an object and is designed for blind people to detect objects in front of them. Inputs A and B are plugged into a distance sensor. Motor 1 is plugged into a piezo element. The distance sensor inputs between 0-255. The piezo can only work with a range between 0-100 which is why the distance data is divided by 3 before being transferred into the variable called distance.

Useful Maker Cards

All maker cards could be useful

Curricular Coverage

Design & Technology NC

NCD2G **NCD2H**

Computing NC

NCC2A **NCC2B** **NCC2C**

Suggested Module Outline

1, Preparation before the module

Have a good look at the MLT1 & MLT2 sheets which list all the inputs and outputs available. Photocopy them preferably in colour and cross out any equipment that you don't have in school. If there are any other devices that you have, write them on the top of the sheet. If you have very limited amount of equipment, you might want to put a x1 or x2 next to some equipment to show that pupils should only include one or two of these in their project. Photocopy these adapted sheets one set between two or three pupils as the amount of equipment dictates.

Do the same for the MLT3 & MLT4 sheets which provide multiple copies of most devices to stick on to their circuit diagram. You won't need these sheets if pupils are going to draw the input and output devices.

You will also need to photocopy MLT5 on which pupils can record their ideas. I recommend recording their planning individually even if they have to choose one project per two or three children due to lack of individual equipment. You will also need either MLT6 or MLT7 depending on which Crumble you have.

Print out the variable role play cards MLT8–13 so that there are enough sheets for one sheet between each pair. Two sets work for classes which are 32 pupils or under.

2, Role play Variables

Explain that in this project they are going to be using lots of variables to transfer information from the sensors into outputs of different types. Open the three person roleplay MLT9 found opposite so that all pupils can see it. Place number cards from 0-1-2-3-4 on the ground in a line and explain that this is a slider. You may want to show pupils a slider and ask them where they have seen one before. A music mixing desk is the obvious one or aircraft controls. Ask one volunteer to be the human slider and move up and down the numbers pausing on a number for a while. Ask for another volunteer to be the variable. Their job is to watch the slider and say whatever number the slider is on. Explain that the information is passed from the slider to the Crumble and stored in the variable. The third person has to read the code and jump slider variable times followed by a 5 second wait. You may want to demonstrate another couple of the role play examples if pupils have not used variables in any other context.

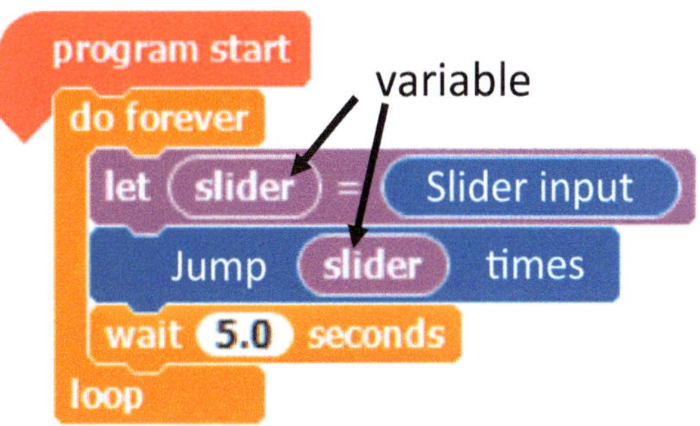
program start
variable
do forever
let slider = Slider input
Jump slider times
wait 5.0 seconds
loop

In this example a slider inputs a number between 0-5 and places it in a variable called slider. The jump output uses that number via the variable slider to determine how many times they should jump.

Direct pupils to work in groups of threes and encourage them to swap roles so they all get an opportunity to read and be the input, variable and code output.

Move the class round eight times so that everyone gets to work with each roleplay opportunity.

While pupils are working with these, look out for misconceptions. You can find some of these on the chart on the following page.

Leave these roleplays where pupils can access them as they are useful if pupils need to think through the code examples later in the project.

Formative assessment questions	Corrective	Enrichment
MLT8 **Temperature** In which part of the code do both conditions need to be met? **Answer:** Less than 80 greater than 30	Point out Boolean **OR AND** in the code. Which sentence suggests you need both? (I need food **OR** water. I need food **AND** water.)	Which part of the program passes the information from the temperature sensor into the variable called temperature? Answer: Let temperature = temperature sensor
MLT9/10/11/12 **Slider, Dial, Distance** If you replaced the number of seconds with the slider variable and the slider input was on 3, how many seconds would you wait? **Answer:** 3 seconds	Trace how the number 3 starts in the slider before being put inside the slider variable (slider=slider input) , used in the jump before determining how long to wait.	Which part of the program passes the information from the slider input into the variable called slider? **Answer:** Let slider = slider input
MLT13/14 **Movement Sensor** What action would happen when the movement sensor has not been triggered? **Answer:** MLT13 buzzer off **Answer:** MLT14 buzzer on	Read the code: if movement variable less than 101 then (depends on card). Point out that this is when it is triggered. Else is when it has not been triggered.	Which part of the program passes the information from the movement sensor input into the variable called movement? **Answer:** Let movement = movement sensor

3, Introduce the project

Explain that pupils will design their own Crumble projects that use a full range of inputs and outputs chosen by them. If pupils did the Maker Lab One, then you might want to mention that this is the full version.

4, Generating big ideas (Top section MLT5)

Give out MLT1, MLT2 & MLT5 and get pupils to start thinking of big ideas. It helps if they are encouraged to collaborate with a partner or small group.

Encourage pupils to fill in the big ideas section of MLT5. It helps if they can come up with three or more ideas but one good idea is fine. If pupils are struggling with a big idea, a sentence scaffold can help with gaps where pupils can insert the input and output and a description of what it might do. However, I recommend giving pupils time to think before introducing this scaffold.

The _________ input passes a number into the Crumble. This is stored in a variable called __________. When the number in the variable is __________ (less that/ equal to/ greater than), it makes _______ output do__________.

The _________ input passes a number into the Crumble. This is stored in a variable called __________ . This number in the variable, called _________, is then used to make output __________ do ______________.

5, Breaking the project up (decomposition) (Middle section MLT5)

The section underneath the big idea is for pupils to take one idea and break it down further using these questions

- What input(s) will trigger what output(s)? *Insist on specific language.*
- What will the input(s) input? If it inputs a number, what is that number? *1-255/1-100/HI or LO (MLT1 & MLT2)*
- At which point(s) (number/HI/LO/>/<) will an output be triggered? *Specific number, <, > or all the time.*
- What will the outputs do when they are triggered? *Specific action.*

- What will you call your variable to pass information from the input to the output if you have one? *Name*

You may want to print the example MLT5A and go through this with pupils who are struggling to understand parts of MLT5 although it is possible they will try to copy this rather than think of their own idea.

The section on the bottom right of MLT5 is asking pupils to think of parts that can be tested before building the whole project. It really help if students know that their inputs and outputs are wired correctly because they have tested them with simple code.

6, Breaking project up by hardware (Bottom section MLT5)

Part of the design phase for their project is to make sure that they can plug in all the inputs and outputs that they need into the one Crumble board. Completing the bottom section of MLT5 allows them to check this. Occasionally, pupils who are using the Crumble Playground forget that there is only one A, B, C & D port and they try and plug in something to the crocodile clip A and something else into the 3.5mm jack plug for A. A quick reminder that only one device can be plugged into any one port can be helpful before they fill in this section.

7, Wiring diagram

The next stage is to use MLT6 or MLT7 to create a wiring diagram. Pupils will need the relevant maker cards to help them decide which ports to use and where wires need to connect.

You can either encourage pupils to draw the equipment or cut out the devices they need from MLT3 & MLT4. Lines need to be drawn with a ruler and a pencil. It can be tempting to encourage the use of colouring pencils but due to the possibility of mistakes I would encourage standard pencils.

Producing detailed wiring diagrams allows them to check if their project is achievable with the hardware they have available and many faults can be avoided or fixed.

8, Check plans

Before pupils go on and connect their devices and start turning their idea into programming, it can be a really good idea to mark their work, paying real attention to their original idea and the answers that they gave to the middle section (section 5 above). Have they linked specific inputs to specific outputs? Remember one input can trigger multiple outputs. Have they answered all the middle questions carefully? If they wired using a playground accessory, did they use a playground socket? If they wired using the classic Crumble, did they use the crocodile clip connections?

9, Wiring

Pupils are now ready to wire and program. They will be able to do this independently using the maker cards and their wiring diagram they created in step 7.

10, Programming

Every project will be different but it can help pupils to look at the variable roleplay sheets (MLT8-13) that are similar to the idea that they want to achieve.

Common debugging hints

- Are you sure your input/output letters on your programming match where you have wired them?
- Have you checked to see if your wiring diagram matches your wiring?
- Are all your wires firmly pushed in (for 3.5mm jack leads on playground)?
- Have you checked to see if the metal on the crocodile clips is touching the metal on another crocodile clips (short circuit)?

- Is your battery pack switched on?
- Did you line up and turn the Crumble in the same manner as the maker card?
- Do your batteries need replacing?
- Are your batteries the right way round?
- Did you send the program to the Crumble by clicking on the green arrow?
- Did you plug the Crumble into the computer using the USB cable?
- Did the program say it was running successfully?
- Did you use more than one starting block?

11, Assessment

There are two assessment sheet options for you. The first MLT16 follows the standard formula of many other modules of having a response form so that pupils can assess their own learning using faces and stick on any problem solving attitude stickers that they gain.

The second sheet MLO15 assesses all their problem solving skills mentioned below. Pupils assess where they are before and after the project. They could stick stickers on the bottom of the sheet and on the back.

Useful Problem Solving Skills to Assess

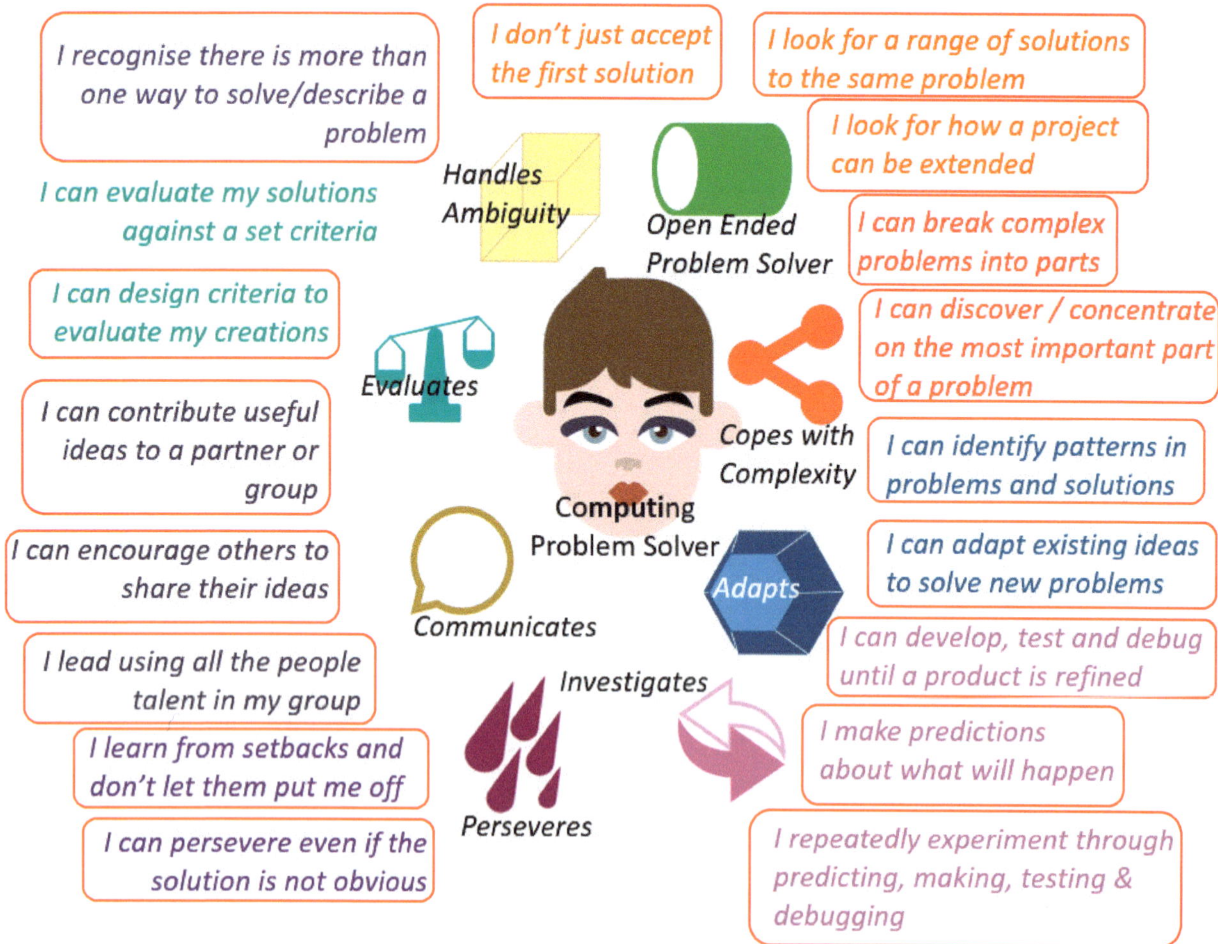

I recognise there is more than one way to solve/describe a problem
I don't just accept the first solution
I look for a range of solutions to the same problem
I look for how a project can be extended
Handles Ambiguity
Open Ended Problem Solver
I can evaluate my solutions against a set criteria
I can break complex problems into parts
I can design criteria to evaluate my creations
I can discover / concentrate on the most important part of a problem
Evaluates
I can contribute useful ideas to a partner or group
Copes with Complexity
I can identify patterns in problems and solutions
Computing Problem Solver
I can encourage others to share their ideas
I can adapt existing ideas to solve new problems
Adapts
Communicates
I can develop, test and debug until a product is refined
I lead using all the people talent in my group
Investigates
I make predictions about what will happen
I learn from setbacks and don't let them put me off
I can persevere even if the solution is not obvious
Perseveres
I repeatedly experiment through predicting, making, testing & debugging

Problem solving skills are adapted from a problem solving rubric created by Mark Dorling and Thomas Stephens that the author worked on helping to define. You can find this at http://code-it.co.uk/attitudes/

Maker Lab Two   Outputs you can use   MLT1

Output Name	Crumble Classic (Crocodile Clip)	Playground (Headphone)	Connections	Notes
Programmable Light		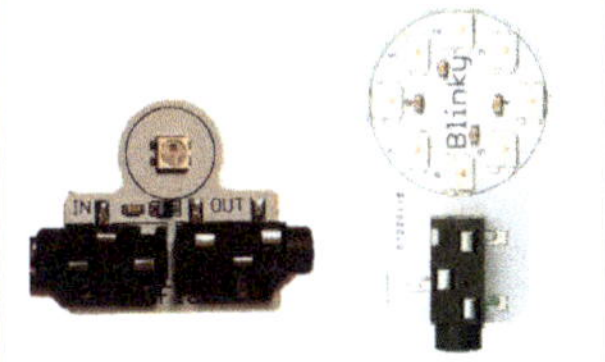	OUTPUT D	OUTPUTS A FULL RANGE OF COLOURS CAN CONNECT 32 LIGHTS TO ONE OUTPUT (D)
LED Light	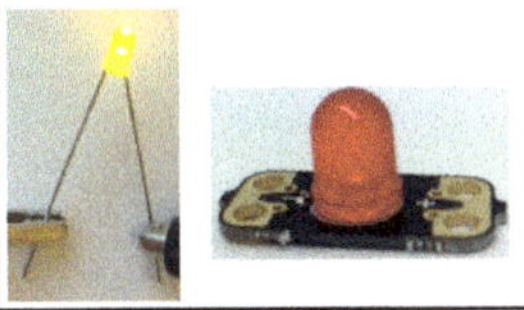		OUTPUT A, B, C or D	OUTPUTS A COLOURED LIGHT ON HI OFF LO
Motor			MOTOR 1 OR 2	OUTPUTS FORWARD OR REVERSE POWER 0-100%
Stepper (Servo) Motor			MOTOR 1 OR 2	OUTPUTS MOVEMENT BACK AND FORWARDS 0-90 DEGREES
Geared Motors			MOTOR 1 OR 2	OUTPUTS FORWARD OR REVERSE SPIN POWER 0-100%
Traffic Lights		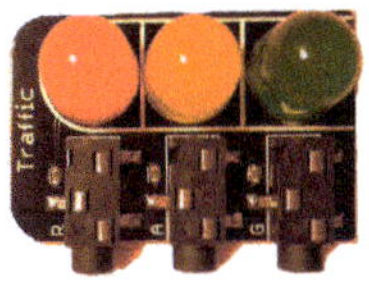	OUTPUT A, B, C or D	RED GREEN AMBER ON HI OFF LO
Buzzer	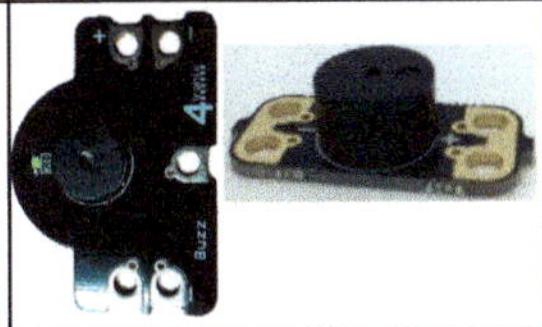		OUTPUT A, B, C or D	OUTPUTS ONE TONE SOUND ON HI OFF LO
Piezo Buzzer			MOTOR 1 OR 2	OUTPUTS DIFFERENT TONE WHEN POWER 0-100% PASSED THROUGH
Number Counter			MOTOR 1 OR 2	OUTPUTS 0-99 VIA MOTOR POWER PERCENTAGE

Input Name	Crumble Classic (Crocodile Clip)	Playground (Headphone)	Connections	Notes
Distance Sensor	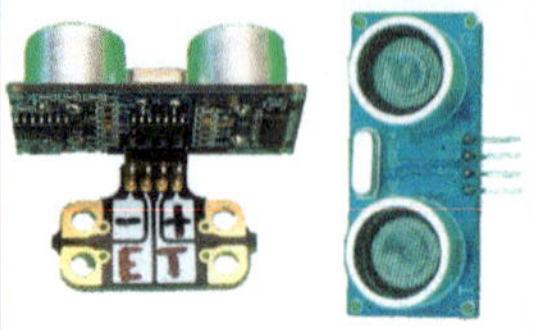		INPUT A, B, C OR D	INPUTS 0-400 These are cm
PIR Movement Sensor			INPUT A, B, C OR D	INPUTS HI (Motion detected) or LO (Motion not detected)
LDR Light Dependent Resistor	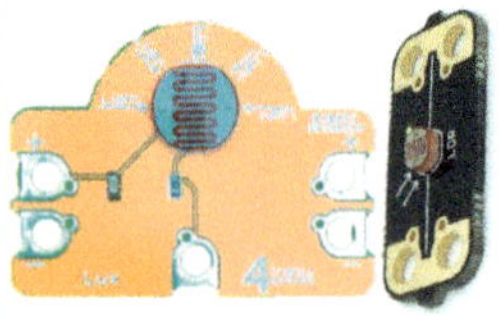	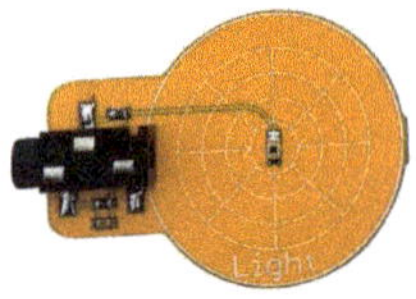	INPUT A, B, C OR D	INPUTS 0-255
Push Button	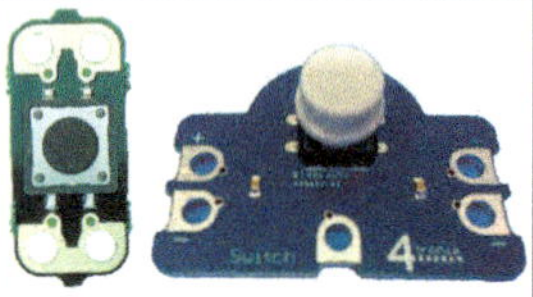		INPUT A, B, C OR D	INPUTS HI (Pressed) or LO (Not Pressed)
Toggle Switch			INPUT A, B, C OR D	INPUTS HI (Connection made or LO Connection not made)
Dial or Slider	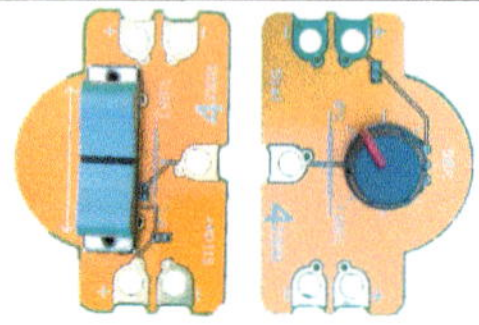	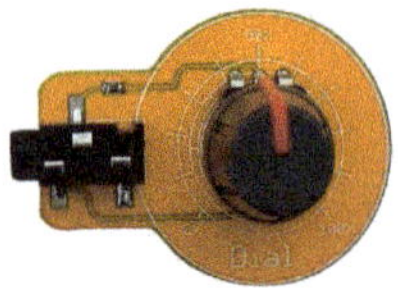	INPUT A, B, C OR D	INPUTS 0-100
Close Proximity Sensor	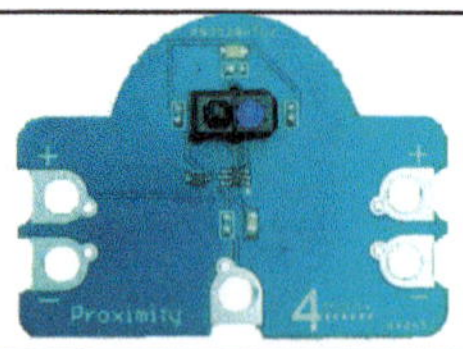		INPUT A, B, C OR D	INPUTS HI OR LO
Accelerometer X, Y, Z	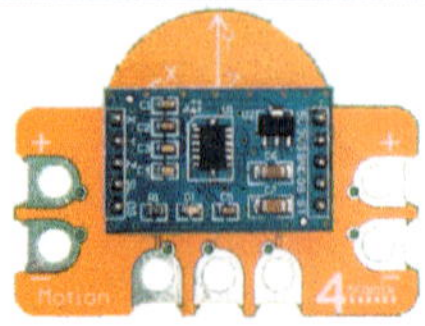		INPUT A, B, C OR D	INPUTS 0-255 ON EACH AXIS X Y & Z
Touch Sensor		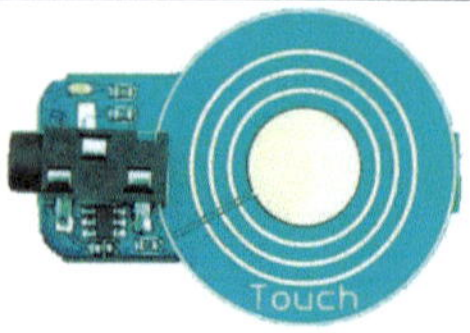	INPUT A, B, C OR D	INPUTS HI OR LO

MLT3

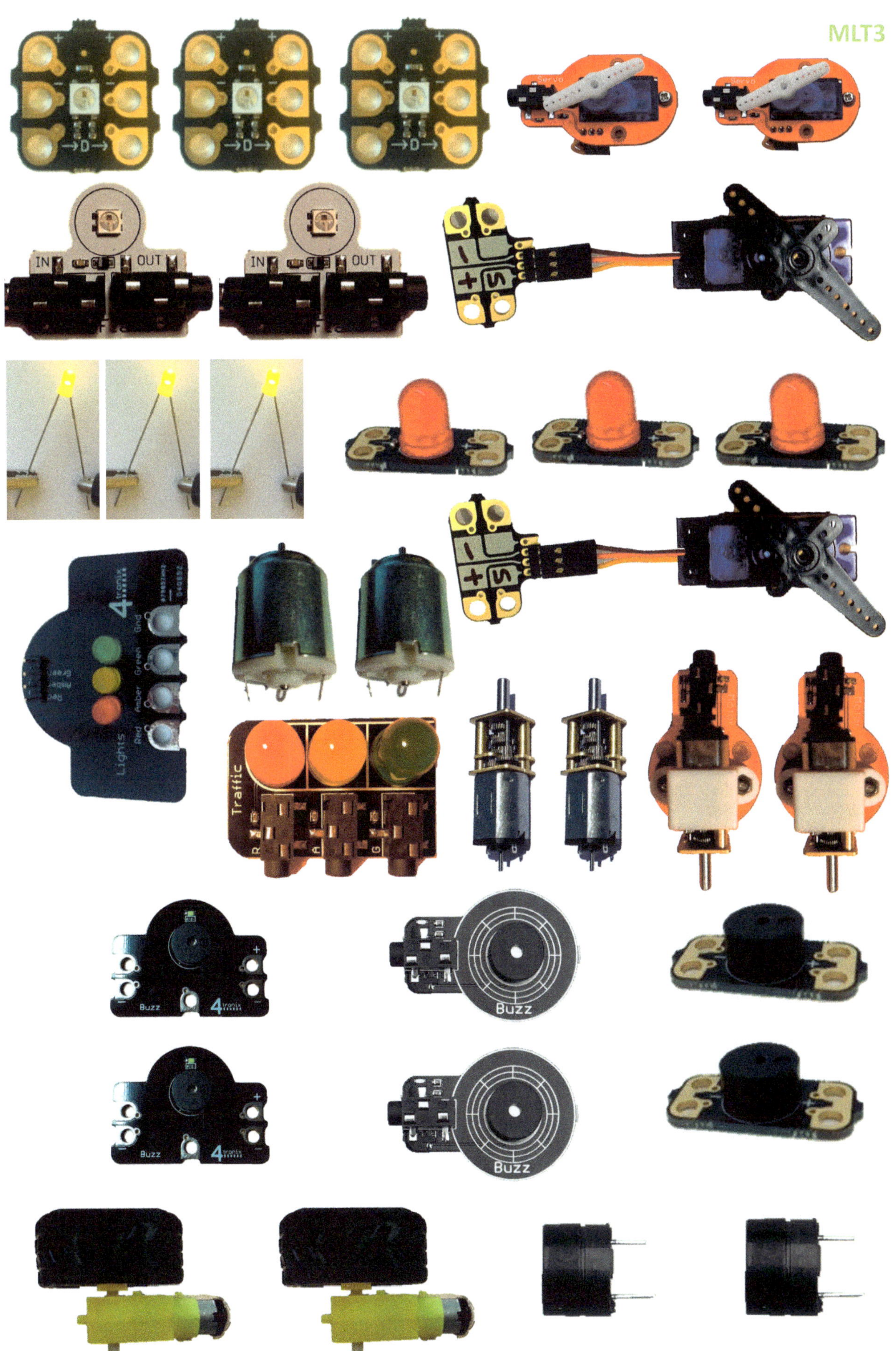
IN
OUT
IN
OUT
Lights
Red
Amber
Green
Gnd
Traffic
R
A
G
Buzz
Buzz
Buzz
Buzz

MLT4

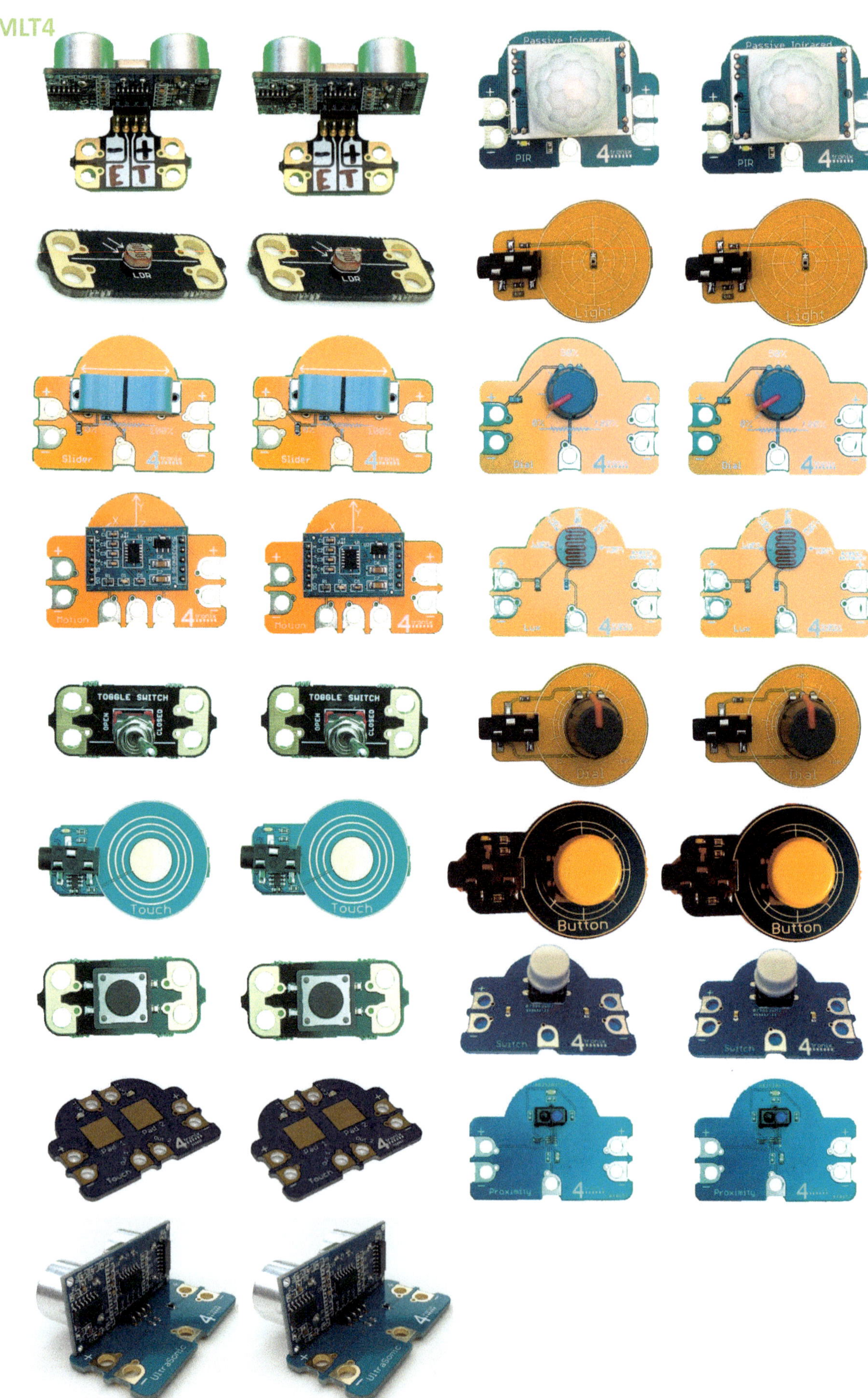

Name ____________________________ Class ___________ Maker Lab 2 MLT5

Planning my Maker Lab Two project.

Big idea 1	Big idea 2	Big idea 3

What input(s) will trigger what output(s)?

What will the input(s) input? (number range/HI or LO) If it inputs a number, what is the range for that number?

At which point(s) (number/HI/LO/>/</all the time) will an output be triggered?

What will the outputs do when they are triggered? How long will the outputs stay on for?

What will you call your variable, to pass information from the input to the output, if you have one?

PORTS	DEVICE	IN/OUTPUT	TYPE INPUT (HI/LO/NUM)
A			
B			
C			
D			
MOTOR 1			
MOTOR 2			

Which parts of your project can be tested separately?

(eg I can test my motor runs before linking it to a sensor.)

Name ____________________________ Class ___________ Maker Lab 2 MLT5A

Planning my Maker Lab Two project EXAMPLE

Big idea 1	Big idea 2	Big idea 3
Automatic Toy My toy car will go forward until it detects something in front of it. It will then back off and turn either right or left. It will then drive away until it detects something else.	Other big idea	Other big idea

What input(s) will trigger what output(s)?

A distance sensor will trigger both motors to stop, go backwards and turn right or left.

What will the input(s) input? (number range/HI or LO) If it inputs a number, what is the range for that number?

The distance sensor inputs between 0-400 cm.

At which point(s) (number/HI/LO/>/<) will an output be triggered?

I will try it first to detect less than 50cm to trigger the back and turn sequence. I might need to change this number.

What will the outputs do when they are triggered?

Stop both motors. Run motor backwards for 1 second, one motor turns off the other runs to turn the toy. Will try and make which direction the toy turns random.

What will you call your variable, to pass information from the input to the output, if you have one?

Motion variable

PORTS	DEVICE	IN/OUTPUT	TYPE INPUT (HI/LO/NUM)
A	Distance Sensor Trigger	input	0-400 cm
B	Distance Sensor echo	input	0-400 cm
C			
D			
MOTOR 1	Motor	output	0-100%
MOTOR 2	Motor	output	0-100%

Which parts of your project can be tested separately?

(eg I can test that my motor runs before linking it to a sensor.)

I will test both motors to see if they run without the distance sensor first.

I will build the back and turn sequence first before linking it to the distance sensor.

Name ______________________ Class __________

MLT6

Maker Lab Two Wiring Diagram

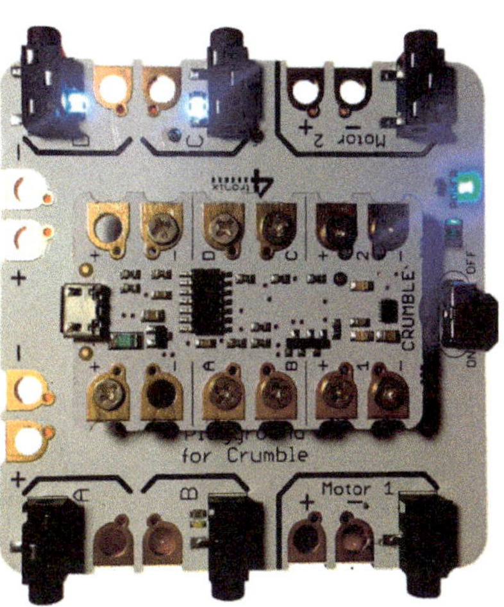

Draw your devices and the wires that connect them.

Name ______________________________ Class ____________ MLT7

Maker Lab Two Wiring Diagram

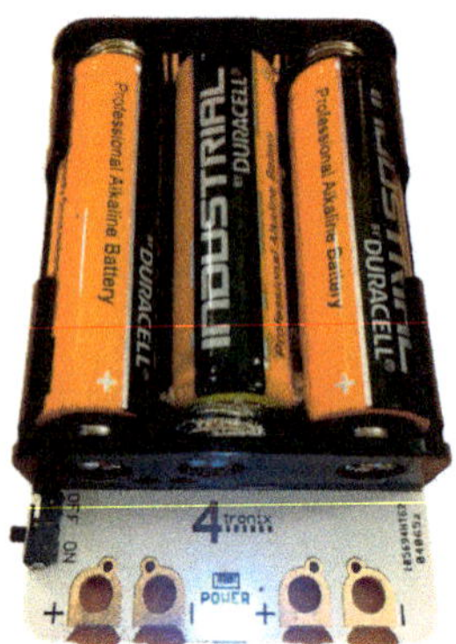

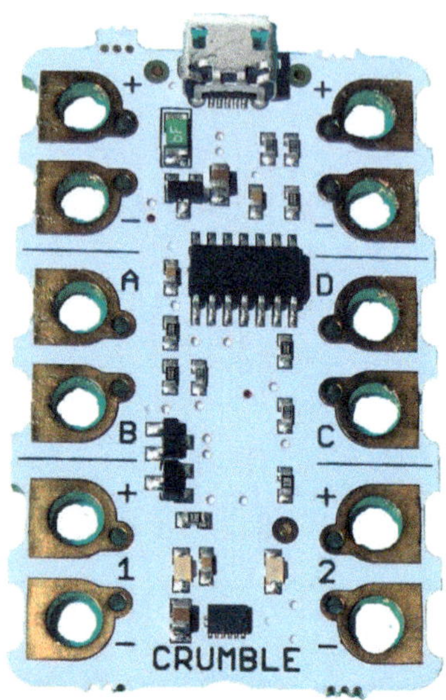

Draw your devices and the wires that connect them.

Temperature

Work in groups of three

MLT8

One person is the temperature sensor **Input** who gives information (temp cards) that goes into the variable.

One person is the **variable** who holds the temperature information given to it by the sensor and says the number.

One person is the **Program** and does what is in the program (holds this code sheet).

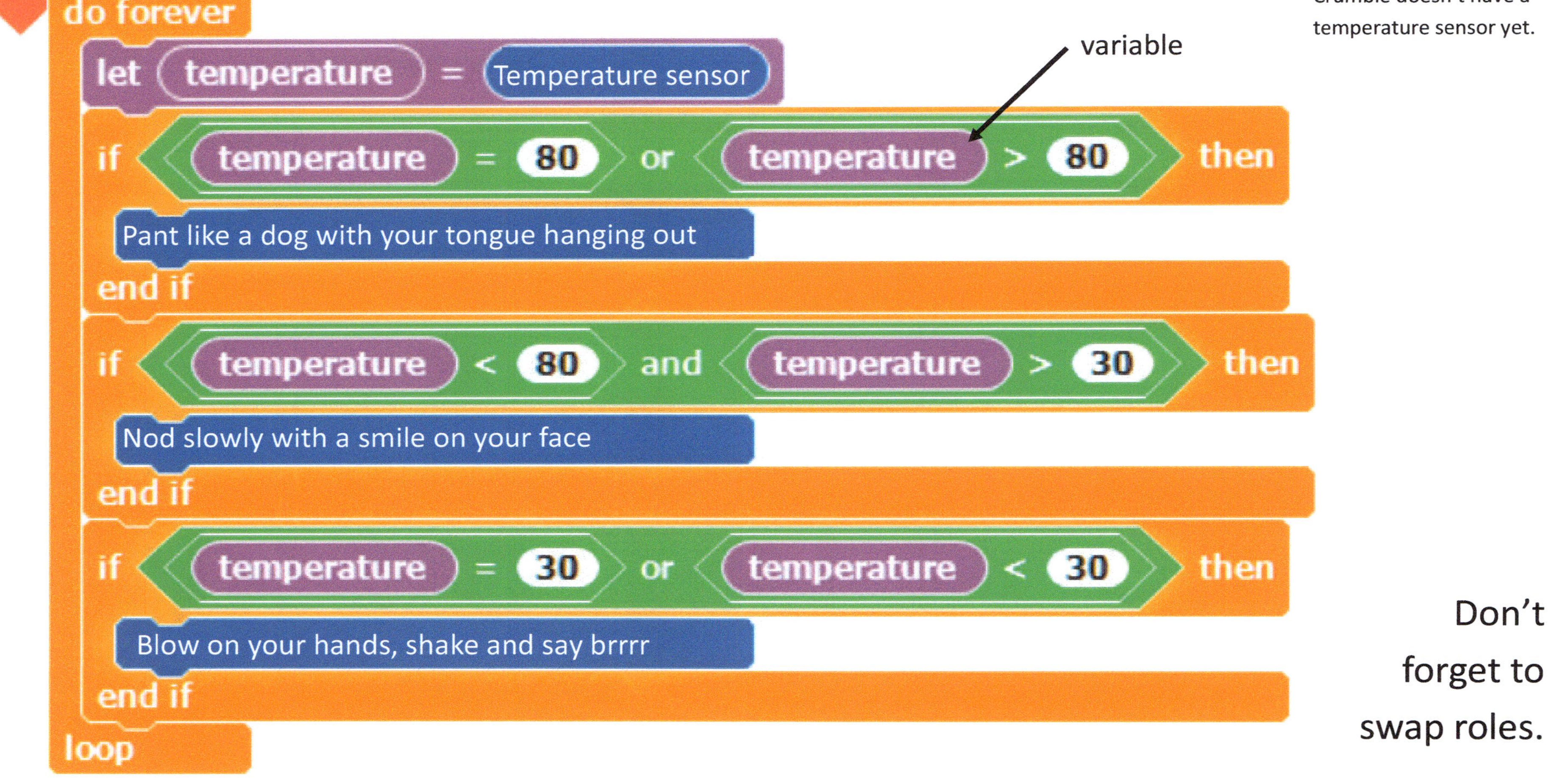

program start
do forever
let temperature = Temperature sensor
if temperature = 80 or temperature > 80 then
Pant like a dog with your tongue hanging out
end if
if temperature < 80 and temperature > 30 then
Nod slowly with a smile on your face
end if
if temperature = 30 or temperature < 30 then
Blow on your hands, shake and say brrrr
end if
loop
variable

Crumble doesn't have a temperature sensor yet.

Don't forget to swap roles.

Temperature Cards to go with MLT8

14	83	31	52	72
05	99	29	43	11

Slider

Work in groups of three

One person is the slider **Input.**

Place 0-1-2-3-4 cards on the floor in a row. Stand next to a number to be the slider stick.

One person is the **variable** who says the slider number information.

One person is the **Program** and does what is in the program (Holds this code card).

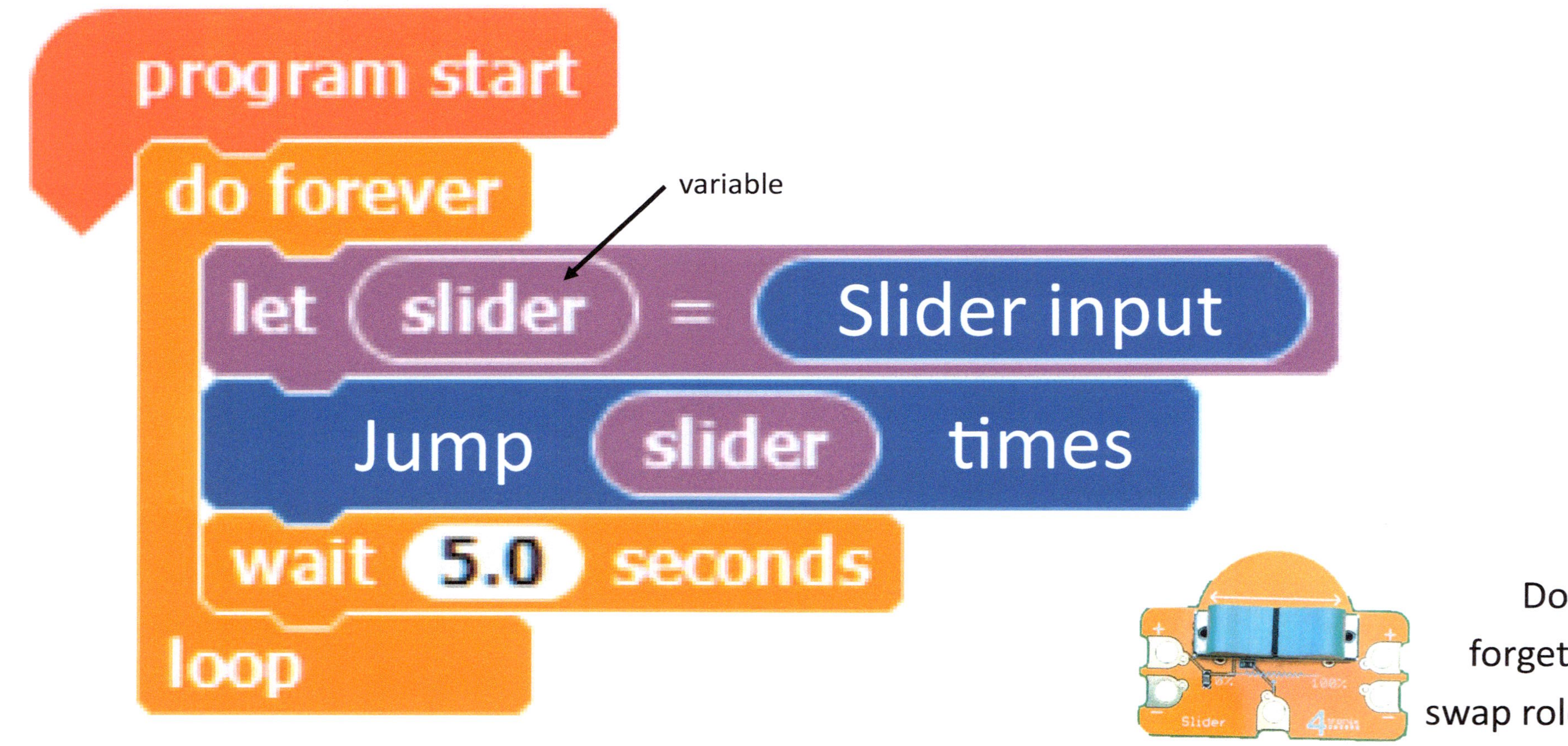
program start
do forever
variable
let slider = Slider input
Jump slider times
wait 5.0 seconds
loop
Slider

Don't forget to swap roles.

MLT10

Dial

Work in groups of three

One person is the dial **Input.**

Place the 0-1-2-3-4 cards on floor in an arc. Point to one number like a dial hand.

One person is the **variable** *(called dial)* who says the dial number pointed at.

One person is the **Program** and does what is in the program (holds this code).

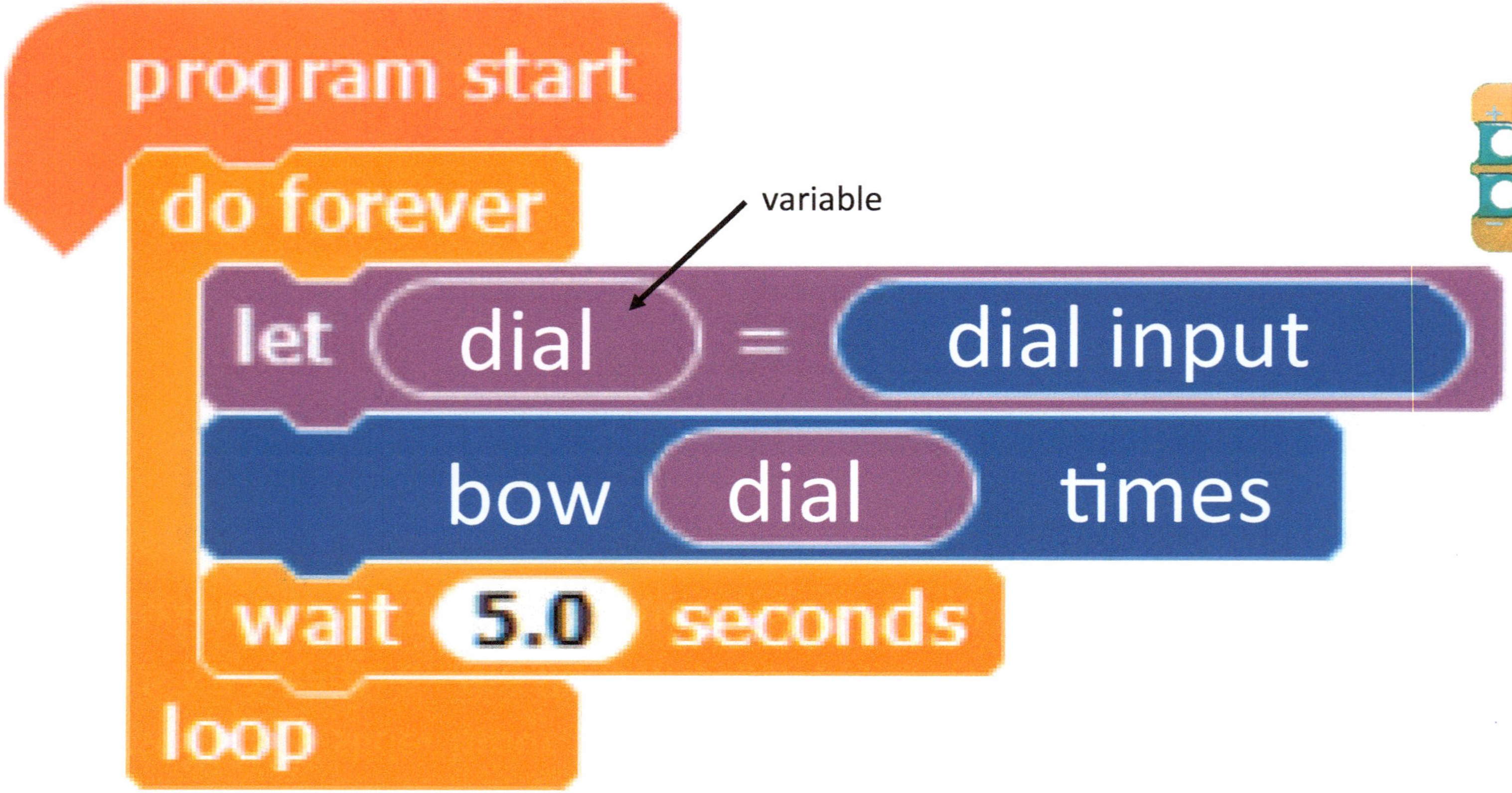

```
program start
  do forever
    let dial = dial input
    bow dial times
    wait 5.0 seconds
  loop
```

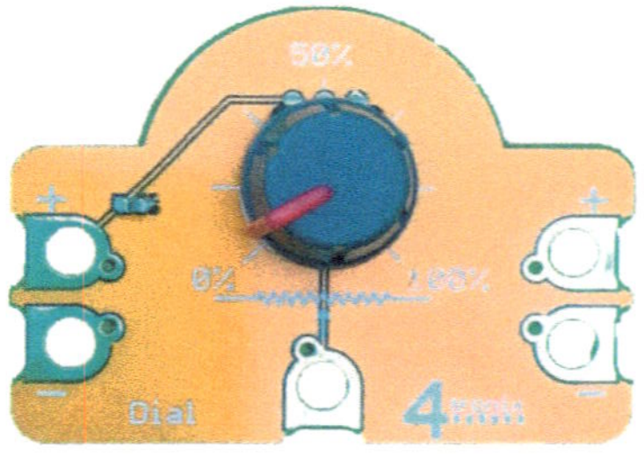

variable

Don't forget to swap roles

Slider & Dial Cards to go with MLT9 & MLT10

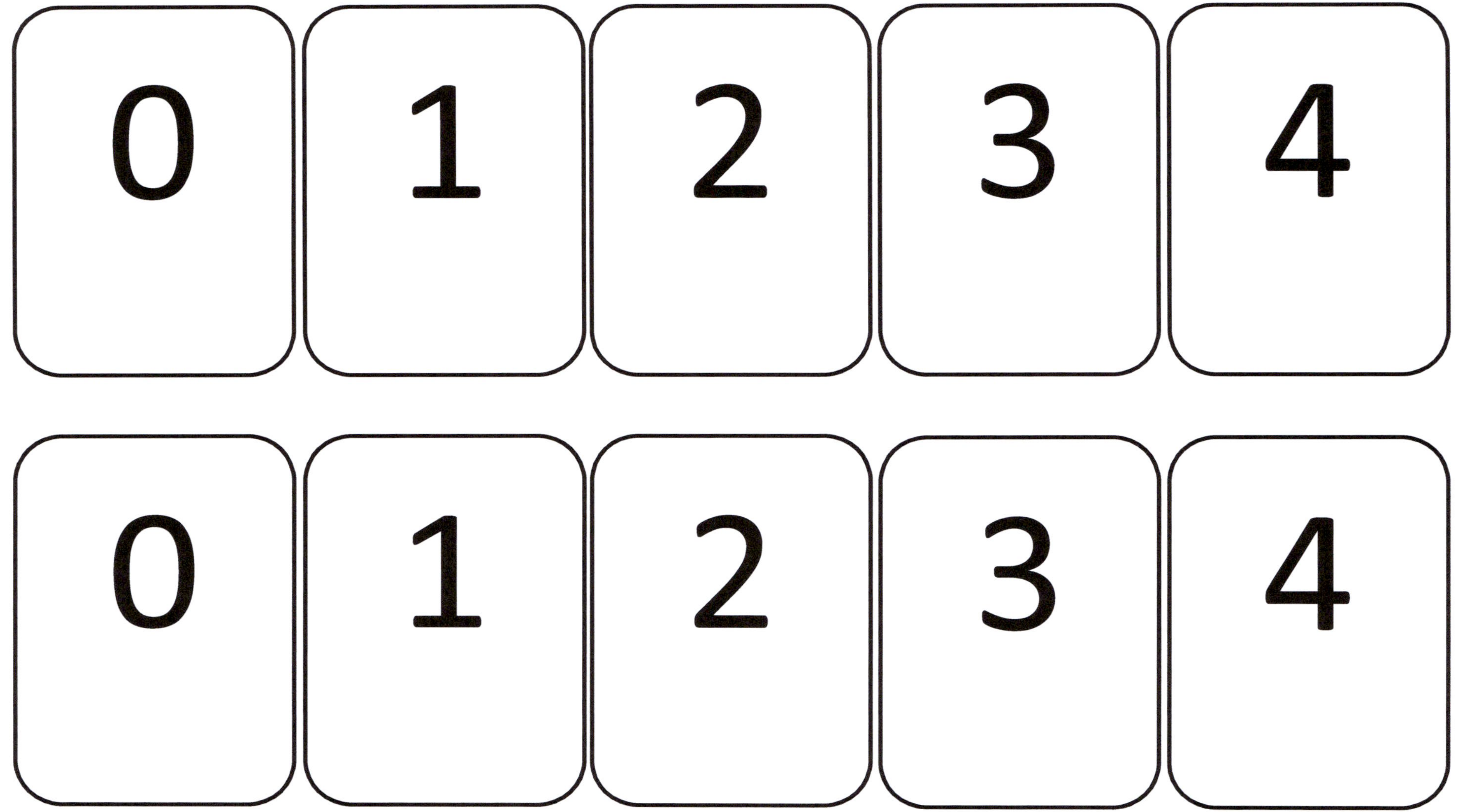

Distance

Work in groups of three

One person is the distance sensor **Input.**

Place the 0-1-2-3-4 cards on floor in a line. Move up and down cards slowly detecting distance.

One person is the **variable** *(called distance)* who says the distance sensor information.

One person is the **Program** and does what is in the program (holds this code).

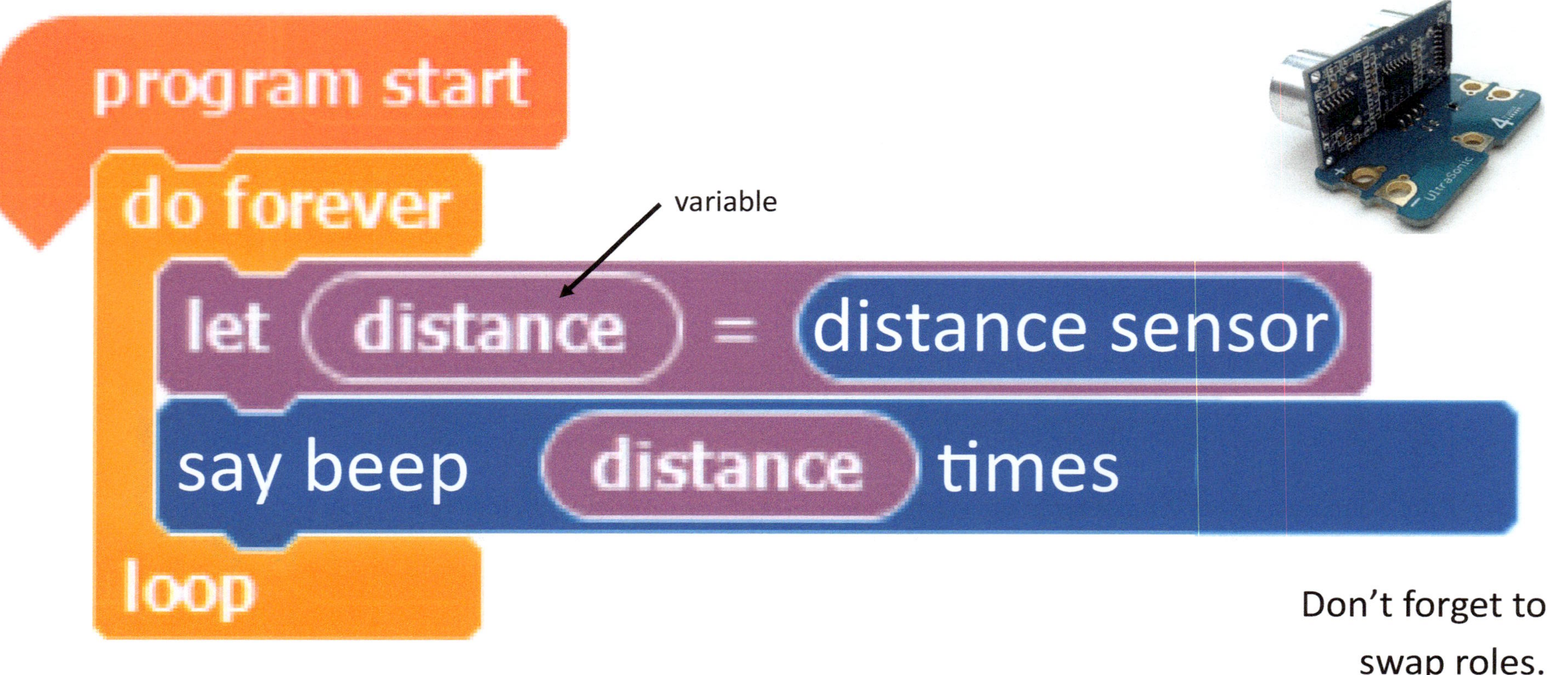
program start
do forever
variable
let distance = distance sensor
say beep distance times
loop
Ultrasonic

Don't forget to swap roles.

Distance 2

Work in groups of three

One person is the distance sensor **Input.**

Place the 0-1-2-3-4 cards on floor in a line. Move up and down cards slowly detecting distance.

One person is the **variable** *(called distance)* who says the distance sensor information.

One person is the **Program** and does what is in the program (holds this code).

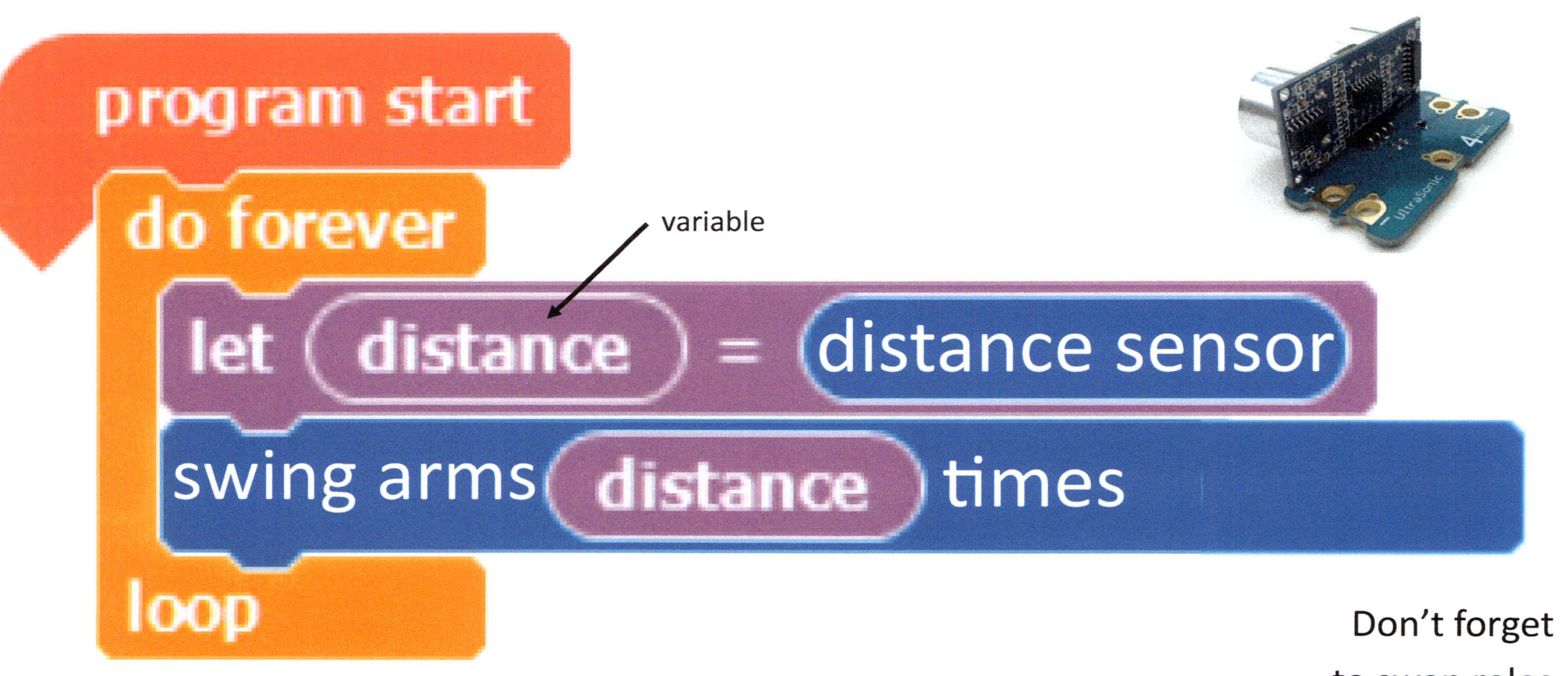
program start
do forever
variable
let distance = distance sensor
swing arms distance times
loop
UltraSonic

Don't forget to swap roles

Distance Sensor Cards to go with MLT11 & MLT12

0	1	2	3	4
0	1	2	3	4

Tilt Sensor

Work in groups of three

One person is the tilt sensor **Input** (attached to X axis)

Place the 98-99-100-101-102 cards on floor in order, move along and stop at a number.

One person is the **variable** *(called tilt)* who says the tilt sensor information from X axis.

One person is the **Program** and does what is in the program (holds code and does actions).

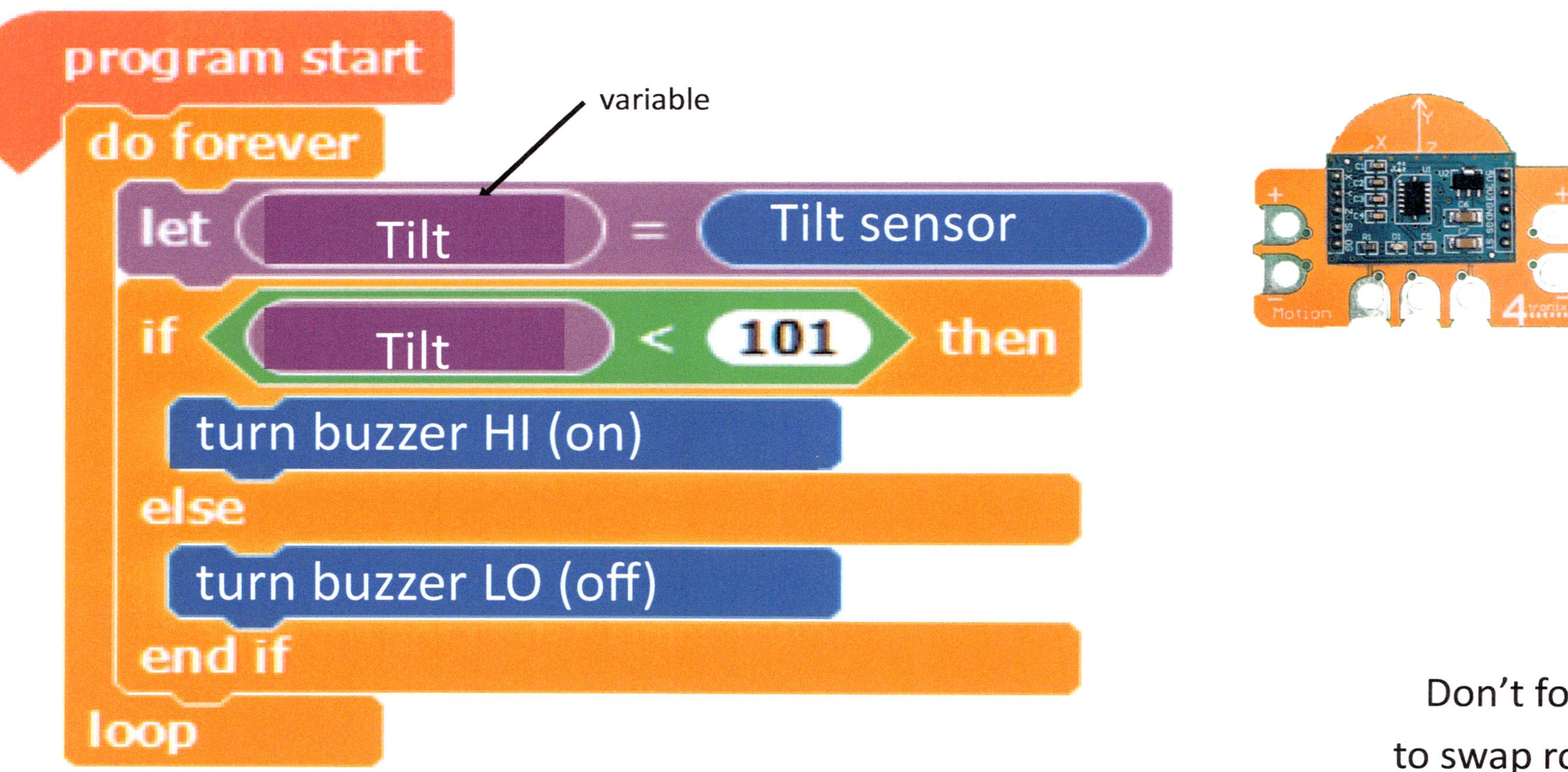
program start
do forever
let Tilt = Tilt sensor
variable
if Tilt < 101 then
turn buzzer HI (on)
else
turn buzzer LO (off)
end if
loop
Motion

Don't forget to swap roles.

Tilt Sensor 2

Work in groups of three

One person is the tilt sensor **Input** (attached to X axis)

Place the 98-99-100-101-102 cards on floor in order, move along and stop at a number.

One person is the **variable** *(called tilt)* who says the tilt sensor information from X axis.

One person is the **Program** and does what is in the program (holds code and does actions).

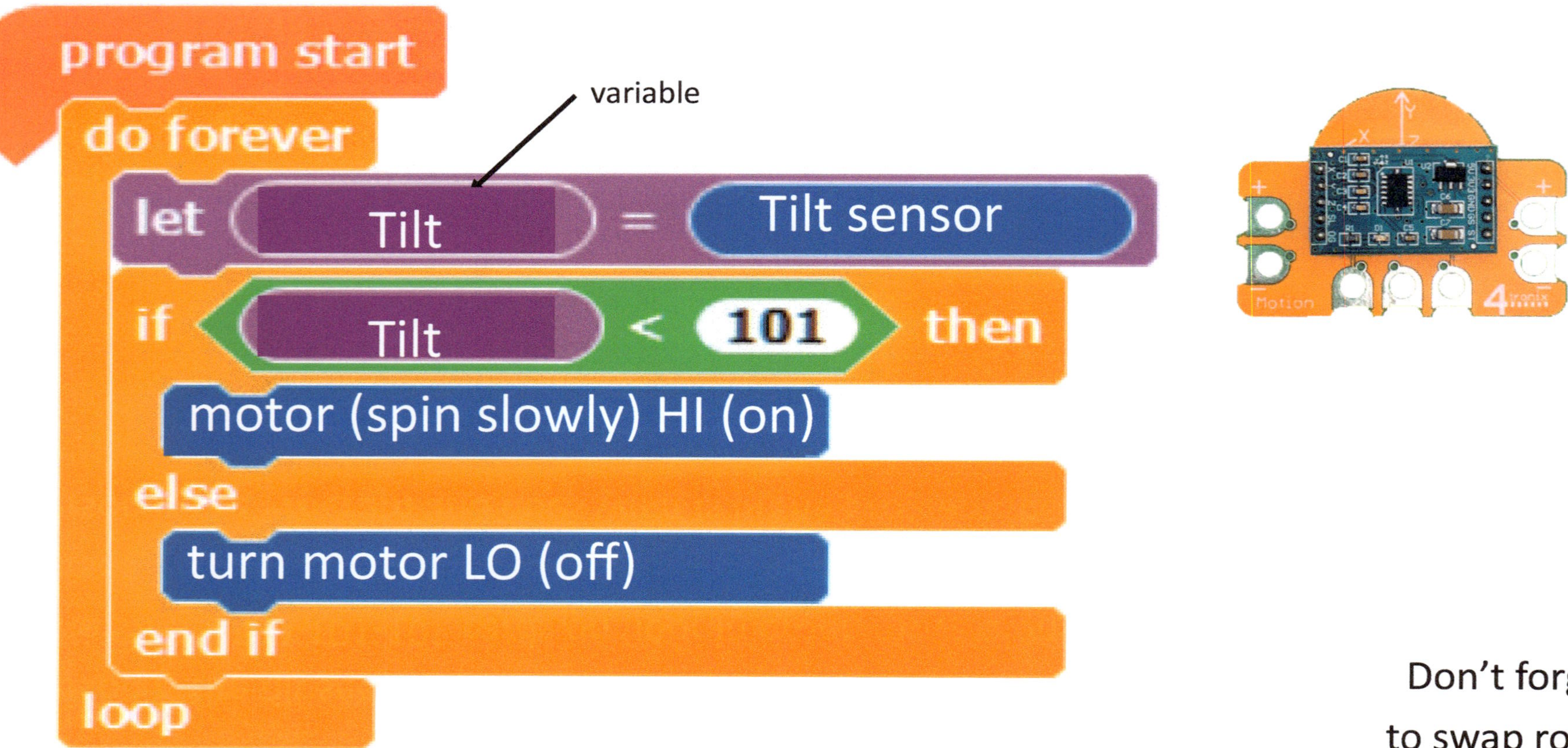
program start
do forever
let
Tilt
=
Tilt sensor
variable
if
Tilt
<
101
then
motor (spin slowly) HI (on)
else
turn motor LO (off)
end if
loop
Motion

Don't forget to swap roles

102	102
101	101
100	100
99	99
98	98

Light Dependant Resistor Work in groups of three MLT15

One person is the LDR **Input.** Place the 98-99-100-101-102 cards on floor in order. Move along range stop at a number.

One person is the **variable** *(called light)* who says the light sensor information

One person is the **Program** and does what is in the program (holds this code and does the actions).

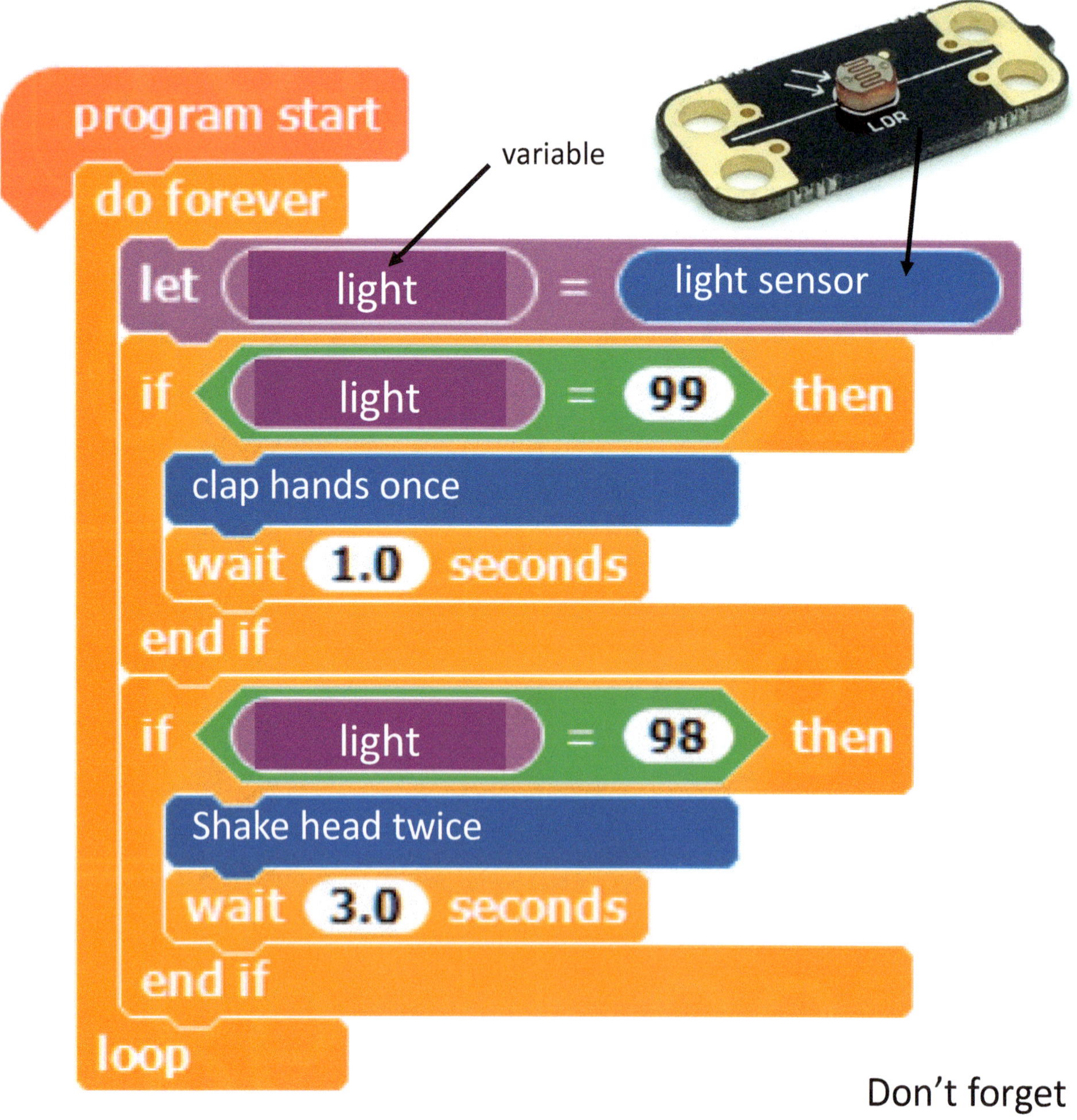
variable
LDR
program start
do forever
let light = light sensor
if light = 99 then
clap hands once
wait 1.0 seconds
end if
if light = 98 then
Shake head twice
wait 3.0 seconds
end if
loop

Don't forget to swap roles.

102

101

100

99

98

Maker Lab Two Assessment Sheet

Name ____________ Group ______

MLT16

I did this well ☺

I did this ok or I did this a little 😐

I tried this but it didn't work or I didn't do this at all ☹

I thought of some big ideas.	
I planned my idea in detail.	
I drew an accurate wiring diagram.	
I wired up my Crumble and accessories.	
I fixed any part of the wiring that wasn't working.	
I programmed my idea independently.	
I tested my idea to see if it worked.	
I added something new after I had got my initial idea working.	
I debugged a part of my program.	

Sticker	I got this sticker for
Sticker	I got this sticker for
Sticker	I got this sticker for

Maker Lab One Assessment Sheet Name ______ Group ______

MLT17 B = Where you are **before** the project A = Where you are **after** the project		I don't understand what it is	I know what it is but don't	I do it a little.	I do it a lot.	I do it a lot and can explain how.
1	I can evaluate my solutions against set criteria.					
2	I can design criteria to evaluate my creations.					
3	I can contribute useful ideas to a partner or group.					
4	I can encourage others to share their ideas.					
5	I lead using all the people talent in my group.					
6	I learn from setbacks and don't let them put me off.					
7	I can persevere even if the solution is not obvious.					
8	I look for a range of solutions to the same problem.					
9	I look for how a project can be extended.					
10	I can break complex problems into parts.					
11	I can concentrate on the most important part of a problem.					
12	I can identify patterns in problems & solutions.					
13	I can adapt existing ideas to solve new problems.					
14	I make predictions about what will happen.					
15	I experiment through predicting, making, testing & debugging.					
16	I can develop, test and debug until a product is refined.					

13. Expanding the Design & Technology Elements

Chapter Aim

This chapter aims to provide planning documents that can be used to extend the design and technology elements of many of the projects.

Sheets Described

DT1 & DT2

These link to **NCD1A** and **NCD2A** which are part of the design section of the Design and Technology National Curriculum in England outlined in chapter one. Pupils are asked to draw a design in detail and label features. Teachers might need to remind pupils of the questions at the bottom of both sheets. Sheet DT2 may also need an explanation of what innovative means.

DT3 & DT4

These link to parts of **NCD1B** and **NCD2B** and asks pupils to sketch possible design ideas. These could be used as part of a generating design ideas session before pupils use sheet DT1, DT2 or DT5 to expand the idea in detail. Sheet DT4 has the added requirement to choose one of the sketch designs and label it.

DT5

These link to **NCD1A** and **NCD2A**. Pupils are asked to draw a surface design in detail and label features on a box net.

Name ____________________________ Class ____________ DT1

My Design

Draw your own design in the centre to hold your wiring. Label the parts and explain how your design works, who it is for and why the user will find it appealing.

Name ______________________ Class __________ DT2

My Design

Draw your own design in the centre to hold your wiring. Draw boxes around the edges to label parts and explain how your design works, who it is for, why the user will find it appealing and how it is innovative?

Name ____________________________ Class ____________ **DT3**

My Design Ideas

Sketch a few design ideas. Don't take too long on any one idea. Don't worry about drawing four ideas, sketch as many as you can in the time.

Name ______________________________ Class _____________ DT4

My Design Ideas

Sketch a few design ideas. Don't take too long on any one idea. Don't worry about drawing four ideas, sketch as many as you can in the time. Choose one that you would like to make (tick the box) and label the parts.

Name ______________________________ Class ____________ DT5

My Box Design Idea

side

side | bottom | side

side

top

Draw your design on this box net to show what it will look like on the outside.

Don't forget to show where electrical components will pass through the box or are mounted on the outside.

Add labels to explain features and identify components.

14. Crumble Educators

Overview

In my travels I have met some great educators who use the Crumble. This is a small selection of the best in their own words and where you can access some of their planning and resources.

Peter Gaynord

I am a full time KS2 generalist primary school teacher and also a CAS master teacher. I host the Cambridge primary HUB and do training events for fellow primary school teachers in Computer science. I have over 20 years of experience in industrial software development before I became a primary teacher and am passionate about the relevance of the Computing curriculum. At the launch of the Computing curriculum in 2014, I was made aware that over 80% of primary schools nationally cover their PPA time with sports coaches. This has the implication for Computer Science in primary schools that there are no men in white suits coming to teach it for primary school teachers. Instead it must be delivered by generalist primary school teachers. This challenge has been my focus as a master teacher for several years now by sharing my own planning and knowledge via CAS and at training events. I have supported generalist teachers by utilising supportive technologies such as video and screencasts to provide complete, ready to go units of work broken down into lesson plans, complete with all resources based around Scratch, TTS Probots, Go, BBC Microbit and more recently the wonderfully primary friendly Redfern Crumble controller.

I have undertaken many projects at my after school programming and electronics club involving the Crumble and automated buggies such as the *Lollibot.*

https://www.youtube.com/edit?o=U&video_id=u8a8yPn8E5s

I especially relish the challenge to plan a unit of work for my colleagues to fit our school's topic based curriculum and am constantly surprised at how many opportunities there are to include physical computing. Below are a couple of those units based around the crumble controller.

The first was with a Year 3/4 topic called *Sunny Hunny.* I made the connection of fairground rides and the seaside town of Hunstanton and planned this unit of work to utilise the schools existing stock of standard non-geared DT motors with some sparkles to make programmable fairground rides.

https://community.computingatschool.org.uk/resources/4759

The second was a Year 5/6topic about India for which I planned a unit of work that culminates in the creation of a river Ganges pollution warning system using an LDR, some sparkles and a buzzer.

https://community.computingatschool.org.uk/resources/5229

I'm always keen to support where I can so please ask for help if needed:

Peter.gaynord@computingatschool.org.co.uk

Peter is based near Oxford

Cobie Van de Ven

For over 35 years I worked as a teacher in primary education;
15 years on Jenaplan schools with children in a group of 6-10 years old.
10 years in a primary school with a classroom system.
10 years teaching ICT to all kids and colleagues in my school and maintaining the website and all equipment.
Cutbacks inspired me to leave my school to start my own company: Digitaal Laboratorium with workshops in Media literacy, Animation, Coding, Website building, and 3D printing at schools, festivals and special events.
My motto: You have really learned something when you can explain it to another person.
I love storytelling and projects with a mixture of analogue and digital elements.
My favourite books on education are:
"Lifelong kindergarten" Mitchel Resnick
"An ethic of Excellence" Ron Berger

I think the Crumble is great, because it can be programmed with a special version of Scratch. So Dutch kids can combine telling their stories with their Crumble things coded in their own language.

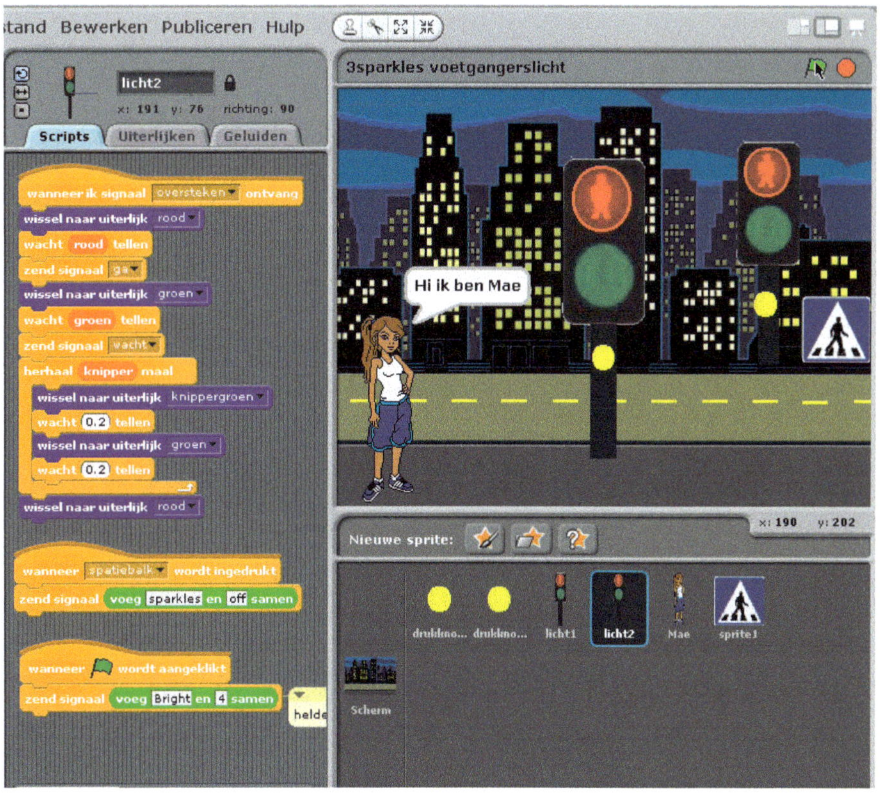

We made a lot of things with the Crumble:
Sending messages with morse from a ship to a rescue helicopter.
Disco lights with music loops.
Led lights with switches made out of copper tape, paper, cotter pins and paperclips.

Some projects are documented with movies on youtube

How to make a Fancar:

https://www.youtube.com/watch?v=K9enBbN1RKc

Later on we used Scratch with Makey Makey to create a start and finish point with which we measure the speed of the cars.

Halloween: Sparkles in a pumpkin and a weirdo soundscape:

https://www.youtube.com/watch?v=VsPDfYud3f8

You can follow Cobie on Twitter as @hetdigilab

You can try out Crumble connected to Scratch using resources created by the excellent Simon Walters @cymplecy

http://simplesi.net/scratchcrumble/

If you want the Crumble programming language translated into your home language contact Joseph Birks who created it via the Redfern Electronic website https://redfernelectronics.co.uk/contactus/

Nic Hughes

Nic is a self confessed IT geek. He is a class teacher, Head of Computing at Latymer Prep School, Primary CAS Master Teacher, CAS Hub leader, a Raspberry Pi Certified Educator, a Pi-Top Champion, a Google certified Educator, a Global Minecraft Mentor Ed and works part-time as an educational consultant for 3BM.

He loves to explore the different ways technology can be used to enhance teaching and learning. He is a massive fan of physical computing and robotics and how they can be used to support the teaching of programming.

In the past he worked alongside the education team in the London Borough of Redbridge as a AST for ICT, running training, supporting schools and writing curriculum. He has been lucky enough to speak at a number of conferences over the years about his work with robots, physical computing and the application of Games Based Learning in the classroom. He is eager for as many teachers as possible to learn more about Computing and how to teach it effectively.

Follow him @duck_star on twitter and he has a blog at nicholashughes.blogspot.com.

His Crumble resources can be accessed at

https://drive.google.com/open?id=0B5Y5ujFyRCfWbm1FcEF4dF9JeGc

OR

http://bit.ly/NicHughesCrumbleResources

Mike Cargill

Mike is a self-confessed crumble addict. He realised its potential as a system through which learners can focus on the outcome and improve their coding skills because they want to enhance the appearance/functionality/engagement of their products. His background in civil engineer took him into teaching Design Technology and Engineering in 1995, since then he's taught on the Isle of Wight and East Yorkshire and since 2009 has developed and run regional and national STEM programmes. He launched UK STEM in 2015 to focus full time on STEM education. He lives with his partner near York and spends his time eating (and cooking), walking, cycling and keeping an old Defender road worthy!

His resources can be accessed at

https://www.ukstem.uk/

Dr Jon Chippindall

Dr Jon Chippindall is a primary school teacher at Crumpsall Lane Primary School in Manchester and SEERIH's Engineering Champion at The University of Manchester, where he also runs the computing PGCE. He is a CAS Master Teacher, was an author of the Barefoot Computing resources and regularly runs Crumble training courses with teachers nationwide.

The first video of nine outlining a robot orchestra project.

https://youtu.be/iVrfDEHDTwc

15. Maker Cards

Crumble Playground Single Cable

MC07

- Programmable Light MC01
- Servo Motor MC02
- Dial MC03
- Traffic Lights MC04
- Buzzer MC05
- Push Button MC06
- Geared Motor MC07
- Light Dependant Resistor MC08

MC03

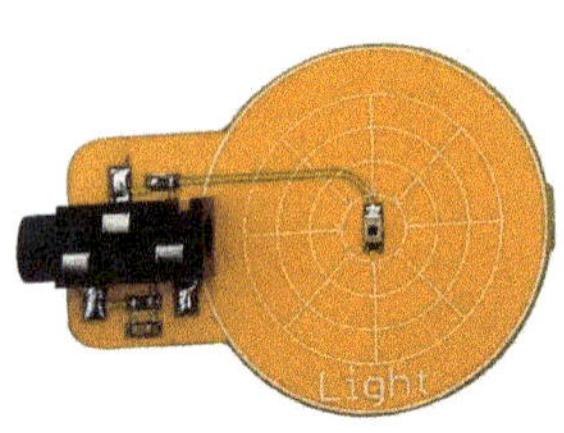

MC08

Crumble Playground Crocodile Cable

- Programmable Light Redfern MC09
- LED Lights MC10
- LED Lights Redfern MC11
- Motor MC12
- Servo Motor 4tronix MC13
- Servo Motor Redfern MC14
- Dial 4tronix MC15
- Slider4tronix MC16
- Traffic Lights 4tronix MC17
- Push Button Redfern MC18
- Push Button 4tronix MC19
- LDR MC20
- LDR 4tronix MC21
- LDR Redfern MC22
- Buzzer 4Tronix MC23
- Buzzer Redfern MC24
- Piezo MC25
- Distance Sensor MC26

MC18

MC16

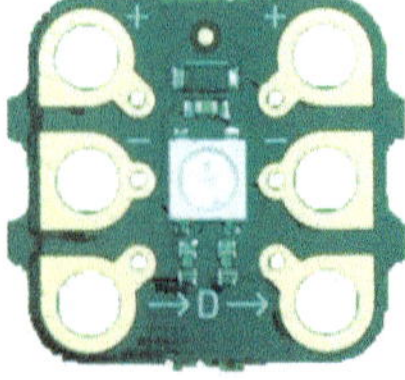

MC09

MC14

- Distance Sensor Redfern MC27
- Distance Sensor 4tronix MC28
- PIR 4tronix MC29
- Number Counter 4tronix MC30
- Tilt Sensor 4tronix MC31
- Close Proximity Sensor 4tronix MC32

MC34

Classic Crumble Maker Cards

- Buzzer 4tronix MC33
- Buzzer Redfern MC34
- Close Proximity Sensor 4tronix MC35
- Dial 4tronix MC36
- Distance Sensor MC37
- Distance Sensor Redfern MC38
- Distance Sensor 4tronix MC39
- Light Dependant Resistor MC40
- Light Dependant Resistor 4tronix MC41
- Light Dependant Resistor Redfern MC42
- LED Light MC43
- LED Light Redfern MC44
- Motor MC45
- Number Counter 4tronix MC46
- Piezo MC47
- PIR Sensor 4tronix MC48
- Programmable Lights Redfern MC49
- Push Button Redfern MC50
- Push Button 4tronix MC51
- Servo Motor 4tronix MC52
- Servo Motor Redfern MC53
- Slider 4tronix MC54
- Tilt Sensor 4tronix MC55
- Traffic Lights 4tronix MC56

MC40

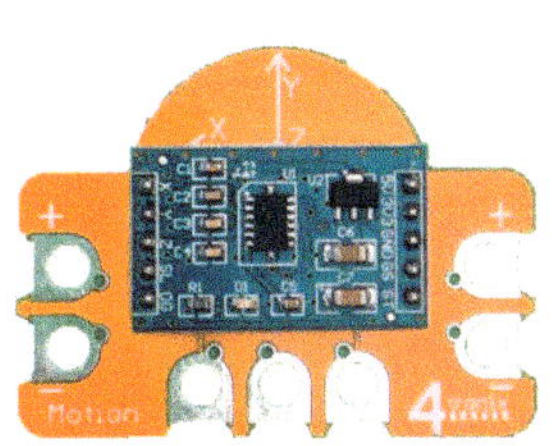

MC31

MC46

MC34

MC51

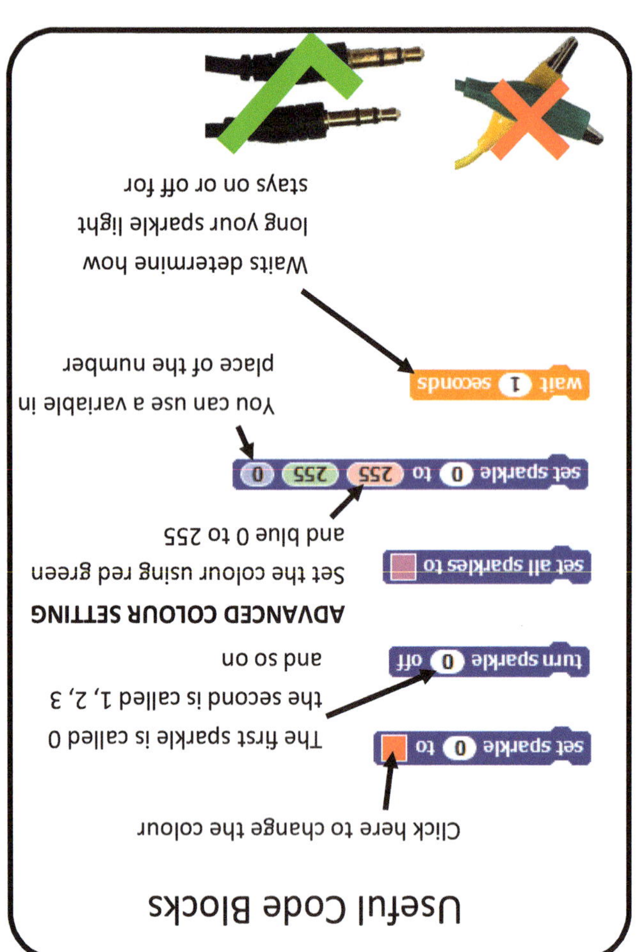

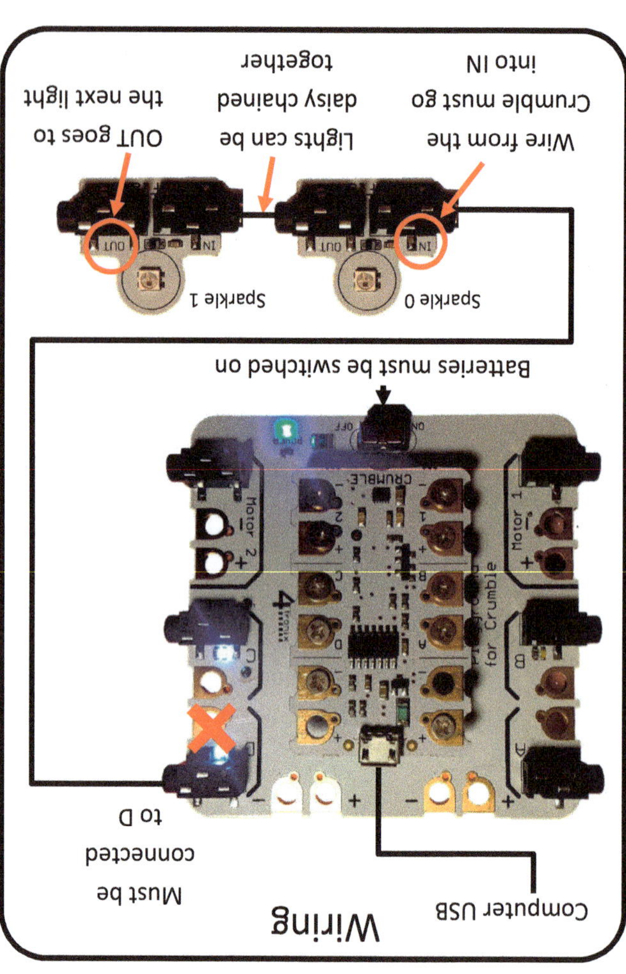

More Information

Lights are outputs. Programmable lights can be very bright. You can reduce this by covering the light with a translucent cover such a piece of white paper.

Up to 36 programmable lights can be daisy chained together.

4Tronix who make this programmable light call it a flame. The Crumble software calls it a Sparkle.

You can program multiple lights on one device with these.

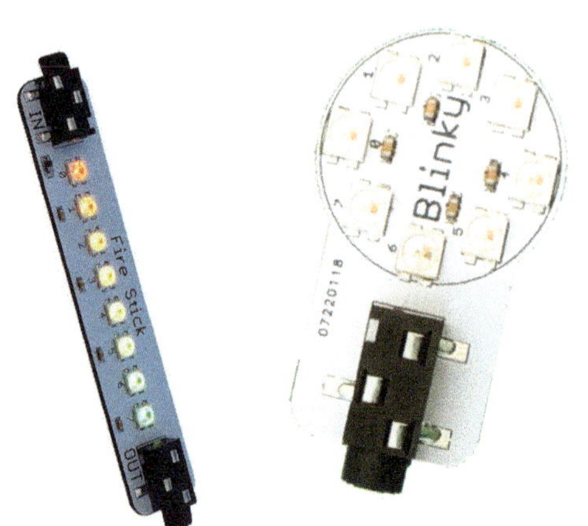

Crumble Playground **Programmable Lights**

MC01

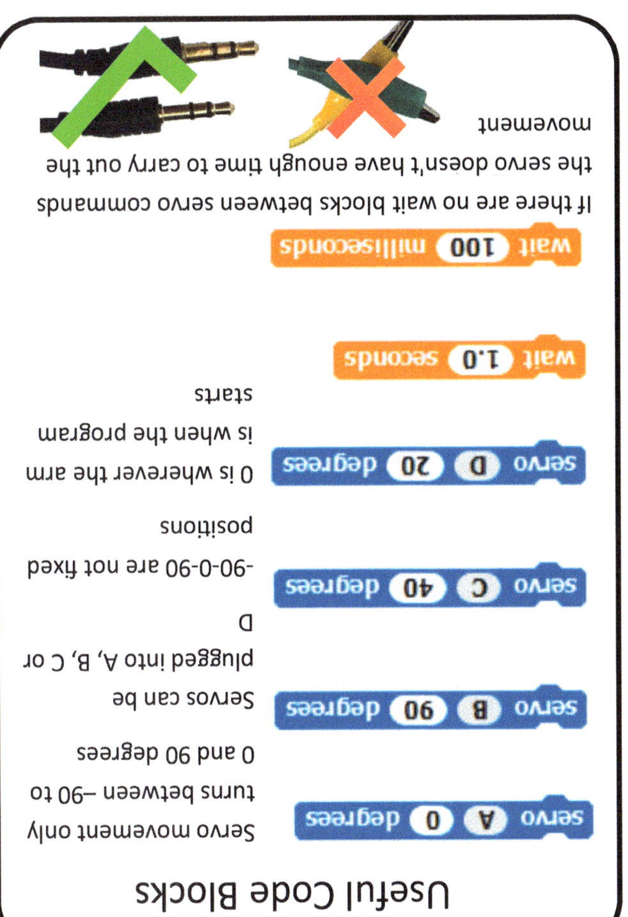
Useful Code Blocks
servo A 0 degrees
Servo movement only turns between −90 to 0 and 90 degrees
servo B 90 degrees
Servos can be plugged into A, B, C or D
servo C 40 degrees
-90-0-90 are not fixed positions
servo D 20 degrees
0 is wherever the arm is when the program starts
wait 1.0 seconds
wait 100 milliseconds
If there are no wait blocks between servo commands the servo doesn't have enough time to carry out the movement

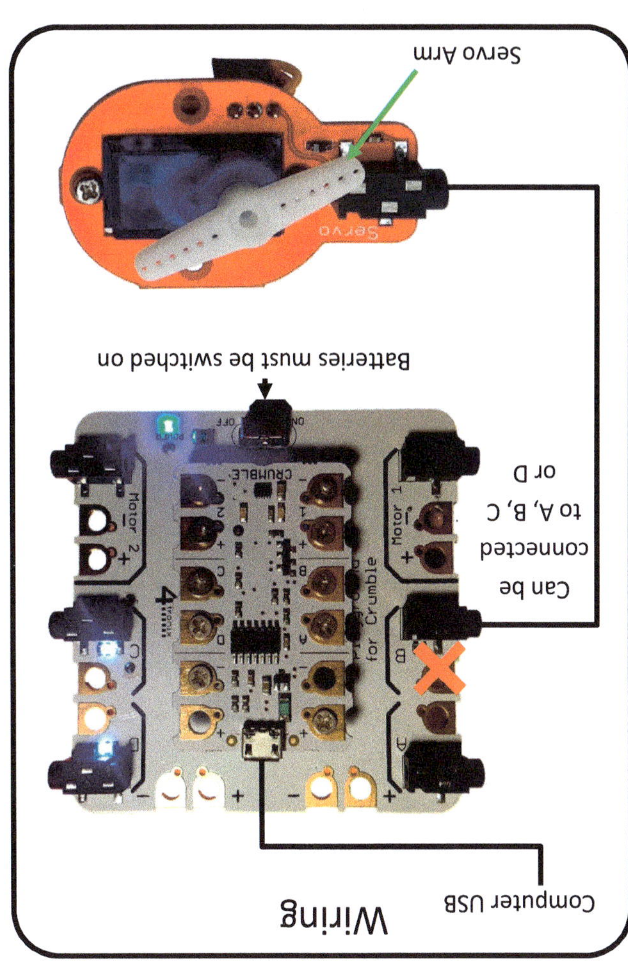
Wiring
Computer USB
Can be connected to A, B, C or D
Batteries must be switched on
Servo Arm

More Information

This sample program would move a servo attached to A from the 0 start position to the 90 degree position and then stop

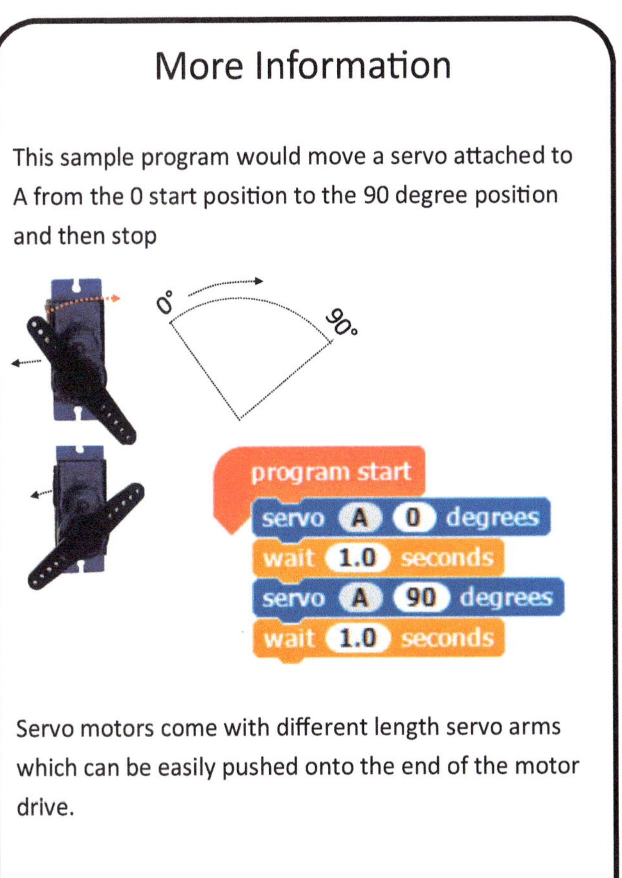
0°
90°
program start
servo A 0 degrees
wait 1.0 seconds
servo A 90 degrees
wait 1.0 seconds

Servo motors come with different length servo arms which can be easily pushed onto the end of the motor drive.

Crumble Playground

Servo / Stepper Motor

MC02

Crumble Playground

Dial

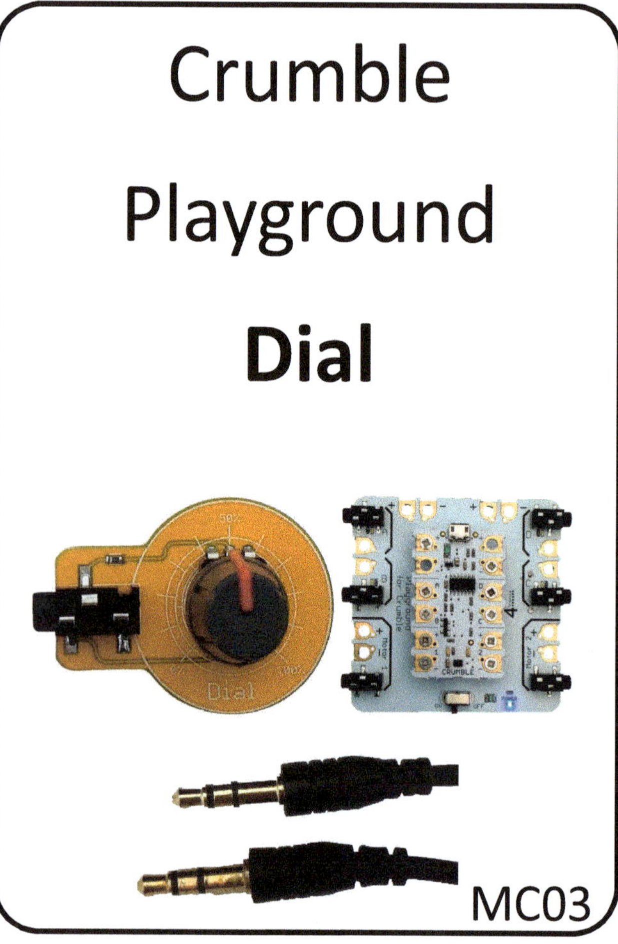

MC03

Wiring

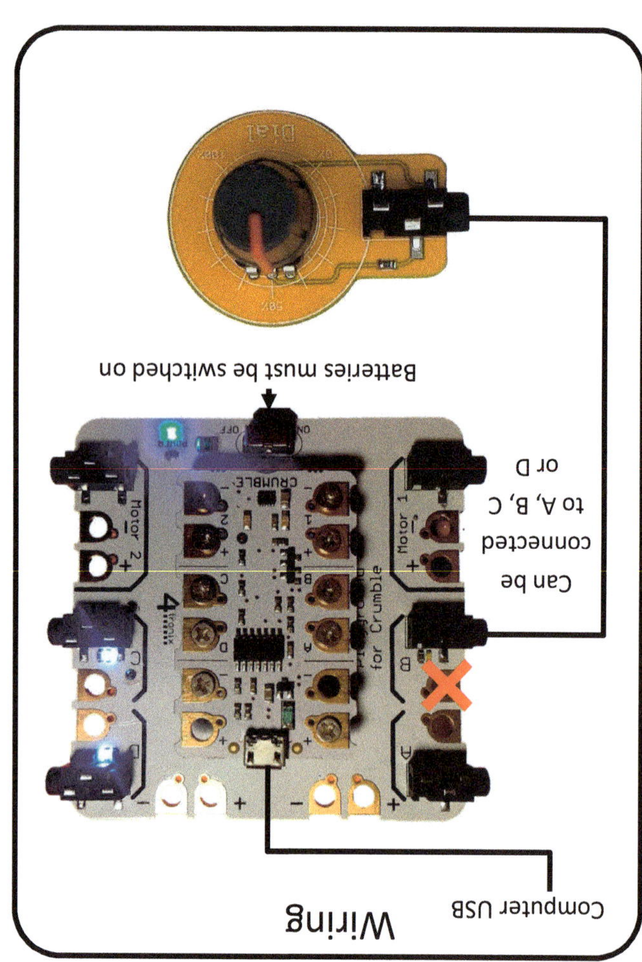

Computer USB
Batteries must be switched on
Can be connected to A, B, C or D

Useful Code Blocks

If you create a variable, you see what is inside it on the Crumble programming screen.

This program transfers the data from the dial (analogue) and puts it inside a variable called dial. It checks repeatedly to see if anything has updated. It is a good program to test to see if the dial is working.

Information is inputted into the Crumble through the analogue block as a number between 0-255. This one shows 0 when the dial is at 0%, 109 at 50% and 220 at 100%.

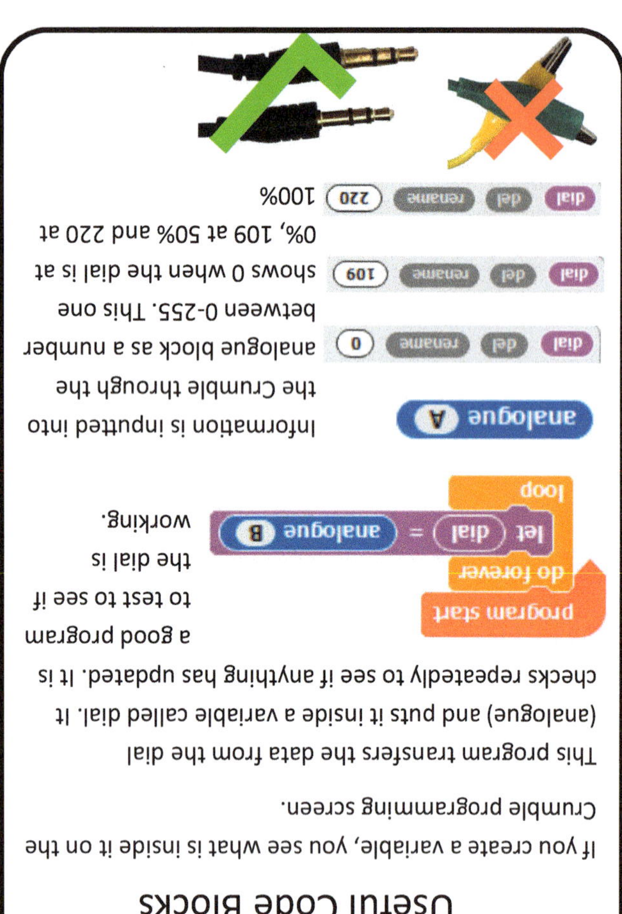

program start
do forever
let dial = analogue B
loop
analogue A
dial del rename 0
dial del rename 109
dial del rename 220

More Information

Dials can be used to adjust the amount of power going into a motor, the colour balance of a programmable light, the tone of a piezo element, The amount of turn a servo moves etc.

It can be used wherever there is a number that could change. Just replace the number with a variable and link the variable to the dial.

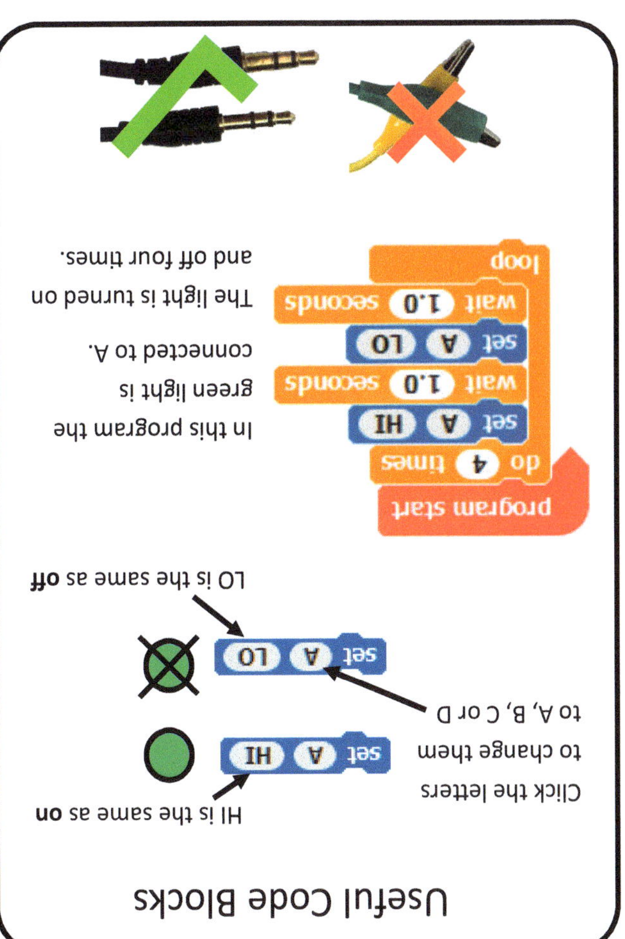
Useful Code Blocks
Click the letters to change them to A, B, C or D
set A HI
HI is the same as **on**
set A LO
LO is the same as **off**
program start
do 4 times
set A HI
wait 1.0 seconds
set A LO
wait 1.0 seconds
loop
In this program the green light is connected to A.
The light is turned on and off four times.

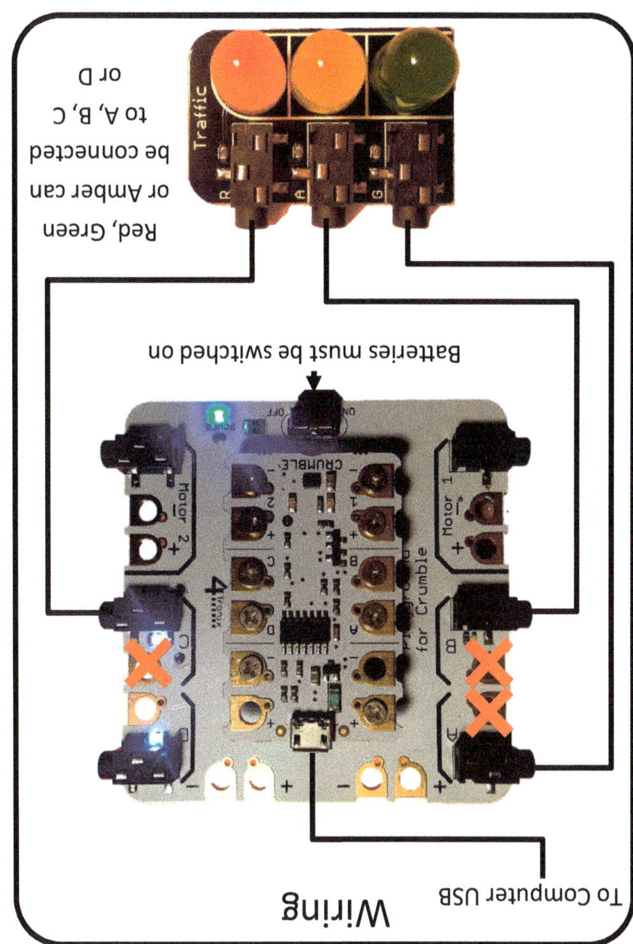
Wiring
To Computer USB
Batteries must be switched on
Red, Green or Amber can be connected to A, B, C or D
Traffic

More Information

LED Traffic lights can be used to program traffic lights or a single LED light on the traffic light can be used to indicate something else.

A green LED could be switched on when the light from an LDR goes above a set number.

Or

A red LED could be turned on when a PIR detects motion.

You don't have to wire every light to use just one.

Crumble Playground

Traffic Light

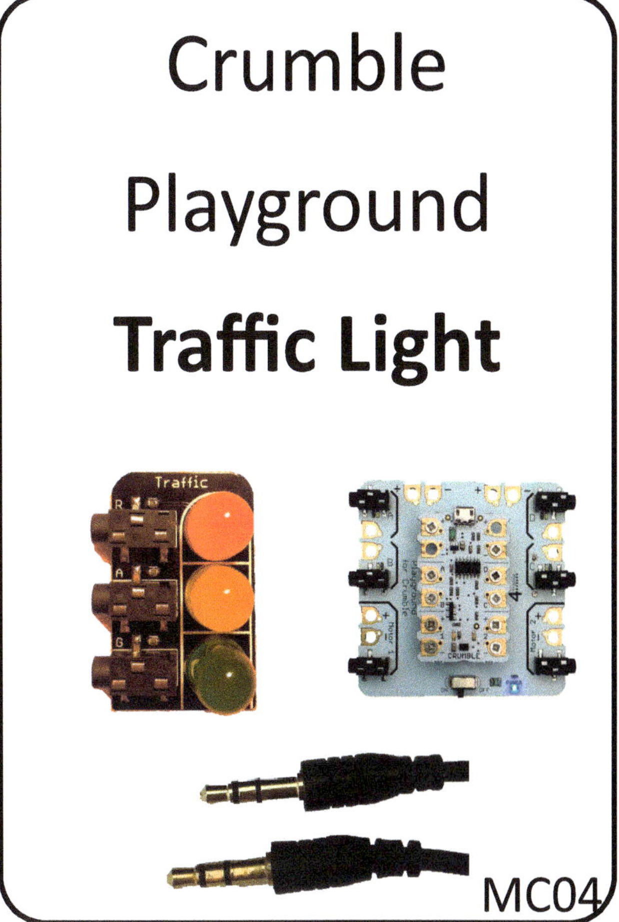
Traffic

MC04

Crumble
Playground
Buzzer
Buzz
MC05

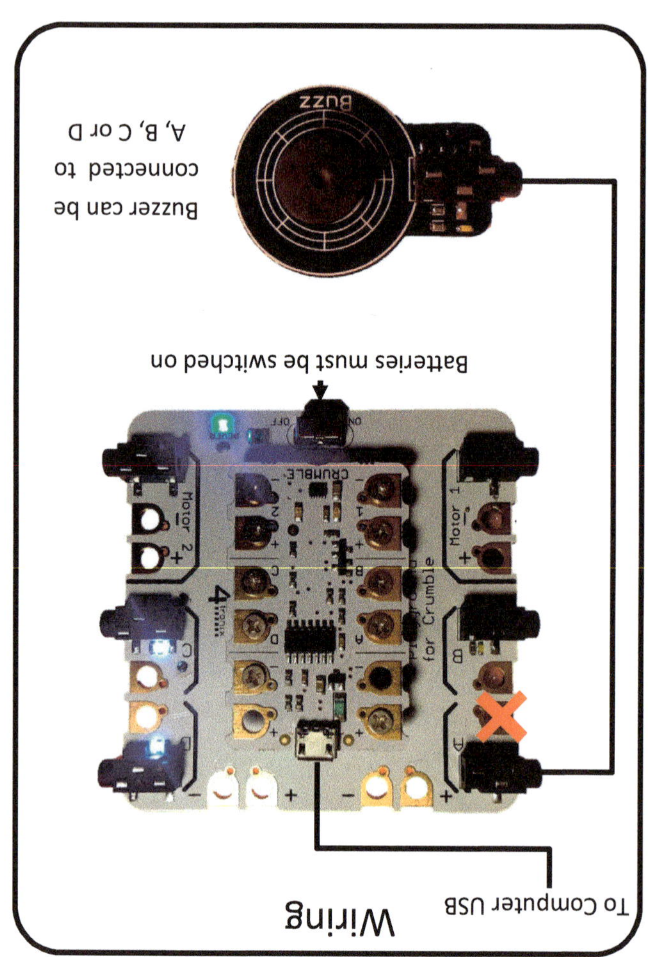
Wiring
To Computer USB
Batteries must be switched on
Buzzer can be
connected to
A, B, C or D
Buzz

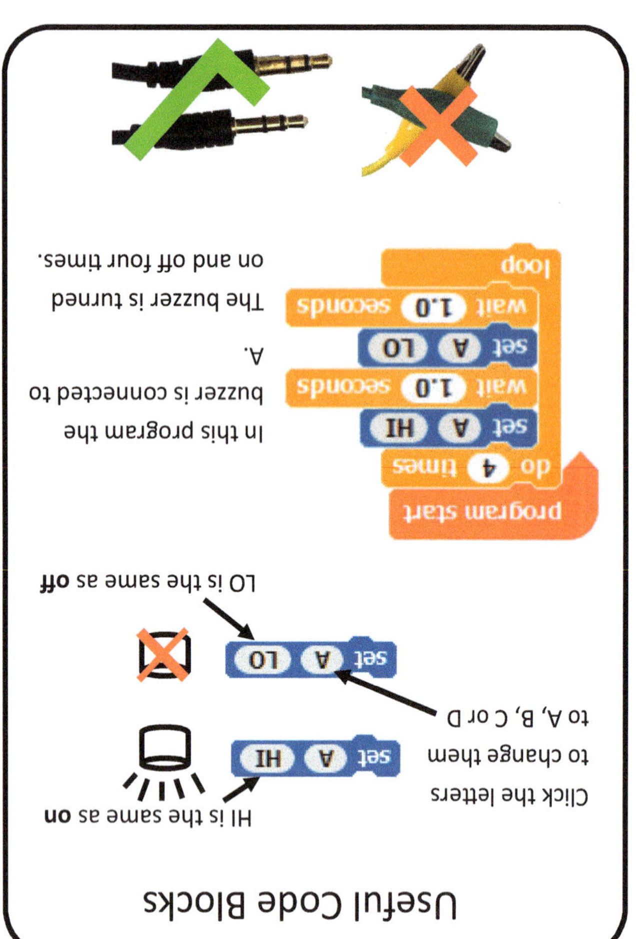
Useful Code Blocks
HI is the same as on
LO is the same as off
set A HI
set A LO
Click the letters
to change them
to A, B, C or D
program start
do 4 times
set A HI
wait 1.0 seconds
set A LO
wait 1.0 seconds
loop
In this program the
buzzer is connected to
A.
The buzzer is turned
on and off four times.

More Information

The part that buzzes on a buzzer is called a piezo. It makes the noise when electricity stretches or compresses the piezoceramic material. Our buzzers are setup for a set voltage of electricity which is why they only make one tone.

Where else can you find piezo buzzers?

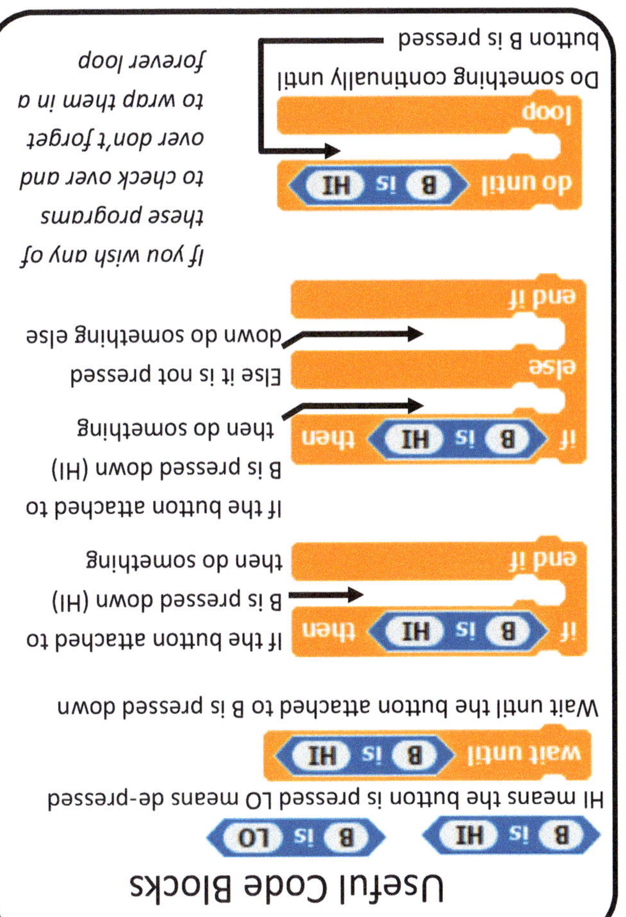
Useful Code Blocks
B is HI
B is LO
HI means the button is pressed LO means de-pressed
wait until B is HI
Wait until the button attached to B is pressed down
if B is HI then
end if
If the button attached to B is pressed down (HI) then do something
if B is HI then
else
end if
If the button attached to B is pressed down (HI) then do something
Else it is not pressed down do something else
do until B is HI
loop
Do something continually until button B is pressed
If you wish any of these programs to check over and over don't forget to wrap them in a forever loop

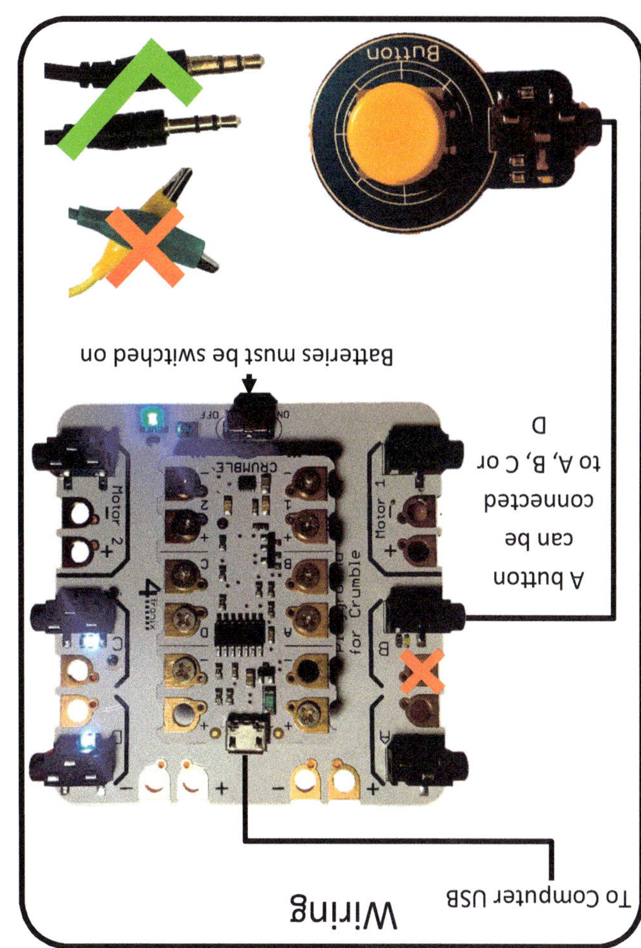
Wiring
To Computer USB
A button can be connected to A, B, C or D
Batteries must be switched on
Button

More Information

Remember you can make things happen when the button is pressed and when the button is de-pressed.

There are other types of switches that don't have to be held down to stay (HI) on.

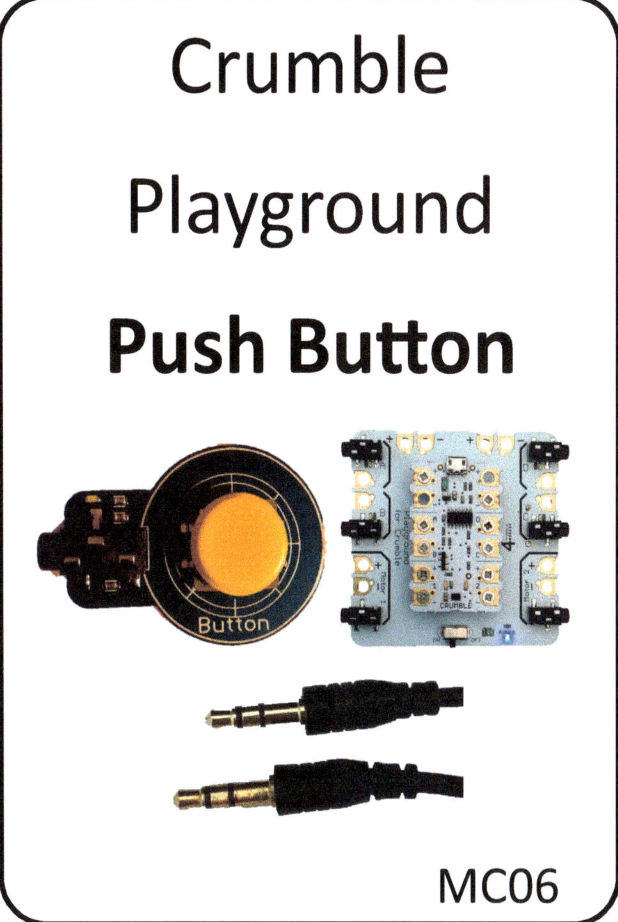
Crumble
Playground
Push Button
Button
MC06

Crumble Playground

Geared Motor

MC07

More Information

Some motors can trip a temporary fuse if they are suddenly switched from full power forward to full power in reverse.

Start your motor at 50% power and adjust upwards you can test if there is anything in the program that trips the Crumble Playground temporary fuse at higher power settings.

Wiring

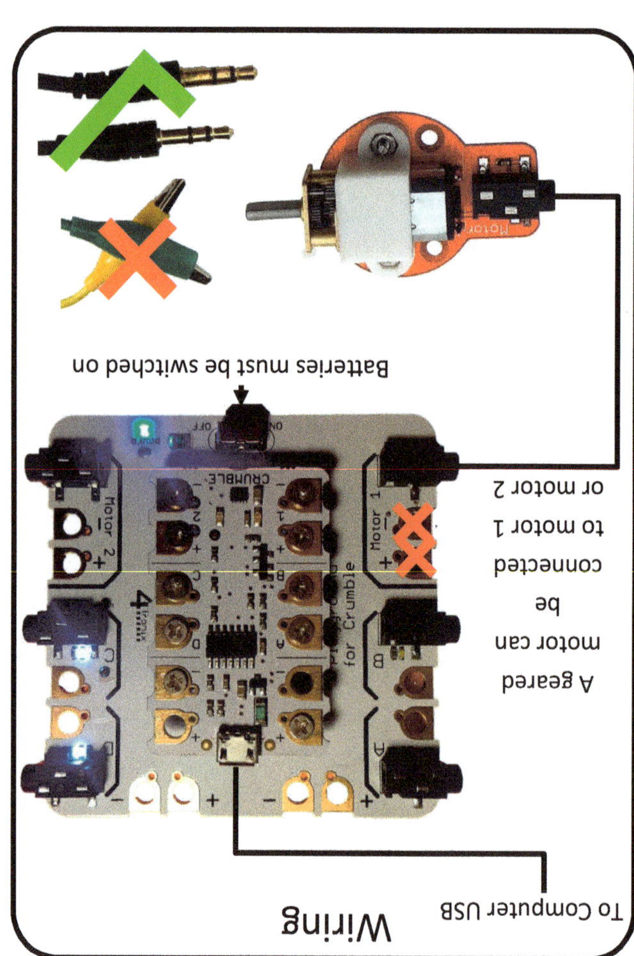
To Computer USB
A geared motor can be connected to motor 1 or motor 2
Batteries must be switched on

Useful Code Blocks

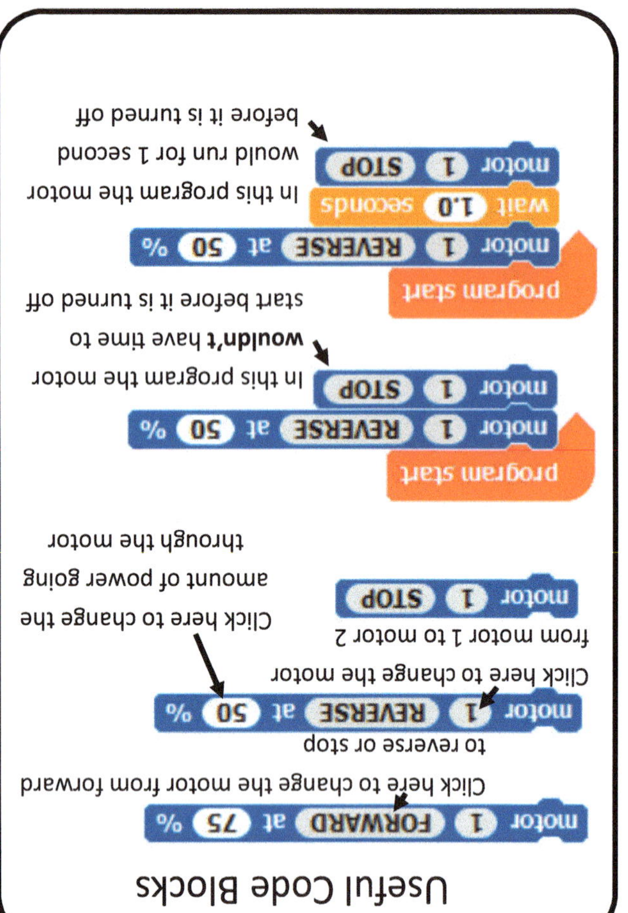
motor 1 FORWARD at 75 %
Click here to change the motor from forward to reverse or stop
motor 1 REVERSE at 50 %
Click here to change the motor from motor 1 to motor 2
Click here to change the amount of power going through the motor
motor 1 STOP
program start
motor 1 REVERSE at 50 %
motor 1 STOP
In this program the motor **wouldn't** have time to start before it is turned off
program start
motor 1 REVERSE at 50 %
wait 1.0 seconds
motor 1 STOP
In this program the motor would run for 1 second before it is turned off

Crumble

Playground

Light Dependant Resistor

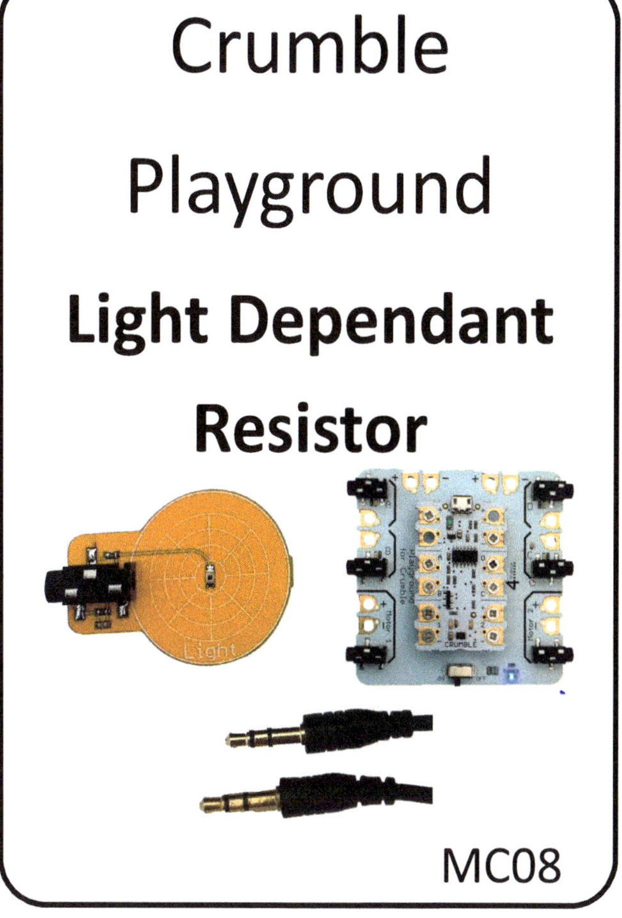

MC08

Wiring

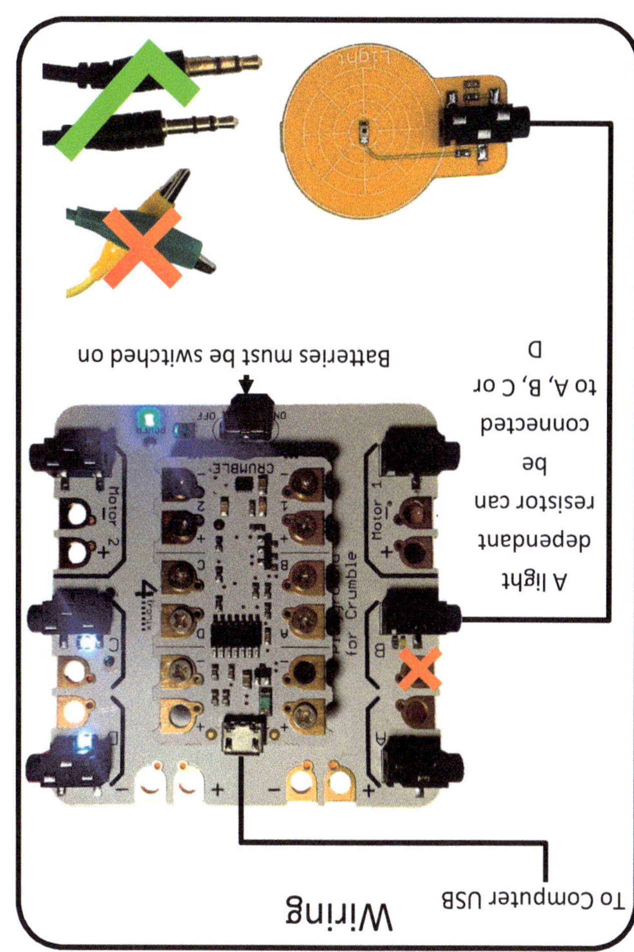

To Computer USB
A light dependant resistor can be connected to A, B, C or D
Batteries must be switched on

Useful Code Blocks

`analogue A`

A light dependant resistor (LDR) inputs between 0 and 255 through the analogue block. 0 would be no light and 255 a very bright light.

```
program start
  do forever
    let LDR = analogue B
  loop
```

To test the LDR its input needs to be transferred into a variable. In this program the LDR attached to port B has been transferred into a variable called LDR. It has been placed inside a forever loop so the input will be updated continually. Equals = means the same as. You can see what number is inside the LDR on the variable page of the Crumble software. It will look like this.

`LDR` `del` `rename` `149`

You can then use this to change other things in your program.

More Information

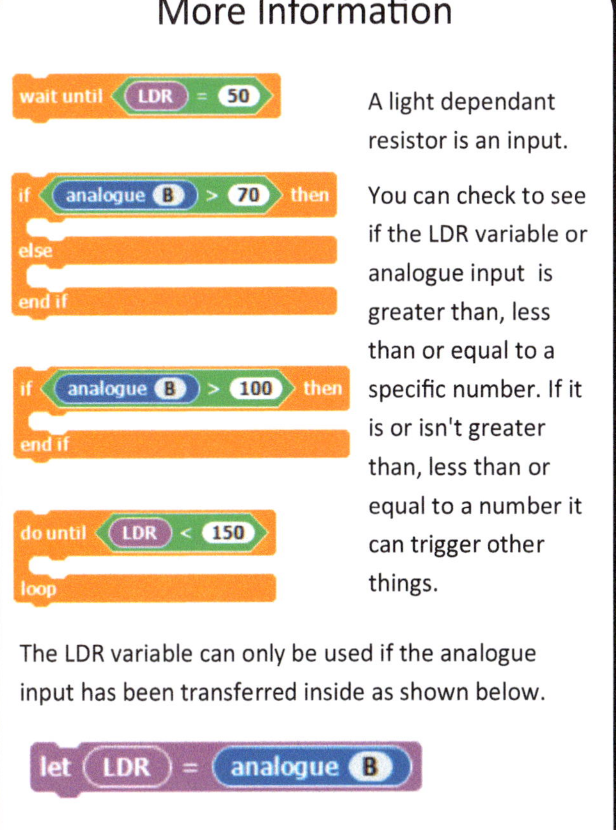

wait until LDR = 50
if analogue B > 70 then
else
end if
if analogue B > 100 then
end if
do until LDR < 150
loop

A light dependant resistor is an input.

You can check to see if the LDR variable or analogue input is greater than, less than or equal to a specific number. If it is or isn't greater than, less than or equal to a number it can trigger other things.

The LDR variable can only be used if the analogue input has been transferred inside as shown below.

`let LDR = analogue B`

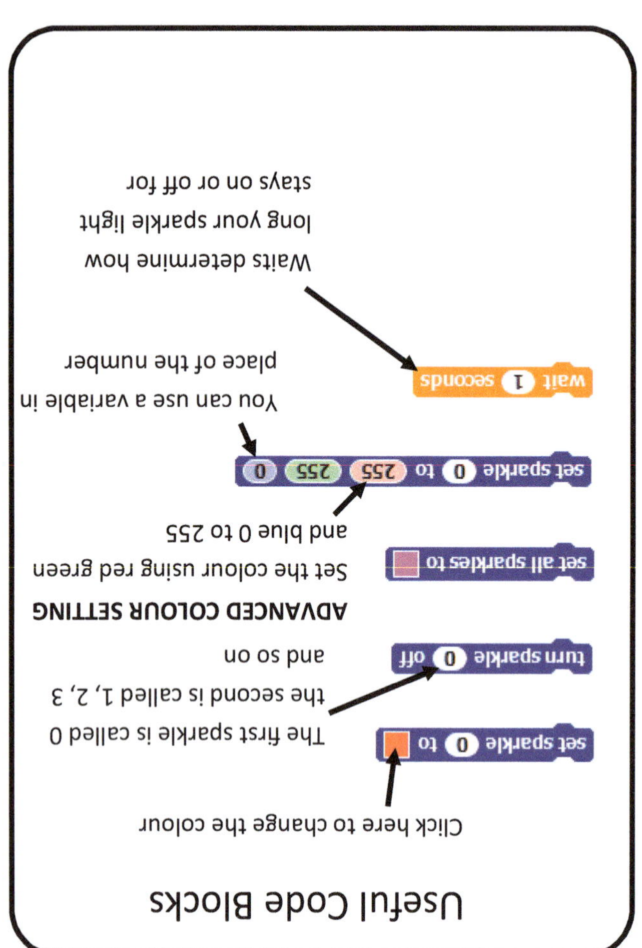

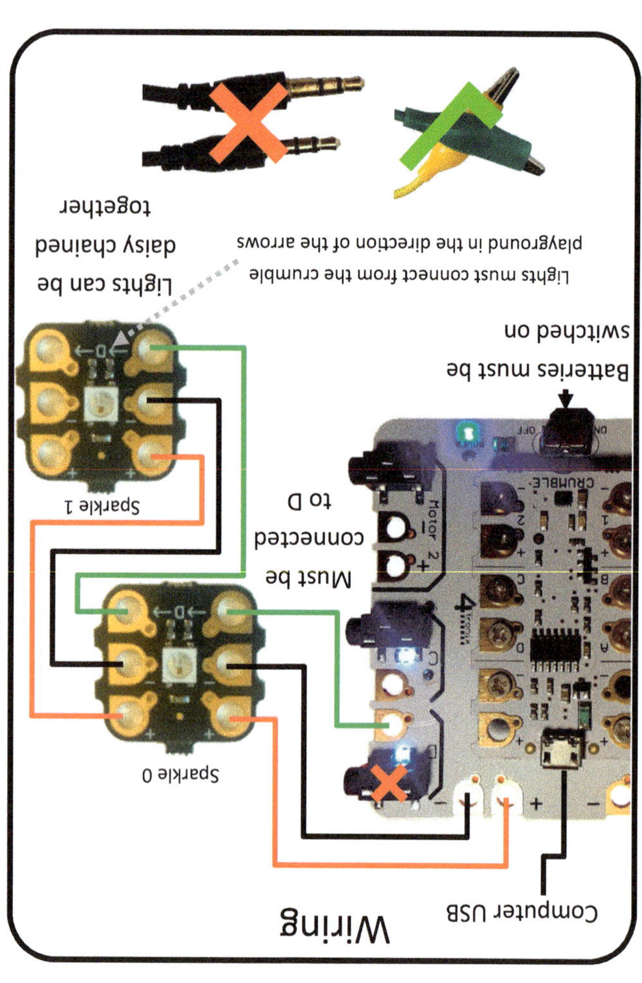

More Information

Lights are outputs. Programmable lights can be very bright. You can reduce this by covering the light with a translucent cover such a piece of white paper.

Up to 36 programmable lights can be daisy chained together.

Redfern Electronics who make this programmable light call it a sparkle.

You can program multiple lights on one device with these.

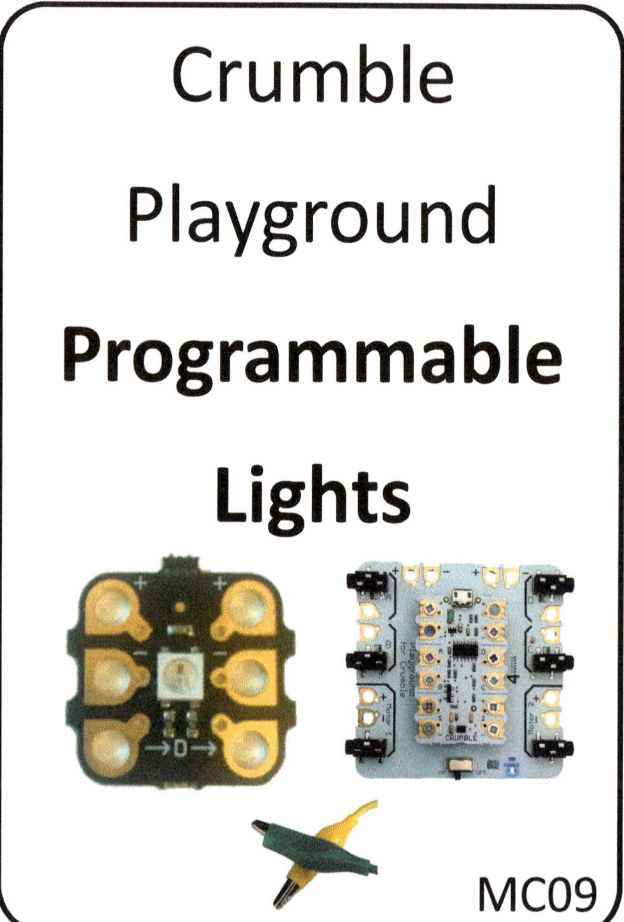

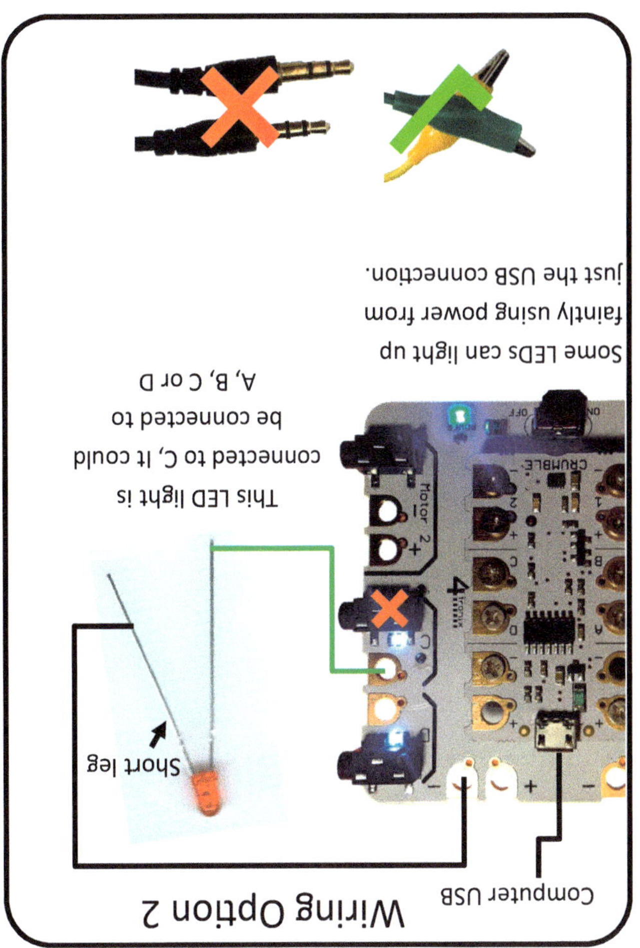
Some LEDs can light up
faintly using power from
just the USB connection.
This LED light is
connected to C, it could
be connected to
A, B, C or D
Short leg
Computer USB
Wiring Option 2

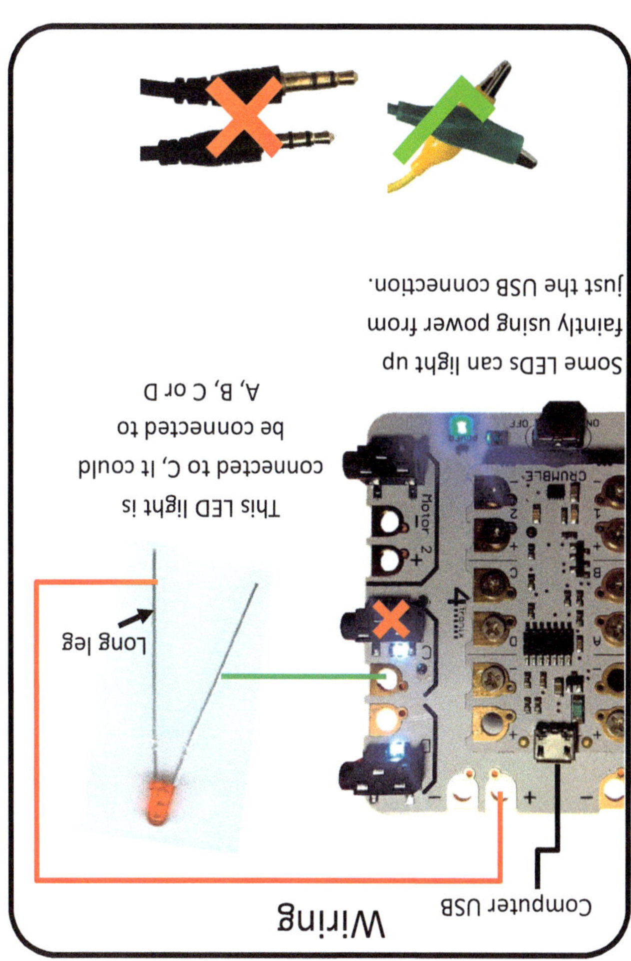
Some LEDs can light up
faintly using power from
just the USB connection.
This LED light is
connected to C, it could
be connected to
A, B, C or D
Long leg
Computer USB
Wiring

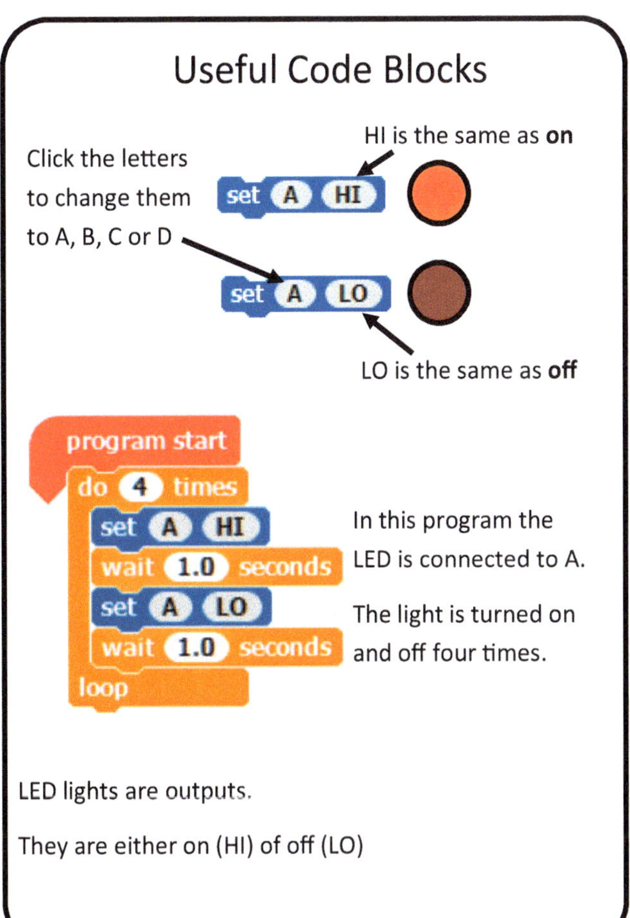
Useful Code Blocks
Click the letters
to change them
to A, B, C or D
HI is the same as **on**
set A HI
set A LO
LO is the same as **off**
program start
do 4 times
set A HI
wait 1.0 seconds
set A LO
wait 1.0 seconds
loop
In this program the
LED is connected to A.
The light is turned on
and off four times.
LED lights are outputs.
They are either on (HI) of off (LO)

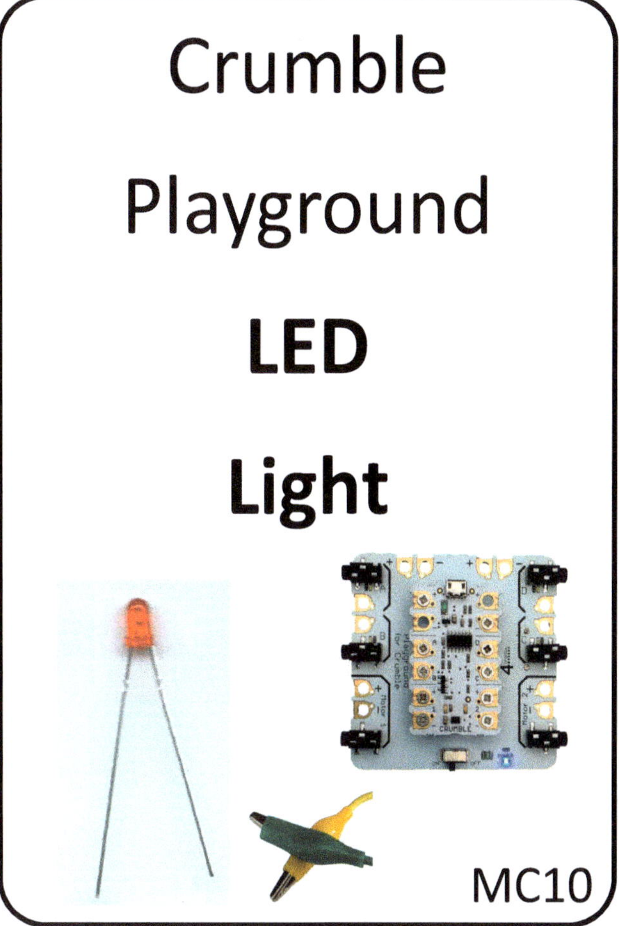
Crumble
Playground
LED
Light
MC10

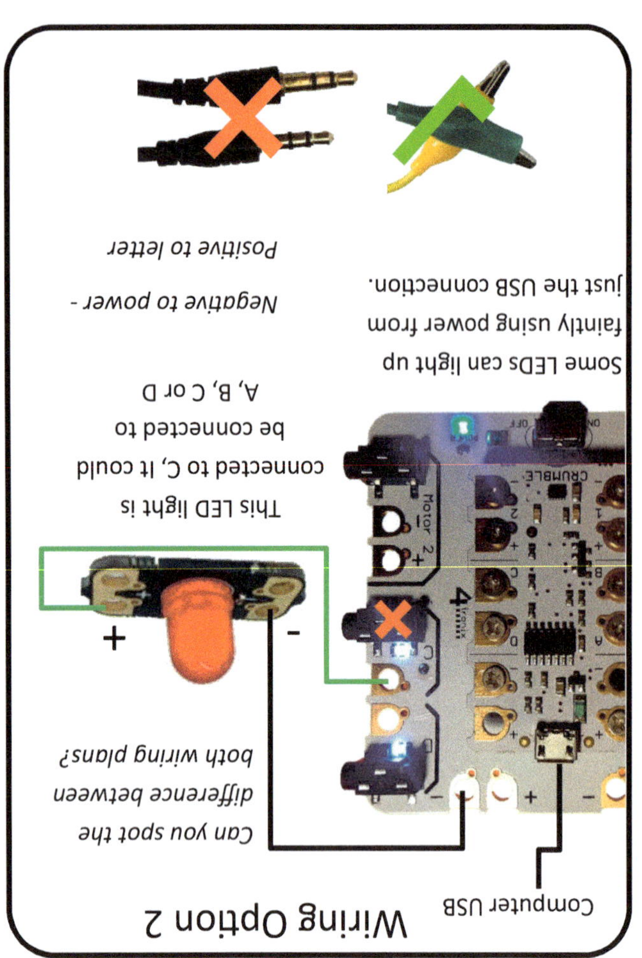
Wiring Option 2
Computer USB
Can you spot the
difference between
both wiring plans?
+
-
This LED light is
connected to C, it could
be connected to
A, B, C or D
Some LEDs can light up
faintly using power from
just the USB connection.
Negative to power -
Positive to letter

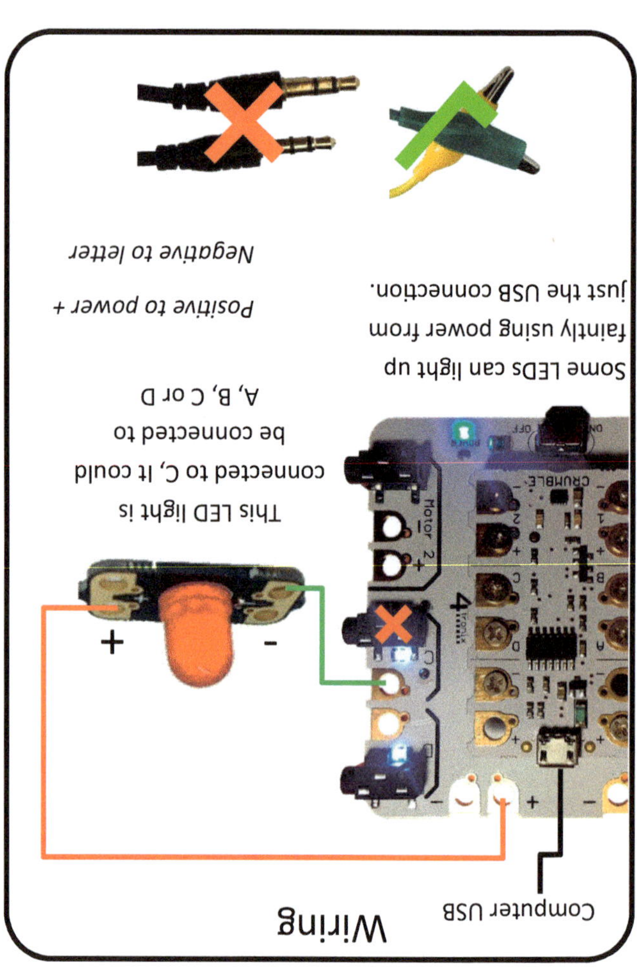
Wiring
Computer USB
+
-
This LED light is
connected to C, it could
be connected to
A, B, C or D
Some LEDs can light up
faintly using power from
just the USB connection.
Positive to power +
Negative to letter

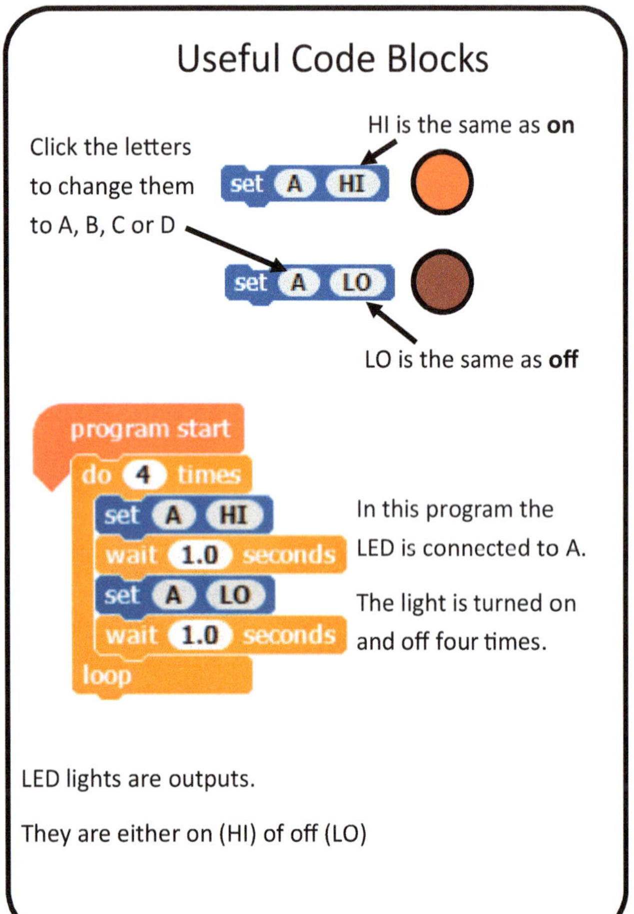
Useful Code Blocks
Click the letters
to change them
to A, B, C or D
HI is the same as **on**
set A HI
set A LO
LO is the same as **off**
program start
do 4 times
set A HI
wait 1.0 seconds
set A LO
wait 1.0 seconds
loop
In this program the
LED is connected to A.
The light is turned on
and off four times.
LED lights are outputs.
They are either on (HI) of off (LO)

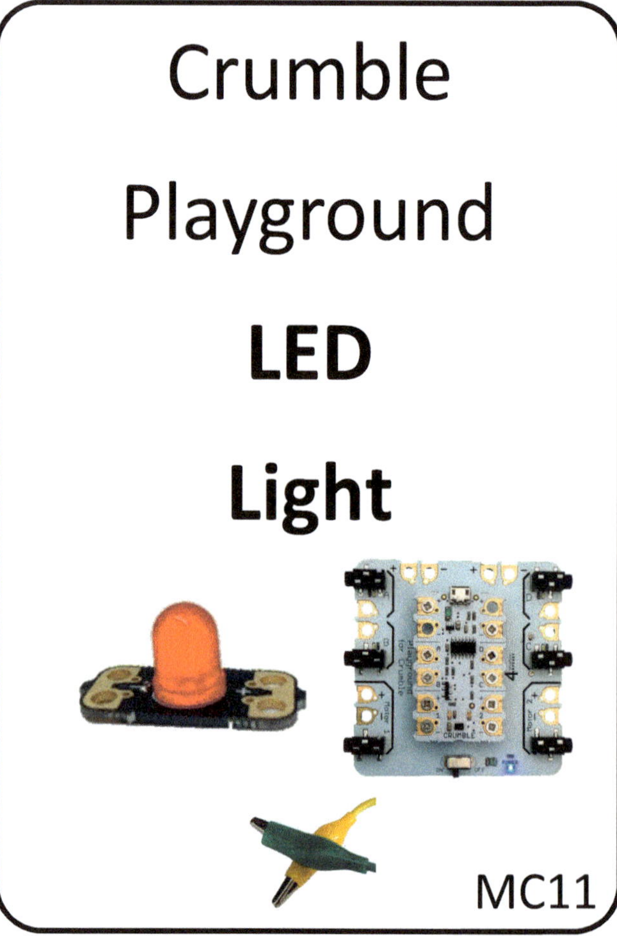
Crumble
Playground
LED
Light
MC11

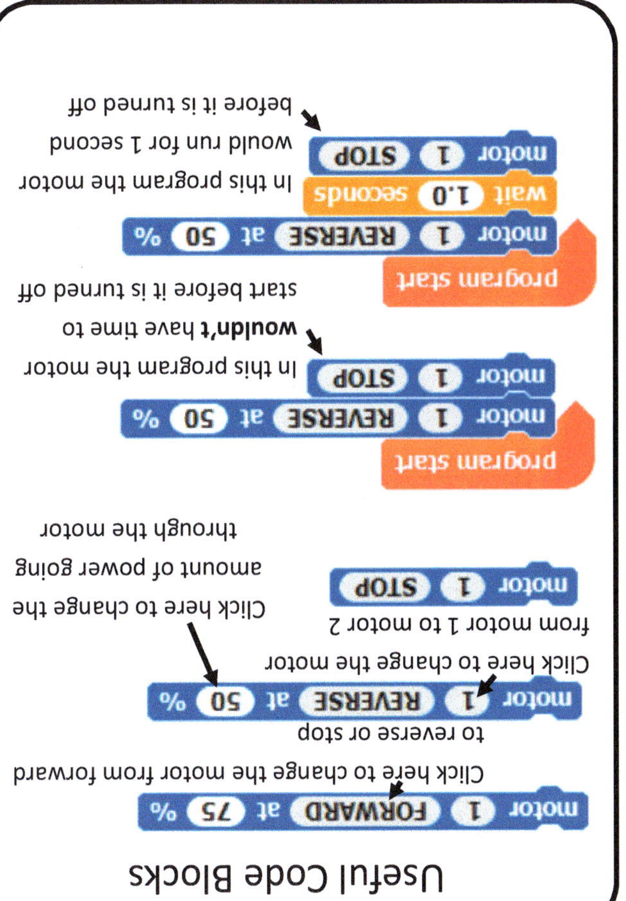

Useful Code Blocks
motor 1 FORWARD at 75 %
Click here to change the motor from forward to reverse or stop
motor 1 REVERSE at 50 %
Click here to change the motor from motor 1 to motor 2
Click here to change the amount of power going through the motor
motor 1 STOP
program start
motor 1 REVERSE at 50 %
motor 1 STOP
In this program the motor wouldn't have time to start before it is turned off
program start
motor 1 REVERSE at 50 %
wait 1.0 seconds
motor 1 STOP
In this program the motor would run for 1 second before it is turned off

Useful Code Blocks

Some motors can trip a temporary fuse if they are suddenly switched from full power forward to full power in reverse.

Start your motor at 50% power and adjust upwards you can test if there is anything in the program that trips the Crumble Playground temporary fuse at higher power settings.

You can manually reverse the direction of the motor by swapping the negative and positive connections on the motor.

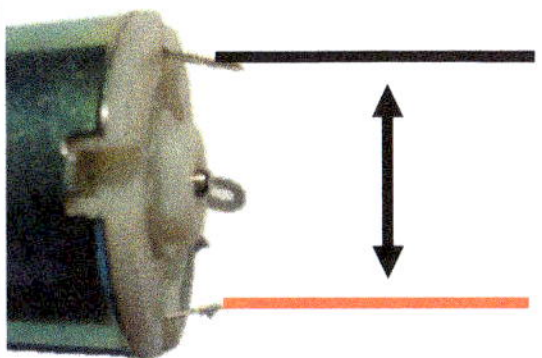

Crumble Playground **Motor**

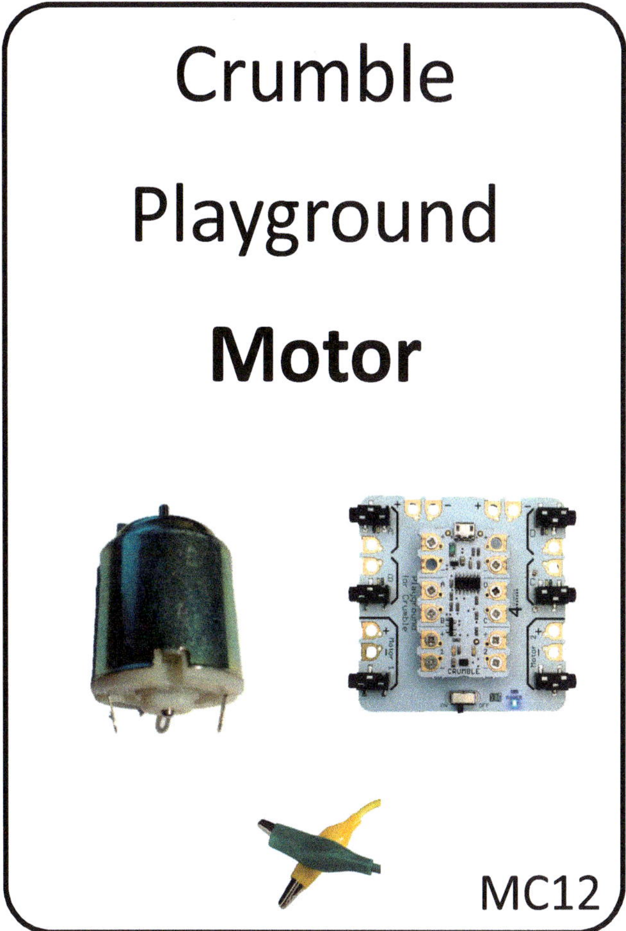

MC12

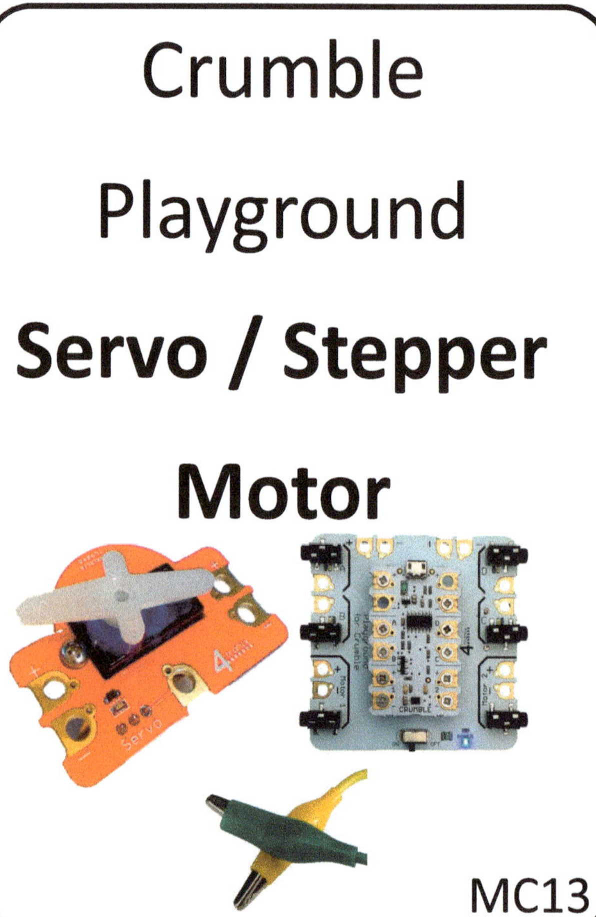

Crumble
Playground
Servo / Stepper
Motor
MC13

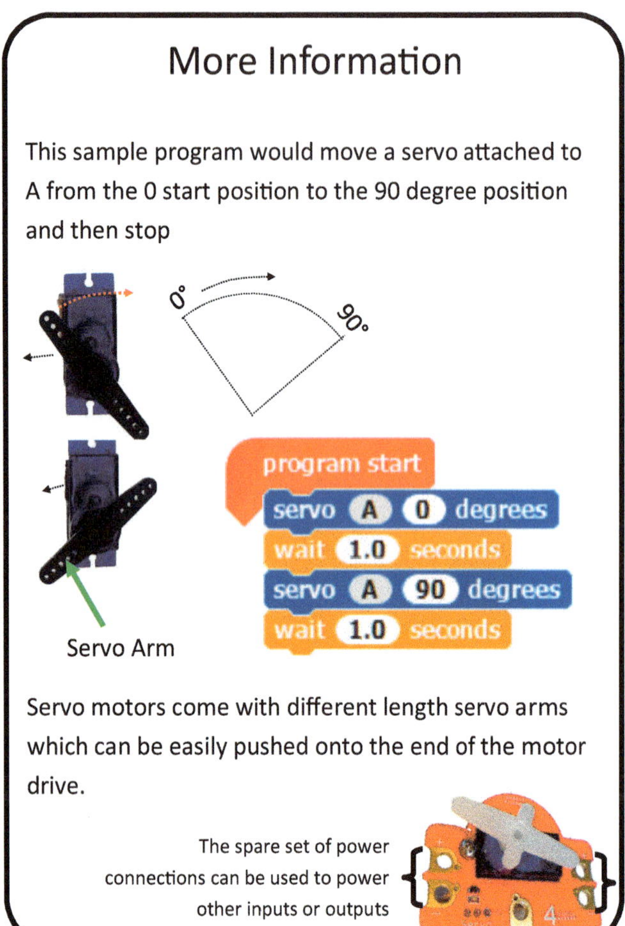

More Information
This sample program would move a servo attached to A from the 0 start position to the 90 degree position and then stop
0°
90°
program start
servo A 0 degrees
wait 1.0 seconds
servo A 90 degrees
wait 1.0 seconds
Servo Arm
Servo motors come with different length servo arms which can be easily pushed onto the end of the motor drive.
The spare set of power connections can be used to power other inputs or outputs

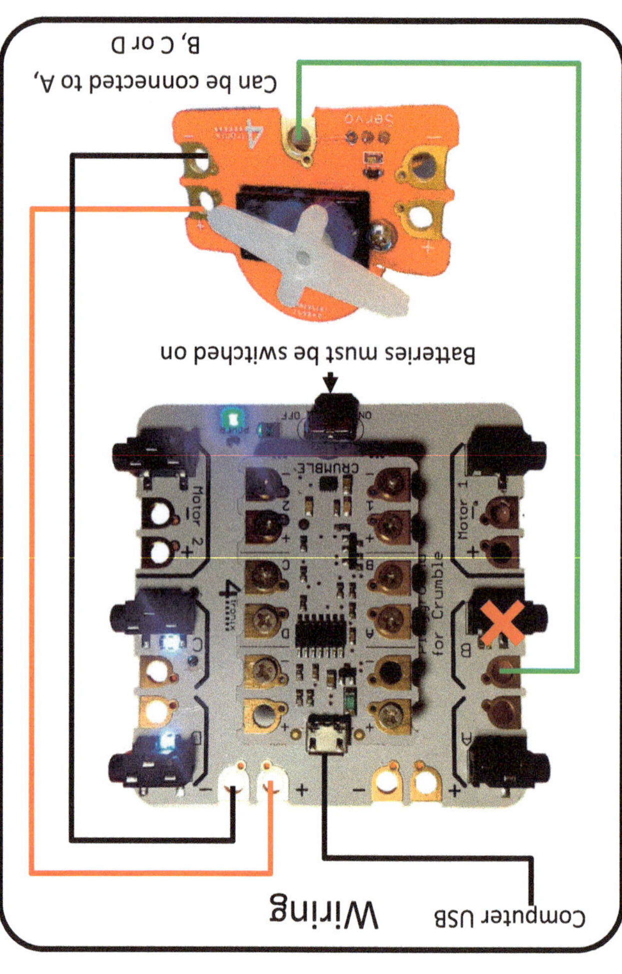

Wiring
Computer USB
Batteries must be switched on
Can be connected to A, B, C or D

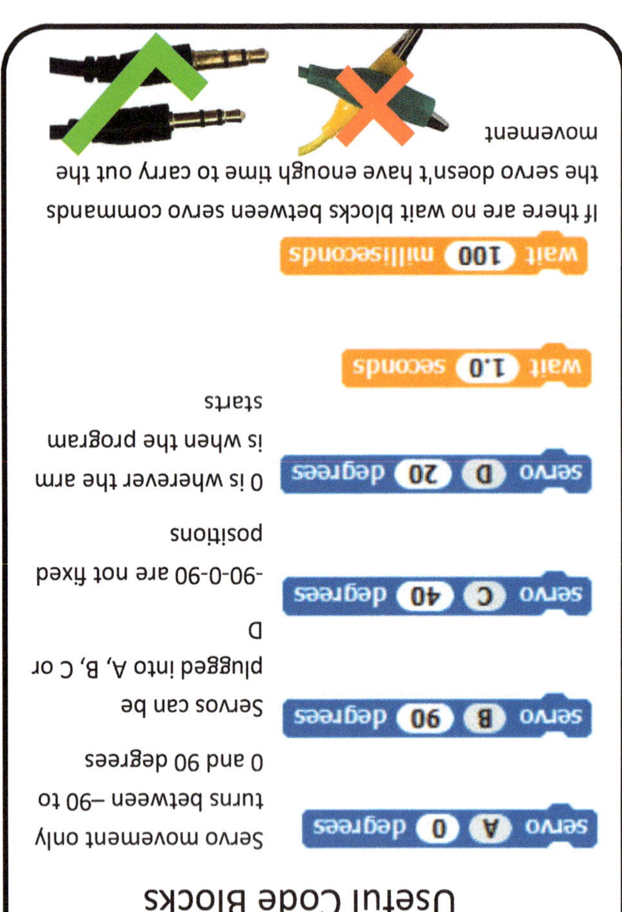

Useful Code Blocks
servo A 0 degrees
Servo movement only turns between –90 to 0 and 90 degrees
servo B 90 degrees
Servos can be plugged into A, B, C or D
servo C 40 degrees
-90-0-90 are not fixed positions
servo D 20 degrees
0 is wherever the arm is when the program starts
wait 1.0 seconds
wait 100 milliseconds
If there are no wait blocks between servo commands the servo doesn't have enough time to carry out the movement

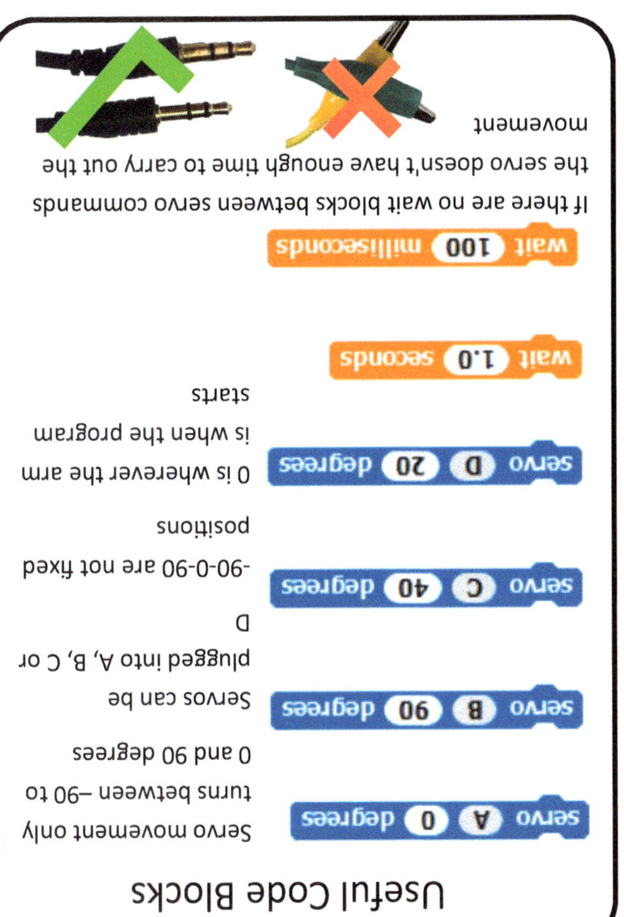

Useful Code Blocks

```
servo A 0 degrees
```

Servo movement only turns between −90 to 0 and 90 degrees

```
servo B 90 degrees
```

Servos can be plugged into A, B, C or D

```
servo C 40 degrees
```

-90-0-90 are not fixed positions

```
servo D 20 degrees
```

0 is wherever the arm is when the program starts

```
wait 1.0 seconds
```

```
wait 100 milliseconds
```

If there are no wait blocks between servo commands the servo doesn't have enough time to carry out the movement

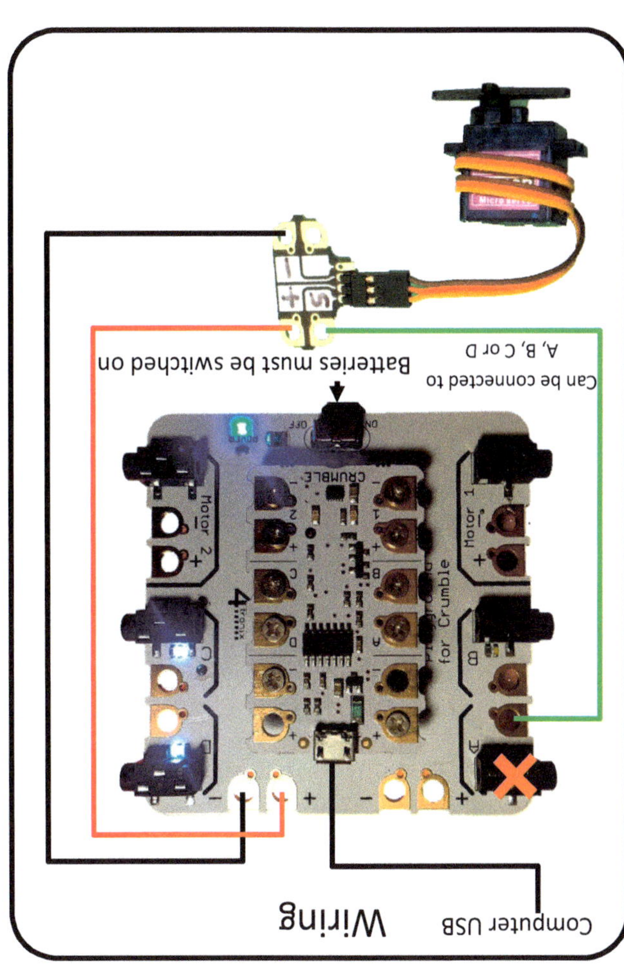

Wiring

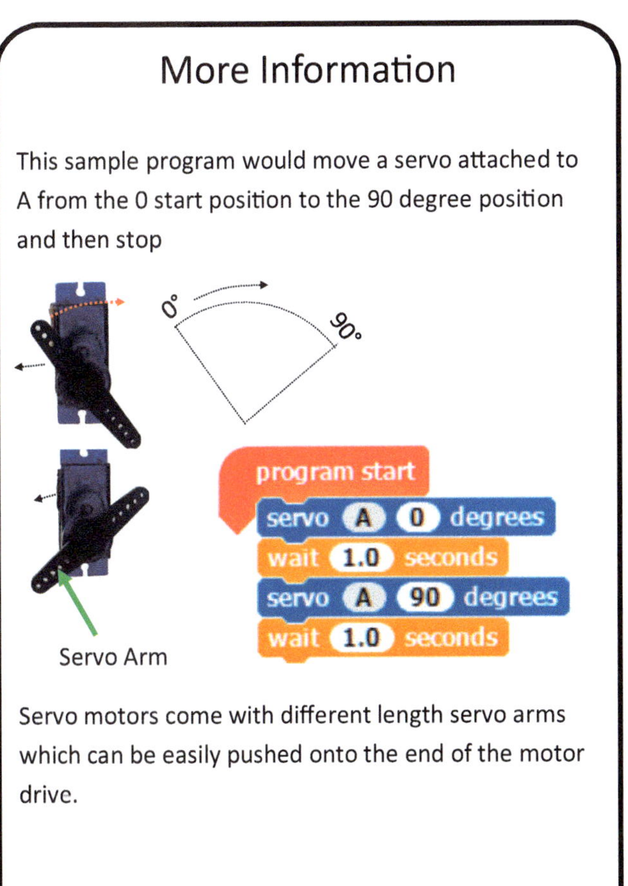

More Information

This sample program would move a servo attached to A from the 0 start position to the 90 degree position and then stop


```
program start
servo A 0 degrees
wait 1.0 seconds
servo A 90 degrees
wait 1.0 seconds
```

Servo motors come with different length servo arms which can be easily pushed onto the end of the motor drive.

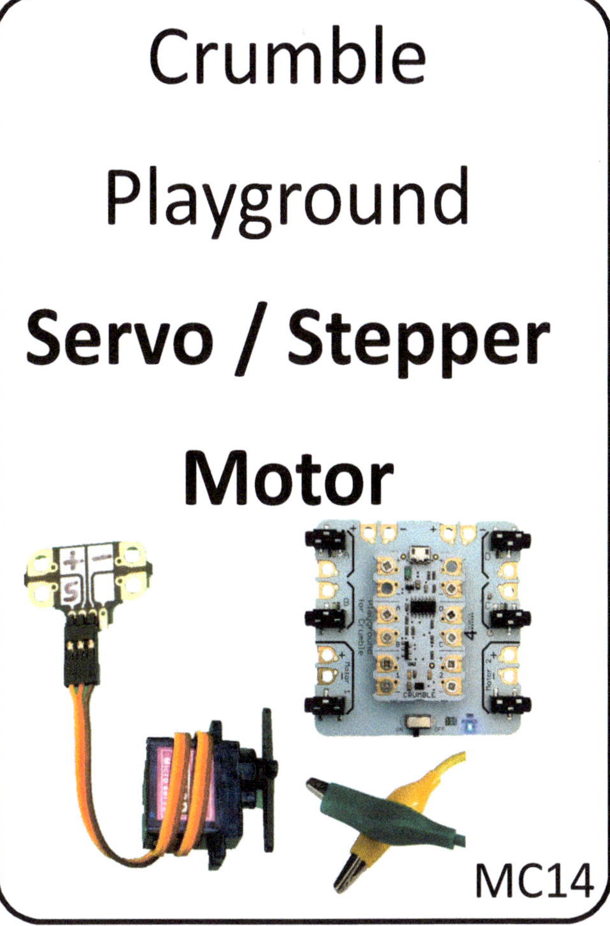

Crumble Playground

Servo / Stepper Motor

MC14

Crumble Playground

Dial

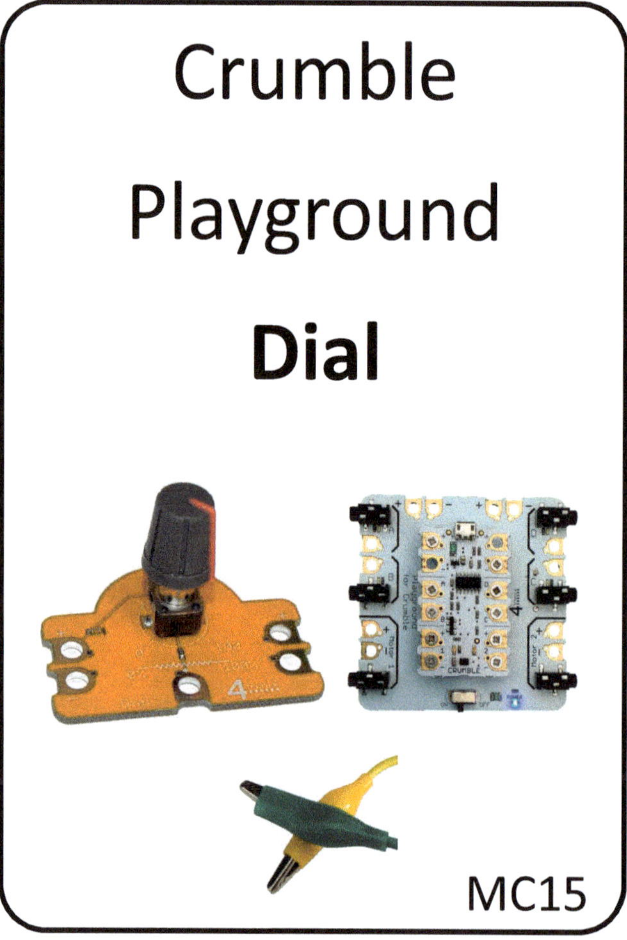

MC15

More Information

Dials can be used to adjust the amount of power going into a motor, the colour balance of a programmable light, the tone of a piezo element, The amount of turn a servo moves etc.

It can be used wherever a number that changes is used.

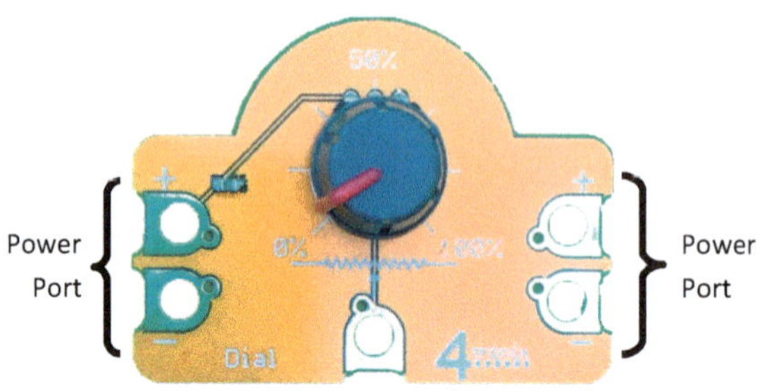

The left over power ports on this dial can be used to power another device.

Wiring

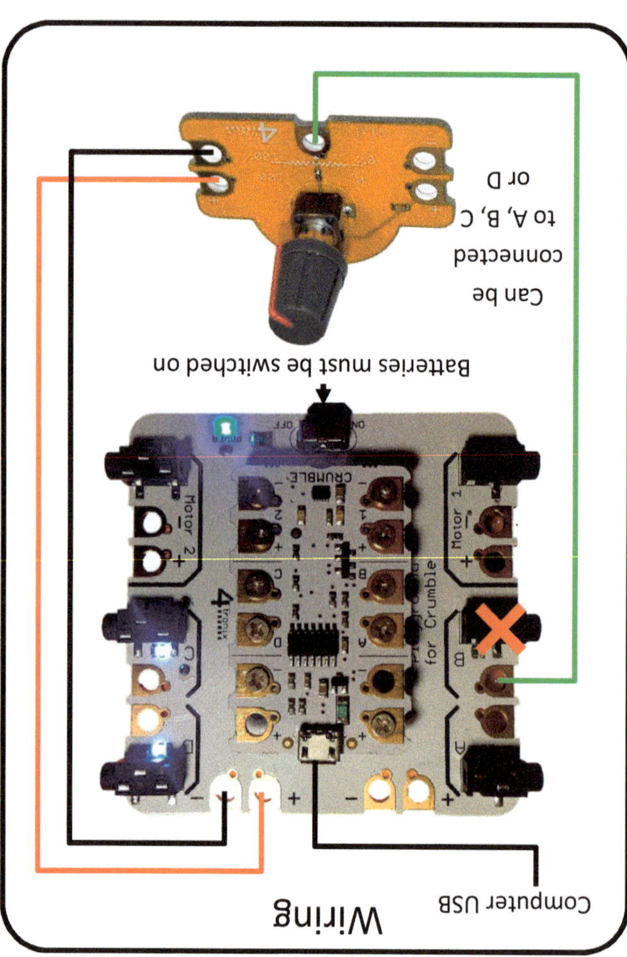

Useful Code Blocks

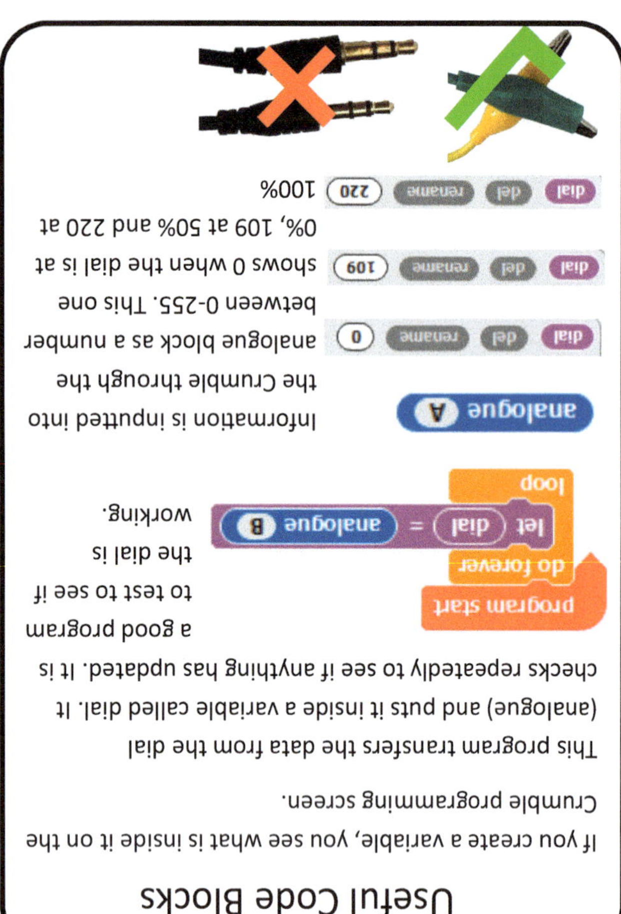

If you create a variable, you see what is inside it on the Crumble programming screen.

This program transfers the data from the dial (analogue) and puts it inside a variable called dial. It checks repeatedly to see if anything has updated. It is a good program to test to see if the dial is working.

```
program start
do forever
  let dial = analogue B
loop
```

Information is inputted into the Crumble through the analogue block as a number between 0-255. This one shows 0 when the dial is at 0%, 109 at 50% and 220 at 100%

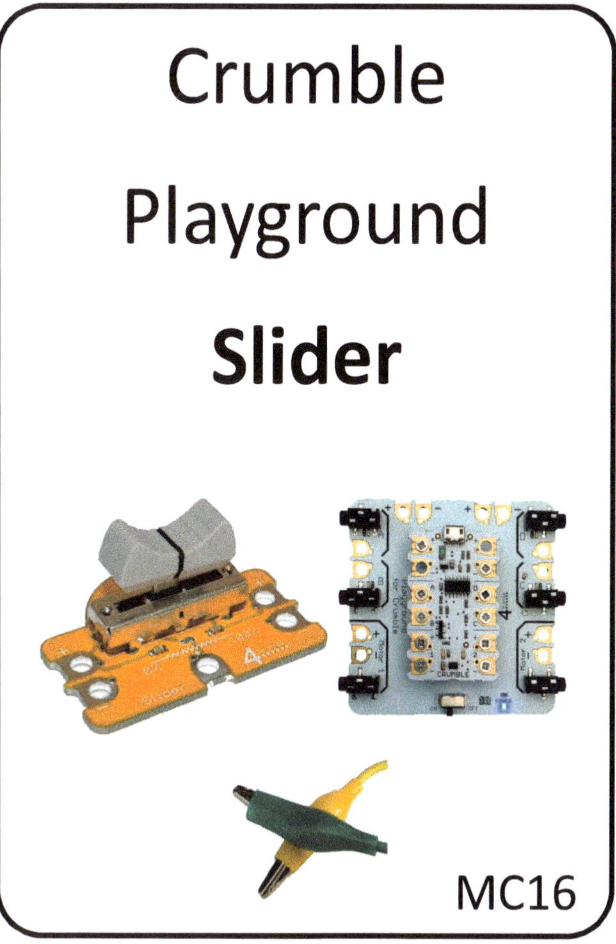

Crumble Playground **Slider**

MC16

More Information

Sliders can be used to adjust the amount of power going into a motor, the colour balance of a programmable light, the tone of a piezo element, The amount of turn a servo moves etc.

It can be used wherever a variable can be used in place of a fixed number.

The left over power ports on this slider can be used to power another device.

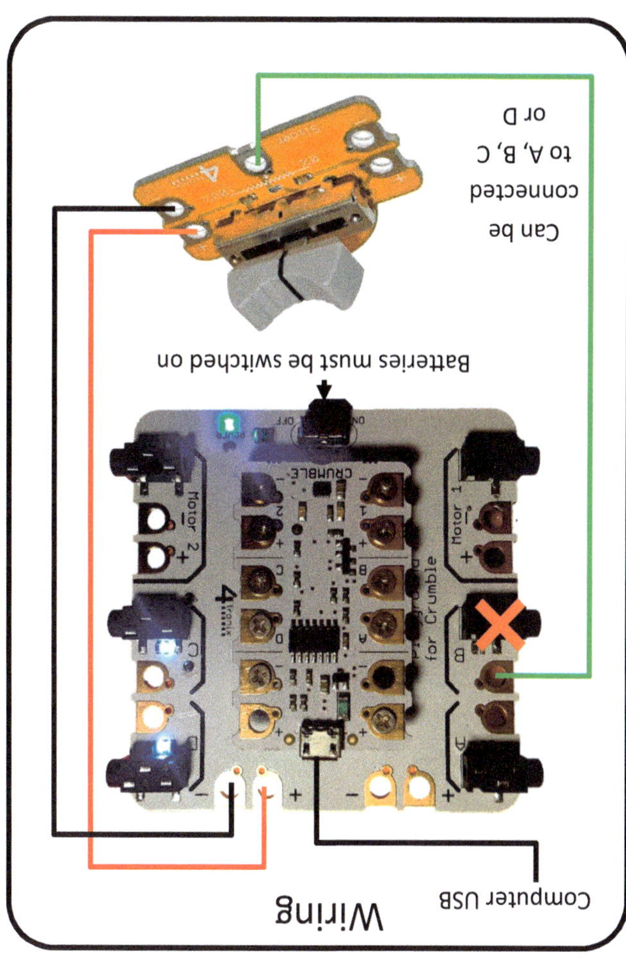

Wiring

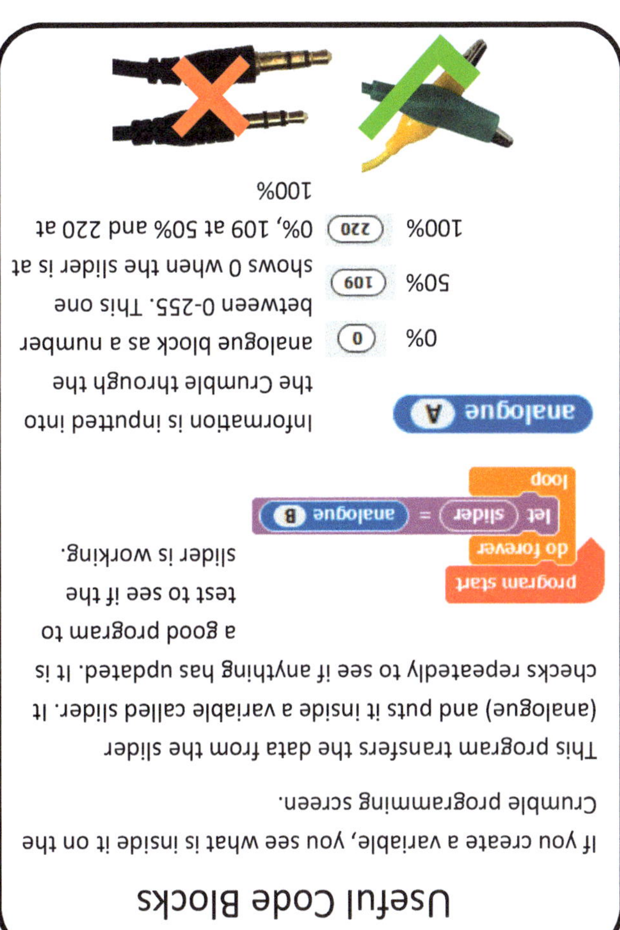

Useful Code Blocks

If you create a variable, you see what is inside it on the Crumble programming screen.

This program transfers the data from the slider (analogue) and puts it inside a variable called slider. It checks repeatedly to see if anything has updated. It is a good program to test to see if the slider is working.

Information is inputted into the Crumble through the analogue block as a number between 0-255. This one shows 0 when the slider is at 0%, 109 at 50% and 220 at 100%

0%	0
50%	109
100%	220

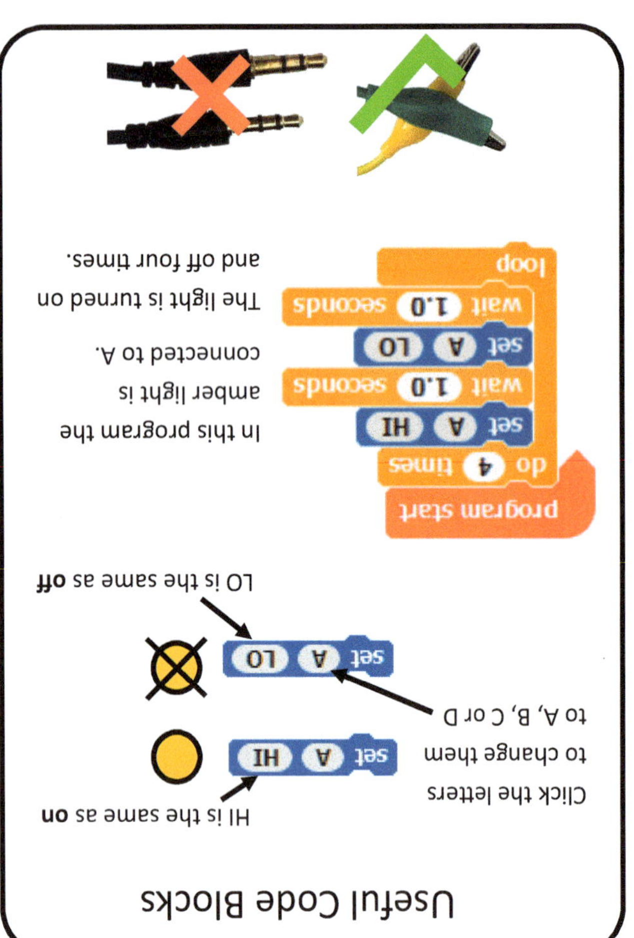

Useful Code Blocks
Click the letters to change them to A, B, C or D
HI is the same as **on**
set A HI
LO is the same as **off**
set A LO
program start
do 4 times
set A HI
wait 1.0 seconds
set A LO
wait 1.0 seconds
loop
In this program the amber light is connected to A.
The light is turned on and off four times.

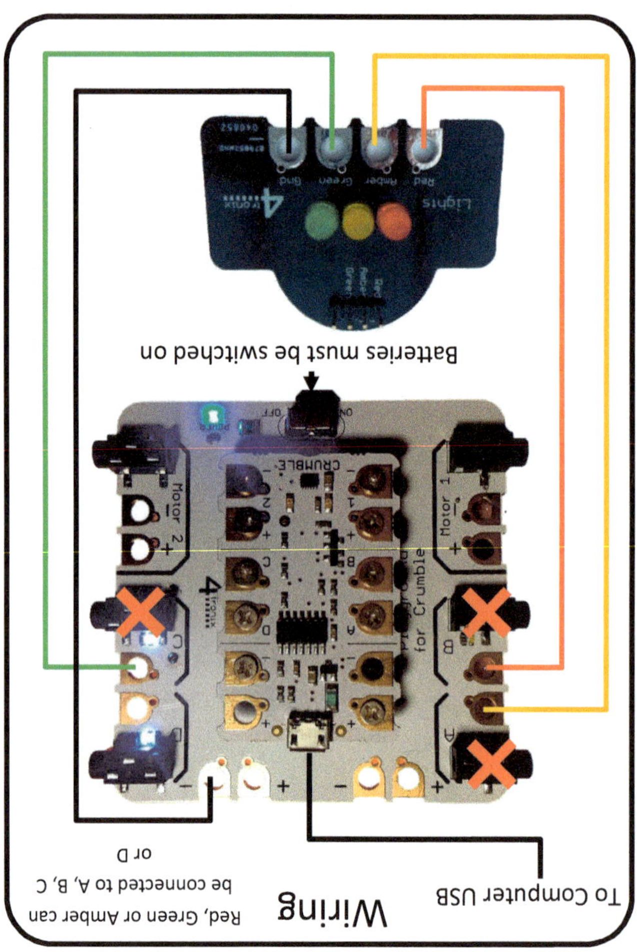

More Information

LED Traffic lights can be used to program traffic lights or a single LED light can be used to indicate something else.

A green LED could be switched on when the light from an light resistant resistor goes above a set number.

Or

A red LED could be turned on when the PIR detects motion.

You don't have to wire every light to use just one.

If you wanted the red light only then red to A, B, C or D and GND to negative.

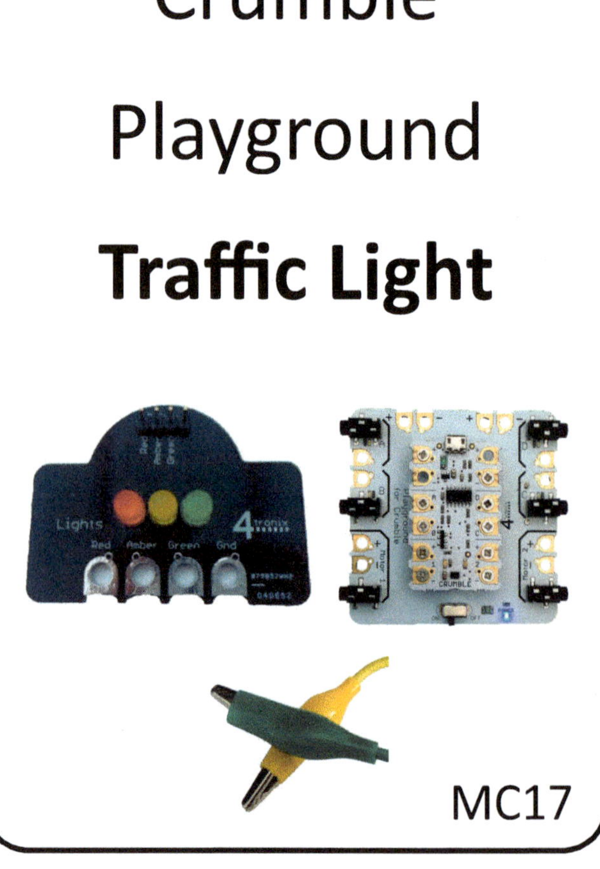

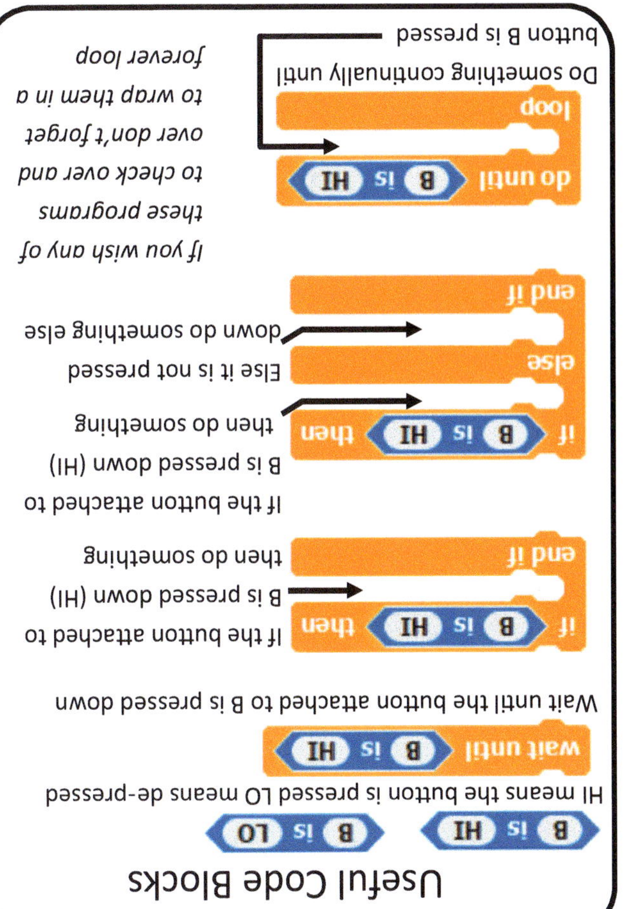
Useful Code Blocks
B is HI
B is LO
HI means the button is pressed LO means de-pressed
wait until B is HI
Wait until the button attached to B is pressed down
if B is HI then
end if
If the button attached to B is pressed down (HI) then do something
if B is HI then
else
end if
If the button attached to B is pressed down (HI) then do something
Else it is not pressed down do something else
do until B is HI
loop
Do something continually until button B is pressed
If you wish any of these programs to check over and over don't forget to wrap them in a forever loop

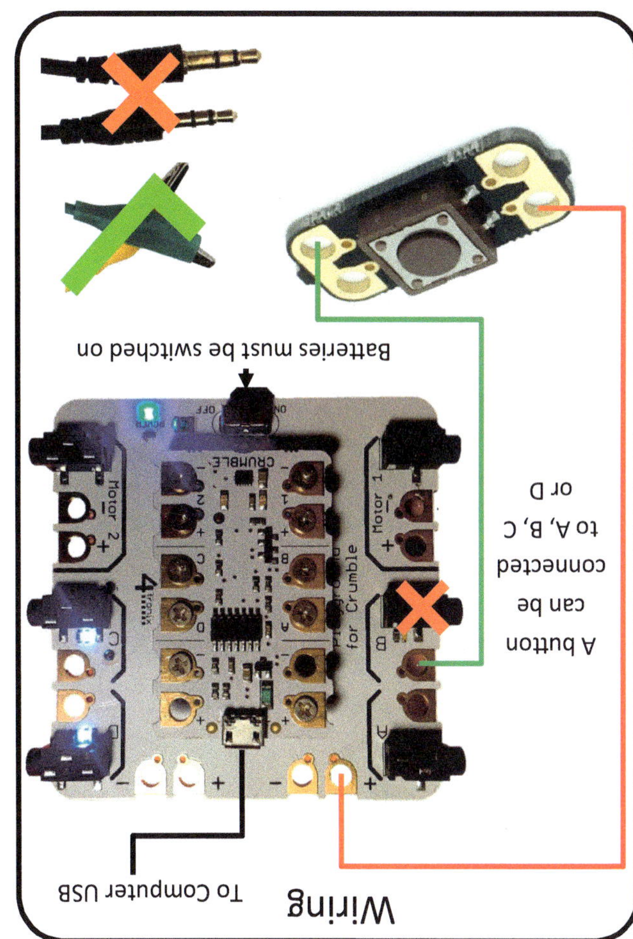
Wiring
To Computer USB
A button can be connected to A, B, C or D
Batteries must be switched on

More Information

Remember you can make things happen when the button is pressed and when the button is de-pressed.

There are other types of switches that don't have to be held down to stay (HI) on.

The colour of the insulation on the wires is to help you easily spot errors. Many electrical diagrams would show + as red and - as black. You can use any colour that is available to you. It will make no difference to the program.

Crumble
Playground
Push Button
MC18

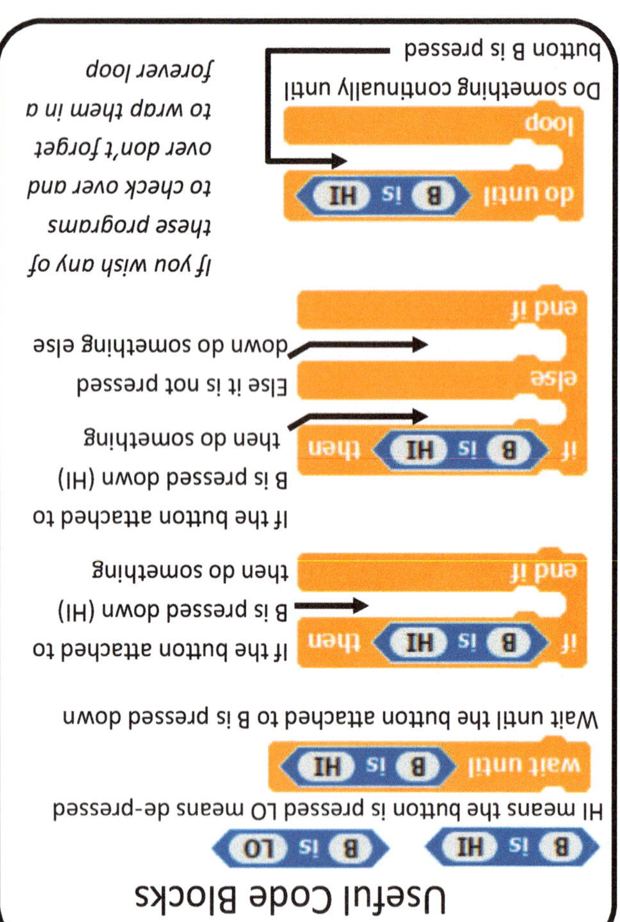
Useful Code Blocks
B is HI
B is LO
HI means the button is pressed LO means de-pressed
wait until B is HI
Wait until the button attached to B is pressed down
if B is HI then
end if
If the button attached to B is pressed down (HI) then do something
if B is HI then
else
end if
If the button attached to B is pressed down (HI) then do something
Else it is not pressed down do something else
do until B is HI
loop
Do something continually until button B is pressed
If you wish any of these programs to check over and over don't forget to wrap them in a forever loop

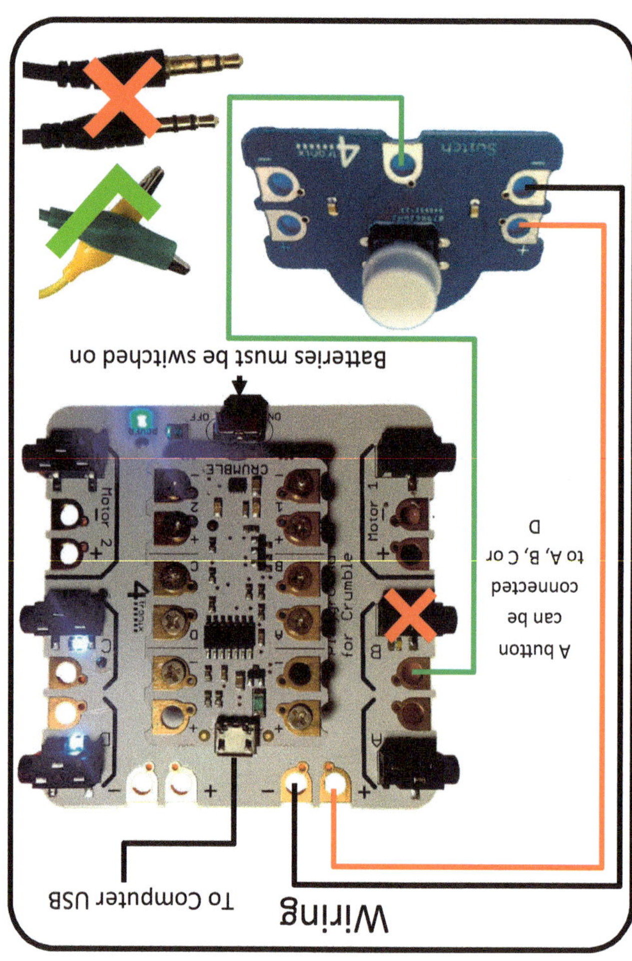
Wiring
To Computer USB
Batteries must be switched on
A button can be connected to A, B, C or D
Motor 1
Motor 2
Switch

More Information

Buttons are INPUT devices

Remember you can make things happen when the button is pressed and when the button is de-pressed.

There are other types of switches that don't have to be held down to stay (HI) on.

The colour of the insulation on the wires is to help you easily spot errors. Many electrical diagrams would show + as red and - as black. You can use any colour that is available to you. It will make no difference to the program.

Switch

Electricity can be passed on to other devices through the extra + and - power connections on this device

Crumble
Playground
Push Button
Switch
MC19

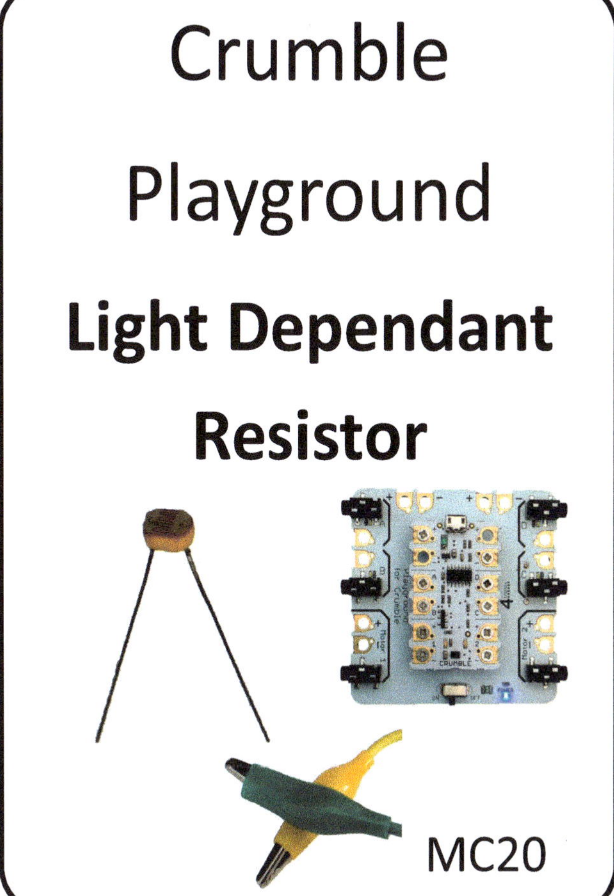

Crumble

Playground

Light Dependant Resistor

MC20

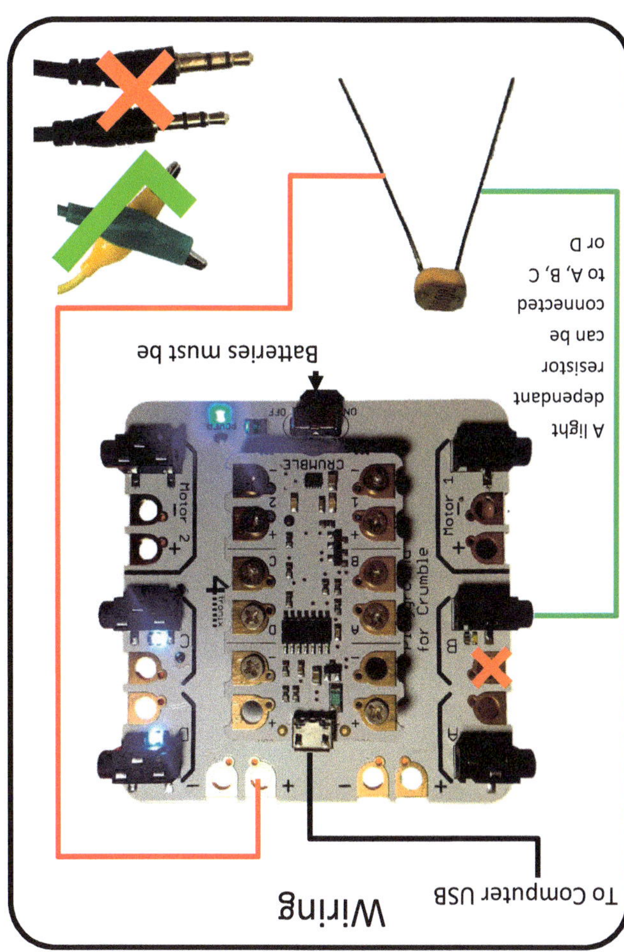

Wiring

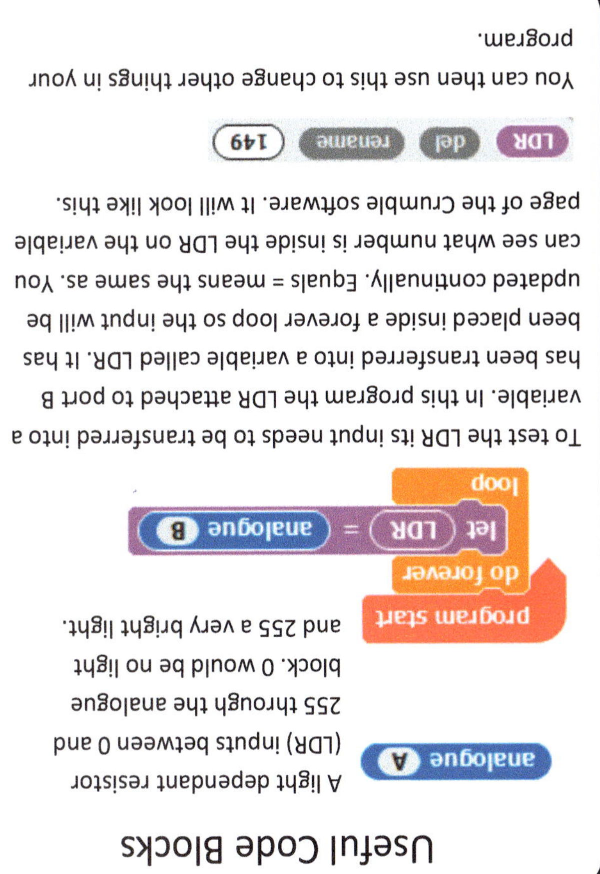

Useful Code Blocks

A light dependant resistor (LDR) inputs between 0 and 255 through the analogue block. 0 would be no light and 255 a very bright light.

To test the LDR its input needs to be transferred into a variable. In this program the LDR attached to port B has been transferred into a variable called LDR. It has been placed inside a forever loop so the input will be updated continually. Equals = means the same as. You can see what number is inside the LDR on the variable page of the Crumble software. It will look like this.

You can then use this to change other things in your program.

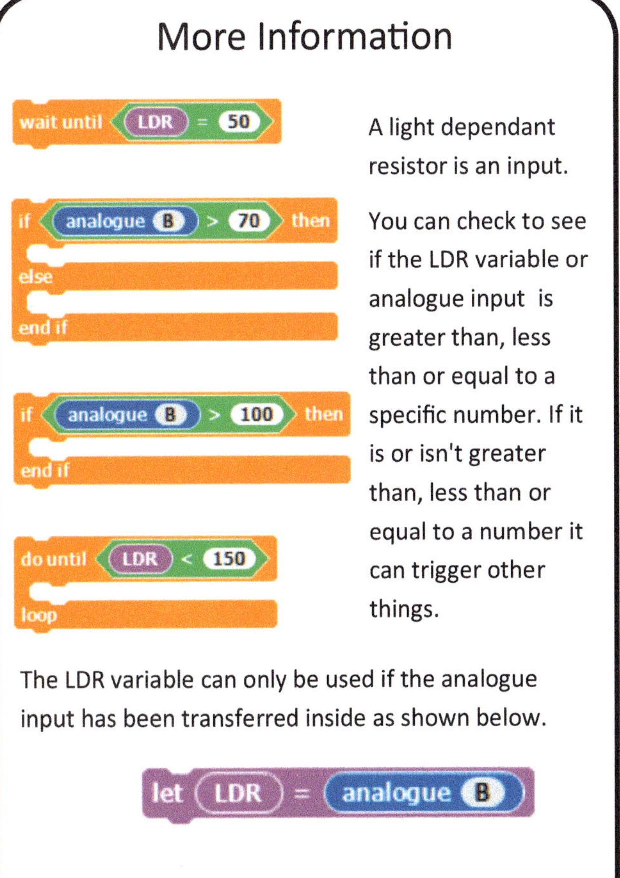

More Information

A light dependant resistor is an input.

You can check to see if the LDR variable or analogue input is greater than, less than or equal to a specific number. If it is or isn't greater than, less than or equal to a number it can trigger other things.

The LDR variable can only be used if the analogue input has been transferred inside as shown below.

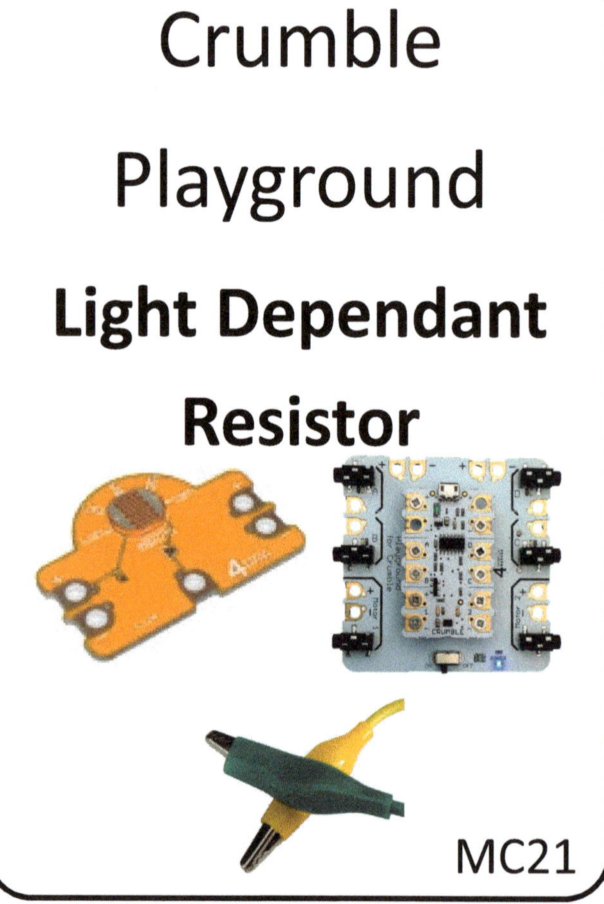

Crumble Playground

Light Dependant Resistor

MC21

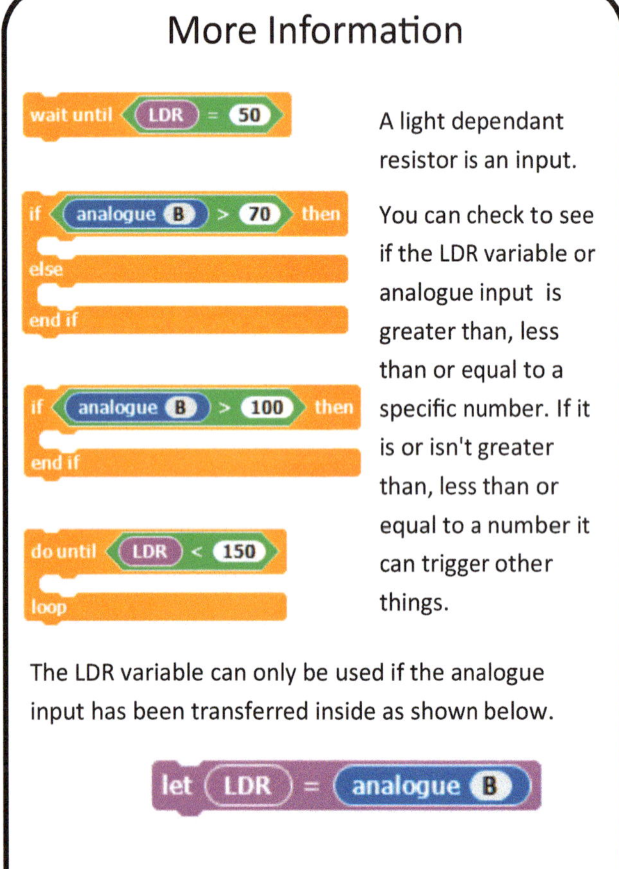

More Information

```
wait until < LDR = 50 >

if < analogue B > 70 > then
else
end if

if < analogue B > 100 > then
end if

do until < LDR < 150 >
loop
```

A light dependant resistor is an input.

You can check to see if the LDR variable or analogue input is greater than, less than or equal to a specific number. If it is or isn't greater than, less than or equal to a number it can trigger other things.

The LDR variable can only be used if the analogue input has been transferred inside as shown below.

```
let LDR = analogue B
```

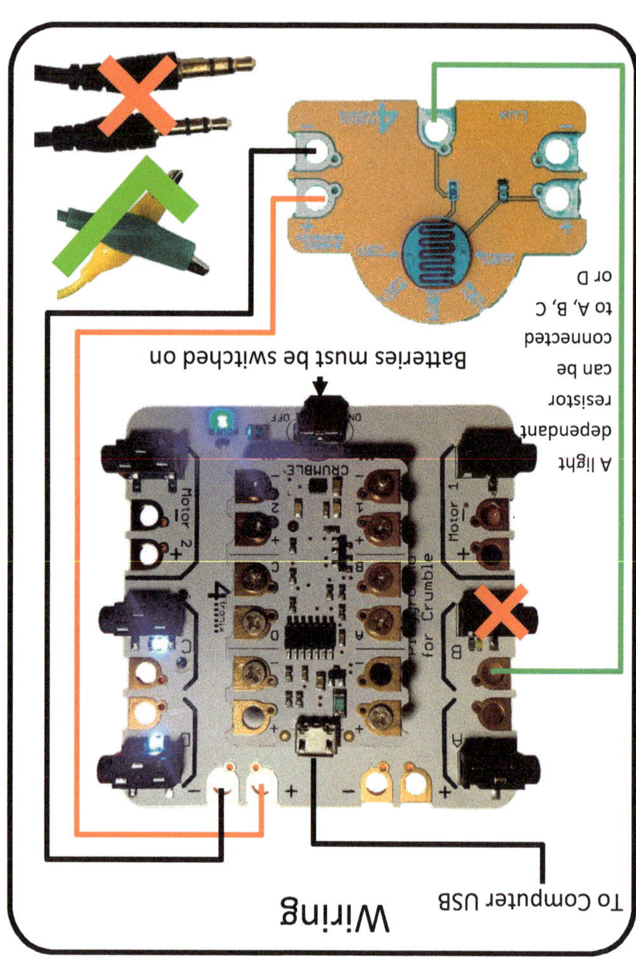

Wiring

To Computer USB
Batteries must be switched on
A light dependant resistor can be connected to A, B, C or D

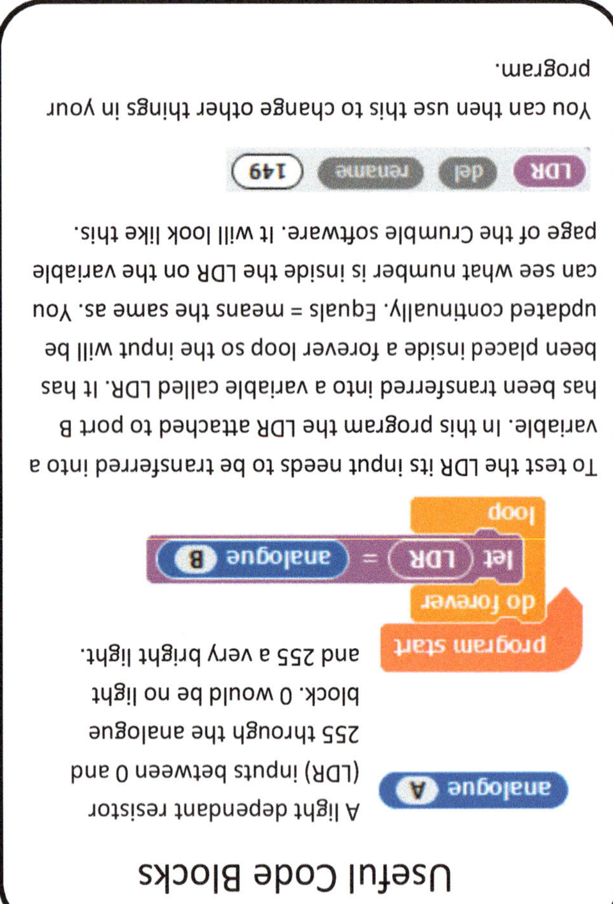

Useful Code Blocks

```
analogue A
```

A light dependant resistor (LDR) inputs between 0 and 255 through the analogue block. 0 would be no light and 255 a very bright light.

```
program start
do forever
  let LDR = analogue B
loop
```

To test the LDR its input needs to be transferred into a variable. In this program the LDR attached to port B has been transferred into a variable called LDR. It has been placed inside a forever loop so the input will be updated continually. Equals = means the same as. You can see what number is inside the LDR on the variable page of the Crumble software. It will look like this.

```
LDR  del  rename  149
```

You can then use this to change other things in your program.

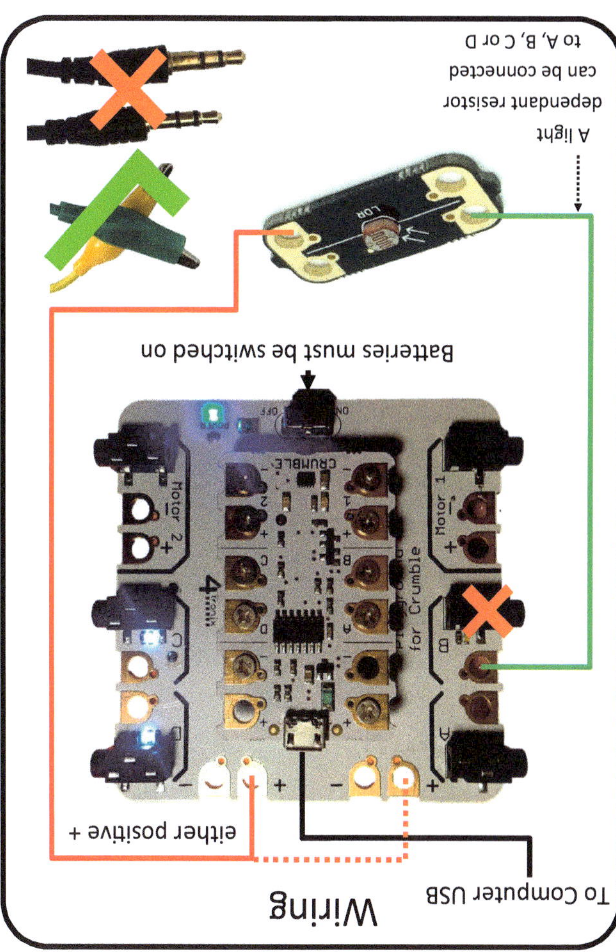
Wiring
To Computer USB
either positive +
Batteries must be switched on
A light dependant resistor can be connected to A, B, C or D

Useful Code Blocks

analogue A

A light dependant resistor (LDR) inputs between 0 and 255 through the analogue block. 0 would be no light and 255 a very bright light.

```
program start
do forever
  let LDR = analogue B
loop
```

To test the LDR its input needs to be transferred into a variable. In this program the LDR attached to port B has been transferred into a variable called LDR. It has been placed inside a forever loop so the input will be updated continually. Equals = means the same as. You can see what number is inside the LDR on the variable page of the Crumble software. It will look like this.

LDR del rename 149

You can then use this to change other things in your program.

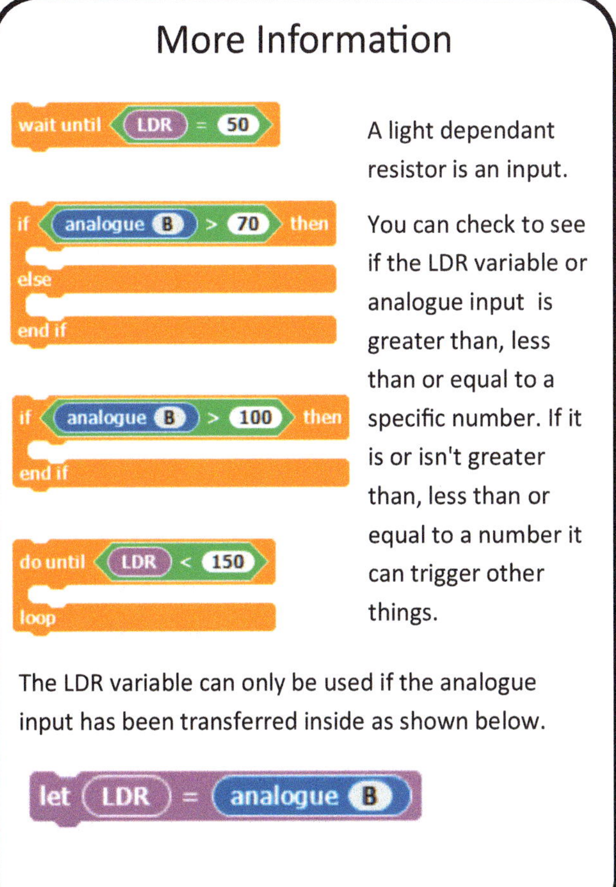

More Information

```
wait until LDR = 50
```

A light dependant resistor is an input.

```
if analogue B > 70 then
else
end if
```

```
if analogue B > 100 then
end if
```

```
do until LDR < 150
loop
```

You can check to see if the LDR variable or analogue input is greater than, less than or equal to a specific number. If it is or isn't greater than, less than or equal to a number it can trigger other things.

The LDR variable can only be used if the analogue input has been transferred inside as shown below.

```
let LDR = analogue B
```

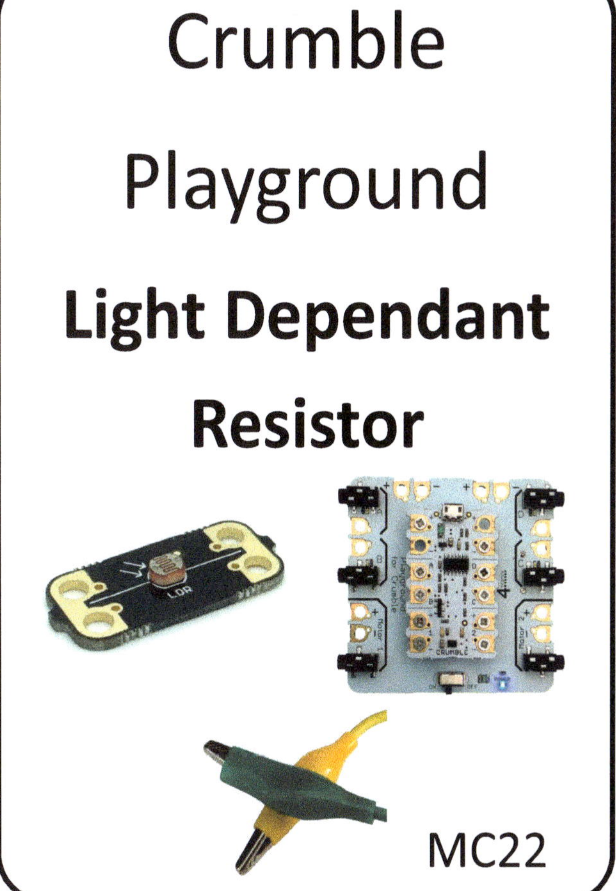

Crumble Playground

Light Dependant Resistor

MC22

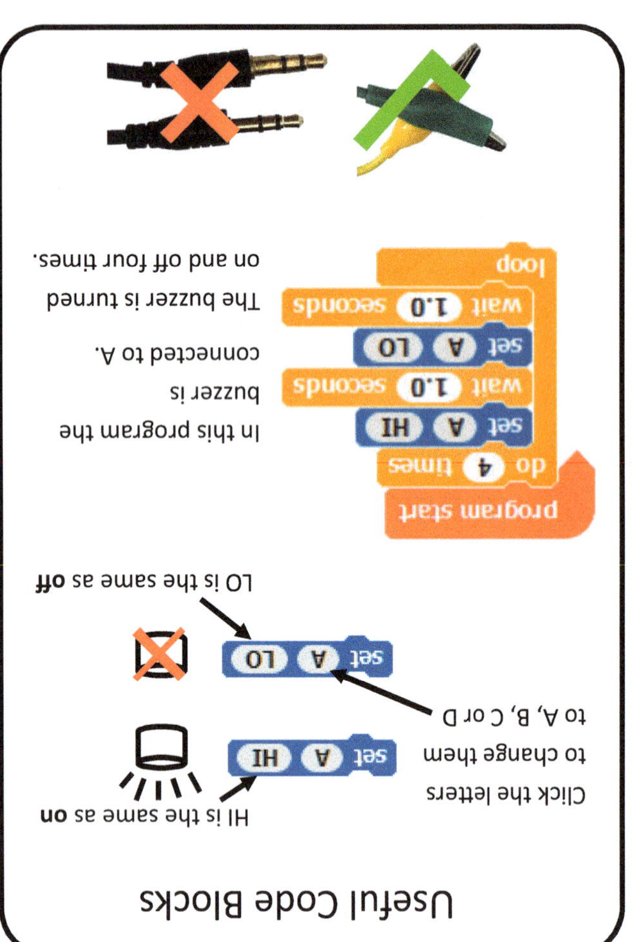
Useful Code Blocks
Click the letters to change them to A, B, C or D
HI is the same as on
set A HI
set A LO
LO is the same as off
program start
do 4 times
set A HI
wait 1.0 seconds
set A LO
wait 1.0 seconds
loop
In this program the buzzer is connected to A.
The buzzer is turned on and off four times.

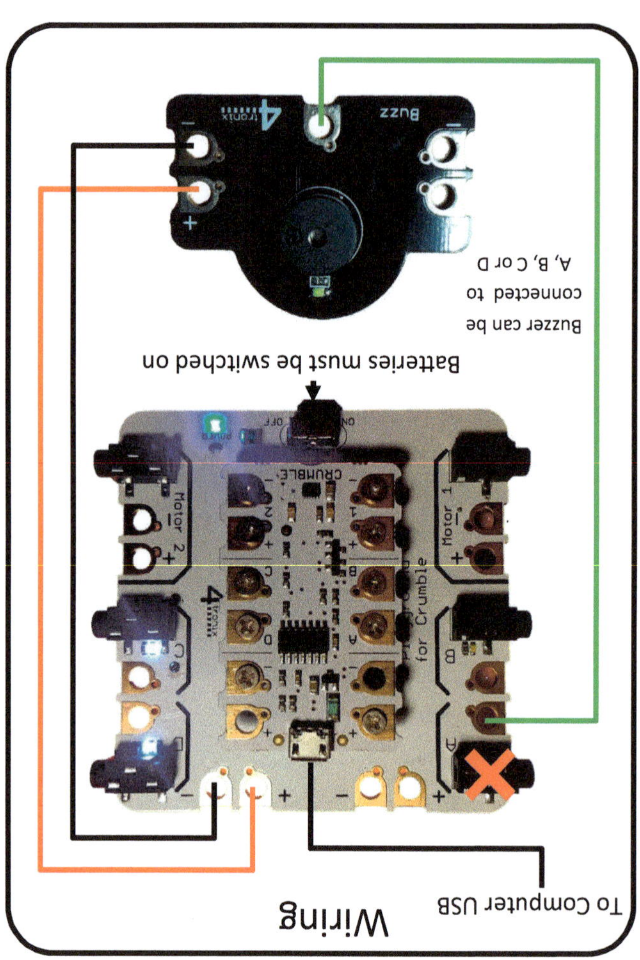
Wiring
To Computer USB
Batteries must be switched on
Buzzer can be connected to A, B, C or D
Buzz

More Information

The part that buzzes on a buzzer is called a piezo. It makes the noise when electricity stretches or compresses the piezoceramic material. Our buzzers are setup for a set voltage of electricity which is why they only make one tone.

Where else can you find piezo buzzers?

Power Port

Buzz

Power Port

The spare power port can be used to pass electricity on to other devices.

Crumble Playground **Buzzer**

Buzz

MC23

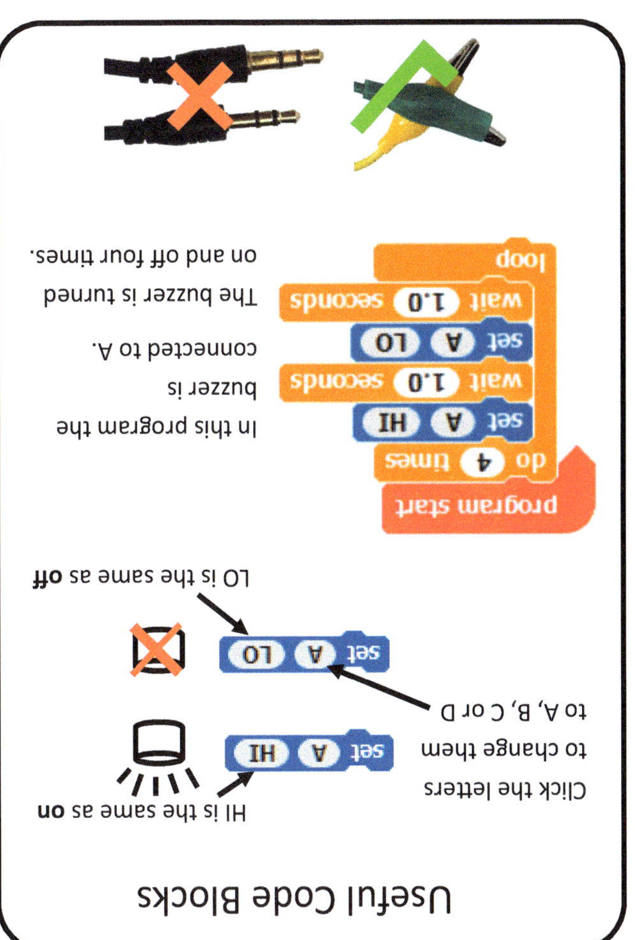

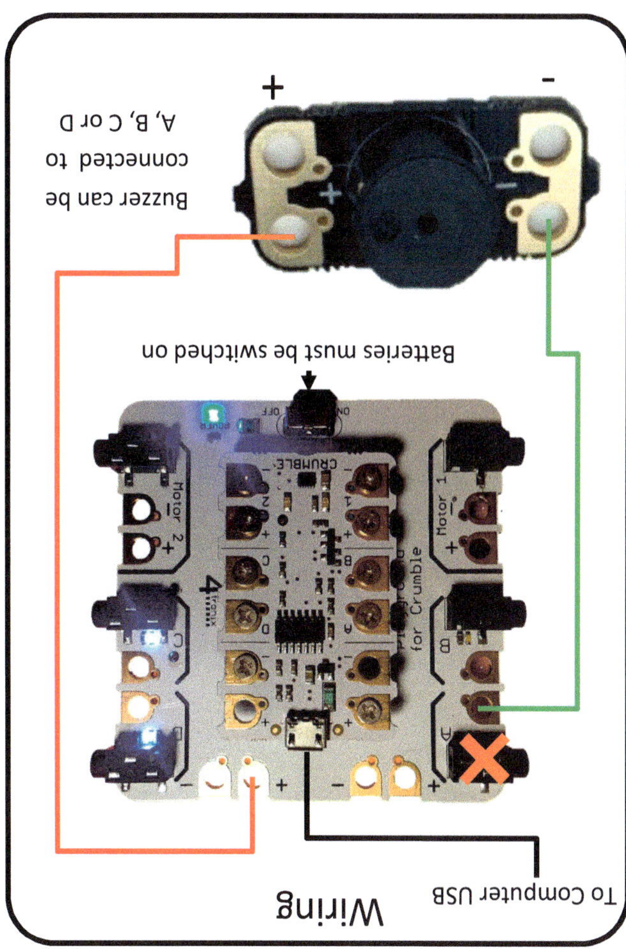

More Information

The part that buzzes on a buzzer is called a piezo. It makes the noise when electricity stretches or compresses the piezoceramic material. Our buzzers are setup for a set voltage of electricity which is why they only make one tone.

Where else can you find piezo buzzers?

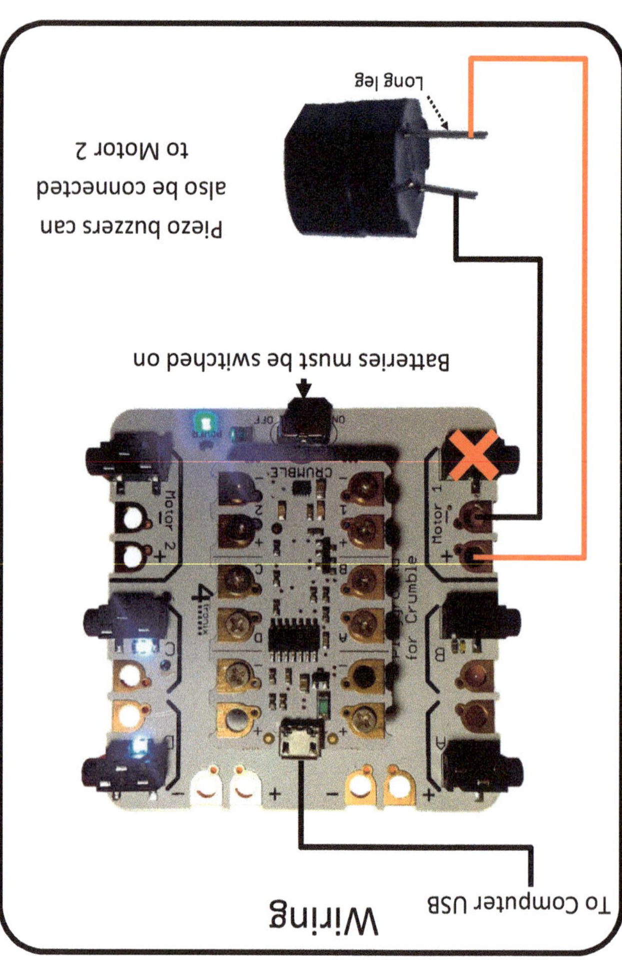

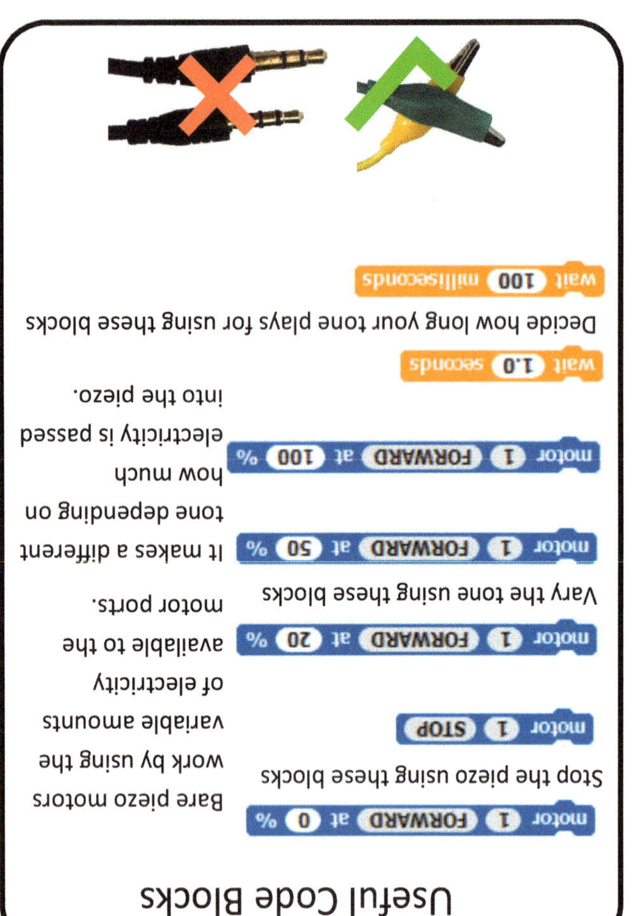

Useful Code Blocks
Bare piezo motors work by using the variable amounts of electricity available to the motor ports.
motor 1 FORWARD at 0 %
Stop the piezo using these blocks
motor 1 STOP
motor 1 FORWARD at 20 %
Vary the tone using these blocks
It makes a different tone depending on how much electricity is passed into the piezo.
motor 1 FORWARD at 50 %
motor 1 FORWARD at 100 %
wait 1.0 seconds
Decide how long your tone plays for using these blocks
wait 100 milliseconds

More Information

The piezo makes the noise when electricity stretches or compresses the piezoceramic material.

Don't forget to remove the sticker before using the piezo.

Where else can you find piezo buzzers?

Crumble Playground

Piezo

MC25

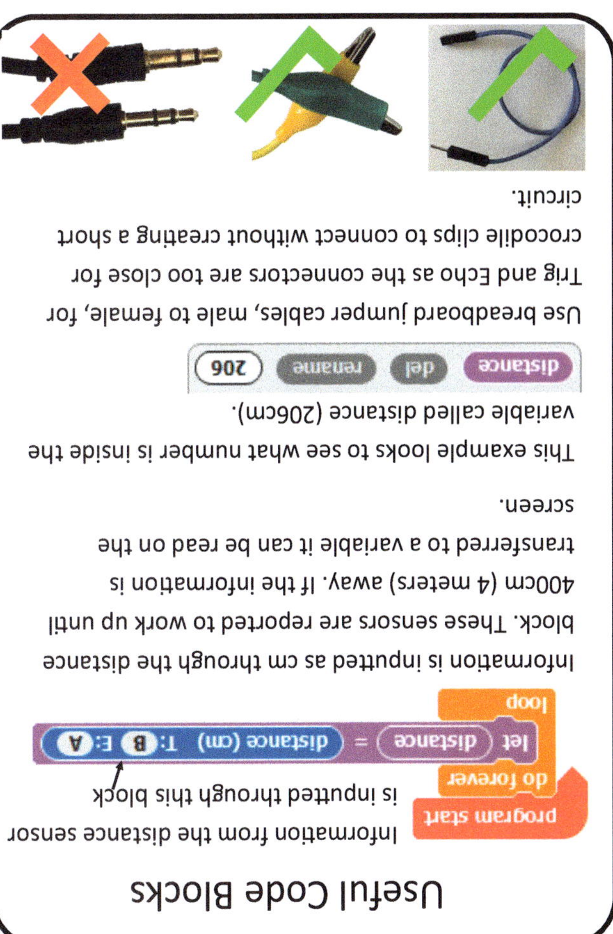
Useful Code Blocks
program start
do forever
let distance = distance (cm) T: B E: A
loop
Information from the distance sensor is inputted through this block
Information is inputted as cm through the distance block. These sensors are reported to work up until 400cm (4 meters) away. If the information is transferred to a variable it can be read on the screen.
This example looks to see what number is inside the variable called distance (206cm).
distance
del
rename
206
Use breadboard jumper cables, male to female, for Trig and Echo as the connectors are too close for crocodile clips to connect without creating a short circuit.

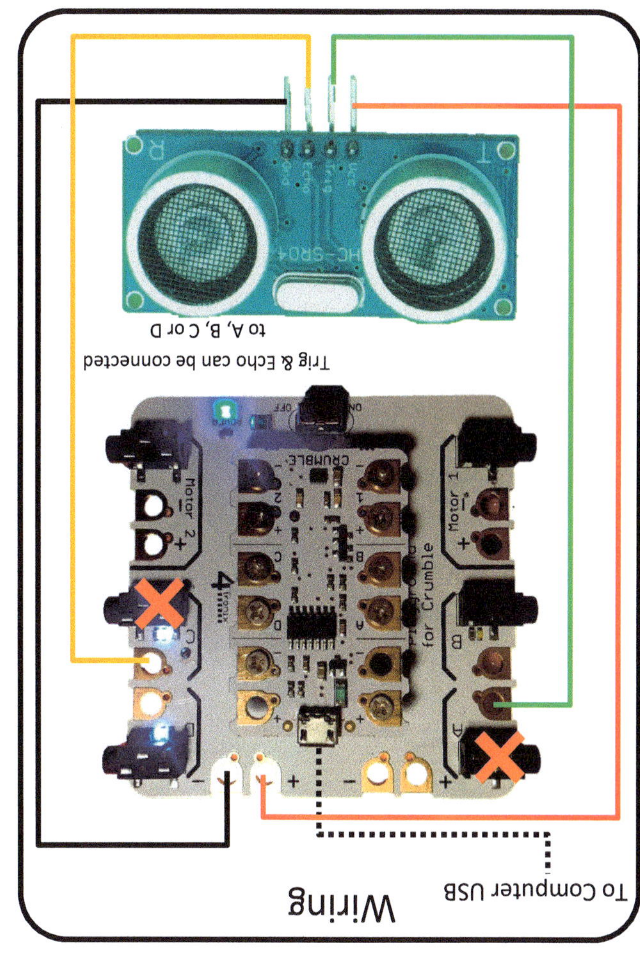
Wiring
To Computer USB
Trig & Echo can be connected to A, B, C or D

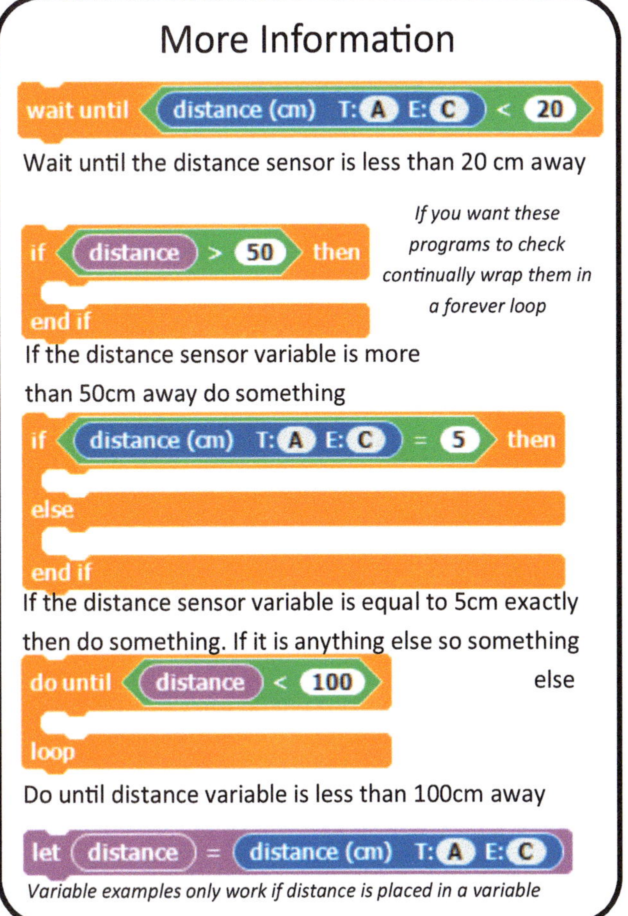
More Information
wait until distance (cm) T: A E: C < 20
Wait until the distance sensor is less than 20 cm away
if distance > 50 then
end if
If you want these programs to check continually wrap them in a forever loop
If the distance sensor variable is more than 50cm away do something
if distance (cm) T: A E: C = 5 then
else
end if
If the distance sensor variable is equal to 5cm exactly then do something. If it is anything else so something else
do until distance < 100
loop
Do until distance variable is less than 100cm away
let distance = distance (cm) T: A E: C
Variable examples only work if distance is placed in a variable

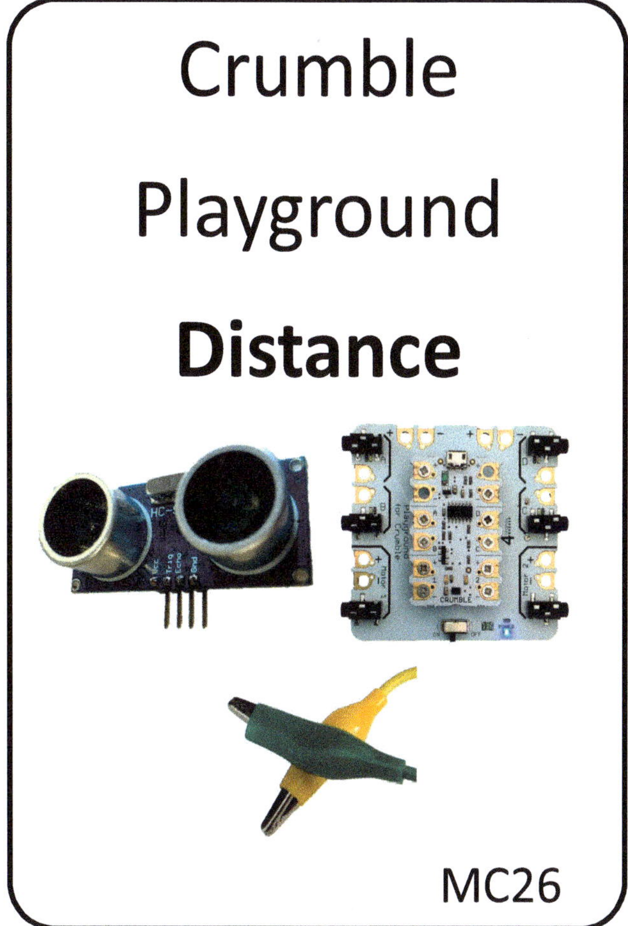
Crumble
Playground
Distance
MC26

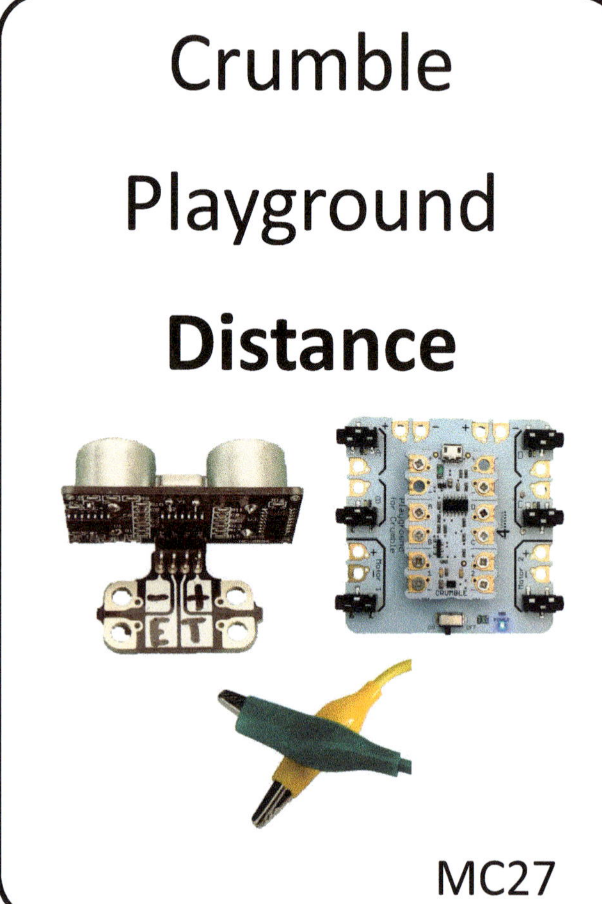

Crumble Playground **Distance**

MC27

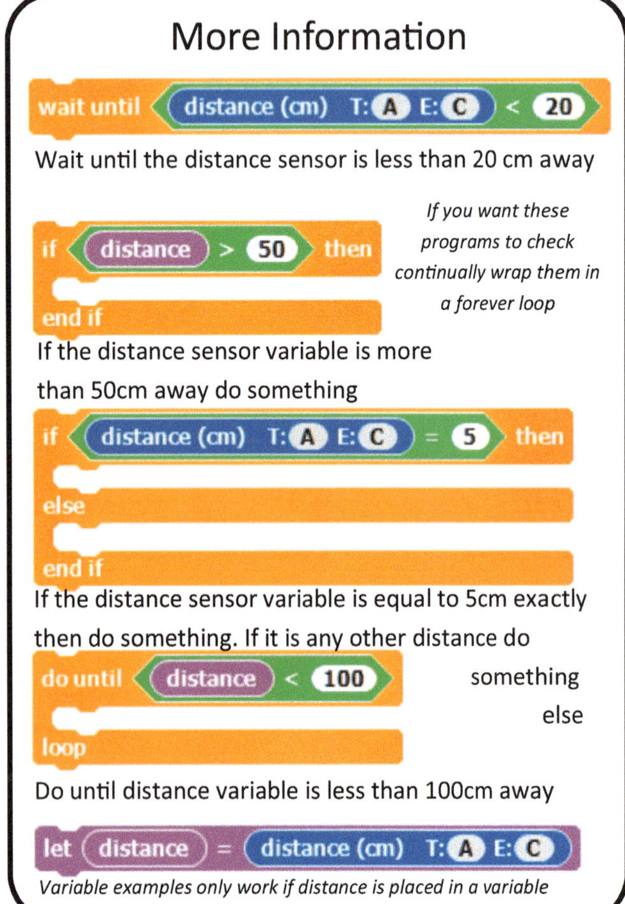

More Information

`wait until ( distance (cm) T: A E: C ) < 20`

Wait until the distance sensor is less than 20 cm away

`if ( distance ) > 50 then` … `end if`

If you want these programs to check continually wrap them in a forever loop

If the distance sensor variable is more than 50cm away do something

`if ( distance (cm) T: A E: C ) = 5 then` … `else` … `end if`

If the distance sensor variable is equal to 5cm exactly then do something. If it is any other distance do something else

`do until ( distance ) < 100` … `loop`

Do until distance variable is less than 100cm away

`let ( distance ) = ( distance (cm) T: A E: C )`

Variable examples only work if distance is placed in a variable

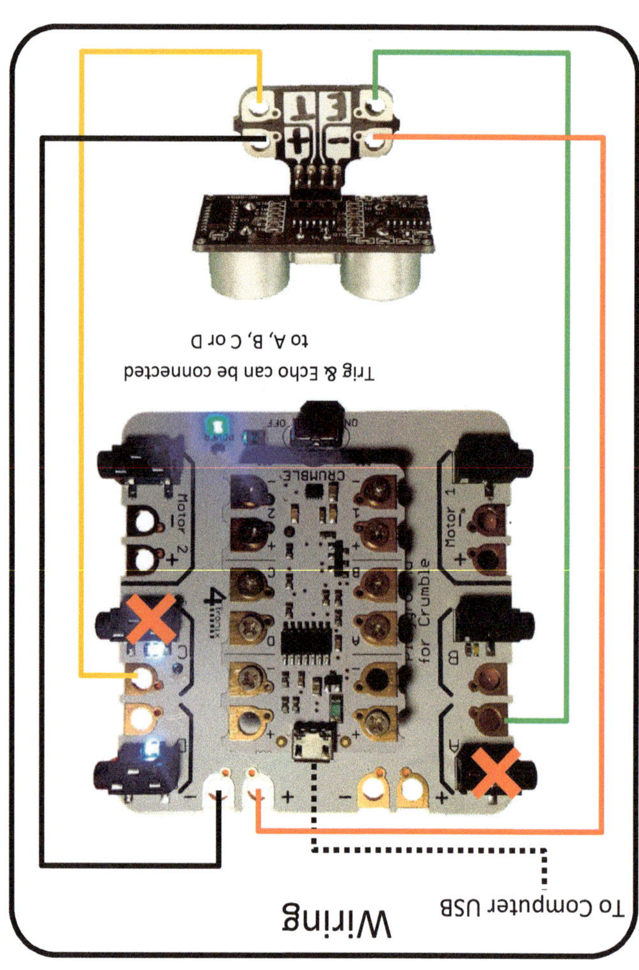

Wiring

To Computer USB
Trig & Echo can be connected to A, B, C or D

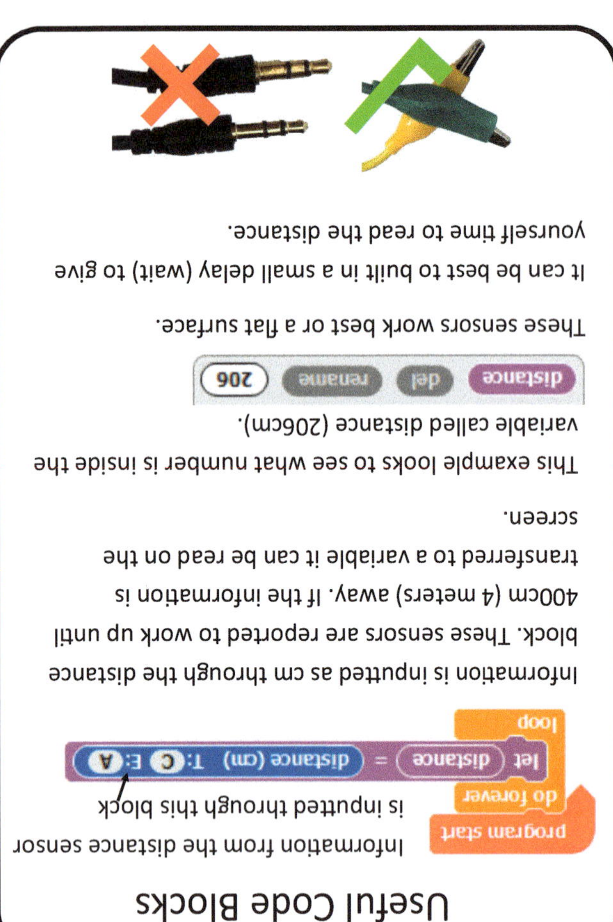

Useful Code Blocks

```
program start
  do forever
    let (distance) = (distance (cm) T: C E: A)
  loop
```

Information from the distance sensor is inputted through this block

Information is inputted as cm through the distance block. These sensors are reported to work up until 400cm (4 meters) away. If the information is transferred to a variable it can be read on the screen.

This example looks to see what number is inside the variable called distance (206cm).

`distance` `del` `rename` `206`

These sensors work best or a flat surface.

It can be best to built in a small delay (wait) to give yourself time to read the distance.

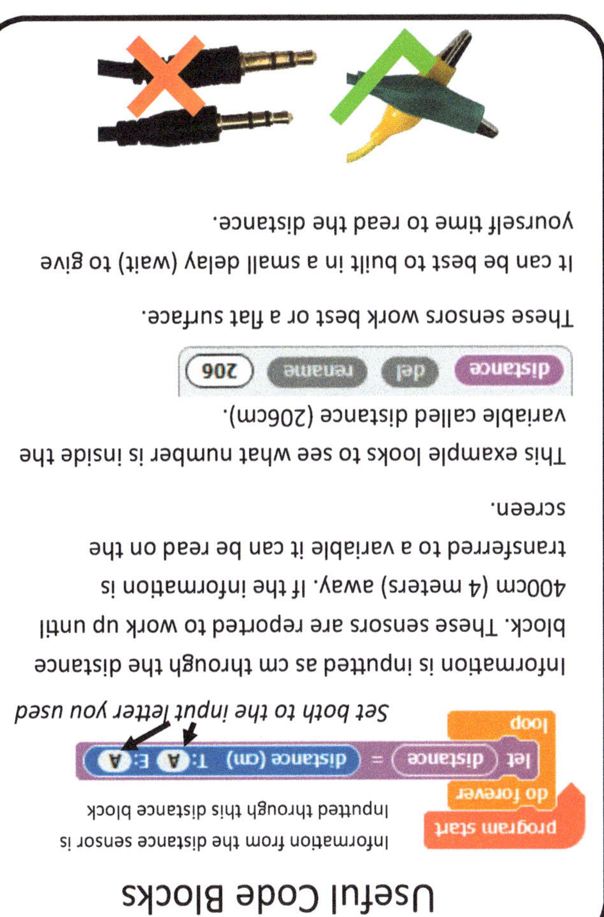

Useful Code Blocks
program start
do forever
let distance = distance (cm) T: A E: A
loop
Information from the distance sensor is
Inputted through this distance block
Set both to the input letter you used
Information is inputted as cm through the distance block. These sensors are reported to work up until 400cm (4 meters) away. If the information is transferred to a variable it can be read on the screen.
This example looks to see what number is inside the variable called distance (206cm).
distance
del
rename
206
These sensors work best or a flat surface.
It can be best to built in a small delay (wait) to give yourself time to read the distance.

Wiring
To Computer USB
Combined
trig and
echo can
be inputted
through A,
B, C or D

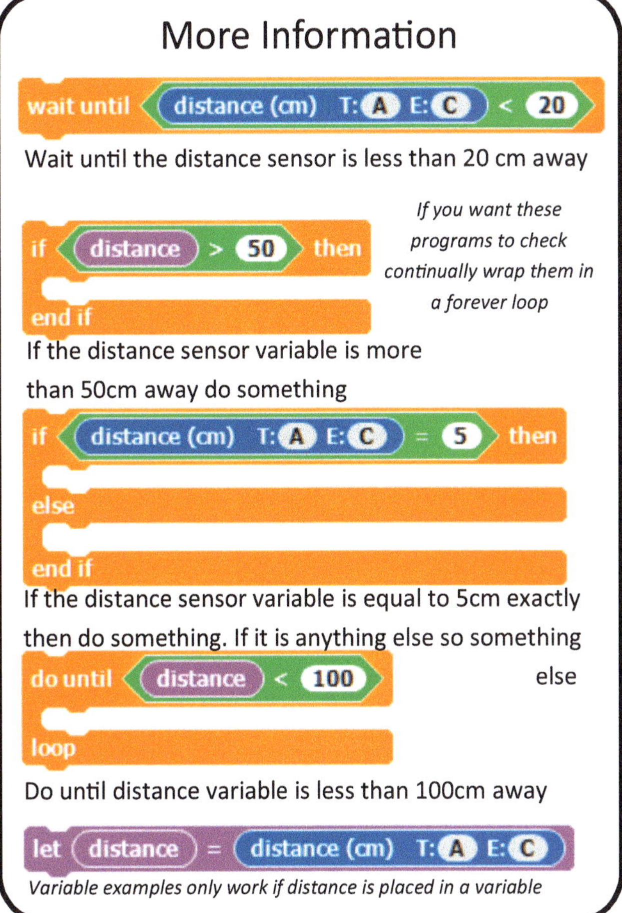

More Information
wait until distance (cm) T: A E: C < 20
Wait until the distance sensor is less than 20 cm away
if distance > 50 then
end if
If you want these programs to check continually wrap them in a forever loop
If the distance sensor variable is more than 50cm away do something
if distance (cm) T: A E: C = 5 then
else
end if
If the distance sensor variable is equal to 5cm exactly then do something. If it is anything else so something else
do until distance < 100
loop
Do until distance variable is less than 100cm away
let distance = distance (cm) T: A E: C
Variable examples only work if distance is placed in a variable

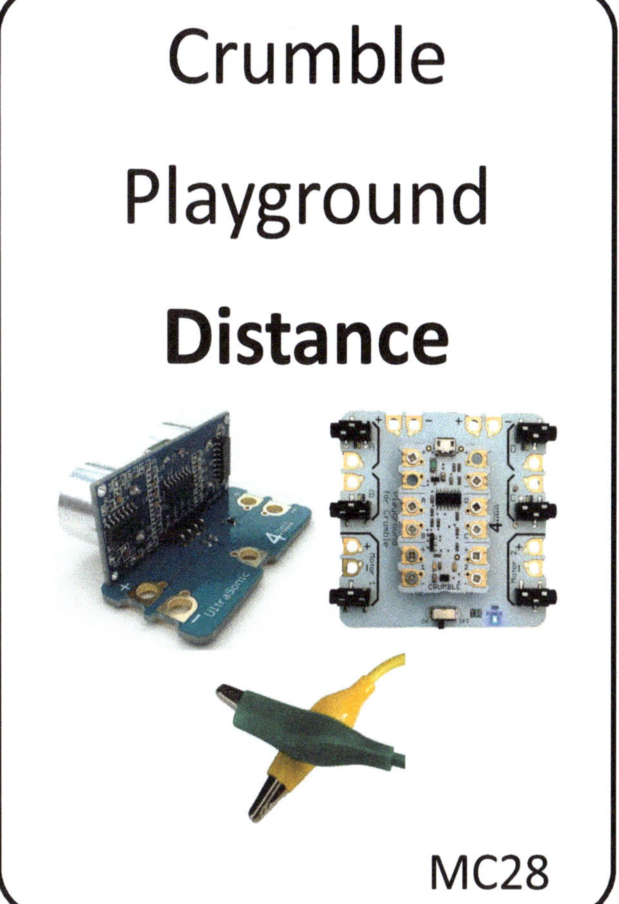

Crumble
Playground
Distance
MC28

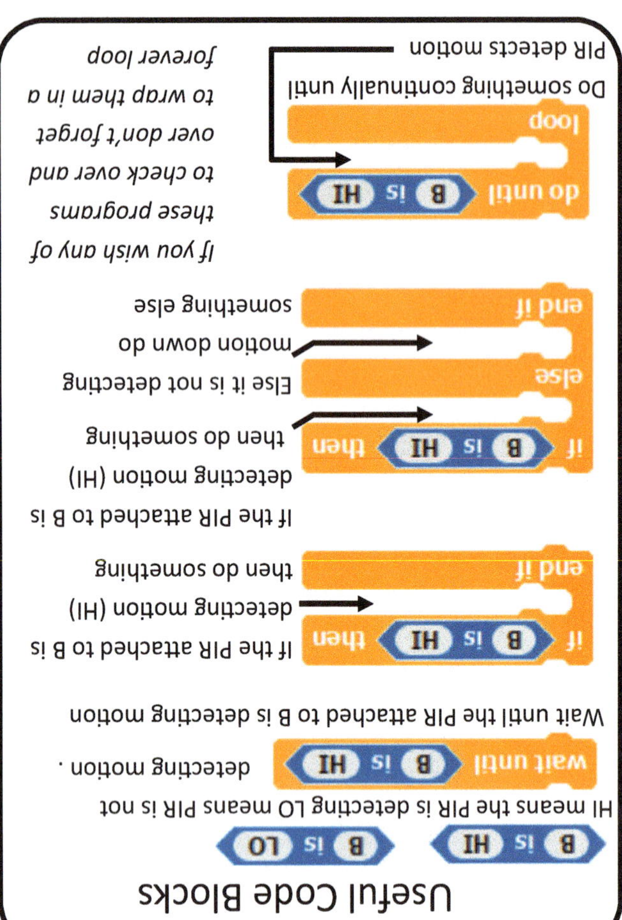

Useful Code Blocks
B is HI
B is LO
HI means the PIR is detecting LO means PIR is not detecting motion .
wait until B is HI
Wait until the PIR attached to B is detecting motion
if B is HI then
end if
If the PIR attached to B is detecting motion (HI) then do something
if B is HI then
else
end if
If the PIR attached to B is detecting motion (HI) then do something
Else it is not detecting motion down do something else
do until B is HI
loop
Do something continually until PIR detects motion
If you wish any of these programs to check over and over don't forget to wrap them in a forever loop

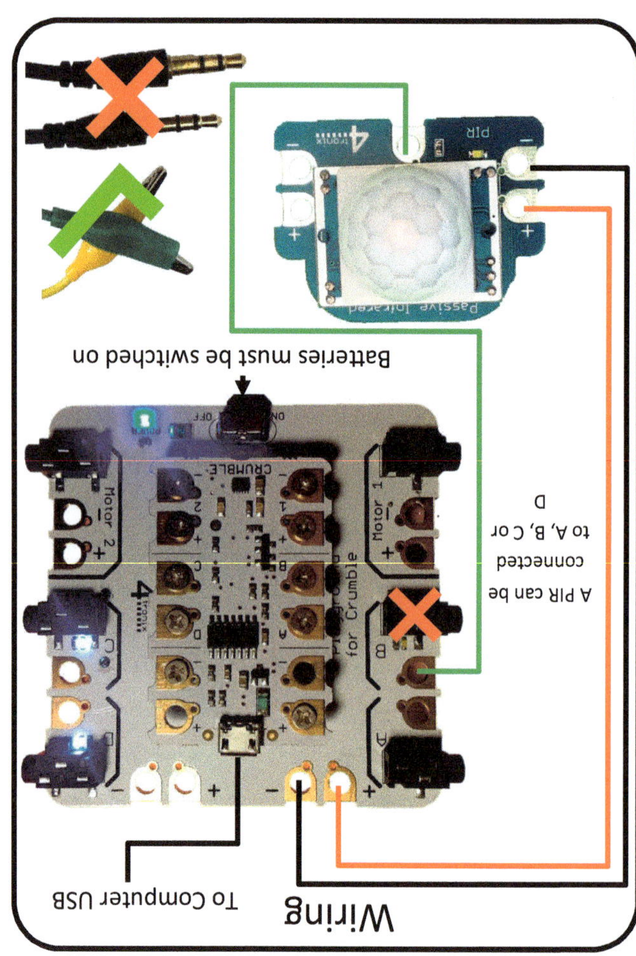

More Information

PIR are INPUT devices

You can make things happen when the PIR detects motion.

There are two small dials on the back of the PIR sensor which can be carefully turned around to adjust the sensitivity of the PIR.

Use a small screwdriver to adjust these.

NOTE PIR are one of the most difficult input devices to make work.

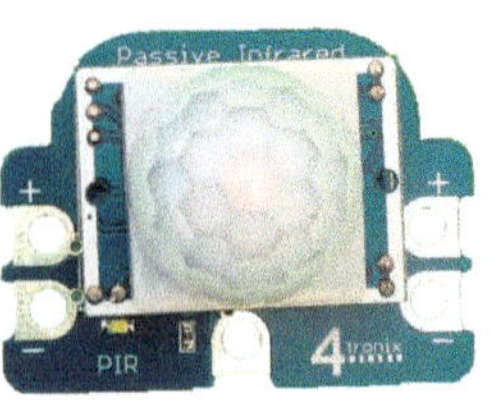

Electricity can be passed on to other devices through the extra + and - power connections on this device

Crumble

Playground

PIR

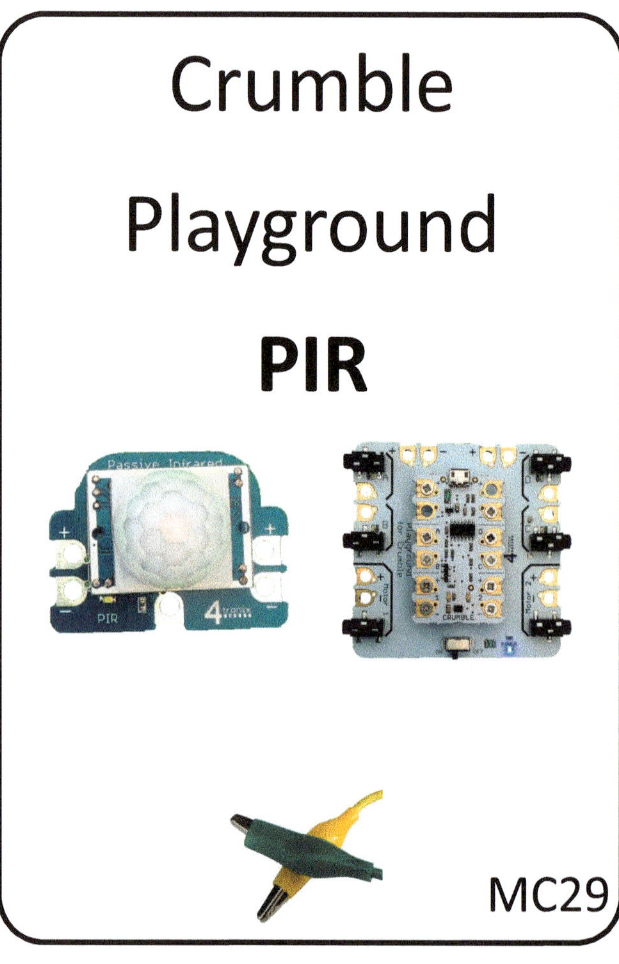

MC29

Crumble

Playground

Number Counter

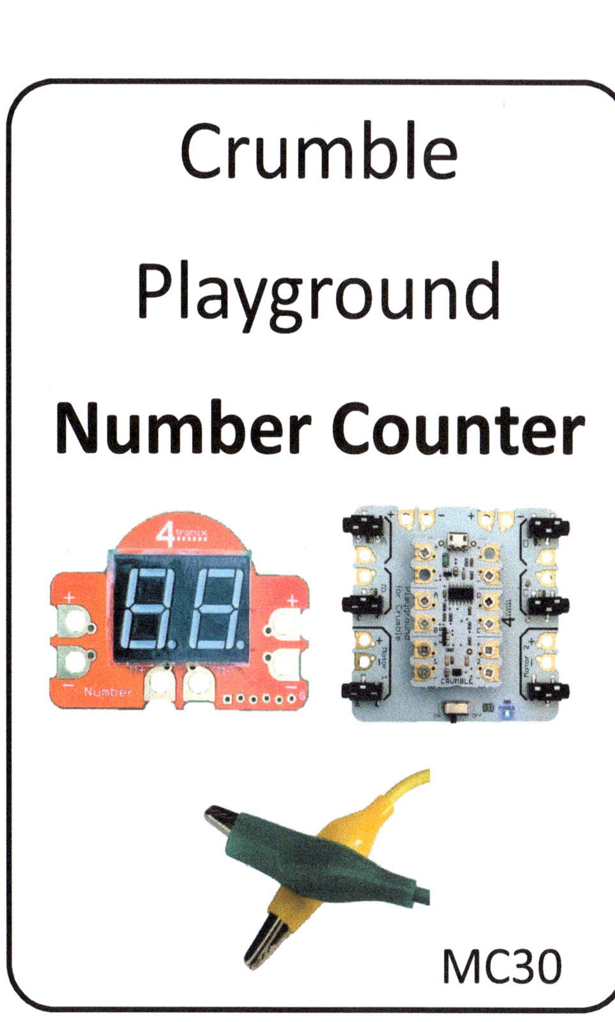

MC30

Wiring

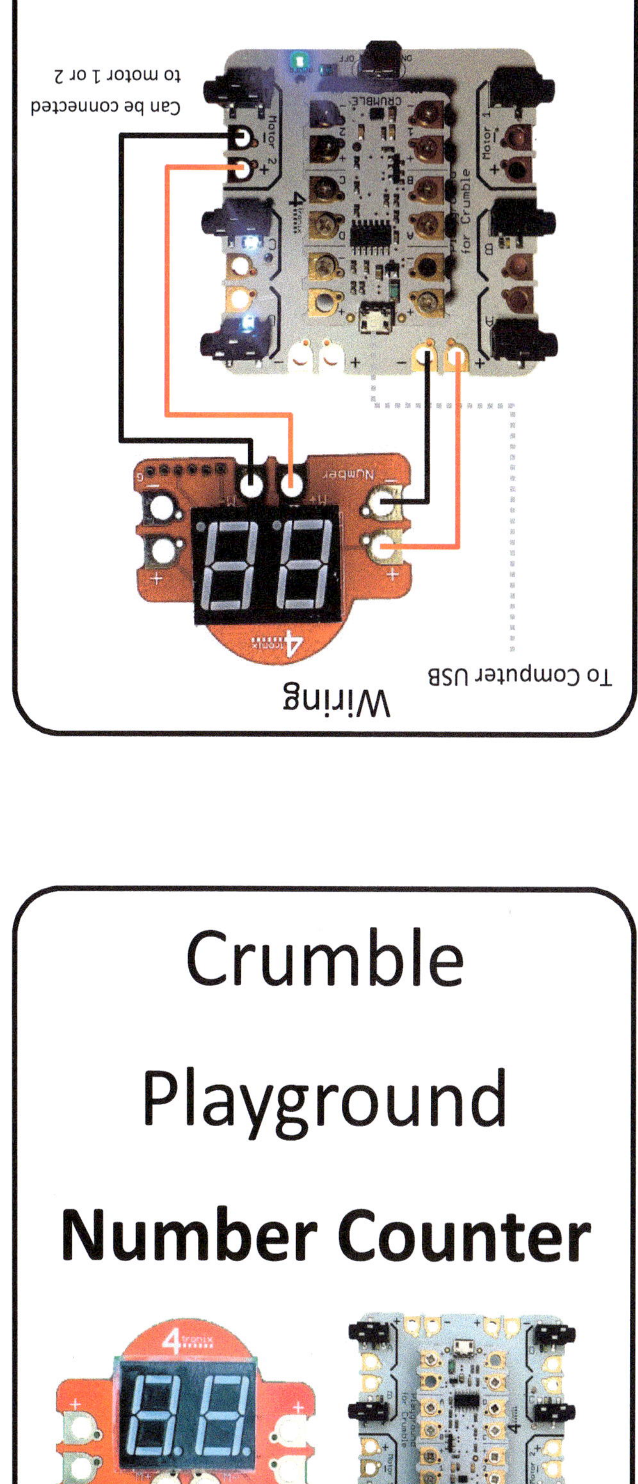
To Computer USB
Can be connected
to motor 1 or 2
Number

Useful Code Blocks

To test the number counter create this small program.

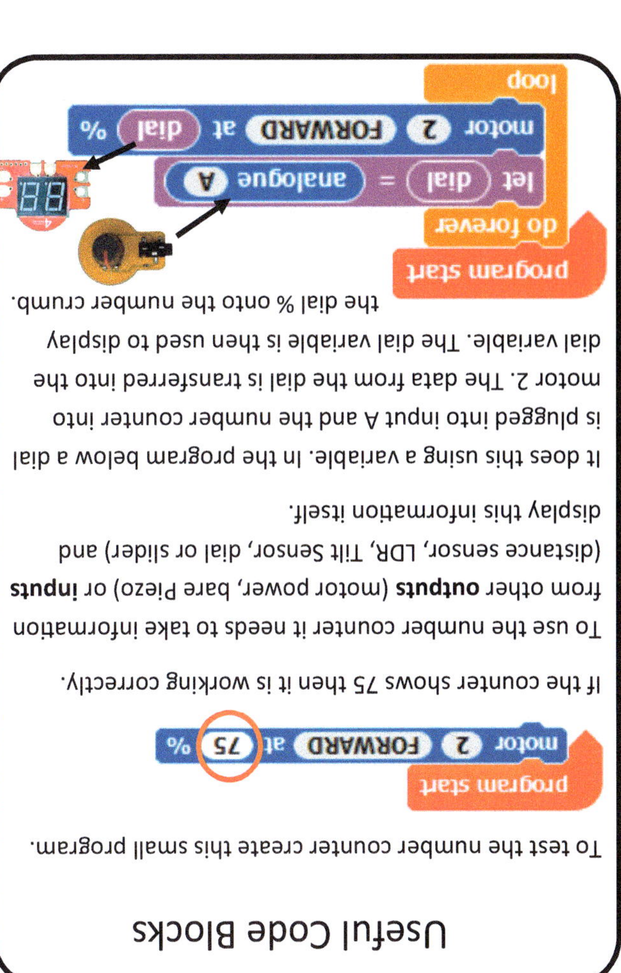
program start
motor 2 FORWARD at 75 %

If the counter shows 75 then it is working correctly.

To use the number counter it needs to take information from other **outputs** (motor power, bare Piezo) or **inputs** (distance sensor, LDR, Tilt Sensor, dial or slider) and display this information itself.

It does this using a variable. In the program below a dial is plugged into input A and the number counter into motor 2. The data from the dial is transferred into the dial variable. The dial variable is then used to display the dial % onto the number crumb.

program start
do forever
let dial = analogue A
motor 2 FORWARD at dial %
loop

More Information

One of the difficulties with the number crumb is that it only outputs numbers between 0 and 99.

This means that any inputs over 99 are not recognised.

The Distance sensor inputs 0-400

The LDR sensor inputs 0-255

The programmer will need to adapt the input number to make it fit inside 0-99 using maths blocks

```
let distance = distance ÷ 4
```

In this example the distance sensor 0-400 has been divided by 4 so that it will almost fit into the number counter.

One digit on the number counter is now equal to 4 cm

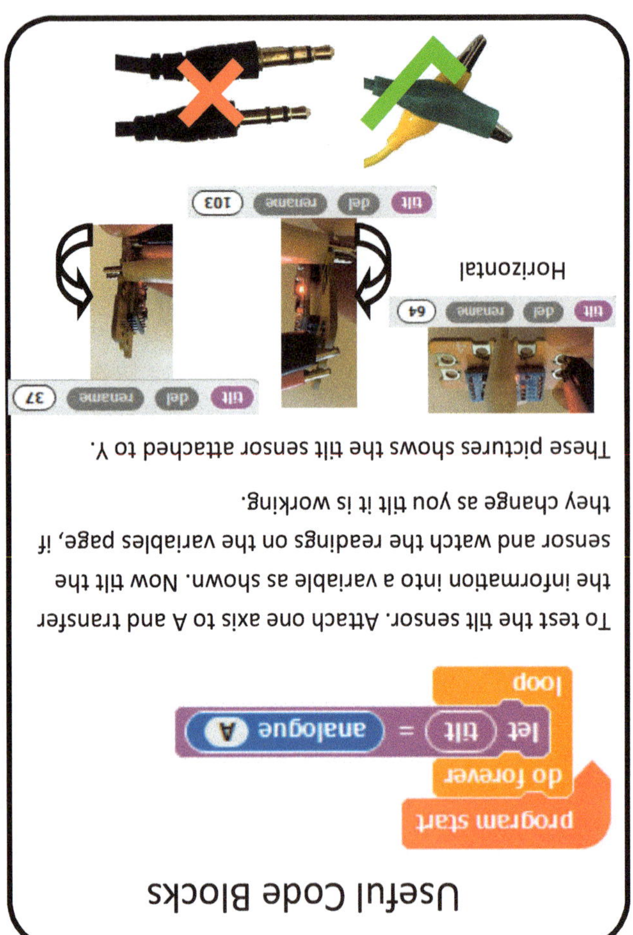
Useful Code Blocks
program start
do forever
let tilt = analogue A
loop
To test the tilt sensor. Attach one axis to A and transfer
the information into a variable as shown. Now tilt the
sensor and watch the readings on the variables page, if
they change as you tilt it is working.
These pictures shows the tilt sensor attached to Y.
tilt del rename 37
tilt del rename 103
tilt del rename 64
Horizontal

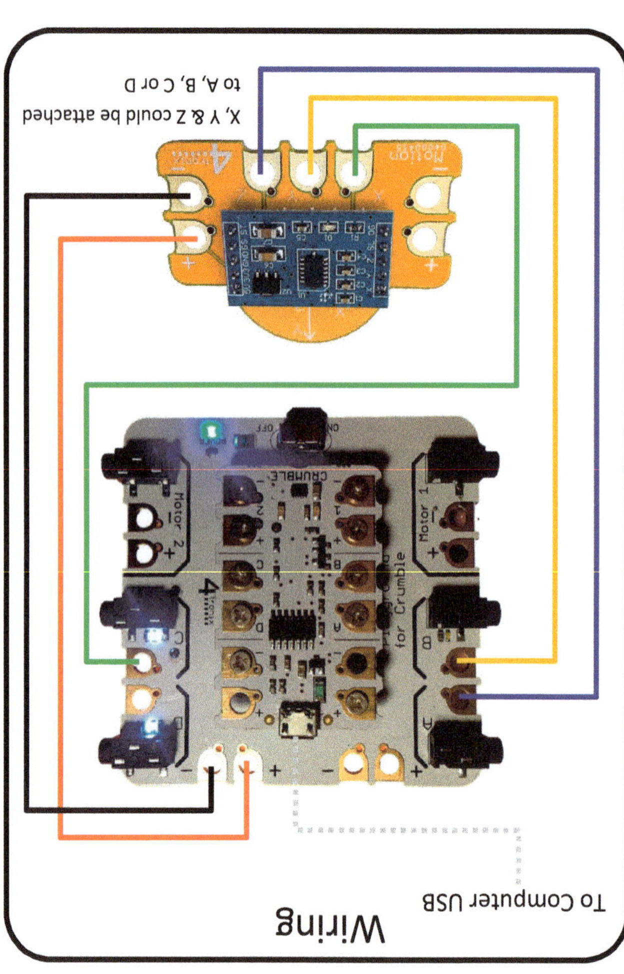
Wiring
To Computer USB
X, Y & Z could be attached
to A, B, C or D

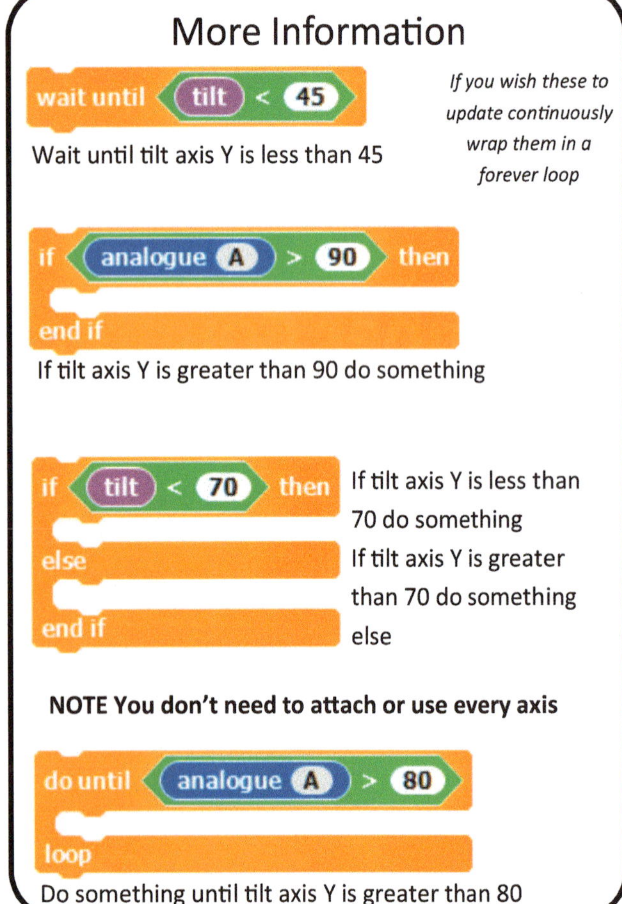
More Information
wait until tilt < 45
Wait until tilt axis Y is less than 45
If you wish these to update continuously wrap them in a forever loop
if analogue A > 90 then
end if
If tilt axis Y is greater than 90 do something
if tilt < 70 then
else
end if
If tilt axis Y is less than 70 do something
If tilt axis Y is greater than 70 do something else
NOTE You don't need to attach or use every axis
do until analogue A > 80
loop
Do something until tilt axis Y is greater than 80

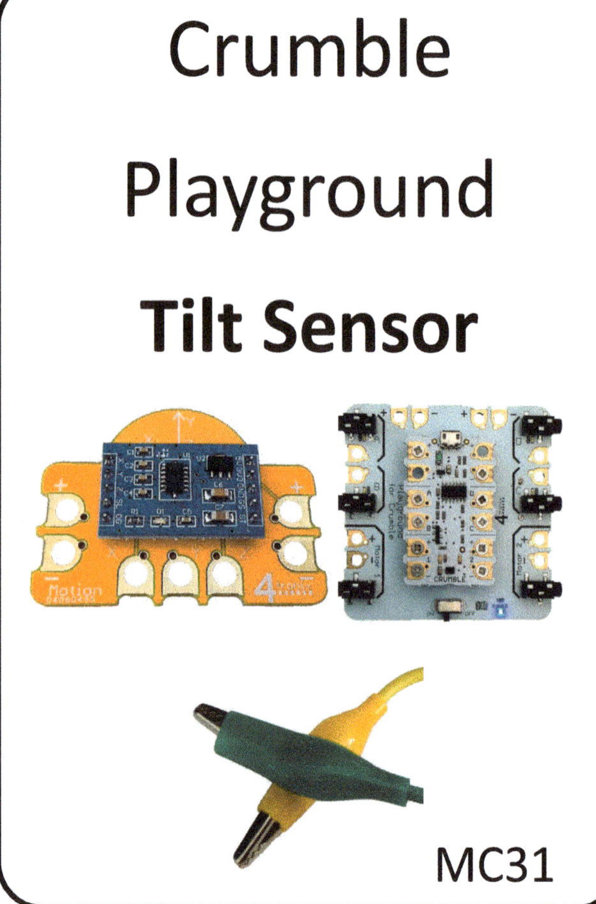
Crumble
Playground
Tilt Sensor
MC31

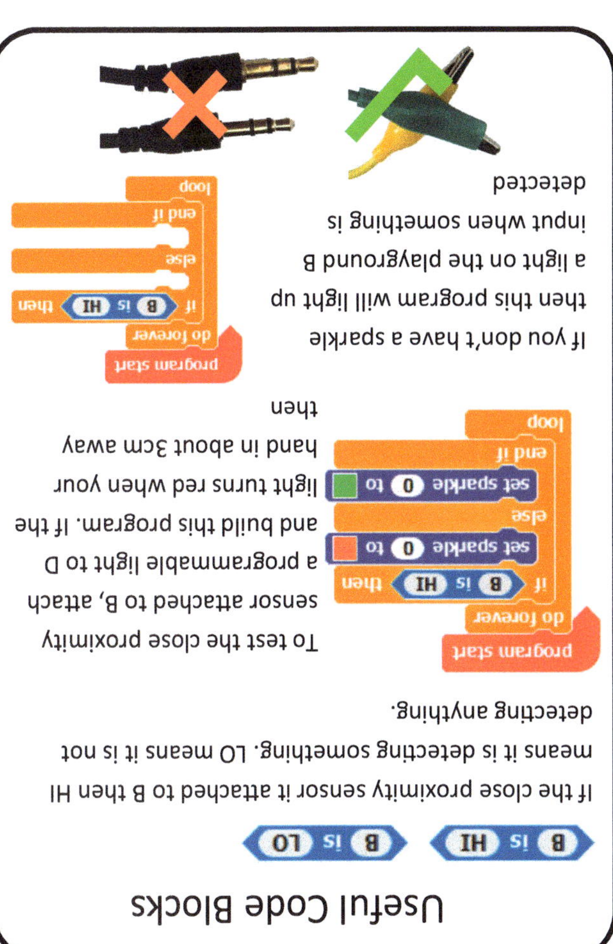
Useful Code Blocks
B is HI
B is LO
If the close proximity sensor it attached to B then HI means it is detecting something. LO means it is not detecting anything.
program start
do forever
if B is HI then
set sparkle 0 to
else
set sparkle 0 to
end if
loop
To test the close proximity sensor attached to B, attach a programmable light to D and build this program. If the light turns red when your hand in about 3cm away then
program start
do forever
if B is HI then
else
end if
loop
If you don't have a sparkle then this program will light up a light on the playground B input when something is detected

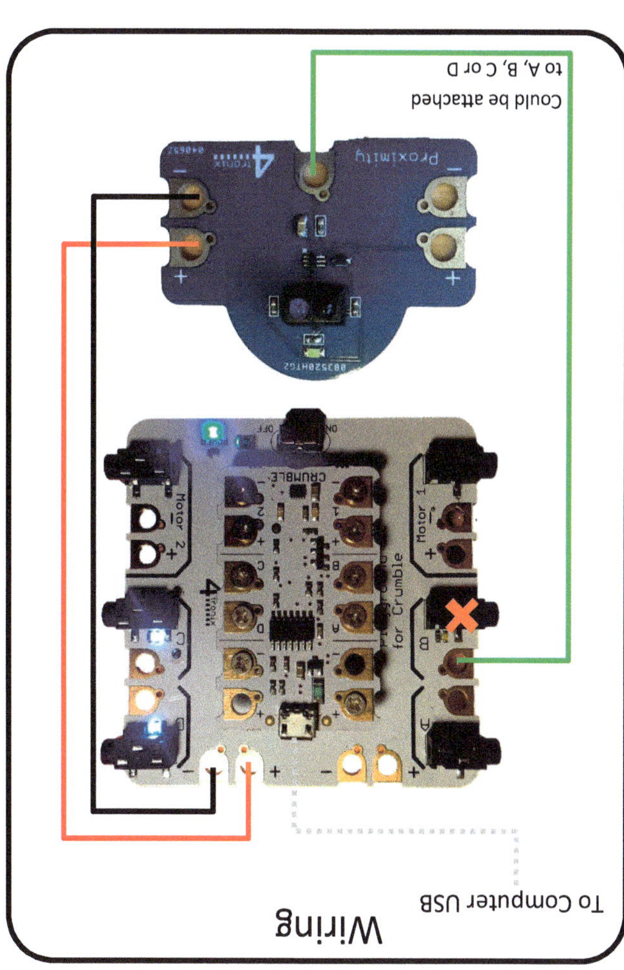
Wiring
To Computer USB
Could be attached to A, B, C or D

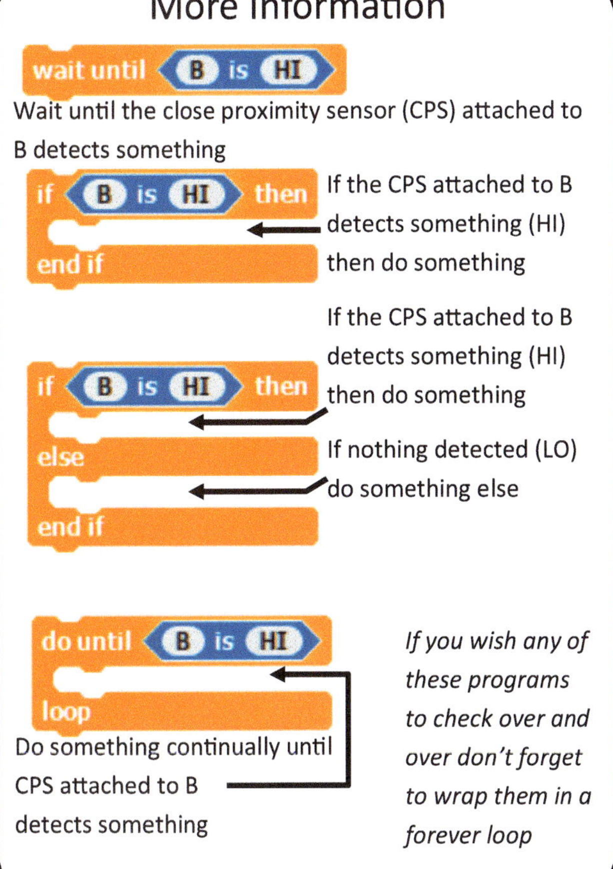
More Information
wait until B is HI
Wait until the close proximity sensor (CPS) attached to B detects something
if B is HI then
end if
If the CPS attached to B detects something (HI) then do something
if B is HI then
else
end if
If the CPS attached to B detects something (HI) then do something
If nothing detected (LO) do something else
do until B is HI
loop
Do something continually until CPS attached to B detects something
If you wish any of these programs to check over and over don't forget to wrap them in a forever loop

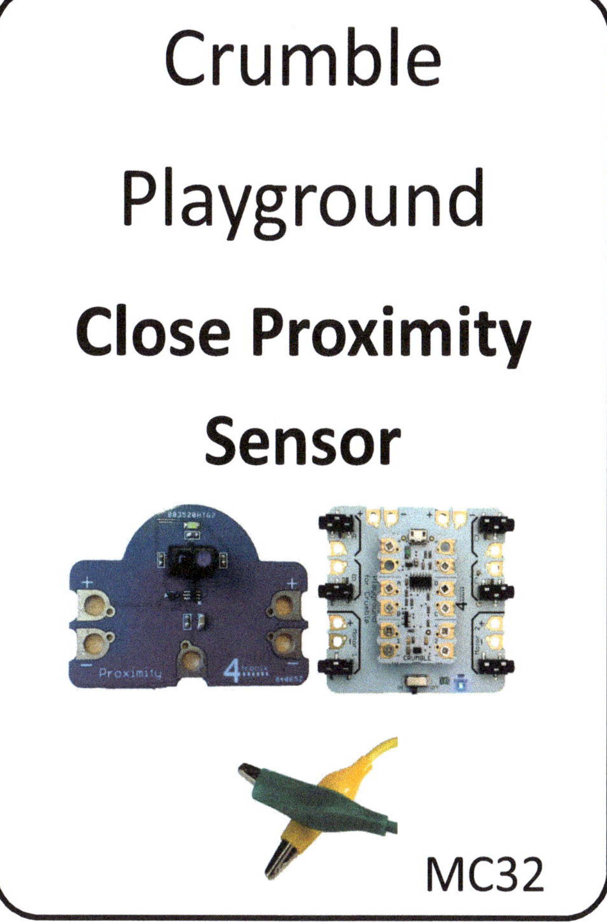
Crumble
Playground
Close Proximity
Sensor
MC32

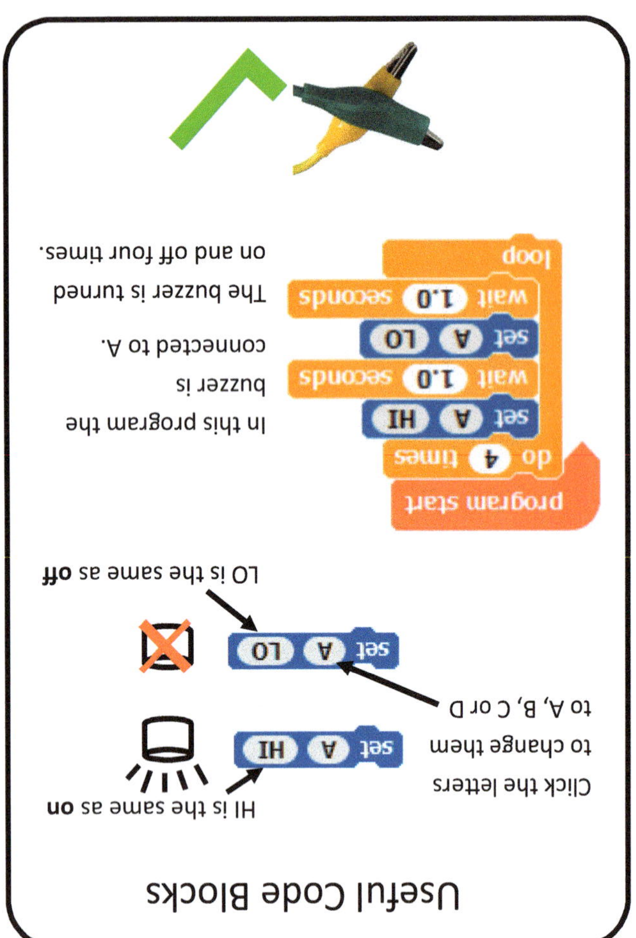

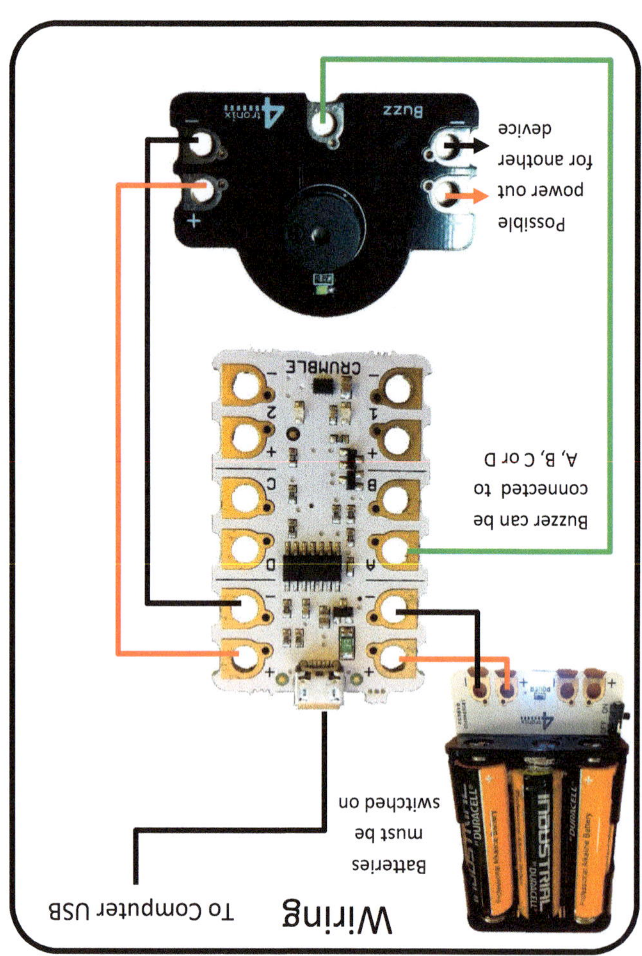

More Information

The part that buzzes on a buzzer is called a piezo. It makes the noise when electricity stretches or compresses the piezoceramic material. Our buzzers are setup for a set voltage of electricity which is why they only make one tone.

Where else can you find piezo buzzers?

The spare power port can be used to pass electricity on to other devices.

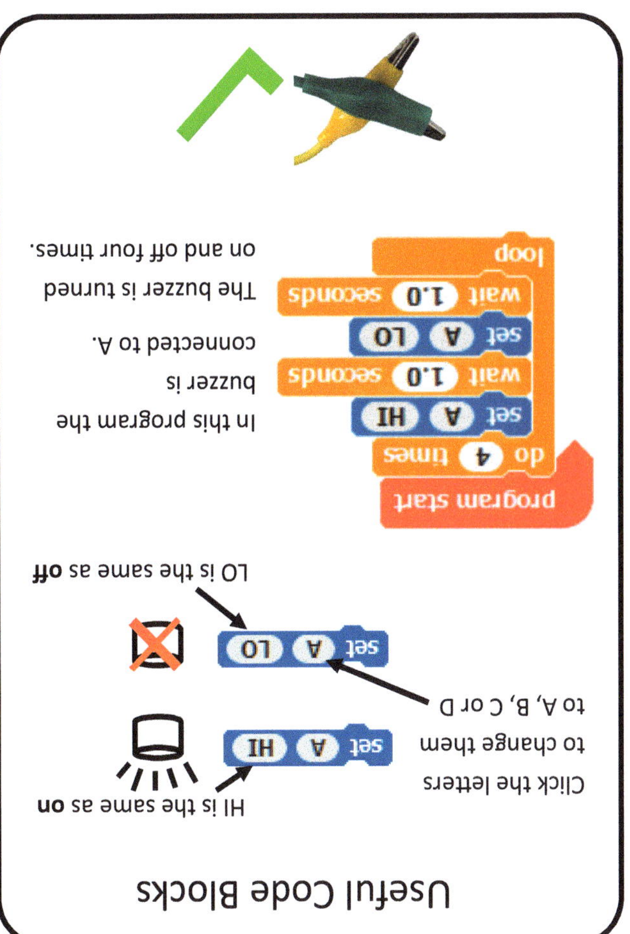
Useful Code Blocks
Click the letters to change them to A, B, C or D
set A HI
HI is the same as on
set A LO
LO is the same as off
program start
do 4 times
set A HI
wait 1.0 seconds
set A LO
wait 1.0 seconds
loop
In this program the buzzer is connected to A.
The buzzer is turned on and off four times.

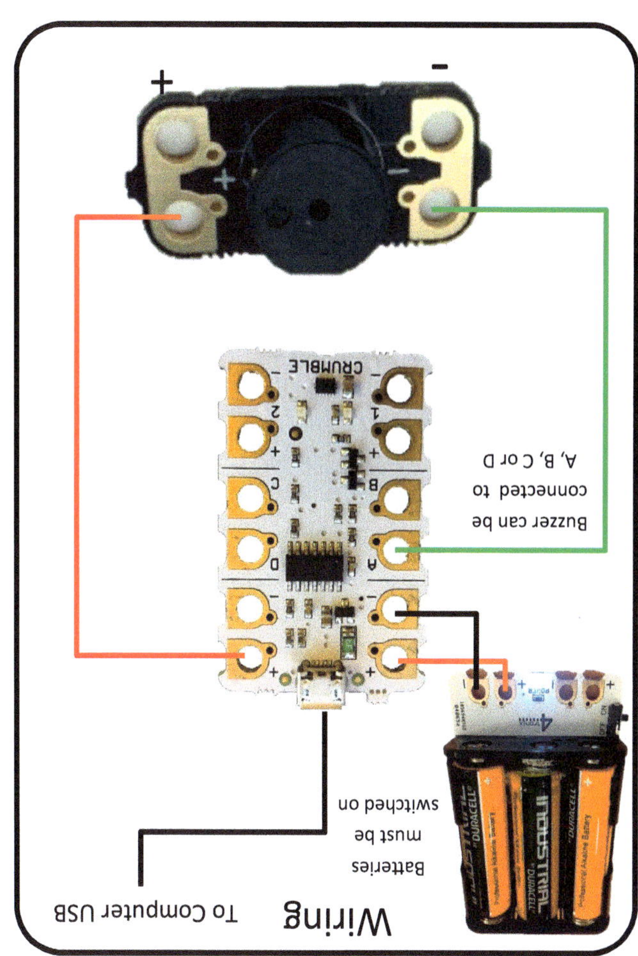
Wiring
+
-
CRUMBLE
Buzzer can be connected to A, B, C or D
Batteries must be switched on
To Computer USB

More Information

The part that buzzes on a buzzer is called a piezo. It makes the noise when electricity stretches or compresses the piezoceramic material. Our buzzers are setup for a set voltage of electricity which is why they only make one tone.

Where else can you find piezo buzzers?

Crumble
Buzzer
CRUMBLE
MC34

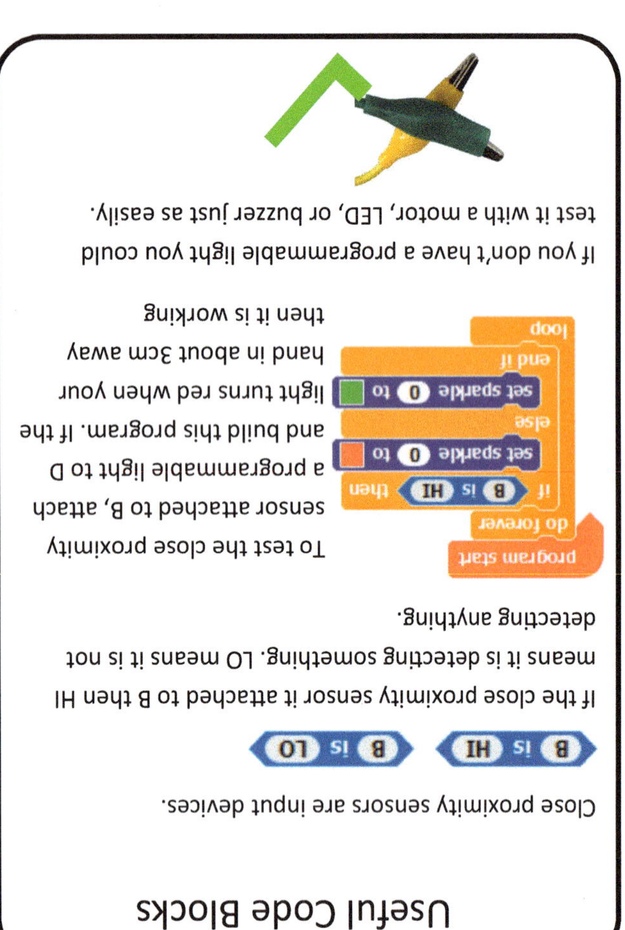

Useful Code Blocks

Close proximity sensors are input devices.

B is HI
B is LO

If the close proximity sensor it attached to B then HI means it is detecting something. LO means it is not detecting anything.

program start
do forever
if B is HI then
set sparkle 0 to
else
set sparkle 0 to
end if
loop

To test the close proximity sensor attached to B, attach a programmable light to D and build this program. If the light turns red when your hand in about 3cm away then it is working

If you don't have a programmable light you could test it with a motor, LED, or buzzer just as easily.

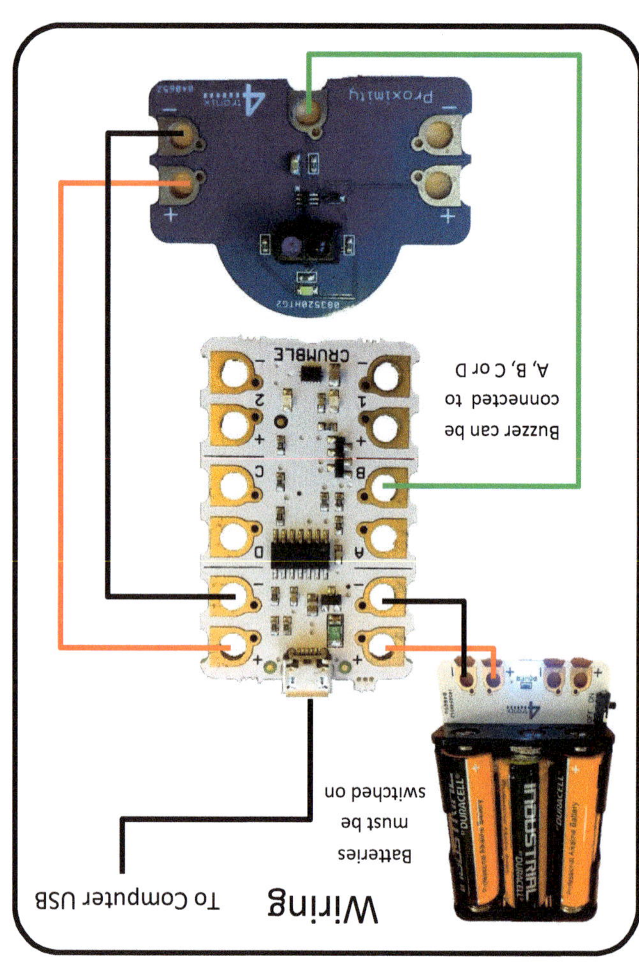

Wiring

To Computer USB
Batteries must be switched on
Buzzer can be connected to A, B, C or D
CRUMBLE
Proximity

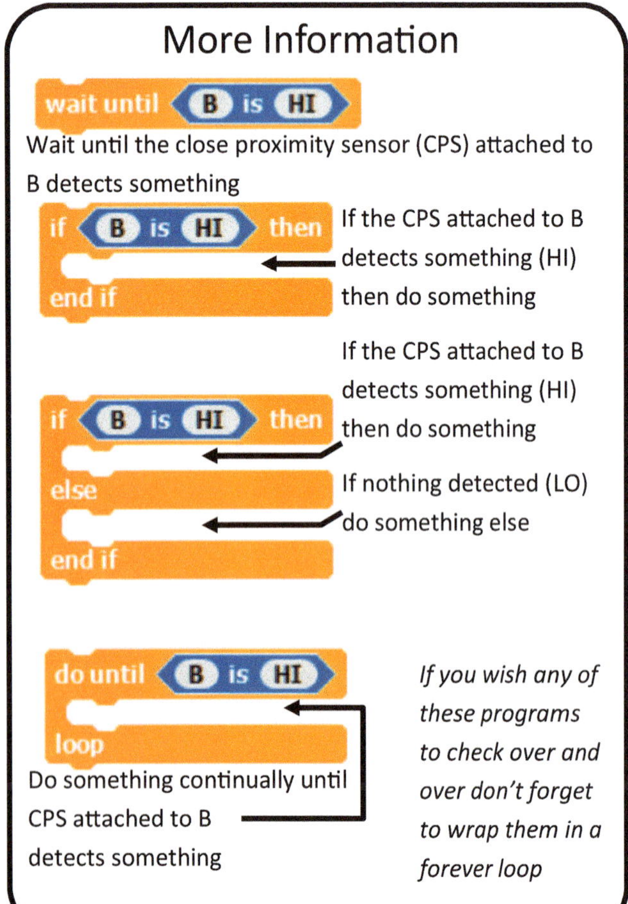

More Information

wait until B is HI

Wait until the close proximity sensor (CPS) attached to B detects something

if B is HI then
end if

If the CPS attached to B detects something (HI) then do something

if B is HI then
else
end if

If the CPS attached to B detects something (HI) then do something

If nothing detected (LO) do something else

do until B is HI
loop

Do something continually until CPS attached to B detects something

If you wish any of these programs to check over and over don't forget to wrap them in a forever loop

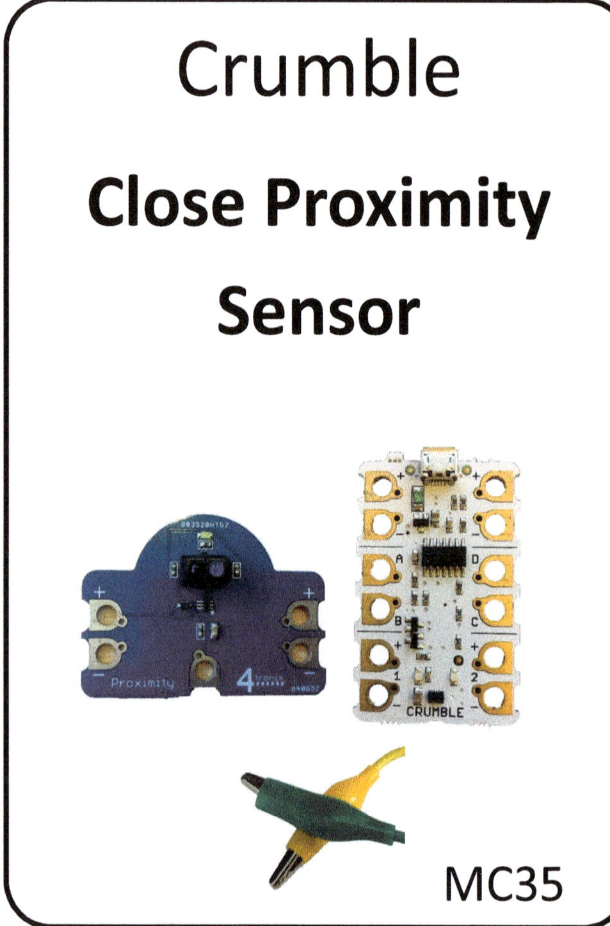

Crumble

Close Proximity Sensor

Proximity
CRUMBLE

MC35

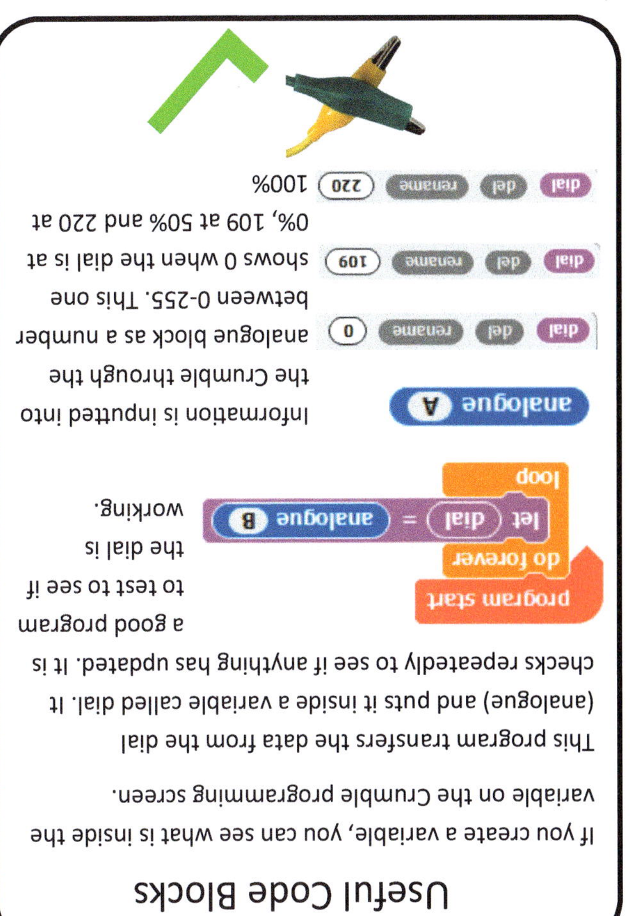

Useful Code Blocks

If you create a variable, you can see what is inside the variable on the Crumble programming screen.

This program transfers the data from the dial (analogue) and puts it inside a variable called dial. It checks repeatedly to see if anything has updated. It is a good program to test to see if the dial is working.

```
program start
do forever
  let dial = analogue B
loop
```

`analogue A`

Information is inputted into the Crumble through the analogue block as a number between 0-255. This one shows 0 when the dial is at 0%, 109 at 50% and 220 at 100%

dial	del	rename	0
dial	del	rename	109
dial	del	rename	220

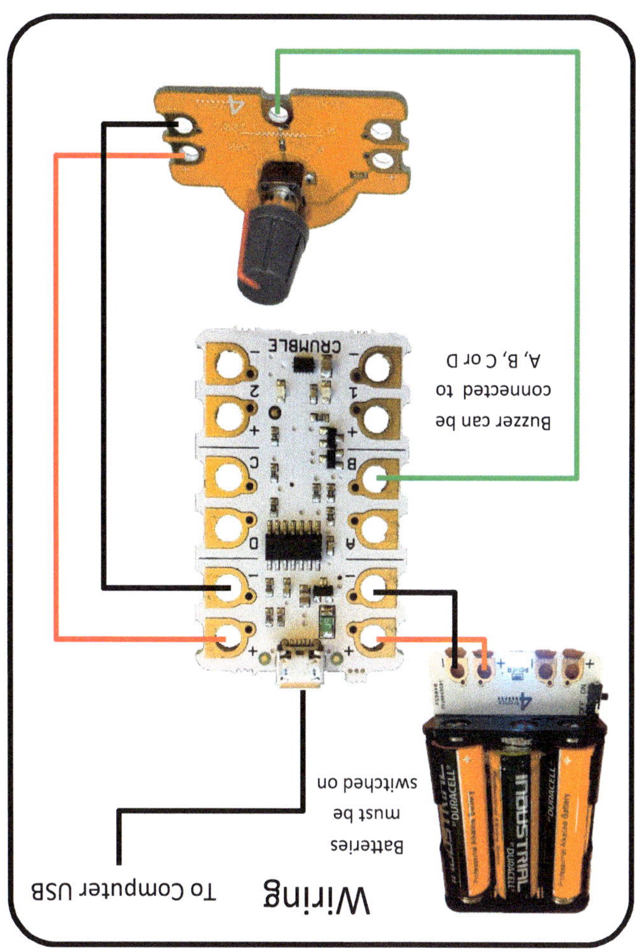

Wiring

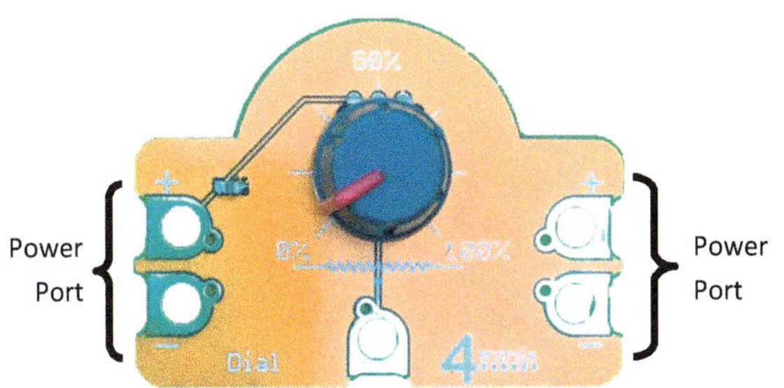

More Information

Dials can be used to adjust the amount of power going into a motor, the colour balance of a programmable light, the tone of a piezo element, The amount of turn a servo moves etc.

It can be used wherever a number that changes is used.

The left over power ports on this dial can be used to power another device.

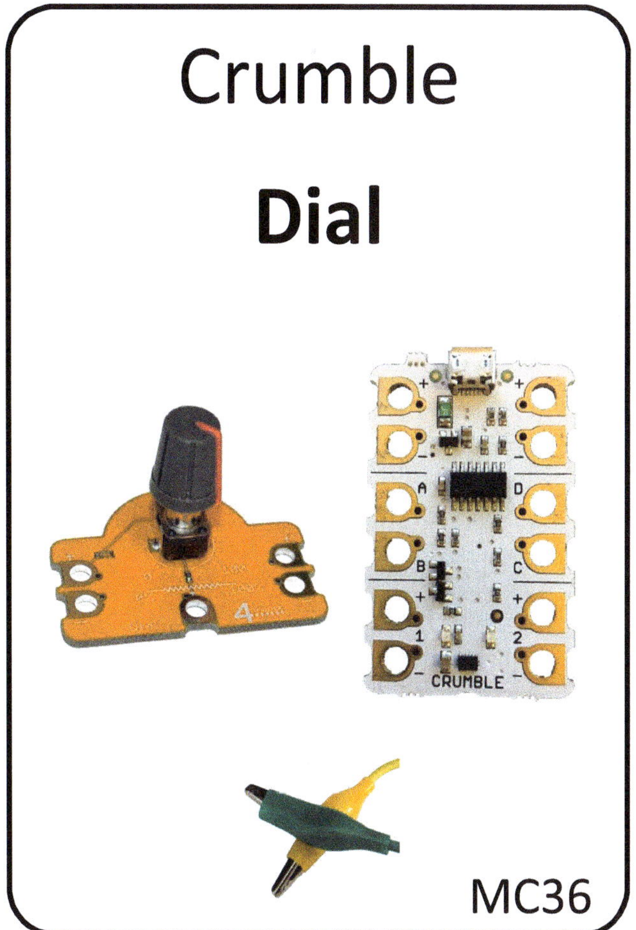

Crumble

Dial

MC36

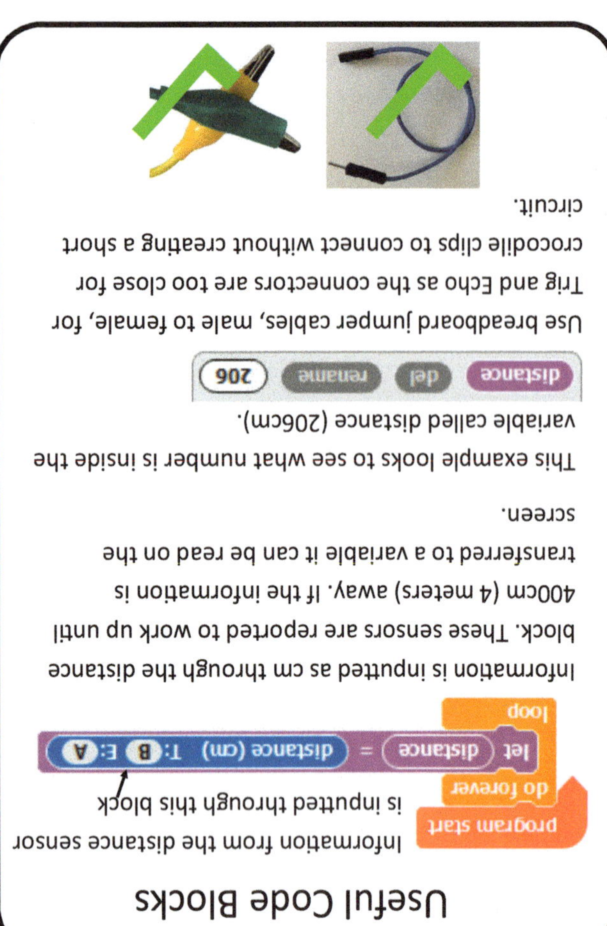
Useful Code Blocks
program start
do forever
let distance = distance (cm) T: B E: A
loop
Information from the distance sensor is inputted through this block
Information is inputted as cm through the distance block. These sensors are reported to work up until 400cm (4 meters) away. If the information is transferred to a variable it can be read on the screen.
This example looks to see what number is inside the variable called distance (206cm).
distance
del
rename
206
Use breadboard jumper cables, male to female, for Trig and Echo as the connectors are too close for crocodile clips to connect without creating a short circuit.

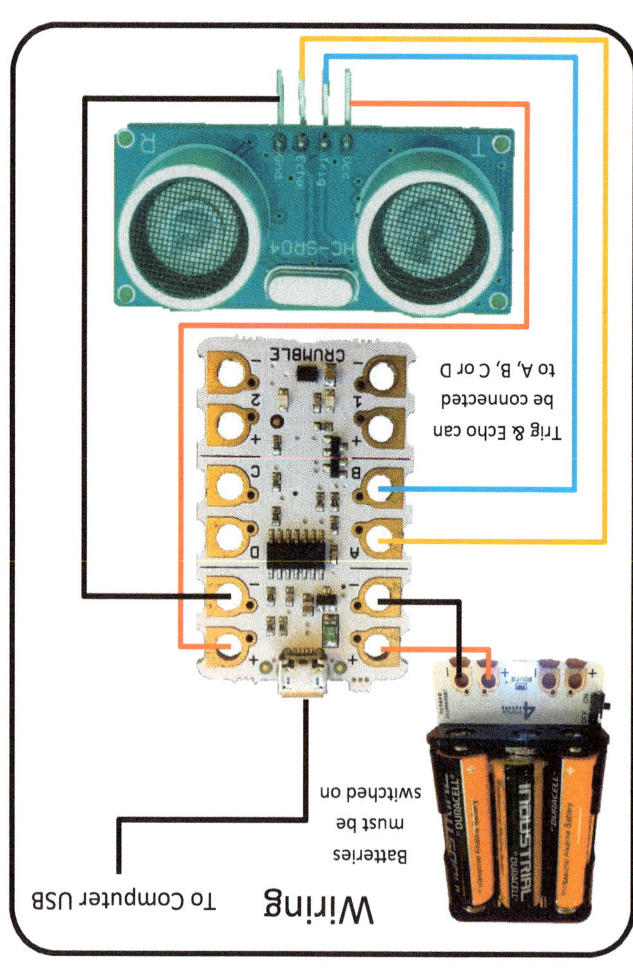
Wiring
To Computer USB
Batteries must be switched on
Trig & Echo can be connected to A, B, C or D
CRUMBLE
HC-SR04

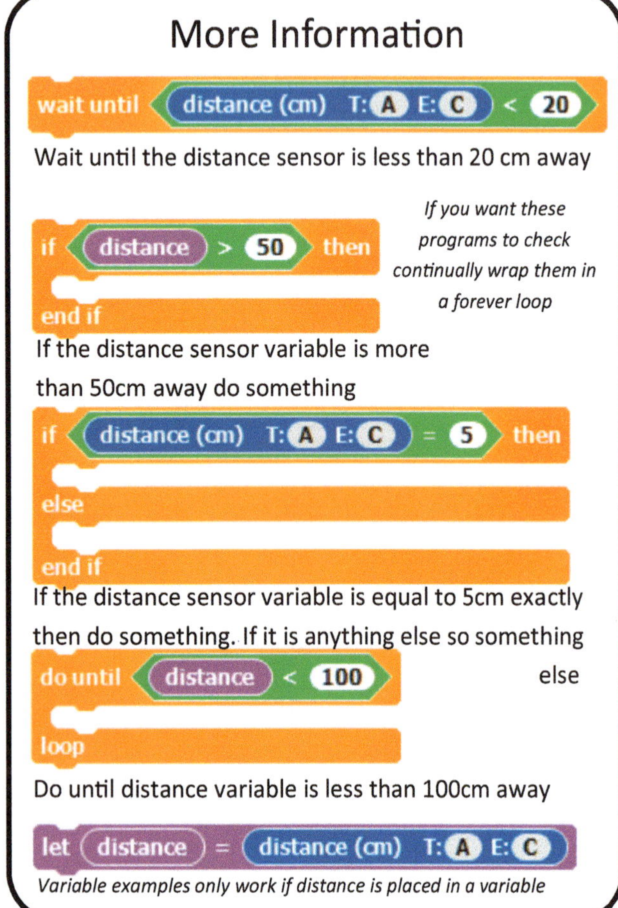
More Information
wait until distance (cm) T: A E: C < 20
Wait until the distance sensor is less than 20 cm away
if distance > 50 then
end if
If you want these programs to check continually wrap them in a forever loop
If the distance sensor variable is more than 50cm away do something
if distance (cm) T: A E: C = 5 then
else
end if
If the distance sensor variable is equal to 5cm exactly then do something. If it is anything else so something else
do until distance < 100
loop
Do until distance variable is less than 100cm away
let distance = distance (cm) T: A E: C
Variable examples only work if distance is placed in a variable

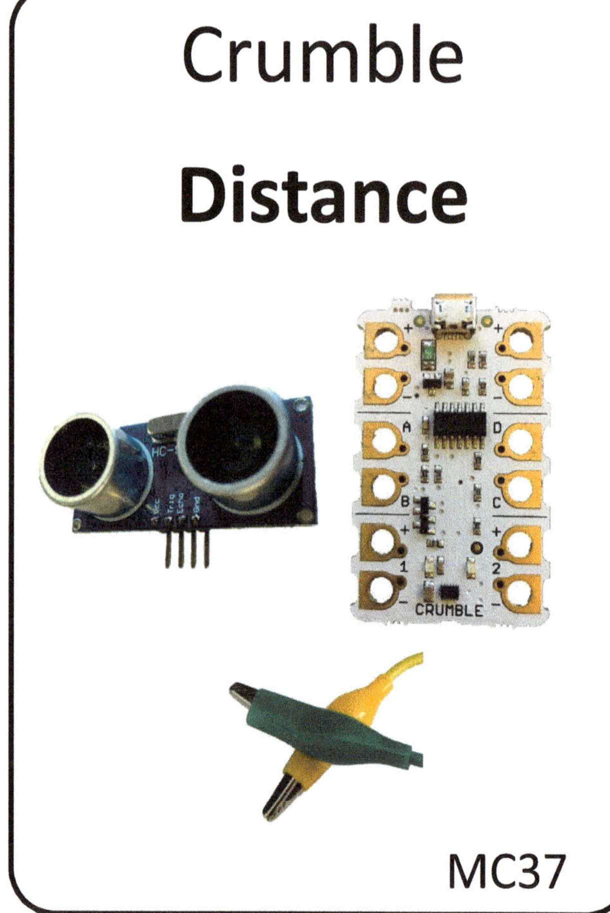
Crumble
Distance
CRUMBLE
MC37

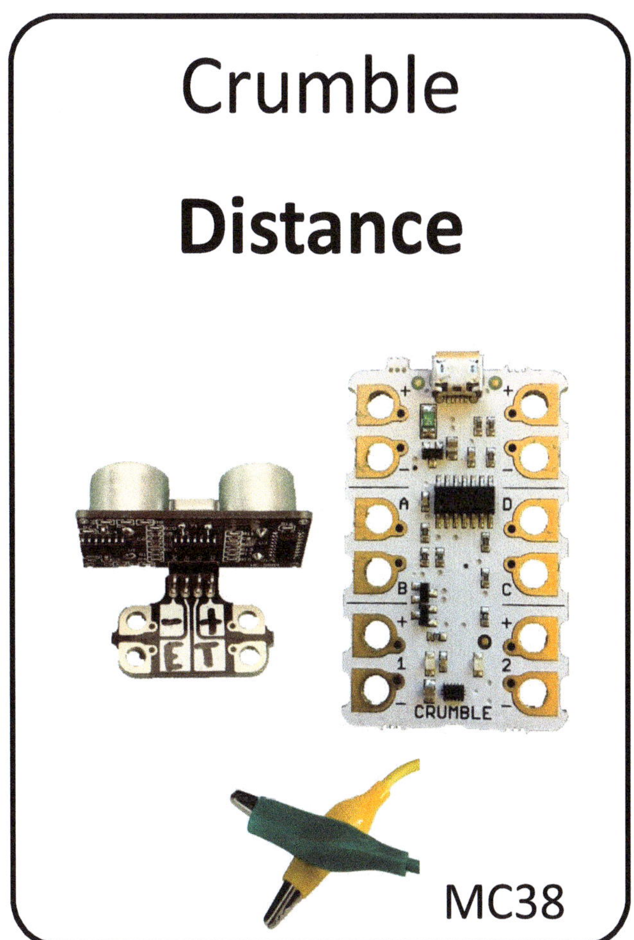

Crumble

Distance

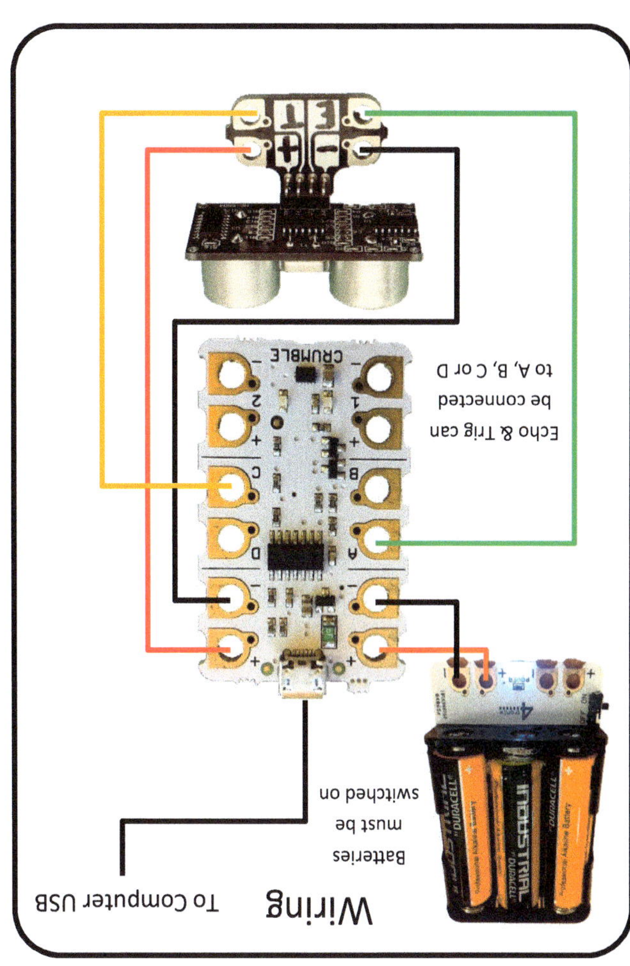

Wiring

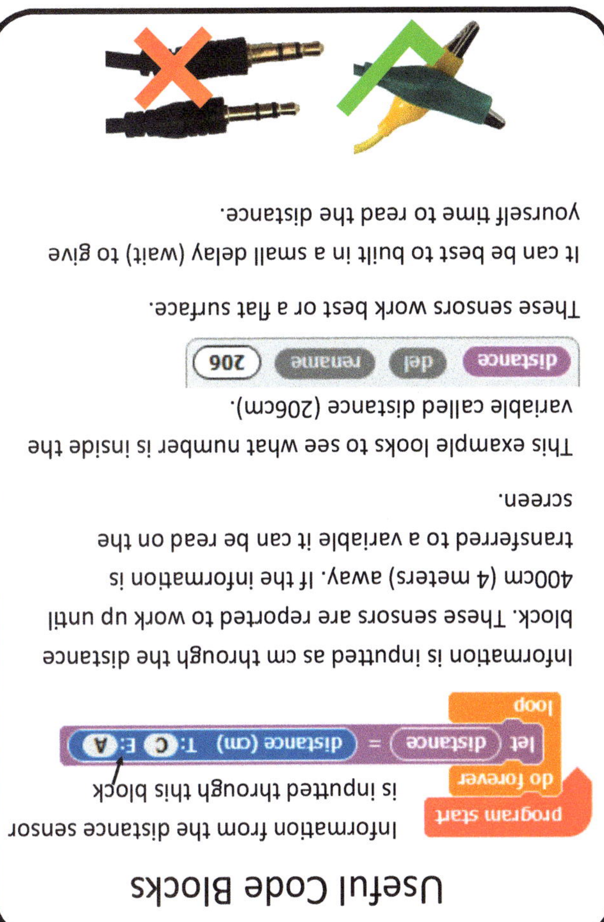

Useful Code Blocks

program start
do forever
let (distance) = (distance (cm) T: C E: A)
loop

Information from the distance sensor is inputted through this block

Information is inputted as cm through the distance block. These sensors are reported to work up until 400cm (4 meters) away. If the information is transferred to a variable it can be read on the screen.

This example looks to see what number is inside the variable called distance (206cm).

distance | del | rename | 206

These sensors work best or a flat surface.

It can be best to built in a small delay (wait) to give yourself time to read the distance.

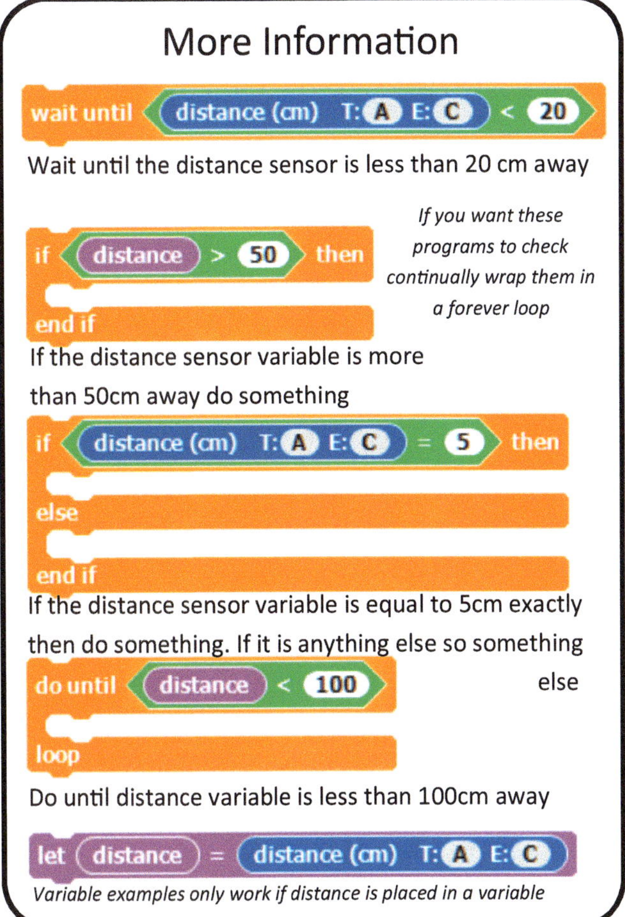

More Information

wait until (distance (cm) T: A E: C) < 20

Wait until the distance sensor is less than 20 cm away

if (distance) > 50 then
end if

If you want these programs to check continually wrap them in a forever loop

If the distance sensor variable is more than 50cm away do something

if (distance (cm) T: A E: C) = 5 then
else
end if

If the distance sensor variable is equal to 5cm exactly then do something. If it is anything else so something else

do until (distance) < 100
loop

Do until distance variable is less than 100cm away

let (distance) = (distance (cm) T: A E: C)

Variable examples only work if distance is placed in a variable

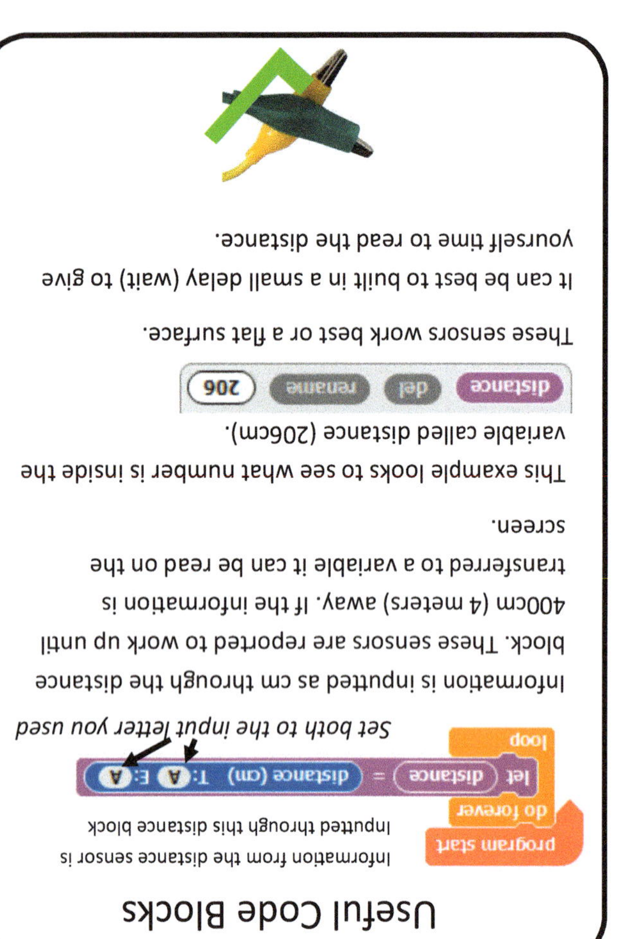

Useful Code Blocks

Information from the distance sensor is inputted through this distance block

```
program start
do forever
  let distance = distance (cm) T: A E: A
loop
```

Set both to the input letter you used

Information is inputted as cm through the distance block. These sensors are reported to work up until 400cm (4 meters) away. If the information is transferred to a variable it can be read on the screen.

This example looks to see what number is inside the variable called distance (206cm).

```
distance  del  rename  206
```

These sensors work best or a flat surface.

It can be best to built in a small delay (wait) to give yourself time to read the distance.

Wiring

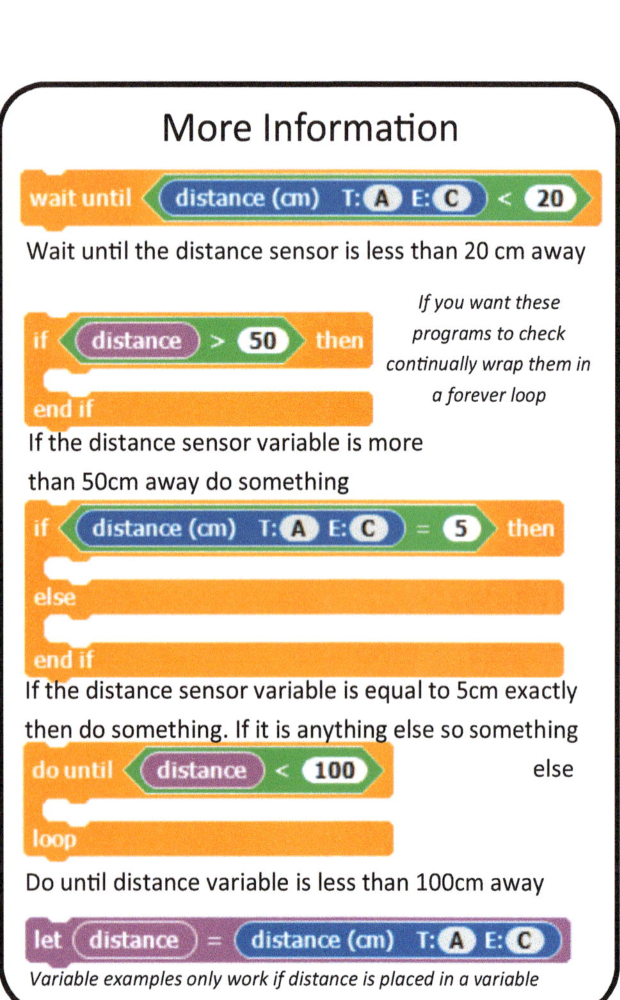

More Information

```
wait until distance (cm) T: A E: C < 20
```

Wait until the distance sensor is less than 20 cm away

If you want these programs to check continually wrap them in a forever loop

```
if distance > 50 then
end if
```

If the distance sensor variable is more than 50cm away do something

```
if distance (cm) T: A E: C = 5 then
else
end if
```

If the distance sensor variable is equal to 5cm exactly then do something. If it is anything else so something else

```
do until distance < 100
loop
```

Do until distance variable is less than 100cm away

```
let distance = distance (cm) T: A E: C
```

Variable examples only work if distance is placed in a variable

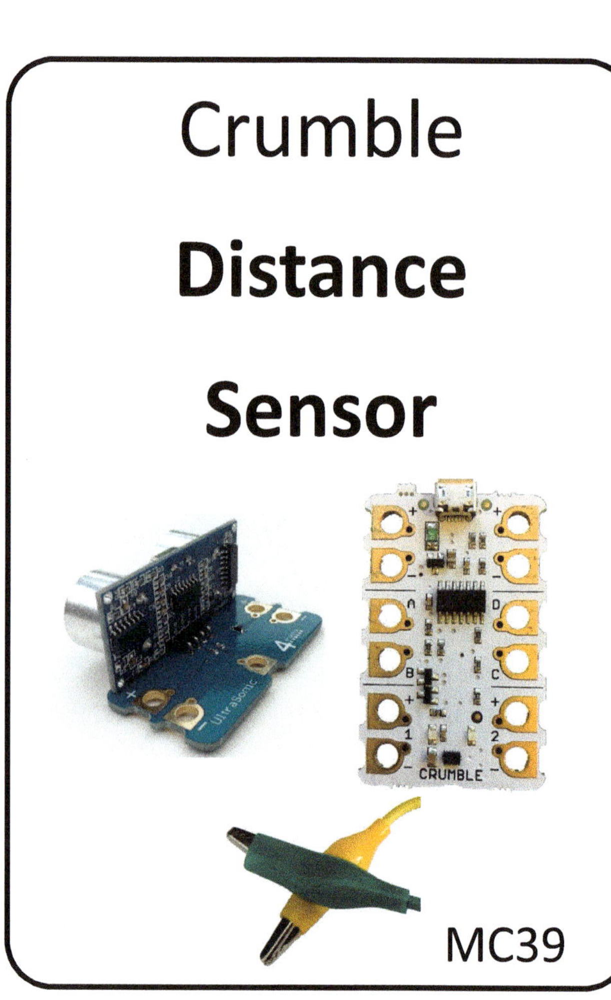

Crumble **Distance Sensor**

MC39

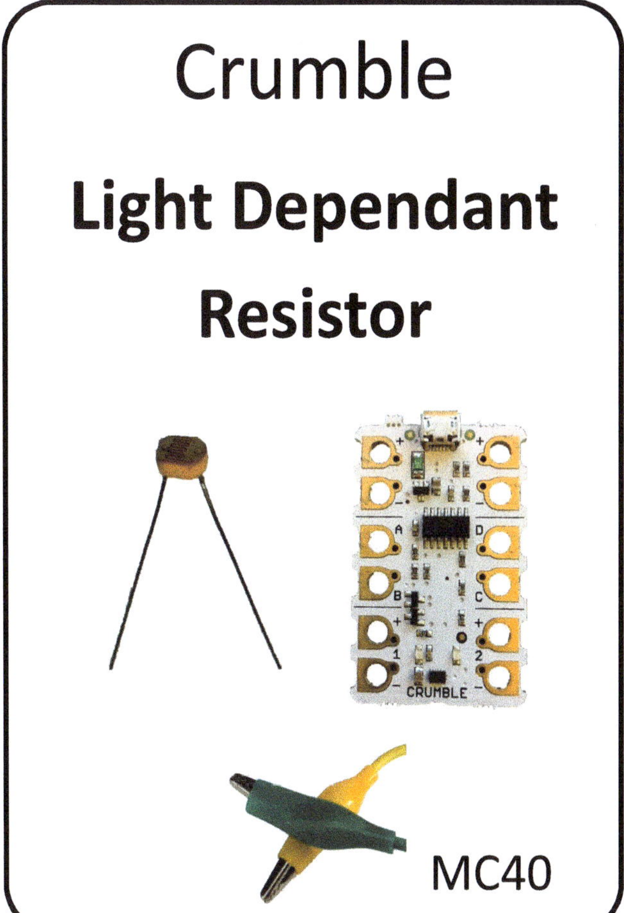

Crumble

Light Dependant Resistor

MC40

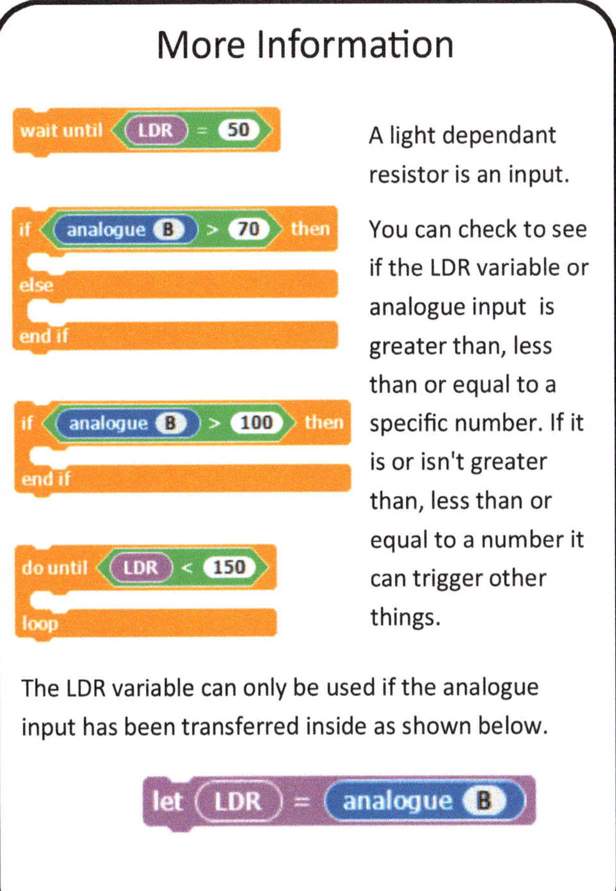

More Information

wait until LDR = 50

if analogue B > 70 then
else
end if

if analogue B > 100 then
end if

do until LDR < 150
loop

A light dependant resistor is an input.

You can check to see if the LDR variable or analogue input is greater than, less than or equal to a specific number. If it is or isn't greater than, less than or equal to a number it can trigger other things.

The LDR variable can only be used if the analogue input has been transferred inside as shown below.

let LDR = analogue B

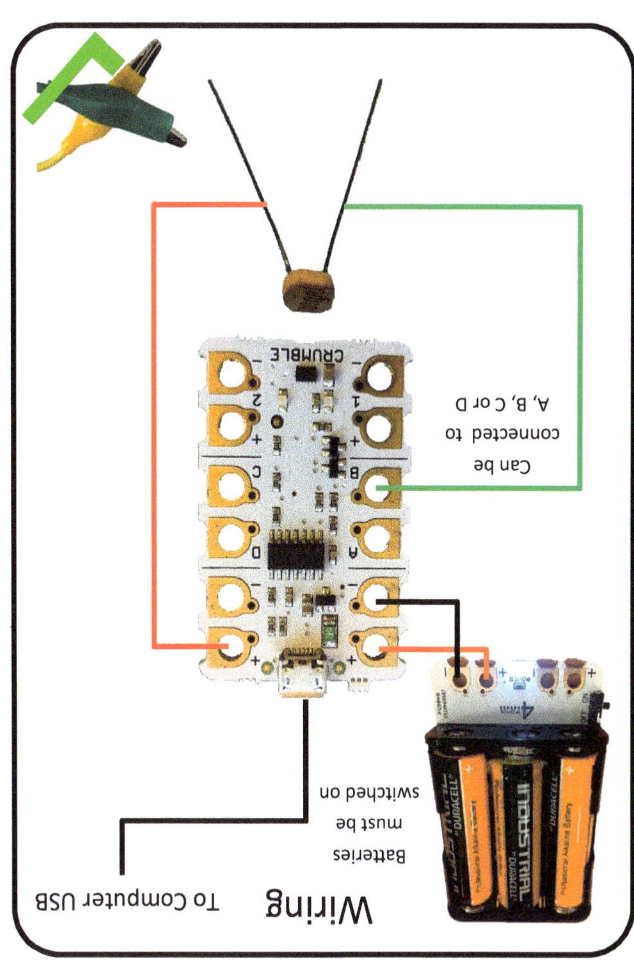

Useful Code Blocks

analogue A

A light dependant resistor (LDR) inputs between 0 and 255 through the analogue block. 0 would be no light and 255 a very bright light.

program start
do forever
let LDR = analogue B
loop

To test the LDR its input needs to be transferred into a variable. In this program the LDR attached to port B has been transferred into a variable called LDR. It has been placed inside a forever loop so the input will be updated continually. Equals = means the same as. You can see what number is inside the LDR on the variable page of the Crumble software. It will look like this.

LDR del rename 149

You can then use this to change other things in your program.

Crumble
Light Dependant Resistor
CRUMBLE
MC41

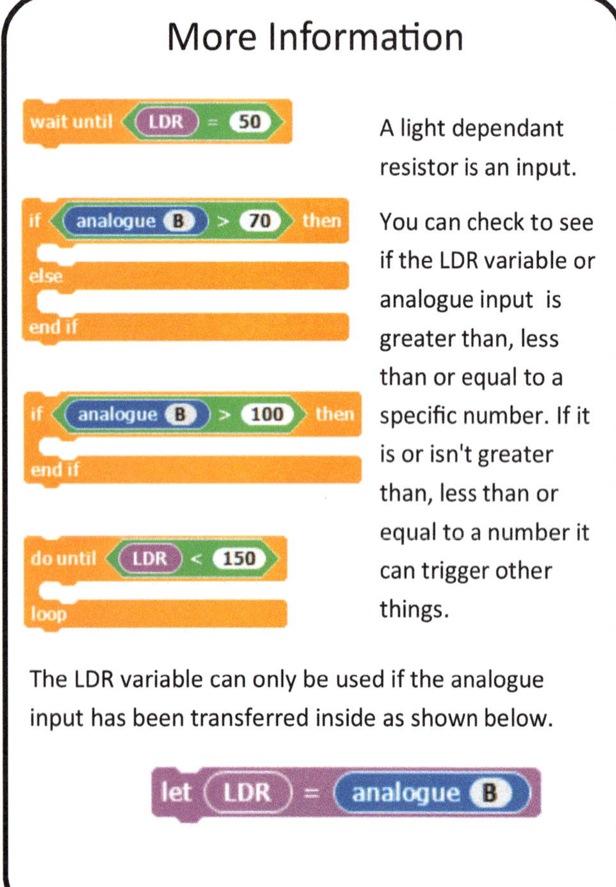
More Information
wait until LDR = 50
if analogue B > 70 then
else
end if
if analogue B > 100 then
end if
do until LDR < 150
loop
A light dependant resistor is an input.
You can check to see if the LDR variable or analogue input is greater than, less than or equal to a specific number. If it is or isn't greater than, less than or equal to a number it can trigger other things.
The LDR variable can only be used if the analogue input has been transferred inside as shown below.
let LDR = analogue B

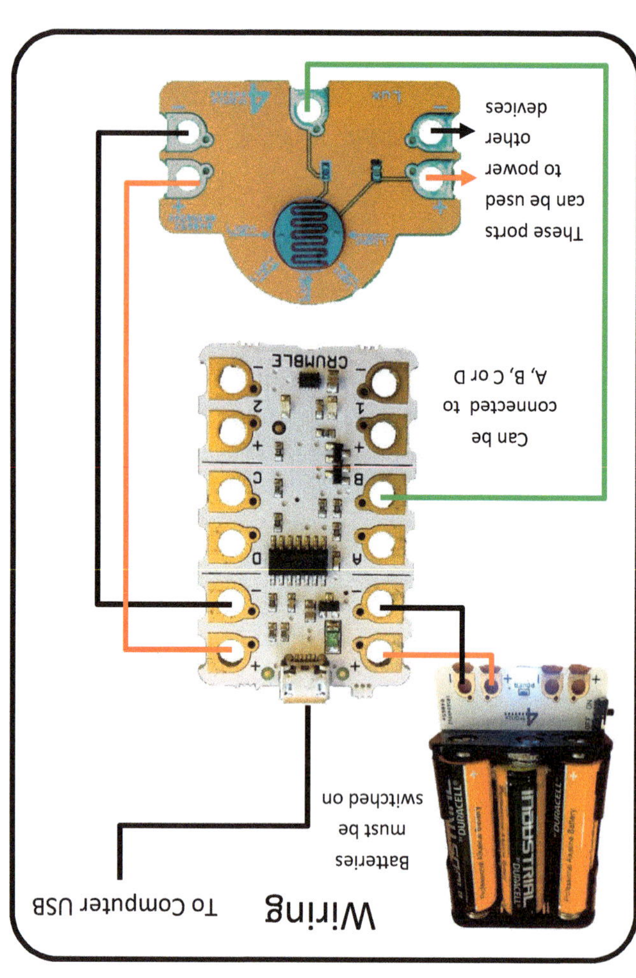
Wiring
To Computer USB
Batteries must be switched on
Can be connected to A, B, C or D
These ports can be used to power other devices
CRUMBLE

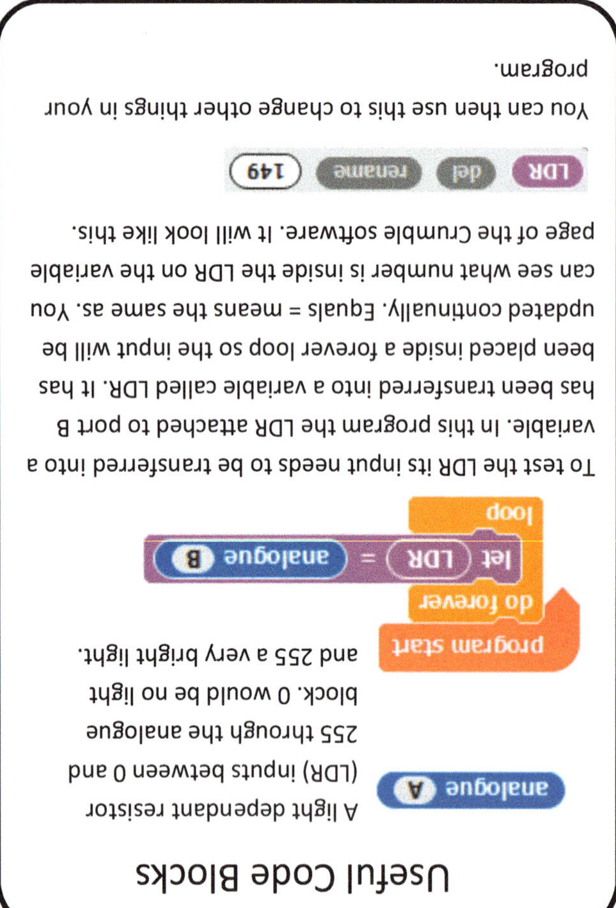
Useful Code Blocks
analogue A
A light dependant resistor (LDR) inputs between 0 and 255 through the analogue block. 0 would be no light and 255 a very bright light.
program start
do forever
let LDR = analogue B
loop
To test the LDR its input needs to be transferred into a variable. In this program the LDR attached to port B has been transferred into a variable called LDR. It has been placed inside a forever loop so the input will be updated continually. Equals = means the same as. You can see what number is inside the LDR on the variable page of the Crumble software. It will look like this.
LDR del rename 149
You can then use this to change other things in your program.

Useful Code Blocks

`analogue A`

A light dependant resistor (LDR) inputs between 0 and 255 through the analogue block. 0 would be no light and 255 a very bright light.

```
program start
do forever
  let LDR = analogue B
loop
```

To test the LDR its input needs to be transferred into a variable. In this program the LDR attached to port B has been transferred into a variable called LDR. It has been placed inside a forever loop so the input will be updated continually. Equals = means the same as. You can see what number is inside the LDR on the variable page of the Crumble software. It will look like this.

`LDR` `del` `rename` `149`

You can then use this to change other things in your program.

Wiring

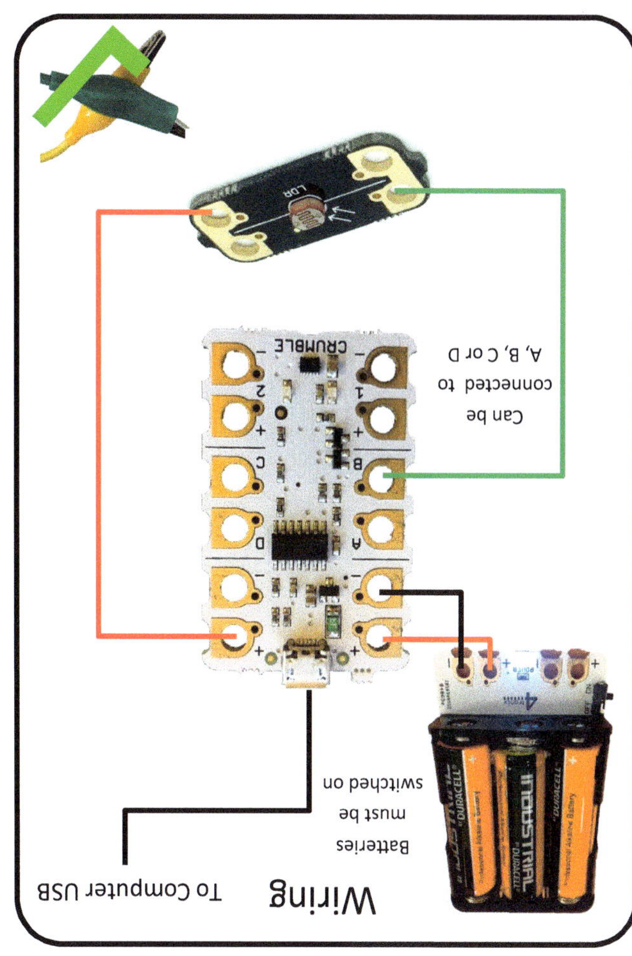

More Information

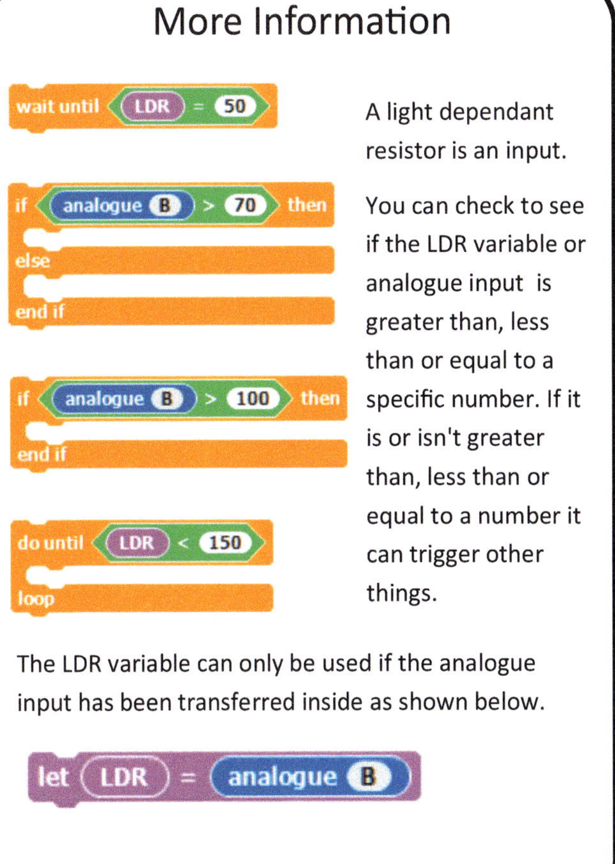

A light dependant resistor is an input.

You can check to see if the LDR variable or analogue input is greater than, less than or equal to a specific number. If it is or isn't greater than, less than or equal to a number it can trigger other things.

The LDR variable can only be used if the analogue input has been transferred inside as shown below.

```
let LDR = analogue B
```

Crumble

Light Dependant Resistor

MC42

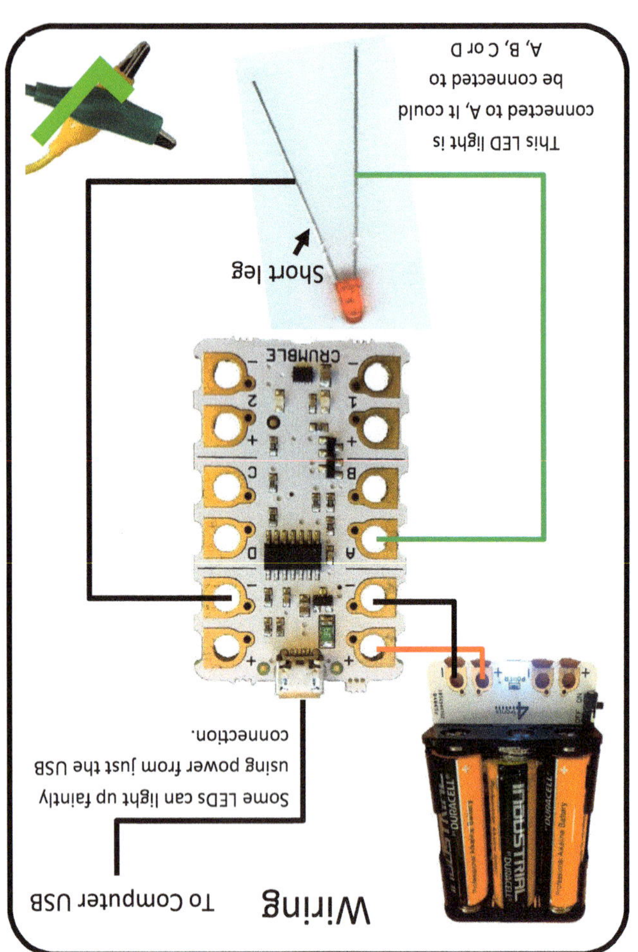
Wiring
To Computer USB
Some LEDs can light up faintly using power from just the USB connection.
This LED light is connected to A, It could be connected to A, B, C or D
Short leg
CRUMBLE

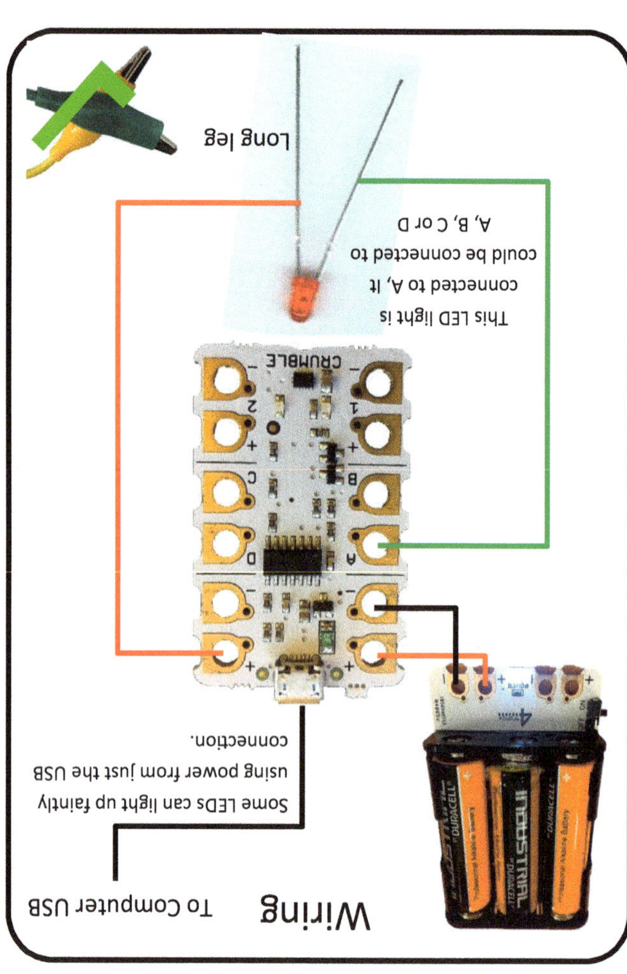
Wiring
To Computer USB
Some LEDs can light up faintly using power from just the USB connection.
This LED light is connected to A, It could be connected to A, B, C or D
Long leg
CRUMBLE

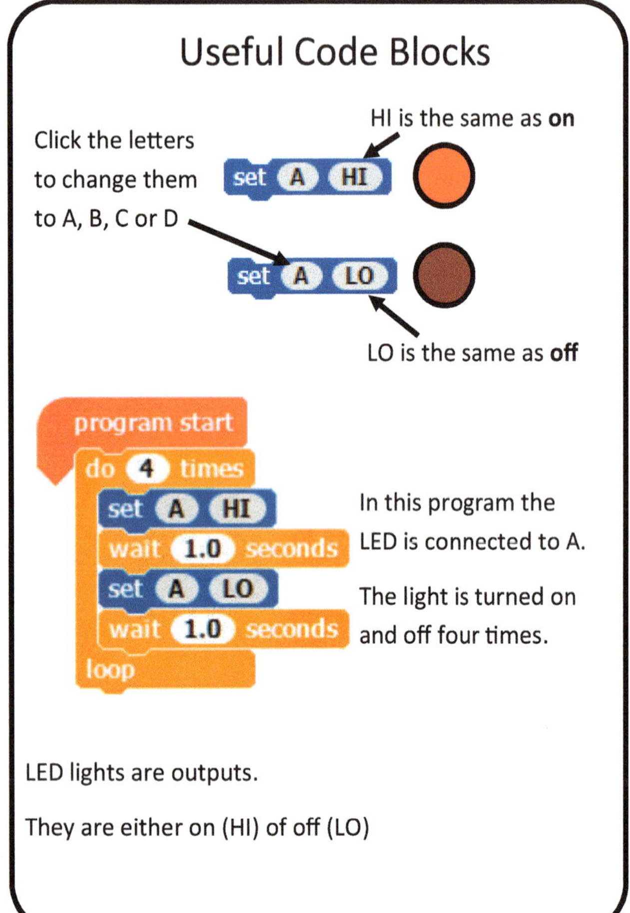

Useful Code Blocks

Click the letters to change them to A, B, C or D

HI is the same as **on**

set A HI
set A LO

LO is the same as **off**

```
program start
do 4 times
  set A HI
  wait 1.0 seconds
  set A LO
  wait 1.0 seconds
loop
```

In this program the LED is connected to A.

The light is turned on and off four times.

LED lights are outputs.

They are either on (HI) of off (LO)

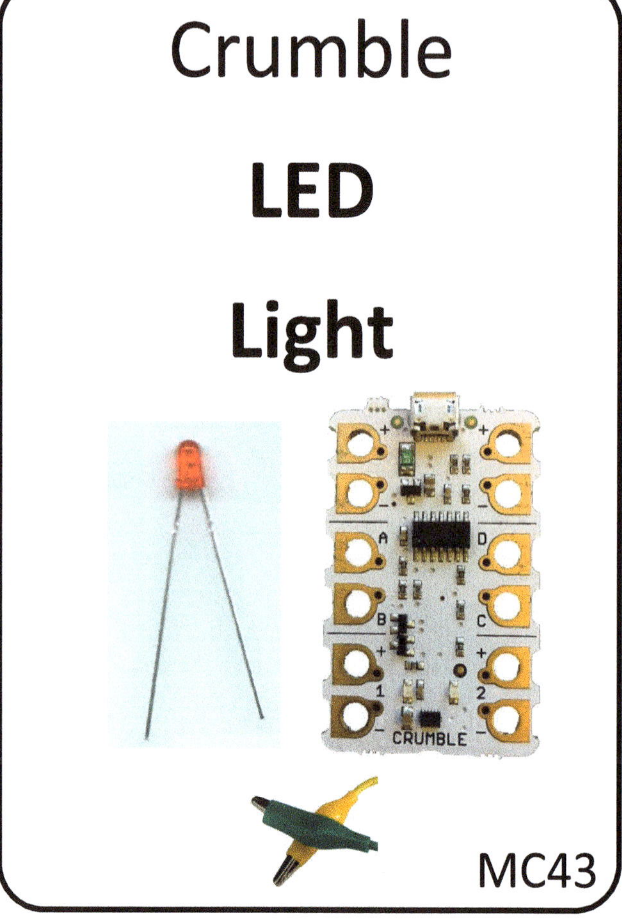

Crumble

LED

Light

CRUMBLE

MC43

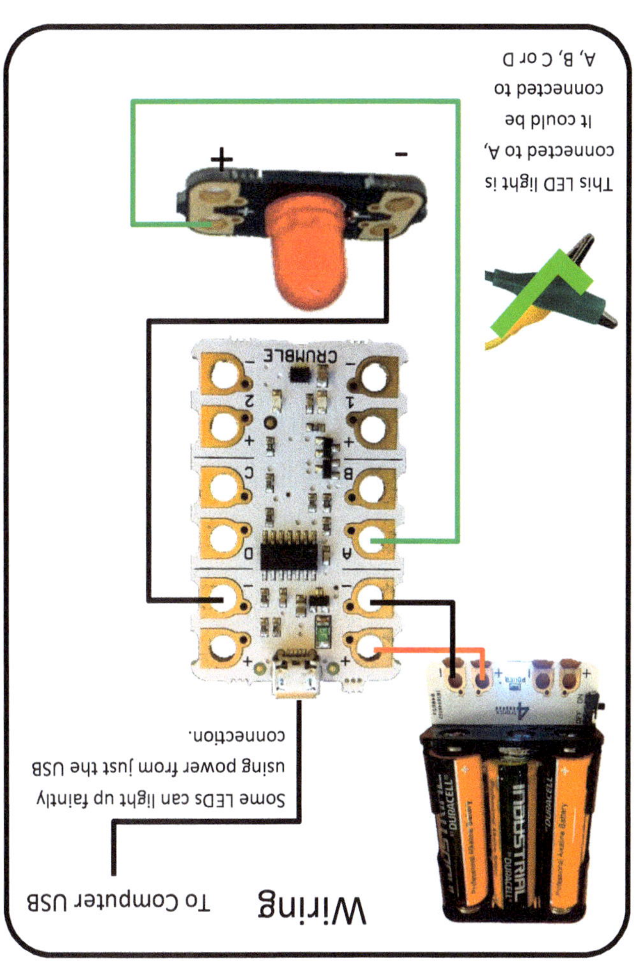
Wiring
To Computer USB
Some LEDs can light up faintly using power from just the USB connection.
This LED light is connected to A, it could be connected to A, B, C or D
CRUMBLE

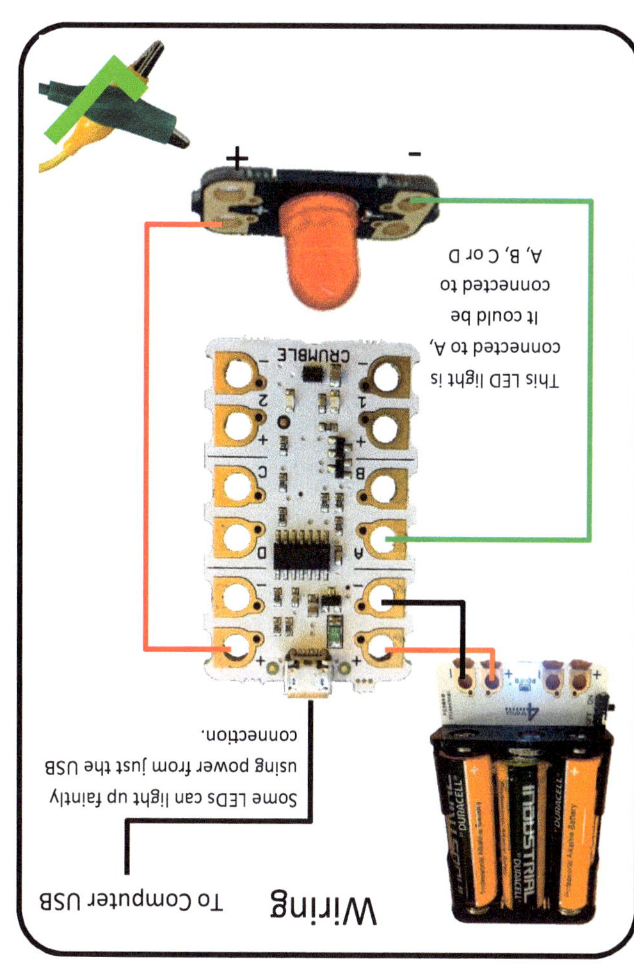
Wiring
To Computer USB
Some LEDs can light up faintly using power from just the USB connection.
This LED light is connected to A, it could be connected to A, B, C or D
CRUMBLE

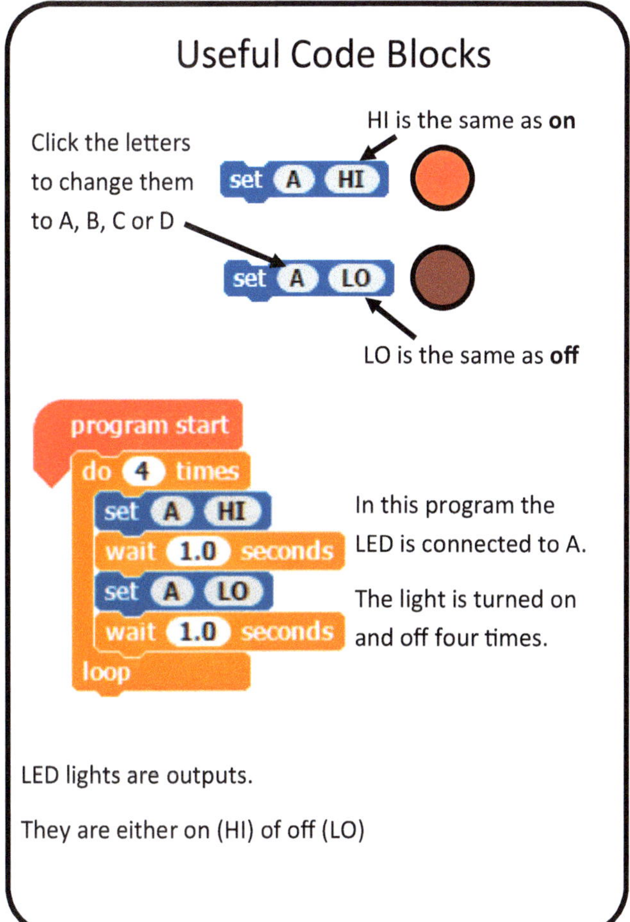
Useful Code Blocks
Click the letters to change them to A, B, C or D
HI is the same as **on**
set A HI
set A LO
LO is the same as **off**
program start
do 4 times
set A HI
wait 1.0 seconds
set A LO
wait 1.0 seconds
loop
In this program the LED is connected to A.
The light is turned on and off four times.
LED lights are outputs.
They are either on (HI) of off (LO)

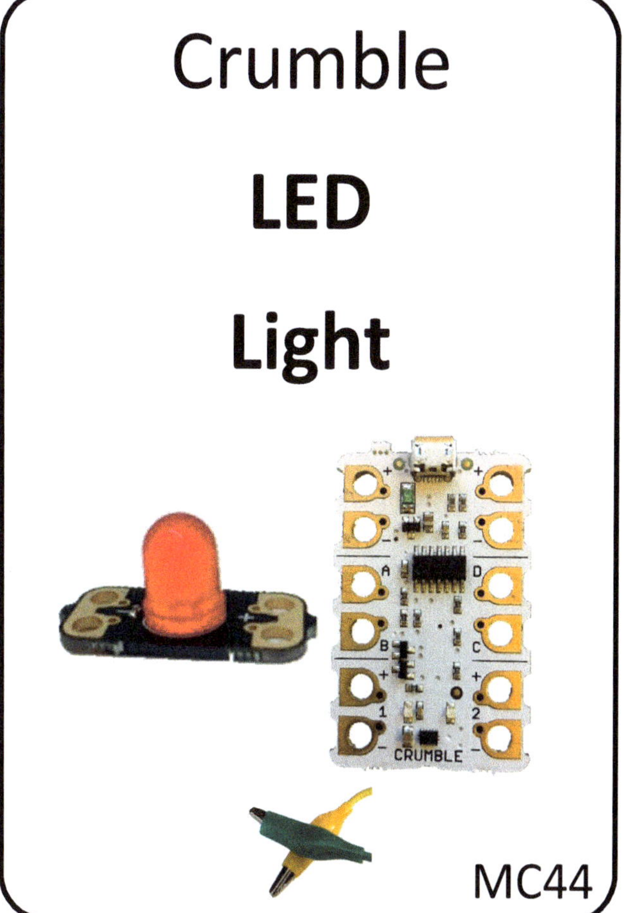
Crumble
LED
Light
CRUMBLE
MC44

Useful Code Blocks
motor 1 FORWARD at 75 %
Click here to change the motor from forward to reverse or stop
motor 1 REVERSE at 50 %
Click here to change the motor from motor 1 to motor 2
motor 1 STOP
Click here to change the amount of power going through the motor
program start
motor 1 REVERSE at 50 %
motor 1 STOP
In this program the motor wouldn't have time to start before it is turned off
program start
motor 1 REVERSE at 50 %
wait 1.0 seconds
motor 1 STOP
In this program the motor would run for 1 second before it is turned off

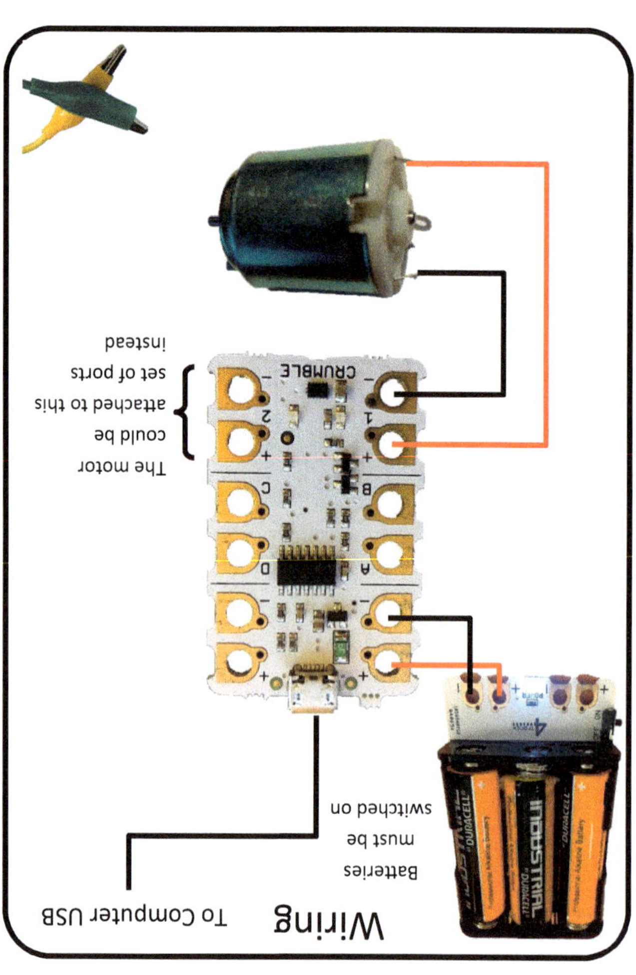
Wiring
To Computer USB
Batteries must be switched on
The motor could be attached to this set of ports instead
CRUMBLE

Useful Code Blocks

Some motors can trip a temporary fuse if they are suddenly switched from full power forward to full power in reverse.

Start your motor at 50% power and adjust upwards you can test if there is anything in the program that trips the Crumble temporary fuse at higher power settings.

You can manually reverse the direction of the motor by swapping the negative and positive connections on the motor.

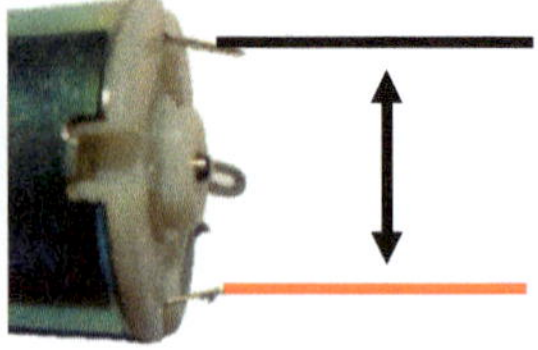

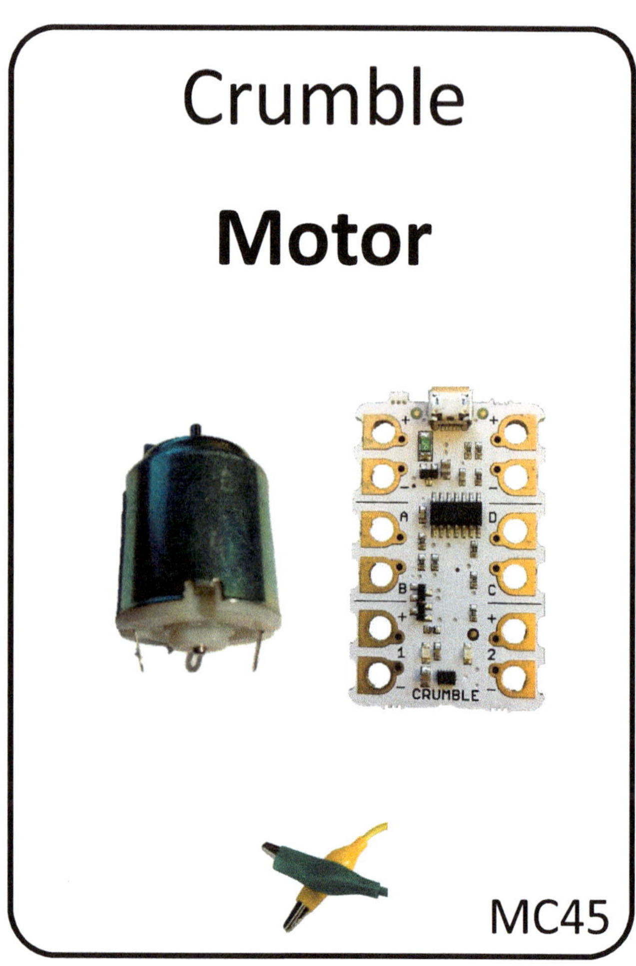
Crumble
Motor
CRUMBLE
MC45

Crumble

Number Counter

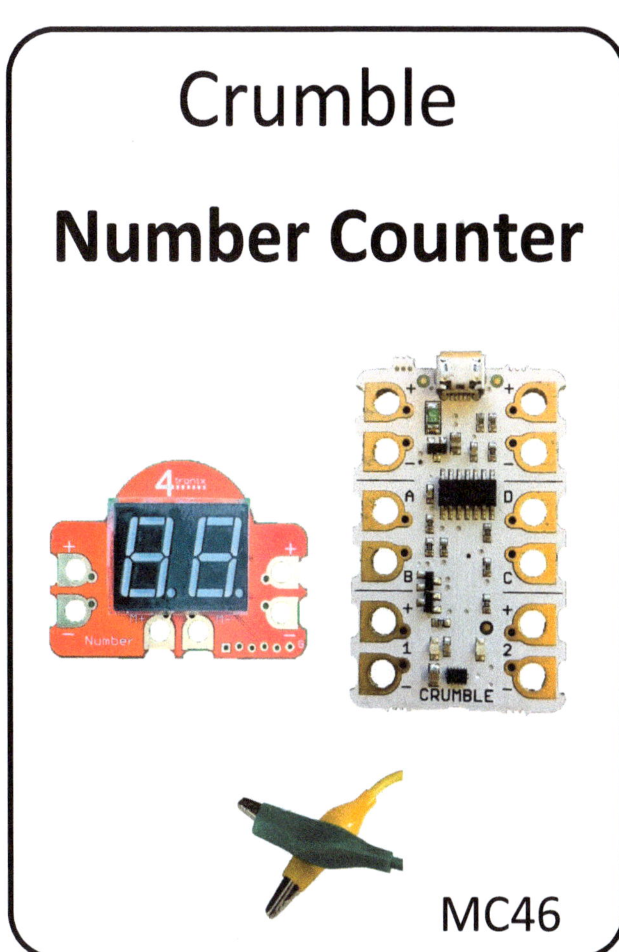

MC46

More Information

One of the difficulties with the number crumb is that it only outputs numbers between 0 and 99.

This means that any inputs over 99 are not recognised.

The Distance sensor inputs 0-400

The LDR sensor inputs 0-255

The programmer will need to adapt the input number to make it fit inside 0-99 using maths blocks

```
let distance = distance ÷ 4
```

In this example the distance sensor 0-400 has been divided by 4 so that it will almost fit into the number counter.

One digit on the number counter is now equal to 4 cm

Wiring

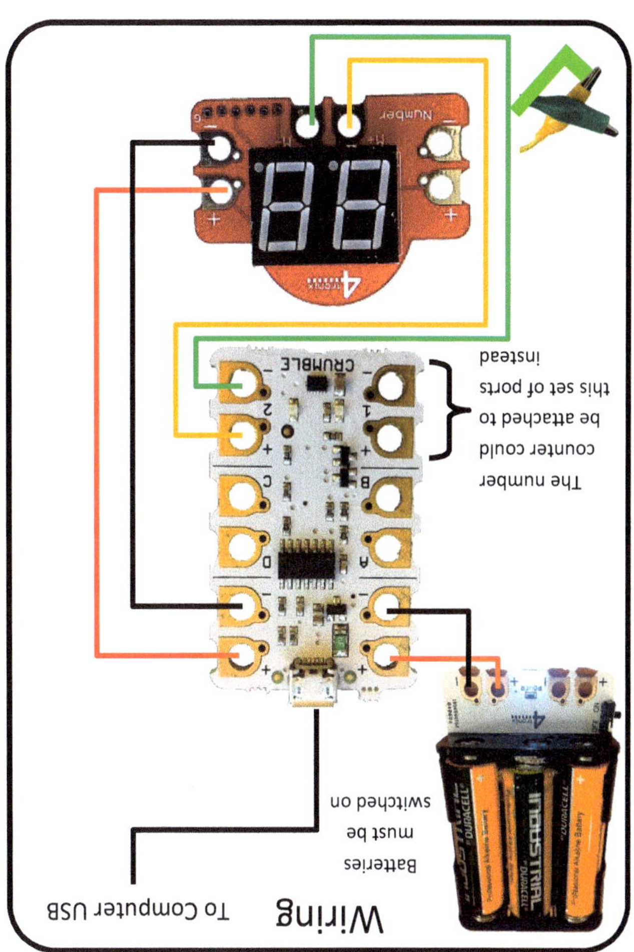

Useful Code Blocks

To test the number counter create this small program.

```
program start
    motor 2 FORWARD at 75 %
```

If the counter shows 75 then it is working correctly.

To use the number counter it needs to take information from other **outputs** (motor power, bare Piezo) or **inputs** (distance sensor, LDR, Tilt Sensor, dial or slider) and display this information itself.

It does this using a variable. In the program below a dial is plugged into input A and the number counter into motor 2. The data from the dial is transferred into the dial variable. The dial variable is then used to display the dial % onto the number crumb.

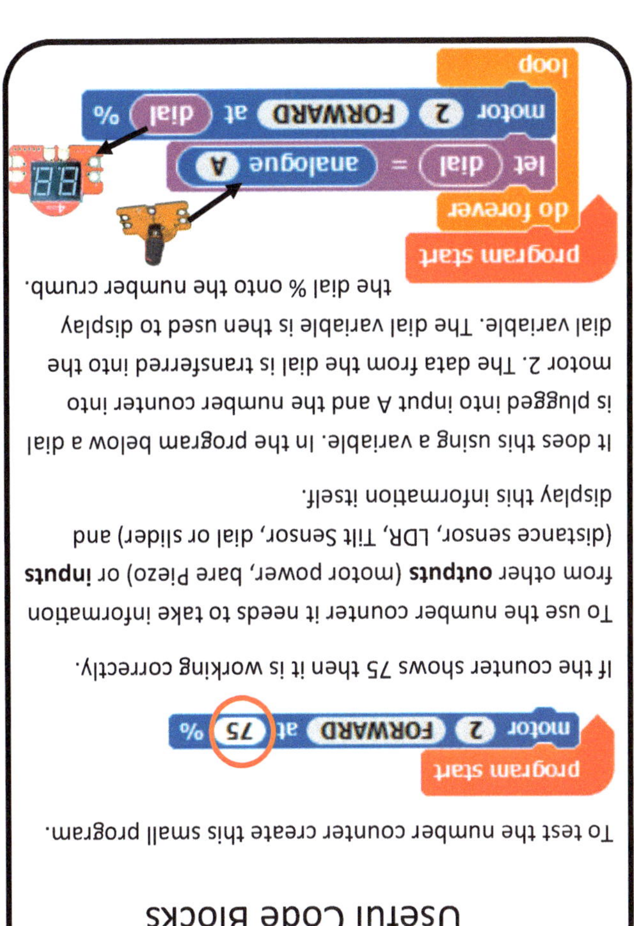

```
program start
    do forever
        let dial = analogue A
        motor 2 FORWARD at dial %
    loop
```

Crumble

Piezo

CRUMBLE
MC47

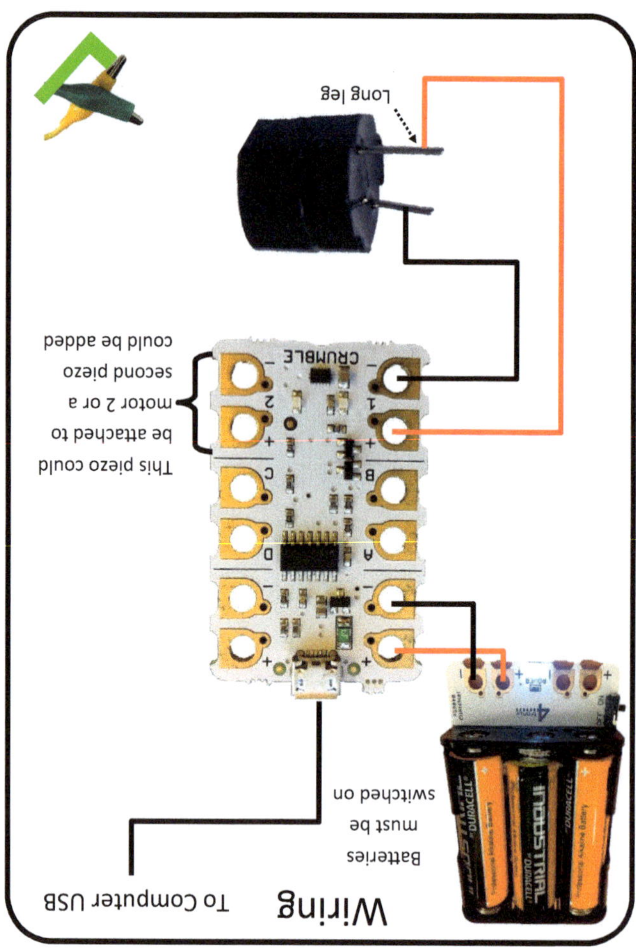

Wiring
To Computer USB
Batteries must be switched on
This piezo could be attached to motor 2 or a second piezo could be added
Long leg
CRUMBLE

Useful Code Blocks
Bare piezo motors work by using the variable amounts of electricity available to the motor ports.
motor 1 FORWARD at 0 %
Stop the piezo using these blocks
motor 1 STOP
motor 1 FORWARD at 20 %
Vary the tone using these blocks
motor 1 FORWARD at 50 %
It makes a different tone depending on how much electricity is passed into the piezo.
motor 1 FORWARD at 100 %
wait 1.0 seconds
Decide how long your tone plays for using these blocks
wait 100 milliseconds

More Information

The piezo makes the noise when electricity stretches or compresses the piezoceramic material.

Don't forget to remove the sticker before using the piezo.

Where else can you find piezo buzzers?

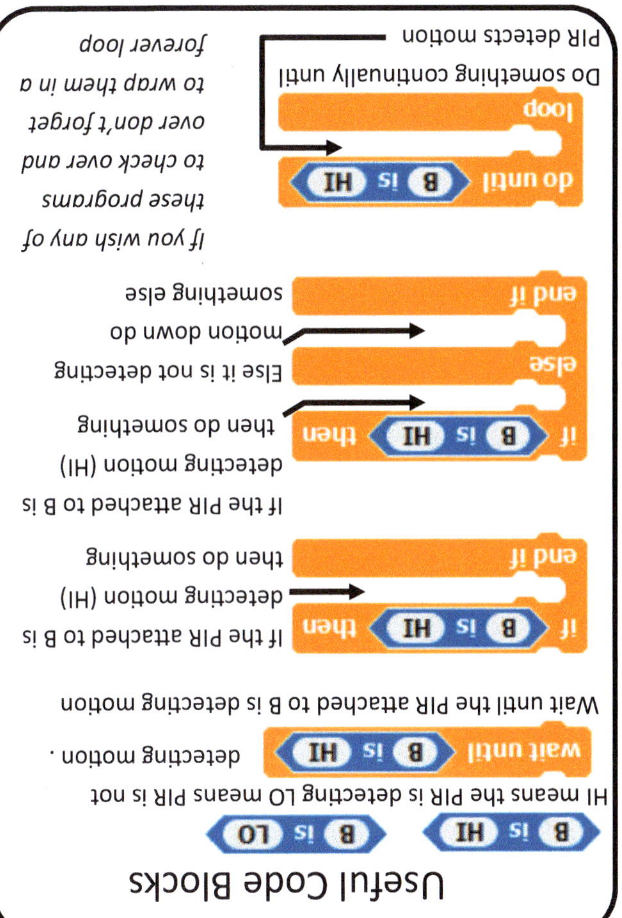
Useful Code Blocks
B is HI
B is LO
HI means the PIR is detecting LO means PIR is not detecting motion.
wait until B is HI
Wait until the PIR attached to B is detecting motion
if B is HI then
end if
If the PIR attached to B is detecting motion (HI) then do something
if B is HI then
else
end if
If the PIR attached to B is detecting motion (HI) then do something
Else it is not detecting motion down do something else
do until B is HI
loop
Do something continually until PIR detects motion
If you wish any of these programs to check over and over don't forget to wrap them in a forever loop

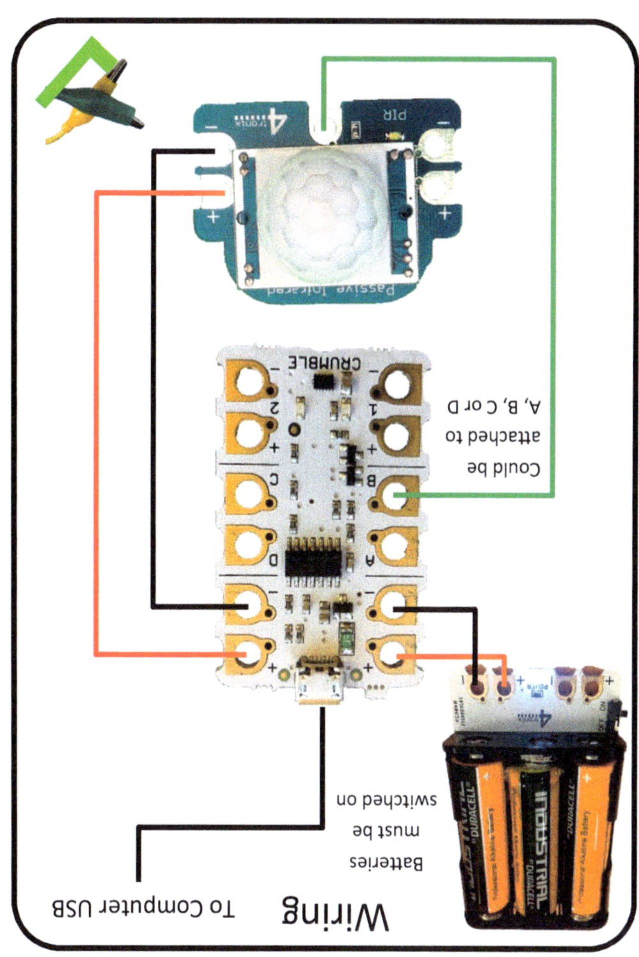
Wiring
To Computer USB
Batteries must be switched on
Could be attached to A, B, C or D
PIR
CRUMBLE

More Information

PIR are INPUT devices

You can make things happen when the PIR detects motion.

There are two small dials on the back of the PIR sensor which can be carefully turned around to adjust the sensitivity of the PIR.

Use a small cross head screwdriver to adjust these.

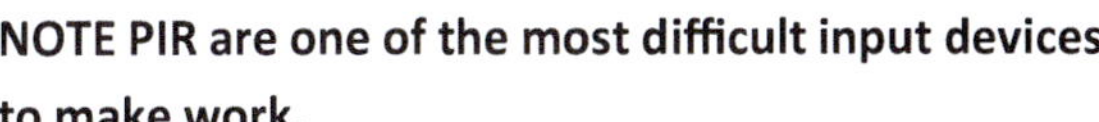

NOTE PIR are one of the most difficult input devices to make work.

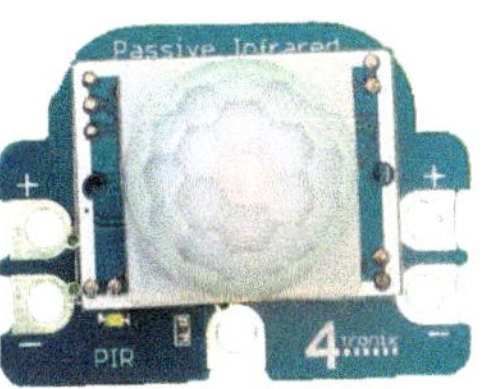
Passive Infrared
PIR

Electricity can be passed on to other devices through the extra + and - power connections on this device

Crumble

PIR

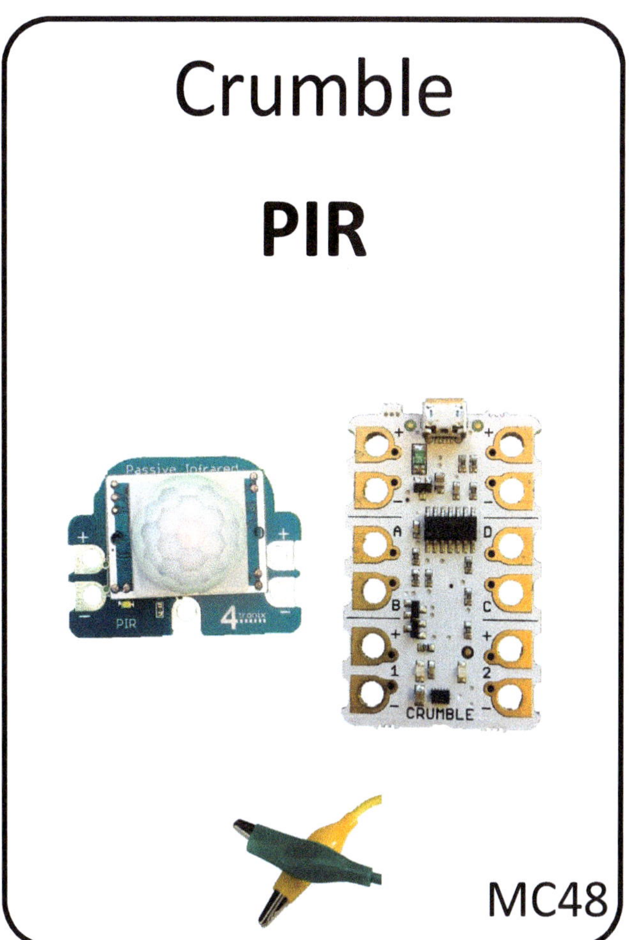
Passive Infrared
PIR
CRUMBLE

MC48

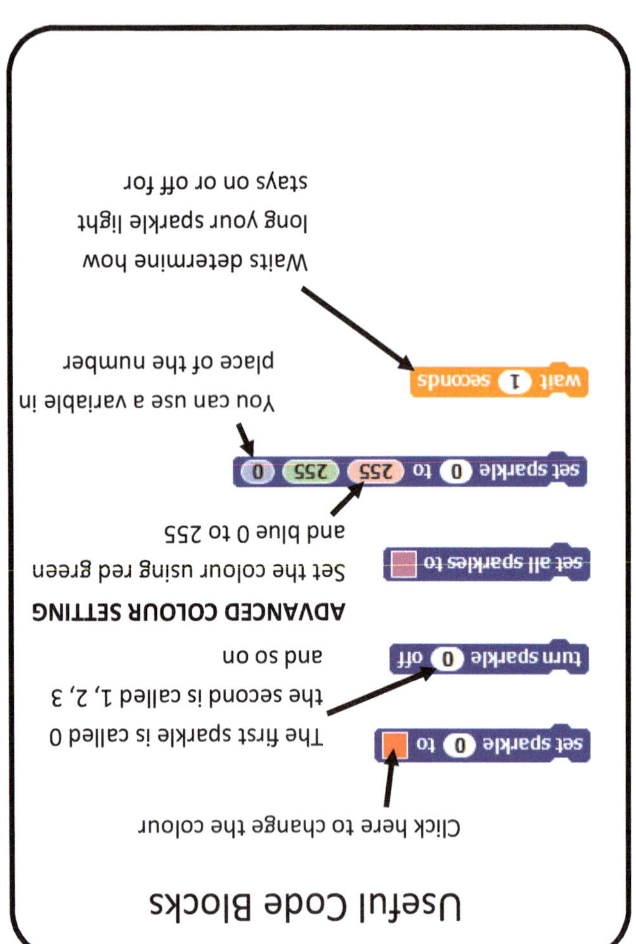

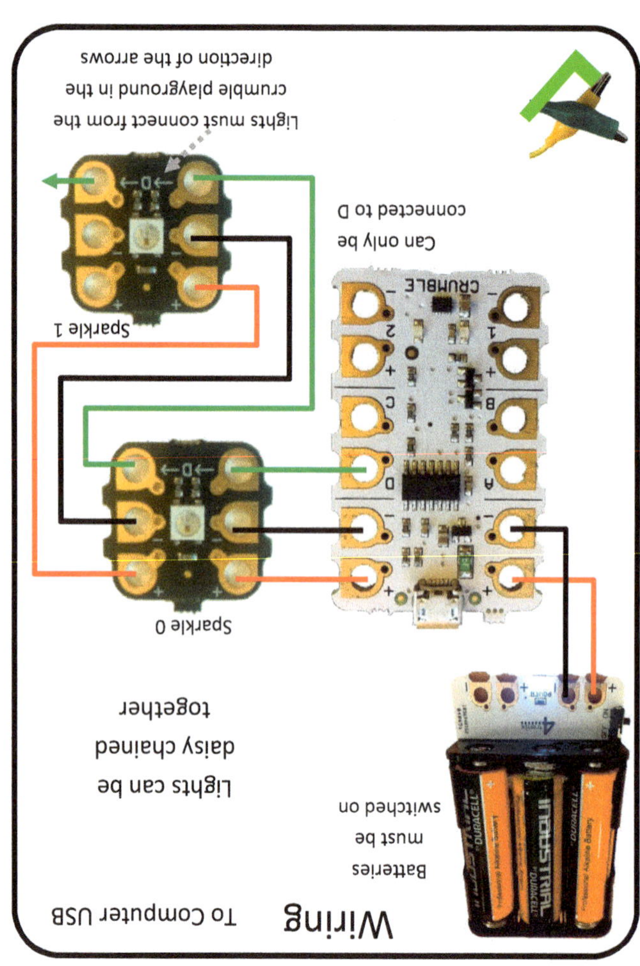

More Information

Lights are outputs. Programmable lights can be very bright. You can reduce this by covering the light with a translucent cover such a piece of white paper.

Up to 36 programmable lights can be daisy chained together.

Redfern Electronics who make this programmable light call it a sparkle.

You can program multiple lights on one device with these.

Crumble

Programmable

Lights

MC49

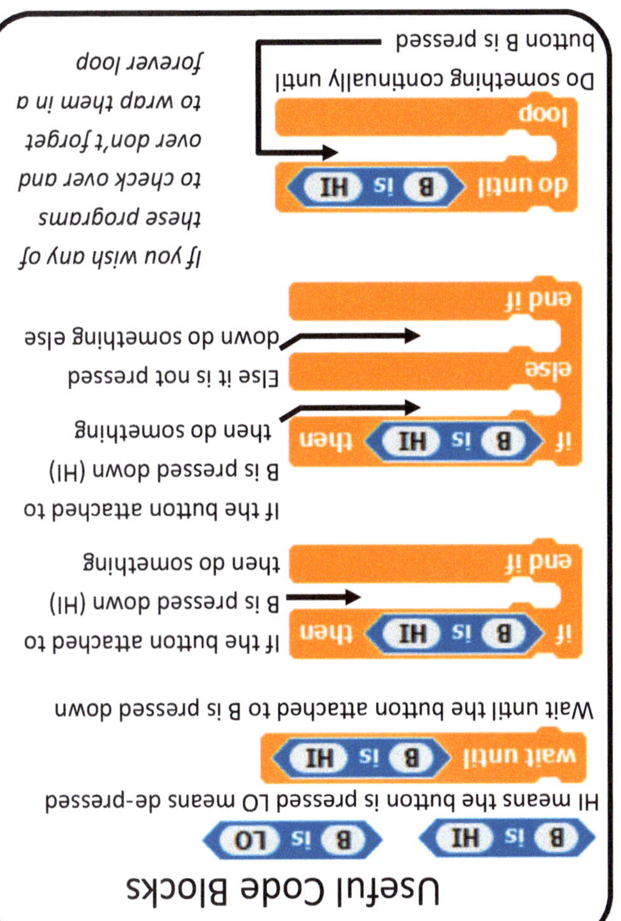
Useful Code Blocks
B is HI
B is LO
HI means the button is pressed LO means de-pressed
wait until B is HI
Wait until the button attached to B is pressed down
if B is HI then
end if
If the button attached to B is pressed down (HI) then do something
if B is HI then
else
end if
If the button attached to B is pressed down (HI) then do something
Else it is not pressed down do something else
do until B is HI
loop
Do something continually until button B is pressed
If you wish any of these programs to check over and over don't forget to wrap them in a forever loop

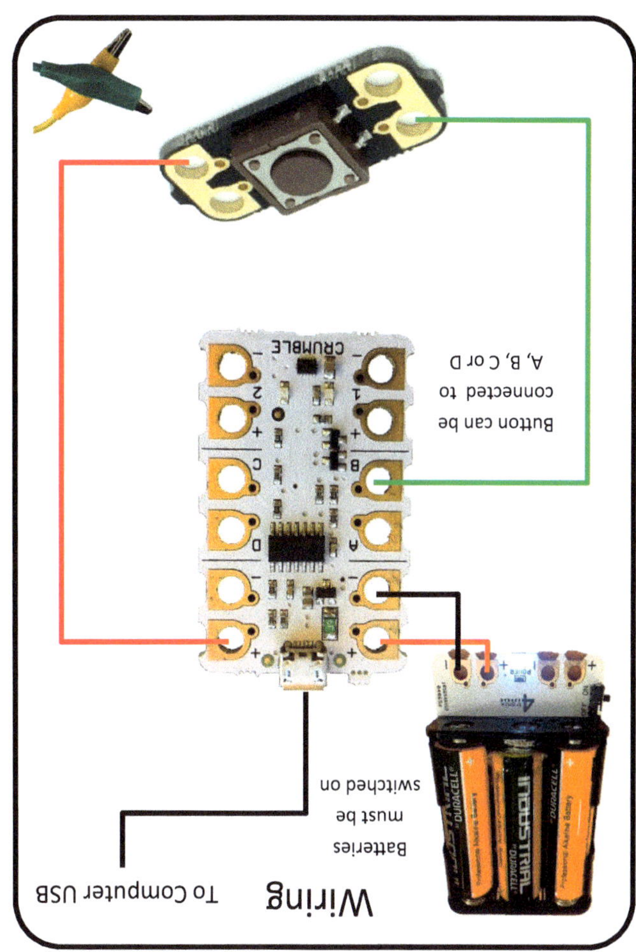
Wiring
To Computer USB
Batteries must be switched on
Button can be connected to A, B, C or D
CRUMBLE

More Information

Remember you can make things happen when the button is pressed and when the button is de-pressed.

There are other types of switches that don't have to be held down to stay (HI) on.

The colour of the insulation on the wires is to help you easily spot errors. Many electrical diagrams would show + as red and - as black. You can use any colour wire that is available to you, it will make no difference to the program.

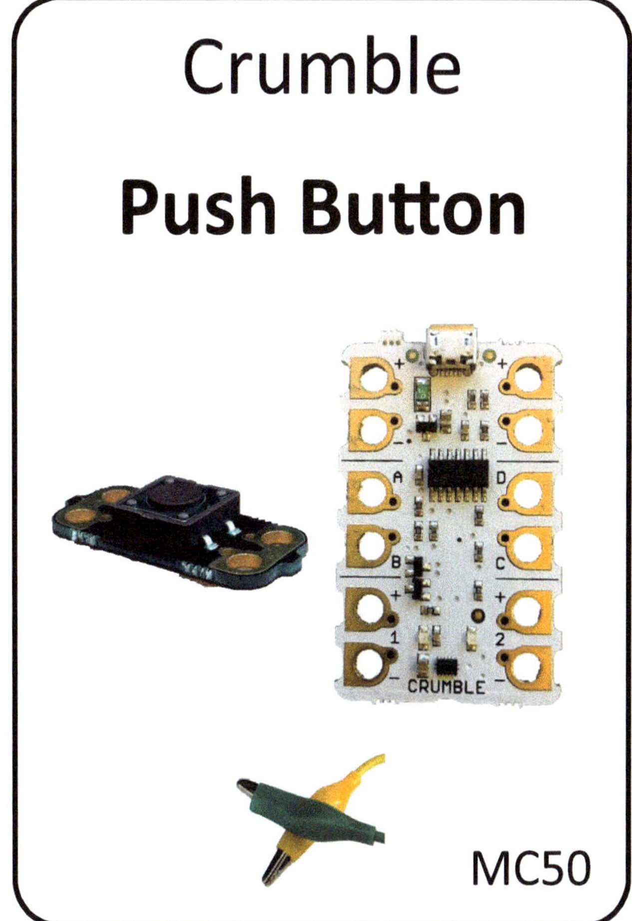
Crumble
Push Button
CRUMBLE
MC50

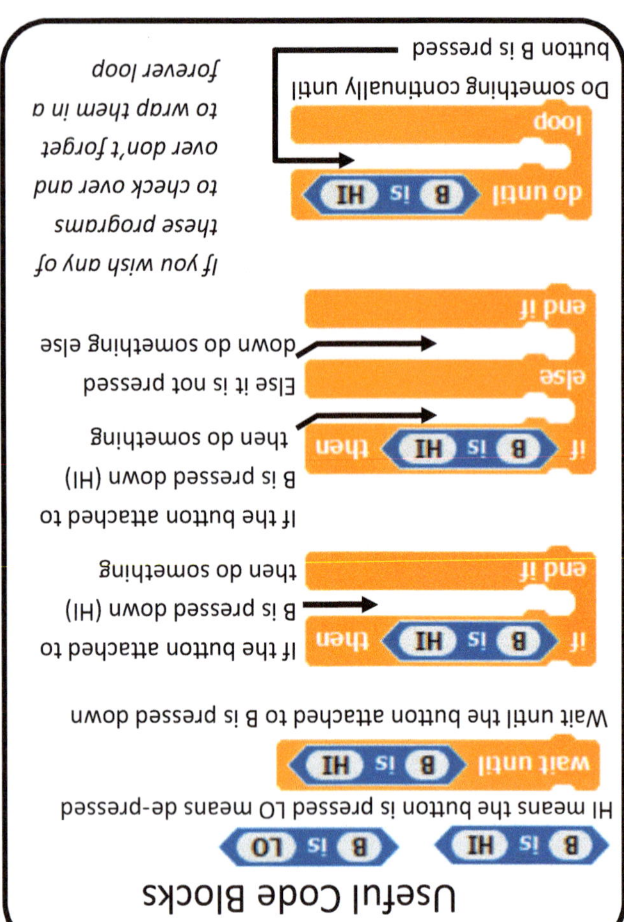
Useful Code Blocks
B is HI
B is LO
HI means the button is pressed LO means de-pressed
wait until B is HI
Wait until the button attached to B is pressed down
if B is HI then
end if
If the button attached to B is pressed down (HI) then do something
if B is HI then
else
end if
If the button attached to B is pressed down (HI) then do something
Else it is not pressed down do something else
do until B is HI
loop
Do something continually until button B is pressed
If you wish any of these programs to check over and over don't forget to wrap them in a forever loop

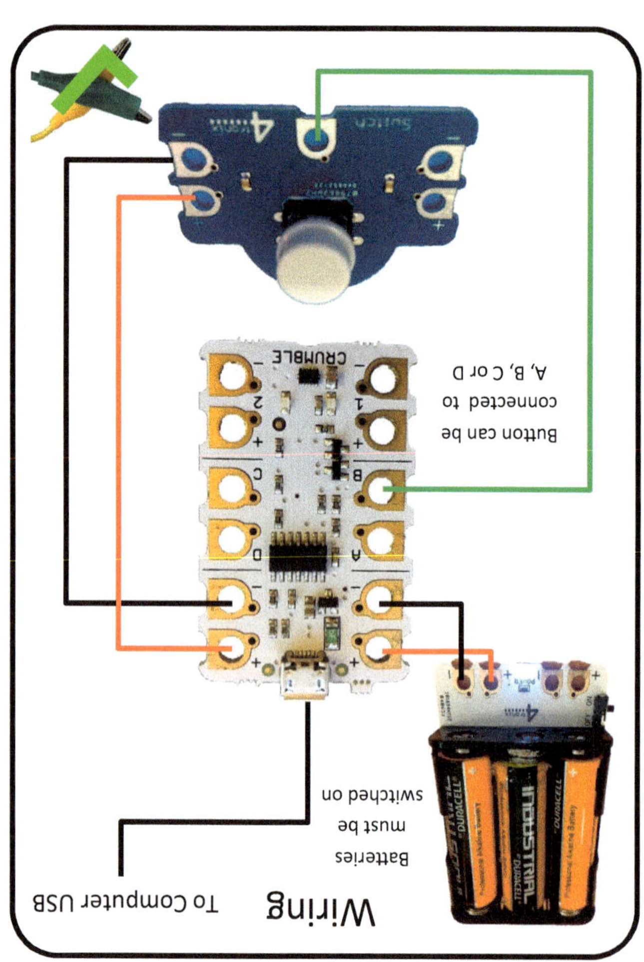
Wiring
To Computer USB
Batteries must be switched on
Button can be connected to A, B, C or D
CRUMBLE

More Information

Buttons are INPUT devices

Remember you can make things happen when the button is pressed and when the button is de-pressed.

There are other types of switches that don't have to be held down to stay (HI) on.

The colour of the insulation on the wires is to help you easily spot errors. Many electrical diagrams would show + as red and - as black. You can use any colour that is available to you, it will make no difference to the program.

Electricity can be passed on to other devices through the extra + and - power connections on this device

Crumble

Push Button

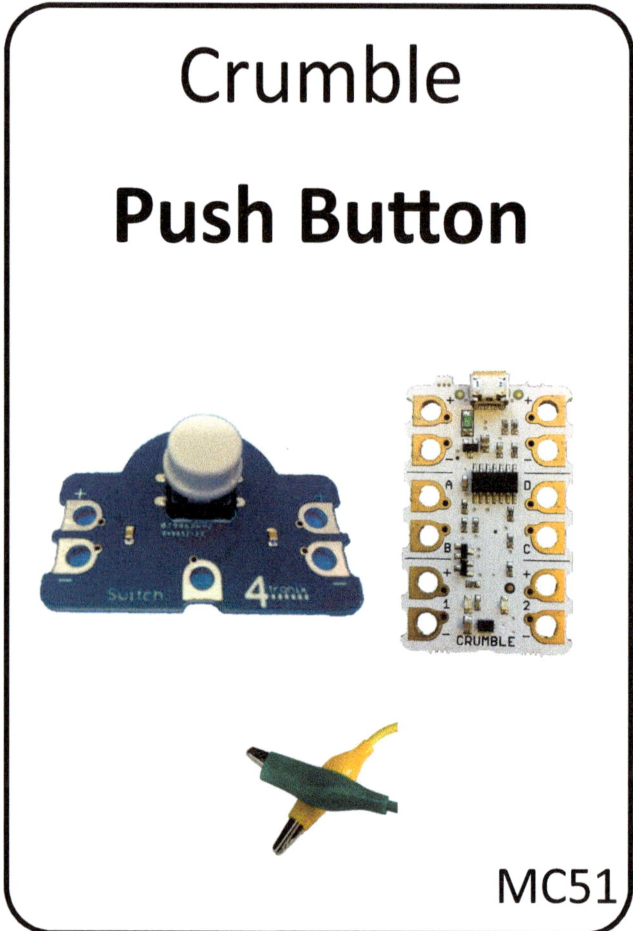
CRUMBLE

MC51

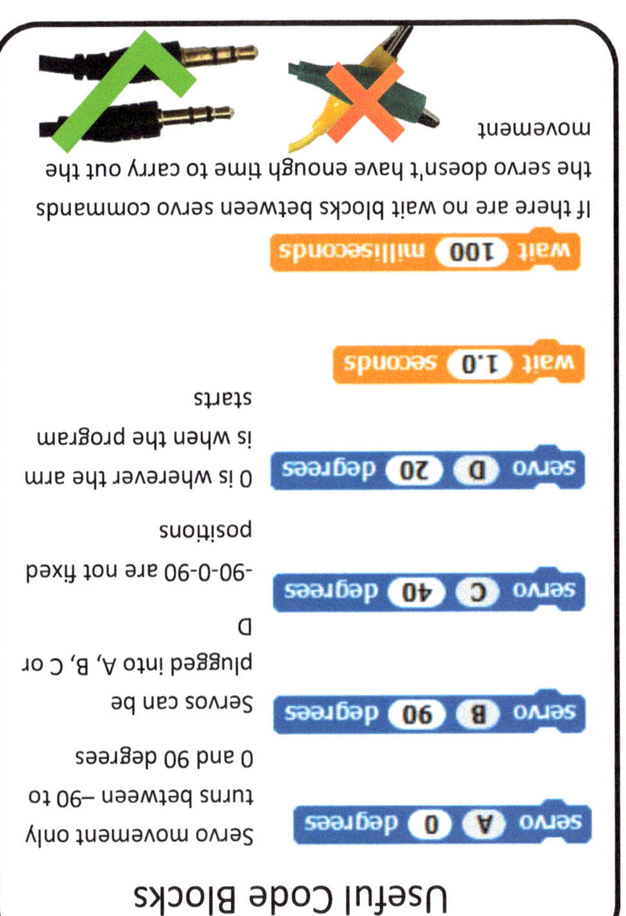
Useful Code Blocks
servo A 0 degrees
Servo movement only turns between –90 to 0 and 90 degrees
servo B 90 degrees
Servos can be plugged into A, B, C or D
servo C 40 degrees
-90-0-90 are not fixed positions
servo D 20 degrees
0 is wherever the arm is when the program starts
wait 1.0 seconds
wait 100 milliseconds
If there are no wait blocks between servo commands the servo doesn't have enough time to carry out the movement

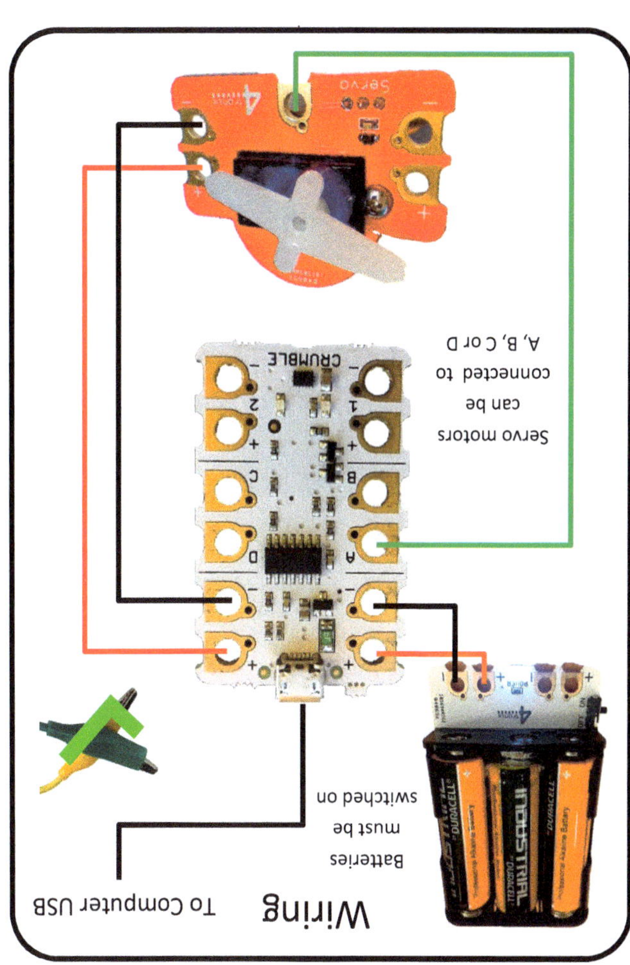
Wiring
To Computer USB
Batteries must be switched on
Servo motors can be connected to A, B, C or D
CRUMBLE
Servo

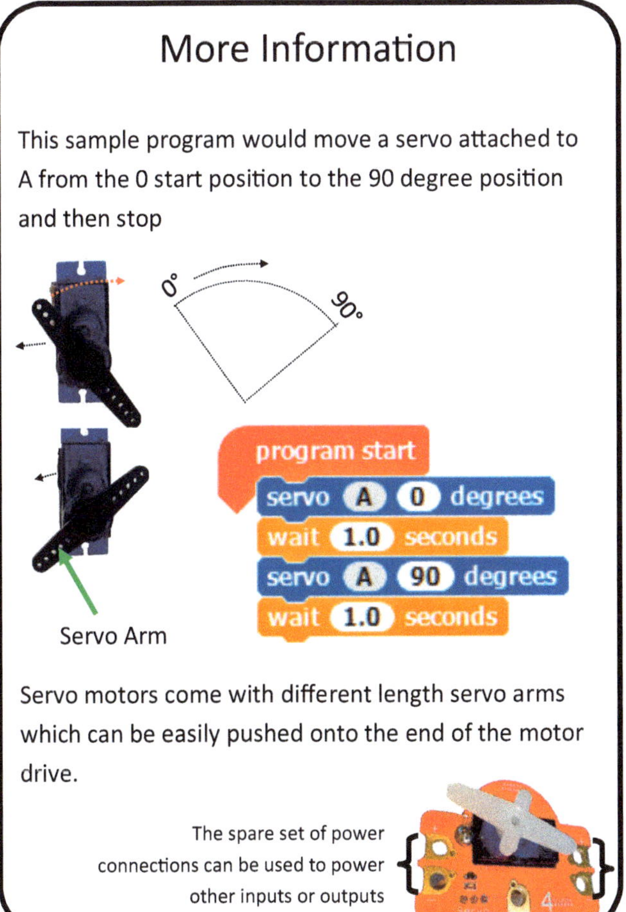
More Information
This sample program would move a servo attached to A from the 0 start position to the 90 degree position and then stop
0°
90°
program start
servo A 0 degrees
wait 1.0 seconds
servo A 90 degrees
wait 1.0 seconds
Servo Arm
Servo motors come with different length servo arms which can be easily pushed onto the end of the motor drive.
The spare set of power connections can be used to power other inputs or outputs

Crumble
Servo / Stepper
Motor
CRUMBLE
Servo
MC52

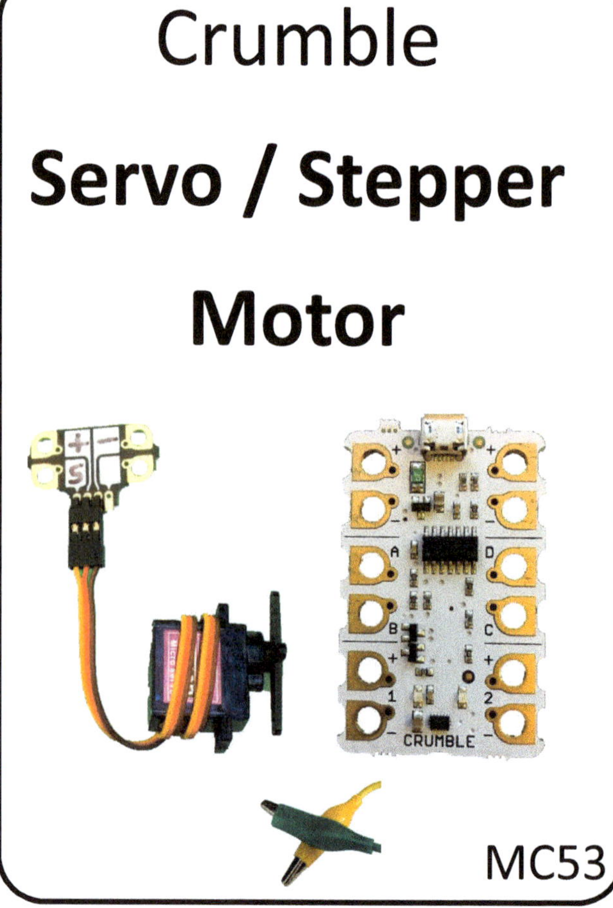
Crumble
Servo / Stepper
Motor
CRUMBLE
MC53

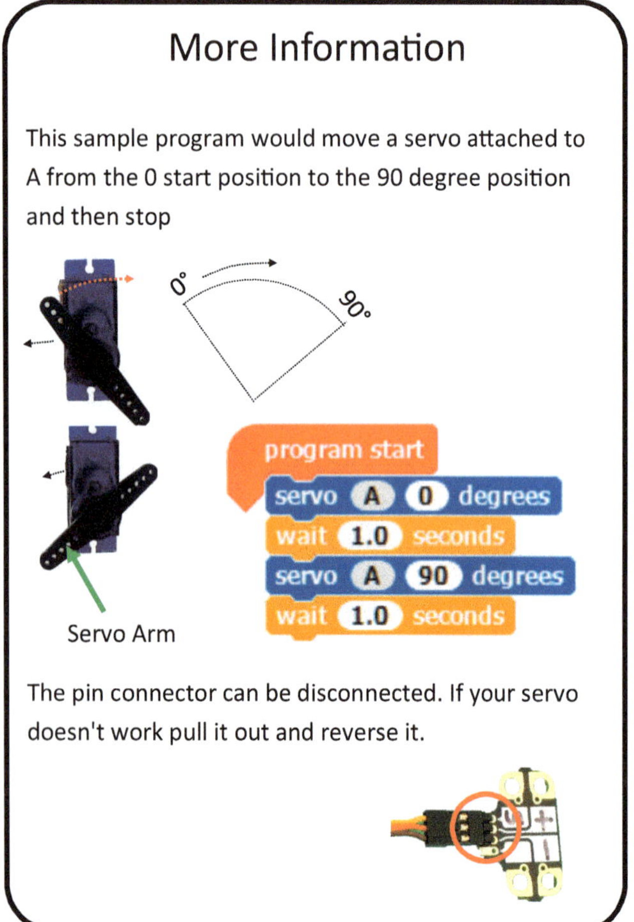
More Information
This sample program would move a servo attached to A from the 0 start position to the 90 degree position and then stop
0°
90°
program start
servo A 0 degrees
wait 1.0 seconds
servo A 90 degrees
wait 1.0 seconds
Servo Arm
The pin connector can be disconnected. If your servo doesn't work pull it out and reverse it.

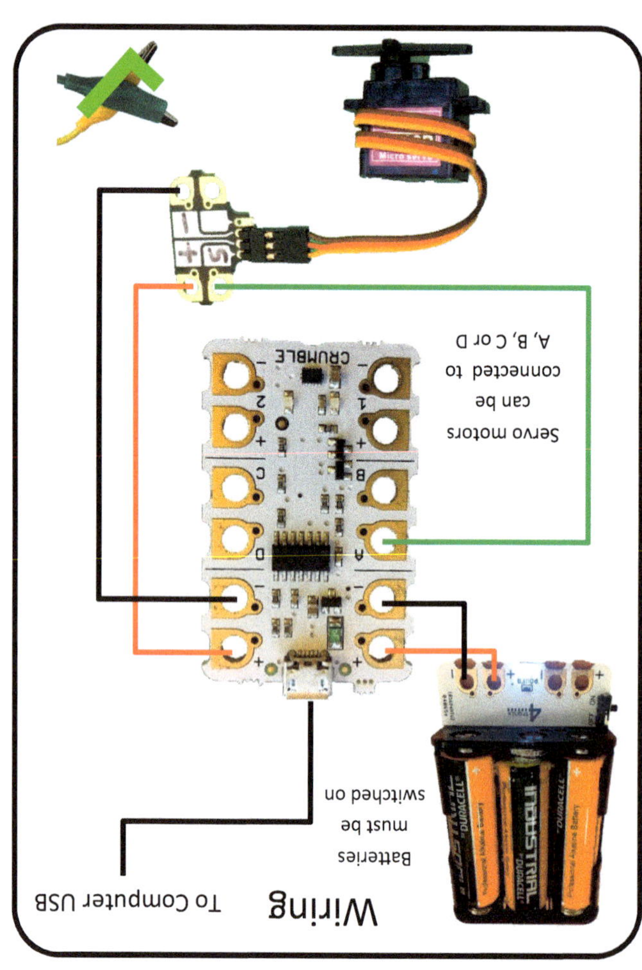
Wiring
To Computer USB
Batteries
must be
switched on
Servo motors
can be
connected to
A, B, C or D
CRUMBLE

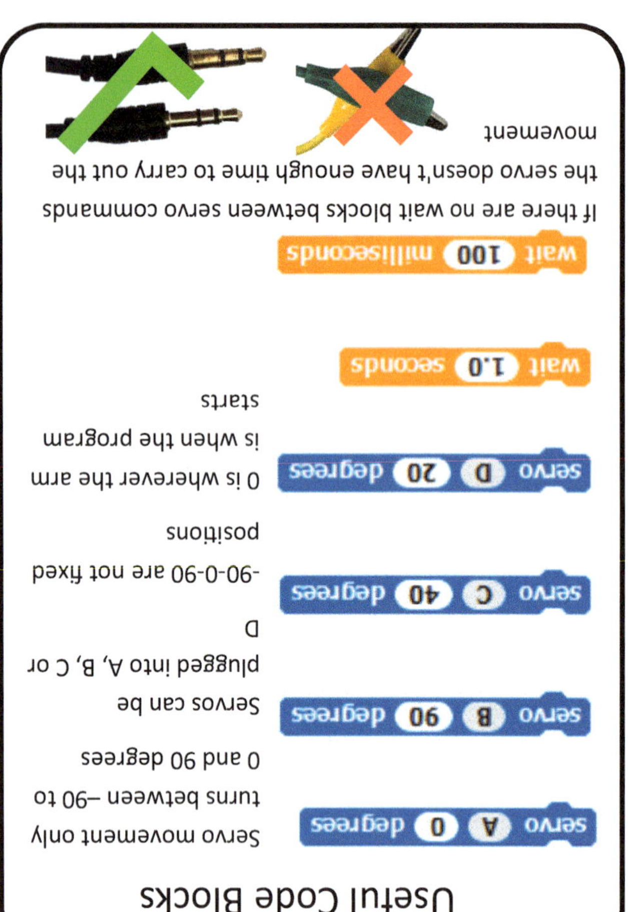
Useful Code Blocks
servo A 0 degrees
Servo movement only turns between –90 to 0 and 90 degrees
servo B 90 degrees
Servos can be plugged into A, B, C or D
servo C 40 degrees
-90-0-90 are not fixed positions
servo D 20 degrees
0 is wherever the arm is when the program starts
wait 1.0 seconds
wait 100 milliseconds
If there are no wait blocks between servo commands the servo doesn't have enough time to carry out the movement

Crumble

Slider

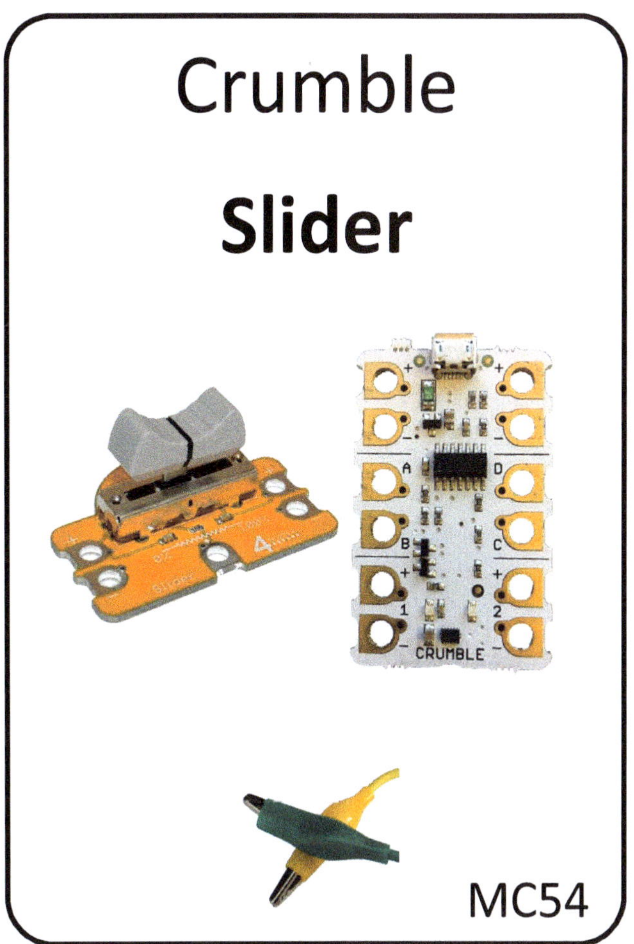

MC54

More Information

Sliders can be used to adjust the amount of power going into a motor, the colour balance of a programmable light, the tone of a piezo element, The amount of turn a servo moves etc.

It can be used wherever a variable can be used in place of a fixed number.

The left over power ports on this slider can be used to power another device.

Wiring

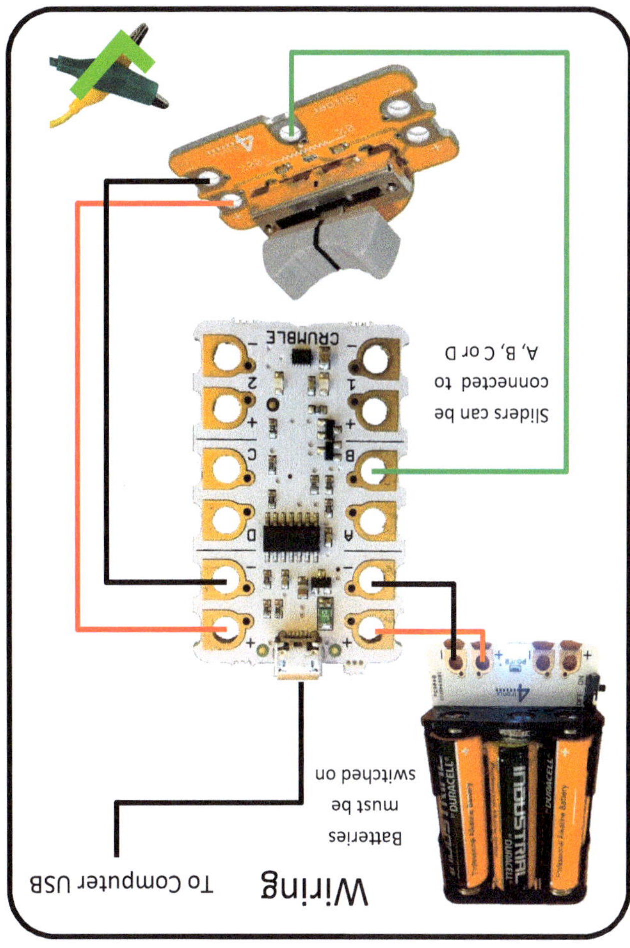

Useful Code Blocks

If you create a variable, you can see what is inside it on the Crumble programming screen.

This program transfers the data from the slider (analogue) and puts it inside a variable called slider. It checks repeatedly to see if anything has updated. It is a good program to test to see if the slider is working.

```
program start
  do forever
    let slider = analogue B
  loop
```

Information is inputted into the Crumble through the analogue block as a number between 0-255. This one shows 0 when the slider is at 0%, 109 at 50% and 220 at 100%

0%	0
50%	109
100%	220

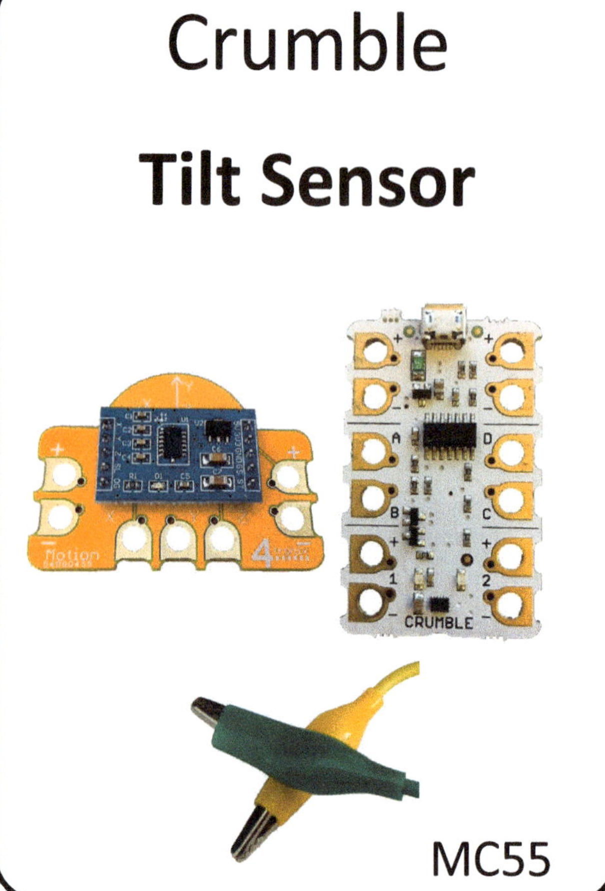
Crumble
Tilt Sensor
MC55

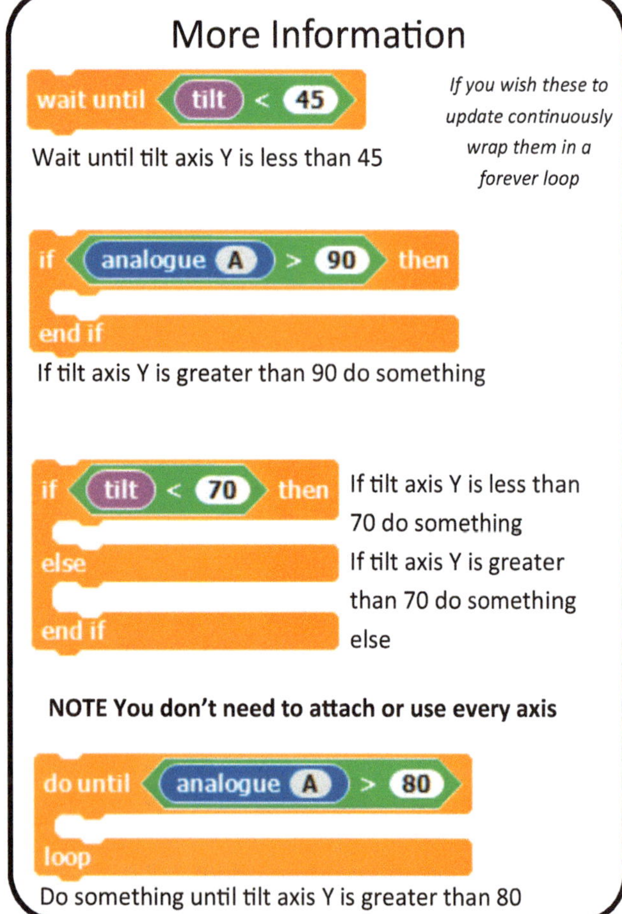
More Information
wait until tilt < 45
Wait until tilt axis Y is less than 45
If you wish these to update continuously wrap them in a forever loop
if analogue A > 90 then
end if
If tilt axis Y is greater than 90 do something
if tilt < 70 then
else
end if
If tilt axis Y is less than 70 do something
If tilt axis Y is greater than 70 do something else
NOTE You don't need to attach or use every axis
do until analogue A > 80
loop
Do something until tilt axis Y is greater than 80

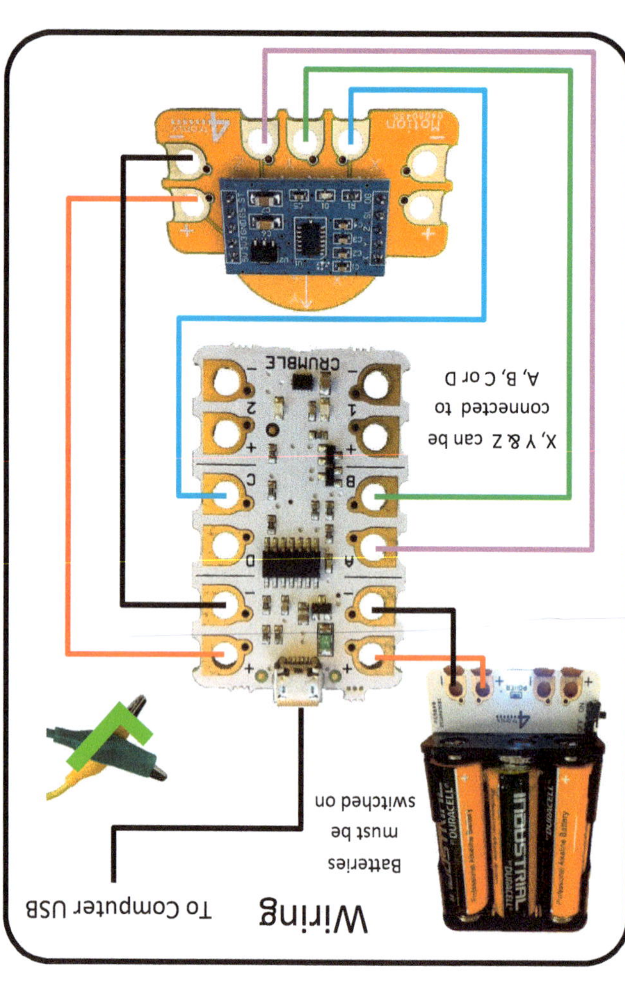
Wiring
To Computer USB
Batteries must be switched on
X, Y & Z can be connected to A, B, C or D

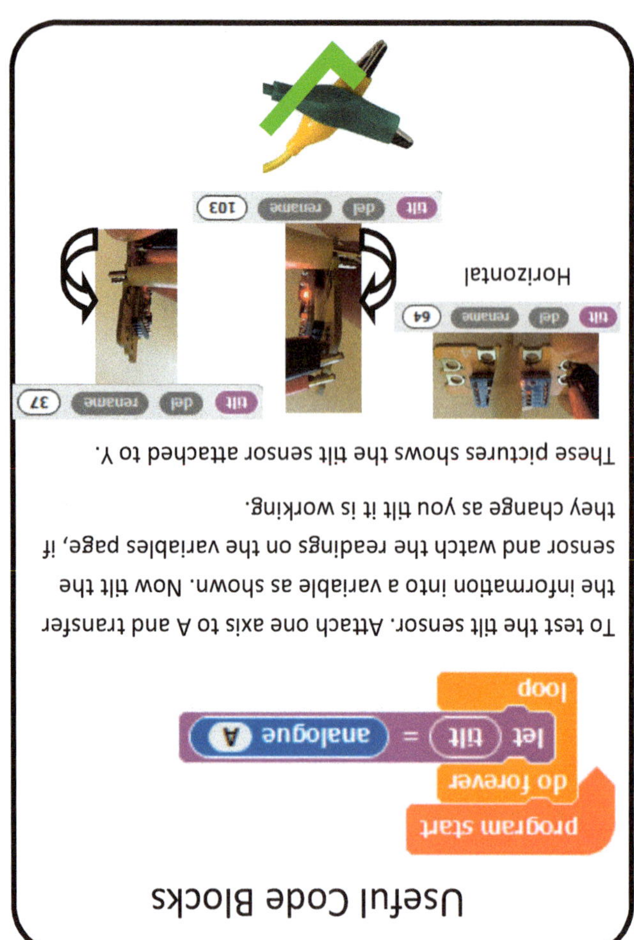
Useful Code Blocks
program start
do forever
let tilt = analogue A
loop
To test the tilt sensor. Attach one axis to A and transfer the information into a variable as shown. Now tilt the sensor and watch the readings on the variables page, if they change as you tilt it is working.
These pictures shows the tilt sensor attached to Y.
tilt del rename 64
Horizontal
tilt del rename 103
tilt del rename 37

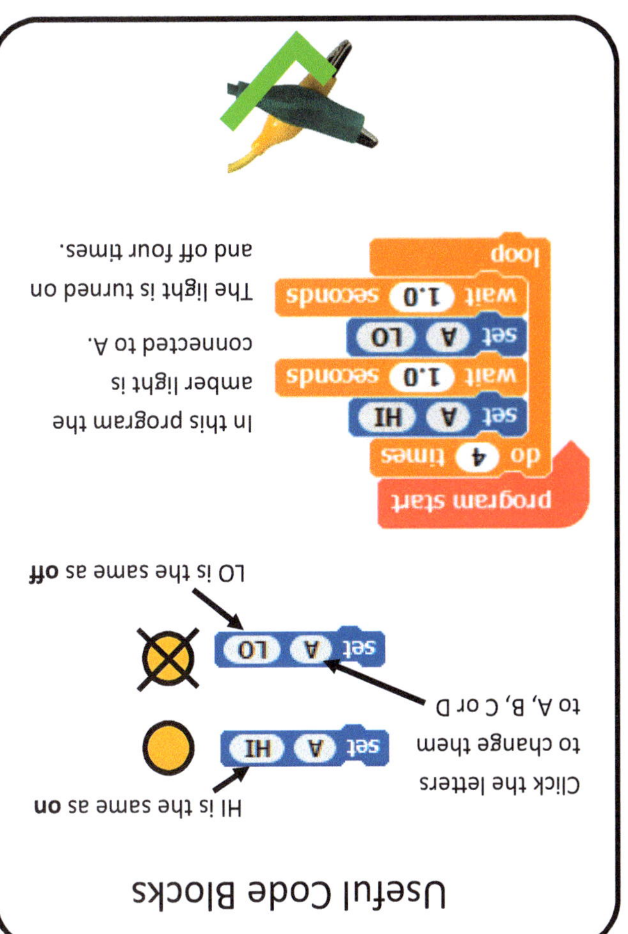
Useful Code Blocks
HI is the same as on
Click the letters to change them to A, B, C or D
LO is the same as off
set A HI
set A LO
program start
do 4 times
set A HI
wait 1.0 seconds
set A LO
wait 1.0 seconds
loop
In this program the amber light is connected to A.
The light is turned on and off four times.

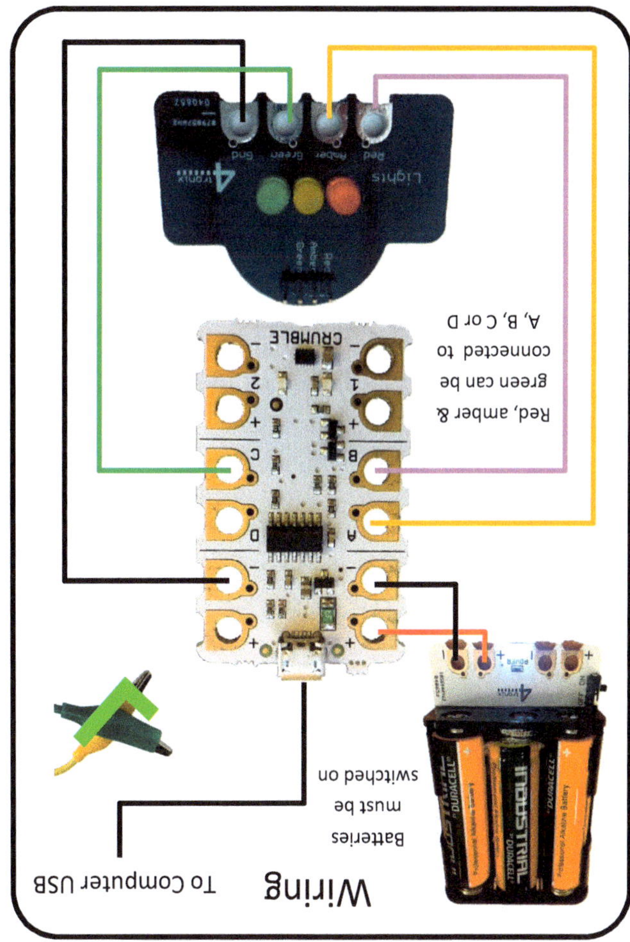
Wiring
To Computer USB
Batteries must be switched on
Red, amber & green can be connected to A, B, C or D
Lights
Red Amber Green Gnd
CRUMBLE

More Information

LED Traffic lights can be used to program traffic lights or a single LED light can be used to indicate something else.

A green LED could be switched on when the light from an light resistant resistor goes above a set number.

Or

A red LED could be turned on when the PIR detects motion.

You don't have to wire every light to use just one.

If you wanted the red light only then red to A, B, C or D and GND to negative.

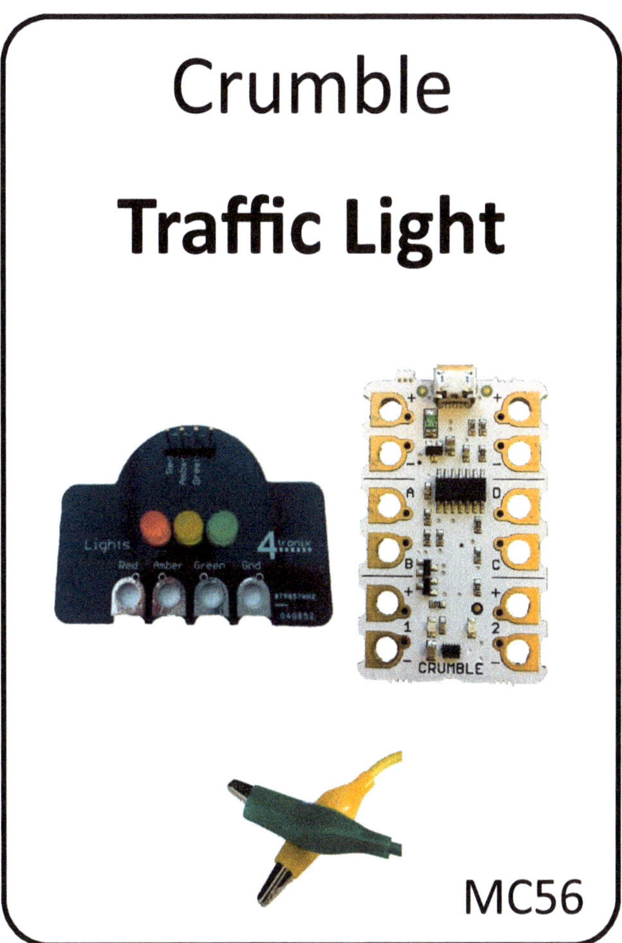
Crumble
Traffic Light
Lights
Red Amber Green Gnd
CRUMBLE
MC56

16. Problem Solving Sticker Templates

These templates were made for printable pages of stickers.

Fourteen stickers to a page
Two columns of seven
Seven rows of two
Slightly rounded edge
Size 99.1mm x 38.1mm

They come in boxes of 50, 100 or 500.

You can find packs of 100 here
https://goo.gl/cHhdK9
You can find packs of 500 here
https://goo.gl/SCTDYQ

I can adapt existing ideas to solve new problems

Code-IT

I can adapt existing ideas to solve new problems

Code-IT

I can adapt existing ideas to solve new problems

Code-IT

I can adapt existing ideas to solve new problems

Code-IT

I can adapt existing ideas to solve new problems

Code-IT

I can adapt existing ideas to solve new problems

Code-IT

I can adapt existing ideas to solve new problems

Code-IT

I can adapt existing ideas to solve new problems

Code-IT

I can adapt existing ideas to solve new problems

Code-IT

I can adapt existing ideas to solve new problems

Code-IT

I can adapt existing ideas to solve new problems

Code-IT

I can adapt existing ideas to solve new problems

Code-IT

I can adapt existing ideas to solve new problems

Code-IT

I can adapt existing ideas to solve new problems

Code-IT

Handles Ambiguity

I recognise there is more than one way to solve / describe a problem

Code-IT

Handles Ambiguity

I recognise there is more than one way to solve / describe a problem

Code-IT

Handles Ambiguity

I recognise there is more than one way to solve / describe a problem

Code-IT

Handles Ambiguity

I recognise there is more than one way to solve / describe a problem

Code-IT

Handles Ambiguity

I recognise there is more than one way to solve / describe a problem

Code-IT

Handles Ambiguity

I recognise there is more than one way to solve / describe a problem

Code-IT

Handles Ambiguity

I recognise there is more than one way to solve / describe a problem

Code-IT

Handles Ambiguity

I recognise there is more than one way to solve / describe a problem

Code-IT

Handles Ambiguity

I recognise there is more than one way to solve / describe a problem

Code-IT

Handles Ambiguity

I recognise there is more than one way to solve / describe a problem

Code-IT

Handles Ambiguity

I recognise there is more than one way to solve / describe a problem

Code-IT

Handles Ambiguity

I recognise there is more than one way to solve / describe a problem

Code-IT

Handles Ambiguity

I recognise there is more than one way to solve / describe a problem

Code-IT

Handles Ambiguity

I recognise there is more than one way to solve / describe a problem

Code-IT

I can encourage others to share their ideas

Code-IT

I can encourage others to share their ideas

Code-IT

I can encourage others to share their ideas

Code-IT

I can encourage others to share their ideas

Code-IT

I can encourage others to share their ideas

Code-IT

I can encourage others to share their ideas

Code-IT

I can encourage others to share their ideas

Code-IT

I can encourage others to share their ideas

Code-IT

I can encourage others to share their ideas

Code-IT

I can encourage others to share their ideas

Code-IT

I can encourage others to share their ideas

Code-IT

I can encourage others to share their ideas

Code-IT

I can encourage others to share their ideas

Code-IT

I can encourage others to share their ideas

Code-IT

Copes with Complexity

I can discover / concentrate on the most important part of a problem

Code-IT

Copes with Complexity

I can discover / concentrate on the most important part of a problem

Code-IT

Copes with Complexity

I can discover / concentrate on the most important part of a problem

Code-IT

Copes with Complexity

I can discover / concentrate on the most important part of a problem

Code-IT

Copes with Complexity

I can discover / concentrate on the most important part of a problem

Code-IT

Copes with Complexity

I can discover / concentrate on the most important part of a problem

Code-IT

Copes with Complexity

I can discover / concentrate on the most important part of a problem

Code-IT

Copes with Complexity

I can discover / concentrate on the most important part of a problem

Code-IT

Copes with Complexity

I can discover / concentrate on the most important part of a problem

Code-IT

Copes with Complexity

I can discover / concentrate on the most important part of a problem

Code-IT

Copes with Complexity

I can discover / concentrate on the most important part of a problem

Code-IT

Copes with Complexity

I can discover / concentrate on the most important part of a problem

Code-IT

Copes with Complexity

I can discover / concentrate on the most important part of a problem

Code-IT

Copes with Complexity

I can discover / concentrate on the most important part of a problem

Code-IT

Copes with Complexity

I can discover / concentrate on the most important part of a problem

Code-IT

I can design criteria
to evaluate
my creations Code-IT

I can design criteria
to evaluate
my creations Code-IT

I can design criteria
to evaluate
my creations Code-IT

I can design criteria
to evaluate
my creations Code-IT

I can design criteria
to evaluate
my creations Code-IT

I can design criteria
to evaluate
my creations Code-IT

I can design criteria
to evaluate
my creations Code-IT

I can design criteria
to evaluate
my creations Code-IT

I can design criteria
to evaluate
my creations Code-IT

I can design criteria
to evaluate
my creations Code-IT

I can design criteria
to evaluate
my creations Code-IT

I can design criteria
to evaluate
my creations Code-IT

I can design criteria
to evaluate
my creations Code-IT

I can design criteria
to evaluate
my creations Code-IT

I can repeatedly experiment through predicting, making, testing & debugging

Investigates

Code-IT

I can repeatedly experiment through predicting, making, testing & debugging

I can repeatedly experiment through predicting, making, testing & debugging

I can repeatedly experiment through predicting, making, testing & debugging

I can repeatedly experiment through predicting, making, testing & debugging

I can repeatedly experiment through predicting, making, testing & debugging

I can repeatedly experiment through predicting, making, testing & debugging

I can repeatedly experiment through predicting, making, testing & debugging

I can repeatedly experiment through predicting, making, testing & debugging

I can repeatedly experiment through predicting, making, testing & debugging

I can repeatedly experiment through predicting, making, testing & debugging

I can repeatedly experiment through predicting, making, testing & debugging

I can repeatedly experiment through predicting, making, testing & debugging

I can repeatedly experiment through predicting, making, testing & debugging

I look for how a project can be extended

Code-IT
Open Ended Problem Solver

I look for how a project can be extended

I look for how a project can be extended

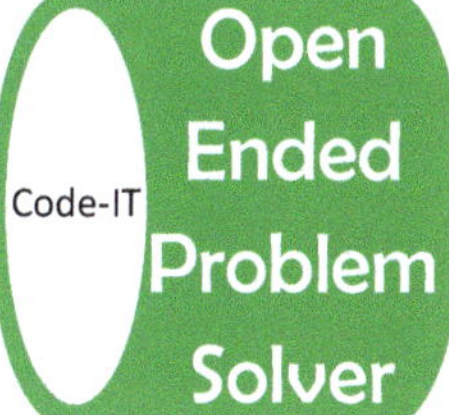

I look for how a project can be extended

I look for how a project can be extended

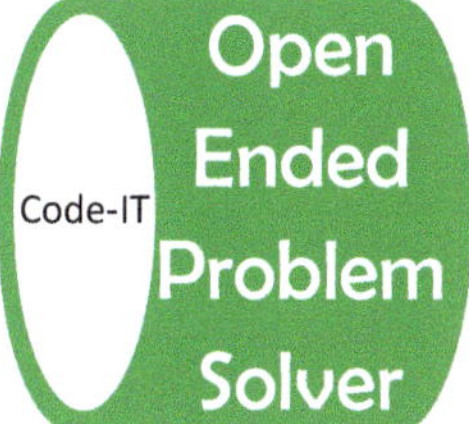

I look for how a project can be extended

I look for how a project can be extended

I look for how a project can be extended

I look for how a project can be extended

I look for how a project can be extended

I look for how a project can be extended

I look for how a project can be extended

I look for how a project can be extended

I look for how a project can be extended

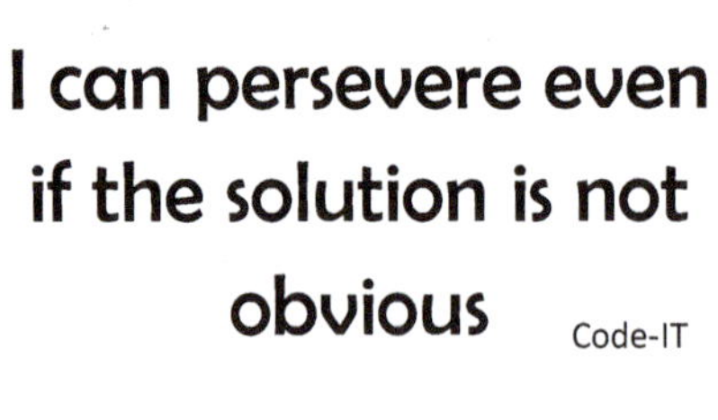

I can persevere even if the solution is not obvious

Code-IT

I can persevere even if the solution is not obvious

Code-IT

I can persevere even if the solution is not obvious

Code-IT

I can persevere even if the solution is not obvious

Code-IT

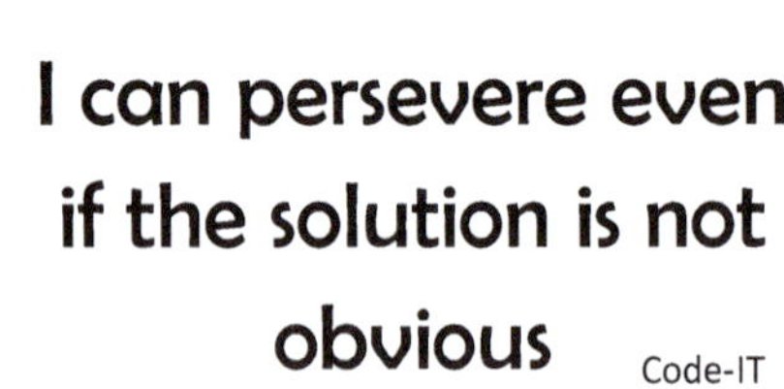

I can persevere even if the solution is not obvious

Code-IT

I can persevere even if the solution is not obvious

Code-IT

I can persevere even if the solution is not obvious

Code-IT

I can persevere even if the solution is not obvious

Code-IT

I can persevere even if the solution is not obvious

Code-IT

I can persevere even if the solution is not obvious

Code-IT

I can persevere even if the solution is not obvious

Code-IT

I can persevere even if the solution is not obvious

Code-IT

I can persevere even if the solution is not obvious

Code-IT

I can persevere even if the solution is not obvious

Code-IT